Cognitive Development

Cognitive Development

Research based on a Neo-Piagetian approach

Edited by

J. A. Keats

Department of Psychology
University of Newcastle
Australia

K. F. Collis

Department of Education
University of Tasmania
Australia

G. S. Halford

Department of Psychology
University of Queensland
Australia

JOHN WILEY & SONS

Chichester · New York · Brisbane · Toronto

0349749

41507

Copyright © 1978, by John Wiley & Sons, Ltd.

All rights reserved.

No part of this book may be reproduced by any means, nor
transmitted, nor translated into a machine language without
the written permission of the publisher.

Library of Congress Cataloging in Publication Data:

Main entry under title:

Cognitive development.

   1. Cognition in children. I. Keats, John
Augustus. II. Collis, Kevin Francis. III. Halford,
Graeme.
BF723.C5C56   155.4'13   77–1717

ISBN 0 471 99505 3

Photosetting by Thomson Press (India) Limited, New Delhi and
Printed by The Pitman Press, Bath.

ABOUT THE CONTRIBUTORS

PROFESSOR JOHN KEATS is the Foundation Professor of Psychology at the University of Newcastle. Following experience in educational research at the Australian Council for Educational Research and his doctorate on formal and concrete operational thinking at Princeton University, he became senior lecturer and later reader in psychology at the University of Queensland where he continued his interest in the application of quantitative methods to the study of cognitive processes. Professor Keats took up his present appointment in 1965 and encouraged graduate students to take an interest in experimental studies of cognitive processes of the kind described by Piaget. Most of the contributors to this volume were at some stage associated with this group of former graduate students.

PROFESSOR KEVIN COLLIS was born and educated in Queensland where he obtained his Master's degree in Education. After accepting a lectureship in that field at the University of Newcastle, Professor Collis completed his Ph.D. in the Psychology Department there in 1972 for studies of thought processes in mathematics based on the development of Piaget's theory of intelligence. He then continued these studies as well as contributing to the development of curricula in mathematics for various groups including students in developing countries in the South Pacific area. Professor Collis worked on a SSRC project at the University of Nottingham and has contributed papers to national and international conferences as well as learned journals. He is currently Professor of Education at the University of Tasmania.

DR. GRAEME HALFORD graduated B.A. with Honours and M.A. with Honours at the University of New England and obtained his Ph.D. at the University of Newcastle. His early interests were in trying to relate cognitive processes to learning processes, a problem which was receiving little attention from psychologists at that time. This background caused him to become interested in the problem of devising a new paradigm for dealing with the role of learning in cognitive development, to which he has been devoted in the last few years. Dr. Halford became a lecturer in psychology at the University of Newcastle in 1965 and a senior lecturer in 1970. In 1972 he accepted an appointment as Associate Professor of Psychology at Queen's University in Canada. His present position of senior lecturer in psychology at the University of Queensland was taken up in 1975.

DR. JOHN SHEPPARD is currently Head of the Department of Behavioural and General Studies at Cumberland College of Health Sciences in Sydney, Australia. The College trains students for the paramedical professions. Before joining the staff of Cumberland College he had been a school teacher, clinical psychologist, and teachers college lecturer. He obtained his Bachelor of Arts degree, Diploma in Education, and Master of Arts degree from the University of New England, Armidale, New South Wales and his Doctor of Philosophy degree from the University of Newcastle, New South Wales. His major research interests are in the areas of child development, behaviour modification, and training in the health professions, and he has published a number of articles in those areas. He is an Assistant Editor of the *Australian Journal of Education*.

DR. DAPHNE KEATS is senior lecturer in psychology at the University of Newcastle. She obtained her B.A. and Dip.Ed. from the University of Sydney and later completed graduate work at the University of Queensland where she was awarded her M.Ed. in 1962 and Ph.D. in 1969 for studies of students from Asia studying at that university. Subsequent research in cross-cultural psychology included a survey of former Colombo plan students who had returned to Asian countries which was published by the Australian National University. With her husband, Professor John Keats, Dr. Keats received research grants from 1971 to study the effect of bilingualism on the development of cognitive concepts. Dr. Keats has lectured in psychology at the University of Newcastle since 1970 and is currently involved in research into the development of values in various Asian and European cultures.

DR. IAN SEGGIE completed his doctoral work at the University of Newcastle, New South Wales, during employment as a psychologist with the Australian Army Psychology Corps. His interest in the general field of problem-solving and cognitive activities dates from an early career involvement in two diverse areas: the investigation of crime in a British police force and engineering research. Since the completion of his doctorate he has taken a more academic interest in complex cognitive activities and has taught at the Mitchell College of Advanced Education, the University of New England, and the University of Newcastle, where he lectures at present. His publications report investigations in the field of concept learning and formal operational thought.

MISS MARGARET JURD is a qualified teacher with teaching experience at infants, primary, and secondary levels. She served as an educational psychologist for eighteen years working with pupils of all ages. Miss Jurd was awarded her M.A. in psychology from the University of Newcastle in 1971 for studies of the acquisition of concepts in the social sciences. She is a lecturer in education at Newcastle College of Advanced Education and is currently undertaking further research into adolescent cognitive development at Newcastle University, Department of Psychology, under a grant from the National Committee for Social Science Teaching.

CONTENTS

0349749

41507

GLOSSARY OF TECHNICAL TERMS

Algorism (or **algorithm**)

A method of calculation, according to fixed rules, which yields effectively the solution of any given problem of some class of problems.

Associativity

A property of an operation which makes the result of two successive applications of the operation independent of the order in which they are performed. Thus if $\circ$ is an associative operation, then $(a \circ b) \circ c = a \circ (b \circ c)$, e.g. addition is associative since $(a + b) + c = a + (b + c)$ for all a, b, c, but subtraction is not associative since $(a - b) - c \neq a - (b - c)$ for all a, b, c.

Binary operation

A principle or rule which assigns or maps all ordered pairs of elements from a set into one and only one element from the same or a different set.

Binary relation

A set of ordered pairs of elements from a set (a binary relation is a subset of a Cartesian product set).

Cartesian product

A set composed of all possible ordered pairs of elements from another set.

Closure

The assignment of single elements to sets of two or more elements, so that each single element is equivalent to the set to which it is assigned; e.g. when a binary operation is performed, such as $3 + 5 = 8$, this is tantamount to assigning the element 8 as equivalent to elements 3 and 5.

Conjunction

A binary connective in symbolic logic, read as *and*. Thus the conjunction of A and B (written as $A \cdot B$) means all the things which have both A and B as attributes.

Disjunction

A binary connective in symbolic logic, read as *or*. Thus the disjunction of A and B (written as $A \vee B$) means all the things which have *either* A or B as attributes.

Far transposition

(See transposition.)

Function

A principle or rule which assigns to every element in a set, one and only one element in another set.

Group

A set of elements which have a single binary operation (alternatively, has the closure property), has an identity element, has an inverse element for every element, and which is associative.

Grouping

A translation of Piaget's term 'groupement', meaning a variety of structure which bears some resemblance to a group, but differs in certain respects (see Chapter 2 for details).

Groupoid

A set with a single binary operation.

Identity

An element which, when combined with any element, produces a result equivalent to that other element alone.

Implication

A binary connective in symbolic logic. If A implies B (written as $A \supset B$) this means that whenever A occurs, B also occurs. Thus A cannot occur without B, but B *may* occur without A.

Inverse

An element which, when combined with an element of which it is the inverse, produces the identity element as a result.

Mapping

A set of assignments of elements to other elements, as in a function or a binary operation.

Operation

(see binary operation.)

Operational behaviour

In contrast to intuitive behaviour (when a pattern is noticed but not internalized) operational behaviour requires internalization and consistent application of a recognized pattern.

Operator

An element which changes a system from one state to another state.

Reversibility

A translation of Piaget's term 'reversibilité', which is the ability of thought processes to compensate for or cancel one another.

Revertibility

A translation of Piaget's term 'renversibilité', which is the observation that an empirical phenomenon can be cancelled or reversed.

'Scanning for recurrent regularities'

The description given by Bruner and his associates (1959) to the strategy used to achieve consistent dealings with the environment. It involves the noting of recurrent regularities and the discarding of certain *apparent* regularities which would lead to inconsistent judgments.

Schema

The figurative component of a cognitive organization.

'Schema of proportionality'

Piaget's term, one form of which can be represented by an equation such as $A/B = xA/xB$. If, to solve such an equation, the expression as a whole must be considered and sequential closure is impossible, formal operation is required. On the other hand, individuals who have attained the level of concrete generalization are able to cope if sequential closures are possible and they are not required to consider the interrelationship between the variables.

Scheme

An organized set of processes underlying a particular psychological function or performance.

Sequential closure

This occurs when there is more than one operation in a problem but each can be carried out independently, in turn. For example, consider the solving of $(2 + 3) \times 4 = ?$ Individuals in the middle concrete operational level can cope with more than one operation if sequential closure is possible.

Set

A collection: it may comprise any kind of elements, with or without a principle of selection. Thus the elements of a set do not necessarily have any attributes in common.

Structuralism

A philosophical approach to science which seeks explanation in relation between events.

Structure

(See Chapter 1.) This is used in this book to refer to a cognitive structure, meaning stored information about relationships between elements of a task or situation, or between cognitive symbols used to represent the task or situation.

Structure d'ensemble

English: 'structured whole'. This concept from the writings of Piaget refers to an integrated set of psychological processes underlying a variety of superficially diverse performances.

Symbol

An element which stands for or represents another element or thing, but which bears no necessary resemblance to the thing represented. The relation between the symbol and the thing symbolized depends on convention rather than on any logical or necessary connection.

System

A set of elements with an organizing principle.

Transformation rule

This is the third variable required for solving problems which are at the formal operational level. The transformation rule consistently relates the operations and variables involved one to another. It becomes part of the 'recurrent regularity' in the relationship which must be found in order to be able to operate at a formal operational level.

Transposition

Refers to transfer of the basis of a discrimination from the training task to a test task. For instance, if a subject is trained to respond to the larger of two stimuli, then tested on a new pair, transposition is exhibited if the larger stimulus is again chosen, even though it may not be similar in size to the larger stimulus in the training pair. Far transposition refers to test stimuli which are very different from the training stimuli, while near transposition refers to test stimuli which differ only slightly from the training stimuli.

Truth table

A table with three or more columns which assigns values 'true or false' to all possible combinations of attributes of two or more dimensions. (See Chapter 1 for examples and explanation.)

FOREWORD

This, as its title proclaims, is a book about cognitive development. Its object is to analyse and to explain whatever changes may be observed in the ways in which children can represent their knowledge and understanding of the world and its phenomena. It is not, save indirectly, a book about theories of cognitive development, and still less a book about one theory, that of Jean Piaget. Its first concern is to establish what are the facts, and to this end each of its seven authors has adduced an impressive and well-founded body of evidence in support of the thesis that there are indeed clear-cut changes in the character of children's thinking and learning occurring between the ages of five and eighteen. Yet the book is certainly not atheoretical, inasmuch as these facts are themselves the outcome of careful observations based on original experimentation carried out in the light of the writers' own theoretical interpretations of the nature of cognitive growth in children.

I have chosen deliberately to use the plural 'interpretations', because the editors have themselves been at some pains to point out that each of the contributors has accumulated his own set of data, working from a partly independent perspective, and addressing himself to a different content area. Also, as will be apparent from the last chapter, there are certain residual differences which separate the conclusions of Sheppard, of Collis, and of Halford.

Nevertheless, much more important than these differences are the areas of agreement. For each of these writers has found evidence in support of a stage theory of cognition, and each is prepared to give prominence to at least three stages, similar in some ways to Piaget's three stages of representation: preoperational, concrete operational, and formal operational (though it should be added that most of Collis' evidence is concerned with important distinctions *within* the last two). It would be quite wrong to suggest that these agreements among the present writers, or indeed their partial agreement with Piaget, are superficial or accidental. Keats and his colleagues have been impressed by the cogency of the Piagetian evidence and it is this that has led them to look for stages roughly corresponding to those outlined by Piaget and Inhelder.

But the stages of which they speak are also different from those of Piaget. Thus, for the present authors 'A stage results, not from the possession of a specific structure or set of structures, but from the possession of sufficient information processing capacity to organize symbolic systems at a particular level of complexity' (p. 416). I would like to refer to this formulation once more towards the end of this Foreword. For the moment I would recall Piaget's repeated insistence on the child's elaboration of structures which then became available for the assimilation of data from different content areas but which (a) transcend this or that content and (b) are not learned by precept, or by imitation, or by reinforcement, or indeed abstracted from empirical (sensory) evidence, but are abstracted from the subject's own actions. Piaget's structures recall the Kantian transcendentals from which ultimately they derive. It seems as if, for Piaget, the eight 'groupments' of concrete intelligence and subsequently the INRC group become a part of the permanent furniture of our minds or brains; whenever the elements of input (i.e. the successive experiences or observations that we make with respect to a particular set-up such as a conservation experiment) match these structures, they are activated, and it is this activation which allows us to reason operationally.

The authors of this volume question these assumptions, preferring to restrict their argument to a description of the moment of the child's thinking when he is actually engaged in problem solving. In doing so, their mode of analysis comes a great deal nearer to that of contemporary cognitive psychologists who tend to favour an information processing analysis in this wide sense, whether or not that analysis also involves them in the construction of computer programs to simulate the behaviour which they find in the human subject. To that extent, the publication of the present volume may be seen as a welcome fusion of what may have been seen as incompatible approaches.

Because the authors of *Cognitive Development* have approached their task from a number of differing perspectives, their work will also have a wider appeal. Its scope is in no way limited to the study of development in reasoning in relation to abstract laboratory tasks. The study of behaviour in these settings is indeed important because the laboratory setting enables the experimenter to devise and control procedures in such a way as to offer the clearest possible test of theory. Halford's work in particular constitutes a fine example of this approach. But many readers will be at least as attracted to the work of Collis and Jurd, whose interests are more applied, and who address themselves to questions which are, or should be, central for teachers and curriculum designers. They have sought to pinpoint the essential characteristics of tasks which are within the scope of children at selected ages and those which are not.

I have no doubt that their insights will help teachers to understand the problems which face their students when attempting to come to grips with the abstract notions that are essential both in mathematics and in history. Nor would I be surprised to find Jurd's notion of a colligatory concept achieving some currency among teachers of history, just as Collis' fine observations of the concrete general mode of thinking introduces a new term which is essential to describe an important differentiation for the theory and practice of teaching mathematics.

I believe it is true to say that in most areas of psychology the partisan stances which characterized the schools of the thirties have given way to more tolerant attitudes loosely united by (a) a common acceptance of the importance of establishing just how far the computer analogy is adequate and where it breaks down, and (b) a preference for limited theories to describe a relatively narrow range of phenomena and a distrust of overriding theories. It is perhaps inevitable that in this context the vast Piagetian enterprise stands out as an indigestible relic of a bygone era. Not only does it comprise an overarching theory, but like early behaviourism and gestalt psychology, it has tended to produce a polarization among psychologists and educationists into opposing camps, one of blind disciples, and the other of wilfully ignorant opponents. As an unfortunate consequence of this polarization, one might point to a proliferation of trivial experiments aimed to prove Piaget right or to prove Piaget wrong.

It is very much to the credit of Keats and his co-authors that they have stood clear of such arid controversy. For in the final analysis, the measure of Piaget's contribution is the fact that he has been able to bring a wide range of behaviours within the scope of scientific observation and experiment and to bring to light a remarkable number of phenomena that are contrary both to common sense and to an oversimplistic learning theory. The present authors have elected to concentrate their research efforts on continuing and extending those observations while at the same time endeavouring to arrive at their own formulation of a theory which might account for at least a part of the phenomena. There is surely an important sense in which, even when they are most critical of the Genevan work, their own impartiality constitutes a more sincere tribute to Piaget as a scientific innovator than the misguided efforts of certain proselytizers.

By the same token, I am sure that the authors of the book would wish to lay particular stress on the challenging experimental and observational results that it contains. The theory of stages which is described in Chapters Six and Thirteen is one interpretation. It is one which is based essentially on an analysis of the psychological demand which faces a subject when formulating an overall strategy to solve a given class of problem. Some might prefer to lay more stress on analysing the changing demands on cognitive processing that are entailed in each successive step of a solution.

Or again, there are those who might quarrel with any formulation in terms of thinking in the child as opposed to categories of problems which the child might be set. The latter is certainly more openended both because the varieties of problem category form more of an 'open' set, and because a formulation in terms of problems does not carry any implication that a child will usually be at the same stage in relation to all problems. However, to this the authors could reasonably argue that provided problems are categorized on the basis of an analysis of the programme of thinking required for their solution, there is at least *prima facie* ground for supposing that some categories of problem will prove too demanding for some groups of solver. Secondly, they can also offer much evidence to indicate that this *prima facie* case is supported by the facts. Third, there is some evidence that children who have not reached a given level of maturity are not only unable to spontaneously solve certain problems but are also unable to profit from generalized instruction which would help them to solve similar problems in the future—though they can be taught an algorithm. Thus although the concept of stage might not be explanatory, save indirectly, it is in an important sense predictive. Finally, the concept is one that may be useful when formulating suggestions for effective educational practice.

Because the present work invites this kind of constructive and dispassionate analysis, it is one which must surely generate more light than heat, even when it chooses to be controversial. For the most part, however, the reader will find here not controversy but a temperate reasoned argument, based on a solid foundation of scholarship and original experiment.

October 1977   E. A. LUNZER
Nottingham

PREFACE

This book reports the results of an extensive programme of research aimed at developing paradigms which are objective but attempt to capture the essence of the psycho-logic approach of Piaget. Some of Piaget's formulations have been varied to be consistent with theoretical and empirical findings resulting from this programme.

The editors and contributors have in common that they were either graduate students or staff members, or both, of the Department of Psychology, The University of Newcastle, Australia during at least part of the decade 1966 to 1976. While most are now affiliated primarily with other institutions, all are continuing work in the area of cognitive development. Those still remaining at the University of Newcastle have now been joined by others with similar interests.

Our gratitude is expressed to various organizations which supported the research programme:

The University of Newcastle, which provided research funds, post-graduate scholarships and background facilities.

The Australian Research Grants Committee.

The Canada Council Grant No. S73–1087.

The Education Research and Development Committee (formerly the Australian Advisory Committee for Research and Development in Education).

The New South Wales Education Department, which provided additional funds for mature post-graduate students and made available school facilities for the research.

The Newcastle Catholic Education Office, which also made school facilities available.

The Australian Department of Education, which provided post-graduate scholarships and supporting finance.

The National Committee on Social Science Teaching.

Universiti Kebangsaan Malaysia.

Among the many scholars who evaluated and encouraged the present work, Professors A. Heron, E. A. Lunzer, B. Neuman, E. A. Peel, and I. K. Waterhouse were of great assistance. Our gratitude is also expressed to the many people both children and adults in Australia, Canada, and Malaysia who contributed to the studies by acting as subjects and also to their teachers who cooperated with us. Finally we thank Mrs C. A. Brown and Mrs S. D. Byron for their editorial assistance and the many typists who prepared the drafts and the final manuscript.

J. A. K.   K. F. C.
G. S. H.   M. F. J.
D. M. K.   J. L. S.
J. L. S.

1

INTRODUCTION: THE STRUCTURAL APPROACH TO COGNITIVE DEVELOPMENT

G. S. Halford

Although the study of cognitive development dates at least from Binet and Simon (1916), for a considerable time the work of Jean Piaget has virtually defined the field. Despite the fact that the importance of his approach has declined recently, along with the growth of other contributions, no alternative approach has challenged his contributions simultaneously in both scope and depth.

This book is not designed to interpret or test Piaget's theories. There are already numerous good interpretive summaries available (e.g. Beard, 1969; Boyle, 1969; Evans, 1973; Flavell, 1963; Furth, 1970; Halford, 1972; Hunt, 1961; Phillips, 1975; and Wadsworth, 1971). A brief introduction to the whole cognitive development field is provided by Flavell (1977) Turner (1975). There are also several sizeable works devoted to a deeper explication or testing of Piaget's theories (Berlyne, 1965; Bruner, Olver, and Greenfield, 1966; Elkind and Flavell, 1969; Furth, 1969; Hayes, 1970; Hyde, 1973; Peill, 1975; and Sigel and Hooper, 1968).

This book is not specifically devoted to a Piagetian approach. It is devoted to a *structural* approach. The concept of structure is considered in more detail later, but for the present we say that a cognitive structure is information, stored within the organism, about relationships between elements or events. It is perfectly possible to disagree with many of the specific theories which Piaget has propounded, while still believing that there are stages in cognitive development which can be distinguished by their structural properties. Those properties may not be the same as Piaget has suggested for each stage, although they are unlikely to be entirely independent of Piaget's characterizations. What is important is that some means be found of specifying structural stage descriptions which can be investigated directly by experimental means. This is not to say, of course, that research should be confined to the study of structure, but there is a problem of specifying structural properties and their consequences; this book is oriented to this problem.

It has often been pointed out that the structures postulated by Piaget are often related to evidence only in a very indirect way. His observations illustrate his theories, and are consistent with them, but do not demonstrate their validity. Furthermore, it has often been difficult to determine just what Piaget's formulations would mean in concrete experimental terms. It is difficult to define them operationally. The apparent stalemate in controversy in the area is probably traceable to this fact. The chapters which comprise this book arise from a sustained effort over about ten years to find research paradigms which capture the essence of structural stage descriptions, which were undoubtedly inspired by Piaget but are certainly not constrained by his views.

There are four stages of cognitive development, defined by Piaget, which are sufficiently well supported by evidence to be regarded as meaningful and which will serve as the stepping-off point for what follows. The stages are as follows.

The sensori-motor stage lasts from birth until about $1\frac{1}{2}$ to 2 years of age. Originally defined by Piaget (1953a, 1954b), this is the stage in which sensori-motor performances become progressively structured into functional systems which form the building blocks of later cognitive activity. The sensori-motor child's behaviour, while organized, is not cognitive since it depends on responding to the stimulus as presented, rather than as represented or interpreted by cognitive activity. Thus sensori-motor behaviour lacks the representational component of true cognition (Piaget, 1947).

The representational processes are thought by Piaget to develop through the internalization of action schemes. However, the schemes cannot represent anything until they are sufficiently organized to reflect the structure of the thing to be represented. An example is the concept of the permanent object, said by Piaget to develop late in the second year of life. Recognition of the permanence of an object depends on being able to distinguish changes in position from changes in state. That is, if an object disappears momentarily from view, it may have ceased to exist (changed state) or it may simply have changed position relative to the observer (changed position). Only in the latter case is it permanent. In order to know which is which, the observer must have a coherent representation of spatial displacements. For instance, if I see an object disappear from view going from left to right at a certain speed, then to make it reappear again I should turn further to the right. If I do this and the object appears, it has only changed position. On the other hand, if the object does not occupy any position in space which could have resulted from movements it has undergone, then it must have changed state or ceased to exist. Only if the observer can represent to himself what these movements are, and the positions which can result from them, can he determine whether the resulting change is one of position or of state.

Piaget (1954b) has traced the development of a child's ability to represent spatial displacements in this way. He finds that in the first two stages, occupying roughly the first four months, the child makes no attempt to recover vanished objects, which Piaget interprets to mean that the child cannot represent the actions needed to recover the object. He then infers that, since the child cannot represent the actions needed to cancel the displacement which the object has undergone, the child cannot know that the object is permanent. Notice that this observation is consistent with Piaget's view that the infant does not have the concept of the permanent object at this stage, but it does not really provide confirmatory evidence for that view.

The child's elaboration of spatial displacement then develops through four further stages. At the next, he can retrieve objects but is limited to extending ongoing movements. At the fourth stage he can retrieve an object which he has just seen hidden, but is led into error if he sees an object hidden several times at one place and then once at a new place. He tends to search for it at the former place. At the fifth stage, he can handle all visible displacements, but makes errors with invisible displacements. This failure, too, is overcome in the sixth stage. Piaget thus infers that the child has the object concept at this stage.

The preoperational stage lasts from two to about six or seven years and is characterized by the rapid development of representational processes. There are six representational or 'semiotic' functions which Piaget (Piaget and Inhelder, 1969) considers to develop during the preoperational period: imitation, play, drawing, mental image, memory, and language. The child at this stage is restricted to recognizing functional relations, has difficulty in distinguishing the general from the particular, and his reasoning is precausal and prelogical. Much of preoperational behaviour is defined by absence of concrete operational achievements like seriation, classification, conservation, transitivity, and spatial and geometrical concepts. An experiment which illustrates the typical abilities and inabilities of the preoperational child uses a weight hung from a string which passes around a pulley to the horizontal plane where it is attached to a spring. As the weight is increased the spring stretches, so the horizontal length of the string shortens while the vertical length increases. The preoperational child recognizes this functional relation between the length of the horizontal string and the length of the vertical string. What he does not realize, however, is that the amount which is subtracted from the horizontal string is necessarily added to the vertical string. He thinks the string would be more affected in the vertical plane, where the weight is acting, which is an intuitively reasonable but logically unreasonable expectation. Hence the latter period of the preoperational stage is referred to as *the intuitive stage*. The performance is tantamount to failure to conserve the length of the string or to recognize that its total length is equal to the sum of the horizontal and vertical lengths.

The concrete operational stage, which has traditionally been thought to last from about seven to eleven years of age, is characterized by the ability to reason logically with respect to concrete things. It is as if the child at this age can apply simple logic in a situation where the kind of logic required is apparent, but cannot systematically determine what logic is needed or choose from two or more alternative logical approaches. A good example arises from performance in transitivity tasks where a concrete operational child presented with a sequence like 'Mary is better than Wendy and Wendy is better than Jane' correctly concludes that 'Mary is best and Jane is worst', something which the preoperational child would fail to do. However, given the problem in the form 'Wendy is better than Jane and Wendy is worse than Mary', the same concrete operational child tends to answer that 'Jane is best, Mary is worst, and Wendy is in between'. The concrete operational child evidently does not recognize that the sequence is not in an appropriate form to apply transitivity and/or is unable to transform it into the appropriate form. He then resorts to processing the question as asked. For an account of the process by which he arrives at the answer he does, see Johnson-Laird (1972).

The transition from preoperations to concrete operations is a period of rapid cognitive growth, with many of the basic tools of reasoning such as classification, seriation, conservation, and transitivity being acquired. Piaget considers concrete operations to be the earliest emergence of pure thought.

The formal operational stage begins, according to Piaget, at about eleven years and heralds the ability to reason about pure possibilities, test hypotheses, and generally to exhibit cognitive behaviour which is qualitatively similar to that of an adult. If we say that at the concrete operational stage the child is able to produce logical thought, then at the formal stage he is able to produce logical thought which is itself about thought. He can logically manipulate his own cognitive processes as well as use his cognitive processes to manipulate concrete things. Thus, whereas at the concrete stage his thought reflects the elementary constraints of reality, at the formal stage the person is able to see reality as a reflection of the logical constraints in his own thoughts.

OTHER CONTRIBUTIONS TO COGNITIVE DEVELOPMENT

While Piaget's work and that of his followers form the largest single body of work in the area, no account of cognitive development can justifiably be based on this approach alone. The other approaches which have been the most significant contributors to the data base in the area will be briefly outlined in this section. There will be no attempt to be comprehensive, but the references given will be sufficient to enable any approach to be followed up as desired.

Bruner (1964) and Bruner, Olver, and Greenfield (1966) have described three stages: the *enactive*, which corresponds roughly to Piaget's sensori-motor stage, the *iconic*, which corresponds to Piaget's preoperational stage, and the *symbolic*, the onset of which seems to coincide with Piaget's concrete operational stage. The use of the term 'iconic' seems particularly fortunate in some ways, since many of the characteristics of the preoperational stage are what we would expect to be associated with the relatively rigid, particularistic and non-general representations which would result from imaginal processes. The symbolic stage is clearly in conflict with Piaget's characterization of behaviour after five, and has been correspondingly more controversial. It implies that it is the availability of symbolic processes *per se*, rather than the organizational structure or what Piaget would call the operational character of symbolic processes, which is responsible for cognitive growth at that point. This raises the complex and long-standing problem of whether conceptual development depends on language development, or vice versa, or whether some other relationship exists. This problem is taken up by Keats and Keats in Chapters 4 and 5.

Luria's (1961, 1967) account of cognitive development in terms of a developing regulatory role of speech is highly relevant here, and is also dealt with in Chapters 4 and 5 as well as in two very lucid but somewhat polemical articles by Wozniak (1972) and Bronckart (1973). In effect, Luria contends that behaviour is brought under the control of verbal processes by about the age of five, corresponding in rough terms to the onset of Piaget's concrete operational stage.

Work on reversal and non-reversal concept shifts has been quite voluminous since Kendler and Kendler (1962) wrote the first theoretical account of the phenomenon. Their original contention that preschoolers do not mediate whereas children over five do is probably false, in view of evidence of mediational processes in intradimensional shifts below the age of five (Brown and Scott, 1972). Furthermore, it is unlikely that the mediational hypothesis, at least in its original form, can account for the phenomenon (Cole, 1973; Cole and Medin, 1973; Halford, 1969a; Kendler, Kendler and Ward, 1972; Wolff, 1967). Nowadays it is more usual to see reversal shifts as a tendency to treat stimuli as attributes on a dimension, and indeed the tendency to make reversal shifts correlates with seriation of stimuli on the same dimension (Johnson and White, 1967; White and Johnson, 1968).

The appearance of far transposition in transfer of discrimination learning after the age of five, reported by Kuenne (1946) and Alberts and Ehrenfreund (1951), possibly also suggests that children respond to stimuli in terms of their relative position on a dimension, rather than in terms of their absolute values. However, Stevenson (1970) has argued that there is more evidence against this effect than for it. It remains to be seen whether this widely accepted finding can be demonstrated in a stable fashion.

White (1965) reports two experiments on discrimination learning which show that variation in the stimulus field is disruptive to discrimination learning by pre-five year olds, but not for older children. It seems that the older children can focus on the invariant features in a field of variance whereas the preschoolers cannot.

White (1965) reviews some twenty-one qualitatively different performances which show a change between the ages of five and seven years. White suggests that this period is characterized by a change from an associative to a cognitive mode of performance, reflecting a tendency for more verbal representation, increased recognition of the invariant or stable features of a situation, increased ability to string together stimulus–response–consequence events to allow inference and prediction, and increased reliance on distance receptors rather than proximal receptors. White's article represents an important landmark in the progress of cognitive developmental psychology, because it demonstrates a convergence of many lines of research, theoretically and methodologically independent of one another, on a single phenomenon. This phenomenon is a stage transition of immense scope which occurs at an age which corresponds roughly to the age of onset of Piaget's concrete operational stage, which consequently should be seen as part of a wider transition. Since White's paper, still more transitions have been discovered in somewhat the same age range, using yet more varied experimental approaches.

One such discovery is the emergence of synthesizing behaviour, demonstrated by Farnham-Diggory (1972). Young children are taught logographs, i.e. graphic symbols representing words, and are then asked to act out short sentences. However, preschool children frequently tend to act out the meaning of each logograph separately, instead of synthesizing them into a sentence. For instance, given the logographs for 'jump', 'over', and 'block', he jumps in the air, makes a sign for over, and points to the block. It seems that the ability to synthesize elements into a single idea is not yet present, a fact which, if confirmed by future research, could have profound implications for our understanding of what happens to a child's cognitive processes between the ages of five and seven years.

In the current decade, memory development has come into existence as a field of study (Belmont and Butterfield, 1969; Flavell, 1970, 1971b; Hagen, 1972; Huttenlocher and Burke, 1976). It is now clear that cognitive strategies for remembering are actively employed in late, but not in early, childhood (see, for instance, Flavell, 1971b, Kreutzer, Leonard, and Flavell, 1975), and memory apparently comes under cognitive control during the five-to-seven shift.

This convergence of a number of distinct approaches on the five-to-seven shift provides powerful confirmation that at least one of Piaget's stage transitions, from preoperational to concrete operational thought, is not an artifact of Piaget's methods. On the other hand, the additional data provided suggest that Piaget's theory, at least in its present form, is inadequate to encompass all that is known about the shift. The confidence that comes from seeing the convergence provides an incentive to push on towards an integrated theory. On the other hand, granted that we will no longer use Piaget's specific theory as our sole research guide, it is necessary to examine the structuralist approach in more general terms to see what its implications are for the aims and methods of future research.

STRUCTURALISM

Structuralism went out of favour in Western psychology with the demise of the Gestalt school and the rise of neo-behaviourism. There appears now to be a resurgence of interest in this approach, one sign of which is the recent volume by Riegel and Rosenwald (1975). A criterial attribute of the structural approach is a commitment to using structure as an explanatory concept. That is, structure is not something which emerges as a result of other processes but is a primitive datum in itself. This is a feature which distinguishes Piaget's work from, say, the reinterpretations of it by Bruner (1964) or Berlyne (1965). Berlyne attempted to show that the structural properties of cognitive developmental processes were the result of response reinforcement, and generalization phenomena. Leaving aside the question of whether this attempt was successful or not, the fact that it was considered worth attempting attests to a point of view which is at variance with structuralism as such.

Beyond its explanatory role, structuralism also implies a commitment to a world view which is less mechanistic and deterministic than in most alternative approaches to science. There is also a tendency to look for complex interactions rather than for discrete functional relations which can be combined additively, and a belief that structure is a dynamic process which is capable of spontaneous growth towards higher levels of functioning. The concept of stability of and equilibrium in systems is another which appears to be of much more concern to structuralist than to alternative approaches. Overton (1975) also mentions the concept of 'equifinality', i.e. ' . . . the fact that the same end state or goal may be attained despite different initial conditions and different routes' (p. 81). This would imply that, for instance, the question of which training procedure would best promote the transition between Piagetian stages may have no solution. This view would probably occasion little surprise among structuralists, and yet to neo-behaviourists it would be virtually self-evident that some such solution must exist and that research should attempt to find it. It is noticeable that studies which compared the efficiency of two or more training procedures have been more popular among neo-behaviourists than among structuralists, and Piaget has referred to the search for the optimal procedure as ' . . . the American question'. Where structuralists have conducted training studies, as in some of the chapters of this book (see Chapters 3, 5, and 8), they have been more concerned to study cognitive growth as an emergent property of cognitive structures. Sheppard (Chapter 3), for instance, reports one of the relatively few studies in the literature which attempts to create a cognitive structure as a means of promoting a stage transition.

Piaget (1970c) defines structure as a system of transformations which involve laws, and states that structuralism implies ' . . . an ideal . . . of intrinsic intelligibility supported by the postulate that structures are self-sufficient . . . ' (pp. 4–5). Thus he appears to regard structures as some sort of dynamic, self-regulating systems. While there is an idiosyncratic element in Piaget's use of this term, his approach is broadly consistent with the structural school as a whole.

THE STRUCTURAL DESCRIPTION OF STAGES

The essence of the structural approach to cognitive development is the attempt to find definable structural characteristics which differ from stage to stage. The problem is that it has never been altogether clear what this means. In order to explicate the approach, we will first outline briefly Piaget's stage descriptions, then compare these with alternative approaches, and finally try to define the structural descriptions by contrast with the others. In this chapter we will avoid the details of theories and concentrate on trying to pinpoint the essence of the formulations.

The sensori-motor stage is characterized by the interrelation of action schemes. Piaget insists that the particular structures formed constitute a group, but he defines the term quite widely. For instance, he states (Piaget, 1954b, p.105):

> A group is a closed circle of operations that return to the point of departure through an operation of the group as a whole. In this respect it is certain that from the observer's point of view every coordinated activity of the subject will involve the existence of displacement groups.

This raises the question of what a group is. The concept is dealt with in more detail by Sheppard in Chapter 3, and for the purposes of our present argument we only need to get the flavour of the idea. We will take the cyclic three-group and illustrate it by means of a concrete example. First, we define three movements around the triangle in Figure 1.1. It is more usual to define the triangle as moving relative to the observer, but it will suit our purposes better in this book to regard the triangle as fixed and then define movements around it. The three movements are: N, a null movement, meaning to stay at the same place; C, a clockwise movement meaning to go from a to b, b to c, or c to a; A, an anticlockwise movement meaning to go from a to c, c to b, or b to a. The three movements are defined in Table 1.1: that is N is shown as a movement from a to a, etc., C is shown as a movement from a to b, etc.

Second, consider what happens if we perform one movement followed by another. If, for instance, we perform C followed by A ($A \circ C$), the result would be equivalent to performing N, which we can write as $A \circ C \to N$. If, on the other hand, we performed N followed by A, the result would be equivalent to ($A \circ N \to A$). There are nine possible combinations of two movements, each of which is equivalent to a single movement. These are shown in Table 1.2, and the resulting system is the cyclic three-group. In common with every other group, it has four properties:

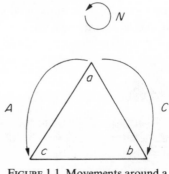

FIGURE 1.1 Movements around a
triangle

TABLE 1.1. Movements from vertex to
vertex around a triangle

| | | Movements | | |
		N	C	A
	a	*a*	*b*	*c*
Initial				
place	*b*	*b*	*c*	*a*
	c	*c*	*a*	*b*

Resulting place

(1) *Closure* Any two elements in the group are equivalent to one and only one element which is also in the group.

(2) *Identity* An identity element is an element which, combined with any element in the group, produces an element which is equivalent to that other element. Thus element N is the identity in Table 1.2, since $N \circ N \to N$, $N \circ C \to C$, $A \circ N \to A$, etc.

(3) *Inverse* Every element has an inverse element, i.e. an element which, when combined with that element, produces a result equivalent to the identity element (e.g. A is the inverse of C because $A \circ C \to N$).

(4) *Associativity* In effect this property means that the order of combination of the elements does not affect the end result; e.g. $(A \circ N) \circ C = A \circ (N \circ C) = N$.

The inverse property is the one which Piaget interprets as reversibility. Where the elements of a group are interpreted as movements or displacements, then the inverse of any element is the element which cancels or reverses that element, so any element and its inverse are equivalent to movements in opposite directions.

A group is an abstract mathematical concept, defined by the relations between the elements. The cyclic three-group, for instance, is defined by the structure shown in Table 1.2, and its status as a group is independent of the specific elements used. Any concrete embodiment of the group is merely a

TABLE 1.2. Cyclic three-group, interpreted
as movements around an equilateral triangle,
as shown in Table 1.1 and Figure 1.1

∘	N	C	A
N	N	C	A
C	C	A	N
A	A	N	C

physical system whose properties happen to correspond to the group. When we choose a particular concrete example which corresponds to a specific group, we are said to 'interpret' the group as that example.

Despite the amount of attention paid to Piaget's work on the sensori-motor child in the recent research literature, his observations of the child's understanding of the group of displacements have received scant notice. Actually, Piaget (1954b) describes six stages of development of the group of spatial displacements in Chapter 2 of his book, but it is more usual to consider Chapter 1 which deals with the object concept. One example from stage 5 is interesting in this connection. He describes (observation 117) how a child walking in the garden discovers that a single path across the diagonal of a square is equivalent to two paths around the sides; i.e. given a set of paths in the garden which form a square $ABCD$, then the path AC is equivalent to the two paths AB and BC (closure). He also recognizes that the movement around the paths AB and BC can be cancelled by walking back along CD and DA (inverse).

The essence of the sensori-motor stage, then, is that it consists of actions which become structured into systems which have the properties of a group. The object concept is considered by Piaget to emerge from this process of structuring into a group. The reason is that all displacements in space form a group (see Chapter 6) and so the child needs to be able to represent the group structure of spatial displacements to distinguish changes of position from changes of state, which, as was explained earlier, is essential to recognition of the permanence of objects.

The second main property of the sensori-motor stage is essentially a non-structural one. It is that this stage is devoid of representational processes. In this respect it contrasts with all the later stages. In contrast to some other theorists such as Bruner (1964), the transition from the sensori-motor stage to the next stage is the only time where Piaget distinguishes between stages on the basis of the presence or absence of representational processes.

The preoperational stage is characterized by the development of representational processes, and the structure of these processes is more primitive than the structure of sensori-motor performance. The structures attained in the earlier stage are retained in sensori-motor performances, but it is not until the formal operational stage that symbolic processes attain the same level of structure as sensori-motor processes have attained by the age of two years.

Specifically, the structure of the preoperational stage is considered by Piaget to be function logic (Piaget and coauthors, 1968). Piaget considers that this function logic differs from the operations which characterize the concrete operational stage in that the former lack reversibility. This is consistent with the priority given by Piaget to the concept to reversibility in all his accounts of cognitive processes, but mathematically there seems to be no reason why functions and operations should be distinguished on this criterion. Operations are not necessarily reversible and functions are not necessarily irreversible.

We will examine the mathematical nature of functions so that they may be contrasted with operations when these are considered in the next section.

A function is a principle or rule which assigns every member of one set to a member of another set. (For a more formal definition, see Ficken, 1967.) The term 'set' simply refers to a collection, and includes a collection of numbers. We will use the task involving a string passing over a pulley with a weight on the end, discussed earlier in relation to the preoperational stage, as an example. The vertical and horizontal components of the string can each take on various values. We will call all the values of the vertical string, set V, and all the values of the horizontal string, set H. Now, knowing that H is a function of V means knowing that for every value of V there is one and only one value of H. This information would be sufficient to allow recognition of the covariation between the vertical and horizontal components of the string. Notice that such a functional relation tells us nothing about the overall length of the string. In fact, such a function could easily exist even if the overall length of the string varied, as would occur if it were made of rubber. To relate V and H to the total length of the string, a binary operation would be required, as we will see in the next section.

The concrete operational stage is defined by Piaget in terms of the presence of what he calls 'groupings', which are structures possessing some but not all of the properties of groups (Piaget, 1953b). The grouping concept has a controversial history and is probably the most complex of all Piaget's notions; it is dealt with at length by Sheppard in Chapter 2. However, Piaget also considers the concrete operational stage to be the beginning of genuine thought which, for Piaget, means that it is the beginning of operations. Piaget's definition of an operation (e.g. Piaget, 1950) is that it is an internalized action which is reversible and governed by laws which apply to the system as a whole.

The process of adding one number to another in thought would be a characteristic example. It is an action which is internalized in the sense that it *could* take place overtly but *actually* takes place internally. For instance, if I want to add 4 to 3, I could take a collection of three marbles, physically add four more, and then determine the result, but in practice I would represent the process internally. Reversibility would imply that if I recognize that $3 + 4 = 7$, then I would recognize that $7 - 4 = 3$.

Once again we find that Piaget's definition of a concept is not altogether consistent with the mathematical definition of it. Mathematically, an operation is not an action but a rule for associating numbers to other numbers. The action of adding one number to another is more akin to what systems theorists call an 'operator', i.e. something which changes a system from one state to another.

A binary operation is a principle or rule which assigns two numbers to another. For instance, the operation of arithmetical addition is a set of assignments or *mappings* of the form $(6, 3) \rightarrow 9$; $(2, 0) \rightarrow 2$, etc. Generally, an operation is a set of ordered pairs of elements in a set mapped into single elements in the set. The concept is illustrated in more detail by Sheppard in Chapter 3.

Applying this concept to the earlier example of the string going around the pulley, we can see that each value of V, combined with each value of H, can be assigned to or *mapped into* a single value S, which represents the length of the string. Of course, in the particular example chosen, every pair of values of H and V would be mapped into the *same* value of S, which is another way of saying that $H + V$ is a constant, or the length of the string is conserved. We can now see, why the preoperational child, being able to represent the process only in terms of functional relations, would be unable to conserve the length of the string, but the concrete operational child, being able to represent the more complex binary operational relations, would be able to conserve the length of the string.

The formal operational stage depends, for Piaget, on the group and the lattice. Formal operations are virtually operations on operations (Inhelder and Piaget, 1958). Piaget does not have arithmetical operations in mind so much as logical operations, of which the most common examples are such things as conjunction, disjunction, implication, and the like. The conjunction of two things, A and B, is anything which includes A and B, and is written $A \cdot B$. Thus the conjunction of things which are red and triangular is all the things which are red triangles. The disjunction of A and $B (A v B)$ is all the things which are either A or B. Thus the disjunction of red and triangle is all triangles, all red things, and all things which are both red and triangle. The implication, A implies B $(A \supset B)$, means that whenever A occurs B occurs also. These and other logical operations are dealt with by Seggie in Chapter 11.

Piaget is not referring to these concepts as they exist in logic, but regards them as operations in thought; i.e. they are part of the person's mental processes. Probably the most profound problem posed by this approach is to determine whether a person has such an operation in his mental repertoire. As was pointed out earlier, Piaget does not attempt to devise objective methods to determine whether a child has these operations, but attempts to 'diagnose' them from unstructured interview-type studies. The result is data which are consistent with the hypothesis that the child has these mental operations but do not actually demonstrate that he does.

It so happens that each logical operation of this kind is a particular set of contingencies between events, which can be summarized in a form which is called a *truth table*. Actually, the whole approach used in this book depends on finding sets of contingencies between events or situations which are equivalent to the hypothetical thought processes and systems which it is desired to investigate. The subject is then tested to determine whether he can process that set of contingencies. Because the truth table is an example of a structure which is important to this approach, it is worth while to consider carefully what it is. The truth tables for conjunction, disjunction, and implication are shown in Table 1.3.

On the left are shown the two variables, A and B. They are variables because they have two possible values, present or absent (corresponding to true or

TABLE 1.3. Truth tables for conjunction (A and B) disjunction (A or B) and implication (A implies B)

A	B	Conjunction $A \cdot B$	Disjunction $A \lor B$	Implication $A \supset B$
1	1	1	1	1
1	0	0	1	0
0	1	0	1	1
0	0	0	0	1

false). Presence of an attribute is signified by 1, absence by 0. All four combinations of presence and absence of A and B are shown. The next column shows whether each combination of values of A and B is consistent with the concept of conjunction. For instance, the first row shows that when A and B are both present, A and $B(A \cdot B)$ is true, as also are $A \lor B$ and $A \supset B$. In the second row, when A is present but B is not, then $A \cdot B$ is not true, but A or $B(A \lor B)$ is true. In the same case, $A \supset B$ is not true, because if A is present but not B, then it cannot be true that A implies B. Considering now the last row, where A and B are both absent, both conjunction and disjunction are both false, but implication is true because this case is consistent with the proposition that A implies B.

Notice that each concept in the truth table is a binary operation in that values of two variables are mapped into a value of another variable. Thus Table 1.3 in effect defines three distinct operations. Actually sixteen such operations can be defined by taking all possible assignments of this kind; these are the sixteen binary operations of propositional logic, which Piaget makes the basic building blocks of formal operations. These sixteen operations are spelled out by Seggie in Chapter 11.

However, our concern at the moment is with what we might call 'operations on these operations'. That is, we can take each of the binary operations in Table 1.3 and negate or invert it, or perform some other transformations on it. Three examples of this are shown in Table 1.4.

The first is an identity or null transformation (I) which preserves the original operation. The next is called the inverse (N), which negates each operation; e.g. it turns A and B into *not A and B*, i.e. not A or not B. The reciprocal (R) reverses the operation in a different way, by inverting the individual terms, so that $R(A \cdot B)$ becomes $\bar{A} \cdot \bar{B}$. The fourth transformation is actually the inverse of the reciprocal, and converts $A \cdot B$ into $A \lor B$, etc. Actually there is a simple rule for each transformation: for the inverse, replace all the 1s in the truth table with 0s, and vice versa; the pattern of 1s and 0s for the reciprocal is a mirror image of the pattern for the original operation, and the correlate

TABLE 1.4. Four transformations which can be performed on the three operations in Table 1.3. The negation sign should be read as 'not', i.e. $\bar{A}$ is read as 'not A'

	A	B	$A \cdot B$	$A \vee B$	$A \supset B$
Identity (I) (original operation)	1	1	1	1	1
	1	0	0	1	0
	0	1	0	1	1
	0	0	0	0	1
Inverse (N)			$\bar{A} \vee \bar{B}$	$\bar{A} \cdot \bar{B}$	$A \cdot \bar{B}$
	1	1	0	0	0
	1	0	1	0	1
	0	1	1	0	0
	0	0	1	1	0
Reciprocal (R)			$\bar{A} \cdot \bar{B}$	$\bar{A} \vee \bar{B}$	$B \supset A$
	1	1	0	0	1
	1	0	0	1	1
	0	1	0	1	0
	0	0	1	1	1
Correlate (C)			$A \vee B$	$A \cdot B$	$B \cdot \bar{A}$
	1	1	1	1	0
	1	0	1	0	0
	0	1	1	0	1
	0	0	0	0	0

can be found by simply taking the inverse of the reciprocal. These rules hold for all the sixteen binary operations, and not just those illustrated here.

Having defined four transformations on logical operations, we now want to determine what happens if we perform one transformation followed by another. We already know that if we perform N followed by R the result is equivalent to performing C. The results of all possible cases where one transformation is performed following another is shown in Table 1.5. This is the group which Piaget calls the *INRC* group. Mathematically, it is called the Klein group. Quite obviously, we have arrived at it by a similar line of argument to that which led us to the three-group in Table 1.2. There is, however, one important difference, and it is exactly analogous to the difference between sensori-motor and formal operational performance. We found the three-group by defining combinations of actual physical actions, but we found the *INRC* group by defining combinations of transformations on operations which, if interpreted psychologically, are transformations of thoughts. This is not to say, of course, that the three-group belongs to the sensori-motor stage and the Klein group to the formal operational stage. As we said before, the group is an abstract concept which is independent of particular interpretations we make of it. Each type of group may appear at any of the four stages, but it will be characterized differently.

Put most generally, the essential structural characteristic of the formal operational stage is the ability to embed logical operations, and other similar structures, in larger systems. We have seen how a set of logical operations can be embedded in a group of transformations. Actually this group is only a subgroup of the group of all possible transformations of the sixteen binary operations (Bart, 1971), but that is not our point at this stage. What is important is that it is possible to define a higher level of structural complexity for formal operations than for the two preceding stages, just as concrete operations were characterized by a more complex structure (the binary operation) than that which characterized the preoperational stage (the functional relation).

Summary of the theoretical stage descriptions

The sensori-motor stage is characterized by a group structure, but it is a

TABLE 1.5. The *INRC* (Klein) Group

	I	N	R	C
I	I	N	R	C
N	N	I	C	R
R	R	C	I	N
C	C	R	N	I

structure of action schemes and not a structure of representational or symbolic processes. At the preoperational stage symbolic processes are structured as functional relations, so that an element in one set is assigned to an element in another set, thus: $a \rightarrow b$. At the concrete operational stage symbolic processes have an operational structure which we have interpreted in terms of binary operations, i.e. assignment rules or mappings of the form $(a, b) \rightarrow c$. Formal operations, on the other hand, are characterized by systems composed of compositions of binary operations. Actually, compositions of binary operations can be defined as ternary operations, so that formal operational structures would be equivalent to mappings of the form $(a, b, c) \rightarrow d$.

ALTERNATIVES TO STRUCTURAL STAGE DESCRIPTIONS

Language is probably the most widely favoured alternative to Piaget's stage descriptions. Bruner (1964) was probably the first to propose that the stages should be reinterpreted in terms of type of representational processes rather than structure. In effect this proposal is tantamount to arguing that the symbolic processes characteristic of each stage should be distinguished by the nature of their elements, rather than the structural relations among elements. However, the theories of Luria, mentioned earlier, also hold that, while symbolic processes are not necessarily all linguistic, a linguistic model describes the basic rules of functioning of symbolic processes. The problem of how language relates to cognitive development is an important and complex one, which is taken up by Keats and Keats in Chapters 4 and 5.

Attention has been proposed as a mechanism mediating cognitive growth, mainly in the form of the hypothesis that young children either attend to irrelevant attributes or are misled by the salient stimulus in the situation (Gelman, 1969; Wallach, Wall, and Anderson, 1967). However, recent theories have tended to concentrate more on the distribution of attention (Pick and Frankel, 1973).

Memory has been proposed as a factor which limits the performance of preoperational children, making it appear that they are less logically competent than they are. The main exponents of this view have been Bryant and Trabasso (1971), who have attempted to show that preoperational children can exhibit transitivity if they are given sufficient training to enable them to retain the relevant information. However, the validity of Bryant and Trabasso's experiment has been challenged by De Boysson-Bardies and O'Regan (1973) and by Halford and Galloway (1977).

Mediation, mainly in the sense of mediating responses, has been used to account for the development of reversal shifts, (Kendler and Kendler, 1962) and also for memory strategies (Flavell, 1970). A mediator in this sense is really a representational process which depends on covert responses, and would include such things as attending to the relevant stimulus or stimulus dimension, naming the relevant stimulus and rehearsing, coding or clustering the to-be-remembered stimulus, etc. The hypothesis is that young children either do not produce the appropriate mediators (e.g. do not rehearse) or do not link them to the final performance (e.g. young children can rehearse but do not recognize when they should do so).

Past learning has been explicitly invoked as an explanation of cognitive development in cumulative learning theories such as that of Gagne (1968), who proposed that children would learn rules for determining volume and thereby come to conserve quantity. However, the rule learning approach has been applied to training Piagetian concepts (e.g. Beilin, 1965) and to a wide variety of cognitive phenomena (Scandura, 1970, 1973). In its most basic form the learning approach holds that the absence of a cognitive process in children of any given age is a reflection of lack of appropriate learning experiences.

Information processing approaches all have in common the hypothesis that a child's cognitive performance reflects the routines, programmes, or systems which he has for processing information. For instance, Simon (1972) accounts for Farnham-Diggory's logograph task performances by postulating two different routines for processing the information. The more primitive routine has three elements: find the next logograph and if there is none, stop; retrieve its meaning; execute the meaning. The more sophisticated routine has the following five elements: (1) find the next logograph and if there is none, go to (2); retrieve its meaning; modify the revised meaning; go to 1; (2) execute the meaning; stop.

The first routine would result in information being retrieved from each logograph independently of the others, and would therefore match the behaviour of the preschool children. The second routine would modify the meaning of previous logographs by adding the meaning of each successive logograph to the total picture. Thus the logograph sentence 'jump over block' mentioned earlier would be read as first 'jump', then 'jump over', and then as 'jump over block', with execution being postponed until all logographs had been read and their meanings added to the meaning of the whole sentence. The output would match the way older children and adults would read such sentences.

The most comprehensive attempt to account for a single feature of cognitive development by means of information processing models is that of Baylor, Gascon, and associates (Baylor and Gascon, 1974; Baylor and coauthors, 1973). They have developed a computer program which perfectly reproduces weight seriation protocols of individual subjects at each of three stages of development. Again, the stages can be distinguished by different information processing routines.

In a similar way Klahr and Wallace (1970, 1973) have attempted to account for classificatory behaviour and Klahr (1973) has done the same thing for conservation, but in both cases without actually running the proposed models on a computer. Both models are based on routines for quantification. Klahr and Wallace account for the acquisition of the inclusion concept in the following way: given three sets, B, A, and A', such that $A + A' = B$, then the more primitive routine counts A first and then B, but without counting any item twice. Thus, when it counts B it in effect excludes all of A, so that it arrives at a quantity for B which is equal to A'. We might say that this routine fails to conserve the set B, and ends up with two mutually disjoined sets A and A'. It consequently outputs the response that $A > B$, an incorrect response which matches the performance of preoperational children. It is well worth comparing this idea with Sheppard's approach to teaching the inclusion concept in Chapter 3. The more sophisticated routine in Klahr and Wallace's model quantifies A first and then returns the elements to the pool to be counted before quantifying B, so that B is conserved. It concludes, correctly, that $B > A$. Klahr's (1973) model of conservation acquisition is based on the idea that children observe transformations of small collections and gradually encode information amounting to a rule that the quantity remains unchanged. This rule is then generalized to larger collections. The implication is that children first learn to conserve with small numbers of objects, but it is doubtful whether this hypothesis, at least in a strong form, is consistent with the data.

However, the purpose of this section is not to evaluate models as such but to pinpoint basic differences between the structuralist and alternative approaches. Perhaps the most striking way in which the information processing approach contrasts with structuralism is in the degree of pragmatism shown. The information processing approach frequently makes no assumptions about underlying psychological processes, but postulates only those processes which are necessary to generate the observed performances. Of course, information processing approaches differ among themselves as much as do structuralist approaches, and the above generalization would be much more true of Baylor and his associates approach than, say, Klahr's. On the other hand, the structuralist and information processing approaches have a very important feature in common. This is that both are concerned with complex interrelationships between task elements. Furthermore, the information processing approach has the power to represent the sorts of complex concepts which appeal to the structuralists. On the whole, the prospects for a convergence of these two approaches are a good deal brighter than for any other two approaches which exist at present. At the conclusion of this chapter some tentative proposals will be made concerning the way structuralist concepts might be translated into information processing concepts and (by implication) vice versa.

The concept attainment paradigm has probably been the single most influential approach in directing empirical research, and its influence has been no less for the fact that it has more often been adopted implicitly than explicitly. It consists nowadays of a complex web of concepts, and the most lucid account of the basic ideas is that by Haygood and Bourne (1965), although Osgood's (1953) account gives illuminating historical insights. There are two aspects of this paradigm which I believe have been specially important in influencing the course of research in cognitive development: the idea that concept attainment is related to discrimination learning and the idea of conceptual rule learning.

Pared to its barest essentials, the neo-behaviouristic concept attainment paradigm implies that a concept is operationally defined by ability to discriminate instances of a concept from things that are not instances. For example, if I have the concept of a ball, this would mean that I would be able to tell whether any particular object presented to me was a ball or not. Thus there is a correlation between possessing a concept and the ability to discriminate instances of the concept from other things. This is not to say that it is necessarily appropriate to define a concept in this way. For instance, I could be taught to discriminate balls without learning to represent to myself the criterial attributes of a ball. I would then be unable, for instance, to see the similarities and differences between the criterial attributes of a ball and a sphere, or a ball and a wheel. There would be a variety of senses in which I did not understand the basis of the concept which I was discriminating. Alternatively, I might have the concept but fail to make the corresponding discriminations for a variety of reasons such as lack of memory, non-attention to the relevant attributes, etc. For this reason some writers have felt dissatisfaction with this paradigm and have sought alternatives (e.g. Rommetveit, 1960).

Basically, a concept attainment paradigm differs from a discrimination learning paradigm in that the former necessarily includes stimuli which vary on more than one dimension, and there must be more than one stimulus in at least one response category. A near-minimal example is given in Table 1.6.

Three concepts are shown. The first is a simple one-dimensional concept, and amounts to discriminating triangles from circles. In a limited way, the subject can then be said to have acquired the concept 'triangle'. The most essential aspect of the task is that the subject learn to make discriminations along the relevant dimension, shape, and ignore the irrelevant dimensions of size and colour. In the other two concepts, a little more is required because there are two relevant dimensions, shape and size. Two different ways of relating the relevant dimensions to each other are also shown: a conjunctive relationship and a disjunctive one. In Haygood and Bourne's terms, these are two different conceptual rules.

Many investigators have assumed the basic concept attainment paradigm

TABLE 1.6. Example of a very basic concept attainment paradigm

Dimensions			Response categories* for three concepts		
Shape	Size	Colour	Simple	Conjunctive	Disjunctive
Triangle	Large	Red	+	+	+
Triangle	Large	Blue	+	+	+
Triangle	Small	Red	+	−	+
Triangle	Small	Blue	+	−	+
Circle	Large	Red	−	−	+
Circle	Large	Blue	−	−	+
Circle	Small	Red	−	−	−
Circle	Small	Blue	−	−	−

* Positive instances of a concept are indicated by (+), negative instances by (−).

in studies of Piagetian concepts such as conservation. Gelman (1969) entitled her training study: 'Conservation acquisition: A problem of learning to attend to relevant attributes'. Thus the basic assumption is that a child fails to conserve (say) liquid quantity because he ignores the relevant dimension of quantity and attends to the irrelevant dimension of height. Two interesting but not altogether explicit applications of this idea are in studies by Gelman (1972) and Beilin (1965).

This approach has a tempting simplicity. Actually it implies an even greater simplification of the problem than it would seem at first, because it assumes that quantity is something which can simply be recognized. Yet quantity is not an obvious physical dimension in the way that shape, colour, and size are. It seems more likely that quantity is a concept which can only be recognized symbolically. This would raise the question of how the subject develops symbolic processes which permit him to represent a concept like quantity.

FACTORS MILITATING AGAINST A STRUCTURAL APPROACH

Outside of the Piagetian school structuralism has not enjoyed great popularity as an approach. Even within the school there appears to have been more attention to non-structural than to structural aspects of Piaget's theory, i.e. there has been more interest in the behavioural phenomena themselves than in the postulated cognitive structures. This is not necessarily a reflection on the validity of the theory, since the current climate of psychological research makes it difficult for structuralism to flourish. Some of the relevant factors in the situation are as follows.

Behaviourism is rarely espoused explicitly as a doctrine nowadays, and it is no longer taboo to talk about mental processes as distinct from behavioural constructs. Holt (1964) has pointed out how imagery has been readmitted to serious scientific study and Paivio (1975) has chronicled the saga which led to imagery being scientifically indexed as a phenomenon. Nevertheless, many of the old attitudes persist not far beneath the surface, and most psychologists are still not entirely free from a little bit of anxiety every time they have to rely on the concept of symbolic processes. As we saw in the last section, a structural approach to cognitive development is inseparable from the idea that a distinction must be drawn between behaviours mediated by symbolic processes and behaviours not so mediated. Yet psychologists are still reluctant to draw that distinction, as Berlyne (1975) has pointed out. This is in spite of the mass of evidence, first assembled by White (1965) and continuing to accumulate since, that the behaviour of the pre-five-year-old child can be distinguished from older people on this basis.

The modularization of psychological research, by which I mean the now virtually universal practice in the Western world of performing small experiments to be reported in single papers, tends to make the study of large-scale systems difficult. There are, it is true, monumental works which have been compiled over a decade or more by individuals or teams (such as Newell and

Simon's (1972) General Problem Solver) and, of course, there is Piaget's own system, but such enterprises are far from common. The structural approach is more likely to be neglected in these circumstances than any of the alternatives we have discussed.

The study of functional relations, more or less in isolation from the systems of which they are a part, is largely a result of this modularization. Piaget (1970c) suggests that movement from this state of affairs to a study of systems has been an historical trend in physics, implying that eventually it will occur in psychology too. But I think this overlocks the fact that, at least in the English-speaking world, psychology has developed into a professional research enter-prise at a much earlier stage of conceptual development than did physics or biology. The modularization and preoccupation with precise determination of parameters entering into specific functional relations is appropriate enough for a science which has reason to be confident of its paradigms, using the term in the sense of Kuhn (1962). When a science's main task, however, is to try to develop those same paradigms, then such a piecemeal approach may be disadvantageous because it is not conducive to integration. It tends to prevent the sustained effort needed to produce formulations which are consis-tent with a wide data base, which surely must be the *sine qua non* of really worthwhile paradigms.

THE ESSENTIALS OF THE STRUCTURAL APPROACH

From this survey it would seem that the structural approach can be distin-guished from all of the others mentioned because it holds that cognitive develop-ment proceeds by the construction of internal, symbolic representations of constraints between elements of a task, situation, or system. The concern with internal representation is shared by language, mediation, and memory approaches, while the concern with constraint between elements, or structure, is shared with the information processing and concept attainment approaches. However, none of the other approaches is concerned with the structure of representational processes as the structuralist approach is.

This definition would include all approaches to cognitive development which are primarily concerned with a child's ability to recognize constraints in a task situation. The argument advanced by Donaldson (1971) that a pre-condition of inference is the ability to recognize constraints between events is therefore clearly a structural theory. The argument below is an extension of Donaldson's, and is presented here to illustrate the sort of deductions which a structural theory permits and also to give a kind of theorem which will be important in some later chapters.

We want to specify the minimum information needed to draw an inference about a state of affairs, Z, in the absence of sufficient direct information about Z itself. The minimum information we need is information about the constraint between Z and some other state of affairs, Y, together with a state-ment about Y itself. Consider, for instance, a situation where I cannot see whether there are clouds in the sky or not, i.e. where I have insufficient information to determine this state of affairs directly. On the other hand, suppose I know the constraint which exists between clouds and rain. I can express this in terms of combinations of events which do and do not occur: a combination of rain and clouds does occur and a combination of rain and no clouds does not occur. Given the further information that it is raining, I can infer that there are clouds.

Notice that constraint is tantamount to combinations of state of affairs which can occur and combinations which cannot. Thus, having an internal representation of constraints in a situation really means having information in some memory store about those combinations of states of affairs in the situation which can and cannot occur. Thus, if I understand the constraint between rain and clouds, which is to say if I have an internal representation of this constraint, this means that I have information in memory store to the effect that rain occurs with clouds but not without clouds, whereas clouds occur with and without rain. It is obvious that a truth table could be constructed to express this constraint, and if I know this constraint then I have stored information equivalent to the relationships in that table. Thus the elusive term 'cognitive structure' really means nothing more than a data base which expresses those combinations of events which can occur and those which cannot. This could well be a most useful point of contact between structural and information processing approaches to cognition.

It now remains to present a more precise statement of the minimum information for an inference in the absence of adequate direct evidence. We will use the symbol $\bar{Z}$ for *not Z*, and T and F for true and false respectively. We can assign values of truth or falsity to states or combinations of states by using statements of the form $Z \rightarrow T$, etc.

Definition The minimum information needed to infer Z, in the absence of direct information about Z, is one or more statements which assign values of T or F to a combination of Z with another state of affairs Y, together with a statement which assigns values of T or F to Y.

By definition we exclude statements of the form

$$Z \rightarrow T \tag{1.1}$$

since they depend on direct information.

However, given that the following assignments were in memory store:

$$Y Z \rightarrow T$$
$$Y \bar{Z} \rightarrow F \tag{1.2}$$

and given that information is currently available that enables a person to determine

$$Y \rightarrow T \tag{1.3}$$

then the person can infer

$$Z \rightarrow T \qquad (1.4)$$

The assignments in (1.2) are entirely internal to the cognitive processes of the person; (1.3), on the other hand, is information direct from the environment; and (1.4) is an assignment which is made internally.

Recall that a binary operation was defined earlier as a principle or rule which assigns to each pair of values of a set, one and only one value from the same or a different set. That is, where A and B are elements of a set, a binary operation assigns to each pair of elements A and B a single element (AB): $A, B \rightarrow (AB)$. Now notice that a binary operation consists of a set of assignment statements of the same form and complexity as the assignments which must be in store to permit inferential statements. If we define concrete operations as that stage where the subject is able to store information about constraints in the form of binary operational assignments, it would follow that the concrete operational stage would permit inferences. If we define preoperations as that stage where children can store information about constraints in the form of binary relational constraints, i.e. mappings of the form $a \rightarrow b$, then it would follow that children at this stage would be incapable of inferences in the absence of direct evidence.

Notice that the above argument means that a system consisting of relationships of the form $(a, b) \rightarrow c$ can generate a relationship of the form $a \rightarrow b$ (e.g. can generate the inference 'Z is true') Remembering that we suggested earlier that formal operations should be defined as compositions of binary operations, or ternary operations, we can now show how such a system can generate a system at the binary operational level. Suppose the person has in memory storage the following set of assignments:

$$\begin{aligned} a\,b\,c &\rightarrow T \\ a\,b\,\bar{c} &\rightarrow F \\ \bar{a}\,\bar{b}\,c &\rightarrow T \\ \bar{a}\,\bar{b}\,\bar{c} &\rightarrow F \end{aligned} \qquad (1.5)$$

If the following event is observed:

$$c \rightarrow T \qquad (1.6)$$

then the following can be deduced:

$$\begin{aligned} a\,b &\rightarrow T \\ \bar{a}\,\bar{b} &\rightarrow T \end{aligned} \qquad (1.7)$$

Notice that (1.7) is similar to the hypothesis 'either a and b or not a and b'. This is the kind of hypothesis that children generate at the formal operational stage (Inhelder and Piaget, 1958). Thus we are able to deduce that formal operational children can generate hypotheses of this form by defining formal operations as stored information about constraints in the form of assignments of sets of three elements into single elements.

So far this discussion of cognitive structures as internally stored information about constraints has dealt mainly with constraints in the form of truth tables. However, nothing need restrict it to this kind of example, and the group structure shown in Table 1.2 can also be thought of as stored information about assignments of pairs of elements to other elements in the form $(N\,C) \rightarrow C$, $(C\,C) \rightarrow A$, etc.

It might be asked whether such a structure, conceived as stored information of this kind, could have sufficient generality to mediate the kind of reasoning and problem-solving tasks with which cognitive developmental psychologists are concerned. It turns out that, once information is stored about the relationships in any example of such a structure, the same set of relationships can be applied to other examples. Consider, for example, the structure shown in Table 1.2. Here we have a structure in the sense that a set of relationships is specified between the elements N, C, and A. The information in the table is general to any set of elements. Suppose, for instance, that we take three new elements, I, X, and D. It only requires a very small amount of information to fit these new items into the structure. Actually all we need is two assignments, such as $(I\,I) \rightarrow X$ and $(D\,X) \rightarrow X$, and we can deduce the rest of the relationships between I, X, and D. (It will be found that the relationships are those which would apply if D, I, and X are substituted for N, C, and A respectively in Table 1.2). Once we know this, we have applied the information in the table to a new task which has no elements in common with the old task. Thus a set of specified relationships between one set of elements can readily be transferred to another set of elements. All that matters is that information about these relationships be available, and it does not really matter what elements are used to store that information.

Thus generality, or the ability to apply a stored structure or system to new tasks, follows directly from the storage of information about relationships between elements in the structure. It is not necessary to postulate a special set of 'abstract' elements in order to provide for representational processes which are truly general in application and which will permit highly mobile transfer. This problem is taken up again in two different ways in Chapters 6 and 7.

To conclude, we can say that Piaget's theories constitute one part of a broad spectrum of approaches to cognitive development, which we might call a structural approach. We define the structural approach, not in terms of the use of logical or mathematical theories, but as a commitment to investigate whether there are stages of cognitive development which may be distinguished by their structural properties. Furthermore, we will apply this approach to a spectrum of content areas, including the comprehension of history dealt with by Jurd in Chapters 9 and 10. We define psychological structure as information, stored somewhere in the person's memory processes, concerning relationships or constraints between elements of a task or situation. This includes, but is not restricted to, the sort of structures that Piaget postulates. For instance, transitivity would be based on internally stored information or a constraint between the elements '*A* relates to *B*', '*B* relates to *C*', and the element '*A* relates to *C*' (that is $ARB, BRC \rightarrow ARC$).

The challenge for researchers is to develop a research paradigm which enables structural stage description to be studied objectively. Piaget's approach has given a wealth of information and insight, but does not really fulfil this criterion. Many of the alternative approaches are based on objective and highly sophisticated methodologies, but are not structural. If it is to survive, the structural approach needs a methodology which is as objective as the others but which permits genuine, non-superficial study of structure. This book consists of chapters which are quite diverse in their approaches, but are held together by this aim.

2

FROM INTUITIVE THOUGHT TO CONCRETE OPERATIONS

J. L. Sheppard

A general account of the four main stages of cognitive development according to Piaget was given in Chapter 1. The purpose of this chapter is to consider the intuitive period of the preoperational stage and the concrete operational stage in detail.

THE INTUITIVE STAGE

Piaget was impressed by the fact that the child may often make statements without using facts to support them and without seeking proof of their validity (Piaget, 1967, p. 29). The child aged from four to seven years is seen to have difficulty in defining the concepts he uses. Instead of being logical he uses intuition, which is an internalization by means of images and mental experiences (Piaget, 1967, p. 30). He is strongly influenced by perceptual appearances. He is able to internalize actions, but they remain at the level of sensori-motor patterns converted to acts of thought. They do not reach a level whereby they become reversible actions. Reversibility helps lift them from the realm of intuitive thought to that of concrete operations. Instances of reversibility will be given later when we consider specific examples of behaviour.

The preoperational period is seen as a time of organization and preparation. The preparation is for concrete operations.

A number of examples will be given of the thought of the child at the intuitive stage. Those chosen happen to be mathematical concepts which are relevant to primary school experiences, but the range of concepts is much wider. They will be considered under the following topics: number, measurement, sets, and shapes.

Number

It has been repeatedly found that preoperational children lack conservation of number. Conservation is awareness of the invariance of material despite

41507

certain transformations. The following is an example of a test item used in research. The child is presented with two rows of five plastic squares each, arranged in one-to-one correspondence. The tester says: 'Here are two rows of plastic squares. This one can be yours and this one can be mine. Have we both the same number of squares or have you more squares or have I more?' (Both the same.) The tester spreads out one row, or arranges it in a circle, or bunches it up. 'Now do you have more or do I have more or do we both have the same number?' (I have more.) 'Why do you have more?' (Because ...)

The preoperational child is influenced by the perceptual features of the stimulus configuration. He may see that one row is now spread out more, so he believes it must have more squares in it. He does not realize that if the squares were moved back again (i.e. reversing the movement) there would be the same number as before, so there must be the same number now that they are spread out. When he develops the idea of reversibility his thought becomes truly operational.

Conservation of number is usually attained around six or seven years of age, but the level of general intelligence (Goodnow and Bethon, 1966), socio-economic status (de Lacey, 1970), and contact with Western culture (Heron and Simonsson, 1969) have been found to affect the speed of development. Conservation is a fundamental requirement in the understanding of number, for without it a child cannot match sets by pairing to establish equivalent sets and may have difficulty with addition. If the child is learning a number sentence like $3 + 2 = 5$ and forms the union of a disjoint set of three counters and another disjoint set of two, the physical movement of the counters into a new pattern may mean he thinks they change in their number characteristics, and though he may recite '3 plus 2 equals 5' he lacks basic understanding.

Measurement

(a) Capacity

This concept is generally referred to in the research literature by the term 'quantity', referring especially to the amount of material that a vessel contains. At the intuitive stage the child does not realize that the quantity of a liquid remains constant if it is only poured from one container to another of a different shape. If two equivalent beakers have an equal quantity of water in them, the child will usually agree they have 'the same amount', but if one is poured into a tall thin beaker (or a short wide beaker) he says the new beaker contains more (or less) than the original untouched one. Children often say that because it is now higher (in the tall thin beaker) it must have more in it. They are influenced by the perceptual impression, and do not reason logically. They lack conservation of quantity.

(b) Substance, weight, volume

Another aspect of quantity is referred to in the research literature as conservation of 'substance' or of 'mass'. Here the emphasis is on the amount of matter in an object. The most usual material employed in the studies is plasticine, or Play-doh. It can be changed easily from a ball into a snake, a pancake, a cross, etc. Preoperational children believe such transformations change the amount of plasticine.

Substance, weight, and volume are usually conserved in that order at about the ages of seven to eight, nine to ten, and eleven to twelve years respectively (Piaget, 1953b, pp. 16–17). Plasticine may be used in the test of each concept. Two identical balls of plasticine are shown on a balance to weigh the same, and one is then deformed in shape. The preoperational child is asked: 'Is yours heavier, or is mine heavier, or are they the same weight?' He will reply that one is heavier and that they are not the same weight.

Volume conservation is assessed in a number of ways, but a simple version is as follows. The child is presented with two identical beakers and he agrees they contain equal amounts of water. He also agrees that two balls of clay are equal in amount. One ball is put in each beaker and he agrees that the water has risen by the same amount in each. One ball is taken out and deformed; e.g. it is made into a sausage, a pancake, a snake, a cross, or several pieces. The child is asked: 'If I put this back in the glass will the water go up to the same level as the other glass, will it go up higher in here, or will it go up higher in there? Why?' Until he is about eleven or twelve years of age the child fails to see that volume is unchanged (Piaget, 1953b).

(c) Length

A young child is shown two sticks placed parallel and he agrees that they are equal in length. When one stick is moved an inch or more in the direction in which it points, he will say that they are no longer equal in length but one is longer. The kindergarten non-conserver measuring with a handspan or a pencil could easily say that an object is longer than his pencil, when in reality it is equal, if he fails to align the pencil and object accurately. He has as yet little understanding of what measuring length can mean.

(d) Area

Here is an example of a test item to measure conservation of area. Two pieces of equal-sized green cardboard are presented and described as paddocks of green grass. A toy cow is placed on each and the child agrees they would have the same amount to eat. Then five small blocks representing houses are placed on each paddock in such a way that the child is aware each gets an equal number. On one paddock the houses are placed in line, adjacent to one another, but on the other they are scattered haphazardly; this gives an illusion of more grass on the first. The child is asked if the cows still have the same amount to eat or if one has more than the other. The child in the junior section of the primary school who lacks area conservation will be deficient in his

0349749

understanding of the meaning of area, even though he may be able to count the number of squares in a rectangle.

(e) Time

While children might appear to be measuring time satisfactorily by devices like a watch or hourglass, until the age of eight or nine they have difficulty with the duration of time intervals, as illustrated by experiments on simultaneity. In one of these, children are shown two identical glasses and water is poured into them from two tubes above, operated by the one tap. They will agree that the water began flowing into both glasses at the same time and stopped at the same time. But if one of the vessels is changed for one that is tall and thin, thereby causing the water to go higher, they will say the water did not stop flowing at the same time for the two glasses, but that the higher-level one went longer. Most intriguing of all is the finding that if the child is given a stop-watch to measure the time of flow he will maintain his stand, rationalising it by saying that the watch went faster for the event that seemed slow. There is in fact a basic inability to comprehend adequately the measurement of time. There may indeed be a confounding of variables in the child's thinking here. He may think, because of his failure to appreciate conservation of liquid quantity, that the tall thin vessel contains more water than the other, and since the flow is at the same rate then he reasons it must have gone on longer.

Sets

Piaget has extensively studied the development of classificatory skills. He found that the child first groups objects according to a graphic configuration (such as to make a representational design) and then has non-graphic collections, which are transitional to true classification, which comes with the onset of concrete operations at about seven or eight years of age. At this higher stage the child can divide geometrical shapes into two classes using one criterion (e.g. shape), then change to another criterion (e.g. size), and then a third (e.g. colour).

One of the more difficult problems with sets is class inclusion, and a test which was administered to Australian children between the ages of five and eleven years will serve as an illustration. The ten and eleven year olds reached a mean score of only 6 or 7 out of 10. A typical item that was used was the following. The child is presented with a white card on which are pasted coloured pictures of sixteen items of clothing, of which nine are trousers, five dresses, one a coat, and one a hat. The tester says: 'What are all these things?' (Clothes.) 'What are these?' (Pants.) 'And these?' (Dresses.) 'Are there more clothes or more pants?' (More pants.) 'How do you know?' (Because there are nine pants and five clothes.)

Preoperational children have difficulty in comparing the total, higher-order class with the one that is within it. It is as if, having counted the pants on one occasion to find the number of pants, they think one cannot count them again

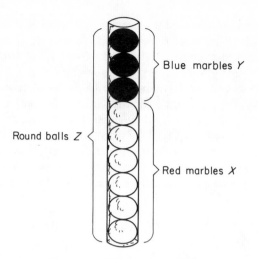

FIGURE 2.1 Marbles in a cylinder

to find the number of clothes. When they are used once, they are used up, so to speak. The child may have no difficulty in seeing the union of sets $A + A' = B$ (pants + dresses, etc. = clothes), but he cannot see that this logically implies the inverse $A = B - A'$ (pants = clothes − dresses, etc.). If he could, he would realize that the whole is conserved and retains its identity, so the whole can be compared with the part as $B > A$ (clothes are more than pants), and the additive composition of classes is achieved. The preoperational child fails, according to Piaget, because of the lack of reversibility in his thinking, and the inability to conceive of the whole and the part simultaneously.

The child's interpretation of fractions will be dependent in part on his handling of class inclusion, for he has to realize that two-thirds, for example, is not as much as or more than the whole. Preoperational children may well argue that there is more in X than in Z (Figure 2.1), because X is greater than Y. Many of the six year olds in first grade were found to do this in the Australian study mentioned earlier. They would do it even when a finger was run along the sides of the cylinder to indicate clearly X and Z. For such children to have a clear understanding that two-thirds is not more than the whole would be difficult. Such problems are compounded by a lack of conservation of quantity and area. In one study (Piaget, Inhelder, and Szeminska, 1960, p. 328) children were required to bisect and trisect one of two equal circular clay pancakes, and preoperational children were found to consider that the sum of the parts did not equal the whole at all. Asked whether they both had the same amount to eat, one child replied that he had more. His answer to 'Why?' was that his was all round and the other was cut up.

Piaget (1952) considers that class inclusion and seriation are necessary and sufficient conditions for a real understanding of number. For this reason a brief consideration of seriation, although it is not an aspect of sets, will be given here.

One of the tests used involved nineteen rods increasing in length by 0·4 cm, from 9 to 16·2 cm. First a staircase is made consisting of ten rods differing by 0·8 cm, and the other nine are to be inserted into the staircase. Three stages are reported by Piaget (1952). At stage I (four years) children can only seriate two, three, or four, but not combine these to get a larger series. At stage II (five to six years) after trial and error the staircase is completed, but the new elements cannot be inserted except by further trial and error. At stage III (seven to eight years) they succeed by selecting the longest or shortest, then by looking for the next closest in length, and so on. They insert the second series because they appreciate the fact that a rod can both be longer than one and shorter than another, thereby indicating what Piaget calls 'operational reversibility'.

Shapes

Historically in mathematics, study has been made of Euclidean, then projective, then topological geometries. Piaget and Inhelder (1956) have found that for the child the order is, instead, the logical one (in that topology is the most inclusive of the three) of topological first (mostly about seven years of age), then projective and Euclidean at about the same time (nine to ten years). Examples illustrating the three areas are given in Table 2.1.

In the topological sphere, it is not until the onset of concrete operations that the child can, for example, tactually discriminate between rectilinear and curvilinear figures kept behind a screen so they are not visible, although he can discriminate an object with a hole in it from one without a hole.

In projective relations, it is not until well into concrete operations that the child can accurately select photographs taken of model mountains seen from several perspectives. For the younger child the viewpoint chosen for the different positions often turns out to be his own.

Euclidean space concepts are illustrated by the finding that understanding of a reference system with horizontal and vertical coordinates is not achieved until the age of nine or ten years. An experiment by Sheppard (1975b) will serve as an example. Children, shown a bottle quarter filled with coloured water and given outline drawings of it tilted in various positions, are required to draw a line indicating the water level, and then to fill in the water. Those at stage I (up to four or five years) show complete lack of the concept of horizontality, and may draw a vague mass, without any line for the level. At stage II (five to seven years) an external reference system is avoided, and the water

TABLE 2.1. Examples of topological, projective, and
Euclidean space

Topological :	proximity, order, enclosure
Projective :	seeing objects from different points of view
Euclidean :	angularity, parallelism, distance

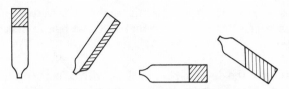

FIGURE 2.2 Some incorrect water level responses

may be drawn parallel to the base, despite the angle of bottle tilt, and may be kept at the base end, so the inverted jar has the water suspended in mid air. With stage III (seven to nine years) correct drawings develop through errors with obliques to immediate success at the age of nine. Examples of some incorrect responses are given in Figure 2.2.

General considerations on the intuitive stage

Three main aspects may be taken to characterize thought at the intuitive stage.

(a) Belief

The child strongly believes in the rightness of many of his errors, and is very resistant to outside pressures which may seek to change him. To him, what he believes *is* logical. The fact that an adult says it is not logical does not impress him. He *knows* he is right. During the course of an experiment in which children were being tested for liquid conservation one girl came to the tester the next day in the school playground and said: 'I was telling my Daddy what I did yesterday, and he said I was all wrong (which she was). He said they had the same amount of water in them and kept pouring them back to show me. I told him I didn't believe him and that if he came to school to see you, you would tell him all about it, so he would know it truly.' The tester had given no indication during testing as to whether the child was right or wrong.

(b) Structure

Prior to concrete operations the child's thoughts are not structured in operational combinatorial systems. Piaget describes this in terms of the theory of the grouping, to be considered later. Only when such systems can be established is there a real order and coherence to the child's cognitions.

(c) Perception

The child at the intuitive stage is dominated by perceptual features in the problems put before him. In the liquid quantity situation, a perceptual illusion is created by the tall thin beaker, and the child responds in terms of these cues, rather than relating an increase in height to a decrease in width. The one dimension which stands out is enough to cause him to make his decision on the answer.

The discussion of the development of these specific concepts has necessarily been cursory. There is a vast number of illustrations that would expand on what has been mentioned; for a fuller appreciation the reader is referred to the many books by and about Piaget that are available (e.g. McNally, 1973; Richmond, 1970). Most of what has been mentioned has been based directly on his findings, but there are many research reports by others, some of them being replication studies, which have in general corroborated his initial work. Further research has gone beyond his position and new perspectives have been adopted.

If his observations and general interpretations are accepted, then it follows that one implication for the teacher is the need to test children individually on the concepts discussed earlier, to find out if the necessary foundations for later mathematical learning are present. So far, while there have been some attempts to produce psychometric tests, little has been provided for the teacher. A paper-and-pencil test for first grade has been constructed by Tanaka, Campbell, and Helmick (1970) which covers conservation, one-to-one correspondence, classification, time, shapes, and spatial relations, but making it a group test diverges from the strict testing method that has traditionally been used in this area. The concepts discussed in this chapter have been described, however, so that a teacher can devise his or her own tests.

THE STAGE OF CONCRETE OPERATIONS

The onset of concrete operations occurs about the age of seven to eight years, according to Piaget, when the child is able to internalize acts in a reversible way. Reversibility is regarded by Piaget as the most important characteristic of concrete operations. For example, with conservation of liquid quantity the concrete operational child can describe how pouring the water into a taller, narrower container can be annulled by pouring it back into the original container. He can understand it is the same water 'because you can pour it back and it would still be the same amount'.

In testing children's understanding of concepts Piaget used a *méthode clinique* which involves much interaction and communication between child and tester. In many research studies, however, a more standardized method of assessment is used, requiring a clear choice of response from the child (e.g. 'they are the same amount') together with a clear verbal explanation of his choice. Examples of some acceptable explanations for various conservations are given below. They apply particularly to conservation of liquid quantity, of substance, and of number.

(1) Subject says the two initial amounts were the same:
e.g. 'They're the same because they were the same before.'

(2) Subject speaks of reversibility:

    e.g. 'If you poured the water back again it would be the same.'

(3) Subject indicates that the same transformation applied to both stimuli produces the same result:

    e.g. 'If you roll them both, they're both the same.'

    'They can be made the same.'

(4) Subject invokes identity:

    e.g. 'Because it's the same stuff.'

    'It's the same water.'

(5) Subject says there has been no addition or subtraction:

    e.g. 'You didn't pour any of it away, so it's the same amount.'

    'You didn't put in any extra ones, so it's the same.'

(6) Subject counts appropriately:

    e.g. 'I can count them and see they are the same.'

    'There are five here and five there.'

(7) Subject points out the equality:

    e.g. 'They are both the same amount of water.'

    'I see the same number.'

(8) Subject says no transformation has been made that will affect the amount:

    e.g. 'You only poured it into the other glass, so it is still the same amount.'

    'You only moved them.'

(9) Subject recognizes the multiplication of relations, compensation:

    e.g. 'This one is lower, but it is also fatter.'

(10) Subject acknowledges partition:

    e.g. 'Because mine is in two little glasses and that's like a big one.'

When the child can show he understands a conservation according to such criteria he is at the level of concrete operations in that particular area. However, he will not necessarily pass in all areas. The concepts appear to develop independently and to be acquired at different times, but they do tend to come at *about* the same time. They are united by common features which Piaget has described in the theory of the grouping (Piaget, 1972a), a structural conception which integrates the diverse phenomena of the concrete operations period. The nature of this structure will be considered in detail in Chapter 3.

At this stage it will be used to classify the phenomena of concrete operations under the eight major forms of grouping which Piaget has described. A grouping is a structure which indicates how the child makes special combinations of ideas in a coherent system. It is most particularly concerned with the way in which these combinations are made.

The phenomena of concrete operations classified according to eight groupings

The concepts discussed under the intuitive stage all apply to concrete operations. It is at this latter stage that success is achieved. However, there are many other concept areas involved, and some of these will be briefly mentioned with their particular grouping. Each grouping will be indicated by a name devised mainly from the set language of union and intersection, with Piaget's term for it given in brackets.

I. Primary union of classes (addition of classes)

This first grouping is applied to hierarchic classifications, such as are found in biology, botany, and zoology, where one class is included in another. For example, labradors and other breeds are included in the class of dogs, which together with other species are included in the class of animals. A hierarchy of classes can thus be developed, each higher level including the lower levels within it. This makes a combinatorial system which is designated as grouping I.

It has been studied particularly in the form of class inclusion (Inhelder and Piaget, 1964). Preoperational children were found by Inhelder and Piaget to be unable to envisage the whole and its parts simultaneously. They did not see the whole as resulting from the additive composition of its parts. Further, they did not appreciate the relevant reversibility and could not carry out the direct operation and the inverse, which are exemplified in the two equations $A + A' = B$ and $A = B - A'$. Operational children could handle the problem. This concept was discussed earlier when considering the handling of sets by the intuitive stage child.

Grouping I has also been involved in tests of classification used by Inhelder and Piaget (1964) when they presented children with collections of objects and asked them to put together the ones that were alike. Their performance was analysed in developmental stages, based on the types of classification made and the strategies used to produce them. Vygotsky (1962) has made a similar kind of analysis in stages.

II. Secondary union of classes (vicariances)

In this grouping the elements are the classes one gets when there are several ways of classifying the one set of materials. For example, a group of people might be classified according to age (children versus adults) or alternatively according to sex (male versus female). Illustrative of this is the crossclassification task used by Inhelder and Piaget (1964). Given sixteen mixed geometrical objects (four blue circles, four blue squares, four red circles, four red squares), operational children could sort them into four boxes, classifying them one way by colour and the other by shape. A version of this test was used in the research to be reported in Chapter 3.

In a further test by Inhelder and Piaget (1964), this time involving reclassification, children who were given red and blue circles and squares of two sizes were asked to make a free classification, to dichotomize the collection, and then to provide other possible ways of making a dichotomy. Successful use of the three criteria of colour, shape, and size was found to be a concrete operational achievement.

TABLE 2.2. Co-univocal multiplication of classes

K_1

	A_2 Brothers	B_2 first cousins	C_2 second cousins
A_1 Sons of	A_1A_2 Sons who are brothers to one another		
B_1 Grandsons of	B_1A_2 Grandsons who are brothers to one another	B_1B_2 Grandsons who are first cousins to one another	
C_1 Greatgrandsons of	C_1A_2 Greatgrandsons who are brothers to one another	C_1B_2 Greatgrandsons who are first cousins to one another	C_1C_2 Greatgrandsons who are second cousins to one one another

(K_2 labels the left-hand rows.)

III. Intersection of subordinate classes (co-univocal multiplication of classes)

The elements of this grouping may be illustrated by a geneological classification in which intersection of classes can occur, producing elements which are simultaneously members of both classes: e.g. 'sons of' intersecting with 'brothers' yields people who are both sons of the 'patriarch' and are brothers to one another (see Table 2.2). 'Sons of' and 'brothers' are said to be multiplied when considered in that way. The inner cells of Table 2.2 result from the multiplication of two outer cells. There has not been much research on grouping III, but in its infralogical or sublogical form (i.e. applying to space and time) it has been discussed with reference to topological, projective, and Euclidean space in terms of one–many multiplication of elements (Piaget and Inhelder, 1956, pp. 466, 473, 480). However, it has not been shown in detail how the grouping applies.

In Table 2.2 three of the cells are empty, because these multiplications do not correspond to anything in reality.

IV. Intersection of subclasses (bi-univocal multiplication of classes)

One element of a series may be paired with one element of another, as in the case where a class C (animals) is subdivided into the classes A_1 (vertebrates) and A_2 (invertebrates). These may intersect with the class D (animals) subdivided into B_1 (land-dwelling), B_2 (aquatic), and B_3 (flying). The multiplications that result are to be found in the relevant cells of the matrix given in

TABLE 2.3. Intersection of subclasses

		C Animals	
		A_1 Vertebrates	A_2 Invertebrates
	B_1 Land-dwelling	$A_1 B_1$ Land-dwelling vertebrates	$A_2 B_1$ Land-dwelling invertebrates
D	B_2 Aquatic	$A_1 B_2$ Aquatic vertebrates	$A_2 B_2$ Aquatic invertebrates
Animals	B_3 Flying	$A_1 B_3$ Flying vertebrates	$A_2 B_3$ Flying invertebrates

Table 2.3. As in grouping III, the product is the intersect of the two classes considered. The product is simultaneously a member of each of the two classes.

There have been several areas of investigation relevant to grouping IV. Piaget (1952) has used one-to-one correspondence of elements in two sets to establish equal numerosity, and Inhelder and Piaget (1964) have found certain matrix tests are passed by children when at the concrete operational level. An example of such an item that parallels Table 2.3 is given in Figure 2.3. The child is required to select one of the six alternatives given on the right, to fit in the missing part of the matrix on the left. The answer is

A similar item structure has been suggested for verbal analogies (Sheppard, 1975a).

The intersect of two classes has been studied by Inhelder and Piaget (1964, p. 174 ff.) with a test using a row of green objects and a row of leaves of various colours, the two rows at right angles to one another as in Figure 2.4. The child was required to fill the empty cell at the point of intersection. The correct answer would be a green leaf. Success was found to come at the age of nine or ten years.

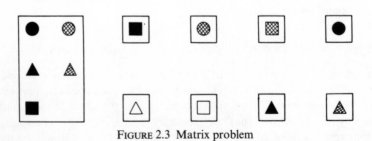

FIGURE 2.3 Matrix problem

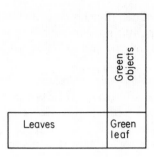

FIGURE 2.4 Intersection of
two classes

V. Addition of difference relations (addition of asymmetrical relations)

Parallel to the addition of classes (grouping I) is the addition of difference relations (grouping V). The elements are the relations between entities (classes, objects, people, etc.) in a series, i.e. with ordered differences. An example would be the increasing lengths of a series of Cuisenaire rods, or heights of steps in a staircase. Measurements in a series are most applicable, but other relations are also relevant, e.g. 'is the father of'.

Seriation has also been studied with time concepts which involve groupings in what Piaget (1950) calls their 'infralogical' form (= spatiotemporal). In one condition subjects are presented with a reservoir of water that has a Y-tube at the bottom and a tap that controls both branches of the Y (Piaget, 1969a). It can pass water into two bottles simultaneously. There are ten such bottles, of increasing capacity and of different shapes, so one cannot visually estimate their filling times. The task is to arrange three or four bottles in increasing order of filling time. This is not achieved until the level of concrete operations.

The solution of the problem is seen by Piaget as involving particularly the transitivity concept—if $A > B$ and $B > C$, therefore $A > C$. Transitivity can be used to establish the middle term (B) which the child comes to see as simultaneously having the relations of 'more than' and 'less than' (more than C and less than A).

The notion of linear order in space is also a concrete operational acquisition. One task used is to require the child to string different coloured beads in one order and then string another set in the reverse order (Piaget and Inhelder, 1956, Chap. 3). This involves grouping V in its infralogical form (Piaget and Inhelder, 1956, p. 463).

Linear order has also been studied with a task that required children to predict the order of three coloured beads on a wire when the wire was to be rotated through 180° (Piaget, 1970a). Success came at the age of seven or eight years.

VI. Addition of symmetrical relations (addition of symmetrical relations)

Symmetrical means that if A is related to B, then B bears the same relation to *A*. Certain genealogical relationships are of this type, e.g. 'brother of', 'sister of', 'first cousin of', but not 'father of', 'son of'. Other examples are 'foreigner to', 'compatriot of', 'friend of', and 'spouse of'. Such are the elements of grouping VI.

Research on this grouping has concentrated on reversibility, using the reciprocal. Preoperational boys may agree that they have a brother, but deny that the other person has a brother too. Being egocentric in their thinking they can only see the relations in a unidirectional way, from their own point of view, and so cannot appreciate that it is a symmetrical relation. Success comes with the development of concrete operations. The intuitive stage child may respond in the following way. Tester: 'Tom, do you have a brother?' Tom: 'Yes, Ian's my brother.' Tester: 'And does Ian have a brother?' Tom: 'No, he doesn't have a brother. It's me who has a brother.'

The same egocentricity has been found in the coordination of perspectives. When asked to select pictures of three mountains seen from different viewpoints the younger child chooses a picture of the view which he himself can see (Piaget and Inhelder, 1956, Chap. 8 and p. 471). This applies to the grouping in its infralogical or sublogical form, as it concerns concepts of space.

VII. Multiplication of difference relations by symmetrical relations (co-univocal multiplication of relations)

An element that could be in grouping V was given as the relation 'is the father of'; one for grouping VI was 'brother of'. The first is a difference relation; the second is a symmetrical relation. In grouping VII elements of those two types may be interrelated by combinations described as multiplication. For example, if John is the father of Robert (*a*) and Robert is the first cousin of James (*b*), then John is the uncle of James (*c*), that is $a*b = c$ where $*$ is the multiplication operation.

As with grouping III, little empirical work is reported on this structure. However, one–many multiplication of relations has been considered to be involved in certain sublogical notions of space, such as ordered series, lines meeting in perspective, or estimates of an angle before measurement (Piaget and Inhelder, 1956, pp. 466, 473, 480).

VIII. Multiplication of difference relations (bi-univocal multiplication of relations)

The elements of this grouping are the relations between objects arranged along two dimensions or series, as in Figure 2.5, where a matrix of objects is depicted so that on one dimension there is an increase in height while on the other dimension there is an increase in width. By removing the objects themselves one is left with the relations shown in Figure 2.6, and these are the elements of the grouping. Figure 2.5 and 2.6 are adapted from Piaget (1972a, pp. 165–166).

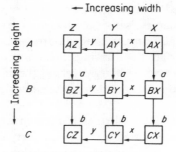

FIGURE 2.5 Matrix with two asymmetrical series, with relations

Figure 2.5 corresponds to a matrix of objects seriated along two dimensions: height and width. In Figure 2.5 those objects under X are all the same width, those under Y are the same width, and those under Z are the same width. But X, Y, and Z are in series of increasing width. A similar analysis applies to A, B, and C. The small letters describe the relations between the objects, and these letters are the elements of the grouping which are to be multiplied (Figure 2.6).

Beakers of various dimensions that would place them in some of the positions of such a matrix have been used by Halford (1970b) to study children's understanding of conservation. Much research has applied to this grouping, particularly on the conservations. In quantity conservation, for example, the operational child appreciates that an increase in height can be compensated for by a decrease in width, and so quantity may remain the same. Here a height relation is multiplied by a width relation.

Similarly, in coseriation problems the grouping applies. In one study (Piaget, 1952), dolls of increasing height had to be paired by one-to-one correspondence with a second dimension, walking sticks of increasing height. Requiring a reversal of the order of the walking sticks made the task even more difficult.

Coseriation has also been studied in the sublogical area of time concepts. Piaget (1969a, pp. 75, 264) has indicated that an experiment on the sequence of temporal events involves grouping VIII. Children were presented with a large container of water with a tap at the bottom. Water was allowed to pass down from it to a narrower and taller container, of the same capacity. The

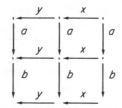

FIGURE 2.6 Matrix of relations extracted from Figure 2.5

flow of water proceeded in six stages from a full top flask to an empty one. Children filled in the water levels in six drawings of the apparatus, to correspond to the movements of the water. Young children about six years of age were found to be able to seriate the drawings if the top and bottom were on the same sheet of paper, but not until they were at the age of concrete operations could they produce a double seriation if the drawings were cut between the two flasks.

The matrix of Figure 2.5 is further illustrated by a study (Inhelder and Piaget, 1964) of multiple seriation in which forty-nine drawings of leaves were to be fitted into a 7×7 matrix varying along the two dimensions of increasing size and increasing colour intensity. Success came with concrete operations.

A sublogical application is seen in children's drawings of a stick that is progressively moved from a vertical position, through tilting away from the observer, until it is horizontal. The two dimensions involved are the distance of the top of the stick from the observer and the apparent length of the stick. The multiplication of 'further distance × shorter stick' produces the correct drawings, indicating a handling of perspective (Piaget and Inhelder, 1956, p. 472).

A further sublogical example is in the development of coordinate systems of reference, the relations being derived from orders of placement and displacement (Piaget and Inhelder, 1956, pp. 416–417, 478–480). The placements are points of reference. Preoperational children have difficulty in drawing horizontal and vertical lines derived from the water levels (or a plumbline) in a tilted bottle. This was discussed earlier when considering the intuitive child's handling of shapes. Various dimensions are involved in multiplication, e.g. parallels, distances, angles, as the bottle is set in a series of positions rotating through $360°$.

A training study illustration

To illustrate a way in which the notion of the grouping has been used to develop experimental procedures, a study on compensation and conservation will be described. It involved grouping VIII. Matrices of containers and of plasticine shapes were designed on the basis of Figure 2.5, above, to provide children with experiences of compensating height and width (Sheppard, 1974b). With one group, training involved pouring water from container to container and predicting water levels; with another it involved deformations of plasticine cylinders and predictions of cylinder heights. A significant number of children acquired conservation of liquid quantity and of substance. The children also generalized their acquired understanding of conservation to the areas of number, weight, and volume.

The dimensions of the cylinders in the matrix varied by height and breadth, as shown in Figure 2.7. Cylinders in the diagonals from the top left to the bottom right were equal in volume, so if a full $B3$ were poured into $C2$ the

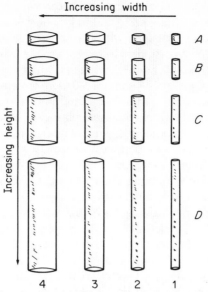

Increasing width

Increasing height

4 3 2 1

FIGURE 2.7 Matrix of cylinders

water would come right to the top, and the same would happen if it were poured into *A*4 or *D*1. Similarly, *A*2 could fill *B*1, *A*3 could fill *B*2 or *C*1, *B*4 could fill *C*3 or *D*2, and *C*4 could fill *D*3. It can be seen that this structure is precisely the same as that outlined above for grouping VIII, where applications were made to the concept of conservation.

The compensations can most clearly be seen with containers of equal volume, e.g. *A*2 and *B*1. The increase in height found in *B*1 is compensated by the appropriate decrease in width that will produce an equal quantity of liquid inside the container. A combinatorial system integrates all the compensations in a groupoid structure based on the judgments of 'less', 'same', or 'more', and will be described in Chapter 3 in more detail.

Children in the group who worked with cylinders of water were shown the matrix of containers, all of which were empty. In a systematic sequence of trials, particular containers were taken as reference containers and compared with every other container in the matrix. For example, container *B*3 might be filled with water; then a judgment would be required about what would happen to that water if poured into each of the other containers in turn. The basic question asked each time by the experimenter was: 'If I pour it into here, where will the water go to—under the top, just to the top, or will it overflow?' Because of the structure of the matrix, *B*3 could exactly fill any one of *A*4, *C*2, or *D*1. When this was discovered or predicted by the child, this observation was emphasized in discussion.

Children working with a matrix of plasticine cylinders were questioned on the effects of pushing down on particular reference cylinders, thereby making them wider and lower, or on the effects of rolling them out, thereby making them thinner and higher. Again each reference cylinder was compared with every other cylinder in turn. The basic kind of question was: 'If I make this one the same fatness as that one, will it become higher, lower, or the same height as that one?' When cylinders were of the same quantity the child found that they could 'turn into each other', back and forth.

From an initial sample of 174 children 80 were selected who lacked understanding of conservation, and these were randomly allocated to four groups: one had containers with water, one had plasticine, one control group had containers without water, and one control group received no intervention activity. The study began with a pretest on conservation of liquid quantity, substance, number, length, weight, and volume, followed by training sessions of from 20 to 25 minutes totalling about $1\frac{1}{2}$ hours, except for the no-training control group. Children were posttested on the six conservation tests on three occasions: in the week after training, two weeks later, and two months later.

Analysis of variance carried out on the obtained data for the two experimental training groups revealed that there were no differences between the two groups, there was significant improvement in conservation performance from pre- to posttests, highest posttest performances were on conservation of number and of substance, and improvements on conservation of substance were at a greater rate than on other conservations. Other analyses showed that pretest performance was comparable to that found in some other studies, and posttest acquisitions were durable over time. At the two months' posttest, 60 per cent of the plasticine matrix training groups were successful on the conservation of substance test.

This study indicates that children lacking concrete operations performance can be assisted to gain understanding of conservation if they are given experiences involving transformations using the matrix structure described by Piaget as constituting the basis of conservation—grouping VIII. However, in the light of what is to be presented in Chapter 3, it is necessary to point out here that it is not intended to use this experiment to support the validity of the notion of the grouping. It will be shown that there are definite conceptual weaknesses with the notion, and a simpler model will be proposed. The conservation training experiment will be conceptualized on the basis of that model, and it will be shown to be based not only on the matrix of grouping VIII but also on a groupoid of quantity judgments involving compensations.

Acquisition of concrete operations

The study just described is concerned with the developmental changes involved in the transition from intuitive thought to concrete operations and focuses on an area which has attracted extensive research interest. Psychologists have sought answers to questions related to the mechanisms of change, the processes of change, the acceleration of change, and the causes of change. Much of the work has involved training studies, in which intervention has been provided in an attempt to produce experimental acquisition of concrete operational thinking patterns. Comprehensive reviews have been provided by Brainerd and Allen (1971) and Beilin (1971b). Inhelder, Sinclair, and Bovet (1974) have given a detailed report of Genevan research in this area, indicating a developing interest in processes, which may be defined as the functioning of thought when there is a transformation from one level of understanding to a more elaborate understanding. Early research studies in the literature found that training had little effect, but there is now a large body of evidence that children can improve in their understanding of certain concepts through training. However, in these studies the usual pattern is that not all subjects respond to the experiences given. Presumably some aspects of individual differences are involved, whether of personality or whether of cognitive status. Assessing various characteristics of 'non-learners' in future research could give valuable insights into the acquisition process. It is apparent that acquisition depends on the way in which the child assimilates his new experiences to the old and that information about the logical operations is not simply fed into the brain; it is dependent, rather, on internal processes of the child himself—on how he goes about organizing the new stimulus input into existing cognitive structures. It has been found that the child can improve significantly in understanding of a logical operation with the passage of a short period of time, if this is a period after initial training experiences have been given. In one study children set to thinking about class inclusion in a new way improved in class inclusion scores over a period of from one to two weeks without training, and in another study children given learning experiences with a mathematical three-group (to be reported in Chapter 3) came back with greater understanding after a rest interval of several hours, a day, or several days. This suggests there could be a threshold point, beyond which it is unnecessary to help a child to learn because from that point he can go ahead and do it all on his own.

If this is the case, then many training studies act as trigger mechanisms, setting off internal processes that consolidate on the relevant structures. This could explain why so many different approaches described in the literature have been successful. A similar argument has been proposed by Halford (1970a, pp. 313–314) and by Beilin (1969, p. 433). Such an explanation is in keeping with Piaget's (1964) notion that development from one level to another proceeds largely by the process of equilibration, with an interplay of assimilation and accommodation.

In the equilibration process the child may be assumed to become aware of the dissonance between his old cognitive structures involving non-conservation, etc., and the structure of the new stimulus information that he is seeking to process. He finally acknowledges that the new information is superior in its explanation of the world, because it is part of a consistent classificatory system and does not involve the ambiguities that are inherent in the old structure. In a class inclusion training study (Sheppard, 1973) some children said that the bottom six red marbles in a cylinder were more than the total of nine round balls in the cylinder (six red plus three blue on top). They then counted the nine and were confronted with the observation that the nine were more than six, yet they had said the six red ones were more. At first, faced with the dissonance between what they had been saying and what they were discovering by counting, they often found it difficult to incorporate the new finding. On subsequent training trials they might still make the erroneous judgment. Yet, when tested later after there had been time for an effective assimilation of the new information into existing structures, correct judgments were forthcoming from a significant proportion of subjects.

The new information is seen by the child as superior in its explanation of the world because it gives a coherent picture of what happens under conditions of change. It sorts out the stable from the unstable. Conservation, for example, is important in human development because it refers to a necessary stability under conditions of change. Without an appreciation of it man could not go beyond a limited awareness of his world.

3

A STRUCTURAL ANALYSIS OF CONCRETE OPERATIONS

J. L. Sheppard

Piaget's theoretical construct for explaining concrete operations is the grouping, derived from the concept of the mathematical group and the semilattice. In this chapter the structure will be analysed, and a further model proposed, the groupoid. Experimental evidence of children's thought that illustrates the groupoid structure will be described.

THE GROUPING

On the basis of Piaget's early formulation (Piaget, 1942, 1949) a grouping may be defined as a set of elements which are structured according to five conditions, four of which are based on the conditions for a mathematical group, while a fifth is based on the mathematical semilattice. The five conditions, using Piaget's terminology, are:

(a) composition, by the direct operation,
(b) the operation of general identity,
(c) reversibility by the inverse operation,
(d) associativity, and
(e) special identities of tautology and resorption.

Five conditions of a grouping

(a) Composition, by the direct operation

Two 'contiguous' classes can be combined to produce a third that is one of the set of classes, e.g. *bananas + other fruit = fruit, fruit + other edible plants = edible plants, edible plants + inedible plants = plants*. However, as Baldwin (1967, pp. 186, 253) has pointed out, there is not complete closure in the system, because only adjacent classes in Figure 3.1 are combined to produce an element of the set of classes. For example, two lines are not drawn to indicate the

48

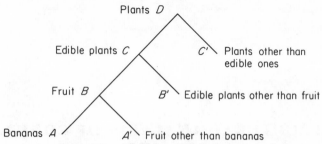

FIGURE 3.1 A hierarchic classification of classes. The classes are related by inclusion

higher class that contains *fruit other than bananas + inedible plants*. Piaget (1972a, p. 107) has discussed this aspect when indicating differences between the set of numbers under addition (a group) and the set of classes under addition (a grouping). However an aspect not particularly emphasized is that this restriction destroys any mathematical concept of closure in the system. The combinativity is selective, and so it is not closed. The importance of closure stems from the fact that the grouping is based on the idea of a mathematical group, which involves a precise form of closure. The lack of closure in the grouping is therefore a significant feature which distinguishes it from a group.

The combinations are effected by the direct operation which may be seen as taking two forms (Piaget, 1972a, p. 104):

(1) the addition of logical addition equations of the form *bananas + fruit other than bananas = fruit* (that is $A + A' = B$), so the complete direct operation might be $(A + A' = B) + (B + B' = C) = (A + A' + B' = C)$; and

(2) the addition of individual classes in the system, for example $+ A; + B; + A'$; producing $A + A' = B$ as the complete direct operation.

For simplicity's sake the second form has been chosen in the present exposition, as Baldwin (1967) has done.

(b) The operation of general identity

Adding a null class leaves the other class unchanged. The identity can be obtained by combining a class with its inverse class.

This means that a new aspect has been added to the system depicted in Figure 3.1—the null class. However, it does not fit neatly on any line. The concept of identity is of great importance in Piagetian research, particularly in the study of the conservation phenomena. The seven or eight year old may know that some plasticine is still the same amount despite various irrelevant transformations, and may know that it retains its identity because, for example, it has been combined with a null class, i.e. nothing has been added or taken away, and combining a transformation with its inverse returns the plasticine to the original identity.

(c) *Reversibility by the inverse operation*

Every combination is reversible, e.g. the inverse of adding is subtracting. If the direct operation is addition, the inverse is the operation which nullifies it, i.e. subtraction. Further, if $A + A' = B$, then $- A - A' = - B$ and $B - A = A'$ or $B - A' = A$, e.g. if *bananas + fruit other than bananas = fruit*, then *fruit − bananas = fruit other than bananas*.

Reversibility is seen as the most significant defining quality of the concrete operations, and there are numerous examples of it to be found in the thought of the child, e.g. in conservation the child says two amounts of liquid are the same after a pouring transformation 'because they were the same before' or 'if you poured the water back again it would be the same'. With reference to Figure 3.1 the child sees that *fruit − fruit other than bananas = bananas*.

(d) *Associativity*

By 'associativity' Piaget means that in operational thought detours may be used, so that the same end result may be achieved by different methods. This usage of the term is in the logical sense rather than the mathematical sense (Piaget, 1950, p. 41). The mathematical meaning is that if a, b, and c are combined by$*$, then $(a * b) * c = a * (b * c)$.

The operations are associative, with, however, the restriction of the special identities, making associativity incomplete so that the form

$$(a * b) * c = a * (b * c)$$

only applies in certain cases (Piaget, 1953b, p. 27; 1972a, p. 105). It does apply, for example, in the case of

$$(A + A) + A' = A + (A + A')$$

since

$$(A) + A' = A + (B)$$

and

$$B = B$$

However, as in the case of closure, mentioned above, the mathematical meaning has been weakened by this restriction, because 'associativity' in a mathematical group means that the condition holds for *all* cases. If, for any one case, it does not hold then there is no associativity.

(e) *Special identities of tautology and resorption*

In Figure 3.1 *fruit* is the smallest class to include both *bananas* and *fruit*, and so it is known as the least upper bound (l.u.b.) or join of *bananas* and *fruit*. Every pair of classes in the figure has a l.u.b. or join, e.g. the l.u.b. of *fruit* and *edible plants* is *edible plants*, for *edible plants* and *plants* the l.u.b. is *plants*. These examples may be symbolized as $A + B = B$, $B + C = C$, $C + D = D$. The first element in each equation makes no change to the second, and so acts as an 'identity element'. This is called *resorption*, where a class combined with its superordinate yields the latter. *Tautology* refers to the fact that a class combined with itself yields itself, and so acts as an 'identity element', for example $A + A = A$.

The structure given in Figure 3.1 is a semilattice. The special identities of tautology and resorption are involved in a grouping because a grouping has a semilattice structure. The semilattice derives from the lattice, which in mathematics is a set of elements structured by a relation so that any two elements have one l.u.b. or join and one greatest lower bound (g.l.b.) or meet. For two classes A and B, the g.l.b. is the largest class that is included in both A and B. The semilattice has a l.u.b. for every pair of elements in the set, but not every pair has a g.l.b. (except for having zero as a g.l.b.). In Figure 3.1 there is no g.l.b., for example, for C and C', or A' and B'. There is only a g.l.b. for some pairs: A and B, B and C, C and D, A and C, A and D, B and D, B and A', C and A', D and A', C and B', D and B', D and C'. Further consideration of the lattice structure will be given in Chapter 11.

Evaluation of the grouping concept

These five conditions are the hallmarks of a grouping as originally proposed by Piaget. For the grouping discussed, Piaget (1949, p. 109) has said that what are combined are equations, although this may be extended to considering that it is classes that are combined (Piaget, 1972a, p. 104). One may assume, then, that the elements of the set are equations or the actual classes. This lack of precision weakens the framework of the conceptual system. If the elements are equations, then within each element are to be found one or more operations ($+$ or $-$ in additive groupings), and again this variability is a weakness in the system.

The direct operation can be regarded as serving two functions: (a) it is part of each element (within an equation) and (b) it is the operation that applies to the grouping as a whole, i.e. it is the operation by which the elements are combined. In the grouping discussed it is addition. If one considers the elements as equations, then the grouping is based on an operation ($+$) on operations ($+ -$). Operating on operations is, however, a description which Piaget reserves for formal operations and not for concrete operations, so this creates an inconsistency in the formulations. If one considers the elements as classes, one still becomes involved with operations, because each class is either a plus or minus quantity, i.e. has been posed or unposed (Piaget, 1949, pp. 99–100) (and these are operations). The inverse operation is always used to create an inverse element, for example $- A$. A is not the inverse element. It is the totality $- A$ that is the inverse element. Therefore, the classes alone are not elements, but rather the elements are classes associated with an operation ($+$) or ($-$). The formulation creates some confusion because an operation can take two forms (a $+$ within an equation or a $+$ combining equations), and as there are addition and subtraction operations there can be a total of four kinds of operation

(+ within an equation, − within an equation, + combining equations, and − combining equations).

Piaget is aware of the fact that he used mathematical ideas in an unusual way. He injected an added psychological aspect into the notion of a grouping which made it refer to the area of human thought patterns. It is a logico-mathematical construct (Piaget, 1950, pp. 37, 40). By taking this orientation he uses group and semilattice as models, so that on an analogy basis he can talk about cognitive events.

Piaget uses his classification of groupings to interrelate his research on concrete operations. He has provided empirical counterparts to the theoretical formulations, but there has been very little research designed to examine the nature of the grouping structures as structures. The most direct recent work has been carried out by Brainerd (e.g. Brainerd, 1972; Weinreb and Brainerd, 1975) and by Osherson (1974), who are critical of the concept.

The conception of an operation is important to the theoretical status of the notion of a grouping. The number of key operations may vary from grouping to grouping, so that the concept of a grouping operation is not unitary. It means different things in different contexts. Again, such variability is a weakness in the conceptual framework. The system can have one operation or two, or three, or four. This will be discussed in more detail later. Piaget does not speak in terms of the number of operations involved and treats the groupings as all being on the same level; yet they do in fact differ in the number and type of operations.

A group has closure and associativity. It has been shown that the grouping is not completely closed nor completely associative, and so mathematically neither concept of closure or associativity is applied precisely to the grouping. This considerably reduces the degree of similarity between the two notions of group and grouping. The resulting lack of similarity between them needs emphasizing and will be taken up again later in the chapter.

Logicians have found difficulties with the construct and various analyses have been made of it, particularly in the French literature. Because of the logical intricacies of the system and mathematical problems, some have attempted to put the concept on a more precise footing (e.g. Wittmann, 1973). On the whole, English-speaking authors have not shown interest in the theoretical ramifications of the concept of grouping, while there have been a number of writings in French (e.g. Apostel, 1963; Granger, 1965; Grize, 1960, 1963, 1967, 1969; Wermus, 1972). Witz (1969) has provided a strictly mathematical interpretation of grouping I, in English. Of greatest significance for the present exposition is his analysis of what Piaget means by the term 'operation'. In discussing grouping I above, Piaget's terminology for the five conditions was used, and from these conditions one can superficially extract three operations:

(1) the direct operation,
(2) the inverse operation, and
(3) the identity operation.

Considering grouping I as represented in Figure 3.1 above, one has simple equations

    (1) $A + A' = B, B + B' = C, C + C' = D,$
    (2) $B - A = A', C - B = B', D - C = C',$ etc.,
    (3) $A - A = 0, B - B = 0, C - C = 0,$ etc.,

which correspond to the three operations just listed. Witz (1969, p. 40) calls each one of these simple equations an operation, while the set of equations of the same form—i.e. all those in (1), all those in (2), and all those in (3)—are general operations or operational schemata. The child's realization that $A + A' = B$ is seen as the performance of an operation. This appears to be an accurate interpretation of Piaget's meaning that is not generally discussed in such a form. Although Witz does not bring out this point, it is really quite a different notion from the mathematical meaning. In mathematics, $A + A' = B$, $B + B' = C$, $C + C' = D$ all involve the one operation, that of addition. Witz is saying that each equation involves a different operation.

The logician Grize has written a number of times on the nature of the grouping and has proposed reformulations of it. An early version (Grize, 1960) was regarded with favour by Piaget and is to be found in a condensed form in Piaget (1966).

This was criticized by Granger (1965), who considered it did not conform to a diagram one can construct to represent grouping I as first enunciated. He offered a different set of definitions, postulates, and theorems, but along the same lines as those of Grize. Piaget and Inhelder (1969, p. 101) have referred to both the Grize and Granger revisions, presumably regarding them with some approval. A further revision was forthcoming from Grize (1967), to culminate in the latest version, published under Piaget's name with the full seal of approval (Piaget, 1972a). This appeared in a second edition of Piaget's (1949) book *Traité de Logique*, in which he clearly outlined the theory of the grouping. The changes in the new edition are minor, when one considers the book as a whole. They consist mainly of altering the symbols used, so that more modern notation is presented, and in introducing Grize's analysis of the grouping. Its major achievements are to establish one main operation for the grouping and to eliminate the idea of incomplete associativity. There is an identity operator and there are special identities forming laws of tautology and resorption. Associativity is not involved. Two 'minor' operations are posing the elements of a class and unposing the elements. This produces the direct operator and the inverse operator, which may be combined under a law of composition (designated by the symbol $\circ$). In effect, then, there is one main operation for the grouping, just as there is one main operation for a mathematical group, the composition operation.

There is, however, a fundamental problem with this formulation: it is not linked in the book with the detailed exposition of all eight different groupings which Piaget postulated, and applied to each in turn, to show its applicability and show how the grouping may be reinterpreted in the light of the new conceptualization. The text is virtually unchanged in the sections detailing the individual groupings. Associativity is still discussed and the details for its application provided, despite the renunciation of associativity. Although the new formulation has one main operation for the grouping, the use of one, two, three, and four major operations for the different groupings is to be found in the unchanged text. There is also a problem of how the new formulation handles the relationship of the inverse to the reciprocal, which is important in Piagetian theory, as they are the earlier stages that lead to part of the *INRC* group of formal operations.

Despite these difficulties, the notion of a grouping is an important contribution to an understanding of the development of operational logic in the child. It emphasizes structure of thought. Thought is not seen as made of isolated units, but as forming wholes. It conforms to a system of interrelationships, of intertwinings, and of interdependencies, this system being a combinatorial one, at the heart of which is the operation on the elements of the system.

THE GROUP

Piaget developed the idea of the grouping from the mathematical structures known as the mathematical group and the semilattice. The latter was discussed above when considering the fifth condition of a grouping, the special identities of tautology and resorption. The characteristics of a mathematical group will now be considered, to show the similarities and differences with the grouping.

A group may be defined as a set of elements closed under an associative binary operation, with one member of the set being an identity element and each element having an inverse element. For example, the rotations of a square form a group. The elements are:

rotation through 0° or 360°,
rotation through 90°,
rotation through 180°, and
rotation through 270° or minus 90°.

If these elements are combined in pairs by the operation 'is followed by', then each resultant would equal one of the rotations in the set. It may be pointed out that this group is actually a subgroup of a more general group, that obtains from rotations through any angle. The group conforms to four requirements of closure, identity, the inverse, and associativity.

Requirements of a group

(*a*) *Closure*

The combination of any two elements produces a third that is in the set, e.g. a rotation of 90° followed by 180° puts the square in a final position that could have been reached by one element, a rotation of 270° or minus 90°,

TABLE 3.1. Multiplication table of
rotations of a square

*	360°	90°	180°	270°
360°	360°	90°	180°	270°
90°	90°	180°	270°	360°
180°	180°	270°	360°	90°
270°	270°	360°	90°	180°

that is $90° * 180° = 270°$, where $*$ is the operation 'is followed by'. All the possible combinations involved can be represented in a multiplication table, shown in Table 3.1.

(b) Identity

There is one element which, when combined with another, produces the same result as the other, e.g. rotating 0° or 360° makes no difference when preceded or followed by another rotation.

(c) The inverse

Every element has an inverse element in the set, so that a combination of an element and its inverse produces the identity element, e.g. rotating 90° and 270° are inverses of one another, while the identity element is an inverse of itself, and so is the rotation of 180°.

(d) Associativity

If the elements are a, b, and c combined by the operation $*$, then $(a * b) * c = a * (b * c)$, i.e. if a and b are combined and the result of that is combined with c, then the same end result is achieved as if a is combined with what results from combining b and c.

For an Abelian group there is an additional characteristic, of commutativity, which states that $a * b = b * a$. This deals with a different aspect of combining. The group given above in Table 3.1 is commutative.

Similarities and differences between the characteristics of a grouping and a group are summarized in Table 3.2. While both structures may involve identity elements and inverses, they differ on all the other points. For the group all elements can be combined within the system (closure), but for the grouping the combinations can occur with only certain elements (composition). The associativity that applies in all cases for the group may apply for only

TABLE 3.2. Characteristics of a grouping and
a group

Grouping		Group
Composition		Closure
Identity	=	Identity
Reversibility	=	Inverse
'Associativity'		Associativity
Special identities		
Variable main operations		A main operation

certain cases for the grouping, a feature that is caused by the special identities which are unique to the grouping. For a group there is one main operation, but for the groupings there is variability in the number of main operations that apply. It has been shown how grouping I has four main operations. The same kinds apply to grouping II (see Chapter 2 for the structure of each of the eight groupings). For groupings III and IV there are three main operations: multiplication, division, and addition. For the overall grouping there is multiplication (which corresponds to intersection) and division (the inverse operation, which is abstracting one class from a product). Multiplication takes two forms: (a) one class multiplied by another, for example $A_1 \times A_2 = A_1 A_2$, (b) two series multiplied together, for example $K_1 \times K_2 = A_1 A_2 + B_1 A_2 + B_1 B_2 + C_1 A_2 + C_1 B_2 + C_1 C_2$ (Piaget, 1972a, pp. 113–114). These are the entries in the cells of Table 2.2. For groupings VII and VIII there are two main operations, multiplication and division. For grouping V and VI there is one main operation, addition of the element relation or of its reciprocal.

THE GROUPOID

With the problems associated with the grouping concept in mind, a further model is proposed for operational thought. It is the mathematical notion of a groupoid.

The mathematical group and Piaget's grouping both involve a more fundamental concept, with fewer requirements and restrictions, with looser structure, and with wider application because of its many developments and variations: the groupoid. A groupoid, the simplest of structures, is a set and a binary operation on that set.

Trotter (1972, p. 120) has pointed out that when Piaget has discussed structure as a system closed under transformation 'the substantial content here is the notion of a set closed under a binary composition'. However, Piaget has not exploited the possibilities of such a conceptualization by analysing operational thought in these specific terms. His analysis has been in terms of a much more rigid system, requiring thought to conform to a tight patterning of rules that has been criticized as imposing too much structure (Flavell, 1963, p. 438).

Reasons for proposing the groupoid concept

In proposing the grouping as a model for thought Piaget moved away from the mathematical precision that is to be found in the concept of a group. As a result both mathematicians (e.g. Witz, 1969) and logicians (e.g. Grize, 1960) have been critical of the concept. To simplify these problems the groupoid has been proposed in this chapter as a model for operational thought. The notion of a groupoid, merely requiring a set and an operation, involves fundamental concepts and is at the origin of the notion of a grouping. The model provides a consistent concept of an operation rather than one which varies under different analyses. It has parsimony in only working with a small number of basic characteristics, yet it allows for expansion because it establishes a framework on which various forms of groupoid can be built, with varying degrees of complexity. For example, the mathematical group is a groupoid. The group merely has certain extra features in addition to those essential for a basic groupoid. The model has applicability to the Piagetian phenomena and may be used for a research programme to investigate development of cognitive structures at the level of concrete operations.

Illustrations of various forms of groupoid

(a) Quantity judgments

An illustration of how the groupoid model may be applied to cognitive events is provided by a structure proposed by Halford (1970a, 1972), who has suggested that the basis of conservation may be found in the pattern of interrelationships represented in Table 3.3. The entries in the cells represent judgments of quantity. One way in which the judgments may be made is to consider the effects of pouring liquid from one container to another, of adding liquid, or of removing liquid. Pouring liquid from one vessel to another is

TABLE 3.3.   A structure for quantity judgments

*	Same	More	Less
Same	Same	More	Less
More	More	More	Same
Less	Less	Same	Less

an identity element, as it has no effect on the quantity of the liquid, which can be judged as 'the same' or of 'equal' quantity. Pouring is also an inverse of itself, because pouring the liquid back again produces the original condition. If liquid is added to a vessel it will be judged to have 'more'. If it is then poured into another vessel it can still be judged as 'more'. The judgments 'more' and 'less' can be conceived as inverses of one another if the quantity of liquid added to provide the judgment 'more' is the same amount of liquid subtracted to provide the judgment 'less'; i.e. adding some liquid can produce 'more' than there was at the beginning, and then if the same amount is withdrawn it produces 'less' than there was before the removal, bringing the quantity back to be the 'same' as at the beginning. Thus, the judgment 'more' combined with 'less' can produce the resultant 'same'. The judgment 'same' or 'equal' is its own inverse, because pouring from one vessel to another can be annulled by pouring back again. The cells of Table 3.3 may be obtained by combinations like the following:

Same * more = more: same—pour liquid from one vessel (A) to another (B)
more—add liquid to that (B)
more—pour that back to A and there is now more than there was at the beginning

Same * less = less: same—pour liquid from one vessel (A) to another (B)
less—remove some liquid from B
less—pour that back to A and there is now less than there was at the beginning

Less * less = less: less—remove some liquid from one vessel (A)
less—remove some more liquid from A
less—A can be known to have less liquid than B

In the terms of the model being proposed in this chapter, the structure is an Abelian groupoid with neutral (identity) element and inverses. It lacks associativity and so is not a group. It does, however, have a characteristic that Piaget has proposed for a grouping, viz. tautology ($a * a = a, b * b = b, c * c = c$).

A number of experiments have been devised to examine implications of this proposed structure. Some of them will be discussed in Chapter 6. At this point three others will be mentioned briefly. In the first (Sheppard, 1973) the combinations involved in one cell of the structure were used in the experimental induction of concrete operational thought in the area of class inclusion. It has been shown above that a single combination of elements can be regarded as an operation if one accepts the view expressed by Witz (1969). He asserted that a child in the act of realizing $A + A' = B$ was exemplifying the performance of an operation. Such a combination of one element with another to produce a third corresponds to one cell in a groupoid table. This idea was adopted for a class inclusion experiment as a preliminary exploration of structures by starting at the simplest level of the groupoid, viz. the combination that produces one cell. The combination was 'same * more = more'. This was chosen as being particularly applicable to Piaget's test of class inclusion, success at which often comes at about the age of seven or eight (Inhelder and Piaget, 1964). A typical test item for the concept is that, presented with twelve roses and five tulips, the child is asked: 'Are there more roses or more flowers?' The child at the intuitive stage who has not yet acquired concrete operations typically says that there are more roses because the twelve roses are more than five tulips. This concept has been discussed in Chapter 2 when considering sets as handled by the intuitive child and in the grouping I of concrete operations. In the experiment it was predicted that children could develop an awareness of class inclusion if they were given materials and questions that assisted them to follow a sequence of logical analysis based on the groupoid cell combination 'same * more = more'. The sequence of logic is illustrated in Figure 3.2. The judgment 'same' is elicited in the first step by obtaining agreement to the numerical equality of two sets of ten roses, A_1 and A_2. In the second step three tulips are added to one of the sets of ten roses (A_2) making a set of flowers, B. The child is led to observe that the flowers (B) are more than the roses (A_1). In the final, third step the child is given the opportunity to conclude that the flowers (B) are more than the roses (A_2), thereby displaying an understanding of class inclusion. The three steps should provide the child with an opportunity to conceptualize a large subordinate class separately from the same one when it is included in the superordinate class.

The sequence can be seen as depending on a combination of two transformations:

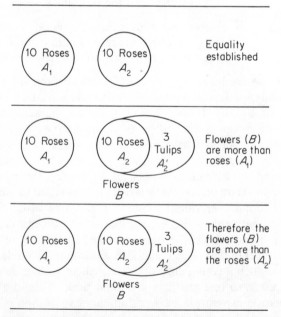

FIGURE 3.2 A sequence of three steps of reasoning, based on the combination 'same * more = more'

(1) identity transformation, i.e. the set of ten roses by themselves (A_1) is the same as another set of ten roses (A_2) which is added to tulips to make the set of flowers (B). This is tantamount to saying a set does not lose its identity by being combined with another set.

(2) the transformation of adding (i.e. plus three tulips).

An identity transformation coupled with an addition must always produce a result of 'more'. It cannot give 'less' or 'the same' as the starting point state. This, then, constitutes the groupoid cell that was chosen.

The assumption was that if a mathematical model of operational thought is conceived in the form of structures like the groupoid, then one can expect training studies which are based on it to produce some significant acquisition of Piagetian concepts. Successful transfer of training from learning sessions to posttests should constitute some support for the applicability of the model. With this in mind, the aim of the class inclusion experiment was to apply the sequence of Figure 3.2 to a training programme.

Training with a series of trials for an experimental group was found to produce significant acquisition of the concept from pre- to posttests, while a control group given no training did not change. Further, for the experimental group there was an improvement from the first to the second posttest, and this was maintained to the third posttest which was given three or four months after training.

In a second experiment which illustrates the quantity judgments groupoid, increased understanding of conservation resulted from a training schedule involving all of the combinations in the groupoid table (Sheppard, 1974b). Some aspects of the study were described in Chapter 2 to illustrate application of Piaget's grouping VIII to an experimental setting. Training involved the use of a matrix of containers and a matrix of plasticine cylinders. The diagram of the matrix is presented again in Figure 3.3 but is slightly transposed for purposes of exposition. (The exact orientation of the cylinders used in the experiment is that which was given in Chapter 2.) Cylinders are shown as increasing in width from left to right and increasing in height from top to bottom, and were of equal capacity in the diagonals running from top right to bottom left. Preoperational children were given training which required them to take a particular cylinder full of water and compare it with every other cylinder to see where the water would come if it were poured into the comparison container.

By making a large number of these comparisons the children were involved with a combinatorial system based on the quantity judgments groupoid. They were continually confronted with the need for quantity judgments that involved combining a change in one dimension, e.g. height, with another dimension, width, which would produce a resultant of a particular quantity of water within the comparison container. For example, if $C3$ in Figure 3.3 were the standard container filled with water and it was being compared with $B2$, the child had to observe that $B2$ was both *less* in height and *less* in

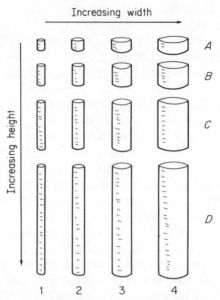

Increasing width

Increasing height

FIGURE 3.3 Matrix of containers. Those in a diagonal from top right to bottom left were equal in volume

width, which produces the resultant of *less* capacity than *C*3. When comparing *C*3 with *D*2, he had to notice that *D*2 was *more* in height but *less* in width, such changes exactly compensating one another so that *D*2 held the *same* amount of water as *C*3. Thus, the combination 'less with less' produced 'less', and 'more with less' produced 'same'. In like manner all the combinations of the quantity judgments groupoid may be obtained. To emphasize the direct parallel between the matrix materials and the groupoid structure the groupoid table has been recast and presented as Table 3.4. The combinations have not been changed, just the order of the sequence of elements. Comparison between Figure 3.3 and Table 3.4 reveals that, with both of them, referring to quantity, in the top left there is 'less', along the diagonal there is 'the same', and in the bottom right there is 'more'. Children given experience with the matrix were able to benefit and a significant number of them acquired conservation.

TABLE 3.4. Quantity judgments groupoid

*	Less	Same	More
Less	Less	Less	Same
Same	Less	Same	More
More	Same	More	More

A third experiment involving the quantity judgments groupoid was a developmental study designed to assess the age at which children could succeed in making the judgments consistently (Sheppard, 1976). Each cell of the groupoid was taken as the basis for a test item, and this nine-item test, together with tests of concrete operations, were given to 100 children aged from six to ten years. The judgments test was group administered, but individual administration was used for conservation of substance, conservation of length, and class inclusion.

The judgments test was an extension of the transitivity paradigm. Wooden rods were compared for length. For example, to test the groupoid combination of 'more * less = equal (same)', children were shown at the classroom blackboard a red rod 39·5 cm long and a brown rod 40 cm long, both placed upright beside each other. They were asked: 'Is this one (the brown one) equal to that one, or is it longer, or is it shorter?' The class was to chorus 'longer' (= more). A small piece of rod 0·5 cm in height was placed on top of the shorter rod (the red one), and it was emphasized that the difference in length was indicated by that chip of rod. The longer brown rod was stood at the extreme left of the blackboard, leaving the shorter red rod in the centre, and the word 'longer' was written on the board near the brown rod. Another brown rod 40 cm long was introduced and placed beside the red rod. Children were asked: 'Is this one (the red one this time) equal to that one (the new brown one), or is it longer, or is it shorter?' The class would chorus 'shorter' (= less), and the chip of 0·5 cm rod was used again to show it was less by the same amount as the first brown rod was more. Then the new brown rod was placed at the extreme right of the blackboard and the word 'shorter' was written on the right of the central red rod.

After chorus repetition of the discovered relationships between the rods the class was asked: 'Now the question is about the two brown ones. Is this one (the left) equal to that one (the right), or is it longer, or is it shorter?' Children recorded their answer.

The other eight items were obtained in a similar way, but with the 0·5 cm chip being unnecessary for all except 'less * more = equal'. The small difference in length between the rods enabled children to discriminate between them when they were placed beside each other, but not when separated and when the crucial final question to each item was asked.

It was found that the level of performance on the judgments test was similar to the performance on the concrete operations tests, and that general success in both areas came at about nine years of age, when one would expect concrete operational thought to be well consolidated.

(b) Transitivity of equivalence

The transitivity paradigm, on which the above nine-item test was developed by extension, is the proposition that if $A = B$ and $B = C$ then $A = C$. If $A = B$ is taken as an element, however, with $B = C$ as a second and $A = C$ as a third,

TABLE 3.5. Multiplication table of
the elements of transitivity of
equivalence

*	$A = B$	$B = C$	$A = C$
$A = B$	$A = B$	$A = C$	$B = C$
$B = C$	$A = C$	$B = C$	$A = B$
$A = C$	$B = C$	$A = B$	$A = C$

they form a closed set under a binary operation of combining and so establish
a groupoid themselves. These elements correspond to Piaget's preliminary
grouping elements on the transitivity of equivalence. They do not form a
group, because there is no identity element, no inverse law, and no associativity.
Table 3.5 gives the possible combinations that could be rationally made.
Success with such transitivity has been found to come with concrete operations.

(c) Geneological classes

Another groupoid can be obtained by analysis of elements described by
Piaget for grouping III. Taking the set of elements 'brother of', 'first cousin
of', 'second cousin of' (with a person P being related to X, Y, and Z), and
applying a combining operation to them, produces the groupoid multiplication table given in Table 3.6. If the geneological classes are abstracted from
the table, the result is Table 3.7. This is a groupoid with an identity element.
It is not associative and there are no inverses.

(d) Mathematical groups

The mathematical group is a groupoid. Group structures have quite wide
applicability. As an example, developmental studies on the group of rotations
of an equilateral triangle will later be discussed in detail. The multiplication
table for such a group is given in Table 3.8.

TABLE 3.6. Multiplication table of three genealogical classes applied to particular
individuals

*	P brother of X	P first cousin of Y	P second cousin of Z
P brother of X	P brother of X	X first cousin of Y	X second cousin of Z
P first cousin of Y	X first cousin of Y	P first cousin of Y	Y second cousin of Z
P second cousin of Z	X second cousin of Z	Y second cousin of Z	P second cousin of Z

TABLE 3.7. Multiplication table of three abstracted genealogical classes

*	Brother	First cousin	Second cousin
Brother	Brother	First cousin	Second cousin
First cousin	First cousin	First cousin	Second cousin
Second cousin	Second cousin	Second cousin	Second cousin

Various mathematical groups are relevant to the development of number, such as the infinite group of integers, or rational, irrational, real, and complex numbers all under addition.

Performance on a mathematical group task has been found to be related to the degree of benefit children gain from training for one aspect of concrete operations, namely understanding the concept of horizontality of water levels (Sheppard, 1974c). Those who had higher understanding of the rotations involved in a mathematical two-group or four-group were later more likely to increase their understanding of horizontality as measured by a special test (Sheppard, 1975b).

(e) Applications to school subjects

Groupoids may be found in a range of experiences presented in the day-to-day tasks of learning in schools. A mathematical example is the problem of combining vectors, or arrows of movement. If a boat is propelled along a river, with the bow pointed straight up the river and a side current pulling to the right, the ultimate movement of the boat will be in between the two vectors. Two movements combine to produce a third. All possible combinations of two such vectors are replaced by a third. In the area of science learning at school, one can consider the mixing of colours on the colour wheel, whether considering pigments or light. Two colours can be seen to combine to produce a third, which is in the total system. In natural science, crosspollination and

TABLE 3.8. Multiplication table of rotations of an equilateral triangle

*	360°	120°	240°
360°	360°	120°	240°
120°	120°	240°	360°
240°	240°	360°	120°

the examination of genetic transmission through generations involves combinations in pairs that produce a third element in a total combinatorial system. In the area of music, two independent tones may be perceived to combine to make a chord, if presented simultaneously, and that chord is itself part of a large system of sounds.

THE GROUPING, THE GROUP, AND THE GROUPOID

The grouping is particularly distinguished from the groupoid by failing to meet either of the defining characteristics of the groupoid, viz. having (a) an operation and (b) a set that is closed under that operation. The notion of an operation applied to the grouping is not of the unitary kind that is applied to the groupoid, and there is no closure.

The terms 'groupoid' and 'mathematical group' refer to concepts that are to be distinguished in quite a different way. The term 'groupoid' can cover a range of structures of varying complexity, one of these structures being a group. Groupoid is a more general classification than group. A structure which has a set and an operation is a groupoid, whether it has further characteristics or not. A group is a groupoid, but a groupoid is not necessarily a group, because it may not meet all the axioms of a group.

Many groupoids have characteristics additional to the essential ones of a set and an operation, such as associativity (a semigroup), associativity and an identity element (a monoid), or associativity, an identity, and inverses (a group). Some of the groupoids given as examples for analysis of Piagetian concepts were of this type. There is a diversity of phenomena to which the concept can apply; it is not intended to refer only to the simplest of structures.

THE NATURE OF AN OPERATION

The groupoid has been described as involving a set and an operation. A set is commonly regarded as a collection of things, although mathematical analyses of it are much more complex than this. As these are not appropriate to the present discussion they will not be examined. However, the meaning of an operation, crucial to Piaget's theory, is of special interest to the present work and so will be treated in some detail.

In mathematics two main views are taken of the concept 'operation'. The first view, stricter than the second, has been described in two different ways, but they amount to the same.

Two versions of the one viewpoint

One version of the first view states, for example, that if ∘ is a binary operation on the non-empty set S then ∘ is a mapping of $S \times S$ into S. This may be illustrated by a set S which contains the two elements a and b. The possible com-

Table 3.9.   Mapping of $S \times S$ into S

binations of these two elements with themselves are

$$aa \quad ab \quad ba \quad bb$$

If aa could be represented by a, ab by b, ba by b, and bb by a, then it is said that there has been a mapping of $S \times S$ into S, as shown by the arrows of Table 3.9.

This table may be converted to another form, representing the combining aspect by a symbol for the combining operation $*$, in the same way as the group multiplication tables have been presented earlier. The result is Table 3.10. The operation involved is determined by the nature of the mapping. In other words, if the cell entries were arranged differently, then it would involve a different operation, as in Table 3.11.

There are many ways in which the cell entries can be arranged: in fact, there are $2^4 = 16$ ways. For a set of three elements there are $3^9 = 19,683$ possible mappings, which means that there are that many possible operations.

A variation of this view of an operation states that an operation on a set of elements is a rule which assigns to every ordered subset of the set a unique element of the set. For a binary operation each subset has two elements. This definition illustrates that the notion of an operation involves closure as a requirement. This is in the sense that one can say that the set S is 'closed under

Table 3.10.   Mapping
of $S \times S$ into S

$*$	a	b
a	a	b
b	b	a

Table 3.11.   A different
mapping and so a diffe-
rent operation

$*$	a	b
a	b	a
b	a	b

the operation ∘' means whenever x and y are both members of the set S there is a unique element z in S such that $x \circ y = z$.

A second viewpoint

The approach discussed so far, with its two variations, is a very strict interpretation of an operation. In mathematics another view may be taken in which closure is not so closely involved (but is there in another form). This view states that an operation on a set of elements is a rule which assigns to every ordered subset of the set a unique element of a differently designated set. Suppose this first-mentioned set is S and the second-mentioned set is T. If T should be S or a subset of S, S would be closed under the operation. Thus the set of integers is closed under the binary operation of addition, as the sum of two integers is always an integer, but the set of integers is not closed under the operation of division, because the division can yield a rational number as its resultant. If S is the set of integers and T the set of rational numbers the set S is not closed under division, but T is closed. So the notion of closure is still involved with the notion of the operation.

Thus, if these two approaches to the concept of an operation are taken, the first (in its two forms) stricter than the second, the notion of closure is found to be important—it applies to the set S or the set T. It can be observed that a combination always has to produce a unique resultant, either in the set of combining elements (S) or in another specified set (T). As there always has to be a resultant, there are never any combinations that are impossible or without a resultant and are still meeting the definitions of an operation—in the sense that if a multiplication table is drawn up to depict the mappings, every cell will be filled in and none left empty.

It is this feature that was not found in the formulation of a grouping. But it is an essential aspect of a groupoid which involves the mathematical interpretation of an operation, and will be shown later in the chapter to be an important feature of children's handling of a mathematical group structure.

The mathematical view applied to operational thought

In this chapter studies will be reported which were designed to illustrate the viability of the notion of operativity that is presented in the form of the groupoid model. The assumption is that the model may be taken as an analogy to the structure of thought and that concrete operational thinking may be analysed in a way that is parallel to well-known and accepted mathematical constructs.

Piaget's view of operational thought has been well presented in his book *Genetic Epistemology*, published in 1970. He attributed four major characteristics to an operation: (a) it is an internalized action, (b) it is reversible, (c) it supposes some invariance or conservation, and (d) it is part of a system of operations, a total structure. The characteristics of such a structure are: (a) laws apply to the whole system, (b) the laws are of transformations, and (c) it is self-regulating and conforms to a principle of closure (Piaget, 1970b, pp. 21–23).

The groupoid model can be seen to have close connections with this point of view. The major changes lie in establishing closure as more important for the groupoid concept, reducing the significance of reversibility (which can be involved with some groupoids that have inverses, but in other cases may not be relevant), and emphasizing the transformation aspect in the form of making combinations of two elements to be replaced by a third in the system.

EXPERIMENTAL EVIDENCE

To illustrate an application of the groupoid model two studies will be discussed which examine children's ability to effect mappings with a mathematical group. The group chosen was the cyclic three-group known as the rotations of an equilateral triangle, the elements of which are: a = rotation through $0°$ or $360°$ (identity element), b = rotation through $120°$, c = rotation through minus $120°$. The appropriate group multiplication table is found in Table 3.12. Here, $*$ stands for the operation 'combined with' or 'followed by'. If three points on a board are coloured brown, blue, and yellow, and arranged to form an equilateral triangle as given in Figure 3.4, then the rotations of Table 3.12 can be applied.

Taking brown as the starting point and rotating around the centre of the circle, a combination of b and b (that is $b * b = c$ in Table 3.12) means moving first to yellow (b) and then to blue (b), which could have been achieved by just going direct from brown to blue (c). All other entries in the cells of Table 3.12 may be obtained in like manner. The nine combinations, with their resultants, are $aa = a$, $ab = b$, $ac = c$, $ba = b$, $bb = c$, $bc = a$, $ca = c$, $cb = a$, $cc = b$. The structure fulfils the four requirements of closure, an identity element, associativity, and each element having an inverse.

A study concerned with the understanding of mathematical group material at the level of formal operations was carried out by Page (1970). It was found

TABLE 3.12. Rotations of an equilateral triangle

$*$	a	b	c
a	a	b	c
b	b	c	a
c	c	a	b

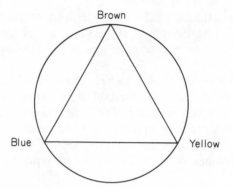

FIGURE 3.4 Equilateral triangle on a circular board

that it could be said, though with some caution, that performance on a cyclic four-group and the pendulum test of Inhelder and Piaget (1958) were related. The four-group used combinations of coloured lights. Formal operational and concrete operational children could be distinguished by their methods of approach and final level of understanding. The older subjects demonstrated understanding of the laws of a mathematical group, but younger subjects had difficulty.

In the two studies to be described in this chapter concrete operational patterns of thought were examined, and so an understanding of the axioms of the mathematical group was not sought. Page's evidence suggests that this would be too difficult. However, making consistent combinations that would establish closure was hypothesized to be within the capabilities of the concrete operational child.

The research was therefore designed to see whether children at the stage of concrete operations could use materials to show they can consistently make the combinations involved in a mathematical group as illustrated with rotations, and replace each combination with a third element. If operational thought at that stage is characterized by a grouping or groupoid structure, then the child should be able to do it.

Exploratory study: the farmhouse test

The subjects were fifty-four boys and girls aged from five to nine years in a parochial primary school situated in a suburb that was in group 2 of a six-group rating of Newcastle suburbs for social status (Newton, 1972). (Group 1 represented the highest status). They were individually administered form B of the Peabody picture vocabulary test (Dunn, 1965), and ten subjects were selected at the ages of five, seven, and nine whose IQ's were within the range 80 to 120. At each age there were five boys and five girls. The mean IQ's and ages were 98·4 (5 years 6 months), 101·1 (7 years 7 months), and 103·8 (9 years 7 months).

A circular board 48 cm in diameter and painted green was used to apply the rotations involved in the group given in Table 3.12. Three small wooden houses were fixed on the perimeter, equidistant from one another, and painted white with red roofs. They were in the positions of the three corners of the equilateral triangle in Figure 3.4. Each house had a window, through which the subject could look and see a small cone 10 cm in towards the centre. For each house there was a separate cone, described to the subject as a hill, and they were distinguished by their colour—brown, yellow, or blue, the colours given in Figure 3.4. The positioning of the coloured hills also formed an equilateral triangle. A small plastic farmer was placed at one of the houses.

To introduce the material, the children were told the following story: 'This is a farmer who works for the ladies who live in these houses. When he goes to a house the lady there tells him what house he is to work at for the day. She tells him by giving him a code message.'

The houses were described by the colour of their adjacent hills, and each subject was shown how he could look through the hole in a house to see its corresponding hill. This gave him a view of 'what the farmer could see when he looked out of the window of the house'. By presenting a card depicting a colour picture of a hill, the experimenter was able to indicate where the farmer was supposed to be, because such a view could only be obtained if the farmer was at that particular house.

The test was divided into four phases.

Phase 1

The subject was required to learn the meaning of the messages. There were three, corresponding to the elements of Table 3.12. They were presented on separate cards, drawn in different colours. For a, the symbol was a circle, referred to as 'stay where you are'. For b, an incomplete circle with an arrowhead at one end was 'go round that way (clockwise) to the next house'. For c, an arrowhead pointing the opposite way was 'go round that way (anticlockwise) to the next house'. If the subject had some difficulty in working out the meanings, after being shown a sequence of movements for b and c he was told the meanings, given practice, and then helped where necessary. The younger subjects all needed assistance. Phase 1 was terminated after the subject demonstrated consistent accuracy of movements in response to all three code messages.

Phase 2

The subject was told that the ladies now gave the farmer two messages at once and that he would do one after the other. The two came from all combinations of two sets of the three messages, viz. ab, ac, bc, bb, aa, cc, ba, ca, cb. These are all the combinations of Table 3.12. Because the group is commutative, the last three are simply the reversed order of the first three.

The subject was asked where the farmer would end up if he did what the two messages told him, executing what was on the first message, and then what was on the second. The messages were presented on nine separate cards in the above order, until two successive sequences yielded complete success. If complete success was not achieved within one hour (broken up into two or three sessions), phase 2 was discontinued and the testing of phase 4 was applied. When errors occurred, subjects were given help in correcting them.

Phase 3

The subject was given the following instructions: 'Here are your cards with the messages (the three codes). The farmer is at brown. The lady gives the farmer two messages together, like this. It makes him end up at one of the houses. Instead of the two messages, the lady could have given him one message, and he would still have ended up at the house she wanted him to. You show me, from your card, what message she could have given him. To work it out, think where her two messages send him and where he ends up, then think how one of your messages will send him there.'

The same cards were presented in the same order as in phase 2, to the same criterion, but each new sequence began at a different colour. Errors again led to correction.

Phase 4

Up to this point subjects had been given every opportunity to become acquainted with the ideas involved and get used to the material. Sessions were really for learning, rather than for testing. Phase 4 was used to assess whether such learning had occurred.

Test 1. The elements The three codes were presented at the three houses and the subject was asked: 'What does he do?' This made nine items.

Test 2. Reversal of elements For the same nine combinations, randomized in order, the experimenter moved the farmer and asked what message he had been given.

Test 3. The combinations in closure The phase 3 tasks were tested in random order.

Test 4. Reversal of combinations The same phase 3 tasks of test 3 were involved, but the subject presented cards containing the two messages to the experimenter, who had to select one message for the two and give it as his answer. The subject had to say whether the experimenter was correct or incorrect, and if the latter, he had to offer the right answer. The experimenter made an 'incorrect' choice on four of the nine items. The selection of the four was made at random.

Tests 1 and 2 concerned the meaning of the elements, which was a basic requirement, while tests 3 and 4 were the main assessments, indicating whether the subject could combine two elements to produce a third, thus making up the entries of Table 3.12.

As much as 1½ hours were required to administer the four phases, so they covered several sessions, usually lasting from 20 to 30 minutes. The order of the three ages tested was randomized.

The findings

As this was an exploratory study, it was intended to gain insight into the child's behaviour rather than to apply rigid quantification procedures. What follows is mainly a descriptive analysis, and the statistics, while considered important, are not intended to be at all comprehensive. Each level of development is discussed in turn, but there is an integration of some statistical comparisons across the ages.

The child at the age of five: appreciation of symbols, success at elementary combining, with failure at complete combining and closure The five year olds were able to learn the code in phase 1 and apply it to the spatial arrangement of the board, though it was necessary to tell them clearly what the symbols meant. Further, simple telling was not enough. They needed trials using them, eliminating errors with help from the experimenter, over a period of about 15 minutes. In the early parts they generally showed some confusion about the translation of the symbols to the actual physical model, but this was finally overcome by all except one. In this one case the following exchange occurred after about 20 minutes.

> *Subject 1* 'Move your hand around the board to show the way he goes round for this message. (She does it correctly). He is at brown. Where will he go if he gets this message?' (She gives the wrong answer.)

While they did learn the code in phase 1 there were often mistakes in phase 2 by reversing the direction of movement from that depicted on the card. They had difficulty in maintaining a consistency of response.

Phase 2 combinations of a with the other two symbols were among the easiest items and led to eventual success. This may be attributed to the fact that the identity element is no movement, so that there are not two displacements required but only one. Five year olds could handle one movement, but were not consistent with two. Errors were compiled for the items that required two movements and those that required one because they had a combination with a. Mean errors are given in Table 3.13. When t tests were applied between one movement and two movements for each age level it was found that at the age of five two movements were significantly harder than one ($t = 2.86$, $df = 8$, $p < 0.05$), but this was not the case at the ages of seven and nine, where both kinds were handled more accurately (age 7, $t = 2.17$, $df = 9$, N.S.; age 9, $t = 0.51$, $df = 9$, N.S.).

Sometimes combinations more difficult than those with the identity element

TABLE 3.13.   Performance at three age levels

Age	N	Mean errors, 1 move-ment, phase 2	Mean errors, 2 move-ments, phase 2	Mean time (min), phase 1 + 2	Mean incon-sisten-cies, phase 2	Number of subjects scoring 7 + out of 9			
						Test 1, ele-ments	Test 2, ele-ments	Test 3, clo-sure	Test 4, clo-sure
5	10	6·70	10·40	52·00	4·44 ($N=9$)	7	0	1	1
7	10	3·90	5·10	35·50	2·80	10	10	9	8
9	10	0·90	1·10	19·00	0·50	10	10	10	9

were correctly made by the five year olds, but not consistently. Children might correctly answer *cc*, but not *bc*, and vice versa, or they might have an item correct on one occasion and get it wrong the next time. In sum, they were unable to show full competence on the combining of two transformations. Consequently, they were not given phase 3, except for two cases.

Inconsistency of response was measured by taking for each age group the average number of times the subjects had an item correct and then on sub-sequent presentation had it wrong. Total possible inconsistencies was 9, as there were nine items. Table 3.13 indicates that there was a decrease in in-consistencies with age, which was found to be significant by a one-way analysis of variance ($F = 8·83$, $df = 2/26$, $p < 0·005$). When *post hoc* comparisons were made using Duncan's multiple range test, five and seven year olds were significantly more inconsistent (at the 5 per cent level) than nine year olds, but five and seven year olds did not differ significantly from one another.

Two behaviours were isolated as reasons for some of these errors on the part of the five year olds. First, difficulty was experienced with the idea that two transformations had to be executed in succession. The following is representative.

Subject 2   Shown *bb* on two occasions he only effects the first transforma-tion and ignores the second. The same happens on two occasions with *cb*. Given *bc* on one trial he takes the first message; on a later presentation he takes the second. With *cc* he treats it as the one movement to be carried out three times. This behaviour persists despite explanations throughout that two elements are to be considered.

Second, children occasionally did not appreciate the necessity of moving on from the point reached by the first transformation. One girl had this sequence.

Subject 3   In explanation of her reasoning when given *cb* with the farmer at brown, she says: 'That one (the first) tells him to go to the blue house (correct), and that one (the second) tells him to go to the yellow house (correct if the starting point is still brown, but it now has to be blue). So he will end up at the yellow house.'

The requirement of closure, where a third element is substituted for the combination of two, was even more demanding, and there was distinct lack of success. In addition to the difficulties mentioned so far one faulty strategy observed for *bb* and *cc* was to select the same message as that which was repeated on the card. Lacking the facility to deal with the task appropriately they selected an easier perception determined response.

Two of the ten children at the age of five succeeded on phase 2 within one hour, and so were given phase 3. They were allowed extra continued sessions to see if, with extended time, they could achieve success. Perhaps the failures of the others were because of a lack of sufficient learning time, rather than a lack of cognitive capacity. One of the two achieved success after a total of two hours, and passed the tests of phase 4. It was accordingly not possible to say that the closure behaviour of phase 3 was definitely beyond the reach of five year olds. However, with the failure of the other child after $2\frac{1}{2}$ hours, at which time he expressed a desire to discontinue, it was clear that success was very rare indeed.

Fisher exact probability tests showed that children aged five differed significantly from those aged seven ($p < 0.005$) and nine ($p < 0.005$) on tests 3 and 4 (closure), while those aged seven and nine were not significantly different from one another. The number of successful subjects is given in Table 3.13. The seven and nine year olds were able to combine all pairs, and get a resultant from them to effect closure, thereby filling in all the cells of Table 3.12. Most of the younger subjects did not achieve this level of performance, and closure was beyond their reach. However, they were able to understand the meaning of the symbols used and were not significantly different from the other ages (on a Fisher exact test) when the material was presented in a familiar way (test 1), but had difficulty when it was slightly changed (test 2)—on Fisher exact tests five year olds differed significantly from children at the ages of seven ($p < 0.005$) and nine ($p < 0.005$). No systematic sex differences were observed.

The child at the age of seven: successful closure after eliminating errors with combining The seven-year-old subjects did succeed with the main task of the test—the closure of phase 3, maintained in the subsequent testing of phase 4. All but one passed on phase 2 in less than an hour, and completed everything in $1\frac{1}{2}$ hours or less. The average time was 1 hour 10 minutes. Some were quite fast: the three quickest took 35, 40, and 50 minutes, with hardly any errors at all. Their IQ's on the Peabody were 100, 93, 120. To compare all three ages, time to completion of phases 1 and 2 was taken as an index of difficulty. Mean times are given in Table 3.13. A significant F in a one-way analysis of variance showed that speed increased significantly with age ($F = 20.29$, $df = 2/27$, $p < 0.001$). *Post hoc* comparisons by Duncan's multiple range test, applying an alpha of 0·05, indicated that the differences between all means (ages five and seven, seven and nine, and five and nine) were significant.

The seven year olds made some of the mistakes of the five year olds, but were able to eliminate them. With experience, for instance, they were able to forego the idea that just the first message in the pair could be enough, or that one did not have to move on from the point reached, or that two like symbols necessarily produced a third that was like them. These difficulties they shared with the five year olds.

What they could do that the younger children could not was the combining of all pairs and getting a product from them to effect closure, filling in all the cells of Table 3.12. In regard to the four laws of a group, in addition to closure they demonstrated facility with the inverse law, by seeing that bc and cb returned the farmer to his starting point and had the same effect as the identity element a, and that there was an identity element which made no change to the other elements. Associativity was not assessed and was not particularly involved.

One subject who had not successfully completed phase 2 after an hour, and hence had not been given phase 3, was nonetheless given the tests of phase 4 (but four days later). Out of the eighteen items in tests 3 and 4 she only had one error. Such development of understanding without being given phase 3 was achieved by no five year old.

A supplementary finding was that many subjects improved their performance after a rest interval of several hours, a day, or several days. There was evidence of this in eight of the ten subjects, and it suggested that a form of rehearsal was involved. A somewhat similar phenomenon was found with the learning of class inclusion, when scores of trained subjects improved significantly after a two-week interval of no training (Sheppard, 1973).

The child at the age of nine: successful closure as with the seven year old, but in half the time Average time for completion was 40 minutes. Generally these subjects made only one or two errors at the beginning of phase 2 and of phase 3, which were immediately overcome. They virtually had direct success, without the need for training and introduction to the general idea. They handled all aspects of the task with ease.

Main study

The exploratory study showed that under the conditions of testing, five year olds generally did not establish closure, while seven and nine year olds did, there being an improvement with age on several measures of the learning process applied to a mathematical group used as a groupoid.

The main study, which is reported in detail elsewhere (Sheppard, 1974a), was designed to extend these findings and examine the data in a more systematic way. A similar learning task was used but it was reduced to very elementary constituents. It did not have the complications of the somewhat extraneous aspect of looking through a window, having a hill plus a house, using colour pictures, and building up a story about a farmer.

Transfer tasks were introduced to assess the question of whether successful subjects had merely displayed rote memory learning or not. They might have demonstrated their facility with the combinations in the same way as they would have learnt lists of paired nonsense syllables, and so would not really be able to combine two elements to produce a third in the system, operating within a group structure. Two additional tests were used to see whether the same structure could be applied with different problem material.

The operational solution of equations was examined, with the elements being derived from the learnt group structure in one case and numbers being used in the other.

Finally, tests of concrete operations were given, so that a more precise index of operational level than age could be applied.

The children who were tested came from a school situated in a suburb that was in group 4 of a six-group rating of Newcastle suburbs for social status (Newton, 1972). (Group 1 had the highest status.) Thirty subjects were chosen from a sample of forty-six, with sixteen rejected because their IQ's on form B of the Peabody Picture Vocabulary Test (Dunn, 1965) were too high or too low. IQ's of the accepted children ranged from 89 to 118. There were ten subjects at each of the ages of six, eight, and ten years. The group IQ's were 99·2 (age six), 98·6 (age eight), and 103·0 (age ten). However, three of the thirty subjects left the school and two failed the initial basic testing situation, so the groups were finally made up of 7 six year olds, 8 eight year olds, and 10 ten year olds.

The mathematical group material was a white card disc with a diameter of 20 cm, a 5-cent coin, and sets of three cards which described the three rotations of the group. The coin could be moved between three equidistant coloured circles that were drawn on the edge of the disc. The subject was told that in the game he was going to play the coin could be on one of the three colours, but could only get there by means of cards that were then placed before him. The first card read 'Around and back again'. The second read 'Next circle' and below it was an outline drawing of a 'clock'. It was a drawing of a stopwatch. A real stop-watch was then produced and used to illustrate the direction in which a clock's hand moved. This card was presented to mean that the coin should move to the next circle on the disc in the direction of a clock's movement. The third card was the same as the second except that a large × crossed out the clock and was interpreted to mean the opposite direction.

Learning sessions were similar to those for the farmhouse test, but adapted to the new materials. There were three learning phases, followed by another three testing phases.

In phase 1 the subject was presented with the three cards, instructed in their meaning, and then required to carry out the rotations depicted on them. The phase was completed when the subject was able to make a perfect sequence of all the rotations. In phase 2 the subject was told that two rotations were to be executed in succession, and two sets of the three cards were combined in all the nine possible ways: *aa*, *ab*, *ac*, *ba*, *bb*, *bc*, *ca*, *cb*, *cc*. For each of these combinations the child was required to state the colour at which the coin would finish. If he did not demonstrate perfect performance on a sequence within one hour (broken up into two or three sessions), phase 2 was discontinued and final testing was administered. When errors occurred, subjects were given help in correcting them, In phase 3 the subject was given a third set of the cards, and instead of naming a colour he was required to point to the one card in his array which could replace the two combined cards in the experimenter's array. Errors again led to correction.

Following the learning session there were the phase 4 tests of the subject's grasp of the mathematical group, using first the learning material, then two transfer tasks, and finally the equations tests. On each task he was first tested on nine items concerning the basic meaning of the cards and the movements (testing of the phase 1 learning), and then on the nine possible combinations that could be replaced by a third rotation (testing of the phase 3 learning). A score of 7 out of 9 on this last test was regarded as a 'pass'. The first transfer task involved the use of three cards which read 'Go right around', 'Clockwise to nearest house', and 'Anticlockwise to nearest house'. These were the three elements of the mathematical group and were to apply to the movements of a small plastic man who could be moved between the coloured houses, set equidistant on a circular piece of wood painted green and 15 cm in diameter. Through initial discussion the experimenter was able to see that the cards were understood. The second transfer task involved three cards which read 'Don't move', 'Next corner like a clock', and 'Next corner *not* like a clock', used to apply to the rotations of a cardboard equilateral triangle with sides 10 cm in length. One corner of the triangle was coloured red and was to be used to orientate the triangle when rotated. The three tests, which will be referred to as 'circle', 'houses', and 'triangle', were all scored in the same manner (7 out of 9 = pass).

The last assessment in the testing session was of equations, the tests being of two types. One involved the mathematical group training material (circles equations), while the other involved numbers (numbers equations). The notion was drawn from research by G. S. Halford (1972, personal communication). The numbers task was to find an unknown, when given other parts of an equation; for example $4 + 2x = 10$ can be solved for x. It is the same as $4 + x + x = 10$. The initial 4 can be regarded as a starting point and 10 as an end point, so the equation can be applied to the group structure material as 'brown + unknown movement + that unknown movement again = green'. This was presented to subjects in the circles equations task as: 'The coin is at brown. It gets to green by doing the same kind of movement twice. What is the movement? It is one of the three cards we use. Pick out the correct one. Which card do you do twice to get to green?'

Some equations involved two unknowns, for example $4 + x + y = 2$. This was presented as: 'The coin is at brown. It gets to green by two different kinds of movement. What are they? You have to pick out two different cards to end up at green.' There were six items, covering all possible combinations used with phase 3, but omitting duplication by commutativity.

TABLE 3.14. Materials and transformations for conservation tests

Conservation	Materials	Item	Transformations
Quantity	Two equivalent transparent beakers with equal quantities of water; a tall, thin beaker; a short, wide beaker; two small beakers	1	Thinner and taller beaker
		2	Shorter and wider beaker
		3	Two small beakers
Substance	Two equivalent balls of plasticine	1	Long 'snake'
		2	A cross
		3	Two small balls
Number	Two sets of five green plastic squares	1	One row spread out
		2	One row arranged in a circular pattern
		3	One row pushed close together
Length	Two pencils of equal length	1	One moved slightly to the right
		2	One moved to make a T
		3	One moved slightly to the left
Weight	Two equivalent balls of plasticine; a small balance	1	Pancake shape
		2	Broken into six balls
		3	Rolling into a snake and joining ends to make a circle

For numbers equations subjects were presented with four red cards and five blue cards. The blue cards were placed before the subject adjacent to one another and on each card was the number -2, -1, 0, $+1$, or $+2$, arranged in that order from left to right. Children were given simple instructions to indicate that the numbers referred to operations that could be made on the red cards, which were arranged in a square pattern on the subject's left. The six equations, without the answer given in brackets, were:

(a) $4 + 2x = 4 (+0)$,
(b) $4 + x + y = 5 (+0, +1)$ or $(-1, +2)$,
(c) $4 + x + y = 2 (+0, -2)$,
(d) $4 + 2x = 8 (+2)$,
(e) $4 + x + y = 4 (+1, -1)$ or $(+2, -2)$, and
(f) $5 + 2x = 1 (-2)$.

A fifth red card was provided for item (f). As an example, item (b) was presented by the experimenter saying and demonstrating: 'You start with 4 (pointing to the red cards) and end up with 5. You do two different things to end up with 5. What two different cards (pointing to the blue cards) will you do to end up with 5, after starting with 4?'

Six months after this period of testing the children were retested on the basic meaning of the mathematical group cards and the rotations, and then on the nine possible combinations that produced a resultant (the phase 3 learning). This was done for the learning material (circles) and the transfer tasks (houses, triangle). This constituted phase 5. In a further session which made up phase 6, they were administered Piagetian tests of operational thinking, covering conservation of quantity, of substance, of number, of length, of weight, seriation, crossclassification, horizontality, and transitivity. The order of these tests was randomized for each subject.

The conservation tests each consisted of three items requiring a judgment and an explanation that conformed to established criteria. Two stimuli were first judged to be equal in the attribute discussed, then one was transformed and a further judgment was elicited. For example, in conservation of number (of plastic squares) the experimenter asked: 'Have you more, have I more, or do we both have the same number?' The materials and transformations are given in Table 3.14.

The materials of the seriation test were a set of ten rods of one colour and a set of nine rods of a different colour that were to be inserted between the rods of the first set. The nineteen rods increased in length by 0·4 cm. For the horizontality test children were first shown a bottle containing some coloured water. The bottle was then removed and the children were required to complete a test booklet of eight drawings of the bottle set at different angles. They were to draw the water line on each bottle outline and 'fill in the water' so it would 'look right'. The materials for the items of the crossclassification test and the transitivity test are given in Table 3.15.

For all tests except seriation and horizontality a satisfactory explanation was required for each item response before it could be marked correct, and if two of the three items were correct then the subject was scored as operational. On horizontality a score of 6 or more out of 8 was regarded as operational, and on seriation the subject was required to seriate at least fifteen rods.

The findings

At all phases the six year olds performed below the level of the older subjects.

TABLE 3.15. Materials for crossclassification and transitivity

Test	Item	Materials
Crossclassification	1	4 blue circles, 4 red circles, 4 blue squares, 4 red squares
	2	Pictures of 4 boys, 4 girls, 4 men, 4 women
	3	4 green rectangles, 4 yellow rectangles, 4 green triangles, 4 yellow triangles
Transitivity	1	Pencils measuring 17·5 cm, 17·5 cm, 16 cm, to involve the logic of $A = B$, $B > C$, therefore $A > C$
	2	Pencils measuring 17·5 cm, 17·5 cm, 19 cm, to involve the logic of $A = B$, $B < C$, therefore $A < C$
	3	Pencils measuring 16 cm, 16 cm, 15·5 cm, to involve the logic of $A = B$, $B > C$, therefore $A > C$

TABLE 3.16. Time and error measures of the learning in phases 1 and 2

Age group	Phase 1		Phase 2	
	Mean time (min)	Mean errors	Mean time (min)	Mean errors
6	13·7	3·4	47·5	41·3
8	4·7	1·6	9·8	1·5
10	2·9	1·3	6·9	2·3

However, at phase 1, in which basic understanding was necessary for subsequent performance, they were able to reach the same standard as the other children when they were given the time and practice. Table 3.16 gives mean time and error measures on the first two phases. Analysis of variance indicated significant differences between the age groups on all four measures except the phase 1 errors. The six year olds, while taking longer to learn the meaning and use of the cards, did not perform with them significantly differently from the eight and ten year olds. When F-tests were calculated for each test of each phase (taking phase 6 as a total test of operativity), there was a significant difference between age groups in each case. The six year olds had consistently more difficulty than the eight and ten year olds, who did not differ significantly from one another.

Time on phase 1 was measured as the time in minutes from beginning the first session to the point where the subject passed all nine items that tested his understanding of the three rotation cards when the coin was set at each of the three colours. Time on phase 2 was the number of minutes from beginning phase 2 until the subject passed all nine items involving combinations of two elements, or until a total of one hour from the beginning of phase 1 was reached, at which point phase 2 was discontinued. The time the experimenter was involved was not constant from child to child, because he corrected individual errors as they arose.

While the eight and ten age groups did not differ significantly on most measures, they did differ on time to completion of phase 3 (t (16) = 2·69, $p < 0.02$). They did not differ in mean score on the circles equations or numbers equations of phase 4. The equations tests were scored out of 6. The means were: circles equations for eight year olds, 4.5, and for ten year olds, 4·0; numbers equations for eight year olds, 4.6, and for ten year olds, 5·2. These indicated that the subjects were quite successful on these two tasks. At the age of eight there was a significant correlation between circles equations and numbers equations ($r = 0.68, p < 0.01$). On the other hand, for a ten year old a Pearson r between circles equations and numbers equations was not significant ($r = 0.12$, N.S.).

When the phase 4 tests of circles, houses, and triangle were given, all eighteen subjects in the eight and ten years age groups passed on all three tasks, while only one of the 7 six year olds succeeded, and then only on circles. Table 3.17 gives

TABLE 3.17. Number of successful subjects on the mathematical group tests and the concrete operations tests

Tests (Age group N)	age group		
	6 years 7	8 years 8	10 years 10
Phase 4			
Circles	1	8	10
Houses	0	8	10
Triangle	0	8	10
Phase 5			
Circles	0	7	10
Houses	0	6	10
Triangle	1	5	10
Phase 6			
Conservation of quantity	2	8	10
Conservation of substance	2	8	10
Conservation of number	4	8	9
Conservation of length	2	8	9
Conservation of weight	3	8	10
Seriation	7	8	10
Crossclassification	2	7	9
Horizontality	1	4	7
Transitivity	1	7	10

the number of successful subjects at each age for the initial testing of the mathematical group (using the later sample size), the retesting, and the tests of concrete operations. The six year olds were generally unsuccessful, but one of the three who reached phase 3 in the learning sessions passed on circles in phase 4, and another one given phase 3 passed on triangle in phase 5. These two subjects were the only six year olds to give a consistent pattern of operational responses on the tests of concrete operations. They both passed eight of the nine tests. The ten year olds maintained perfect success, while the eight year olds almost did so. Only one subject failed to maintain accurate solutions on circles, two failed on houses, and three failed on triangle. Almost every eight and ten year old was scored as being at the concrete operational stage on almost every test of operativity administered. The one eight year-old who did not score at the concrete operational level on at least eight of the nine tests (she succeeded on seven) was the one who also failed on the mathematical group circles, houses, and triangle. Solving the mathematical group was therefore closely related to operativity level.

The Fisher exact probability tests on the Table 3.17 frequencies for the three age groups on the tests of the mathematical group in phase 4 and the retesting in phase 5 showed that the six year olds were significantly less successful than the eight and ten year olds (who did not differ from one another), except for the comparison between the six and eight years age groups on the phase 5 retesting of triangle. The significant Fisher exact probabilities were $p < 0.01$ for the six and eight years age comparison. The eight and ten year olds evidenced complete transfer from the teaching material to the new material on phase 4, with only a slight loss for the eight year olds on phase 5 retesting. No systematic sex differences were observed.

The relation between concrete operations performance and success at the various tests of the mathematical group throughout the phases was examined by the Fisher exact test. If a child succeeded on seven of the nine tests of concrete operations he was classified as operational; if he passed one or two only of the nine he was preoperational. This classification incorporated all of the subjects. For the tasks of each phase the children were classified as pass or fail. Thus, for each test a 2×2 contingency table could be drawn up, and these are given in Table 3.18. Except for phase 1, when all subjects were successfully acquiring the basic understanding of the material, there was at

TABLE 3.18. Contingency tables relating operativity and mathematical group solution

Task	Operativity	
	Operational	Preoperational
Phase 1		
Pass	20	5
Fail	0	0
Phase 2		
Pass	20	1
Fail	0	4
Phase 3		
Pass	19	0
Fail	1	5
Phase 4 circles		
Pass	19	0
Fail	1	5
Phase 4 houses		
Pass	18	0
Fail	2	5
Phase 4 triangle		
Pass	18	0
Fail	2	5
Phase 5 circles		
Pass	17	0
Fail	3	5
Phase 5 houses		
Pass	17	0
Fail	3	5
Phase 5 triangle		
Pass	19	0
Fail	1	5

each test a strong correlation between operativity and performance on the mathematical group task, significant at $p < 0.001$.

Concrete operations and solving the mathematical group

Taking the two studies together, one can say that closure in the mathematical group eluded most of the five and six year olds, but they also had difficulty with simpler tasks, such as the combinations of phase 2. However, many of the seven and eight year olds had the same difficulties, though less pronounced. The five and six year olds showed that they did understand the nature of the task on phase 1 by their success with it. It just took them longer to be able to remember the meaning of the elements. Similarly, they took longer on phase 2, but their error responses were of the same type as those errors made by the seven to ten year olds. The difference was in their failure to achieve consistently accurate solutions. On this basis the younger subjects may be taken to have understood the rudimentary aspects of the mathematical group task, but to have failed to go significantly beyond them.

While different age groups were used in the two studies, it was nevertheless possible to compare some of the effects of learning-task difficulty. On the time taken to the end of phase 3 and final closure test performance on the mathematical group, there were no significant differences between the ages of seven and eight, or nine and ten when tests were applied. On the qualitative side, five year olds did appear to have more difficulty than six year olds on understanding the symbols, but they did not have significantly different time scores on phase 1. Overall, the farmhouse test was not particularly more difficult than the circles test.

The equations tests were used to explore further the depth of understanding achieved by those who had shown they could solve the mathematical group task. The notion was drawn from the quantity judgments structure of 'same', 'more', and 'less' proposed by Halford (1972) and discussed earlier in this chapter. Making use of these elements in a combinatorial system, the child is assumed to come to know, for example, that 'same' plus 'more' yields 'more'. If water from one of two *identical* beakers is poured into a third of different shape (*same*) and then *more* water is poured into the third on top of that (*more*), the child of a certain age appreciates that the third holds *more* water than the original which has not been touched (*more*). Halford (1972, personal communication) has further proposed that this combination of 'same + more = more' has a direct parallel in mathematics, with $0 + 3 = 3$, or $0 + 5 = 5$, or $0 + 1 = 1$, etc. If the preoperational child is unaware of the 'meaning' of the first element ('same' or 0), and for him it is an unknown x, then we have $x + $ more = more, or $x + 3 = 3$. In both cases one can solve for x. With continued experience of such equations, the child can discover that x is an identity element which effects no change.

The assumption is that attainment of concrete operations involves the solution of equations, of varying form. In the light of this, the main study investigated whether subjects who were at the stage of concrete operations could handle such equations in mathematical form and, more importantly, as transformations. Having learnt the mathematical group, the children were found to be capable of solving these equations, and at the age of eight at least, there was a correlation between handling numbers and handling spatial displacements.

However, the equations are not seen to exist in isolation, but rather as part of a larger combinatorial system (such as the groupoid or mathematical group) which links the elements. This applies equally to the mathematical group of integers under addition, the groupoid of 'same', 'more', and 'less', and the mathematical group of rotations of an equilateral triangle. The equations form part of the system by the law of closure, which requires any two elements to be mapped into a single element that is a member of the set, i.e. there is a form of coding and all elements are interrelated. For the closure to occur, however, the child first has to appreciate that elements can be combined, a feature which is central to the nature of operational thought. For instance, in conservation there is a combination of relations, such as height and breadth of containers; in class inclusion of number one set combined with another produces the whole, which is larger; in classification the elements combine according to various criteria that establish different sets; etc. The preoperational child, in failing to make such combinations in a consistent manner, does not discover the principle of closure. Instead, he is influenced by extraneous features and may respond particularly to perceptual cues. Such a perceptual dominance was observed with the younger subjects, who often thought that the combination of an element with itself was mapped into itself ($b * b = b$, $c * c = c$) in phase 3 of the farmhouse test. Seeing an element repeated on the card they chose that element to be repeated again, i.e. the perceptual configuration had a dominant effect on their response.

While most of the five or six year olds, at the age of preoperational thought, were unable consistently to form the image of a transformation and store it in memory so that a second could follow it in sequence, they did, however, have success at elementary combining, evidenced by higher performance of the five year olds when the identity element was to be combined with another element and by their consistently correct appreciation of some of the combinations (although not all). They were also able to handle the meaning of the symbols, a basic requirement for the higher level of achievement. On the other hand, those who were seven years plus, at the age for concrete operations, could with practice combine two elements to produce a third in closure. Further, in the second study, those who succeeded on the mathematical group tasks were at concrete operations in the phase 5 testing, and presumably were operational also when tested at phase 4 six months earlier, because they were average in IQ and passed almost all of the tests of concrete operations when they were given. The consistently obtained correlations between operativity and mathematical group solution (except for the basic phase 1 comparison) indicated that consistent mapping in closure, with two combined elements replaced by one, came with concrete operations. The groupoid model, using a mathematical group, was relevant to such a developmental analysis.

CONCLUSION

The detailed analysis of a mathematical group has been provided as an illustration of one form of groupoid which can have a direct bearing on the nature of operational thought as presented by Piaget. When the mathematical group study is related to the experiments on the quantity judgments groupoid discussed earlier, it is to be noted that being able to make the combinations in closure coincided with the onset of concrete operations, and that preoperational children had difficulty. It can be asserted that what essentially distinguishes operational thought is that it involves the combining of two elements to be replaced by a third in a closed mapping, and that this is not performed at the preoperational level. This is the achievement of concrete operations that makes it a new stage in the child's development: he can now perform an operation in its real sense; he can combine and map.

This achievement has been described in another way by Lunzer (1960, p. 31), who refers to the child's examining two judgments at the same time and coming to a conclusion. The two judgments to be examined are like the two elements to be combined in the groupoid, and the conclusion reached is like the resultant in the groupoid mapping. McLaughlin (1963) has described it in terms of processing of concepts. As he has illustrated it, in solving the class inclusion problem operationally the child demonstrates that, as well as being able to classify eighteen beads as 'brown wooden' and two others as 'white wooden', he can simultaneously think of a third concept 'wooden of any colour'. The younger child can handle the two classifications together, but generally does not integrate the third with them. As a result he tends to say that there are more brown beads, when asked whether there are more wooden beads or more brown beads.

The proposal that concrete operational thought can be regarded in terms of a mapping in closure is considered to be the major outcome of the research reported in this chapter. The evidence points to difficulties with closure experienced by the preoperational child in various conceptual areas and to the success with which the concrete operational child can meet tasks which require it for satisfactory solution. Collis (1972) has also found it a significant variable in his analysis of operational thought, at the level of formal operations.

Possible future research

Brainerd (1972) has proposed to examine other forms of structure as models for operational thought, and such an approach would be an appropriate sequel to the research reported in this chapter. Increasingly more complex groupoids, like the semigroup, monoid, group, quasigroup, field, and ring could be investigated in various ways, but particularly in developmental studies. Also, other groupoids of the type discussed earlier could be specified and examined developmentally. New tests could thus be devised from the groupoid model to assess levels of cognitive development. The nature of an operation as interpreted in the model also bears further scrutiny. Tasks that involve the closed mappings of an operation could be compared with ones that do not, and a task analysis of the basic mechanisms involved in an operation could be made. These mechanisms could be graded in order of difficulty, to assess developmental changes. Some mechanisms would be typically concrete operational; others formal operational. Collis (1972) has done this with mathematical material.

Such a research programme would throw some light on how the various cognitive experiences of the child and adolescent are integrated, and could lead to possible reformulations of the Piagetian position at the theoretical level. If a task analysis of cognitive mechanisms is carried out together with examination of structures, there would be some integration of the 'automaton' and 'competence' models specified by Flavell and Wohlwill (1969).

4

THE ROLE OF LANGUAGE IN THE DEVELOPMENT OF THINKING— THEORETICAL APPROACHES

J. A. Keats and D. M. Keats

From a phylogenetic point of view it is tempting to equate language and thinking. Both spoken language and operational thinking occur for the first time in human beings and so it is natural to link the two. Furthermore, from the ontological point of view of developmental psychology, both show rapid increases between the third and seventh years of age, which also suggests a ielationship. It is because of this rapid early development that chapters on this topic are introduced here, following those on the earliest stages of operational thought. Many of the scholars who have carried out studies on the role of language in thinking have tended to consider subjects in this age range.

Theorists have been grouped here into five categories: first, those who follow Piaget in considering language development as dependent on cognitive development; second, those who take the Russian view that thinking is inner speech and thus a development from language; third, those who see thinking as constrained by the characteristics of language either in its structure or lexicon; fourth, those whose position derives from developments of Chomskyan psycholinguistic theory; and, last, those who explain the relationship between language behaviour and cognitive activity in terms of biological development. In this chapter the theories will be presented and related to the Piagetian view. In the next chapter the research evidence will be evaluated in terms of the types of question which these theoretical positions generate, and some empirical studies using a different approach will be described.

PIAGET'S THEORY OF LANGUAGE AND THOUGHT

From the Piagetian viewpoint (Furth, 1969; Piaget, 1923, 1954a, 1963; Piaget and Inhelder, 1969; Sinclair, 1971, 1973) the development of language and the growth of the child through the various stages of the development of logico-mathematical reasoning are not indivisibly linked. For Piaget, cognitive development is the independent and language development the dependent variable: the essential component of intelligent functioning is symbolic representation, of which language is regarded as but one special kind among many. This interpretation does not deny the importance of language or the existence of close positive relationships between language and thought, especially in their higher forms, but rather aims to show that the symbolic functions which are essential to logical operations may be developed independently of language.

For explication of this view Piaget turns first to evidence from early childhood. The earliest evidence of intelligent functioning is seen at the sensorimotor level, well before the apprearance of language in any form. For example, the child may grasp for distant or hidden objects. However, these 'constructions' or 'action-schemes' are made without the use of any type of symbolic representation. They are based on perceptions and movements, and do not show any indication of representative evocation of an object or event which is not present. Thought in the sense of representational thought does not appear until the second year, when the child first shows signs of 'semiotic functioning'.

The semiotic functions

The early semiotic functions include deferred imitation, symbolic play, drawing, mental images, and verbal evocation, which begin to appear almost at the same time in the second year. They differ from the earlier responses to signals and signs of the sensori-motor stage of the first year, where the signal or sign is undifferentiated from what it signifies, in that for the first time it is not necessary for the object or event to be present for the representative evocation to occur. This is an important step because it means that the child has developed 'differential signifiers' which enable him to refer to elements not perceptible at the time as well as those which are.

Piaget considers that the level of semiotic functioning reached shows the level of intelligent functioning achieved. The semiotic functions continue to develop in the child as he proceeds through the preoperational to the operational stages. Language develops at the same time, but the logical level at which the child is functioning produces the logical level of the language used—not the other way around. Thus it could be said that thought can be independent of language, but not that language is independent of thought.

(*a*) *Deferred imitation*

This is the first to appear and the least complex. Piaget notes that imitation may occur in the sensori-motor stage when a model is present, but it is not until the postsensori-motor stage that it occurs *after* the model has departed. Piaget regards deferred imitative behaviour as constituting the beginning of representation and the imitative gesture as evidence for the beginnings of a differentiated signifier.

(b) Symbolic play

The second in complexity of the early semiotic functions is symbolic play, in which the child represents a person or situation in play after the event. This behaviour does not occur at the sensori-motor level. Both objects and actions may be clearly symbolic and used to express emotions and behavioural responses to persons or occurrences which are no longer present. It is not purely imitative.

(c) Drawing

The third of the early semiotic functions is drawing, which rarely appears before two or two and a half years. Piaget regards this development as occurring at a stage intermediately between symbolic play and the fourth of the early semiotic functions, the mental image.

(d) Mental images

Piaget finds no trace at all of mental images at the sensori-motor level. He argues that, were mental images present at that stage, infants would have less difficulty than they appear to experience in regard to the permanence of objects temporarily obscured from their perceptual field. The importance of the mental image increases as it continues to be used in the operational stage. Piaget considers that at that stage two main types of mental image become distinguishable, the reproductive, which is an evocation of an object or situation in the past, and the anticipatory, which requires prior imagining of an as yet unrealized process (Piaget and Inhelder, 1971). The anticipatory type is not evident in the preoperational stage, which is characterized by the more static reproductive type.

In none of the four semiotic functions discussed above is there the necessity for language; indeed, they may appear before the use of nascent language. However, they are regarded by Piaget as early equivalents of thinking. Piaget discounts the notion that these forms are not thinking by pointing to the motor and perceptual nature of many of the operations of later stages in which mental imagery of a motor or visual-perceptual kind plays a particularly important part. Operations are 'actions interiorised'. Moreover, the ways in which young children use these symbolizations to reenact situations which are new, to emit behaviour which can be interpreted as emotional responses, and to varify object permanence when the object is out of the visual field are all regarded as evidence of intelligent behaviour in the preoperational child.

Language as a semiotic function

The evolution of language in the growing child follows a pattern which begins with spontaneous vocalization, appearing almost universally at between six and eleven months, followed by differentiation of phonemes by imitation at about eleven to twelve months, then one-word sentences which may express desires, emotions, and observations, leading to the use of two-word sentences at about the end of the second year. The next stage of this evolution is reached with the use of short complete sentences having neither declension nor conjugation, and finally there is the gradual acquisition of grammatical and syntactical structures which proceeds through the concrete operational stage until language is fully developed.

Although verbal evocation may arise in association with deferred imitation, linguistic behaviour as communication develops relatively late among the semiotic functions. Nascent language in this sense does not appear until verbal representation is added to the deferred imitation, permitting verbal evocation of events that are not occurring at the time. It may be noted that this interpretation implies a use of language which goes beyond the mere labelling of persons and objects and is concerned with relationships, classificatory systems, and actions.

Piaget stresses the distinction between the symbolization of the image and the symbolization function of language: what a mental image brings forth is the thing itself, whereas the word can represent a class or relationship as well as the thing itself. The distinction made in language between the signifier (the word) and what is signified (the thing) does not occur in mental images, where there is a correspondence between thing and image. However, the correspondence is not necessarily one to one, as perceptual schemata tend to be used to organize images (Piaget and Inhelder, 1971). In preoperational children the distinction between symbol and sign may not be drawn. The child tends to think that the object named could not bear any other name: the name is seen as part or characteristic of the thing itself.

The language use of preoperational children was observed by Piaget and his associates (Piaget and Inhelder, 1969) in studies which led him to describe it as egocentric rather than social. He described the phenomenon of preoperational children who talk at the same time rather than hold a conversation. This language is not socialized in that its purpose is not to provide information or ask questions. It consists rather of 'collective monologues', in the course of which everybody talks to himself without listening to the others.

Piaget found that children of this age have great difficulty in explaining things to other children, in giving directions, and retelling a story. They appear unable to put themselves in the role of the listener, and it is not until the concrete operational stage that this is finally achieved.

An important contrast is drawn between the socially given nature of language and the egocentrism (autism) of other semiotic functions such as deferred imitation, mental imagery, and symbolic play. Unlike images and other semiotic instruments, which are created by the individual as the need arises, language is given to the child by another person in a social communication. That communication already contains a socially elaborated notation for an entire system of cognitive instruments including relationships and classifications, which are available to the child for use in the service of thought. The individual acquires the system from others, but having learned it proceeds to enrich it himself (Piaget and Inhelder, 1969). Language helps to detach thought from action by differentiating the signifiers, the words, from their significates, the actions or things which the words represent. In this regard it is one of the semiotic functions. The distinction between the socially given nature of language and the autism of the other semiotic functions is further emphasized by Piaget's use of the terms 'sign' for the symbols of language and 'symbol' for the symbols of other semiotic functions.

Role of language in concrete operations

The acquisition of grammatical structures and syntactical complexity is a gradual process which, together with elaboration and extension of vocabulary, may proceed through the concrete operational stages. The facilitative function of language becomes apparent in that now not only does the child use language in its social function for communication but his increased use of language may also increase his powers of thought in range and rapidity. However, Piaget continues to emphasize the level of the logic reached rather than the linguistic level. There is still much evidence of the perceptual-motor side of operations, and mental images may play a very great part in these operations. Piaget maintains that it is controversial whether logico-mathematical structures are themselves linguistic or non-linguistic in nature. But language is regarded essentially as a tool, and Piaget considers that the logico-mathematical structures can be considered separately from the language in which they are either acquired or expressed.

Two types of data source are cited to support this position: on the one hand, studies in which deaf-mutes were shown to be able to attain conservation, albeit somewhat later than normal children who had language, as shown in the studies of Furth (1966), Oléron (1971), and Vincent and Affolter (Piaget, 1963); and on the other hand, the systematic comparison of linguistic progress with the development of intellectual operations in the normal child, as shown in the work of Sinclair (1967, 1969, 1971). These studies are discussed in more detail in the following chapter. Although Sinclair found a relationship between the language employed and the mode of reasoning and a close connection between the stages of development of seriation and the terms used, the interpretation given to these findings was that the mastery of certain expressions does not structure operations and nor does their absence impede their formation. The child acquires the expressions and makes their use functional according to a process similar to the mode of structuring of the operations themselves. The contribution of language is seen as directing attention to pertinent factors of a problem. Thus, language could prepare an operation but was neither sufficient nor necessary to the formation of concrete operations. Piaget considers that the use of expressions of the higher linguistic level is acquired by training. The child at first does not understand their usage; then at the preoperational level he understands but does not use them; and then he uses them himself after having reached the concrete operational level, but not spontaneously. If the preoperational child is taught higher-level expressions, he learns them with difficulty and the training rarely influences his notions of conservation. Seriation, on the other hand, can be improved by verbal training, because in seriation the linguistic process also relates to the act of comparison and therefore to the concept itself.

For Piaget, the acquisition of language alone is not sufficient to ensure the transmission of operational structures ready made. The child does not receive the structures ready made from outside through the medium of linguistic constructs. Rather, the mastery of higher orders of language is dependent on reaching the level of concrete operations. For example, the child does not master the use of inclusive definitions by genus and specific difference until seven to eight years, i.e. at the level of concrete operations, as is shown in the way such items have been used in the Binet test. Classifications in general are not mastered until the concrete operational stage, and verbal expressions that refer to the inclusion of a subclass within a class are not mastered until the concept of class inlcusion has been acquired. Piaget also points out that saying numbers is not of itself sufficient to ensure conservation of numerical wholes, nor conservation of equivalence by bi-univocal correspondence.

It is clear that in this interpretation Piaget is, as always, placing the emphasis on the logico-mathematical operations rather than on the language used to elicit whether they are present or not. Piaget also emphasizes the important role played in these operations by mental images of a perceptual-motor kind. When the child can handle the materials himself, he is able to show conservation sooner than if he has to express the relationships through language alone.

Role of language in formal operations

At the formal operational level the role of language becomes more complex as the child becomes able to carry out operations on operations. There is no doubt that language is the principal mode for doing this, but even so Piaget still does not consider that language is a sufficient condition for thought, though it may be a necessary one. In formal or hypothetical deductive operations the operations are no longer confined to manipulations of the objects themselves. The child is now able to handle propositions usually expressed verbally in terms of hypotheses, which requires not only a greater use but also a more advanced level of language. The importance of language in this level of thinking is recognized by Piaget; in fact he finds it hard to conceive how propositional operations elaborated at this level would reach an advanced stage of development without the use of language (Piaget, 1963, in Furth, 1969). However, the ability to use complex linguistic forms does not of itself ensure that the child has reached the formal level of thinking, because at that level the structures of propositional operations may be more complex than the language forms and thus go beyond the linguistic structures. Such structures need the support of verbal behaviour for their elaboration, but the current language alone may be inadequate for expressing the concepts, and an arcane supralanguage, e.g. mathematical symbols, is invented for indicating relationships, function, and such concepts as probability. Piaget considers that language could conceivably have an active influence on operations of the complex thought systems of the formal level by providing an efficient coding system which allows for the precorrection of errors occurring between encoding and decoding, but not by the transmission of ready-made structures.

Implications and problems

The theme of Piaget's writing on the relationship between language and thought is that of the independence of thought from language. Thus concepts and the language through which they are acquired may be considered independently. Piaget strongly rejects any view that language is more than a tool, albeit an efficient one. On the contrary, he considers that in the early stages of development language is neither a necessary nor a sufficient condition for thought, while at both the concrete operational and formal stages it may be necessary but is still not sufficient.

The first problem in accepting this view lies in the question of whether the relatively primitive non-verbal symbolic representations of the preoperational child can be considered as equivalent to thought. However, Piaget insists on the continuity and integration of these structures into operations at the later concrete level, stressing the important role played by mental images and motor and perceptual symbols in these operations. At the same time he points out that mental images are not of themselves thinking, though like language they may have a facilitating role (Piaget and Inhelder, 1969).

In regard to the concrete operational stage, there are objections which can be raised as to the meaning of the data Piaget uses to support his argument. For example, while the deaf children cited in the studies by Furth (1966), Oléron (1971), and Vincent and Affolter (Piaget and Inhelder, 1969) were shown to be able to master the operations of classification, seriation, and perspective (using tests of shadow), they were considerably retarded compared with the hearing children who had language. The facilitative effect of language is thus apparent. Nevertheless, its presence does not have to be a necessary condition for the operations as the deaf children *did* acquire the concepts, albeit more slowly.

At the formal level, Piaget himself is less clear in his exposition because of the increased role played by language in the formulation of propositional structures, but the distinction he makes between the assistance given to logico-mathematical structures by language and the independence of those structures from the language through which they are expressed is an important one. The need for precise language is greater when the operations no longer are performed directly upon the objects themselves, but become operations upon operations. Such operations are frequently couched in verbal terms or mathematical symbols, which Piaget regards as being psychologically equivalent to a language. The difference between the signifier (the word or symbol) and the significate (what is being represented) now becomes of prime importance. Piaget would argue that such signifiers are only invented to meet a need which has arisen because of the logical level of operations achieved.

Piaget's distinction between the terms 'sign' used for the symbols of language and 'symbols' for the symbols of other semiotic functions has been criticized, principally by Furth (1969), as unnecessary and misleading. Furth claims that it arises from the use of these terms by the structural linguists, particularly Saussure, who were influential in the 1920s at the time of Piaget's early writings on language. Furth's criticism derives from Piaget's findings that the young child's language is characterized by ego-involved, subjectively motivated factors, whereas the structural linguists' approach was derived from the assumption that language was a finished product which was studied in a static classificatory manner without regard for its developmental aspects. Furth points out that Saussure assumed *a priori* that language is the essential instrument by which thinking is structured into an organized, rational whole. Language signs were therefore called conventional or arbitrary 'signs' and separated from other self-motivated 'symbols', a distinction which Piaget adopted. Whereas the child at the preoperational level may not yet have developed this distinction, there does seem to be a case for maintaining the distinction at later levels to point up the fact that the signifier–significate difference is understood and used.

A final difficulty in regard to Piaget's evidence for the independence of thought from language is, unfortunately, that all Piaget's own data have been obtained by verbal methods, generally using question-and-answer situations. This aspect of Piaget's theory could be tested by endeavouring to establish examples of formal operational thinking in which there is *no* evidence of facilitation by language and *no* use of language in the task or the responses. At present Piaget remains unique in his insistence that language is not a sufficient condition for this level of functioning.

THE RUSSIAN THEORY OF LANGUAGE AND THOUGHT

The Russian attitude to the language-and-thought question derives from the emphasis Russian psychologists have placed on the physiological reflex. Pavlov (1949) distinguished between a first and a second signalling system. The first, the 'objective', dealt with the reflexes and the conditioning that was possible with these, while the second, the 'verbal', dealt with the more abstract thought processes. In the second signalling system, Pavlov included those segments of the brain associated with speech. Current writers, e.g. Sokolov (1972), make it clear that this system includes not only the afferent but also the efferent motor aspects of speech, both central and peripheral. The notion seems to be that as children develop they learn to inhibit overt speaking of their thoughts but think with the aid of an embryonic articulation of words.

This theory is attractive for two reasons. First, it has commonly been observed that young children can complete a series of tasks only if they repeat the instructions aloud as they carry them out. At a later stage the repetition is not voiced, but lip movements indicate clearly what is happening. Finally all outward signs of repetition disappear. Second, the two most obvious differences between man and the other primates are (a) that man has a well-developed language system and (b) that he is far superior in his abstract thinking. It is tempting to think that the latter characteristic arose as a derivative of the former.

Luria (1961) attributes to Pavlov the suggestion that speech introduced 'a new principle in nervous activity, that of abstracting and generalising innumerable signals coming in from the external environment'. He summarizes Pavlov's findings with animals in the following four ways:

(1) In animals a new link is formed when a signal (to be conditioned) is accompanied by a constant unconditioned reinforcement. The development of the link may be slow, particularly if it is fairly complicated and involves differential excitatory and inhibitory reactions. It may also proceed through several stages from an initial generalization of reactions to similar stimuli to a subsequent differentiation. The sequence of stages is determined by a gradual concentration of highly irradiated nervous process.

(2) The new link becomes strong only gradually and may be extinguished by eliminating the constant reinforcement.

(3) Reshaping a system of links (conditioned reflexes) in animals often means remaking every firmly established link (both excitatory and inhibitory) by means of fresh reinforcements. Thus a firmly established system of temporary links is highly inert in that, for example, it is difficult to convert it to a system of opposite links.

(4) While a new system of temporary links is being developed the animals respond to concrete signals and their visual relationships, but experience great, if not insuperable, difficulty in responding to signals in an abstract form e.g. a precise sequence of (say) long and short signals.

None of these generalizations applies fully to the formation of new links in human beings, because of the operation of speech which may be used as an intermediary. Pavlov referred to speech as 'the second signalling system' because in the majority of cases this system plays a decisive part in the formation of new links with human subjects. Thus human adults tend to invent and apply rules for responding to the stimuli presented, which now become more than mere signals and take the form of items of generalized information. Responses to such stimuli depend more on the system of rules into which they are taken than on their physical properties. Human beings may be contrasted with animals with regard to the four generalizations above in that (1) they form new links; (2) these links do not extinguish once a rule has been formulated, even though reinforcement ceases; (3) reversal of links is readily possible in adults and school children; and (4) human subjects can form systems of responses to signals in an abstract form. These differences are attributed to the abstracting and generalizing function of speech, i.e. to the second signalling system.

Three Russian psychologists, Luria (1961), Sokolov (1972), and Vygotsky (1962) are commonly quoted as having investigated aspects of the relationship between language and thinking. Luria adopts a developmental approach and uses a methodology closely linked to the classical conditioning model. In Sokolov's work, which is mainly with adults, the preferred experimental approaches make use of both interference techniques and physiological measures. Vygotsky's work, which mainly preceded that of the other two, was particularly concerned with the development of classificatory behaviour and the effect of various types of psychopathologies on such behaviour.

The above generalizations tend to stress the differences between these three contributors, although of course there was some overlap. For example, Luria did work with adults with brain lesions. However, they did have the same theoretical approach stemming from Pavlov and each may be thought of as explicating various portions of Pavlovian theory. Thus Luria was most concerned with the role of the second signalling system in learning at different age levels, Sokolov explored the correlation between inner speech activity and problem solving, and Vygotsky studied the development of classificatory systems using language and the effect of brain lesions on these systems.

To follow Luria's analysis of the role of speech in the formation of links between stimulus and response, one must first distinguish between afferent auditory speech signals and efferent motor speech. Afferent auditory speech is effective in assisting in the development and consolidation of links even as early as the second year after birth by supplying a second, auditory, dimension to the stimulus. At this stage it is not the content of the speech that is significant but the added stimulus dimension. For example, a one year old child will have difficulty in discriminating between a red and a green box to obtain a sweet, but saying the word 'red' in connection with that box greatly facilitates the building up of the link. Presumably, however, saying the word 'lab' would work as well.

At a later stage, between three and five years of age, the content of the language can be used to establish an excitatory link. For example, 'Press the button when the light goes on' is effective in obtaining that response to a light. However, such instructions are not effective in producing the implied inhibitory response of not pressing when the light is off. It is almost as if the child is superlogical at this stage, arguing that as the experimenter said nothing about not pressing when the light is off that must be permissible.

That he is not superlogical is demonstrated by the fact that inhibitory responses cannot be established in these children directly by using verbal instruction. The instruction, 'Press the button when the light goes on', followed by the instruction, 'Do *not* press the button when the light is off', does not produce the desired discrimination at this age. Inhibitory instructions seem to lead to confusion, in this example leading to no pressing at all or to ignoring the second instruction. Inhibitory responses, however, can be conditioned with the aid of language at this age by reinterpretation of the task in such a way that the subject will interpret some aspect of the signal as feedback information, telling him when to stop responding. In the present case the instruction, 'When the light comes on press the button to put it out', can lead to the required discrimination.

Afferent auditory speech signals proved effective in assisting the two year old to discriminate, but, it was argued, only because they provided a second dimension to help discriminate between the stimuli. In the case of the three to five year old the content of auditory speech is still not very effective in assisting discrimination between more abstract stimuli such as geometrical shapes. In fact physical manipulation providing additional tactile and motor dimensions is more effective than the additional auditory stimulation for this age group.

Finally, beyond the age of five years verbal instruction and description can lead to the rapid and permanent establishment of quite complicated chains of stimuli, excitations, and inhibitions. Thus the development of the use of the afferent aspects of the second signalling system is by no means straightforward, and is in fact more complex in detail than the above general account suggests. In the case of the efferent, motor aspects of the second signalling system, the development of its use is even more complicated, as a distinction must be made between the impulse aspects of the motor activity, on the one hand, and the significative aspects, on the other. The development of inner speech must also be considered.

The basis for the distinction between the unspecific, impulse aspects of speech as opposed to its specifically significative connection is well illustrated by variations in the task, discussed earlier, in which the child learns to press a button in response to a light. There are many experiments of a similar kind which, Luria claims, show that it is the 'impulse' aspect rather than the 'significative' or content aspect that is dominant at the three to five-year-old level. Towards the end of this period and with older children the dominant regulatory function shifts from the impulse aspect to the significative.

Luria finds it most interesting that at the time of the change from the impulse aspect to the significative aspect the mode of speech itself shifts from external to internal. Thus the child begins to whisper the instructions to himself and finally only a tremor of the lips reveals the presence of inner speech, unless an electronic aid is used to detect muscle potentials. However, when faced with a complicated task, the five to seven year old will revert to external speech, but the significative aspects will dominate in regulating his behaviour. It is at this stage that verbal analysis of the situation begins to play an important role in establishing new connections.

The apparently facilitative role of externalizing speech is noted by Sokolov, who concentrated his research effort on the problem of the relationship between inner speech and thought. From the theory of the primary role of language in the second signalling system it seemed clear that the mechanisms of inner speech as an activity were closely linked with, if not identical to, the mechanisms of thinking. If this were so, at least two hypotheses would arise for testing: (a) activities which interfere with the activity of inner speech should also interfere with thinking, and (b) muscle and nerve activity associated with inner speech should always accompany thinking. Sokolov proceeded to investigate these two hypotheses.

In the case of interference it is possible to specify a gradient of activities which should have greater and greater effect on the mechanisms of inner speech and thus on thinking. First, any activity, such as pressing a bulb, may affect any other activity, such as inner speech and thus thinking. However, such effects are likely to be very small if indeed they are noticeable at all. At the next level, clamps applied to the tongue should have the effect of interfering with the peripheral organs of inner speech during counting sequentially, and reciting verse from memory should progressively occupy more of the total inner speech mechanism.

The sequence of activities just specified all relate to the progressive interference with the efferent, motor aspects of inner speech. However, Pavolv and later writers included both the afferent and the efferent aspects in the definition of the second signalling system. On this theoretical basis Sokolov predicted that listening to spoken prose with the aim of remembering it would also engage most, if not all, of the inner speech mechanism, and so should interfere with the process of thinking.

On the basis of these explications of the theory of the relationship between inner speech and thought, Sokolov and his associates carried out a research programme to test the various hypotheses. The results of this programme (see Chapter 5) tended to support the theoretical predictions both as to the occurrence of interference and the order of effectiveness of this interference. Furthermore, primary school children were more affected by the more peripheral interferences than adults. Sokolov took these results to be a confirmation of his theoretical analysis and stressed not only the role of inner speech in thinking but also its necessity for fixing material in memory and recalling it later. He describes inner speech as being 'telegraphic' and a 'language of semantic complexes', differing from adult speech but in some ways resembling that of young children.

Thus for Sokolov language behaviour and thinking are the same process. To test this theory further he sought to demonstrate with the aid of physiological measures that thinking is always associated with electrical activity in the organs, muscles, etc., involved with inner speech. He stated his theoretical propositions as follows: 'The principal physiological role of motor speech stimuli ... consists in setting up excitation in the second signal system ... thereby maintaining the system's working tonus (speech "dominant") which is necessary for the functioning of thought process ...' and '... voluntary fixation of perceived stimuli with their subsequent retrieval from memory with the aid of motor speech impulses' (Sokolov, 1972, p. 186). Sokolov sought to test these propositions by using electromyographic equipment to record the electrical activity in muscles associated with inner speech during problem-solving tasks. However, all that such recordings could show is that there is continuous inner speech activity during the time it was reasonable to assume the subject was thinking about the problem. Even if this were true, which it is not, as his own data showed (see Chapter 5), the only conclusion that can be drawn is that inner speech normally accompanies thinking—not that it is necessary for thinking.

Vygotsky, more than the other Russian writers, produced a theory to account for the development of language from the earliest appearance of speech to adult use of language. Like Piaget's theory of intelligence, this is a stage-wise theory. Unlike the Chomskyan syntactic theories of language development, Vygotsky places great stress on the *development* of the meaning of a word, i.e. words are not initially learned with their final meaning but the meaning used by the child gradually approaches this ultimate meaning. A description of the stages makes this point clearer. They are not linked to particular age levels as the age will differ from child to child, but are intended to be sequential in that the child proceeds from one level to the next in the prescribed order.

Stage 1. Syncretic conglomeration of individual objects

At this stage, the beginning of language, heaps of objects are grouped under one word meaning. The basis of this grouping is at least in part casual associations the child has observed, but the important point is that words may refer to many objects, e.g. 'car' may refer to anything that moves or is red or makes a noise.

Stage 2. Thinking in complexes

At this stage bonds between pairs of objects in a group are established by concrete properties they have in common, even though no other pair in the group has that property in common. This represents a considerable advance from the egocentricism of stage 1. Different types of complexes have been observed by Vygotsky in his work with children faced with the task of categorizing blocks when one member of a particular category is identified by name. These types are as follows:

(a) The *associative* complex tends to group objects which have at least one trait in common with the specimen or its opposite, or are nearer to it, or have some other circumstantial connection.

(b) The *collective* complex consists of objects which differ from the specimen and others, and so complement each other.

(c) The *chain* complex is indicated by grouping objects by one characteristic (e.g. colour) and then suddenly switching to another (e.g. shape) as the basis for adding further objects to the chain, and so on.

(d) The *pseudo-concept* complex has been observed by Vygotsky in the categorization task. If the named object is red but redness is not the basis of the category, the child may form a collection of all of the red blocks of different sizes and shapes. On being shown that one of the blocks does not have the right names the child indicates that he is not thinking in concepts by simply that block and suggesting that all red blocks except the one removed will form a category. It can be seen that such behaviour could seve as a link between thinking in complexes and thinking in concepts.

Thinking in complexes is also referred to as concrete thinking because the basis of the complex are concrete physical characteristics of the object. Examples of this type of thinking are included in most language, e.g. synonyms that derive from different concrete characteristics of the same object—the automobile, motor car and horseless carriage. The distinction between 'the neck of a bottle' and 'a bottleneck' is also given by Vygotsky as an example of an effect of thinking in complexes, and he claims that language creation in general is to some degree analogous to complex formation in children. From the point of view of the development of language and thought these studies indicate how the meaning of words changes as the child proceeds from thinking in complexes to thinking in concepts. This stage in the development of the meaning of words is very important to Vygotsky's theory. His analysis of thinking in complexes also helps to explicate Piaget's preoperational stage in that it reveals some of its positive aspects whereas Piaget tends to stress the negative.

Stage 3. Thinking in concepts

As in the previous stage, this stage may be broken down into substages. First, the child tends to lump together objects that are maximally similar, e.g. blocks which are red and triangular, etc. However, in Vygotsky's studies no two blocks are identical, so the child at this stage must also learn to ignore at least one of the other attributes. This first substage is followed by an ability to abstract a single attribute, e.g. redness, and categorize on this basis. Notice that this second substage is very much like that of pseudo-concepts, but differs critically from it in that a given categorization is not persisted with once it has been shown to be wrong but a new categorization based on a different attribute is set up. Finally, before the child reaches the final stage of thinking in concepts, he passes through a stage in which he is able to use them to solve problems but has difficulty both in describing the abstract concept and in applying it to new situations. It is only when these difficulties have been overcome, usually not until adolescence, that the subject may be described as thinking in concepts on Vygotsky's task.

Vygotsky's theoretical stages correspond at least to some extent with those of Piaget. The stage of thinking in complexes corresponds to Piaget's intuitive stage which precedes that of concrete operations, and, in Piaget's theory, the beginnings of thinking in concepts occur at the beginning of concrete operations.

The distinction between concrete operations, which are logical operations based on concrete attributes, and thinking in complexes, which makes use of concrete attributes to form complexes which are not logically defined, must be remembered. In some ways the description of thinking in complexes can be regarded as a further explication of the intuitive stage which Piaget tends to define in the negative terms of what the child cannot, or at least does not, do. The child thinking in complexes gives every word equal value. For example, if the word 'flower' and the word 'rose' have the same status to the child he cannot make the logical distinction between class and subclass necessary to answer the class inclusion question. However, Piaget's distinction between concrete and formal operations does not correspond to a particular stage differentiation by Vygotsky. One possible explanation for this is that in the task used by Vygotsky the identification of a conjunctive concept was required for the child to succeed. Had he also used the identification of a simple one-dimensional concept and contrasted performance on it with performance on a conjunctive concept, he might well have seen the necessity to divide his stage of thinking in concepts into two stages.

Despite their similarities and the complementary nature of the two theories, Vygotsky criticizes Piaget on two major points: his failure to consider the role of inner speech and his emphasis on spontaneous learning resulting from the child's informal activities as opposed to formal learning in schools.

As noted above, Russian psychologists place great stress on the role of inner speech in thinking. Vygotsky claims that the behaviourists imply a sequence from vocal speech to whispering to inner speech, whereas Piaget assumes a sequence from vocal speech to egocentric speech which gradually disappears. Vygotsky considers that the behaviourists are wrong because, even though it is possible to train very young children to whisper, it has not proved possible even with somewhat older children to complete the sequence from whispering to inner speech. But he also considers that Piaget is wrong in not concluding that the disappearance of egocentric speech occurs because it is transformed into inner speech. There are a number of strands to this argument. First, Piaget does assume that children's actions are internalized to form the basis of concrete operations, but he does not allow for the internalization of egocentric speech. Vygotsky notes the gradual separation of social speech from egocentric speech and observes that the latter gradually develops characteristics which are similar to inner speech in that the subject of the sentence is dropped and the speech becomes more and more predicative. For these reasons, as well as orthodox Pavlovian theory, Vygotsky concludes that inner speech arises from a gradual internalization of egocentric speech. According to Vygotsky, the child learns to think in words when he develops inner speech.

The second important criticism Vygotsky makes of Piaget is that Piaget confines his attention to spontaneous learning and ignores formal school learning. In the case of spontaneous learning the child starts with common everyday objects and develops logical thinking with these, and then generalizes to objects more remote from these, whereas with school learning the child is taught for the first time to think logically with objects remote from his everyday experience. The difference is well brought out in a study in which the children were asked to complete sentences with a clause beginning with 'because'. Vygotsky reported that children gained a higher score when the sentences contained content from social science lessons than when the sentences related to everyday experiences and objects.

Vygotsky's findings concerning the relationship between thought and word may be paraphrased as follows:

(1) Word meaning is the unit of verbal thought. From the point of view of psychology the meaning of every word is a generalization or a concept.

(2) Word meaning is a phenomenon of thought (since it is a concept) only insofar as thought is embodied in speech and of speech only insofar as speech is connected to thought—it is a phenomenon of verbal thought.

(3) The fact that word meanings evolve leads the study of thought and speech out of a blind alley. These meanings change as the child develops and also with the various ways in which thought functions.

(4) From the point of view of external speech the child begins with one word and then in time connects two or three words to form a sentence. However, from the semantic point of view the single-word sentence, supplemented at times by gestures, conveys the whole meaning. Development takes the form of differentiating this one meaning into separate meaningful units. These two contrasting developments proceed to maturity, interacting with each other at each stage, and thus they may be regarded as different aspects of the same process.

(5) In a similar way, but at a later stage, the semantic and the grammatical aspects of language interact. In fact, it is possible to distinguish the psychological as opposed to the grammatical subject or predicate. The former changes from situation to situation for the same sentence.

(6) The child must learn the difference between semantics and phonetics. Initially the word is part of the object it signifies: to the child only the nominative function exists and semantically only the objective reference.

(7) The child's analysis leads from phonetic to semantic to inner speech to thought. Inner speech is a specific formation, differing from speech in that it is personal as opposed to social. It appears disconnected, incomplete, telegraphic, predicative (in that the subject and its qualifiers are not needed), abbreviated, and sometimes coded. It is very rapid. In inner speech there is a preponderance of 'sense' over meaning, where 'sense' includes the psychological events aroused by the word. There is also combining of words, as in German, and the incorporation in one word of many implied meanings and senses which would require hundreds or words to make the meaning clear in written form.

From this summary it seems clear that Vygotsky was to some extent departing from the other Russian writers in that he was not equating inner speech with thought but regarding it as a bridge structure between the semantic aspects of language and thought itself. According to Vygotsky's approach, overt speech arises from the thought via inner speech, the semantic system, and the phonetic system.

LINGUISTIC RELATIVITY

In contrast to Piaget, supporters of the theory of linguistic relativity have in common to varying degrees a basic insistence that language and thought are interdependent. If there is seen to be a dependent variable in this relationship, thought is regarded as being dependent upon language rather than language upon thought. It is generally considered that the theory was expressed most explicitly by Whorf (1956) and therefore it is frequently referred to as the Whorfian hypothesis, but the view was not new for it precedes even Sapir (1921), whose statements Whorf elaborated, and was evident in the writing of European linguists in the late nineteenth century. Probably adherents of this view or variants of it are more numerous than the adherents of the independence approach, and they include linguists, sociolinguists, and anthropologists as well as psychologists.

In brief, the Whorfian theory of linguistic relativity proposes that the language used by a person produces a culturally idiosyncratic way of looking at the world—one's *Weltanschauung* or world view. Thus it could be expected, for example, that in cultures in which colour words are not finely distinguished people would be less able to discriminate between the colours themselves, or in cultures such as that of the Hopi Indians in which there are many ways of expressing time there would be greater sensitivity to temporal aspects of the environment and more precise methods of measuring time units and the passing of time than in cultures such as those of Europeans who have fewer words for time in their languages.

The distinction between structure and function was not made clear in the formulation by Whorf. The need for making the distinction was brought out particularly by Fishman (1960) and Hymes (1966, 1967), who both proposed paradigms for examining the Whorfian hypothesis which distinguish the structural and functional aspects of language. Hymes suggested two types of relativity—one related to structure, the other to use—which may vary from culture to culture and within which variations may occur in one component while the other remains invariant between the cultures being compared. Fishman's paradigm separated structure from function but also distinguished lexical from syntactic structural elements, again proposing variation within any of the components.

So much debate has been generated by the Whorfian hypothesis that it is important to distinguish between the original statements and later extensions. Sapir and Whorf were both much more reluctant to impute causative relationships than their successors have been. What Sapir and Whorf both proposed was a correlation rather than a cause.

Critics of the linguistic relativity theory (Miller and McNeill, 1968) have pointed out that the reality base is wanting—that the Hopi Indians, whom Whorf found to have so many ways of expressing time and who, Whorf speculated, might have discovered relativity earlier than Europeans because of this, did *not* discover relativity and had virtually no physics. Comparative studies of colour perception and colour naming over a large group of American Indian tribes have shown minor variations but not basic inabilities to recognize and distinguish colours or communicate about colour fairly efficiently (Lenneberg and Roberts, 1956; Ray, 1953). See Chapter 5 for a more detailed discussion.

The distinction between function and structure would seem to be an important one in regard to the question of the role of language in thinking. The selective uses to which the language is put show variations in how people habitually express certain things by means of language, and how and when language is used as a communication mode in preference to other modes such as gesture, action, graphic illustration, or dance, but do not necessarily refer to the role of language in the thinking process itself. But if the structural properties of the language are such as to *prevent* the thinking processes from occurring in respect to certain kinds of subject matter, then one might conclude that in those cases the Whorfian hypothesis is supported. However, as yet there are many unresolved problems in choosing appropriate tasks and subject matter in order to elicit evidence of whether thinking is occurring or not. This is especially so when working with non-literate languages. The extent to which both semantic and functional equivalence can be achieved has to be considered: transliterations of Western tests and tasks do not necessarily convey the same intentions in each culture. On the other hand, applications of the semantic differential (Osgood, 1964) suggests that lexical equivalents are also semantic equivalents in a very large number of languages (Osgood, 1965; Tanaka, 1967). In its extreme interpretation, the Whorfian hypothesis should mean that languages are not really translatable; in its weaker form (Hockett, 1954), it merely suggests that languages differ not so much in regard to what it is possible to say but in what it is possible to say easily.

Bruner's theory of language as instrumental to thought

Proponents of the relativity hypothesis have generally been concerned with the limits and constraints of linguistic forms rather than with the verbal processes involved in cognitive tasks or their implications for cognitive development and concept learning. Cognitive operations of a relatively complex type, such as formal operations, have received little attention. One example of an application of the relativistic approach to the development of thinking in the child is Bruner's (Bruner, Olver, and Greenfield, 1966; Greenfield and Bruner, 1966) theory of language as instrumental to thought. Bruner himself regarded his views as being less extreme than those of Sapir or Whorf and as having been strongly influenced by both Vygotsky and Chomsky; nevertheless,

Bruner's theoretical stance must be regarded as being in the main derived from the linguistic relativity hypothesis.

Bruner regards symbolic activity as stemming from 'some primitive or protosymbolic system' species-specific to man only. This system includes symbolic activity of any kind, not language alone. Three modes of representation are posited: the enactive, which is kinaesthetic and can be related to Piaget's sensori-motor activity; the iconic, which is perceptual, involving mental imagery; and the linguistic mode. The minimum properties of such a symbolic system are categoriality, hierarchy, predication, causation, and modification, without which *any* symbolic activity, and especially language, is logically and empirically unthinkable.

Bruner recognizes that the development of language and the development of the other specialized expressions of symbolic activity may not proceed at the same pace. The child reaches syntactical maturity relatively early; consequently, the syntactical maturity of a five year old may seem to be unconnected with his ability in other spheres of symbolic activity. Though the child can use words and sentences with a confident mastery of highly abstract rules, he cannot organize the things words and sentences stand for. This 'asymmetry' is also evident in the child's semantic development, which may lag behind his syntactic development (Bruner, 1966).

In this regard Bruner at first might appear to be suggesting the separation of language and concept, in that, though the child has acquired the grammatical structures, he still may not be able to organize the empirical implications of what the words and sentences stand for. But this interpretation is offset by Bruner's often-quoted interpretation of the relationship between thought and language: 'One is thus led to believe that, in order for the child to use language as an instrument of thought, he must first bring the world of experience under the control of principles of organisation that are in some degree isomorphic with the structural principles of syntax' (Bruner, 1966, p. 47). In other words, the child has to learn to bring his thinking and his empirical experiences into line with what he has acquired linguistically. For this he needs special training in the symbolic representation of experience, which schooling generally provides, and without which he would continue to adulthood still dependent on the enactive and iconic modes of representing and organizing the world, no matter what language he speaks. The implications of this notion are that the enactive and iconic modes can represent experience symbolically but at best less efficiently than language and that schooling is the principal means of providing this special training in the representation of experience. As Bruner points out, it is no accident that schooling involves so much verbal interchange.

Bruner's claim that his position is not as extreme as the Whorfian hypothesis rests on the fact that he does not concur that it is the lexical richness of a language which makes for 'superior' cognitive development. It is not the labels *per se*. According to Bruner's theory the presence in a language of superordinate class words like 'colour' and 'shape' will strongly influence the use of those attributes for equivalence grouping tasks. Thus it is the availability of hierarchical lexical structures rather than the richness of the vocabulary in the lexicon that is the significant factor in how language may shape thought. Bruner considers that the correspondence between linguistic and conceptual structure relates not to words in isolation but to their depth of hierarchical embedding, both in the language and in thought, and to the presence or absence of higher-order words that can be used to integrate different domains of words and objects into hierarchical structures.

Bruner was influenced by Chomsky in his conceptualization of the structure of language, in particular the separation of the learning of the semantic aspect from the learning of the syntactic. The syntactic sphere is regarded as autonomous, which leads Bruner to look favourably on Chomsky's theory that language is an innate pattern based on innate 'ideas' that are gradually differentiated into the rules of grammar.

PSYCHOLINGUISTIC THEORY

Recent developments in the study of linguistics (e.g. Fillmore, 1971; Halliday, 1973; Lakoff, 1971; and McCawley, 1971) have increasingly emphasized the psychological, interpretative aspects of language use. Since Chomsky's (1957) first version of generative transformation grammar Chomsky himself has made two substantial variations on his original theory (Chomsky, 1965, 1972) and other writers have taken up and modified his ideas. It is beyond the scope of this chapter to give a definitive treatment of the current state of psycholinguistic theory: we shall take up only those aspects relating to cognitive development and consider their relevance to the interpretation of the language–thought relationship.

Chomsky (1972) has maintained strongly that the study of language is a branch of cognitive psychology. He sees the role of his particular interpretation of linguistics as that of bringing together the disciplines of philosophy, psychology, and linguistics in an attempt to discover fundamental relationships between language and mind. His aim is to reveal and formalize the universal grammatical structure basic to all language. The basis of this structure, according to Chomsky, is innate rather than acquired solely through conditioning or other purely social means. It is also species-specific, the sole property of humans, and not shared by even the most complex of other animal sound systems. Whereas even the sound systems of birds are finite, the number of sound combinations which the human speaker could develop is regarded as infinite.

Chomsky does not regard other symbolization systems as either equivalent to or even precedents to speech. To Chomsky the potentiality for speech is biologically determined; he rejects the notion that language consists of a set of habitually patterned response sets. According to Chomsky, not only is the ability to acquire speech innate but so also are the structures themselves. He does not present specific neurological evidence for this position, but it must be said in support of Chomsky's theory that it is presented as a hypothesis which is available for testing by others with a physiological orientation.

If the structures are innate and species-wide as Chomsky proposes, then it follows that there must be a universally shared language basis common to all languages. Three aspects of universality are involved: a universal phonetics system, universal semantic features, and universal syntax, which together make up the three components comprising a universal grammar. Attempts have been made by Chomsky and his associates (Chomsky and Halle, 1968) to develop a 'universal feature set', a phonetics system which would identify all possible combinations of speech sounds, but these attempts have met with criticism by some linguists and phoneticians.

The notion of universal semantic features implies that there are laws common to all languages which govern the interrelation and permitted variety of semantic features. The notion of a universal syntax requires that there are laws to which all languages adhere, relating the surface structure (i.e. the superficial structure) and the deep structure (also called latent or inferred structure) which includes what is implied but not superficially explicit. Universal grammar is defined as the study of the conditions that must be met by the grammars of all languages (Chomsky, 1972). That proposed by Chomsky is called a generative grammar in that it does not assume that any language is fixed but rather that any language is capable of infinite variations, whereby a speaker may generate new sentences without limit. However, the means by which this variation is achieved are finite. The way in which deep structures are converted to surface structures is through a number of transformations (hence the term 'transformational grammar'). These transformations can be shown to be organized as branching patterns of phrases which can be grouped and regrouped as the transformations are carried out. (For a detailed statement of the early form of the theory see Chomsky in Lenneberg, 1967, or, for the later form, Chomsky, 1972).

Chomsky's construct of universal biologically-based language structures must be distinguished from the mere location of a language area in the brain, which would not necessarily involve any structural organization of grammatical features, universal or otherwise. To emphasize this point Chomsky retrieves the term 'mind' as used by Descartes to stress that what he is proposing is systematic and organized rather than physiologically static and finite.

In another variation of this idea McNeill (1966) proposed an abstract 'Language Acquisition Device', which creates a grammatical system from the input of a corpus of speech. Though the inputs from different languages may differ, the 'Language Acquisition Device' itself would be universal because it must have an internal structure which enables it to acquire any natural language. The neurological basis of such a device was not spelled out.

The question of whether a biologically-based universal grammar is demonstrable empirically is of considerable importance to the problem of the relationship between language and thought. Such a set of universal semantic and syntactic laws should make possible the translation of any language, past, present, or future, and the fact that the pattern is there awaiting development would explain why a child may learn any language apparently with equal ease. However, Chomsky's references to the neurological bases of these structures are implied rather than specific, and it is not clear how the structures would be explained neurologically, although he is optimistic that they will be (Chomsky, 1972). His adoption of the term 'mind' does not really meet this problem. In this his principal aim would appear to be to emphasize his refutation of the relevance of Skinnerian behaviourist interpretations of learning to the acquisition of language.

Chomsky's position appears to assume that language exerts a powerful influence upon thinking because of the way in which sentence structure shapes the presentation of ideas, as evidenced by the transformation from deep structures to surface structures. The linguistic structure as proposed by Chomsky is both abstract and complex, and universal because it is innate and species-specific. What then is the relationship between language and intelligence? According to Chomsky (1968, pp. 52–53), the systems are not the same:

> ... to account for the normal use of language we must attribute to the speaker-hearer an intricate system of rules that involve mental operations of a very abstract nature, applying to representations that are quite remote from the physical signal. We observe, furthermore, that knowledge of language is acquired on the basis of degenerate and restricted data and that it is to a large extent independent of intelligence and of wide variations in individual experience.

This statement seems to indicate a view somewhat less 'Whorfian' than is often attributed to Chomsky. Many of his followers in psycholinguistics appear to take a stronger line.

Problems, implications, and later extension

In his early formulations Chomsky emphasized syntactic structure and almost ignored the semantic aspects of language; although later criticism led him to a revision of the former position he continues to place his greatest emphasis on syntactic structure. Influential among those who emphasize semantic aspects are Katz and Fodor (1963) and Lakoff (1972), who adopted a viewpoint questioning another of Chomsky's basic ideas, namely that the syntactic grammar could be studied apart from language use. Increasingly, now, psycholinguists are turning to include contextual aspects. In doing so, they are trying to account for what are essentially cognitive processes, of interpretation, of underlying concept formation, and of concept learning. Some like Maclay (1971) have put forward an almost entirely cognitive interpretation which is very similar to that of Piaget, in that language is seen as but one of many products of the underlying cognitive process; but, as Kess (1976) points out, this view is not as yet widely received by psycholinguists.

Also, the more readily accepted psycholinguistic models have not yet been able to account for the role that language plays in more complex thinking tasks such as those of formal operations. Linguistic models are unable to account for qualitative differences between difficult and simple conceptual relationships on a linguistic basis alone, and are inadequate in regard to descriptions of the psychological process mechanisms. This failure has been attacked by Brenner and Hjelmquist (1974), who point out that Chomsky's dichotomy into competence (i.e. knowledge of language) and performance (i.e. language behaviour) explicit excludes memory processes, motivational processes, and decision processes from competence and subsumes them under performance. In Brenner and Hjelmquist's opinion this is due to a confusion between competence (the knowledge), mechanism (the cognitive processes), and performance (the result of the processes). They prefer a threefold data reference base giving distinctions between (a) performance as manifest data, (b) mechanism (how the system functions in producing performance data, i.e. cognitive processes and other inner processes), and (c) competence (the knowledge of the system, what it can and cannot do). From each of these data references different domains of data could then be studied. Brenner and Hjelmquist argue that Chomsky confuses these three data reference bases and that he never makes clear, in early or later writings, that he ever recognized that a theory of cognitive structures and process must take account of the level of mechanism. They argue that this fact invalidates Chomsky's claims for the relevance of his theory to psychology.

In sum, they consider that the main contribution of Chomsky has been that the psycholinguistic theory arising from his work draws attention to the creative process of language production and brings out the distinction between surface and deep structure. It might be added that it has also drawn attention to child language development as a profitable way of studying language. However, the psycholinguists' domain of discourse, as will be seen in more detail in the discussion of evidence in Chapter 5, has not really thrown much light on the language–thought relationship controversy, because it does not deal with the thinking processes adequately. For example, in psycholinguistic theory there is no conceptual difference between a child's labelling or naming of an object and his naming of the correct answer to a problem. Recently psycholinguists have shown more concern for this aspect (Maclay, 1971), but have a tendency to confound semantic knowledge with conceptual knowledge. To use the much-quoted psycholinguistic example from Bloom (1970), the child who says 'Mommy sock' both to indicate that the sock belongs to the mother and, indiscriminately, that the mother is putting the sock on the child, could be described as having demonstrated merely an associative link between the two concepts, 'Mommy' and 'sock'. Such 'thinking' is at a very early stage indeed and would barely meet the criteria for Vygotsky's stage of thinking in complexes.

LENNEBERG'S BIOLOGICAL THEORY OF LANGUAGE DEVELOPMENT

It is interesting to note the sympathetic treatment of Chomsky's ideas by Lenneberg, whose own theoretical position contrasts so strikingly with that of Chomsky in its biological and neurological approach. Also, Lenneberg and Piaget's positions are not opposed but have considerable common ground.

Lenneberg's theoretical stance is a biological maturational one. His theory rests upon five, major, general, biological premises (Lenneberg, 1967):

(1) Cognitive function is species-specific.
(2) Specific properties of cognitive function are replicated in every member of the species.
(3) Cognitive processes and capacities are differentiated spontaneously with maturation.
(4) At birth man is relatively immature; certain aspects of his behaviour and cognitive function emerge only during infancy.
(5) Certain social phenomena among animals come about by spontaneous adaptation of the behaviour of the growing individual to the behaviour of the individuals around him.

Premise (1) states the more general case of cognitive function, under which the language function is subsumed. Thus language is also regarded as species-specific. It is implicit throughout Lenneberg's theory that no other animals could acquire language. In premise (2) is assumed the innateness of the capacity for language in every normal member of the species. Premises (3) and (4) set out the basis for the delay in the appearance of language in humans and the length of time required for its development, while premise (5) is the basis for how Lenneberg accounts for the social aspects of language acquisition.

As language is regarded by Lenneberg as but a manifestation of species-specific cognitive propensities, it follows that language is regarded as dependent on cognitive function, rather than vice versa. In this he is with the Piagetian school. The basic cognitive process underlying language is one of categorization and extraction of similarities. Categorization includes the subdivision of broad categories into ordered sets of narrower categories and the building of comprehensive categories, while similarities may be extracted both from physical stimuli and from categories of underlying schemata. Words are thus equivalent to labels, indicating that a categorization has been made.

The limits to the range of possibilities in natural language are set, on the one hand, by specialized anatomical features of the human body such as the shape of the palate, ear, and velum, but these aspects do not explain the phylogenetic development of language. On the other hand, the limits are set by the biological properties of the human form of cognition. Within these limits, Lenneberg, like Chomsky, regards the possibilities for variation as infinite and, also like Chomsky, thus accounts for the great variety of language forms while still maintaining that the underlying type remains constant.

Lenneberg's interpretation of how language develops stresses its dependence on the more general maturation of cognitive function. The maturation of the language function is an unfolding of the language capacity, given the appropriate social conditions, rather than the result of the child's being a passive recipient of what is passed on to him by another. Maturation brings cognitive processes to a state of language readiness. If the conditions are appropriate, or as Lenneberg puts it the relevant 'raw material' is available, the organism will then go on to develop language. The course of language unfolding is prescribed by the maturational path traversed by cognition. The state of language readiness is described as a state of 'latent language structure' and the unfolding of language as a process of 'actualisation', in which latent structure is transformed into realized structure.

Links with both Piaget and Chomsky are evident here. The concept of language readiness and its dependence upon the development of more general cognitive functions is consistent with Piaget's ontogenetic theory. The relationship between latent structure and realized structure parallels the relationship between the constructs of universal and particular grammars as proposed by Chomsky, latent structure being responsible for universal grammar and realized structure for particular grammar and the unique aspects of grammar of any natural language.

Lenneberg distinguishes between the actualization process and merely beginning to say things, and Piaget's distinction between early verbalization and nascent language may be noted. Latent structure will not become actualized if the proper raw material is not available. Included in this raw material are external physical stimuli, such as the sounds made by others, and internal conditions, such as the development of the relevant anatomical features related to hearing and speech production. Like Chomsky, Lenneberg rejects the idea that the adults surrounding the child are the causative or shaping agents that determine language onset or its course of development. But the raw material itself is not the cause of the developing structure of language. Like Piaget, Lenneberg considers that the primitive language of the young child is too different from adult language to be regarded merely as a direct mirroring of what the adult is attempting to communicate to the child.

The maturation of cognitive processes, and hence of language, is seen as a process of progressive differentiation, in which highly unstable states are traversed. These unstable states, which Lenneberg refers to as states of disequilibrium, lead to rearrangements which bring about new disequilibria, producing further rearrangements, and so on until the relative stability known as maturity is reached. Language readiness is regarded as an example of such a state of disequilibrium. The period of disequilibrium of language readiness is seen as being of limited duration, beginning at about the age of two and lasting until the late teens, when the disequilibrium declines and the capacity for primary language synthesis is lost. By this time the cognitive processes are firmly structured.

Replication of the language potential and the latent language structure in every healthy human being occurs as a consequence of cognitive processes which are uniquely human and common to all men. There is therefore an inner form of structure of a single type common to all languages which is evidenced by universal grammar, which enables every child to learn any language as easily as any other.

But how is it that the child learns one language rather than another, and what is the role of the social setting in this learning? Lenneberg introduces the metaphorical concept of resonance to answer this question: 'In a given state of maturation exposure to adult language behaviour has an excitatory effect upon the actualisation process in much the way a certain frequency may have an excitatory effect upon a specific resonator: The object begins to vibrate in the presence of the sound' (Lenneberg, 1967, p. 378). The energy required for the resonance comes from the individual, but slight variations in the frequency may affect the quality of the resonance. The range of possible frequencies of the resonator is like the total range of possible languages, and each natural language is like a selected frequency band within this range. There is activation of the child's language behaviour through the social setting and he 'harmonises' his language function with that of others, but the child can and does construct language by himself rather than merely copy what is handed on through the culture. Individual differences in language performance arise from variations in the formation of the latent structure, which occur because of variations in cognitive function or the course of maturation, and from variations in the process of actualization from latent structure to realization, which occur mainly because of variations in peripheral anatomical function or structures.

How does Lenneberg view the role of language in thought? Early work by Lenneberg and associates (Lenneberg and Roberts, 1956) using colour naming has sometimes been quoted in support of the Whorfian hypothesis, but the more general tone of Lenneberg's position is not to support but to reject the Whorfian view, although acknowledging the creativeness of Whorf's ideas.

RELATIONSHIPS AMONG THE FIVE THEORIES

The main theme of this book is to present theory and data on cognitive development inspired by the work at Geneva. The fact that the typical Piagetian task involves a substantial verbal component in its stress on explanation makes the question of the relationship between language (use) and thinking an important one. Whereas elsewhere in this and many other writings in this field it is quite clear what the products of thinking are, the processes of thinking are not self-evident but have to be implied. Often they are unfolded through verbal probing. Can one then distinguish between those contributions to the final 'knowledge' which arise from the purely 'linguistic' side and those which arise from the purely 'cognitive' side?

From the brief statements of the five major groups of writers discussed above it is clear that there is a great deal of controversy about the relative weight of these contributions. The lack of agreement begins with lack of agreement as to what constitutes language. Is it only the act of spoken communication or also written communication? Does it include *what* is said or written as well as the *act* of speaking or writing or reading? Should the study of language stress the structural aspects, such as syntax or grammar, or should it be more concerned with the semantic aspects? How is the semantic meaning of the words used differentiated from the concepts the words stand for?

None of the theories deals with all of these questions. Partly because of their particular orientations, cognitive, cultural, linguistic, or physiological, they stress different aspects. They break down most strongly into those which seem to support the notion of the independence of language and thinking and those which see thinking as dependent upon language. Piaget's view is that, at least for the preformal stages of thinking, language development is not a necessary condition for the development of thought processes, whereas the Russian theorists seem to take the view that thinking *is* inner speech and therefore completely dependent on language for its development at all levels. Other theorists (Bruner, Chomsky, and Lenneberg) seem to take a more interactionist view than these two extremes. In the following chapter we shall review the evidence and relate it to the Piagetian and other positions.

5

EVIDENCE SIGNIFICANT IN THE LANGUAGE–THOUGHT RELATIONSHIP

D. M. Keats and J. A. Keats

The theoretical positions outlined in the previous chapter may be regarded as originating from five distinct areas of research: Piagetian studies of cognitive development, studies explicating Pavlov's notion of the second signalling system, studies of social and cultural differences, psycholinguistic studies, and studies of the effects of damage to the speech areas of the brain. This research evidence is voluminous in quantity and extremely diverse in aims and methodologies. Not all of it stems from an explicit stance on the relationship between thought and language, although obviously much comes from workers who have adopted a particular point of view. Some of the evidence we shall discuss has become available because of attempts to establish which theory is more predictive in a certain situation, and some is relevant to several theoretical approaches, but other evidence we shall be considering, e.g. the factor analytic, has become available from studies concerned with other theories and so is theoretically neutral to this controversy.

Because of the large amount of evidence available, it will be helpful to classify it in some way. Even so, some omissions will be unavoidable. Rather than duplicate the structure of the previous chapter by presenting the research relevant to the five approaches in turn, we shall treat the evidence according to the issues to which it relates most directly. Seven such issues, and therefore classes of evidence, have been distinguished. Finally, we shall attempt to evaluate the contribution the evidence makes to a resolution of the controversy and present some empirical studies based on a new approach.

(1) The first issue is concerned with whether language structures and the development of language are universal, and, if universal, also innate. If innate, then by what means can these innate structures be described— by direct neurological evidence, by inference from neurological evidence, or by inference from some other type of evidence such as the way the child acquires language? If demonstrable, then how are these innate language structures related to thinking, and in particular to the development of the kind of cognitive structures dealt with in this book?

(2) The second issue is to what extent the development of thought processes is impeded by deprivation of language. If it could be shown that, where language is absent or severely retarded in either its input or output processing, the normal development of thought processes either does not occur at all or is severely delayed in appearing, then it could be argued that thinking is dependent upon language. It might also be expected that the longer the language deficit continued, the greater the cognitive deficit should become.

(3) The Whorfian theoretical position and its offshoots in sociolinguistics raise the issues of the degree to which social and cultural differences in language may affect thinking and how such influences can be demonstrated in behavioural phenomena. As a research problem the question is whether the relevant social variables can be adequately controlled or isolated so that one can consider the language effects as distinct from the effects of material culture, education, social class, ethnicity, innate factors, and the like. Another question raised by the Whorfian view is whether some languages are inferior to others as vehicles for expressing complex concepts, and hence whether the speakers of such languages are inhibited from full cognitive development because of syntactical or lexical shortcomings. If so, there should be evidence that either no people using those weak languages would exhibit advanced levels of thinking or the absence of certain concepts would be paralleled by the absence of words, or effective phrases, or sentence constructions which could express those concepts. Such languages should have a paucity of abstract terms for hierarchical classification and should lack ways of expressing operations upon operations.

(4) The fourth issue raised is the effect of language activity upon learning. Under what conditions can language activity have a facilitatory or an inhibitory role? From the Russian point of view language activity should be present in all thinking. What evidence is there for thinking occurring without language activity?

(5) An important question concerns the neurological basis for the relationship between language and thinking. Modern devices make it possible to detect muscle potentials associated with the speech organs, and with the aid of these devices experimenters have been able to detect the occurrence of subvocal speech. The extent to which subvocal speech is associated with thought processes has been used by some experimenters as evidence in favour of the claim that thought processes are dependent on inner speech. In a similar way attempts have been made to use electroencephelogram recordings to provide evidence of activity of language areas of the cortex during problem solving. Data from this source are very complex, but modern analytic devices enable some clarification of their interpretation.

(6) The main issue raised by the factor analytic approach is whether verbal or language factors can be effectively demonstrated, and, if so, in what

kinds of task the differential effects of a language are most evident. This class of evidence has been ignored by nearly all of the theorists whose points of view are discussed in Chapter 4, but for different reasons. Russian psychologists are opposed to the notion of individual differences in cognitive ability and so evidence from this source is ignored by them. Piaget and his followers and those working in linguistics tend to criticize such an approach as dealing entirely with the products of intellectual activity rather than with the process. However, seventy years of research concerned with the structure of abilities, and in particular the relationship between verbal activity and other forms of abstract reasoning, can hardly be ignored as a source of evidence on the relationship between language and thought.

(7) The final issue, and hence type of evidence, concerns the effects of experimental manipulation of either the language or the concept inputs. The question is whether training designed to influence the acquisition of higher linguistic forms can also influence the acquisition of operational concepts, or, alternatively, whether training on the concepts may lead to the acquisition of higher linguistic forms.

EVIDENCE RELATING TO THE INNATENESS AND ACQUISITION OF LANGUAGE

Support for the Chomskyan view of the innateness of language structures is based on two main sources of evidence. One is the analytico-deductive type which Chomsky himself uses to justify his case for universal generative grammar, and the other is the evidence obtained from a variety of empirical and descriptive studies of the ways in which the child acquires language.

Chomsky's own evidence for the universality and hence the innateness of language structures was based upon examples from English and only a very small number of other languages. However, he himself does not regard this as a drawback in any way; indeed, he believes that a single language can provide strong evidence for a universal grammar. He points out that a child acquires a generative grammar of his language on the basis of a very restricted access to the language. Chomsky argues that, had the process been purely associative as in the Skinnerian (Skinner, 1957) reinforcement interpretation, both the grammar and the vocabulary learned would be much more limited than the range the child can use. In this, Chomsky is supported by McNeill (1966, 1970). This evidence rests mainly on the logic of the analysis (Chomsky, 1968).

The case against the Chomskyan notion of the innate universality of language structures was most explicitly stated by Skinner (1957) in his treatment of language as behaviour and by Broadbent (1970) who criticized the Chomskyan position for its lack of empirical evidence. The main premise of the innateness approach, which both Piagetian and Skinnerian theories reject, is not so much the postulated idea that there is some kind of latent ability base with an as yet unspecified neurological location but that there is mapped into it some kind of syntactic ability already programmed for syntactic activity alone, rather than a general readiness for language which would be developed in the same way as other intellectual abilities develop. There is no problem in regard to the existence of a language base which is innate, but such a base does not necessarily make language competence available to all. The reinforcement and the Piagetian views are in agreement that the child requires social reinforcement to develop competence. Thus differences in performance are differences in levels of competence, rather than competence and performance being completely different concepts. Slobin (1971), after a summary of evidence, concluded that there would appear to be more evidence against the reinforcement approach than there is direct evidence in support of Chomsky's contention that the construct of innate language structures is the only real alternative to the inforcement learning approach. Whether such structures are innate, or universal, or not, has relevance to the language–thought problem but does not do much to resolve it. Nor is there any direct empirical evidence, neurological or otherwise, to demonstrate the existence of Chomsky's hypothetical construct as a psychological mechanism, though the construct may well be a creative and effective method of describing underlying meanings in linguistic structures.

Many empirical studies of child language acquisition have been generated by Chomsky's ideas and have been regarded by many psycholinguists as providing evidence for the innateness hypothesis. A remarkable number of similarities have been reported in the way in which children acquire language in widely differing social and cultural environments (Clark, 1973; Lenneberg, 1967; Slobin, 1971). Many of these studies involved the intensive observation of one or two children over a period of many months (see, for example, Bellugi and Brown, 1964; Bloom, 1970; Brown, 1973; McNeill, 1966, 1970; Slobin, 1973). They produced some common findings in regard to the word order 'Noun–Verb–Noun' (N–V–N). One of their major contributions was to demonstrate the creativeness of the child in making up new word-constructions to convey grammatical structures, such as past tense in a way they could not have heard from their elders. It was as if the child was hypothesizing a grammatical rule. It is inferred from such behaviour that there is some inborn 'Language Acquisition Device' (McNeill, 1966) by which such structures are able to be generated. Gleitman, Gleitman, and Shipley (1972) claim that even young children may reveal a capacity 'to reflect on' linguistic structure. In one of their studies, in which children were asked to say whether a sentence was 'silly' or not and give their corrected version, even some two year olds could tenuously follow the instruction in a role-modelling situation. These children were able to isolate what was wrong and often gave partially corrected paraphrases. But in a number of these corrections the linguistic is not distinguishable from the cognitive; it seems quite likely that the child is rejecting the silly sentence on the grounds of its cognitive implausibility rather than its semantic anomaly.

However, there is also some conflicting evidence. Clark (1974) reported observations of her own child in Edinburgh which suggest that this child used many different levels of linguistic structure concurrently. For example, the child would incorporate immediately prior utterances intact into his own utterances or he would extend his repertoire of structures by combining two existing structures without reordering any of the elements to match adult syntax.

In a review of similar type of research in socialist countries, Průcha (1974) finds evidence of some differences in regard to word order. Průcha reports work by Zarebina describing early language development in three Polish children aged between two and three years in which word order appeared to be very variable in declarative sentences and even in questions. Průcha comments that this result seemed to confirm one of the universals in the ontogenesis of grammar suggested by Slobin, namely that word order in child speech reflects the word order in the input language, in this case the relatively free word order of Polish. It would seem to be a strange argument in support of an innate universal language structure, that the child reflects the word order of the parental language. Surely there ought to be a common universal word order at the beginning of language learning if not in the full adult speech. Another example cited by Průcha was work by Meggyes in Hungary, which involved the analysis of the speech of one girl from 21 to 26 months. Meggyes' findings on the child imitation of adult utterances did not fully support Bellugi and Brown's (1964) hypothesis of selected imitation, in which it was claimed that the child imitates (for English) mainly 'content words' from the adults' sentences while other words were omitted. Meggyes found that the words repeated by the child were those which had the greatest communicative importance, mainly nouns, pronouns, and verbs, while adjectives were left out. The ideology of socialist countries is to reject notions of inborn differences, but they do not deny entirely the role of biological factors in language acquisition. As stated by Průcha, their view is to accept that certain psychophysiological mechanisms are inborn but to insist that a decisive role in language ontogenesis is played by the child's active learning and its sociocultural and historical determinants, and they therefore emphasize educational and learning factors.

Whereas the earlier work concentrated on syntactic aspects, following on Chomsky's view, later studies have become more interested in the semantic. This change brings the psycholinguistic explanations of language and thought closer to the positions of Vygotsky and Piaget. For example, instead of explaining two-word sentences in terms of pivot and open words the pair of words is seen as being increasingly differentiated, but the order and the way of combining the two words are not seen as being as fixed as was previously thought. In this regard the Vygotsky explanation seems just as appropriate as that of McNeill or Chomsky.

As the stress on syntactic forms has given way to a greater stress on the semantic aspects, psycholinguists have entered the field of the cognitive rather than the purely linguistic. In trying to explain language development in terms of non-linguistic strategies (Clark, 1973), which are supposed to occur in the virtual absence of (linguistic) comprehension, and in stressing the diversity of routes to concept mastery (Nelson and Bonvillian, 1973), they have come closer to the separation of language and thought as independent, in the Piagetian fashion. Edwards (1973), for example, compared semantic clause types used to describe relational meanings which are expressed in the two-word speech of young children with concepts of the sensori-motor stage. The concepts dealt with were object permanence, spatial relations of objects, persons as physical objects, persons as active beings, and persons as causers of change in positional relations of objects. Edwards found a close correspondence between the child's semantic and conceptual development, and argued from these results that the nature of sensori-motor intelligence was such as to constrain the range of relational meanings which the child could express. Psycholinguists are also beginning to insist on the separation of the extra-linguistic (i.e. such features as the sociocultural, the environmental, knowledge of the world, and the universe of discourse adopted by the informant) from the linguistically pertinent (Boon, 1973), and they are realizing that meaning is conveyed, especially in conversation, by other than and more than either the surface or deep structure of the sentence (Barr, 1975).

Overall the contribution of the psycholinguistic evidence to the language–thought relationship must be described as circumstantial. Chomsky himself offers no tangible support for his idea of innate universal structures. Studies of child language acquisition have shown similarities but not an essential basic underlying universal which could not be accounted for otherwise. Also, much of the evidence produced from the child language acquisition studies rests upon very small numbers, and, even though these children were studied intensively, the disconfirming examples (Clark, 1974; Průcha, 1974) must be given serious consideration. The concentration on language acquisition understandably directs attention away from other symbolic functions developing at the same time, namely deferred imitation, mental images, and drawing. Work such as that of Clark (1973), Nelson and Bonvillian (1973), and Edwards (1973) brings out the ways in which other strategies are used and hence comes closer to both the Vygotskyan and Piagetian positions. In all, the evidence produced is consistent with interpretations other than the innateness of language structures hypothesis, which is not necessary to explain the common features of language acquisition.

EFFECTS OF LANGUAGE DEPRIVATION ON THOUGHT PROCESSES

Situations of failure to achieve language competence, as in the congenitally deaf and children deprived of access to verbal communication in early childhood, all provide a valuable source of evidence regarding the relationship between language and thought.

Studies with the deaf

It is well known that hearing deprivation generally produces early and extensive language deficits. Unless they have been given special training, deaf children up to the age of six years may attain a vocabulary of only between 10 and 50 words: the deaf six year old usually has no self-initiated lip-reading skills (Lenneberg, 1967). The extent to which language deficits are associated with deficits in thought processes may vary greatly according to the age of the child and the nature of the tasks used as criteria. For this purpose language is considered as social communication and is distinguished from egocentric production of speech sounds. Lenneberg (1967) has shown that congenitally deaf infants make the same sounds as hearing infants, despite the fact that they do not have auditory models for these sounds. Tape-recordings were made of the spontaneous noises made during play of eighteen deaf children over an eighteen-month period. Two of the children who were born to deaf parents were recorded from the first month onwards, and sixteen with hearing parents were recorded between their second and fifth year. Lenneberg found that all eighteen children vocalized often during play and, although they did not develop words, the order in which cooing, babbling, laughter, and sounds of discontent occurred was the same as for hearing children. Many of the deaf children produced sounds which were identical to well-articulated speech sounds. The deaf children, however, tended to persist in certain types of noise, whereas the hearing children seemed to have wider range of babbling sounds and apparently enjoyed going over their own repertoires. The hearing children were also much more vocal in the presence of others than were the deaf children. Observations of the play of deaf and hearing preschool-age children by Lenneberg showed that unless there was also some generalized neurological or psychiatric disturbance the almost total absence of language did not prevent deaf children from engaging in imaginative and intelligent play. On the other hand, Lenneberg observes, mentally deficient children may have a much greater degree of language development at five years than the peripherally deaf, but their language advantage is not associated with a more sophisticated level of play. It may be noted that Lenneberg presents these statements as observations from his experience, but they could be empirically tested and form the basis of manipulative experiments.

Testing was conducted by Lenneberg on preschool deaf and hearing children using the Leiter scale, a relatively language-free concept formation test in which pictures have to be sorted in accordance with various criteria which range from simple to complex and require both conceptualization and reasoning. No difference was found between young deaf and hearing children, and similar results were obtained with older children. In both cases, as long as there was no psychiatric or neurological disturbance, the scores depended on maturation rather than on the presence or absence of language skills (Lenneberg, 1967).

The work with deaf children by Vincent, Affolter, and Oléron of the Genevan school has often been referred to by Piaget in support of the independence of thought and language (Piaget, 1954a, 1963; Piaget and Inhelder, 1969). Oléron (1971, 1962) found no appreciable difference between deaf and hearing children on learning tasks based on the concepts of sameness or difference. The performances of thirty-eight deaf and thirty-eight hearing children aged four and seven were compared using stimulus discrimination involving shape, object, colour, weight, size, and speed. From the age of five onwards a majority of both deaf and hearing children succeeded on these tasks.

Concept transfer tasks in which subjects are required to shift the basis of classification successively have frequently been used to compare deaf and hearing subjects. Early results on such a task by Hoefler (1927) using the weight sorting test showed that only four out of thirty deaf shifted spontaneously. Macandrew (1948) used a restructuring situation in which social pressures were used to get the subjects to change. Subjects were deaf and hearing children aged from nine to fifteen years. All normals changed, but only four out of twenty four deaf subjects changed. Oléron (1951, 1953), using subjects with a mean age of fifteen years and a similar task with training trials on blocks and transfer trials on drawings, found differences between the normal and hearing subjects, although not so markedly. The order of shifting in the hearing subjects was object → colour → number, but no predominant order occurred in the deaf.

In another study, Oléron (Furth, 1964) devised transfer tasks in which manipulations were carried out on tests involving size, size with form varied, weight, and two speed tasks. Subjects were 4 seven-year-old deaf and hearing children. No differences were found on size, with form varied, or weight, but results on the speed tasks were varied, the deaf being poorer on one than on the other measure.

The role of language in contributing to the evidence of deaf children's poorer performance on conservation tasks was tested in studies by Oléron and Herren (1961) and Furth (1964) using non-verbal methods. Oléron and Herren devised a set of pictures which the subjects learned to use as equivalents to verbal responses on weight and volume conservation tasks. The ages at which the hearing subjects succeeded were 8·5 on conservation of weight and 10.5 on the conservation of volume, but for the deaf there was a retardation of about six years on both problems. Furth replicated this experiment but modified the pretask training by using a miming procedure with a horizontal hand position to indicate 'equal' and a downward movement of the hand for 'heavier'. Again the normal children performed better, but the obtained discrepancy, about two years, was much less than that found by Oléron and Herren. The deaf children performed more like six than eight year olds, and were more hesitant and inconsistent in their responses than six-year-old hearing children.

On the other hand, Oléron found deaf children aged from five to seven years solved a manipulatory problem both quantitatively and qualitatively as easily as hearing children of the same age. The result contradicted an earlier finding on similar tasks (Furth, 1964).

Studies by Furth (1961, 1964, 1966, 1971), Furth and Milgram (1965), and

Furth and Youniss (1971) with deaf children and adults using various concept learning tasks have produced results which, Furth and Youniss argue, show the specific effects of linguistic deficits but not the effects of any deficit in the basic development and structure of intelligence.

In one group of experiments (Furth 1961) 180 deaf and 180 hearing subjects, thirty subjects for each age group from seven to twelve years, were given three non-verbal concept learning tasks. Results confirmed predictions that the hearing subjects would not be superior to the deaf subjects in performance on tasks involving sameness and symmetry but would be superior on problems involving opposites, in which language experience was thought to be more relevant. Furth related this finding to Vygotsky's notion of pseudo-concepts. The hearing children's superior results were interpreted as showing evidence not so much that they had superiority on the concept but that on this task their performance was facilitated by their familiarity with their mother tongue.

In a related group of classification experiments Furth and Milgram (1965) compared the performance of normal, retarded, and deaf children on a series of verbal and non-verbal classification tasks in which verbal and non-verbal input and output were varied. Ages ranged from six to sixteen years. The experiments involved four conditions of a classification task: picture sorting, picture verbalization, word sorting, and word verbalization.

In the first experiment subjects were thirty-eight normal subjects with a mean age of 9·1 and thirty-seven retarded children of the same age with mean IQ's of between 64 and 78. Results showed that, with pictures, sorting was easier than verbalization while, with words, verbalization was easier than sorting. On the picture tasks low inelligence depressed the score on verbalization without affecting sorting, but on the word tasks sorting was more severely affected than verbalization. The substitution of verbal instead of pictorial elements in the input made the task more difficult for both normals and retarded, but to a greater extent for the retarded.

In the second experiment in the series two groups of deaf children of eight and sixteen years of age were given the picture sorting test using the same sets of pictures as in the previous experiment, but with a variation in stimulus presentation and use of gestures and sign language. The younger deaf children were found to be inferior to the normal controls on total score, and particularly on the first part of the test, but there was no difference between the older deaf and normal groups, both on the easy initial part of the task and on the more difficult second part. Furth interpreted this result as showing that the young deaf children lacked general cognitive experience.

Furth and Youniss (1971) and their associates (Furth, Youniss, and Ross, 1970; Robertson and Youniss, 1969; Youniss and Robertson, 1970) developed a series of tasks to measure the growth of operational thinking from the concrete to the formal level. In one of these studies (Furth and Youniss, 1971) three tasks at the formal operational level were given to groups of deaf, disadvantaged rural, and middle-class suburban adolescents. One was a symbol logic test, the second tested probability, and the third tested combinational reasoning.

Additional information was available on the deaf subjects' language competence and reading. Training sessions were given over a five-week period and results obtained before and after training. Although the overall group results favoured the hearing samples over the deaf sample, particularly in the symbol logic task, nevertheless there was evidence of many deaf subjects reaching the higher-level scores. Furth and Youniss also pointed out some striking cases of high achievement accompanied by extremely low linguistic performances such as reading ages equivalent to second and third grade. The findings clearly supported the notion of the independence of thinking of this type from language. It was argued that linguistic use, especially reading, which clearly favoured both the hearing groups, would have a facilitating effect on the symbol logic task, but was not a prerequisite for and hence not a causal determinant of formal operational thinking.

Furth and Youniss conclude from these experiments that when thinking tasks are devised that are not couched in verbal terms the same basic manifestations of logical thinking are present in the deaf as in the hearing, without any important structural deficiencies. Furth argues that in a deprivation experiment even one bona fide case of non-impairment would be valuable evidence, whereas evidence of impairment could be expected, but it could arise from other irrelevant sources as well as from linguistic deficit. Furth and his colleagues did not find the deaf equal to the hearing on all tasks, but there were a number of tasks on which there were no differences. The tasks on which the deaf failed were not consistently related to specific logical operations but seemed to be due to problems of familiarity, difficulty with grasping instructions, and not being ready to take an intellectual initiative, all of which Furth regarded as arising from inadequate social experience rather than inadequate logical functioning. The deficit did not increase with age.

According to this interpretation, the language deficit of the deaf is of a specific kind. As a direct result of linguistic incompetence, the deaf are poor at all verbal tasks and those non-verbal tasks in which linguistic habits are directly advantageous, and as an indirect result they are frequently deficient in intellectual experience—they lack factual information; they do not show intellectual curiosity; they have less opportunity and training for thinking; they are insecure, passive, or rigid in unstructured situations. These deficiencies may possibly be reducible by making greater use of non-verbal methods of instruction, as Furth suggests. In sum, the studies with the deaf show substantial support for the independence of language and thought, but not conclusive support.

Deprivation resulting from social isolation

A number of well-known cases of children who survived alone in the forests, or who were placed in deprived environments without social or verbal contact, have been reported from time to time (Mann, 1970) and may also shed some light on the language—thought relationship. Reports of efforts to teach these children after extended periods of deprivation show that to learn verbal communication is one of the most difficult tasks. It seems improbable that such children could have survived at all had they not been able to think in such a way as to cope with their own environment. It has been proposed by Lenneberg (1967) that there is an age, probably up to five years, beyond which the acquisition of language becomes extremely difficult. Such cases appear to support the notion of language being socially acquired rather than there being ready-programmed, innate grammatical structures. If such structures did exist, then it could be expected that after the initial trauma of return to a more normal environment the language structures would be quickly triggered off. This does not occur.

EVIDENCE RELATED TO THE LINGUISTIC REALITY HYPOTHESIS

The evidence in relation to the Whorfian hypothesis comes from a variety of fields. These include Sapir and Whorf's studies in comparative philology, attempts to test lexical and syntactical aspects of the theory, social applications in which social class or ethnic differences have been investigated, studies of cognitive performance of bilinguals in their two language modes, and cross-cultural studies of groups with differing languages.

Evidence from comparative linguistics

The source of Sapir and Whorf's observations on the influence of linguistic habits upon habitual modes of thinking lies in their work in comparative philology, particularly that of Sapir on American Indian languages which he recorded and analysed. So great and varied are Sapir's achievements in this area, encompassing also Indo-European, semitic, and many other language groups, that it is difficult to pinpoint particular sources of evidence. However, the following three examples may serve to illustrate. In his discussion of the different ways of saying that a stone falls, Sapir drew from comparative studies of German, French, English, Russian, Latin, Kwakiutl, Chippewa, Nootka, and Chinese. In this example he showed how the differences between reference systems may reflect different ways of analysing and reporting the same experience.

From his study of the speech of the Nootka tribe on Vancouver Island, Sapir (1915) showed how the Nootka language used variations on consonants and diminutive affixes to express a mixture of mocking pity and affection. The same or very similar diminutive forms were used when referring to someone small in stature and to someone suffering from speech or eye defect, or other physical disability. Not only the attitude of the speaker, but the characteristic response of a person to his affliction could be expressed in this way.

The third example comes from his studies of the Yana language carried out over some years from 1910 onwards. Sapir found that in Yana there were two distinct language forms, a male form used between males and a reduced female form used between or about females. The sex-role differences among the Yana were related to language forms in a way which suggested that the majority of the female language forms had become no longer merely linguistic particles used to denote sex but 'a conventionalized symbolism of the less considered or ceremonious status of women in the community' (Sapir, 1929, in Mandelbaum, 1949, p. 212).

It may be noted that all three of the above examples are drawn from the syntactic rather than the lexical aspects of the language. Sapir did not regard the richness or otherwise of vocabulary as relevant to ways of thinking. If the language was formally complete in the sense of having a well-defined and exclusive phonetic system into which forms all expressions could be fitted, new words could be borrowed or invented. He regarded the language forms as providing a complete frame of reference through which experience can be expressed, in much the same way as a number system is a complete reference system of quantitative reference. Shifting into another language was therefore like changing references systems: although the environment may remain the same, the system of interpreting one's experience of it will differ.

Tests of the Whorfian hypothesis—lexical aspects

The use of the colour spectrum as a means of testing the lexical aspects of the Whorfian hypothesis has considerable appeal because the psychological determinants of recognition, naming, etc., can be related to the invariant physical properties of the colours by whatever names they are known. Typical of experiments of this kind are those of Ray (1953), Brown and Lenneberg (1954), and Lenneberg and Roberts (1956). More recently work has been directed more towards the use of Osgood's semantic differential (Osgood, Suci, and Tannenbaum, 1957), to elicit semantic similarities across a variety of languages. Examples are the studies of Osgood (1964), Nordenstreng (1970), and Tanaka (1972).

Ray (1953) showed how in ten North American languages representing sixty different cultural groups, there was very little common ground in terms of the cutoff points on the colour spectrum by which names were given to colours. However, he found no difficulty in perceiving any colours in any group. Nor did environmental explanations account for the differences: e.g. one group, the Atka, had no word for the violet categories, but those colours were predominant in their environment. Ray concluded that the category names were arbitrary and pragmatic and there was no physiological, psychological, or anatomical basis for the differences in colour systems.

In the Brown and Lenneberg (1954) and Lenneberg and Roberts (1956) experiments codability was distinguished from discriminability of colours. Codability meant that there was a word to match the colour and discriminability that the subjects could distinguish between the colours. The materials used were the Munsell colours. In Brown and Lenneberg's experiment the subjects were American college students; in Lenneberg and Roberts' they were Zuni

Indians. The American college students were tested tachistoscopically, recording response times, and in the study of the Zuni a field adaptation of these methods was used. All subjects were screened first for colour-blindness.

Within both the student and Zuni groups there was fairly high agreement as to codability. In both Zuni and the student subjects codability was found to be related to recognition. If a colour name required a long word or a group of words it was also likely to take longer to recognize, both between and within persons, within the linguistic community, and from one testing to another. A factor analysis (Brown and Lenneberg, 1954) yielded only one general factor on these measures, namely codability. The measure contributing most to this general factor was found to be the reliability of the naming response among those who spoke the same language. The codability of a particular colour was also found to be related to the ability to recognize colours. For example, the Zuni colour lexicon has only one term for orange and yellow. The American student subjects never made recognition errors in relation to these two colours, but the Zuni frequently confused the two stimuli. Bilingual Zunis who also spoke English made this error less often than Zunis who spoke only Zuni, but more often than the Zunis who were only English-speaking. Brown and Lenneberg (1954) suggested from these results that there may be general laws relating codability to cognitive processes to which all cultures could conform, although they might differ among themselves in the values the variables assume in particular regions of experience.

Two further studies using the Munsell colours, by Burnham and Clark (1955) and Lantz and Stefflre (1964), qualified the Brown and Lenneberg findings. Burnham and Clark, using the Framework–Munsell Test Colours, found that colours differed in recognizability, but that the errors differed in systematic ways. It appeared that naming habits were used to restructure the colours into anchors or boundaries between name maps. For example, instead of remembering all the different greens, the subject remembered the point at which green changed to yellow or blue. Lenneberg (1967) considered that the combined effect of these experiments was to suggest that semantic structure influenced recognition only under certain experimental circumstances, namely when a task was difficult and the stimuli were chosen in a certain way. If it were possible to obtain a positive as well as a negative correlation between codability and recognizability, it would also be possible to select stimuli in such a way that codability would have zero correlation with recognizability of a colour. Lenneberg concluded therefore that both the Brown and Lenneberg experiment and the Burnham and Clark experiment were special cases (Lenneberg, 1967).

Lantz and Stefflre (1964) looked at relationships between communication accuracy and recognition. The findings were that when the communication accuracy is determined for every colour in a given array of colour stimuli there is a close relationship, but codability predicts recognizability only in special cases in particular contexts with particular stimulus arrays.

Crosscultural studies using the semantic differential to elicit affective meanings depend to a great extent upon the translatability of concepts. Data obtained by Osgood (1964) and Tanaka (1967, 1972) suggest that there is a great deal of semantic similarity shared across a very large number of languages. Interactions between subject and scale and between concept and scale have been found (Miron and Osgood, 1966; Tanaka and Osgood, 1965), but after a rigorous testing (Nordenstreng, 1970) it was concluded that these effects are minimal even if interesting compared with the demonstrable generality of meaning which the semantic differential appears to evoke.

Overall, the Whorfian hypothesis is not given strong support by these findings. The semantic structure of a language is seen as having only a 'mildly biasing' effect (Lenneberg, 1967) upon recognition. In special circumstances limitations of vocabulary may be overcome by the creative use of descriptive words.

Tests of the Whorfian hypothesis—syntactical aspects

Tests of the grammatical aspect of the Whorfian hypothesis were carried out by Carroll and Casagrande (1958) using Navaho Indians in a series of experiments in which characteristic ways of expressing and perceiving similarities of form in English and Navaho were related to the tendency, found in European and American children, to distinguish objects on the basis of size and colour rather than on the basis of how they were handled. Carroll and Casagrande hypothesized that the Navaho children would learn to discriminate the form attributes rather than the colour of objects earlier than would European–American children. Subjects included two Navaho groups, one predominantly Navaho-speaking and the other predominantly English-speaking, living on the same reservation. Each child was asked to pick the two objects of three presented which went best together. The type of objects included a rope, a stick, a cube, a sphere, and an oblong block, in colours of either yellow or blue. In each trial a pair could be made on the basis of colour, or another could be made on the basis of form. In both the Navaho groups grouping on the basis of colour gave way to grouping on the basis of form with increasing age, but earlier for the Navaho-dominant than in the English-dominant group who did not reach the level of the Navaho-dominant group although the difference between the two groups tended to decrease over time. Comparisons with middle-class white European and black Harlem American children, however, showed that the white middle-class children resembled the Navaho-dominant more than the English-dominant Navahos, while the black Harlem children resembled the English-dominant Navahos more than the Navaho-dominant.

Carroll and Casagrande's interpretation of this result introduced a consideration of environmental factors, but in addition to the linguistic effects rather than instead of them. They suggested that the white middle-class children's performance may have been influenced by their early experience with toys, blocks, and puzzles. It would seem, however, that if these kinds of experience are sufficient to offset the effects of grammatical characteristics of the language, perhaps the poorer performance of the Negro slum children and the English-dominant Navahos on attention to shape rather than colour might also be explained just as well on an experiential as on a linguistic basis. Also, perhaps the traditional attention to form in Navaho culture was being transmitted more effectively in the Navaho-speaking groups than in those who had so lost their Navaho traditions as to be English-dominant in their speech habits. The Carroll and Casagrande study is probably the only strongly confirming experimental evidence for the syntactic aspects of the Whorfian hypothesis.

Social applications of the Whorfian hypothesis

Language deprivation of a social kind has been found in cases in which the language used by or available to some speakers is restricted in some way. Under certain social conditions the language mode commonly employed does not make use of the entire range of the language, but is limited in vocabulary and syntax to a relatively small segment of the total usages. Such conditions may include, for example, class or ethnic minority membership, and geographical or institutional isolation. To what extent is there evidence that socially-based limitations on linguistic development interfere with thinking processes or not?

One source of such evidence which has had considerable influence and excited some controversy is the work of Bernstein (1958, 1959, 1960, 1965, 1971, 1973). Bernstein proposed that there was a relationship between the mode of linguistic expression and the mode of structuring ideas and feeling in the middle classes versus the lower classes. He saw these two groups as differing fundamentally. The middle classes possessed a cognitive and affective awareness of the importance between means and long-term ends; they were disciplined to orient their behaviour toward certain goals and values, and at the same time placed a premium on individual differentiation; they had an instrumental attitude to social relations and objects; they were sensitive to structure rather than content; and they discouraged direct expressions of feeling, particularly feelings of hostility. In the middle classes words were used as mediators between the expression of feeling and its approved social recognition. Thus a value was placed upon the verbalization of feeling. The attitudes of working classes and the semiskilled, on the other hand, were non-instrumental and more sensitive to content than structure. They expressed feelings directly and more often through action than through words (Bernstein, 1958).

Bernstein considered that these tendencies were universal to all societies where such class structures are to be found. The important determining factor was seen as being the nature of the words and the type of language-use, not so much in the size of vocabulary as in the way that a particular social emphasis might mediate the relation between thought and feeling. In terms of the Whorfian hypothesis he was following the weaker form of Hockett (1954), Fishman (1960), and Hymes (1964) rather than the purely lexical version.

The 'restricted' code, more typical of the lower classes, was said to be characterized as follows (Bernstein, 1959):

(1) Short, grammatically simple, often unfinished sentences, a poor syntactical construction with a verbal form stressing the active mood.
(2) Simple and repetitive use of conjunctions ('so', 'then', 'and').
(3) Frequent use of commands and questions.
(4) Rigid and limited use of adjectives and adverbs.
(5) Infrequent use of impersonal pronouns as subjects ('one', 'it').
(6) Statements formulated as implicit questions which set up a sympathetic circularity, e.g. 'Just fancy?', 'It's only natural, isn't it?', 'I wouldn't have believed it'.
(7) A statement of fact is often used as both a reason and a conclusion, or more accurately, the reason and conclusion are confounded to produce a categoric statement, e.g. 'Do as I tell you', 'Hold on tight', 'You're not going out', 'Lay off that'.
(8) Individual selection from a group of idiomatic phrases will frequently be found.
(9) Symbolism is of a low other of generality.
(10) The individual qualification is implicit in the sentence structure; therefore it is a language of implicit meaning. It is believed that this fact determines the form of the language.

In contrast, the 'elaborated code' of the middle classes is characterized by:

(1) Accurate grammatical order and syntax regulate what is said.
(2) Logical modifications and stress mediated through a grammatically complex sentence construction, especially through the use of arrangement of conjunctions and relative clauses.
(3) Frequent use of prepositions indicating logical relationships, and temporal and spatial contiguity.
(4) Frequent use of impersonal pronouns such as 'it', 'one'.
(5) A discriminate selection from a range of adjectives and adverbs.
(6) Individual qualification verbally mediated through the structure and relationships within and between sentences.
(7) Expressive symbolism which distributes affectual support rather than logical meaning to what is said.
(8) A language use which points to the possibilities inherent in a complex conceptual hierarchy for the organizing of experience.

These characteristics are relative to those of the restricted code. It would seem that Bernstein is suggesting a continuum rather than different dimensions and also that the restricted code as he describes it above is rarely found in a pure state. However, it is clear that he regards the restricted code as both less precise and less conducive to expressing affective states. Bernstein (1959, p. 318) suggests that learning is affected because a correlate of such a code is a

... low level of conceptualisation—an orientation to a low order of causality, a disinterest in processes, a preference to be aroused by and respond to that which is given rather than to the implications of a matrix of relationships, and thus, it is suggested, partly conditions the intensity and extent of curiosity, as well as the mode of establishing relationships.

Bernstein's evidence for these claims was mainly derived from studies carried out with 300 male adolescent apprentices of the lower class in London (aged from fifteen to eighteen years). The boys were tested using the Raven Progressive Matrices, 1938 (RPM 38), and the Mill Hill Vocabulary Test. Results of the first stage of this study showed that scores on the RPM 38 ranged from 71 to 80 IQ to 121 to 126. This group came from skilled and semiskilled backgrounds, randomly distributed geographically in inner and outer suburbs (295 had left school at the age of fifteen). It was predicted that the higher the score on Matrices the greater the difference between the Progressive Matrices and Mill Hill scores. Results supported the hypothesis (Bernstein, 1958). In the second stage of this study (Bernstein, 1960) two extreme social groups were used: sixty-one students, all of whom were employed as messenger boys and none of whom had had a grammar school education, and forty-five subjects matched for age and sex with the former, all pupils of major public schools with a cross-section of scholastic attainment and educational interests. Subjects were given the Raven Progressive Matrices 38 and Mill Hill Vocabulary tests as before and a similar result was obtained. The language scores of the working-class group tended to remain depressed in relation to their higher Progressive Matrices scores, but for the middle-class group there was relatively no difference between the levels of vocabulary and Progressive Matrices at each IQ level.

In regard to the relationship between the language and cognitive measures, Bernstein concluded from his results that the lower-class boys were disadvantaged on the language measure. However, while the results in the two groups clearly differ, there are some problems in accepting Bernestein's interpretation. It could be, for example, that the increasing discrepancy at the upper levels of the lower-class group illustrates not dependence of thinking upon language but independence, an interpretation at odds with the Whorfian aspects of Bernstein's basic predictions. Also, it might be argued that the choice of the Mill Hill Vocabulary Test was inappropriate for eliciting differences in language performance because this test can show only *recognition of vocabulary*, not use of either vocabulary or syntax. The presence or absence of formal language devices, as set out in Bernstein's description of the elaborated code, therefore would not be tapped. What Bernstein claims to be universal characteristics may well be culturally endemic and limited to special groups of disadvantaged speakers of English. Despite these problems, Bernstein's notions are provocative and testable, and since the original statement much research has taken up the question of how socially-based linguistic styles may affect thinking. The result is some qualified support for the hypothesis from studies in England (e.g. Lawton, 1968; Robinson, 1965; Robinson and Rackstraw, 1972, 1975) and some contrary evidence from Australia (Owens, 1976; Poole, 1972a, 1972b) and the United States (Labov, 1972).

Lawton found such differences in syntactic structures in written material. He argued that the restricted code was adequate for expressing and describing concrete things and events rather than ideas and reflections upon events. Although Robinson and Rackstraw (1972) found differences in speech patterns between working-class and middle-class children, they argued that social class can have no causal significance (Robinson and Rackstraw, 1975) and planned a programme of assistance to working-class mothers aimed at helping them to respond more effectively to their children's questioning.

Poole (1971), 1972a, 1972b, 1973) carried out a series of studies of the oral and written language used by university students in Australia. For the oral language Poole used structured interviews which were subjected to detailed linguistic analysis. She found that students from middle-class backgrounds used sentences of greater length and complexity, a wider variety of adjectival qualifiers and adverbial modifiers, more egocentric references, and fewer fragmented or repetitious sentences. However, lower-class students did not use a higher proportion of non-specific and sociocentric speech as was predicted from the Bernstein hypothesis (Poole, 1971).

The written language was examined using the Cloze method. In terms of lexical and structural predictability, the middle-class messages were more difficult to predict than the lower-class messages, which were more stereotyped and limited in lexicon, but overall support for the Bernstein position was limited. Poole suggests that some conformity tendencies in completing the Cloze items might have accounted at least in part for the findings. Unfortunately the relationship between linguistic performance and general academic performance was not tested, but it should be noted that as all subjects were university students they had already shown evidence of academic superiority.

The work of Owens (1976) has provided an extremely thorough and rigorous testing of the Bernstein theory in regard to syntactic aspects of written language. Owens used a sample of 240 boys and girls from Grade 5 (primary school) and Forms I, III and V (high school) in Sydney, Australia. The sample was balanced on grade, sex, and upper and lower socioeconomic status. Owens collected compositions on three topics all in the narrative descriptive mode, and gave a brief test of cognitive development designed to elicit intuitive, concrete or formal operational thinking, and some transitional categories, from the comprehension of short verbal passages. The test was devised originally by Peel (1966, 1967a) but incorporated some local modifications by McNally (1968) and others. From this testing Owens obtained a group of 128 subjects from Forms III and V such that there were equal numbers of each sex, equal numbers of middle-class and lower-class socioeconomic status, and equal numbers of concrete and formal operational thinkers. IQ was treated as a covariate. Social class was assessed on the basis of parents' occupation and education. Four indices of syntactic development were devised: clause-to-sentence development; depth of subordination; subordinate clause type, i.e. use of adverbial, adjectival, and noun clause; and use of passive voice. These indices were based directly on work arising from the Bernstein theory. Clause-to-sentence development was defined operationally as the 'T-unit', the minimal terminal unit, namely one main clause with all its subordinate clauses. Depth of subordination was related directly to the work of Loban (1963) and Lawton (1963, 1964). The use of passive was also justified on the basis of Lawton's work. In accord with the Bernstein position it was predicted that the lower class would be inferior on all indices and on the cognitive task.

The analysis failed to support any of the eight major predictions. There were no social class differences on any of the indices of psychosyntactic development and there was no relationship between either social class or syntactic develop-ment and cognitive level. Nor were there any significant interaction effects between the major language and class variables. In the case of the analysis by cognitive level, some interactions between level, sex, clause length (T-unit), and use of passive verbs were obtained such that boys at the formal operational lever were superior to girls on the syntactic measures. At least for these Austra-lian adolescents on this task there can be no support for the Bernstein position. Two problems suggest themselves, however. One is that the use of school compositions as the sample of written English would be biased towards the use of the elaborated code. The bias would necessarily favour the lower SES since good writing style also sets limits to the number of subordinate clauses, sentence length, and use of passive. The other is that as the cognitive screening test was itself a verbal test it could be a possible source of confounding, in that children who did well on a verbal comprehension test would also do well in a written task. In Bernstein's original work the lower-class boys performed differently on the Mill Hill test from the RPM but the middle class did not. On the other hand, the use of a verbal task would seem to have been an appro-priate instrument to detect evidence of the cumulative developmental lag proposed by Robinson and Rackstraw (1975). Even had individual testing been carried out the problem of the verbal content of explanations would still have remained.

The work of Labov (1972) on negro speech in the United States also provides a contrary case. After examining the nature of the speech of socially disadvantaged and middle-class negroes, Labov concluded that they indeed suffered a language disadvantage. However, the disadvantage did not arise from any lack of richness or creativeness in the lower-class negro speech but rather from its being different from the standard American English, favoured by, if not necessarily always spoken by, their middle-class negro and white teachers. Labov would agree with Bernstein that such differences could lead to a break-down in communication between a lower-class negro child and his teacher, hence poorer performance might be expected of such speakers.

Social class-based and ethnically-based deficiencies in language may be compared with those studies of peripheral language deficit in the deaf, described above, The language input and output are restricted in each case, but in different ways. Yet in both types of work there is at least some evidence that performance on tasks generally considered to reflect the presence of intellectual functioning need not necessarily be impaired. That impairment does occur may depend on many factors other than language. Indeed, the importance of Labov's findings lies in showing the compounding of the effects of social disadvantage which arise from an interaction between class and ethnicity with those of language disadvantage, or language difference, whichever way one may interpret the non-standard use of English by negro speakers.

Evidence from crosscultural studies

Bruner argues that it is not so much the lexicon of a given language as its capacity to develop linguistic terms for hierarchical superordinate classifications that can contribute to the development of classificatory abilities in the speakers of that language. Much of the evidence for his view is derived from Greenfield's studies with the Wolof children in Senegal (Greenfield, 1966), using classificatory tasks requiring subjects to make equivalence groupings.

In one experiment with unschooled village children (thirty subjects) ten objects obtained from the African market in Dakar were laid out on a table and each child was asked to indicate those that were alike and the reason for his choice. The ten objects could be grouped by function, form, and colour: a sandal, a blouse, a pair of shorts, and a scarf—all to wear; an onion, a ball of indigo dye, a glass bead, and a rubber ball—all round; a plastic drinking cup and a pencil—both coloured red, as were also the scarf and the ball. Greenfield reports that these children were able to make groupings based on a criterial attribute, but they did not change away from colour as that attribute nor did the percentage of reasons expressed in superordinate language increase with age.

In a further experiment with the Wolof subjects Greenfield again used the equivalence grouping task, but this time with a set of pictorial materials rather than objects and with a much larger number of subjects. Three sets of three pictures each were used, such that they could be grouped on the basis of function, shape, or colour. Subjects were asked to show the two pictures in each set which were most alike and were then asked the reason for their choice. No type of pair appeared twice in the same position. The picture displays included set 1, a clock, an orange, a banana; set 2, a sandal, a bubu (a Wolof robe), a guitar; and set 3, a bicycle, a helmet, a car. The 212 subjects in this experiment consisted of unschooled and schooled children from village and urban environments from age groups from six to adult.

In a third study, results from the above groups were compared with those of a group of children from the French schools of Dakar, all of whom spoke French as their first language and were mainly the children of French nationals living in Dakar. The children ranged from nursery school to sixth grade. The sixth-grade children were matched with the Wolof children (N was not given).

Greenfield found that the use of non-superordinates declined with age among all Wolof children. The unschooled children could not identify pictures as well as could the schooled children in any age group. Almost no failures were reported among the schooled, even in the younger groups, but failures did occur in the older unschooled. The schooled children used superordinate language structures far more than the unschooled; these usages increased with age and to a greater extent in the urban than in the rural school. For the unschooled there was no increase with age. When the use of superordinate terms was further broken down into generalized types (they are all X) and itemized types (this is X, this is X) the age differences showed increases in the generalized terms for the schooled groups but not for the unschooled. As before, the urban group was superior to the rural group.

The urban children also showed a developmental trend in the direction of using somewhat more functional concepts with age, but the bush school children showed almost no development of functional groupings. Greenfield also claims that the urban children tended towards using more nominal concepts, although this does not seem justified by the data as presented. For the schooled children the use of colour as a basis for grouping decreased and the use of form as a basis increased, but for the unschooled children colour groupings increased with age but the use of form and functional attributes was virtually non-existent—at any age. However, the number of children showing an increase in functional groupings was small.

The comparison with the French-speaking children was used by Greenfield to look at the findings from the point of view of testing the Whorfian hypothesis. The idea that the results depended upon lexical characteristics of the Wolof language was rejected. Because terms for the colour groupings had to be taken from the French language, it was not possible by using the Wolof language alone to make explicit the three colour groupings which were possible in the picture grouping task. Lexically the colour word deficiencies in Wolof, namely that the French *bleu* had to be used for 'blue' and that the Wolof language did not distinguish orange from red, did not prevent either Wolof children or adults from using colour as the most common criterial attribute. Greenfield concludes that the role of language in terms of specific lexical considerations is not great and that factors other than the lexicon determine the dimensions of equivalence, but that a specific lexicon may influence the range of categories within a given dimension.

The use of superordinate class terms in the sense of hierarchically organized labels—in this case the words 'colour' and 'form' (shape)—was found to be related to the ability to vary the choice of grouping attributes, and occurred more frequently in the French-speaking children than in the Wolof children tested in either French or Wolof. Use of the sentential mode, as against the ostensive and labelling modes, was more frequent in the schooled group than in the unschooled and in the schooled Wolof children tested in French than the schooled Wolof tested in Wolof. In all the schooled groups the use of the sentential mode increased with age and the use of labelling decreased, but for the unschooled the percentage of labelling remained much the same. Bruner's general conclusion from these results was that the main differences were those which arise from schooling, which forces the child to learn to use language as an implement of thought and to rely on linguistic coding as a means of communication.

Two final points may be made in regard to the findings. First, why there was a preference at all for shape over either colour or function is not really explained, either in terms of the child's levels of conceptualization or in terms of language. Second, the attributes of colour and shape (or form) are both perceptible attributes of objects whereas function is not, an aspect which is not taken into account either in the analysis or in Bruner's interpretation of the findings.

Bilinguals

Studies with bilinguals have been useful in considering whether using one or other of the two languages is more conducive to effective cognitive performance. If it could be shown that bilingual persons with equal competence in two languages performed better on cognitive tasks in one than in the other, such findings, given appropriate controls over social and experiential variables, might well show support for the Whorfian view of the language–thought relationship.

The effect of language medium in conservation tasks has been examined by Kelly (1970), Philp and Kelly (1974), and Tenezakis (1975) in studies using bilingual Greek-speaking children in Sydney, Australia. The Greek children were migrants who had lived at least four years in Greece and at least two in Australia; they attended an Australian school at which they were treated linguistically as other Australian children. The tests were conservation of length using sticks and conservation of substance using plasticine. Each test consisted of an initial establishment of equality, a transformation (position or shape), a return to equality, a second transformation, a third transformation, and a final equality. The subjects were pretested in both English and Greek; all twenty subjects reached a satisfactory level of performance in both languages and were all included. They were then tested in both the sets of conservation tasks— first in English, then in Greek, and then again in English. Of the total, thirteen demonstrated conservation to criterion, five failed to conserve on the initial testing in English but attained conservation on the testing in Greek and the second testing in English, and two failed to conserve in English but attained conservation in Greek and failed again in the second testing in English. The small numbers in the sample, the absence of an Australian control group, and the failure to control for the order in which the different media were employed are limitations of these studies.

Following on Kelly and Tenezakis' work with the Greek migrant children, Gallagher (1971) used bilingual Greek children in Victoria, Australia, in conservation tasks. The first aim was to find whether there was any evidence that there would be bilingual children who could conserve in one language but not in the other. Gallagher was also interested in examining the relationships proposed by Bruner between syntactical structures and language. It was predicted that the relationship between syntactic competence and conservation would be greater than that between semantic competence and conservation. The subjects (forty) were randomly selected from Grade 1 classes. Ages ranged from

6 years 2 months to 7 years. All came from relatively low socioeconomic status brackets. Three conservation tests, conservation of number, conservation of discontinuous quantity, and conservation of continuous quantity were used. A pretest was used to check that they understood the concepts of 'more', 'same', etc., in each language. The design of this experiment allowed for two groups of subjects randomly allocated, in one of which the testing was given first in Greek and then in English, and in the other the testing was given first in English and then in Greek. Pretesting was in each case in the same language as the testing. The semantic aspect was tested using the Peabody Picture Vocabulary Test (in English) and the syntactic aspect was measured using the grammatical closure test of the ITPA (also in English).

Gallagher found that for all the cases in which the subject was a conserver in one language and a non-conserver in the other conservation was attained on the second test administered. There was a greater difference between the two sets of results in those who were non-conservers in Greek and transitional in English than there was between the two results in those who were transitional in Greek and non-conservers in English. Correlation between PPVT and the total conservation scores was 0.51 ($p < 0.001$) and the correlation between raw scores on the grammatical closure test and total conservation score was even higher (0.62, $p < 0.001$), the difference between the two being significant ($p < 0.05$). Gallagher concluded that essentially the results favoured the Piagetian view on both counts, there being no contentious issue in the finding in regard to grammatical closure from this view. Inhelder and Sinclair (Sinclair-de-Zwart, 1969) also report a much closer link between syntactical structure and operativity than between vocabulary and operativity.

In a study by Kelly (1971) in New Guinea a sample of 216 subjects was obtained from village environments without schooling and 216 attending English-medium schools. Four different language or cultural groups were represented; age ranges (estimated) were from seven to 15 +. Kelly carried out all the testing, but children who had themselves acted as subjects were used as interpreters to the village sample, so that it could be said that it was conducted in the vernacular. A check on these children showed virtually no change in their responses after acting as interpreters. Unfortunately, there was no way of checking on the effects of the interpreters upon their subjects' responses, but the problems of obtaining a trainable bilingual tester-interpreter of an older age group would have been very great.

The subjects were tested for conservation of length, using sticks, and quantity, using rice. The procedure was as before, from equality through the transformation returning to equality for three transformations. The language medium was the same throughout.

Surprisingly, the village children performed better than the children in school. Possibly this was because the village children were tested in the vernacular and the school children's command of English was inadequate. However, no data are available for school children tested in the vernacular which would clarify this point. These results may be contrasted with those obtained by

Greenfield and Bruner in which school children appeared to have the advantage over those not in school. The native languages spoken by the New Guinea children were non-literate. Again there were no native English-speaking controls.

Studies of French-English bilinguals in Canada provide a setting in which there can be no question of the inferiority of one language over the other in terms of syntactic or semantic richness and in which both languages are widely spoken. Work by Lambert (1972), Lambert and Macnamara (1969), and Bain (1974) give some evidence of superior performance by bilinguals over monolinguals, but there is little to suggest that information learned in one language is not available in the other. Lambert and his associates have carefully followed the progress of a group of English-speaking children who attended French-speaking schools and a group of French-speaking children who attended English-medium schools and compared it with that of matched groups of monolinguals. There has been no indication of impairment in cognitive performance; indeed, the evidence for enrichment appears to be greater. Bain tested balanced bilinguals matched carefully with monolingual children for discovery learning in a problem-solving task and sensitivity to emotional expression. The bilinguals appeared to have some small advantage over the monolinguals on the first task, but a significantly greater advantage on the second.

Kolers' (1968) work was concerned with retrieval and storage of information. He devised experiments in reading aloud, comprehension, word association, and recall, such that in various interference situations input was in one language and production was required in the other, or was itself varied. German–Spanish, Spanish–English, and Thai–English combinations were used. Kolers concluded that some information such as certain objects and physical experiences could be coded into a common linguistic system, but that some abstract terms and more culturally determined concepts were coded into one linguistic system only.

In general, the studies reviewed above showed little effect of bilingualism on concept acquisition. Where differences were found they were often contradicted by other studies.

THE INFLUENCE OF LANGUAGE ACTIVITY ON LEARNING

Because of their concern with the second signalling system Russian psychologists have carried out many experiments in learning in which language has been used as an experimental variable. Some of these have been referred to while discussing Luria's work in the previous chapter, and these need not be mentioned in detail here. However, Luria refers to many such experiments in which learning is facilitated by language; these will be reviewed, together with similar experiments by workers not committed to Pavlovian theory. The results from three to five year olds reported by Luria clearly show the relevance of this distinction and the relative importance of the two aspects at this level. The child is assisted in learning to press a button when a light comes on if he says 'Go!' at the instant the light appears. Similarly, he can learn to press twice each time the light appears by saying 'Go! Go!' Having learned the above, he is then instructed to say 'I shall press twice' to each light and press twice. He usually presses *once* while saying he will press twice.

Luria (1961) reports that it is quite possible for a child aged from three to five years to learn to press a bulb in his right hand if a red figure on a grey background is presented and to press a bulb in his left hand if a green figure on a yellow background is presented. When this learning is complete it is easy to demonstrate that the child is responding to the colour of the figure by presenting (say) a red figure on a yellow background and noting that the child presses with his right hand. The figure appears to be the dominant aspect of this complex stimulus.

Suppose now that an attempt is made to make the child respond to the background and not to the figure. With older children, i.e. six years and above, a simple verbal instruction is usually enough to make the change, but with three to five year olds this instruction is not very effective. However, language can be used to restructure the situation. For example, if the figure is an aeroplane the child can be told to signal to the pilot with his right hand if the weather is grey and so not good for flying and with his left hand if it is sunny (yellow) and so good for flying. The child aged from three to five years who has learned the first part of the task by responding to the colour of the background with these instructions will respond to the background in the second part of the task. Thus language can be effective, even at this age, in changing the basis of the response by changing the structure of the task.

The fact that language on its own is not always effective in facilitating learning is shown by an experiment by Ruzskaya which is quoted by Luria (1961). Children were first taught to press a button with their right hand if a triangle was presented and a second button with their left hand if a square was presented. Correct responses were confirmed by the appearance of a toy car coming out of a garage; if the response was incorrect the doors of the garage stayed shut. Children aged from three to five years could learn this task when a particular triangle and square were used, as of course could older children.

Children who had learned the above task found generalization to triangles and quadrilaterals of different shapes very difficult, even at six to seven years. When the figures were given a verbal label ('triangle' and 'quadrilateral') and the task was thoroughly explained, considerable improvement was found in the six to seven year olds, but much less with younger children. However, if the children had been given previous experience in handling the figures, counting the points and sides, and learning the names, generalization was very effective, even with three to five year olds. Thus, with these children under six years of age, verbal instruction on its own did *not* help them learn the generalized concept, but haptic experience did. Thus it appears that language alone facilitates learning in some situations only after a certain stage of development.

While attempts to reproduce the work of Russian psychologists in this area have not always confirmed their findings, the majority have. It would not be possible to review them all here. The study by Hartig and Kanfer (1973) is one of the more recent and has some interesting points of interpretation not fully developed in their discussion. The basic situation is one in which the children are asked to help the experimenter by looking at some toys and telling him which ones they like. Before the toys are shown the experimenter says he has to do something else for the moment and the child is left alone with the toys but is told *not* to look at them until the experimenter returns. The child is observed until just after he looks at the toys or for ten minutes, whichever is shorter, when the experimenter returns after knocking at the door and shows the toys to the child. The basic measure is the time before the child first looks at the toys after being left alone.

Five random groups were distinguished for each of two age groups; 3 years 4 months to 5 years 5 months and 5 years 6 months to 7 years 4 months. The control group was subjected to the basic treatment and one other group, the verbal control, had the added instruction to recite 'Hickory dickory dock, etc.' while waiting. The three experimental groups were each told to repeat the words, 'I must not turn round and look at the toys', while one group had the added words, 'If I do not look at the toys I will be a good boy (girl)', another the added words, 'If I look at the toys, I will be a bad boy (girl)', and the third had no words added to the self-instruction.

In general, the three self-instruction groups waited longer before looking at the toys than either control group, and the younger children who overtly verbalized waited longer than those who did not. Younger children overtly verbalized less than older children, but for those who did the three self-instruction groups did not differ from the verbal control. Hartig and Kanfer (1973, p. 265) comment: 'These data suggest that for younger children the effects of reciting a nursery rhyme and of giving task-relevant self-instructions were not different, but the same conditions affected the older children differentially.' This suggestion is in agreement with earlier suggestions that the role of the content of language in controlling behaviour increases from three to seven years of age.

Many of the Russian findings with regard to inner speech were replicated by Kohlberg, Yaeger, and Hjertholm (1968) who found that with younger children of average ability overt private speech increases in frequency before beginning to decrease at five years (approximately). Furthermore, private muttering increased from five to nine years while other forms of speech decreased. In problem-solving situations the amount of egocentric speech increased with the difficulty of the task for four-and-a-half to five year olds. In addition, private muttering tended to be replaced by overt self-questioning as the difficulty increased. Taken as a whole the results of their studies tend to support the Russian view that inner speech arises from egocentric speech and is associated with cognitive activity.

The influence of language on learning can also be studied by examining the extent to which irrelevant language activity interferes with learning. In these interference experiments it is commonly assumed that the use of the organs of speech involved not only the peripheral nerves and muscles but also those central areas of the cortex responsible for monitoring speech. It is further assumed that these cortical areas control inner speech and so it should not be possible for the subject to use inner speech for learning or problem solving while he is articulating or even listening to irrelevant verbal material. Thus interference experiments have been seen by Sokolov (1972) and others to provide important evidence on the role of inner speech.

One experiment reported by Sokolov requires the subject to recite a well-known nursery rhyme repeatedly while listening to the experimenter read from an unfamiliar book. The subject has been instructed that he will be required to write down as much as he can of the material read to him. After he has done this, the subject is also asked to describe his experiences while trying to learn the passage when reciting. Experimental effects can be varied by having the subject repeat the experiment with the same material with various amounts of intervening practice in reciting the verse.

Sokolov reports findings for adult subjects who were staff or graduate students of the Institute of Psychology on two descriptive and two discursive passages. For the descriptive passages subjects were unable to recall more than a few points they picked up during breaks at the end of the verses. They reported hearing the noise of the experimenter's voice but mostly they could not even understand the words. After several trials with the same material interspersed with considerable separate rehearsal of the recitation, the subjects reported they could understand the words read by the experimenter but tended to suffer an instant amnesia and were still unable to recall very much of the descriptive passage.

It seems clear from his description that Sokolov did not use a tape-recorder to control such variables as the speed and loudness of the experimenter's reading. Furthermore, by using two channels, the subjects' reciting could have been matched against the material being read to discover the effects of pauses in recitations. Finally, the use of padded earphones could have controlled any auditory interference that occurred because the subject could hear his own voice as he listened to the experimenter. A repetition of this experiment with a suitable tape-recorder seems worth attempting.

Comparisons between the descriptive and discursive material revealed that the discursive seemed easier in that the subject had fewer specific details, and once the general area was reorganized he could reconstruct large sections from a few clues. However, all subjects attempted the descriptive task first, and practice at this might have made the discursive task easier. Some practice effects had been noted by Sokolov within each set of material.

Emperimental factors that can be varied in such an experiment are the interfering conditions and the material to be learned or the problem to be solved. Sokolov reports results using the following conditions: (a) clamping the tongue to prevent movement; (b) sequential counting; (c) free articulation (e.g. 'la-la', etc.); (d) squeezing a ball without the need to control pressure; (e) squeezing a ball to maintain a constant visual reading; (f) recitation; and

(g) listening to a passage to be remembered. Tasks to be performed included the addition of numbers, remembering geometrical figures, and learning details of passages read.

With adult subjects recitation produced the greatest interference to adding numbers as measured by the time taken, and this effect was greater as the number of numbers to be added was increased. Perhaps this latter effect is due to the greater amount of information to be stored and utilized. Other interfering conditions (a, c, d, and e above) produced little effect. Further experiments showed that listening to a passage to be remembered had as great an effect as recitation and that younger children were affected by tongue clamping but older ones were not.

Other experiments reported by Sokolov studied the effect of interference on the accuracy of remembering pictures and words. The general accuracy of remembering pictures was least affected, and accuracy of remembering abstract as opposed to concrete words was most affected by irrelevant articulation and by listening to a passage for later recall. Children were usually affected more than adults by interfering activity. In the case of paired associates learning, in which subjects had to learn which two words or which two pictures formed a pair, there was little difference between pictures and concrete and abstract words in the time taken to learn under interference conditions. This was true even though both reciting verse and listening to a passage for later recall created considerable interference effects in all cases.

From Sokolov's experiments it is clear that both reciting verse and listening to a passage to be recalled later affect such aspects of thinking as recalling pictures and words presented visually, learning paired associates, carrying out arithmetical operations, and translating from a foreign language. If the subject is not told that he will be asked to recall the passage he is listening to, the interference effect is very small. Mechanical interference such as tongue clamping produces interference only in first-grade children for whom inner speech is presumably still more closely linked to articulated speech than it is for older children and adults. In these experiments it would have been interesting to relate the errors in reciting, or the extent of recall of the passage listened to, to the degree of interference on an individual or a group basis.

The social learning experiments of modelling by observation of Bandura (1969) introduce another source of evidence on the role of verbal activity in cognitive tasks. Bandura proposed that effective observational learning depended to a considerable extent on the degree to which the observer forms and stores symbolic representations, mainly in the form of visual imagery and verbal description, which he may use as guides to later reproduction of the behaviour. Studies by Bandura, Grusec, and Menlove (1966), Coates and Hartup (1969), and Kemp and Perry (1976) give some support.

In a developmental study of children from four to seven years of age Coates and Hartup found that, when asked to repeat verbal descriptions of modelled events, observational learning increased in the younger but not the older group. Coates and Hartup argued that the younger children did not spontaneously produce relevant verbalizations whereas the older children did.

In a study using children aged from six to eight years Bandura, Grusec, and Menlove showed that observational learning was less effective when the children engaged in a verbal activity during the modelling period if that activity was such as to interfere with the production of verbal associates of the modelled behaviour.

Kemp and Perry investigated the effects of verbal activity introduced as interference and control conditions in a variety of observational learning given to groups of children aged from four to seven years—163 in all. The children observed a film of a male model performing novel activities. While they watched, subjects either engaged in an activity designed to interfere with verbal coding of the behaviour being modelled or performed a control activity. In the verbal interference condition the experimenter read the numbers 'one', 'two', or 'three' aloud to the subjects at the rate of one every six seconds. Each number was read an approximately equal number of times, but in random order, and subjects had to press the button when the same number was said twice in succession. The control condition required the subjects to press the button whenever they heard the experimenter tap a pencil on the table. The taps and pairs of numbers occurred equally often and at the same time during the film. For a four-minute period after the film was shown they engaged in one of four kinds of activity: preventing verbal rehearsal of the modelled behaviour, preventing visual rehearsal, preventing both visual and verbal rehearsal, or preventing neither visual nor verbal rehearsal. Subsequently, they were tested for recall of the modelled behaviour. Children assigned to the verbal interference treatment condition recalled fewer of the behaviours than the controls in both age groups, but the postobservation rehearsal manipulations did not affect recall in either age group. Older children did better than younger in all conditions. Kemp and Perry concluded that observational learning in children as young as four years is to some extent dependent upon verbal coding, but observational learning in older children may be less dependent on verbal coding than previously believed.

The significance of this type of study in the present context lies in the possibilities it opens up for the experimental control of language variables during performance of cognitive tasks which are patently non-verbal. In these results the interference effects of irrelevant language are evident, but they are offset by the facilitative effects of relevant language. Also the age differences show some unexpected features. Although older children do better in general on the observational learning tasks than the younger children, it would seem that both younger and older subjects can be affected by the interference. The importance of the interference occurring during the observation period rather than immediately afterwards is also brought out. It would be interesting to link this type of study to the physiological studies on the establishment of hemispheric dominance described later in the chapter.

A final example which provides a somewhat different focus on this question is the work of Kearins (1975) on visual memory skills in desert Aboriginal children in Western Australia. Kearins devised a series of tasks of the Kim's game type in which a set of twenty objects was first displayed, scrambled, and then had to be replaced by the subjects in their original position. The arrays included naturally occurring objects, such as sticks, stones, and leaves, and unnatural objects, which were sets of small bottles. The arrays could be set out as combinations of natural versus unnatural and same type (e.g. all stones) or different. The Aboriginal children were matched as far as possible with a comparable group of white children. Several age groups from seven to fourteen years have been used in later variations of the original experiment, with similar results. In all cases the Aboriginal children showed a remarkable superiority over the white children, but it is the difference in style which is of particular interest here. Observations of the children's behaviour during the task showed the Aboriginal children and the whites to differ markedly. The Aboriginal children appeared to become absorbed in the task, sat very still, and were not seen to move their lips, etc., during the viewing period. They worked silently and efficiently on the replacement task, often holding an object for some time while scanning the board before placing it in position. The white children moved about on the chair, picked up objects and turned them over, muttered a great deal and made comments, asked many questions about naming the objects, and made many tentative moves before deciding on a placement. It is, of course, possible that some kind of inner speech accompanied the Aboriginal children's thinking but was not apparent to the observer, though that seems not to have been evident; it certainly seems extremely likely that verbal accompaniment was an important aspect of the white children's less efficient thinking strategy. Whether eidetic images were used or not it would seem that in the case of these desert Aboriginal children we have an example of thinking without strong effects of language. Although Drinkwater (1976) did not obtain the same results in a repetition and variation of the experiments with Aboriginal children in island and coastal communities in Queensland, the Kearins results are nevertheless striking for the subjects used, whether the explanation be cultural or genetic-ecological.

The evidence presented in his section shows clearly that relevant language may facilitate and irrelevant language may interfere with learning and other thought processes. This seems to be true whether the source of the language is the experimenter or the subject. There is some evidence of at least an interaction between language and thinking for adults and children over six years of age. For younger children, the facilitative effect of language is somewhat uncertain, leading some to make the distinction between the impulsive as opposed to the controlling role of language in relation to behaviour. Although some of the findings need to be confirmed and clarified, it seems to be almost certain that the basic finding of at least an interaction between language and thinking will not be overthrown. Whether findings of the kind reported in this class of evidence could establish the identity between thinking and language, either in the form of inner speech or of some other kind, is doubtful. To demonstrate that A influences B, both positively and negatively is not to prove that A is B, as some appear to be suggesting.

PHYSIOLOGICAL EVIDENCE RELATED TO THE LANGUAGE AND THOUGHT RELATIONSHIP

Studies have been of three principal types: those involving the monitoring of the muscles of the tongue, lower lip, and throat during cognitive activity; studies of language disorders; and neurological studies relating verbal activity to hemispheric dominance.

Monitoring of muscle potential

As noted in the previous section Sokolov (1972) reports physiological studies carried out to test further the hypothesis that language in the form of inner speech is the basis of thought. The basis of these studies lies in the ability of electrodes placed in the mouth or on the lower lip to detect muscle potentials related to the organs of speech. Other devices used in these studies included transducers attached to the tongue which transformed both transverse and longitudinal tongue movements to variations in electric current.

After a series of pilot studies, Sokolov concluded that both tongue movement and muscle potentials revealed covert speech movements during various tasks. In the case of muscle potentials it was shown that these were 'linked with the verbal fixation of tasks, logical operations on them, retention of the intermediate results of these operations and the formulation of the final result mentally' (Sokolov, 1972, p. 185). Tasks studied included arithmetical calculations and problems involving several steps, the reading and translation of texts in a foreign language by subjects not well versed in that language, paraphrasing, memorizing, and mental recall of prose. These tasks were considered to be relatively difficult and were associated with more muscular activity than tasks such as reading to onself in one's own language. Individual subjects differed considerably among themselves in the extent to which muscle potentials were associated with those activities.

On the basis of these preliminary findings Sokolov proceeded with more controlled experiments using more refined techniques. The crude myograph recordings were found to be sensitive to pulse effects and the effects of asynchrony or synchrony of impulses in neighbouring muscles. For these reasons integrated potentials were used after demonstrating that these gave more sensitive readings than raw myographic readings. Readings from the integrator gave the total energy and duration of motor speech, and the ratio of total energy and duration provided an intensity measure.

In one experiment using this methodology two university students were chosen who differed greatly in their ability to do mental arithmetic. Integrated myographic recordings were made while each subject solved five mental arithmetic problems, for example $(23 \times 13) \div 4$. Results showed a significant difference between subjects in both the time taken and the total energy recorded during solution. The person with greater ability required less time and showed a recording of less total energy. The mean intensity difference failed to show a significant difference ($p < 0.10$) between the two subjects, but when maximum mean intensities were compared significant differences were obtained even though minimum values were almost identical. The mean intensity values also distinguished between the more and less complex problems.

Similar results were obtained using much younger (second-grade) subjects and much simpler problems. The more able subjects required less time and showed less mean intensity in recordings from the lower lip. Less complex tasks differed from more complex in the same way, and it was also found possible to discriminate more automatic tasks from less automatic. When problems were presented visually they required less time and yielded less intense records than when auditory presentation was used. However, it seemed that the subject could retain the written form for the full period of solution. A third condition in which visual presentation was for the same time duration as auditory presentation may have been a useful control.

In a study of silent reading it was found possible to examine similar variables by comparing slow and rapid readers, and reading in one's own language with reading in an imperfectly mastered foreign language. Subjects were university students and scientific workers who showed considerable individual differences in reading rate. Reading materials used were a Russian novel and a simple and complex prose passage in English. Intensity was integrated over sentences and an average per typographical unit was obtained. Subjects were instructed that they would be asked questions about the material they had read after the reading session. Sokolov found essentially the same results for silent reading as he had obtained for mental arithmetic and concludes, 'Both represent verbal mental operations, and these are impossible without a hidden articulation of words, if only in a very reduced form' (Sokolov, 1972, p. 211).

A final experiment in this series made use of the Raven Progressive Matrices, which Sokolov classifies as requiring 'concrete' thinking 'because the basic premises can be presented directly in a visual manner' (Sokolov, 1972, p. 213). The subjects, who were university students, were individually tested, presented with items one at a time and asked to point to the correct alternative. If the subject pointed to an incorrect alternative the experimenter indicated this and asked the subject to try again. After completion of the items subjects were invited to describe their methods of solution. In addition to the myograph records used in the previous two studies, galvanic skin response and electroencephalograph recordings were also taken from the occipitotemporal and Roland areas.

Since the items within each series increased in complexity, correlations with this rank order were taken as correlation with complexity. Time to solution correlated substantially with complexity, but mean intensity of muscle activity produced lower coefficients, some of which were not significant. There were considerable individual differences between subjects in intensity of muscle activity, so much so that Sokolov refers to visualizers as opposed to verbalizers. For some subjects there were virtually no readings on some of the earlier items. According to Sokolov, these subjects were visualizers for whom it was not necessary to translate the visual information into the second signalling system by means of inner speech. Solutions obtained without detectable intensity were discovered in much less time than other solutions. Neither galvanic skin response data nor electroencephalogram recordings yielded substantial results.

Evidence from studies of Aphasia

Evidence from cases of acquired aphasia has been used by Lenneberg (1967) to support his theory of age limitations to language acquisition. Whereas in adult patients in general there is a complete restoration of physiological function with their language intact after a recovery period, it would appear that very young children have to relearn the language acquisition. If aphasia caused by a lesion on one side occurs at about four years of age there is evidence of two intermingling processes. On the one hand, there are the interference phenomena produced by the lesion as in adult patients, while, on the other hand, the language-learning process may still be active or may be quickly reinstated. From the age of four to ten the symptoms are similar to those of adult patients, but such children generally recover and show little or no aphasic residue. This recovery period may last longer than that of an adult, showing a steady but slow improvement until puberty. But if the aphasia occurs in a very young child during or immediately after language is acquired (20 to 36 months), the patient will become at first totally unresponsive but then will go through all the phases of acquisition again in the same order as before.

An example of peripheral deficit in the speech area is an extreme case of language deprivation studied intensively over four years by Lenneberg. The case was that of a child suffering from congenital anarthria, a rare inability to coordinate the muscles of the vocal tract sufficiently to produce intelligible speech. Although unable to babble, or to say anything at all up to the age of nine years, it was well documented by film and records that the child had complete understanding of English. He was able to follow commands and, by Nodding, answer questions about a quite complex short story told to him and was able to follow instructions from a tape-recorded voice on earphones without the examiner being present.

The significance of this case lies in the dissociation of having knowledge of a language from speaking it. The case is relevant also to the role of inner speech in thinking. Lenneberg considers that since knowledge of a language may be established in the absence of speaking skills, having the knowledge must precede and be simpler than the ability to speak which entails capacities which are accessory rather than critical for language development.

Cortical localization of verbal and other abilities

The importance of the left hemisphere in right-handed people is now well established. Studies of the effects of lesions (Luria, 1970; Milner, 1971; Zangwill, 1960) and of developmental aphasia (Eisenson, 1970; Lenneberg, 1967) have clearly demonstrated the functional localization of speech and language areas in the left hemisphere of right-handed people and the functional location of spatial–visual areas in the minor hemisphere. Early interpretations of these findings were inclined to describe these localizations as rigidly autonomous, but more recent work has shown that the overall organization of left and right hemispheres is more interdependent than previously thought. Studies carried out by Sperry and his associates (Gazzaniga, 1972; Gazzaniga and Sperry, 1967) on patients who had undergone surgical separation of the hemispheres by transection of the corpus callosum and the anterior and hippocampal commissures have shown that both hemispheres can function independently and that many verbal functions can be carried out by the minor hemisphere. Older patients appear to need some time in which to develop these functions, but in younger patients the function develops rapidly.

Moscovitch (1973) used reaction time to visual stimuli presented to the left and right visual fields to study hemispheric dominance effects in normal subjects. He found a definite dominance of the major hemisphere over the minor, and no evidence of an interaction between preferred hand use and reaction time for processing verbal responses.

Neurological evidence also has shown the minor hemisphere to be superior in adulthood in functions such as processing visual, spatial, and non-verbal acoustic information. It has been shown (Marshall, 1973; Moscovitch, 1973) that people in whom language is poorly lateralized, such as the left-handed and right-handed individuals who developed right hemisphere speech as a result of early birth injury to the left hemisphere, generally do not perform as well as pure right-handers on tests measuring visual–spatial skills, but do normally on tests measuring verbal abilities. Thus when language functions are not restricted to one hemisphere, they seem to interfere with the development of the non-verbal capacities in the other hemisphere. Moscovitch suggests that these findings show that the lateralization of language functions is a prerequisite for the lateralization of non-linguistic functions.

More precise evidence has been obtained from EEG exploration. Fenelon (1976) studied the neurological basis of severe reading disabilities using EEG recording. A group of primary school-age children with reading problems was matched with a group of those with a behaviour problem and another of normal children. Audio signals (pure tones) and visual stimuli (light flashes) were administered under controlled conditions and durations. The auditory signals were delivered to the left, right, and both ears, and the visual stimuli to the left and right half-fields and the centre field. Evoked responses were collected at two anterior and two posterior scalp sites.

Differences between the problem readers and the normal readers were apparent. Compared with the normal readers the brain responses of the problem readers to visual stimulation were weakly associated, especially in the right hemisphere and under right hemifield stimulation, and there were temporal disparities in response between hemispheres. On the auditory stimulation task the problem readers were somewhat less differentiated between sites than the normal readers, and lacked strong similarity between right hemisphere posterior and anterior sites for all stimulation conditions.

Fenelon's interpretation of the differences on auditory stimuli was that in the problem-reader group the cerebral responses to auditory stimulation were insufficiently differentiated in the left hemisphere, while the low coefficients in the right hemisphere suggested overinvolvement of that hemisphere in processing incoming signals. Fenelon suggests that it is possible that the functional efficiency in the language hemisphere is interfered with by the right hemisphere activity. In the trials with combined visual–auditory stimuli the results also suggested weak and perhaps interfering interparietal responses and poor right hemisphere coordination of response in the problem-reader group. The major features of the reading disability children were as follows (Fenelon, 1976, p. 195):

(1) Weak responses, especially in the right hemisphere, to right hemifield stimulation, with temporal disparities in hemispheric response suggesting, as one possible explanation, slow transcommisural transfer of signals.
(2) Poor response differentiation of auditory signals in the 'language hemisphere.'
(3) A presumptive over-involvement of the right hemisphere in active auditory signal processing, leading to interference with left hemisphere processing and functional efficiency; this applies also in combined visual–auditory stimulation.
(4) Weak development of left parietal CNV to auditory stimulation.
(5) Lack of the adult-CNV maturation pattern of correlation between activity at various sites.

In all there was 'a suggestion of a poorly co-ordinated and differentiated right hemisphere functionally competing with, and reducing the efficiency of, processing in the left hemisphere. The left hemisphere, moreover, may lack the normal degree of functional maturation in posterior association areas.'

Relevance of physiological evidence to the language–thought relationship

The relevance of these studies to the language–thought relationship is twofold. First, the separation of verbal from other functions which could be described as cognitive has been demonstrated, but there seems strong evidence that both major and minor hemispheres can control verbal activity. Second, the ontogenetic development of lateral dominance relates to the development of cognitive abilities of the concrete operational kind, lateral dominance not being strongly developed until six to ten years.

The observations of Luria and Sokolov on the presence of overt verbal activity in cognitive tasks before giving way to 'inner speech' suggest that in the former case the hemispheric dominance is not yet fully established in the normal child.

Fenelon's findings of uneven dominance and delayed timing in severe reading problems add weight and precision to the above. Whereas the specific localization would be a more clear-cut case for independence, nevertheless

Gazzaniga and Sperry's concept of functional lateralization is consistent with Moscovitch's findings and would also explain the situations where other cognitive activities and verbal activities are closely related. It is not inconsistent with Furth's statement of the role of language at the formal operational level.

The interpretation of Sokolov and Luria that thinking and speech are identical is not supported by the neurophysiological evidence: there is more support for the view that verbal processing is but one of several kinds of processing, all localized but having functional connections reinforced through the normal development of lateral dominance.

CONTRIBUTION OF FACTOR ANALYSIS

The factor analytic method has arisen from the study of individual differences which began in the late nineteenth century. The initial observation was that there were considerable and reliable differences between people on a wide range of cognitive tasks. Later it became clear that in the vast majority of cases cognitive tasks were positively related in the sense that subjects who obtained relatively high scores on one task tended to obtain relatively high scores on others. The relativity was with respect to the group for whom performances on these tasks were available. Spearman (1904) was the first to argue from these positive relationships that they could be due to one very general cognitive factor which was used to varying extents in the specific cognitive tasks. In the development of this idea Spearman devised a measure (factor loading) of the extent to which a cognitive task required the operation of the general factor. The best measures of individual differences on the general factor were those with the highest factor loadings. These tended to be highly abstract diagrammatic reasoning tests such as the Raven Progressive Matrices.

For several decades discussion took place as to whether one general factor with one or two additional minor factors was the most justifiable way of representing the observed relationship, or whether more independent factors with no general factor produced more meaningful representations. This dispute led to substantial empirical studies which were greatly assisted by the development of electronic computers. The general factorists elaborated their theory and methodology to include hierarchies of overlapping group factors. At the same time the group factorists developed the notion of second-order factors which were more general and subsumed several group factors. It soon became clear that there was a possible reconciliation between the two approaches.

Several attempts have been made to organize the results of factor analytic studies into a comprehensive framework. French (1951) attempted to do this for the purpose of providing reference tests for people carrying out further studies. Guilford's (1967) studies increased the number of possible factors enormously, but some independent attempts to isolate these highly specific factors have not been successful. Neither French nor Guilford had occasion to work with second- or higher-order factors, and so are not concerned with hierarchies. On the other hand, Royce (1973) reviews findings related to these higher-order factors and concludes that Spearman's general ability factor is a fourth-order factor, i.e. the most general which may be differentiated through third- and second-order to first-order factors, the most specific cognitive factors.

The question of the relationship between language and thought can be formulated in factor analytic terms. If language and thought are identical then language must be the operation behind the general ability factor. In this context it seems inappropriate to claim that factor analytic evidence is irrelevant because it deals with the products rather than the processes of intelligence. The products obtained must depend on some operations, and the extent to which the evaluations of the products are dependent on the efficiency with which language is used will determine the degree of relationship between the evaluations of the various cognitive tasks. It seems clear that the argument that language and thinking are identical leads to the notion of a general factor and to that extent agrees with factor analytic findings. However, it would be a particular kind of general factor.

If the equating of thought with language is to be substantiated by the results of factor analysis, one would anticipate that the general factor would be best measured by tests of language proficiency such as vocabulary and verbal comprehension. Furthermore, one would expect that the third-order factors which generate the general factor would comprise largely verbal group factors. Neither of these two predictions can be substantiated from the factor analytic literature.

In his view of factor analytic findings Royce (1973) postulates on the basis of numerous studies that the fourth-order general intelligence factor is composed of third-order factors of verbal, non-verbal, and speed factors. The verbal factor is 'the ability to acquire and utilize language elements, i.e. words, symbols, ideas, meaning, etc.', whereas the non-verbal factor is defined as 'the ability to effectively interact and structure nonverbal elements of the environment within the context of a defined problem or goal'. The speed factor is defined in terms of 'intellectual speed, motor speed and motor tempo'. In addition, Royce cites nine studies which support the notion that the WAIS and WISC intelligence scales divide into verbal and non-verbal components.

None of these studies supports the notion that tests with high language content are better measures of intelligence than non-verbal tests. If language and thinking were identical it would be expected that the most general factor would first divide on the basis of types of verbal performance and then later on the basis of separate tasks which are *less* dependent on language content. This is clearly not the case on the basis of many studies carried out by different experimenters in different countries.

In an attempt to relate factors to various regions of the brain, Royce notes that the evidence suggests that verbal behaviour tends to be associated with the left hemisphere and abstract reasoning with the right. Sokolov (1972) agrees with the general location of verbal behaviour but does not comment on the location of abstract reasoning. Of course, the question of the degree of localization of cognitive processes is still open, but the present evidence (described above) does suggest a separation of verbal from non-verbal reasoning in the left and right hemispheres. Thus when factor analytic results are related to studies of brain damage confirmation of the separation of verbal from non-verbal reasoning seems to be obtained.

EXPERIMENTAL TREATMENTS OF LANGUAGE AND OPERATIONAL ACTIVITY

Manipulative studies (e.g. Bearison, 1969; Gelman, 1969) have sometimes been successful in inducing concrete operational concepts, and some of these have looked also at the effects of such training on language behaviour. Alternatively, studies have sought to induce such concepts by verbal explanation of the concepts involved.

Effect of level of language on concept acquisition

The aim of these studies has been twofold: to compare the type of descriptive language used by children without conservation with that used by children who had conservation, and to observe whether training in relative linguistic terms improved the performance on conservation tasks by children who previously did not have conservation. Significant studies in this area are Sinclair's work with Inhelder (Sinclair-de-Zwart, 1967, 1969; Sinclair, 1971, 1973) on children's use of comparatives and with Ferreiro (Ferreiro and Sinclair, 1971) on the use of terms showing temporal relationships.

The method used by Inhelder and Sinclair (Sinclair-de-Zwart, 1967, 1969) at Geneva was to ask children to describe actions carried out by the experimenter using dolls or toys. The child's understanding of the experimenter's descriptions was first checked. Ages ranged from four to seven years. Training on relevant linguistic forms was given after the first response, and the children were also tested on conservation of liquid and seriation. In the first stage the child was given to dolls and to each of the dolls the experimenter gave either some marbles or plasticine which were varied as equal, more, or less *(moins)* amounts. The child was asked whether this was fair and whether both dolls were happy; if the child said 'no' he was asked 'Why not'. Or the child was asked to tell the experimenter the difference between two pencils which were varied on length and thickness. The next step was to ask the child to carry out directions using comparative terms such as 'less' and 'more', differentiated terms such as 'long/short and fat/thin', and coordinated descriptive terms using the comparative such as 'shorter but thicker' and 'longer but thinner'.

The children's answers were compared for three groups divided on the basis of their responses on the conservation tasks, namely total conservation, marginal conservation, and totally preoperational levels. There was no difference between the three groups on the response to directions, although the children did not all use these terms themselves in their own descriptions.

The only difficulty noted was with younger children who had trouble with the 'longer but thinner' construction. On the descriptive tasks, however, the conserves used more advanced forms more often than the non-conservers. Seventy-one per cent. of the conservers used comparatives without adjectives for the description of the amounts of plasticine and all used comparatives for the different number of marbles. Children without conservation used absolute terms in 90 per cent. of the cases. Also, the non-conservers used comparatives for discrete units (for marbles) more than for quantity (for plasticine). Sinclair notes that conservation of number precedes conservation of continuous quantity. The children with conservation all used different terms for different dimensions and used two pairs of opposites, whereas 75 per cent. of the non-conservers used undifferentiated terms for the two dimensions, i.e. they would use the same word 'gros' for 'big' and 'fat' and 'petit' to indicate both short and thin. The children with conservation used only two sentences to describe two objects differing on two dimensions coordinating the dimensions, but the non-conservers used four separate sentences or described only one dimension.

Sinclair and Inhelder then tried to teach the non-conservers the linguistic forms used by the conservers, namely comparative terms, differentiated terms, and coordinated description of a difference in two dimensions. After the verbal training the children were again tested on the conservation tasks. All learned the use of differentiated terms quite easily, but it was more difficult for them to learn to use the comparatives 'plus' and 'moins' (25 per cent. did not) and extremely difficult for them to learn the coordinated structure 'long et (mais) mince' and 'court et (mais) gros'. Even for children who learned to use the expressions there was little change in conservation—only 10 per cent. acquired conservation. However, there was a change in the language used—more than half of those who did not acquire conservation used the higher verbal forms in the posttest. They noticed and described the covarying dimensions of the higher level and the narrower glass and they sometimes explained that the liquid went up higher in a narrower glass, but they did not give the conservation responses. In an experiment with retarded children Sinclair found that if she used the descriptive terms used by conservers the retarded children did not respond, but they did when she used the expressions used by the non-conservers. Similar results were obtained on a seriation task.

A further series of experiments was conducted by Ferreiro and Sinclair (1971) on children's use of verbal constructions to express temporal relationships. Ages were from four to nine years. Ferreiro and Sinclair studied the children's comprehension of sentences in which two events take place simultaneously or successively without being causally connected. The children were asked to act out the sentence using toys and describe two events acted out by the experimenter with the toys. In the first condition of this task the child could describe the action in any way he wished; in the second condition the experimenter asked the child to start his sentence with the event or object which had occurred last in the free description. The inverse-order descriptions required the use of temporal words such as 'when' and 'after' and the use of different tenses. After each the child was asked: 'When did, etc., ...?' Variations of this task involved simultaneous acting out of more than one event followed by the same actions in quick succession.

Three main categories of responses were distinguished. In category I the children described the events in two independent but weakly linked propositions, generally evoked by 'and' and 'then'. Both verbs were in the same (i.e. present) tense and the order of statements corresponded to the order of the events. For the inverse-order task the children either reiterated their previous statement or reversed the order of the two without adding any temporal indication. In response to the 'when' question their most frequent response was 'now', producing a link with the speaker but not between the two events. In category II the children gave their free choice description using the same tense for each two statements, but also used adverbial expressions and the order of enunciation was always the same as the order of events. For inverse-order description these children could always begin with the name of the action in the second event but could not give words for temporal indicators. They would make up curious variations which violated the temporal order of the events but they had no trouble with the 'when' questions. The children in category III gave correct answers to all three types of problem and used 'when' and 'before' in their free choice description. Ferreiro and Sinclair relate these findings to the concept of reversibility which was reached in conservation of liquid by category II respondents but not by category I.

An application of Sinclair's (1967) method was carried out by Tenezakis (1975) using Greek- and English-speaking children in Sydney, Australia. The children, 162 bilinguals and 136 monolingual English speakers were from first-, second-, and third-grade classes and were of low socioeconomic status. The monolinguals were tested once and the bilinguals twice (approximately one half in Greek first and in English second; the other half in English first and Greek second), with an interval of approximately three weeks. Testing was by native speakers. Language production, language comprehension, and conservation of quantity, using rice, were tested. On the conservation task the proportion of conservers was approximately the same for the monolinguals, the Greek children when tested in Greek, and the Greek children when tested in English. As in Sinclair's findings there were no differences on the language comprehension task. On the language production task results were in the predicted direction but not as strong as in the Genevan results. Overall, however, these results tend to confirm the Genevan findings.

A CROSSCULTURAL MANIPULATIVE STUDY WITH BILINGUAL CHILDREN

Although the performance of bilinguals in their different languages on various tasks has been studied extensively (see above), their potential for a manipulative approach to studying the language–thought relationship has not yet been fully explored. Not only can the language factor be accounted for but to a great extent controlled by the variation of the language medium used for training. Thus one can manipulate both concept and language as experimental variables, rather than engage in fruitless efforts to control the language factor either by attempting to remove it, as in non-verbal tasks, or by using variations from normal language, as has been attempted in studies using artificially contrived symbol languages (Rimoldi, 1971).

In discussing Kolers' work (above), Kess (1976) remarks that much can be learned about the mind in general by investigating the operations involved in the acquisition, storage and retrieval of language information, and, in the case of bilinguals, because they have internalized two sets of symbols, both in highly coded systems, 'one wonders what the outcome is when information is acquired in one language and tested in another' (p. 232). This approach was used by the present authors in a series of studies with bilingual children in Australia (Keats and Keats, 1974) and Malaysia (Keats, Keats, and Wan Rafaei 1974a, 1974b, 1976, 1977). The aim was to determine whether and to what extent logical concepts acquired by a training programme in one language could be transferred to a second language. It was argued that if this transfer was relatively complete then the concepts could be considered as relatively independent of the language in which they were acquired, and hence provide support for the Piagetian view of the independence of thought and language. If, on the other hand, the transfer either did not occur or subsequent performance in the language not used for training was very poor, then the Whorfian view of the dependence of thinking upon language would be supported.

The Polish-German study

The first study was carried out with a group of 100 four to seven year olds in Australia, consisting of one group of thirty-five who spoke Polish and English, another of thirty-one who spoke German and English, and a control group of thirty-four English-speaking monolinguals. The bilingual subjects were the children of families who had migrated to Australia. The language groups of Polish and German were chosen partly because of the availability of subject, but more particularly because they provided a contrast to each other. Although these countries are culturally similar in the northern European tradition, the two languages are linguistically dissimilar, Polish being much less like English than is German.

All the children used were selected on their inability to conserve weight in one of their languages and ability to count to ten. Each was matched with a bilingual child in the other language group and an Australian control, matched on sex, age (as far as possible), socioeconomic status, school or preschool attended, and location of home. To obtain this sample preliminary testing was carried out on a total of 142 children as shown in Table 5.1. Subjects in the bilingual groups were randomly allocated to one of two subgroups, maintaining the matching within the subgroups, and the language medium used for testing was varied as set out in Table 5.2. Bilingual testers were selected and trained,

Table 5.1. Selection of subjects by pretesting

Language group	Number pretested	Number selected	Number rejected
Australian	52	34	18
Polish (tested in English)	21	17	4
Polish (tested in Polish)	22	18	4
German (tested in English)	20	15	5
German (tested in German)	27	16	11
Total	142	100	42

and allocated to testing and testing-and-training sessions in such a way as to give as much control as possible over biases arising from tester effects.

Form A of the Peabody Picture Vocabulary Test was translated into both Polish and German and back-translated into English again as a check on the original translation. Each child in the experimental groups was given this test in each of his languages. The counting test was as used in the Binet test. Pretests were given on the concepts of conservation of number, discontinuous quantity, weight, and volume, and the concept of class inclusion. The training procedure followed that of Bearison (1969) but was adapted to the conservation of weight

Table 5.2. Tests and language media employed for each group

	German (G) I	II	Polish (P) I	II	Australian (E) I	II
Peabody picture vocabulary test form A or B	G(A)	E(B)	P(A)	E(B)	E(A)	E(B)
Counting test	G	E	P	E	E	E
Pretest	G	E	P	E	E	E
Peabody picture vocabulary test form A or B	E(B)	G(A)	E(B)	P(A)	E(B)	E(A)
Counting test	E	G	E	P	—	—
Training	E	G	E	P	E	E
Posttest (1)	G	E	P	E	E	E
Child's questionnaire	G	E	P	E	—	—
Posttest (2)	G	E	P	E	E	E
Posttest (3)	E	G	E	P	—	—
Interview with parents	E(+G)	E(+G)	E(+P)	E(+P)	—	—

rather than quantity. The posttest was the same as the pretest and in the same language, and was followed by a short questionnaire related to the child's preferences for one language over the other in different situations. A follow-up posttest in both languages was administered one month after the first posttest. An interview was conducted with one or other, or both, of the bilingual children's parents to obtain some factual information about the child's background in the two languages. The parent interviews were conducted mainly in the parent's own home or sometimes at the University of Newcastle, in English but assisted if necessary by a Polish or German speaker.

Each of the subjects was tested individually at home, at school or preschool, or at the University of Newcastle. Before the experiment and between testing sessions, plasticine, books, coloured pencils, and paper and toys were available for the children to play with to offset fatigue.

The training procedure consisted of the following six phases.

Phase 1

Equal and unequal numbers of identical plasticine balls were placed on each of the pans of a beam balance to make the subject aware of the possibility of a numerical justification for weight relations. In this and the following phases, the subject was questioned both before and after the balls had been placed on the balance.

Phase 2

The experimenter pushed three of her plasticine balls into a sausage which was treated as a unit and compared with various numbers of the subject's balls. Correct explanations in terms of the number of balls on each side were accepted.

Phase 3

This phase was similar to phase 2 except that both the experimenter and the subject had three balls pushed together to form a sausage and these sausages were compared with each other with one, two, or three additional balls added to either side. Again explanations in terms of numbers of balls were accepted.

Phase 4

In this phase, the original-shaped balls were dispensed with and three of the experimenter's and three of the subject's balls were rolled into a sausage. On each trial of this phase either the experimenter's or the subject's sausage was transformed in shape with or without the addition of another ball. After each trial, the original sausages were restored. Again explanations in terms of number were accepted.

Phase 5

New plasticine of a different colour was now introduced in the shape of two sausages of identical weight. One or both of these sausages were transformed in shape using either the whole or parts of each, and comparisons of the weights of these new shapes were sought both before and after they were placed on the scales. Explanations in terms of the number of balls were now no longer possible or acceptable. This phase was essentially the same as the standard test of conservation of weight with the addition of feedback after each question. In this and the earlier phases failure to master the tasks of the phase was met by going back to an earlier phase and retracing the steps.

Phase 6

This phase was concerned with class inclusion and followed a procedure adapted from one used by Sheppard (1973) but with fewer examples. Three red balls of plasticine were each placed in front of the experimenter and the subject and a further black ball was added to the subject's collection. The subject was asked whether the plasticine balls were heavier or the red balls were heavier. The effect of class inclusion on weight was sought by making appropriate comparisons, asking questions, and checking on the balance. A parallel task using green and white plastic squares and the balance was also used.

The subjects were given a total pretest score out of a possible 33, made up of a response score out of 11 (1 for each item correct) and an explanation score of 22 (2 for each item for a completely conserving explanation, 1 for each item for a transitional explanation, and 0 for each item for a non-conserving explanation). The scores for the German and Polish groups were based on testing in either English or the foreign language. The pretest response scores were found to be positively correlated with explanation scores. The regression line of explanation score on the response score showed that an average of approximately 1 was scored on the explanation scale for each correct response.

All the children were posttested immediately after training, but for the German and Polish groups the tests were given in the language other than the one in which they were trained. The conservation of weight scores were divided into a response score (out of 2) and an explanation score (out of 4). There was significant improvement in response. The language used for training or testing had no effect on response scores, but in the case of explanation scores for the first time a significant difference between the two Polish experimental groups appeared. The mean explanation score for the group trained in English and tested in Polish was significantly greater than the mean for the group trained in Polish and tested in English. No such difference applied in the German group.

Although the immediate posttest indicated that the training received had an effect on the response score, the longer-term effects of this training are of greater interest. The delayed posttests were given in both English and the relevant foreign language, so that any difference in the means of explanation scores noted in the immediate posttest for the two Polish groups could be further examined. The repeat reliability over a four-week period was measured by correlating the immediate posttest score with the delayed posttest score in the same language and found to be satisfactory, and a total criterion score was therefore obtained using all sub-tests combined.

The regression line of explanation score on the response score for the Australian sample indicated that on the average an explanation score of 1·5 was obtained for each response score, which may be compared with the corresponding figure of 1 explanation score for each response score in the pretest. Thus the training had the effect not only of increasing the number of correct responses but also of raising the average level of explanation per correct response. The German group produced a very similar graph whether the data from the delayed post test were taken in English or German. For the Polish group, however, the regression slope for the data from the testing in Polish was almost exactly the maximum value of 2. Unlike the others, the regression line for the English-trained when tested in English, showed substantial curvilinearity. When the Polish children were tested in Polish they gave correct explanations for almost every item for which they gave a correct response, but when the same children were tested in English their level of explanation per correct response was low, except for some children in the English-trained group who had very high response scores.

Apart from the correlation between response and explanation scores, the inclusion of all subtests in a total criterion score was justified by the fact that almost all subtests intercorrelated positively and in most cases these correlations were significant. These correlations also suggested that there was generalization from the conservation of weight to other concepts. Group means on total criterion scores are shown in Table 5.3. For the Australian monolingual group there was a significant increase from the pretest to the immediate posttest and an increase, but not significant, from the immediate posttest to the delayed posttest. For the Polish-speaking children both the English training and Polish training produced scores which were significantly greater on the immediate posttest than the pretest. For the English-trained group the delayed posttest mean was almost the same as the immediate posttest mean and was also significantly greater than the pretest. It can be argued that the performance

TABLE 5.3.   Means on criterion scores

Group	N	Pretest	Immediate posttest	Delayed posttest (English)	Delayed posttest (German/Polish)
Polish (trained in English)	18	6·2	14·06	12·4	13·9
Polish (trained in Polish)	17	6·8	11·5	9·2	12·4
German (trained in English)	15	8·3	14·1	15·5	16·2
German (trained in German)	16	7·2	15·1	18·4	19·7
Australian (group I)	17	8·4	13·2	14·5	—
Australian (group II)	17	7·0	12·1	13·5	—

in Polish on the delayed posttest was as high as that on the immediate posttest. However, for the Polish-trained group, the delayed posttest mean was lower than the immediate posttest mean. The difference just failed to reach significance. The delayed posttest mean was not significantly greater than the pretest mean. Thus for this group the improvement in English performance resulting immediately from the Polish training was substantially lost during the four weeks between the immediate and the delayed posttests. A closer examination of the data showed that the loss was not in the concept of weight conservation, for which the mean increased slightly, but in the scores on the other concepts, which decreased significantly. The delayed Polish score for the group trained in English was greater than the delayed English score for the group trained in Polish, but this difference was not significant. The route from English to Polish tended to be more effective than the route from Polish to English in the longer term.

For both the English-trained and German-trained German-speaking children there was significant improvement from pretest to immediate posttest and an increase in mean from immediate to delayed posttest, although for the English-trained group this increase was not significant. The mean of the delayed English scores for the group trained in German was not significantly greater than the corresponding mean for the English-trained group when tested in German. It could not be argued that the English–German route was superior to the German–English route, or vice versa.

To examine the relationship between the scores obtained and the children's background in English, three language measures were obtained: scores on the Peabody Picture Vocabulary Test; a measure of the child's use of English, based on totals from the child's questionnaire; and a measure of the use of English in the home, based on totals of relevant items in the interview with parents. As correlations between the child's use of English and the use of English in the home were both positive and significant, these two scores were added together to produce a combined English-usage score.

On the Peabody Picture Vocabularly Test the Australian group correlation between Forms A and B were positive and significant, but neither form correlated significantly with the criterion score. For the Polish and German groups the correlations between the Peabody scores on English and the translated versions and English-language usage measures, as well as the criterion scores, are shown in Table 5.4. The extent of the child's use of English and of the use of English in the home were significantly and positively related to the Peabody score in English and negatively related to the Peabody score in Polish and German. The only significant correlation with the criterion was for the Peabody score in English when correlated with both the Polish and the English criterion scores for the Polish group.

Tests of the relationship between English-language usage and performance showed that the mean score of the German group was significantly higher than the Polish group on the combined English-language usage measure, but this could be traced to the greater use of English in the home. Correlations of the

Table 5.4. Correlation between Peabody scores and English-usage and criterion scores

Group	N	Child's use of English	Use of English in the home	Combined English usage	Criterion (Polish/English/German)	
Polish (English)						
Form A (in Polish)	35	− 0·34[a]	− 0·31	− 0·39[a]	0·22	0·23
Form B (in English)	35	0·48[b]	0·43[a]	0·54[b]	0·43[a]	0·49[b]
German (English)						
Form A (in German)	31	− 0·49[b]	− 0·27	− 0·46[b]	0·28	0·23
Form B (in English)	31	0·39	0·41[a]	0·46[b]	− 0·06	0·03

Australian monolinguals correlation between form A and form B, 0·59[b]

[a] Significant at 0·05 level of confidence.
[b] Significant at 0·01 level of confidence.

combined English-usage scores with the criterion and the response and explanation scores taken separately were all non-significant. Correlations between combined English usage and errors in training were non-significant for all groups.

The mean age at which the children learned English was lower for the German group than for the Polish group, but there were no significant differences in the number of years of learning English. Years of learning English correlated positively with the English version of the Peabody Picture Vocabulary Test

Table 5.5. Correlation of age and years of learning English with Peabody and criterion scores

	Age of learning English		Years of learning English	
	Polish	German	Polish	German
Peabody form A	− 0·37[a]	0·23	− 0·34	− 0·11
Peabody form B	− 0·30	0·17	0·51[b]	0·57[b]
Criterion tested in Polish or German	0·05	0·43[a]	0·43[a]	− 0·23
Criterion tested in English	0·01	0·53[b]	0·43[a]	− 0·23

	Polish	German	Australian
Mean age at testing	6·09	5·86	5·87
Mean age of learning English	3·84	3·32	
Mean years of learning English	2·31	2·48	
N	35	31	34

[a] Significant at 0·05 level of confidence.
[b] Significant at 0·01 level of confidence.

(Form B), and significantly and negatively with the Polish version (Form A), but the age of learning English correlated significantly only with the Polish version. For the Polish group there was no relationship between age of learning English and the criterion, but for the German group this correlation was positive and significant. Years of learning English correlated positively with both Polish and English criterion scores for the Polish group but negatively (though not significantly) with the corresponding scores for the German group. These results are set out in Table 5.5. In sum, the degree of background in English, as measured by Peabody scores or by use of English in the home, was not a directly relevant factor in producing the results on the operational tasks.

The Malaysian study

Although these findings gave some support to the Piagetian view, some problems remained. It was possible that one of the findings, that the earlier the German-speaking (but not the Polish-speaking) children had learned English the poorer was their performance on the concept acquisition tasks, could have been an effect which arose partly from the linguistic similarity between English and German compared with that between English and Polish. On the other hand, the results may have arisen partly because the children were migrants in a society in which speaking English is the norm. A further problem arising from the former study was the methodological one that no further use had been made of subjects who showed conservation in one language. Hence those who were included constituted a somewhat select group, and it was possible that this selection could have had the effect of reducing the magnitude of any correlations between pretests which could be examined. Also, there were no children included who were not given a training programme, so that it was possible that although improvements occurred after training these could have been the result of maturation which would have occurred in any case. Finally, there was the theoretical question of whether a training programme based on Piagetian theory of concept acquisition, which had been designed originally for American children and adapted for European migrants to Australia, could also have validity in a completely non-European milieu.

With its many language and cultural groups, Malaysia offered an ideal contrast to the Australian setting in which to follow up these questions. Its three principal local languages, Malay, Chinese, and Tamil, are different from English and from each other. Also, Malaysian bilinguals are not migrants but permanent members of a prevailing multicultural, multilingual environment in which the use of English is widespread, and bilingualism with English as one of the languages is a common phenomenon. Of more general interest was the applicability of Piagetian cognitive theory to Asian settings which has not yet been fully explored.

The children were five year olds who were bilingual in Malay and English and in Chinese (Cantonese dialect) and English, almost all of whom attended kindergartens in Kuala Lumpur. The criterion for selecting subjects was their inability to conserve weight in *either* of their languages and their ability to count to ten in one language. Preliminary testing on sixty-eight Chinese/ English bilinguals gave fifty-four non-conservers and on seventy-five Malay/ English bilinguals gave fifty-four non-conservers. There was no significant difference between the groups in the number rejected as conservers. Subjects in the two bilingual groups were randomly allocated to one of four groups comprising two experimental and two control groups, maintaining matching between the groups on age, sex, socioeconomic status, and kindergarten attended. A team of Chinese and Malay bilingual testers was selected and trained to administer the tests and carry out the training. The instruments were translated into Bahasa Malaysia and Chinese by the testers, and back-translated by members of the Unit Bahasa-Bahasa of Universiti Kebangsaan Malaysia and by one of the experimenters.

The procedure for the experimental groups involved four main stages: pretests in both languages, training in one language on the conservation of weight only, immediate posttests in the language other than the one used for training, and delayed posttests in both languages. The control groups received no training and the experimental groups differed on the language of training and immediate posttest. Otherwise the tests used and the procedure were the same as in the previous study. The Peabody Picture Vocabulary Test was given in both languages and a questionnaire was given to the child about his use of English and his other language. Testers were allocated so as to minimize tester effects—Malay and Chinese testers trained and tested both Chinese and Malay children in English and both male and female testers were used. The design is set out in Table 5.6 and the results are summarized in Table 5.7.

No statistically significant difference between Malay and Chinese groups was found on performance on the operational tasks on the pretests. Malay children did significantly better in Malay than in English on the operational

TABLE 5.6.   Tests and language used—Malay and Chinese

	Malay groups (M)				Chinese groups (C)			
	I	II	III	IV	I	II	III	IV
Pretesting								
PPVT form A	M	M	M	M	C	C	C	C
PPVT form B	E	E	E	E	E	E	E	E
Pretest (1)	E	M	E	M	E	C	E	C
Pretest (2)	M	E	M	E	C	E	C	E
Counting test	E	M	E	M	E	C	E	C
Training	M	E	—	—	C	E	—	—
Immediate posttest	E	M	—	—	E	C	—	—
Child's questionnaire	E	M	E	M	E	C	E	C
Delayed posttest (1)	E	M	E	M	E	C	E	C
Posttest (2)	M	E	M	E	C	E	C	E

TABLE 5.7. Summary of means

	Group I (trained in Malay or Chinese)	Group II (trained in English)	Group III (no training)	Group IV (no training)	Conservers
Malay subjects					
Pretest in					
Malay	10·92	7·54	7·71	12·46	20·10
English	10·17	6·47	6·57	8·77	16·10
Immediate posttest					
Malay	——	21·92	——	——	
English	17·08	——	——	——	
Delayed posttest					
Malay	20·08	19·17	25·17	22·67	
English	21·50	18·17	24·50	22·55	
Chinese subjects					
Pretest in					
Chinese	9·07	5·54	7·69	9·69	18·57
English	8·73	7·77	9·46	11·23	15·86
Immediate posttest					
Chinese	——	11·38	——	——	
English	17·07	——	——	——	
Delayed posttest					
Chinese	21·67	20·58	21·92	25·67	
English	18·75	18·33	20·50	24·00	

tasks. The Malay background score correlated significantly with the Malay vocabulary score, but neither of these correlated significantly with performance on the operational tasks. The English form of the vocabulary task correlated significantly with English background for the Chinese sample, but not for the Malays, and significantly and positively with performances in English on the operational tasks for both groups, but Chinese background was negatively and significantly correlated with performance on operational tasks in Chinese. The order of acquisition of concepts showed that volume, weight, and quantity were acquired in that order in three of four groups and in the fourth the order was quantity, volume, and weight.

On the immediate posttest both the Malay and Chinese children showed an improvement over their pretest scores, whether trained in Malay, Chinese, or English. The greatest improvement was in the Malays trained in English and tested in Malay and the least in the Chinese trained in English and tested in Chinese. Overall on the immediate posttest the Malays performed better than the Chinese, but there was a significant interaction between the language of testing and the cultural group, the Malays performing better in Malay and the Chinese better in English.

On the delayed posttest both the experimental and control groups showed improvement over their pretest scores in the same language. Correlations between scores in the two languages were both high and significant for both the Malays and the Chinese and there were no significant differences between the groups. For Malays trained in English the delayed posttest scores in both Malay and English were slightly, but not significantly, lower than the immediate posttest scores in Malay, but for the Chinese trained in English the delayed posttest means were significantly higher than the immediate posttest means in Chinese. In the groups trained in Malay and Chinese the delayed posttests means were slightly, but not significantly, higher than the means on the immediate posttest.

An improvement also occurred in the relationship between response and explanation on the immediate posttest for the trained groups and for all groups on the delayed posttests in both languages. There was also evidence of some generalization to other tests after training. This improvement did not extend to the class inclusion task, which remained the most difficult task for all groups. The training programme thus appears to have been effective for both Malay and Chinese groups, whether trained in English or in Malay or Chinese.

When these two studies are considered together the results on the immediate posttest give strong support to the validity of the training method in a variety of contrasting cultural settings. There is also clear evidence that when trained in one language the children could produce the appropriate response in their other language. The significance of the evidence for the occurrence of generalization is that the learning of conservation concepts was not confined either to the weight task alone or to the language in which the weight task was learned. The failure of any group to obtain any improvements on the class inclusion task, and its overall greater difficulty for all groups in both studies, suggests that the task is essentially different from the other conservation tasks. Such a finding is not inconsistent with the results obtained by Ferreiro and Sinclair (1971), discussed above, and those of Inhelder, Sinclair, and Bovet (1974) on their training studies using class inclusion. The interaction effects are complex, perhaps in keeping with the complexity of the language–thought relationship. Overall they suggests that whereas learning may take place in either language, testing performance is slightly better in the home or native language, particularly when social conditions favour its use. In sum the results give more support to the Piagetian than to other interpretations of the language–thought relationship.

EVALUATION OF THE RESEARCH EVIDENCE AND CONCLUSION

Almost all of the research evidence produced in connection with the language and thought controversy has been collected from static studies using intact groups of naturally occurring types of subjects. Such groups include age groups within a culture, handicapped groups such as deaf and aphasic subjects at different age levels, and groups from different cultures such as indigenous people speaking non-literate languages. These studies may be criticized because they have seldom examined factors other than language which could affect cognitive performance. For example, indigenous groups are associated with other cultural differences besides language but observed differences in cognitive performance are often attributed to language, or alternatively such groups are tested in English and any differences obtained are attributed to cultural factors without any study of the degree of mastery of English and its observed relationship to cognitive performance.

A more general criticism of the types of research evidence produced is that the evidence does not arise from the crucial testing of a theory. For example, evidence put forward for the claim that thinking *is* 'inner speech' often simply demonstrates that activity of speech organs often, but apparently not always, accompanies cognitive processes. Of course, it is not easy to devise crucial experiments and to implement all the controls required, but more effort in this direction seems necessary.

One important way to learn more about cognitive development would appear to involve the study of factors which influence that development. The Geneva group were slow to appreciate the scientific significance of such studies and tented to deprecate them by reference to 'the American problem', by which term they seemed to imply that these studies were relevant only to the applied problem of hastening the development of cognitive abilities. More recently Piaget has admitted the value of such studies for elucidating aspects of cognitive development (Inhelder, Sinclair, and Bovet, 1974).

It is not surprising in view of the wide range and large number of studies which have been carried out that there is a great deal of conflicting evidence dealing with the language–thought relationship. It has been called a controversy with some justification. Jenkins (1969) humorously posed a multiple choice question along the lines of, 'What is the relation between language and thought?: (1) Language is dependent on thought, (2) Thought is language, (3) Language is dependent on thought, (4) None of the above. Or perhaps, all of the above' (p. 212). The correct answer, according to Jenkins, is 'All of the above', and it is true that some support can be found for nearly every type of relationship. The present authors, after reviewing the evidence, are of the opinion that the weight of evidence is in the Piagetian direction, at least up to the concrete operational stage, but that at the formal operational stage the evidence is not sufficient to come to any definitive conclusion. Nevertheless, there are some qualifications to full support for the Piagetian view.

Piaget would appear to be wrong in his claim that egocentric speech gradually disappears. The Russian view that egocentric speech gradually becomes internalized as inner speech seems to have considerable support from a number of independent sources. Piaget's claim is surprising in that egocentric speech is disappearing at the stage when according to his own theory other operations are being internalized to form the basis of structures typical of concrete operational thinking. There appears to be no justification for arguing that egocentric speech does not follow this pattern. It is theoretically more convincing to explain the disappearance of egocentric speech *and* the appearance of inner speech in terms of internalization of operations. Studies which demonstrate that egocentric speech can be reactivated by manipulating task difficulty are consistent with this view.

However, inner speech is not the same as thought, as the Russians claim, because other operations are internalized at approximately the same age as speech. There appears now to be ample evidence that training in the use of these other operations and the structures they generate can affect language, but training in relevant language does not facilitate the use of these structures. Furthermore, recent training studies with bilingual children have shown a ready transfer from one language to another without loss of performance in most cases. Perhaps the most significant finding is that, despite the fact that correlations between performances on the vocabulary tests in the two languages used are of zero order, performances on the concrete operational tasks in two languages correlate almost as well as the reliability of such tests would permit. It would appear that, after the relevant structure has been activated by training, the results of its operations can be expressed equally well in either language. Any statistically significant differences observed were so small that the generalization that concrete operational thinking is largely if not entirely independent of language seems justified.

From the point of view of the writers of this book, the significance of the above conclusion lies in the notion that if linguistic structures are not the significant ones for operational thinking, various structures based on alternative, internalized operations should be explored and compared. Sheppard (Chapters 2 and 3) has already proposed that the groupoid is a more viable structure than the grouping proposed by Piaget. In later chapters other structures are proposed and evaluated by Halford, Collis, and Seggie, while Jurd shows the generality of this approach by applying it to studies of concepts in history.

6

TOWARDS A WORKING MODEL OF PIAGET'S STAGES

G. S. Halford

FOUR STAGES OF DEVELOPMENT

A brief descriptive account of the stages of cognitive development was given in Chapter 1, and the problem now is to try to determine some of the factors which might underly such a developmental sequence. Whereas the course of cognitive development is easy enough to understand descriptively, the almost universal difficulty which is experienced in understanding any underlying reasons for the development sequence has led to scepticism, or to the view that the concept of the cognitive developmental stage is theoretically intractable. There are, however, a number of concepts which can be related to basic characteristics of the stages and which, when their deeper meaning is considered, do help to provide underlying reasons for the stage progressions.

The organization of symbolic processes appears to be a largely unrecognized area of common ground between numerous investigators of preschool children's thinking. First, it appears to be a common factor underlying all of Piaget's investigations of this period. For instance, his demonstrations that preoperational children cannot orient objects to the horizontal, as in the water-level task, or coordinate the perspectives of a mountain reflect an inability to organize the symbolic processes in a way which adequately reflects the structure of the task. Lack of seriation must reflect, in some sense, an inadequate representation of the relationships between the elements to be seriated. All the Piagetian tasks which depend on inference, including conservation and transitivity, reflect, in the most general sense, the child's ability adequately to represent to himself the constraint between the elements of the situation. The same would be true of children's inability to recognize contradiction (Donaldson, 1971).

The concept of organization of symbolic processes also seems appropriate to deal, in the most general way, with the work of Olson (1970) and Halford and MacDonald (1977) on the failure of preschool children to reproduce two-dimensional patterns. Children's ability to make reversal concept shifts (Kendler and Kendler, 1962; Wolff, 1967) is now usually interpreted as a reflection of their tendency to respond to stimuli individually rather than as attributes on a dimension. As will be suggested in more detail later, the use of dimensions reflects the ability to organize symbolic processes into specific types of system. In general, preoperations can be distinguished from concrete operations by the higher level of organization of the symbolic processes which comprise the later stage.

Preoperational children can represent relations, if taken one at a time. Even casual observation suggests that preschool children have a lively interest in encoding relations between things and events in their environment. Everyday speech of preschool children includes things like 'Cars go on roads, boats go on water', 'Big people eats lots', and 'I'm big, Johnny's small'. On conservation tests they readily recognize one relation at a time (e.g. the relative heights of two containers of liquid), and they also recognize relative lengths of single pairs of objects in the transitivity test. Thus the representational processes which are developing in the preoperational peiod appear capable of handling one relation at a time.

In general, the concrete operational stage is characterized by a greatly increased ability to represent relations between elements of a task. Thus the child can symbolize elements in two-dimensional space, can treat stimuli as values on dimensions, can relate a part to the whole, and can draw inferences. As Donaldson (1971) has pointed out, ability to reason by inference depends on comprehension of certain constraints in the situation. Much of this chapter will be devoted to the task of specifying just those structural properties of a task which a concrete operational child can represent symbolically and a preoperational child cannot.

Along similar lines, we can think of Piaget's *formal operational stage* as depending on ability to construct multiple representations of a task structure. Thus the ability to reason by hypothesis or to perform operations on operations might be thought of as a process of using multiple symbolic representations, each of which is organized in the manner which is characteristic of concrete operations.

CONCRETE OPERATIONS AND THE CONCEPT OF A SYSTEM

Recall that the transition from preoperations to concrete operations coincides with what White (1965) calls the five-to-seven shift. It seems only reasonable, therefore, that any account of the preoperational–concrete operational transition should be consistent with what is known of this larger shift.

We can regard the shift as comprising four classes of acquisition:

(1) *Generality* There is a shift from representations which are mainly related to particular things, and therefore lacking in generality, to representations which are less specific, more general, and more strongly related to other representations.

(2) *Inference* There is the new appearance of ability to decide certain

questions inferentially, in the absence of adequate, immediate perceptual input, as in transitivity.

(3) *Invariance* There is the ability to recognize invariance in a field of variance, as in conservation and in certain tasks used by White (1965).

(4) *Integration* There is the ability to integrate various components of a situation into a structured whole, as in the perspectives of a mountain task.

It will be apparent that there are both points of agreement and of disagreement between this list and that given by White (1965). The list proposed here is an attempt to synthesize the Piagetian concept of the preoperational–concrete operational transition with White's concept of the five-to-seven shift. There is correspondingly more emphasis on structural or organizational considerations and less on perceptual and encoding considerations than in White's list. The influence of a further eleven years of literature accumulation is also reflected, of couse, in this current account of the transition.

The four acquisitions of the five-to-seven shift mentioned above can be dealt with under a single concept—the concept of a *system*. Essentially, a system is a set with an organizing principle (Ficken, 1967). (A binary operation is an excellent example of an organizing principle, so a groupoid, i.e. a set with a single binary operation as discussed by Sheppard in Chapter 3, would be an example of a system.) A good introduction to the system as a psychological concept is provided by Emery (1969).

One property of systems which is of relevance in this context is that its elements are defined by their distribution or arrangement within the system, rather than by properties inherent to them as elements (Angyal, 1941). This means that the system can remain invariant despite drastic changes in the elements.

One type of system, the mathematical group, introduced in Chapter 1 and discussed further by Sheppard in Chapter 3, provides a useful way of illustrating this property. Consider the cyclic three-group in Table 6.1(a).

TABLE 6.1. (a) The three-group and (b) a set with all different elements but still the same group

(a)		a	b	c
	a	a	b	c
	b	b	c	a
	c	c	a	b
(b)		X	Y	Z
	X	X	Y	Z
	Y	Y	Z	X
	Z	Z	X	Y

The same group is shown again in Table 6.1(b) with a completely different set of elements, but the group or system is unchanged by the change in elements. We might say the systems remains *invariant* across the change in elements. This occurs because the elements are defined, so far as the system is concerned, by their relations to one another.

There must be an organizing principle for the system as a whole, and a relation between two or more elements does not of itself constitute a system. A good guide is whether the system would remain intact, irrespective of the particular elements, or whether it is dependent on qualities inherent in the elements themselves. In the latter case it is best thought of as a relation or a compound relation rather than a system, as pointed out by Angyal (1941). Consider, for instance, a set consisting of a large white triangle and a small black square. Numerous relations exist within the set; the elements are related to one another by size, shape, and colour, but even this set of three relations does not constitute a system. If one of the objects in the set was changed the relations would also be changed and there would not be an invariant system. Thus the term 'compound relation' would describe this example better. On the other hand, the three vertices of a triangle are related to one another in a way which is independent of the vertices themselves. It would not matter whether the vertices were formed by intersecting straight lines or by placing pins in the table. The relations between them would still be the same, as would the system they form.

A certain similarity is apparent between the properties suggested as basic to the five-seven shift and the properties of a system. The characteristics of behaviour after the shift are consonant with what we would expect if a child's representational processes became structured as a system. A variety of systems have been used in the research programme reported later in the chapter, and this argument will be illustrated where appropriate with each of them. However, all four characteristics of behaviour after the shift will be first illustrated with a single system, the cyclic three-group, in order to give the flavour of the argument.

Increased generality results from the fact that the elements of a system are independent of their properties as elements. This enables a wider range of examples to be recognized as instances of the same system. For instance, the two examples in Table 6.1(a) and (b) can be seen as instances of the same system, although their elements have nothing in common. Thus the generality of a concept such as the cyclic three-group derives mainly from structural relations among its elements. Thus we see how the generality of a concept is increased when it acquires structural properties.

Inference is made possible because of constraints created by the structural properties of the system. For instance, referring to Table 6.1(b), if we know that X combined with Y yields Y ($X \circ Y \to Y$) and that $Y \circ Y \to Z$, then we know that $X \circ Y \circ Y$ gives Z and therefore $X \circ Z$ must give Z also, because two occurrences of Y must be equal to a single occurrence of Z. Thus the mapping $X \circ Z$

is constrained by the two mappings $X \circ Y$ and $Y \circ Y$. The form of this inference closely resembles the form of the inference involved in transitivity.

Another type of inference which is important to some of the arguments that follow is the interpretation of an unknown element. Suppose we have an unknown element U, such that there is inadequate perceptual information to unable us to determine whether U should be identified with element a, b, or c. Suppose now we know that $b \circ U \rightarrow a$. Referring to Table 6.1(a), we can see that only element which, combined with b, will produce a is element c. Therefore the nature of the system determines that element U must represent element c.

The property of invariance results from the identity element possessed by certain systems such as groups. The important point here is that an element's status as an identity element derives from its relations to other elements, independently of whether we know anything about qualities inherent in the element itself. Consider the element X in Table 6.1(b). We know nothing of this element other than its position in the system as defined by the table. Yet this information alone is sufficient to determine that the element is an identity element. Notice that when X is combined with any element, including itself, the result is the same as that element alone, that is $X \circ X \rightarrow X$, $X \circ Y \rightarrow Y$, $X \circ Z \rightarrow Z$. This is what gives X its status as an identity element, i.e. an element which does not alter another element. (For a discussion of the properties of groups, including identity, see Chapter 1.)

The property of integration results from the existence of an organizing principle which subsumes all the elements. It is as if the place of every element in the system is guaranteed by the structure itself. Thus there is no way that the system in Table 6.1(a) can exist without three distinct elements corresponding to the three types of element, a, b, and c. Analogously, there is no way that a spatial arrangement such as the mountain used by Piaget in his perspectives of the mountain task can exist without all the perspectives being integrated into a single unit. Thus a passage around the mountain guarantees that each perspective must appear in the perceptual field in its proper sequence. It is evidently a child's failure to integrate the various perspectives into a single system which prevents his realization of this.

So far this discussion of systems has been essentially abstract. It remains to show that the concept of a system can have any psychological reality. It turns out that learning sets have a basis which has the essential properties of a system, so it is to learning sets that we now turn.

LEARNING SETS AND LEARNING SYSTEMS

There are several points of resemblance between a learning set and a system. First, since a learning set is an efficient performance on an invariant problem form with varying items, it tends, like a system, to be independent of the specific elements which compose it. Second, the elements of a learning set are defined by their relations to one another, rather than by qualities inherent in them as elements. For instance, in a simple discrimination learning set, the stimuli are defined relative to one another in a relationship of mutual exclusion: if one stimulus is associated with reward, the other is not. In a discrimination reversal learning set, the stimulus which was previously positive is now negative, and vice versa. Thus the constant or invariant factor in learning set tasks is not the task elements themselves, but the interrelations among the elements. This similarity between systems and learning sets makes them a good task to use as the basis of a paradigm for the study of behaviours based on systems.

Parenthetically, there is another reason why learning sets warrant consideration as the basis for such a paradigm. A stage-wise theory of cognitive development demands that we be able to measure ontogenetic differences in a way which is independent of specific task features. Certain kinds of learning sets, specifically discrimination reversal learning sets, have been found to be uniquely useful in measuring phylogenetic differences in this way, as the work of Bitterman, Wodinsky, and Candland (1958), and Bitterman (1960) has shown. They may also prove successful in measuring ontogenetic differences in the same way if learning set tasks which are capable of discriminating normal human subjects over a wide age range can be found. Most learning set tasks used so far have been designed for use with animals (e.g. discrimination learning, reversal learning, oddity, etc.) and discriminate between humans only at the very lowest levels of intellectual development.

Some learning set experiments will be considered now which illustrate the learning of a system which is relevant to human cognitive processes. The experiments were performed by Halford (1975b) on adult human subjects, and the task was based on the cyclic three-group, as shown in Table 6.1(a). The group is a key concept in much of mathematics, and is also relevant to cognitive activity in humans (Dienes and Jeeves 1965, 1970; Lamon, 1969; Sheppard, 1974a). As pointed out earlier, a group is an example of a system in the sense that its elements are defined by their positions within the group, i.e. by their relations to other elements, and independently of their properties as elements.

Experiment 6.1

The task was constructed by using nonsense syllables in place of the elements on the left of Table 6.1(a) and geometric figures in place of the elements on the top of the table. An example of the task which results is shown in the left-hand side of Table 6.2 under the heading 'experimental task'. The stimulus for each item had two components: a nonsense syllable and a geometric figure. The response was also a nonsense syllable. The stimuli were presented one at a time on cards, the subject was presented with a card telling him the three possible correct responses for that problem, and he was then asked to select the response he thought would be correct for that item. Feedback was given by turning the stimulus card around to show the correct response on the back.

TABLE 6.2. Experimental and control tasks used in cyclic three-group experiments

| Experimental (structured) problem | | | Control (unstructured) problem | | |
Stimuli		Responses	Stimuli		Responses
BEJ	Triangle	BEJ	BEJ	Triangle	BEJ
BEJ	Circle	ZAS	BEJ	Circle	ZAS
BEJ	Square	POB	BEJ	Square	POB
ZAS	Triangle	ZAS	ZAS	Triangle	POB
ZAS	Circle	POB	ZAS	Circle	BEJ
ZAS	Square	BEJ	ZAS	Square	ZAS
POB	Triangle	POB	POB	Triangle	ZAS
POB	Circle	BEJ	POB	Circle	BEJ
POB	Square	ZAS	POB	Square	POB

The experimental task in Table 6.2 embodies the structure of the group in Table 6.1(a). BEJ, POB, and ZAS correspond to the elements a, b, c respectively on the left-hand side of Table 6.1(a) and triangle, circle, and square correspond respectively to the elements a, b, c on the top of Table 6.1(a). The responses BEJ, ZAS, and POB correspond to the elements a, b, c within the table. Thus the stimulus 'POB circle' has 'BEJ' as the correct response. This corresponds to that part of Table 6.1(a) in which element b on the left combined with element b on the top of the table yields element c within the table. Notice that the item BEJ triangle in Table 6.2 has BEJ as a response. In fact whenever triangle occurs, the response nonsense syllable is the same as the stimulus nonsense syllable. Thus the element triangle has a constant meaning equivalent to 'maintain the same syllable'. Now notice that if circle occurs with BEJ the response is ZAS, if it occurs with ZAS the response is POB, and if it occurs with POB the response is BEJ. Thus circle in effect 'transforms' BEJ to ZAS, ZAS to POB and POB to BEJ. Square, on the other hand, 'transforms' BEJ to POB, POB to ZAS, and ZAS to BEJ. Thus the experimental task has a structure or set of interitem relations.

The control task parallels the experimental task in all respects except that because of a slight rearrangement of the stimulus–response contingencies, it has no interitem structure. Taken item by item the experimental and control tasks should be of equal difficulty. If, on the other hand, they are learned as integrated systems rather than as individual items, then the experimental task should be much easier. Equal numbers of subjects were allocated to experimental and control tasks and given six learning set problems; i.e. problems with the same form but different items.

The results are fully reported in the original paper (Halford, 1975b), but there are two findings which are relevant in the present context. The first is that the experimental task was much easier than the control task throughout the series. Thus the structure variable had an effect right from the beginning of training, rather than emerging gradually with experience over problems, as had been expected. The second, and more important, finding from the present point of view concerned transfer from one problem to another, as measured by performance on the first trial of each new problem. The experimental group improved significantly from a mean first-trial error rate of 5·56 on problem 1 to 1·67 on problem 6. Since the control group did not improve significantly (5·89 on problem 1 and 5·22 on problem 6), then interproblem learning by the experimental group can presumably be attributed to the task structure.

It would be useful now to consider how this kind of transfer is produced. To the extent that transfer depends on the subject recognizing the constraints between the items, then it depends on the use of a system. We can illustrate how these constraints might operate to facilitate learning a new problem by taking a randomly chosen example from the experimental task in Table 6.2. Suppose that items 7 and 5 were the first to be presented, i.e. 'POB triangle → POB' and 'ZAS circle → POB'. Knowing the task structure, we can see that triangle means 'leaves the nonsense syllable unchanged', so the response syllable should be the same as the stimulus syllable. Then since circle transforms ZAS to POB, the task structure requires that it must transform POB to BEJ and BEJ to ZAS. The remaining geometric figure, square, must effect transformations in the opposite direction to circle, so it must transform ZAS to BEJ, BEJ to POB, and POB to ZAS. Thus, given items 7 and 5, the correct response to all the rest can be predicted. In general, it can be shown that any two different items are sufficient to predict the rest in a problem with this structure. Since the error probability is 0·67, the expected first-trial error rate would be 1·34. The expected rate if there were no structure would be approximately 5·33. The obtained rate of 1·67 is clearly much closer to that expected when the subjects use the task structure.

What is the nature of the system which mediates transfer in this way? Actually the same system can be represented in several different forms. It could be a geometric representation and the subject's employment of the system could be mediated by an image of the geometric model. A suitable model would be an equilateral triangle with the nonsense syllables POB, ZAS, and BEJ at the vertices, with the cue 'triangle' meaning 'stay at the same place', 'square' meaning 'go clockwise from POB to ZAS, ZAS to BEJ, and BEJ to POB', and 'circle' meaning 'go anticlockwise from BEJ to ZAS, etc.' Most readers will probably find that the experimental task in Table 6.2 becomes easy to learn if represented in this way. Alternately, the 'structure' might be represented by means of a set of verbal rules. However, the problem was investigated by Halford (1975b) and there was certainly no clear evidence either for the use of imagery or for consciously rehearsed verbal rules.

Actually the mode of representation may not be of crucial significance. Structural theories are often made vulnerable on the question of what it means to say that a subject has a particular cognitive structure, but the vulnerability may be unnecessary. However, there clearly is a need to define what it means for a subject to have a system. In the present case we will say that the subject has a system if:

(1) The subject has a stored representation of the relations between the elements of the task.
(2) This stored representation is independent of the nature of the specific elements.
(3) The information can be accessed readily in any problem to which the subject recognizes the system as being applicable, irrespective of whether the specific elements have been experienced before or not.

One implication of this definition is that it does not matter how the information is stored, provided the storage is such that all three principles hold good. There appears to be no reason why the three principles cannot hold for both verbal and imaginal storage processes.

Now notice that the system can operate without knowing the right answers for any particular item. It can work by hypothesizing answers for items and then checking to see whether the relations between these items are consistent with the system as a whole. In most cases this implies that items cannot be compared with the system one at a time, but must be checked in sets of at least two items at a time. Consider the item 'BEJ circle → ZAS'. The system provides no indication as to whether the response ZAS is correct or not. When considering one item in isolation, the correct response can be determined only by information supplied from outside, e.g. by feedback. Consider, however, the two items 'BEJ circle → ZAS' and 'ZAS circle → BEJ'. These two items are inconsistent with the system. Either the first item must be changed to 'BEJ circle → POB' or the second item must be changed to 'ZAS circle → POB'. That is, if a particular response is correct to any given item, this will constrain the other items to some extent. Thus this type of task imposes the requirement that the subject select responses which are consistent with the system as a whole.

SYSTEMS, LEARNING SETS, AND COGNITIVE DEVELOPMENT

In this section we will consider some specific examples of systems which can be linked to aspects of cognitive development. First, a system will be considered which seems to be about the simplest possible which could be related to concrete operational performances. An abstract representation of the system is given in Table 6.3. It has two kinds of elements: states and operators. An operator transforms one state into another, according to the mappings (or rules) embodied in the table. For instance, operator N transforms a into a and b into b, etc., so it is a null operator or identity element. Operator R transforms a into b, b into c, etc., while operator L transforms b into a, c into b, etc. The elements of the system can, of course, be changed without changing the nature of the system itself.

A concrete representation of the system is shown in Figure 6.1. There are five houses placed in a line, each house corresponding to one of the states $a, b, \ldots, e$. In this embodiment of the system, operator R is interpreted as a

TABLE 6.3. Systems used in
Experiment 6.2

		Operators		
		N	R	L
Initial state	a	a	b	—
	b	b	c	a
	c	c	d	b
	d	d	e	c
	e	e	—	d

Final state

movement one step to the right, operator L is interpreted as one step to the left, and operator I is interpreted as no movement either way.

The next step is to determine how well children learn a system of this kind, and then to determine how well they can transfer it to new items, use it to interpret ambiguous information, etc. To do this, an experimental procedure was designed which required the child to perform several distinct tasks. These will be considered in turn.

Experiment 6.2

Array training was so called because it began by presenting the child with an array of five cardboard houses arranged as shown in Figure 6.1. The houses were approximately 3 inches wide by 3 inches high, were all white, and were identical to one another. The aim of the task was simply to teach the meaning of the three operators which were represented by three cue-cards (samples of which are also shown in Figure 6.1), each containing a different geometric figure. The figures were randomly drawn from a pool, and randomly assigned one to each of the operators I, R, and L.

A toy truck was placed in front of one of the houses, chosen at random, and

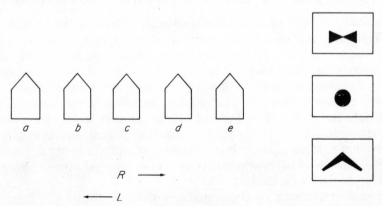

FIGURE 6.1 Concrete embodiment of the system used in Experiment 6.2

the child was told that the three cue-cards were signs which told the truck-driver where to go. The child was then shown one of the cue-cards, and told to move the truck where he thought the driver should go. If an incorrect house was selected, the truck was replaced, and the child was told: 'No, that's not right, try again.' This trial-and-error correction procedure was employed for up to three attempts, after which the child was told the correct response. The truck was then placed in front of the new house, the next cue-card was presented, and the procedure was repeated. Training was continued for up to six trials, or until one error-free trial was achieved (i.e. until all thirteen items were correct).

A new problem was then presented by randomly drawing three new cue-cards, without replacement, from the pool. This problem was then taught in the same way, and learning set training continued in this way for six problems.

The inference task required the child to interpret a single ambiguous cue-card. The task was presented immediately following the last array training task, and the last three cue-cards used were retained. The experimenter introduced an ambiguous cue-card, the same colour as the other cards but without a geometric design.

The child was told that this card meant the same as one of the training cards. The truck was then moved in accordance with one of the operators, *I*, *R*, or *L*, and the child was told that the truck-driver was doing what the ambiguous cue-card told him to do. He was then asked to say which of the three cue-cards meant the same as the ambiguous card. For instance, if the truck was moved from house *b* to house *c*, the ambiguous card would mean the same as the cue-card representing operator *R*.

Symbol allocation was really the reverse of array training, with the experimenter suggesting movements from one house to another and the subject selecting a cue-card for that movement. Specifically, the child was asked to select a cue-card to '. . . tell the truck-driver to go from this house . . . (pointing) to that house . . . (pointing)'. The purpose of the task was to measure the extent to which the children would allocate a cue-card consistently to a particular class of action.

Operator training presented the subject with the same contingencies used in array training, but the houses were not placed on the table in the correct position before training began. Instead, the subject had to arrange the houses on the table in a way which was consistent with the system. Five different coloured houses, red, yellow, blue, grey, and green, were used. The colours were allocated at random to each of the states *a*, *b*, *c*, *d*, *e*, a separate allocation being made for each problem. In effect, the subject had to determine the correct order in which to place the houses while learning the task.

The house which had been randomly selected as a starting point was placed on the table in front of the subject (the exact position varying randomly) and the truck was placed in front of it. The child was given the remaining four houses to hold. The first cue-card was then presented and the child was asked to select the house to which the truck-driver should go. The same trial-and-error correction procedure was used as with array training. When the child had selected the correct house, he was asked to place it on the table '. . . where he thought it should go'. No comment was made on the placement. Therefore the child received feedback for the selection of the house, but no feedback concerning its location on the table. When all five houses were correctly placed, they would form a row as for array training.

Whereas in array training the child had to interpret the cue-cards, representing the operators, on each new problem, in operator training he had to interpret both the cue-cards and the houses. Thus both state and operator elements of the task were unknowns, and the child had to interpret them in a way which was consistent with the system in order to make any sense of the task. Each child was given 2 six-trial problems. Before continuing with details of the experiment and results, we will consider how this task relates to cognitive development.

Relation to concrete operations

This task requires the child to learn a simple system in the array training phase; it then requires him to use the system for reasoning and further learning. Thus, in the most general sense, it would be true that if, as suggested in earlier sections, the onset of concrete operations is attributable to emergence of ability to organize symbolic processes into systems, then it should follow that concrete operational children should be able to construct a symbolic representation of the system used in this task. The existence of such a system would then in turn enable the child to interpret unknown or ambiguous elements of a task in a way which was consistent with the system. However, the link established with concrete operations in this way is a very general one.

A more specific link can be recognized because of the fact that any concrete operational performances require the child to recognize dimensions such as quantity, number, length, weight, etc. In fact seriation, transitivity, and conservation may all be seen as testing a child's ability to deal with stimuli as values on the relevant dimension. Now a dimension is basically an ordered set of objects or values. It takes little imagination to see how this basic feature of dimensions is incorporated into the learning set task used in Experiment 6.2. In effect, the five states a, b, c, d, e are equivalent to five ordered values. Instead of interpreting the states as houses, we could have interpreted them as five quantities, five lengths, or five values on some other dimension, with a as the lowest value and e as the highest. Suppose, for instance, that we interpreted the states a, . . ., e as five discontinuous quantities, as shown in Figure 6.2. Operator R would then be tantamount to adding one unit, operator L would be equivalent to reducing by one unit, and operator N would be equivalent to no change, and would thus be the quantity-conserving operator.

The operator training task is partly analogous to seriation in that it requires the child to place the houses in the correct order. The inference task is analogous to conservation in that it requires the child to interpret an ambiguous action

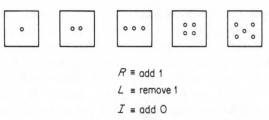

$R \equiv$ add 1

$L \equiv$ remove 1

$I \equiv$ add 0

FIGURE 6.2 A second interpretation of the system in
Table 6.3

performed upon a quantity. On the other hand, there is no direct analogue
of transitivity in the task as it is set up at present. The reason is that no operator
corresponds to two or more other operators. For instance, if operator R
was applied twice, starting at state b, the resulting state would be d (that is R
applied to b would yield c, then R applied again to c would yield d). However,
there is no single operator which can be applied to a to yield d in one step.
To incorporate transitivity into the task there would have to be a single operator
which was equivalent to two successive applications of the other operators.
Since transitivity is a necessary condition for seriation, the task is an incomplete
analogue of seriation.

Subjects

There was a sample of kindergarten and elementary school children and
a sample of preschool children in Eastern Ontario. The school sample comprised
six children at each level, (kindergarten, Grade 1, and Grade 2) in each of
three schools, giving fifty-four children in all. One of the schools was semiurban,
one was rural and rather underprivileged, and the third could be described
as rural improved, since it was housed in a modern building with excellent
facilities and a highly trained staff. The preschool sample consisted of 9 four
year olds and 5 three year olds from a preschool in the working-class section
of a moderate-sized Eastern Ontario city.

Predictions

The expectation was that all the children would learn the array training
tasks to criterion. This is necessary to ensure that the subject learn all the
components of the task. Failure on operator training can then be attributed
with greater confidence to an inability to treat the task as an integrated system.

Since the operator training task requires the children to organize the task
elements in a way which is consistent with the system as a whole, and since
we have argued that ability to construct an internal representation of a system
develops during the five-to-seven shift, then we would not expect preschool
children to succeed on the operator training task. Thus this task should discriminate between the preschool and the school sample.

In order not to overtax the willingness of the three year olds to cooperate, they were not given the inference task or the symbol allocation task; the four year olds were not given the symbol allocation task for the same reason, but were given the inference task. It would be predicted that the school-age children would succeed on the inference task, whereas the four year olds would not. The prediction for the symbol allocation task would be that the school-age children would allocate cue-cards to actions consistently. (This would not have been expected for the preschoolers, but this prediction cannot be tested at the present time.) The inference task and symbol allocation task should be thought of as pilot investigations at this stage.

Results

The results showed that all the school sample reached criterion on both operator training problems and, with one exception, on all array training problems. (The exception was one subject who failed to reach criterion on one array problem only.) This result was suprising only in the degree of regularity obtained.

What was surprising was that all the four year olds reached criterion on all array and all operator training problems. Of the three year olds, only two could be persuaded to return for enough sessions to complete array training, but these two subjects reached criterion on all array training problems and also went on to reach criterion on all operator training problems.

The learning rates did not vary very much from one group to another, but the semiurban and rural-improved sample did learn operator training significantly faster than the rural-unimproved sample, and the four year olds were significantly slower than the kindergarten children. There were no significant differences for array training.

In the inference task, the four year olds made only 6·8 per cent. correct responses, consistent with the prediction that they would not be able to handle this task. The school sample had an overall mean of 75·9 per cent. correct responses. The semiurban children performed significantly better (mean of 90·8) than the two rural groups (overall mean of 68·5). The school sample therefore also had the level of success which was predicted for them.

For symbol allocation, performances were analysed by calculating the information transmitted from cue-cards to actions. The average value for all groups was 1·132 bits, out of a maximum of 1·595 bits, or 71 per cent. consistent. No significant age or SES effects were found.

Discussion of Experiment 6.2

The main predictions concerning the school sample were borne out. There is, however, a major discrepancy between predictions and results for preschoolers on the operator training task. At first sight it would seem that they can handle a task which requires them to deal with a system after all. However, an alert research assistant realized that the children were taking a short-cut in performing this task.

This is possible because of a point which was made earlier; the operators *R* and *L* consist of only one step. Thus if a cue-card means to move to the right, it means to move to a house *immediately* to the right. In these circumstances, the only relationship between houses which must be determined from cue-cards are right and left. There is no relationship equivalent to two steps left, three steps left, etc.

The effect of this is that the child need out consider more than one relationship in order to place the houses appropriately. Thus the operator training task is not fully analogous to seriation of objects on a dimension, because it requires only one relation to be used to fix the position of an item in a series, whereas seriation requires two. For instance, the fact that a stick *x* is more than another sick *b* means that *x* should go to the right of *b*, but it does not mean that *x* should be *immediately* to the right of *b* or next to *b*. For *x* to be placed next to *b*, *x* must both be longer than *b* *and* shorter than any other stick which is longer than *b*. Thus seriation requires the coordination of two relationships at a time.

The point was made earlier that a system is more than a single relation. Thus a task which permits the subject to succeed while using only a single relation as was the case in this experiment, does not force him to use a system. The task was based on a system, but the subject was not forced to use it. This may well account for the unexpected success of the three year olds.

The main value of this experiment, then, is that it has provided a task which can be mastered even by preschoolers as young as three years. It may therefore be the basis of a test procedure for investigating learning set performance as a function of age, with the procedure held constant across ages. It also turns out that this kind of task can be used with systems at several levels of complexity. In the next experiment advantage will be taken of these features of the task to study learning set performance as a function of both age and system complexity, while holding all procedural factors, including number of items to be learned, constant.

Experiment 6.3

The purpose of this experiment was to contrast a task which requires the child to represent relations with a task which requires him to represent a system. The procedure is similar to that used in Experiment 6.2. It was expected that, in the relations task, preschool children would be successful but, in the systems task, only children five years and older would be successful.

The two tasks used are shown in Table 6.4, and the spatial arrangement used to present the tasks is shown in Figure 6.3. The four states are interpreted as the four corners of a square. Both tasks have a null operator and an operator *C* which corresponds to a movement one step clockwise, such as *ab*, *bc*, etc. Task 1 has an operator *A* which corresponds to one step anticlockwise: *dc*, *cb*, etc. Task 2 has an operator *D* which corresponds to two steps clockwise or anticlockwise, or to one step across the diagonal.

Four array training and four operator training tasks were given with the

TABLE 6.4. The two tasks used in Experiment 6.3

		Level 1 task					Level 2 task		
		Operators					Operators		
		N	C	A			N	C	D
States	a	a	b	d	States	a	a	b	c
	b	b	c	a		b	b	c	d
	c	c	d	b		c	c	d	a
	d	d	a	c		d	d	a	b

same procedure as Experiment 6.2. In operator training, the child would have to consider only one relation for the level 1 task, but the level 2 task requires the child to consider two relations at a time, and thus necessitates that a system be employed. The reason for this can best be explained by means of a concrete example.

Suppose that a particular operator training task has four houses, red, green, blue, and yellow, and that there are three cue-cards containing the figures circle, cross, and triangle. It makes no difference where the first house goes, since it is the positions of the houses relative to one another, rather than to any external position, which matters. For convenience, we will assume that the red house is placed at position a in Figure 6.3. Now suppose the cross cue-card is presented and the correct response is for the truck to go to the blue house. We can represent this item thus: 'red, cross → blue'. Having ascertained that blue is the correct response, the subject's task is to decide where to place the blue house. Again there is no external criterion, but it is necessary that the position of blue should not be inconsistent with further items in the task. It is at this point that the level 1 task differs from the level 2 task; we will consider the level 1 task first.

In the level 1 task both operators C and A correspond to movements around the sides; referring to Figure 6.3, they correspond to movements from a to b, b to c, c to d, and d to a, or the reverse of these, that is a to d, etc. There are no movements across the diagonal. The cross cue-card in the item 'red, cross →

FIGURE 6.3 Spatial arrangement used in Experiments 6.3 and 6.4. The letters a, b, c, d are shown here for convenience, but were not present on the apparatus

blue' must correspond to one of the possible operators in the task. Since red is at *a*, blue cannot be placed at *c*, because cross would then represent a movement across the diagonal and there is no such operator in the task. Therefore blue must be placed at either *b* or *c*, and triangle must represent *C* or *A*.

To carry the argument further, a sample set of items for the level 1 task is shown in Table 6.5. Two arrangements which would be consistent with this task are shown in Figure 6.4a, and two which would be inconsistent with it are shown in Figure 6.4b. The essential point is that for any set of items, based on the level 1 task, a spatial arrangement consistent with the task structure can be produced by taking one item at a time. This requires the subject to cognize only one relation at a time, so he is not required to construct an internal representation of a system.

In the level 2 task it is not possible to determine a spatial arrangement which is consistent with the task structure by taking movements one at a time in this way. To illustrate, consider the set of items for the level 2 task in Table 6.5. Suppose that the first item presented is 'red, cross → blue'. In this task a movement can occur either clockwise, anticlockwise, or across the diagonal. If red is at *a* as before and blue is placed at *c*, the placement will be inconsistent with a set of items in which cross represents a non-diagonal movement. This is illustrated in Figure 6.5b. However in order to determine whether cross represents a diagonal or a non-diagonal movement, we need to consider two items jointly, such as:— 'red, cross → blue' and 'blue, cross → yellow'. This means that cross represents non-null movement, a movement which is not its own opposite, and

TABLE 6.5.   Hypothetical sets of items in Experiment 6.3

Level 1 task

		Circle	Cue-card Cross	Triangle
Initial house	Red Blue Yellow Green	Red Blue Yellow Green	Blue Yellow Green Red	Green Red Blue Yellow

Resulting house

Level 2 task

		Circle	Cue-card Cross	Triangle
Initial house	Red Blue Yellow Green	Red Blue Yellow Green	Blue Yellow Green Red	Yellow Green Red Blue

Resulting house

the only operator which has this property in the level 2 task in Table 6.4 is *C*. Therefore triangle must represent operator *C*.

The general point about the level 2 task which is illustrated here is that some of its elements can be interpreted only by taking two items at a time. The interpretation of the elements, so far as this particular task procedure is concerned, occurs by placing the houses on the square in a way which is consistent with the system in Table 6.4. This can only be done by considering items in pairs. The operator training task can only be performed by coordinating pairs of relations, which amounts to constructing a system. Consequently, it would be predicted that, in operator training, preschool children would succeed on level 1 tasks but not on level 2 tasks. As before, it would be predicted that all children would succeed on array training at both levels.

Subjects

There were 12 three year olds and 12 four year olds from a working-class nursery school in Kingston, Ontario, and 12 five year olds and 12 six year olds from a rural school near Kingston. Half the children in each group learned the level 1 task and half learned the level 2 task.

Results

The number of operator training tasks on which each group of subjects

(a)

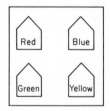

(b)

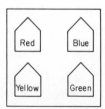 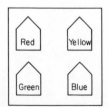

Figure 6.4 Spatial arrangements for Experiment 6.3 which would be consistent (a), and inconsistent (b) with the Level 1 problem in Table 6.5

(a)

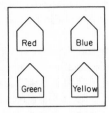 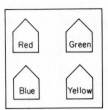

(b)

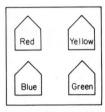 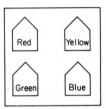

FIGURE 6.5 Spatial arrangements for Experiment
6.3 which would be consistent (a), and inconsistent
(b) with the Level 2 problem shown in Table 6.5

reached criterion for each task is shown in Table 6.6. (All subjects reached
criterion on all array training tasks.) The three year olds failed on all tasks,
whether level 1 or level 2. Thus the prediction that they would fail on level 2
tasks is supported, but they have not succeeded as predicted on level 1. The
four year olds have performed more in accordance with prediction, and they

TABLE 6.6.   Number of problems
mastered in Experiment 6.3

	Problems mastered				
	0	1	2	3	4
Age 3					
Level 1	6	0	0	0	0
Level 2	6	0	0	0	0
Age 4					
Level 1	0	0	0	1	5
Level 2	4	2	0	0	0
Age 5					
Level 1	0	1	1	1	3
Level 2	0	2	1	1	2
Age 6					
Level 1	0	0	0	1	5
Level 2	0	0	1	4	1

succeed much more often on the level 1 task than on the level 2 task. This difference between the two tasks is significant for the four year olds at the 0·005 level by the Fisher exact test. In most cases the five and six year olds have mastered both level 1 and level 2 tasks.

Just why the level 1 task is too difficult for the three year olds is a mystery, particularly since another (admittedly much smaller) sample of three year olds succeeded on a similar task in Experiment 6.2. It is possible that they found the process of placing the coloured houses on the square too distracting, but a more likely possibility is that they could not match movements to the task structure, even one at a time.

It is quite possible that the current theoretical notions need to be revised in light of the fact that three year olds might not be able to utilize symbolic processes which adequately represent even single relations. More data are needed on this. For the present, however, it appears that the theory is right about the contrast between four year olds on the one hand and five and six year olds on the other. Four year olds succeed on the level 1 task, which requires them to match external movements to symbolically represented relations, but cannot match pairs of movements to a system which is more complex than a single relation, as can five and six year olds. Thus an interaction between age and the complexity of the system with which the child can work has been demonstrated, while holding the procedure, number of items to be learned, etc., constant. The next question is to determine whether a similar difference can be demonstrated between six to ten year-old children and eleven-to thirteen-year-old children (i.e. between concrete and formal operational children in Piaget's terms), using the same technique.

Experiment 6.4

The two tasks used are shown in Table 6.7. Task 1 has two parts, identified by ϕ and * in the top-left corners of the respective tables. The apparatus and procedure was the same as for Experiment 6.3, with array training followed by operator training in each task. However, in this experiment, each subject was taught all tasks. The two parts of task 1, ϕ and *, were taught separately, * first, then ϕ. The subject was taught both array and operator training on one part before moving to the other.

When both parts of task 1 had been mastered, the subject was moved on to task 2. The components of task 2 are drawn from task 1, so that there is an additional dimension, ϕ or *, representing the original system from which the operator came. On the cue-cards, this dimension was represented by the presence or absence of diagonal stripes, with stripes indicating ϕ or * at random for each problem. There were thus four cue-cards, comprising all combinations of two geometric figures and two backgrounds. In task 2, therefore, the subject has three kinds of unknown elements to interpret at the beginning of a new problem: states, operators, and the system from which the operator is drawn.

Task 1 is essentially a level 2 task with four operators instead of three, so

TABLE 6.7. The two tasks used in Experiment 6.4

Task 1

	ϕ	Operators					*	Operators			
		N	C	A	D			N	C	A	D
States	a	a	b	d	c	States	a	a	b	d	c
	b	b	a	c	d		b	b	c	a	d
	c	c	d	b	a		c	c	d	b	a
	d	d	c	a	b		d	d	a	c	b

Task 2

		Operators			
		ϕC	ϕD	$*C$	$*D$
States	a	b	c	b	c
	b	a	d	c	d
	c	d	a	d	a
	d	c	b	a	b

it would be expected that children from six to eleven years of age could perform it. Prediction of performance on task 2 depends on relating it to formal operations. Recall that most formal operational tasks require the subject to consider alternative systems; i.e. they demand that the subject investigate alternative ways of relating variables together. Task 2 imposes the same requirement, and so it should be attainable only by children of eleven years and older.

It can also be shown that task 2 requires the child to match movements to the system three at a time in order to interpret certain elements. For space reasons, only one example of this can be given here, but all cases can be checked out using essentially the same kind of reasoning. Consider a hypothetical sequence of items such as 'red, striped triangle → green', 'green, plain triangle → blue', and 'blue, plain triangle → green'. Since an item begins with the initial house already in position, we will assume that red is at d to begin with (the placement of the initial house has no significance in itself, as was pointed out before). Now consider what can be inferred from successive items. The first item, 'red, striped triangle → green', allows nothing to be inferred, and green could be placed at a, b, or c, without apparent inconsistency. When the second item is presented, it can be inferred from the two items jointly that triangle represents operator C, but it cannot be determined whether stripes represent ϕ or *. The reason for this is that if green is placed at b, interpreting triangle as a diagonal movement, blue would then have to go at either a or c, so that triangle would then be either a clockwise or an anticlockwise movement. But there is no operator in the system which can be both a diagonal and a non-diagonal movement, even allowing for the change of background (see task 2 in Table 6.7). Thus triangle must represent C. When the third item is presented, we know that plain triangle represents a movement from green to blue and back again. We already know (from items 1 and 2 jointly) that triangle does not represent the diagonal movement D, so plain triangle must represent $* C$, since this is the only non-diagonal movement which can be its own opposite. Therefore all elements on the cue-cards can be interpreted, and the green house must be placed at either a or c and the blue house at b. This cannot be determined, however, with less than three items.

Subjects

The subjects were twelve children aged from eight to ten years and twelve children aged from eleven to thirteen years from an Eastern Ontario rural school.

Results

The number of problems of operator training in task 2 on which criterion was reached by each age group is shown in Table 6.8. All the subjects reached criterion on all array training problems, and nineteen of the twenty-four subjects reached criterion on all operator training problems for task 1. The remaining five subjects, who were evently distributed over the age range, failed on only one problem each. A more complete analysis of the data is given elsewhere (Halford, paper in preparation).

Significantly more children in the older group reached criterion on all three problems than in the younger group (the Fisher exact probability is less than 0·05). Thus task 2 has discriminated between children under eleven and children over eleven years, while task 1 failed to do so. Thus it appears that a task which requires the subject to represent two alternative systems distinguishes children under eleven from children over eleven years.

Experiments 6.3 and 6.4, taken jointly, seem to be consistent with the following conclusion: children can cognize a level 1 system before the age of five, a level 2 system after the age of five, and a level 3 system after the age of eleven. Thus systems at levels 1, 2, and 3 appear to be within the capacity of preoperational, concrete operational, and formal operational children respectively.

SYSTEMS AND CONSERVATION

The conservation task has become widely known through Piaget's (1952) use of it in his explorations of a child's understanding of number. In the last fifteen years a great deal has been written on it, and it is now almost certainly the most-analysed concept in the cognitive development field. Careful analyses of the logical and empirical basis of conservation have been published by Wallach (1969), Halford (1970a), Klahr and Wallace (1973), and Peill (1975). While the problem is far from solved, a certain amount of concensus about its basis has emerged.

TABLE 6.8.   Number of operator-training
problems mastered in task 2 or Experiment
6.4 by each age group

	Problems mastered			
	0	1	2	3
Age 8 to 10	3	3	4	2
Age 11 to 13	2	0	2	8

The core of the problem is for the subject correctly to interpret the transformation. For instance, in a test for conservation of number a row of eggs might be matched with a row of eggcups so that the subject can see they are equal. Then one row is transformed; e.g. the eggs might be spaced out into a longer row. The preconserving child then says there are more eggs than eggcups. Similarly, in a test of liquid quantity, the child is first presented with equal amounts of liquid in two identical vessels. Then one quantity is poured into (for instance) a taller and narrower vessel. Again, the preconserving child says there is more.

The non-conserving response can easily be seen as a misinterpretation of the transformation. The child does not recognize that the transformation is actually null with respect to the relevant dimension or that it produces no change in that dimension. But the precise nature of the error is not easy to spot. The immediate situation really provides no clue that the quantity is actually the same, especially in the case of liquid conservation (Peill, 1975; Wallach, 1969). Thus the transformation is essentially an ambiguous one. How, then, does the child come to interpret the transformation as a null (conserving) one?

The answer which I want to propose is that the ambiguous transformation could be correctly interpreted, in the absence of sufficient immediate evidence, if the child could embed it into a system. Recall that in Experiments 6.2 and 6.3 the child sometimes had to interpret items in a way which was consistent with the system as a whole, although there was insufficient information in any single item to enable this to be done. We should now ask what kind of system would enable the child to interpret the transformation of a quantity?

Quantity is a dimension, and a dimension is a kind of system. Actually, a dimension is a set of values which are ordered with respect to a transitive relation. Thus a system for interpreting transformations of a quantity would consist of a set of quantities, with the transitive relations between the quantities as the organizing principle. Any action performed on a quantity can be interpreted as a relation between two quantities. Thus any action which increases a quantity makes it 'more', an action which decreases it makes it 'less', and one which makes no change makes it 'same'. Thus the task of interpreting an action on a quantity is basically a matter of determining which relation in the system the action should be identified with.

However, a system which consisted of a set of values on which only a single relation was defined would not be adequate to permit conservation. This is because conservation requires that the subject at least be capable of distinguishing transformations which leave quantity unchanged (null acts) from transformations which increase quantity (adding acts) and those which decrease it (subtracting acts). Thus conservation would require that the subject have a system consisting of a set of values with at least these three implicit actions or operations. The system in Table 6.9 consists of these three operators, and is essentially the system proposed elsewhere (Halford, 1970a, 1975a) as a possible basis of conservation.

Essentially this system would enable a subject to integrate the various quantity values and the operators applied to them in much the same way that the systems described in Experiments 6.1 to 6.4 allowed the subjects to integrate the elements of the various tasks. Such integration would permit subjects to realize the contradiction inherent in treating a particular transformation, or operator, as an adding operator, when in fact it is a null operator so far as the system is concerned. This contradiction arises from the fact that if a particular operator increases a quantity, then that quantity would have to be more on all future occasions than it would have been if the operator had not been applied. This will sooner or later turn out to be contradicted by subsequent experience. That is, the child will eventually recognize that he has no more material as a result of having made that transformation than if he had not made it. Thus the apparent increase was in the short term. Experience in the long term contradicts it. It would follow, therefore, that conserving judgments would eventually result from a shift from a short-term view of the effects of the transformation to a long-term view. (For a more fine-grained version of this argument, see Halford, 1975a.) The function of the system in Table 6.9 then would be to enable the child to integrate actions on quantities over time.

A non-conserving judgment is tantamount to interpreting a null transformation as an adding transformation. This may be likened to interpreting a cue-card in a task such as Experiment 6.3 as implying a larger step than it does. In both cases, the incorrect response leads to no immediate contradiction, but does result in contradictions in the long term. Consider the item mentioned before from Experiment 6.3: 'red, cross → blue'. 'Cross' represents a movement

TABLE 6.9. Hypothetical system

		Null (N)	Second act Add (A)	Subtract (S)
First act	Null (N) Add (A) Subtract (S)	Null (N) Add (A) Subtract (S)	Add (A) Add (A) Null (N)[a]	Subtract (S) Null (N)[a] Subtract (S)

Resulting act

[a] True only if amounts added equal amounts subtracted.

one step clockwise, as shown in Table 6.5. Suppose, however, that it was interpreted as a diagonal. Since a diagonal movement is equivalent to two movements clockwise (e.g. a move from a to c is equivalent to a move from a to b followed by a move from b to c), then this would be tantamount to interpreting 'cross' as a larger movement than it should be. Again, no contradiction would arise in the short term and 'blue' could simply be placed diagonally opposite 'red'. But in the long term this interpretation is inconsistent, as shown in the level 2 problem in Figure 6.5(b). Contrast this with the consistent interpretation in Figure 6.5(a). The inconsistency of the interpretation shown in Figure 6.5(b) is really due to the fact that 'cross' would have no consistent relations to the other operators in the task. With the consistent interpretation shown in Figure 6.5(a) 'cross' would have a consistent relation to both the other cues/operators in Table 6.5. That is, four repetitions of 'cross' are equivalent to the null operator, 'circle', and two repetitions of 'cross' would be equivalent to the diagonal operator, 'triangle'. No such consistent relations to other operators can be found if 'cross' is interpreted as in Figure 6.6(a), and such an interpretation is therefore inconsistent with the system as a whole.

The essence of the argument, then, is that conservation judgments would result when children develop a system for integrating actions on quantities over time. The system shown in Table 6.9 would really be the most primitive which could serve that function. The specific process of bringing a conserving judgment into being would be the recognition that a non-conserving judgment was inconsistent with the system as a whole, in the same way that incorrect interpretations of operators in Experiment 6.3 would be changed when it was discovered that they were inconsistent with the system as a whole.

It follows from the reasoning so far that conservers should differ from non-conservers in that they integrate acts performed on a quantity into systems, whereas non-conservers should be restricted to interpreting acts in isolation from one another. This was tested in a series of experiments in which children were shown a sequence of acts performed on a quantity and were asked to interpret the result in a way which was consistent with the system shown in Table 6.9. For instance, if a null act was followed by an act of adding to the quantity, the system indicates that this would be equivalent to an act of adding. Experiments 6.5 and 6.6 were carried out by Halford (1975a), Experiment 6.7 by Braggert and Halford (unpublished study, 1972), and Experiment 6.8 by Johnson and Halford (1975).

Experiment 6.5

Subjects

Three groups of children were used. One of these consisted of those who were decidedly preoperational in their thinking and who would not be expected to become conservers for approximately another two years (mean age 4 years, range 3 to $4\frac{1}{2}$ years). There were two other groups, both from the same classes at school, who were divided into conservers and non-conservers on the basis of four pretests. The mean age of the conservers was 5 years 11 months (range 5 to $6\frac{1}{2}$ years) and of the non-conservers 5 years 7 months (range 5 to $6\frac{1}{2}$ years). There were thirty-two children in each group, and the groups were equally divided into experimentals and controls.

Procedure

The children were shown two successive transformations of a quantity in the following way. Two identical, cylindrical, clear-plastic vessels of rice, A_1 and A_2, were placed in front of the child, both full, and his agreement obtained that they held the same amount. Then A_2 underwent two transformations, of the kind shown in Table 6.9. For instance, it might be poured into a second vessel B (null act), and then into a third vessel C, but with something added (i.e. further material was added to C after the material from B was poured in). This sequence comprises two acts, null and add, which are jointly equivalent to a single act, add. The child was then asked what would happen if the material was returned to A_2: 'If I pour the rice back here (to A_2) will it just fill it up, will there to too much (so it will overflow) or will there not be enough to fill it up?' Notice that the child was not asked to interpret the acts, but only to predict the actual physical result of pouring back. There were eighteen items, comprising two from each of the cells in Table 6.9, and the dimensions of the containers were varied considerably through the series. The control groups were given the same procedure as the experimentals, using the same vessels, except that they never saw the actual transformations. Instead, the vessels were emptied into a jug and the next vessel filled from another jug. Thus the scores of the control subjects serve as a baseline for judgments based on perceptual cues without the transformation.

Results

These showed that the experimental conservers were 79·5 per cent. correct, while the kindergarten non-conservers were only 64·2 per cent. correct, and the preschool non-conservers had 50·3 per cent. correct. By contrast, the differences between the control groups were all non-significant (43·1, 43·4, and 37.5 respectively).

We can see that there are marked (and significant) differences between the conservers, the school non-conservers, and the preschool non-conservers in the case of the experimental group, and small and non-significant differences between the control groups. Thus there is prima-facie evidence that ability to interpret actions performed on a quantity in a way which is consistent with the system in Table 6.9 does develop between about four years of age and the time children become conservers. The fact that kindergarten non-conservers performed significantly better than their corresponding controls is consistent with the idea that ability to interpret transformations as part of an integrated system develops before the children become conservers. Thus children who are close to conserving are already halfway to acquiring the system.

Experiment 6.6

It was then decided to check the results in a further experiment, using a simpler procedure with fewer steps and without misleading cues, in order to determine how far the error rate can be reduced. The material was initially in two identical vessels, A_1 and A_2, as before, and A_2 was transferred to C behind a screen, with addition or subtraction as appropriate to the item. The height of the screen was such that the transformation was clearly visible but not the quantity which resulted in C. Then a screen was placed in front of the now-empty A_2 and the material poured back to it from B, again with addition or subtraction as appropriate to the item. Nine items (one from each cell in Table 6.9) were given in this way to a further three groups of children, similar to those in Experiment 6.5. Their ages were: preschool non-conservers, mean 4 years (range 3 years 7 months to 4 years 7 months); school non-conservers, mean 6 years 5 months (range 5 years 4 months to 7 years 6 months); school conservers, mean 6 years 5 months (range 5 years 4 months to 8 years 2 months). The children were asked simply whether the material was now more than, the same as, or less than in A_1, which had not changed.

The mean correct responses were: for conservers, 94 per cent.; school non-conservers, 78 per cent.; and preschool non-conservers, 28 per cent. Furthermore, 27 out of 30 conservers had perfect or near-perfect scores (8 or 9 out of 9), 14 out of 30 school non-conservers did so, but none of the 20 preschool non-conservers did so. Of this last group none had scores better than 6 and most had 5 or lower.

Thus from two independent samples, with slightly different procedures, evidence emerges that ability to interpret pairs of transformations in a way which conforms to Table 6.9 develops gradually from four years to the age when children become conservers. The ability to conserve was not required by the items used in these tasks, because in the first experiment children were not asked the actual amount of material after the transformations and in the second experiment misleading perceptual cues, a key feature of conservation tests, were eliminated by screening.

Experiment 6.7

The next question concerns the reasons why non-conservers do not seem to be able to predict the result of pairs of transformations of a quantity. One obvious possibility is that they simply forget them. There are two main ways of checking this possibility. One is to train the children to remember all the transformations and see if this produces a corresponding increase in correct predictions. A second way is to simply check memory scores, along with their prediction scores, and see whether younger children can consistently remember sequences longer than those for which they can correctly predict the result. The first approach was used in Experiment 6.7, which was carried out by Mrs. Catherine Braggert.

A group of thirty-six non-conservers (mean age 5 years 1 month, range 4 years 10 months to 5 years 4 months) was randomly divided into three groups. All were pretested for ability to predict the results of each pair of transformations from Table 6.9, using the procedure of Experiment 6.6. Then one group, called the prediction training group, was taught to predict whether there would be more material, less, or the same after two transformations had been carried out. The second group was simply taught to remember the transformations (memory training group). The third, the control group, was given no training. Then all groups were given a posttest for ability to predict the results of transformations, the same as the pretest. The mean scores (out of 9) on the pretest were: control, 4·50; memory training, 4·00; and prediction training, 4·25; and on the posttest the corresponding scores were: 5·25, 4·16, and 7·25. Only the prediction training group made significant gains, although the memory training group had no trouble learning to recall the transformations. Thus, inability of the younger children, the non-conservers, correctly to predict the results of two successive transformations is not attributable entirely to memory failures.

Experiment 6.8

This experiment was designed to refine and extend the previous three studies. First, transformations were used which, taken individually, should be interpreted errorlessly by all the children. Second, sequences of 1, 2, 3, 4, 5, or 7 transformations were used, so the ability of children to interpret series of acts of different lengths could be studied. Third, a separate test was performed to see whether children were able to remember the transformations performed.

The experiment was conducted by Wayne Johnson as a project for his M.A. qualifying work at Queen's University, and has been more completely reported elsewhere (Johnson and Halford, 1975). Three groups of eight children each were used: non-conservers (mean age 5 years 4 months, range 5 to 6 years), transitionals (defined by the ability to predict that a quantity would be the same after a transformation but failing to maintain equality after seeing the transformation—mean age six years 1 month, range 5 years 10 months to 6 years 5 months), and conservers (mean age 7 years 2 months, range 6 years 10 months to 7 years 7 months).

The procedure was to show the child two fishbowls, each containing five ping-pong balls. Then one of the bowls was placed behind a screen and the child saw a sequence of acts performed on it. The acts were of three kinds: stirring the balls with a wooden ladle (null act), adding one ball, or removing one ball. For instance, a sequence of four acts might be: $+1, 0, -1, +1$. The sequences were selected so that the number of balls never increased or decreased by more than one ball throughout the entire sequence. There were six sequences

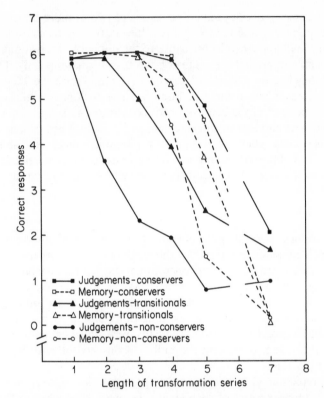

FIGURE 6.6 Performance in Experiment 6.8. Copyright (1975), Canadian Psychological Association. Reprinted by Permission

of each length. At the end of each sequence the child was asked to say whether the number of balls was the same as, more than, or less than those in the other bowl, which had not been changed.

The memory test was conducted in the same way, except that instead of being asked to judge the number of balls resulting the child was asked to reproduce the sequence of transformations in the other bowl. His performance was judged correct if he performed all the same transformations in the same order. The mean number of correct responses out of 6 for each sequence length is shown in Figure 6.6.

The implications of the results are quite clear. First, non-conservers can remember sequences of three transformations perfectly, yet they make errors on judging the results of sequences of two. This occurs in spite of the fact that their performance is virtually errorless on sequences of one, showing that it is not the individual transformations which is the cause of the difficulty. Conservers, on the other hand, can both remember and interpret sequences of four transformations. Transitionals can remember three and can interpret two transformations reliably.

Thus the conservers can predict the results of two or more transformations, but non-conservers cannot, and neither the individual transformations nor the memory load appear to be the cause of the difficulty. Transitional children seem to be able to predict the results of two transformations only. This would mean that they had the system in Table 6.9 in minimal form; i.e. they can apply it to sequences of two transformations but not to longer sequences. If the system is important in the acquisition of conservation, as was argued earlier, we would expect children to show evidence of it slightly before they conserve. Thus transitionals, who are presumably potential conservers, should have the system, but children who are not yet potential conservers should not have it. The observations seem to be quite in accord with these expectations.

Experiment 6.9

Having adduced a fair amount of evidence that children have an operational system which enables them to predict the result of two or more transformations by the time they reach the concrete operational stage, it now becomes important to determine whether they can use this system to interpret an ambiguous transformation. A further experiment was therefore carried out, again using two fishbowls, but this time with one ping-pong ball in each. The only other change in basic procedure was that the balls were added or removed by means of a pair of kitchen tongs, and the null act consisted of inserting and withdrawing empty tongs.

In the prediction task, the child was shown series of one, two, or three transformations, six series of each length. He was asked whether the number of balls resulting was more, less, or the same, as for the Johnson and Halford experiment (Experiment 6.8). In the interpretation task, one of the transformations was concealed (so the child could not see what was done), but the screen was removed at the end of the series so that the subject could see how many balls resulted. The child was then asked to say what the concealed transformation must have been. For instance, if the sequence was a concealed transformation followed by adding one ball, and the result was more balls (it could always be only one ball more or less, or the same number), the correct inference would be that the concealed transformation must have been null ('you didn't put any more in or take any out').

As a check on the possibility that the experimenter might have inadvertently provided a cue as to the concealed transformation, a six length-two transformations series was carried out, with one transformation concealed and the result *not* visible. Performance on this task was not better than chance, indicating that the children could not circumvent the inference task by using such a cue.

The subjects comprised four age groups of twelve children each: 3 years to 4 years 11 months; 4 years to 5 years 11 months; 6 years to 7 years 11 months; and 8 years to 9 years 11 months.

Performance on this task presumably reflects the ability to infer what transformation must have taken place. The inference would have to be based

TABLE 6.10. Mean correct responses in Experiment 6.5 (maximum of 6), with table of significant F values

	Sequence length					
	Prediction			Interpretation		
Age	1	2	3	1	2	3
3 years to 4 years 11 months	$5 \cdot 083^{a,b}$	$4 \cdot 250^{a,b}$	$3 \cdot 583^{a,b}$	$5 \cdot 000^{a,b}$	$3 \cdot 500^{a,b}$	$2 \cdot 250^{b}$
5 years to 6 years 11 months	$5 \cdot 000^{a,b}$	$4 \cdot 583^{a,b}$	$4 \cdot 500^{a,b}$	$4 \cdot 833^{a,b}$	$3 \cdot 333^{a,b}$	$2 \cdot 750^{b}$
7 years to 8 years 11 months	$5 \cdot 250^{a}$	$5 \cdot 250^{a}$	$5 \cdot 583^{a}$	$5 \cdot 083^{a,b}$	$4 \cdot 667^{a,b}$	$3 \cdot 417^{a,b}$
9 years to 10 years 11 months	$6 \cdot 000^{a}$	$5 \cdot 917^{a}$	$5 \cdot 583^{a}$	$6 \cdot 000^{a}$	$5 \cdot 250^{a}$	$5 \cdot 583^{a}$

[a] Significantly better than chance (0·05 level).
[b] Significantly worse than perfect score (0·05 level).

ANOVA

Source	df	F	p
Sequence length (1)	2,80	45·584	< 0·001
Prediction versus interpretation (2)	1,40	65·973	< 0·001
Age (3)	3,40	16·187	< 0·001
1 × 2	2,80	11·992	< 0·001
1 × 3	6,80	5·640	< 0·001
2 × 3	3,40	4·299	< 0·025
1 × 2 × 3	6,80	2·220	< 0·05
2 × 3 × 4	3,40	7·134	< 0·001

jointly on the visible transformations and the final result. The performance required is essentially similar to that of a person who must employ the rational number system (or a part of it, such as the natural number system) to solve a hypothetical problem such as the following.

A child sees a bag containing an unknown number of marbles poured into a box. The child knows some marbles were poured in, but does not know how many. Thus this pouring is an ambiguous act, much like the transformations used in conservation tasks. The child then sees three more marbles added to the box. He is then allowed to look inside the box, sees that there are seven marbles there, and is asked how many must have been poured in from the bag. In effect he is being asked to interpret an ambiguous act (pouring an unknown number of marbles from a bag into a box) in a way which is consistent with a system of operations on numbers—the (rational) number system.

Thus Experiment 6.9 confronts the child with a task which requires him to interpret an ambiguous act in a way which is consistent with a system. In this sense the logic of the task resembles the hypothesized process which leads the child to conserve. The task demands of the immediate situation are superficially very different from those of the conservation task, to be sure. Thus we should expect no more than a very general correspondence between the ability reliably to perform the task of Experiment 6.9 and the age at which conservation occurs.

The mean correct responses are shown in Table 6.10. We find that the preschool group makes significantly worse than a perfect score on all the tasks. On the interpretation task they get 3·5 correct out of 6, even on sequences of two, i.e. where the ambiguous transformation was accompanied by only one another transformation. This is the shortest sequence which requires an inference to be made on a basis which goes beyond the immediate situation. In the oldest group, the inferences are indistinguishable from a perfect score. Thus the results are consistent with the idea that the ability to infer what transformation must have occurred from a system comprising quantities and transformations on quantities develops gradually during the concrete operational stage.

As a task, the procedure in Experiment 6.9 would have one advantage over conservation procedures, in that the child is not misled as to the nature of the transformation. The transformation is simply concealed and he is asked to use his quantitative knowledge to infer what it was. If Piaget is right in saying that the true significance of quantity conservation is that it reflects the child's understanding of operational quantification, then this procedure, if sufficiently refined by further research, may test this knowledge more directly and with less confounding than the traditional conservation task.

SYSTEMS AND RECOGNITION OF PERMANENT OBJECTS

Experiment 6.10

A demonstrational experiment will now be described to show how the concept of 'permanent object' (Piaget, 1954b) can be defined in terms of a system of actions. Subjects will be required to distinguish 'permanent' from 'impermanent' objects using such a system as their only cue. First, we must create a situation where the subjects do not know what objects are permanent—not an easy thing to do, because every normal person can distinguish all objects from non-objects in the environment. Coloured slides of three hypothetical houses were used. Actually, the houses are all identical, being photographs of the same drawing. To identify the houses we give each one an owner who has a distinctive appearance and a first name. Thus the houses could in principle be distinguished by their owners, who are used as identifying cues in preference to natural cues because the subjects would know the natural cues in advance and we could not then give them a problem. The problem is created by always having a visitor with the owner at each house. The visitor is drawn from the same pool as the owner, and there is so far no way of knowing which are owners and which are visitors. (The six people are Pam, Anne, Sue, Ken, Bill, and John.) Actually, the owners can be distinguished from the visitors only by the fact that they conform to the cyclic three-group, as we shall see.

There were also three actions, which are identified by nonsense names, DAT, VUG, and HOX. The actions represent movements from one house to another. For instance, the task begins at the house with Pam and Anne present. We do not know, of course, whether Pam or Anne is the owner of the house.

The action DAT is performed, and the result is the house at which Pam and Ken are present. The subjects were given the following instructions: 'This is a game with three houses and some people. The people are Bill, John, Ken, Anne, Sue, and Pam. Three of the people own one house each. The houses all look the same, but you know which house is which because the owners always stay with their houses. We will pretend that there is a travelling salesman who goes from house to house. As he leaves each house he gets a sign in a strange language telling him what house to go to next. Sometimes the sign might mean to stay at the house where he is already. The idea is for you to learn whose house the salesman will be at next'.

The stimuli were projected onto a screen by means of two Kodak Carousel slide projectors. The first projector showed a slide of two people in front of a house, with the names of each person printed beneath the figure. After 10 seconds, the other projector projected the 'sign' which was a nonsense syllable indicating which of the three actions was being performed. After a further 10 seconds, the 'sign' was switched off and the first projector changed to a slide with two more people standing in front of a house. If the reader would like to decide who the owners are, a sequence of people and instructions as shown to the subjects is in Table 6.11.

The 'location' of the mythical salesman could be determined only by reference to the 'owner' of the house, and the owners were distinguished by one feature only: for the owners, the three signs and the actions which they represent form a simple system, the cyclic three-group, as shown in Table 6.12. For the visitors, the instructions were inconsistent. In fact the reader has probably already recognized that the owners belong to a system which is isomorphic to the experimental task in Experiment 6.1, while the visitors belong to a system which is isomorphic to the control task.

The subjects were tested in small groups. When each 'instruction' was presented, the subjects wrote down the 'owner' whom he thought would occur next. When the next pair of people was presented, the subject wrote down the one he thought was the owner.

Most university students can solve the problem within about half an hour. The problem has also been given to high school students, and the results of second-form students at a high school (of intermediate socioeconomic level) in Newcastle, N.S.W., are shown in Figure 6.7.

Each subject was given three scores for each block of ten items. Score A was the number of owners correctly predicted when the instruction was presented. Score B was the number of either owners or visitors predicted. Score C was the number of owners correctly recognized when the subject (S) saw the two people who resulted from a particular instruction.

Examination of individual protocols shows that five out of fourteen subjects were able to positively identify the owners on the last block of trials (as shown by a C score of 10 out of 10). One subject misidentified the visitors as owners. Four subjects handed in records which either failed to comply with instructions or were incomplete. Hence the results in Figure 6.7 are for nine subjects.

TABLE 6.11. A sequence of people's names and instructions as shown to subjects in Experiment 6.10

PAM		ANNE
	DAT	
KEN		PAM
	VUG	
JOHN		BILL
	DAT	
JOHN		BILL
	VUG	
SUE		ANNE
	VUG	
PAM		JOHN
	HOX	
SUE		KEN
	DAT	
KEN		SUE
	VUG	
PAM		JOHN
	BUG	
ANNE		BILL
	VUG	
JOHN		SUE
	DAT	
SUE		JOHN
	VUG	
ANNE		PAM
	VUG	
BILL		JOHN
	HOX	
PAM		KEN
	HOX	
SUE		ANNE
	DAT	
KEN		SUE
	HOX	
ANNE		BILL
	HOX	
ANNE		PAM
	HOX	

TABLE 6.12. Cyclic three-group composed of trigrams used as instructions in Experiment 6.10

	DAT	HOX	VUL
DAT	DAT	HOX	VUG
HOX	HOX	VUG	DAT
VUG	VUG	DAT	HOX

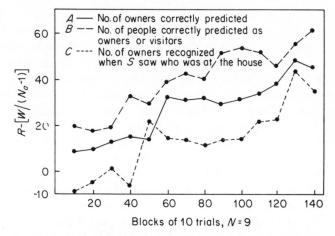

FIGURE 6.7 Scores on Experiment 6.10. Each score is corrected for guessing according to the formula $R - W/N_a - 1$, where R is the number of correct responses, W is the number of wrong responses, and N_a is the number of alternatives

The reader probably had no difficulty in sorting out who were the owners and who were the visitors. In fact the owners were Pam, Bill, and Sue. The only difference between the owners and visitors lies in the relationships between the actions performed with respect to them. The owners always remain the same after DAT occurs. VUG means go from Pam to Bill, Bill to Sue, Sue to Pam; HOX means go from Pam to Sue, Sue to Bill, Bill to Pam. For the visitors, the actions are consistent with respect to any one pair. For instance, DAT always means go from Anne to Ken, VUG means go from Ken to John, etc. However the actions are not consistent with respect to one another if Anne, Ken, and John are taken as the beginning and end points of each action. The relations between actions do not have a consistent interpretation with respect to the visitors, and this factor alone was sufficient to enable the subjects to distinguish owners from visitors.

Relative to the owners, the actions conform to a group (the cyclic three-group), but for the visitors the actions have no consistent structure. The owners, artificially used as cues for points in space, can be distinguished from the visitors, artificially used to represent impermanent, shifting features of the environment, solely by the use of the group structure.

The purpose of the experiment was to demonstrate how a group structure would enable a subject to discriminate (permanent) objects from (imperma-nent) non-objects. This is the first step towards creating a paradigm for experimentally explicating and testing Piaget's theory of the object concept (Piaget, 1954b). There is now an experimental procedure which seems to capture at least part of what Piaget's theory means.

TOWARDS A WORKING MODEL OF STAGES

The purpose of this section is to distil out the essence of stage characterizations which were offered in earlier sections, and thereby to lay what we may hope is a foundation for a working model of the last three stages: the preoperational, the concrete operational, and the formal operational. These last three stages differ from the sensori-motor stage in that they are all characterized by symbolic activity. The progression from preoperational to formal operational may be thought of as a progressive elaboration of symbolic processes into more complex systems, whereas the sensori-motor stage has systems which do not include symbolic processes in any essential role.

We can lay the groundwork for the argument by specifying two kinds of element and three kinds of relation which are important to the kinds of system we are considering. The two kinds of element are *environment elements* and *symbolic elements*. Environment elements include all objects and all aspects of the external world, and all actions other than those of a purely mental character. Thus the external aspect of an action performed by the person on the environment is an environment element for that person, since it is not a part of his mental processes. Symbolic elements are those which are created by and belong to the person's mental processes. They would include images, internal correlates of words, and stimulation arising from the person's own actions. These symbolic elements (the briefer term 'symbols' will be used for convenience) may represent environment elements, but do not always do so. For instance, I can mentally create the symbol 'green cow', but it does not represent any environment element that I am aware of. The three kinds of relation are:

(1) relations between environment elements,
(2) relations between symbolic elements, and
(3) relations between environment elements and symbolic elements.

We will consider each kind of relation in turn. It is commonplace that there are relations between environmental elements. For instance, a mountain is *above* the sea, a man is *bigger than* a mouse, Australia is *south of* China, etc. All these are simple binary relations, but more complex relations exist as well; an ovum and a sperm *combine to form* a zygote (fertilized ovum), etc. There obviously is no limit to the complexity of possible relations between environment elements. Furthermore, environment elements include our own actions, e.g. the action of walking south is *opposite of* walking north, etc.

Relations between symbolic elements include such things as *the knowledge that* three is *more than* two, a mile is *longer than* an inch, a movement one mile north combined with a movement one mile east is equivalent to a movement 1·34 miles northeast, etc. Here we are referring to relations between thoughts, not to relations between things. Thus the relation which exists between the snark and the boojum in Lewis Carroll's famous poem (the snark *is a* boojum) is one which exists only between thought elements or symbols.

The most common relation between environment elements and symbolic elements is the representation of environment elements by symbolic elements; for instance, the thought 'hat' represents the object hat and a certain class of buildings is represented by 'shop'. The same symbolic element may represent two quite different sets of environment elements; e.g. a walk one mile north followed by a walk one mile south might be represented by the same symbolic element used to represent the action of filling a pail and them emptying it again. We are aware, I am sure, of the feature these two actions have in common, yet there does not appear to be a readily available word which exactly expresses this feature. Yet the fact that we are aware that a common feature exists shows that there is a symbol element which can represent it. This is an illustration of the general point that, while many symbolic elements coincide with words, a symbolic element may exist which does not correspond to a word. Of course, the majority of symbolic elements which we discuss in print will correspond to words, simply because these are the easiest to talk about, but it does not follow that symbolic elements are to be identified with words.

Levels of complexity need to be defined for relations between environment elements and between symbolic elements. For present purposes it will be sufficient to define three levels (binary relations, binary operations, and compositions of binary operations), although in theory other levels are possible but are of no interest in the present context.

Binary relations are relations between two elements; e.g. a is larger than b, a is brighter than b, and a is to the left of b are all examples of binary relations. Actually, a binary relation is defined as a set of ordered pairs. Suppose we take a set of four elements:

$$S = \{a, b, c, d\}$$

We can now take what is known as the Cartesian product, (CP), which consists of the set of all ordered pairs in the set above, thus:

$$CP = \{(a,a), (a,b), (a,c), (a,d), (b,a), (b,b), (b,c),$$
$$(b,d), (c,a), (c,b), (c,c), (c,d), (d,a), (d,b),$$
$$(d,c), (d,d)\}$$

Now we take a subset of this Cartesian product set, e.g.

$$R = \{(a,b), (a,c), (a,d), (b,c), (b,d), (c,d)\}$$

This subset is a relation, so we have called it R. In general a relation is a subset of a Cartesian product set.

To relate this idea to a concrete example, suppose that a,b,c,d were four wooden blocks such that a was the largest, b the next largest, and d the smallest. Then the relation *larger than* defined on this set would consist of the set of ordered pairs in R (that is (a,b), (a,c), $\ldots$, (c,d)). In general the relation *larger than* consists of all ordered pairs such that the first member of the pair is larger than the second. (See the glossary for a more technical definition.)

Binary operations, which were discussed in detail by Sheppard in Chapter 3, are actually a composition of two binary relations. A binary operation consists of a set of mappings of the Cartesian product set into the set itself; for example,

$$* = \{(a,a) \to a, (a,b) \to b, \ldots, (d,c) \to b, (d,d) \to a\}$$

TABLE 6.13. A binary
operation, the cyclic
four-group

*	a	b	c	d
a	a	b	c	d
b	b	c	d	a
c	c	d	a	b
d	d	a	b	c

The full mapping is shown in Table 6.13. This particular operation is actually the cyclic four-group. If it is compared with the systems in Table 6.7, then it can be seen that it was used to construct one of the tasks used in Experiment 6.4. More formally, we can say that a binary operation on a set S is defined as $S \times S \to S$, but in this account we are not aiming for rigorous formalization so much as a reasonably deep understanding of the underlying ideas. It is also worth noting, however, that whereas a binary relation is a set of ordered pairs a binary operation is a set of ordered triples. Thus it is purely a matter of convenience whether we write

$$* = \{(a,a) \to a, (a,b) \to b, \dots\} \text{ or } * = \{(a,a,a), (a,b,b), \dots\}.$$

Compositions of binary operations can be created by defining a relation between two binary operations. An example of this is given in Table 6.14, where we have two operations identified by ϕ and *, corresponding to the Klein group and the cyclic four-group respectively. The additional symbol, ϕ or *, specifies the operation to be used, so that, for instance, $d\phi b \to c$ but $d*b \to a$. This is analogous to arithmetic, where we have two operations, addition and multiplication, defined on the set of rational numbers, so that $3 \times 2 \to 6$ but $3 + 2 \to 5$. Another example, which is familiar in terms of Piagetian theory, but by no means exclusive to Piaget, is shown in Table 6.15. Here we have two operations, disjunction and joint denial, and the relation between them is the inverse relation (which Piaget symbolizes by N, and which is one of the elements in his *INRC* group). The four elements I, N, R, and C in Piaget's theory of formal operations are in fact four relations between binary operations. They are discussed in detail by Seggie in Chapter 11. Whereas a binary relation

TABLE 6.14. A composition of binary operations, the Klein group and the cyclic group

ϕ	a	b	c	d		*	a	b	c	d
a	a	b	c	d		a	a	b	c	d
b	b	a	d	c		b	b	c	d	a
c	c	d	a	b		c	c	d	a	b
d	d	c	b	a		d	d	a	b	c

TABLE 6.15. A second composition of binary operations, the operation of disjunction and its inverse, joint denial

a	b	$a \vee b$	a	b	$\bar{a} \wedge \bar{b}$
1	1	1	1	1	0
1	0	1	1	0	0
0	1	1	0	1	0
0	0	0	0	0	1

is a set of ordered pairs and a binary operation is a set of ordered pairs mapped into a single element (i.e. a set of ordered triples), a composition of binary operations is a set of ordered triples mapped into a single element (a set of ordered quadruples).

The concept of cognitive stage emerges from the application of these three levels of complexity to the three kinds of relations defined earlier. We will define a stage of cognitive development by the most complex type of structure which exists between the symbolic elements. We will identify symbolic elements structured at the level of binary relations with the preoperational stage, symbols structured as binary operations with the concrete operational stage, and symbols structured as compositions of binary operations with the formal operational stage. The purpose of what follows is to explain this. To do so, we will use the tasks in Experiments 6.3 and 6.4 as examples.

The level 1 task used in Experiment 6.3 was designed to force the child to use a binary relational structure, while the level 2 task was designed to force the use of a binary operational structure. Table 6.4 shows the relations between environment elements in the two tasks. The environment elements are four places a,b,c,d (corresponding to the four corners of the square in Figure 6.3) and the *movements* are stay at the same place (N), go one step clockwise (C), go across the diagonal (D), and go one step anticlockwise (A).

The minimum symbolic processes needed to perform operator training in the level 1 task would be elements representing the three possible types of movement. Recall that a child could succeed on this task provided that he interpreted each cue-card as indicating one of the possible movements in the task. To represent such movements adequately, a symbolic process would need to represent the beginning and end of each movement. That is, it would have to consist of symbols related to one another in pairs. For instance, the clockwise movement C can be represented by the set of ordered pairs ab, bc, cd, and da, signifying that any movement from a to b or b to c, etc., would be recognized as a clockwise movement. Such a symbolic process belongs to the lowest level of organization between symbols—a set of ordered pairs—and hence is called 'level 1'.

Actually all the possible movements in Experiment 6.3 can be represented as sets of ordered pairs:

$$N = (a,a), (b,b), (c,c), (d,d)$$
$$C = (a,b), (b,c), (c,d), (d,a)$$
$$A = (a,d), (b,a), (c,b), (d,c)$$
$$D = (a,c), (b,d), (c,a), (d,b)$$

It is now apparent that the level 1 task is so called because it requires level 1 symbolic processes. In particular, it requires symbolic processes sufficiently complexly organized to recognize the type of movement which each cue-card represents. Similarly, level 2 and level 3 tasks are so called because they require level 2 and level 3 symbolic processes, i.e. symbolic processes organized at the level of binary operations and compositions of binary operations respectively.

To relate this task to more general considerations concerning the preoperational stage, we will now suggest that all preoperational tasks depend basically on level 1 symbolic processes. Level 1 symbolic processes comprise all structures which consist of ordered pairs, which includes binary relations and simple functional relations. A function is a mapping of a set into a set, and therefore can be thought of as a set of ordered pairs. It is well established that preoperational children recognize one relation at a time and can reason in terms of simple functions (Piaget and coauthors, 1968).

Level 1 symbolic processes would permit two types of relationship. One type would be relations between symbols, or S–S relations, and the other would be relations between symbols and environmental events, or S–E relations. A typically Piagetian example of an S–E relation would be the preconcept, which consists of a word (one type of symbol) identified with an external object (e.g. the word 'slug' identified with the object slug—Piaget, 1950). An example of S–S relations would be the attempts which preoperational children can often be observed to be making to relate one idea to another, as when I recently heard a three year old say: 'Cars go on road, boats go on water.' Here we have juxtaposition of two relations, or what Angyal (1941) calls a 'compound relation'. We have 'car' related to 'road' ($S_{car} - S_{road}$) and 'boat' related to 'water' ($S_{boat} - S_{water}$).

An important point is that S–E identifications at level 1 can only be made on the basis of direct evidence. For instance, one either knows that the word 'slug' belongs to the object slug or one does not—there is no way this can be inferred or arrived at indirectly. Similarly, the movement ab in Figure 6.3 must be seen to be an instance of a clockwise movement, and there is no way its nature can be inferred in the absence of direct evidence using only level 1 symbolic processes. As we shall see, such indirect inferences are possible with level 2 processes, so that symbols need not be identified with specific environmental elements for level 2 systems to work.

The level 2 task in Experiment 6.3 was designed to force the child to use binary operational structures among symbol elements. These are structures of the form $(S,S) \rightarrow S$, i.e. where ordered pairs of symbolic elements are mapped into single elements. Recall that criterion performance on level 2 operator training required the child to identify *pairs* of movements. For instance, given items such as 'red, triangle → green' and 'green, triangle → blue', it can be determined that 'triangle' represents a clockwise (or anticlockwise) movement, but not a diagonal movement. This could not be determined from either item alone. The symbols for these movements, N, C, A, and D, are all equivalent to binary relations. What is needed in the level 2 task is relations between two such symbols. For instance, the child must recognize two occurrences of C or the occurrence of C and another symbol, etc. Two occurrences of C result in a house which is different from both of the last two, as seen in the example above, where the second occurrence of 'triangle' results in a new house, 'blue'. Two occurrences of D, on the other hand, result in a return to the starting point.

This requirement is formally equivalent to representing the single movement to which any pair of movements is equivalent. Table 6.15 shows the mappings of every ordered pair of the elements N,C,D,A into the equivalent single element. In effect, the level 2 task in Experiment 6.3 imposes the requirement that the environment elements (actions) must be identified with the symbol elements in such a way that the relations between the symbol elements correspond to the relations between the actions. For instance, since C and A are defined as opposites (inverses) of each other, they must be matched to two actions which are opposites of each other. In terms of Table 6.16, since A and C are equivalent to the null element N, then they must be matched to a pair of actions which are equivalent to a null movement. Provided this structural correspondence is achieved, there is a certain amount of freedom about the manner in which specific symbols are related to specific environment elements. For instance, it does not matter whether a clockwise movement is related to symbol C or to symbol A, provided that the anticlockwise movement is related to the other of these elements, so that A and C will represent opposite actions.

Similarly, in Experiment 6.1, it did not matter whether the transformation cue circle (Table 6.2) is identified with the group element b (Table 6.1) and the cue 'square' with element c, or whether 'circle' was identified with c and 'square' with b. All that is important is that one of these pairs of identifications must be made, because they are the only identifications which are consistent with the structure of the task.

Notice that in the case of level 2 tasks symbol elements need not be identified

TABLE 6.16. A binary operation (cyclic four-group) mapping pairs of actions into single actions

	N	C	D	A
N	N	C	D	A
C	C	D	A	N
D	D	A	N	C
A	A	N	C	D

with specific environment elements, but *pairs* of symbol elements must be identified with pairs of environment elements. Thus the requirement that specific symbol elements must be identified with specific environment elements, which is necessary at level 1, no longer applies. This is how a level 2 system provides the increased generality which was one of the four properties mentioned earlier as characteristic of behaviour after the five-to-seven shift.

A second property which emerges at level 2 is that elements can be interpreted by inference, in the absence of direct evidence. For instance, if we have an element X such that X combined with C produces a return to the starting point and we know that C represents a clockwise movement, then we can infer that X must represent an anticlockwise movement. This identification is the only one which is consistent with the structure of the system, which requires that X combined with C is equivalent to N. Since conservation tests require an action (environment element) to be identified with a judgment of the same, more, or less (symbolic element) in the absence of direct evidence, it would follow that this could only be done if the symbolic elements were related to one another in a level 2 fashion, i.e. as a binary operation. The evidence from Experiments 6.5 to 6.9 is that conserver status exists only in children who have a binary operational system for interpreting quantity transformations.

The level 3 task in Experiment 6.4 was designed to force the subject to use symbolic processes organized at the level of a composition of binary operations. Recall that the level 3 task requires the subject to identify pairs of actions which might be drawn from either of two binary operational systems. The systems are shown in terms of relations between environment elements in Table 6.7, and the more abstract systems on which they are based are shown in Table 6.13. The system designated by the operational symbol * is the same system that was used in Experiment 6.3. The other system, designated by the operation symbol ϕ, is new in this context and involves some movements which are different from those used in Experiment 6.3. The movements represented by operators ϕN and ϕD are the same as $*N$ and $*D$ respectively, but ϕC and ϕA are new. Operator ϕC represents a movement from a to b, b to a, c to d, and d to c, and ϕA represents movements from a to d, b to c, c to b, and d to a. Thus we can define two new binary relations in the same manner as before:

$$\phi C = (a,b),\ (b,a),\ (c,d),\ (d,c)$$
$$\phi A = (a,d),\ (b,c),\ (c,b),\ (d,a)$$

It was also pointed out earlier that identification of all the new elements of a new level 3 task requires information from at least three items. The additional information is made necessary by the fact that the cues 'plain' versus 'striped' must be identified with the systems * versus ϕ. It is interesting to consider what might happen if a subject who had only a single binary operational symbolic system was presented with a level 3 task such as the one which was used in Experiment 6.4. Referring again to the hypothetical item used in the introduction to Experiment 6.4, consider a pair of items such as 'green, plain triangle → blue' and 'blue, plain triangle → green'. A subject who had only a level 2 symbolic system, such as system * as used in Experiment 6.3 would conclude that triangle represented operator D and would place 'blue' diagonally opposite 'green'. But we know from the account of Experiment 6.4 that sooner or later the item 'red, striped triangle → green' would be presented, and no consistent interpretation of these three items could be found with 'blue' placed diagonally opposite 'green'.

What would this performance amount to? It would really be a form of premature closure. The subject could be interpreting the elements of the task in a way which was consistent with a smaller system, but did not take account of the extra dimension and greater number of operator elements in the enlarged system. In effect, concrete operational children respond to formal operational tasks in terms of a system which is too small. A formal operational task differs from a concrete operational task in that it requires the child not only to identify the task elements with the elements of a binary operational system, which is also required in concrete operational tasks, but to determine what binary operation matches the task.

In effect, the concrete operational child behaves as if only the former were required, and thus makes interpretations which would be valid only in the more restricted situation.

The traditional Piagetian tests of formal operations have, as their lowest common denominator, the requirement that the subject determine the nature of the system which is embodied in the phenomenon the children are expected to understand. For instance, whether the task be the behaviour of the pendulum, the law of flotation, or any of the other traditional tasks (Inhelder and Piaget, 1958), the subject has to determine how one or more operators combine to form a system. Operators may be such things as weight, force, or size (size is an operator in flotation because of the amount of fluid displaced). Seggie deals with these considerations in much greater detail in Chapters 11 and 12. Similarly, Collis' work on formal operations in school mathematics, described in detail in Chapters 7 and 8, has shown that concrete operational children can cope with individual arithmetical operations but have difficulty when they have to relate one operation to another, as when they have to handle both addition and multiplication in a single system.

Lunzer (1973) and Collis (1972) have analysed formal operational thought in considerable depth and have suggested that a fundamental requirement is the ability to 'accept lack of closure'. This means that the child must be willing to suspend interpretation of a task element until he has tested sufficient relationships to make the interpretation with certainty. In dealing with a level 3 system this would mean that he would have to identify three symbol elements with three environment elements. A subject whose symbolic processes included only level 2 systems would tend to identify elements prematurely.

The essential point here is that inability to accept lack of closure would follow whenever a subject is confronted with a task which demands a higher-level system than he has available. It would be observed if a subject with a level 1 systems was dealing with a level 2 task, and also if a subject with level 2 systems was dealing with a level 3 task. Not only can concrete operational reasoning on Piaget's formal operational tasks (Inhelder and Piaget, 1958) be interpreted as due to failure to accept lack of closure, but the preoperational child manifests a similar failure when dealing with concrete operational tasks. For instance, in seriation a preoperational child tends to regard objects as seriated with respect to (say) size, if (for instance) $A > D$, $B > E$, $C > F$, etc. He makes use of information from non-overlapping pairs of elements and ignores the information in the further comparisons (D, B) and (E, C). To coordinate this information with that in the pairs (A, D), (B, E), and (C, F) would require a binary operation or a composition of two relations, which is a level 2 system. The same thing is observed in classification, where pre-operational children consider one aspect of the task and ignore the rest. For instance, they might classify on the basis of size and ignore colour or shape.

INFORMATION PROCESSING REQUIREMENTS OF STAGES

In preceding sections the problem of how symbol systems are related to the structure existing among environment elements has been considered with respect to examples from Experiments 6.3 and 6.4. Three levels of symbolic processes were defined: level 1 in which symbols are related to environment elements one at a time (S–E relations), level 2 in which symbols are related to environment elements in pairs ($S \times S$–$E \times E$) and level 3 in which symbols are related to environment elements in sets of three ($S \times S \times S$–$E \times E \times E$). It is clear that the higher the level of the system, the more information is required to make the identification. This was illustrated for Experiments 6.3 and 6.4, where it was pointed out that an environment element could be identified on the basis of one item for a level 1 task, two items for a level 2 task, and three items for a level 3 task.

Now consider the actual number of units of information which are required for each level of task. At level 1 there are two chunks (where a chunk is a single discrete signal, irrespective of the number of bits of information it contains). One chunk is contributed by the environment element and one by the symbol element. At level 2 there are four chunks, two from the environment and two from the symbols, and at level 3 there are six chunks, three from the environment and three from the symbols. In fact, for a system of level N, the number of chunks of information required to identify symbol elements with environment elements is $2N$.

In the previous section, levels 1, 2, and 3 were identified with the preoperational, concrete operational, and formal operational stages respectively. We now find that these levels require 2, 4, and 6 chunks respectively. This brings us to a curious correspondence with memory spans of children at the relevant ages. If we accept the norms for the Binet and Wechsler tests of childhood intelligence, it turns out that children have a digit span of 2 at the age of two,

4 at the age of five, and 6 at the age of eleven. It seems that the youngest ages of entering the respective stages for average children are two years for the preoperational stage, five years for the concrete operational, and six years for the formal operational. It may be nothing more than coincidence, but it is a striking coincidence, nevertheless, that the number of chunks of information required at each stage is exactly equal to the number of chunks which a child can readily recall at the minimum age of onset of that stage.

At the present time it is not possible to determine the reason, if there is a reason beyond sheer coincidence, for this correspondence. However, it should be useful to indulge in some informed speculation about possible reasons. First, the construction of the symbol systems at each stage would be dependent on noticing recurring correspondences between environment elements and symbol elements. It would not be possible, in most cases, systematically to test the systems belonging to a particular stage, because by definition the child does not have such systems available until he has reached that stage. Second, hypothesis testing would in any case be difficult, if not impossible, because of the fact that the set of elements which defines a particular relationship in a system cannot be reduced to a simpler set. For instance, if the system is a binary operation, the minimum number of elements which has any meaning is two. In such a case, no relations can be identified between symbol elements and environment elements taken one at a time, because no such correspondence exists. That is, the question of whether a particular environment element should be identified with a particular symbol element in a binary operational system will depend entirely on how at least one other identification is made. This was illustrated earlier with respect to both Experiments 6.1 and 6.3. The effect of this is that the child is required to handle all the information necessary to make a particular identification in a single leap.

The problem is, of course, that we do not know how to estimate how much information a person, adult or child, can utilize in such a task. Digit span itself is not a pure measure of the capacity of any theoretical memory store, at least so far as extant theories of memory are concerned (e.g. Norman, 1970). Even recent work on the role of memory in problem solving such as that by Greeno (1973) does not help to answer this specific question. There is a need for more research on the role of memory in thought. We are all familiar with the experience of being unable to solve a problem because of the inability to 'hold on' to sufficient information at once. But what is the nature of that limitation? How does it relate to other kinds of memory? The present research cannot answer that question. Rather it has been devoted to the prior problem of whether the Piagetian stages should be identified with the systems which are here identified with levels 1, 2, and 3.

COMPARISON WITH OTHER APPROACHES

The information processing analysis of Piaget's stages presented by Pascual-Leone (1970) and Pascual-Leone and Smith (1969) depends on first making a semantic-pragmatic analysis of Piaget's tasks. The task is analysed by assessing the number of independent 'schemes' necessary to solve it. For instance, Pascual-Leone and Smith have analysed Piaget's quantification of inclusion task (Piaget, 1952), and find that it requires six independent schemes for a correct response to be generated. They show how, if one of these schemes was omitted, the commonly observed incorrect answer ($A > B$, where $AU \sim A \equiv B$), would result.

Pascual-Leone then postulates a central information processing space, M, such that $M = a + 2$ at the late preoperational stage, $a + 3$ at the early concrete operational stage, $a + 4$ at the late concrete operational stage, and $a + 5$ at the formal operational stage, where a is an empirical constant. The value of the M-space is assessed independently of Piaget's own tasks (see Case, 1972a, 1972b; Pascual-Leone and Smith, 1969) and then the ability of the child to perform a Piagetian concrete operational task is predicted. Impressive accuracy has been obtained in these predictions.

The comparison between Pascual-Leone's model and the one proposed in this chapter corresponds in many respects to the distinction between a performance and a competence model. If a child has a system of a given level of complexity, he still needs to be able to apply the system to the specific task presented. For instance, it might be found that a child can construct and use a level 2 system at the age of five, but he might not perform correctly on the inclusion task until about seven or eight years of age, even though this task requires a level 2 system, in the sense that it depends on the binary operation of disjunction. What Pascual-Leone's theory does is to provide a way of accounting for the lag between the ability to construct the necessary system and the ability to apply it to the task. However, Pascual-Leone's model says nothing about how the system is constructed in the first place.

The theory as presented in this chapter is not, so far, intended to account for the differential difficulty of different tasks at a given level. It is obvious that several different level 2 systems could be constructed. For instance, instead of using the level 2 system in Table 6.4, a larger system such as the operation designated* in Table 6.7, which is also a level 2 system, could be used, thereby increasing the number of items which the subject would have to learn. The form in which the items were presented would also affect difficulty by altering the ease with which the subjects could obtain and code the necessary information, while the number of items would affect the amount of learning, which in turn would invoke motivational and attentional factors. If the system is to be used in a problem-solving context, as with most of Piaget's tasks, then the complexity of the problem as presented needs to be distinguished from the complexity of the underlying system which needs to be employed in solving it. This is particularly true if the task is presented in verbal form or if it involves any kind of misleading cues.

Although the discussion so far has been concerned with systems of different complexity, the paradigm presented here also permits tasks of different difficulty to be presented while holding the complexity of the system constant. This means that the factor of task difficulty can be studied within this paradigm. For instance, what is the effect of varying the number of items to be learned? In terms of the present theory, the effect should be on learning rate rather than on asymptote, which should be a function of level alone. What would be the effect of presenting the items without a spatial array to help the subject code and coordinate the items? These questions are analogous to questions such as: 'Is it harder to seriate seven objects than four objects?' or 'Is it harder to seriate weights than lengths?', and 'If so, why?'

The proposal of McLaughlin (1963) is probably closer to the present one than is Pascual-Leone's. McLaughlin proposed that a child's digit span must be equal to the number of concepts which must be considered simultaneously, and that preoperational performance requires $2^1 = 2$ concepts, concrete operational performance requires $2^2 = 4$ concepts, and formal operations require $2^3 = 8$ concepts. The present proposal clearly differs from McLaughlin's in that it implies that formal operations require a memory span of 6, not 8. However, a more fundamental difference lies in the account given of the stages in terms of systems of different degrees of complexity, and in the provision of a research paradigm for testing the propositions of the theory. Both of these features are missing from McLaughlin's account.

Simon (1962) made some tentative proposals concerning a possible link between cognitive stages and information processing algorithms. His three levels of algorithms were: 'find next', 'find circular next', and 'find circular next carry'. Simon did not trace the link with stages in detail, and his proposal does not appear to have been followed up. It is interesting primarily because it is the first suggested link between cognitive stages and specific information processing systems.

There are numerous other information processing accounts of cognitive developmental phenomena. There is the collection of studies edited by Farnham-Diggory (1972) and there is an information processing account of conservation by Klahr and Wallace (1973) and of classification by Klahr and Wallace (1970). There are also computer simulation or information processing accounts of seriation by Baylor and his associates (1973) and by Baylor and Gascon (1974). There are general information processing approaches to cognitive development by Neimark (1970) and to learning by Biggs (1968). However, only the accounts by Pascual-Leone and Smith, McLaughlin, and Simon have attempted to explain each of the major stages, and the differences between the stages, in terms of information processing considerations.

STAGES OF THOUGHT AND MATHEMATICS LEARNING

It is necessary to compare the present account of concrete and formal operational thought with Collis' account of school mathematics. In many respects Collis' argument is consistent with the idea that concrete operations require the subject to use a single binary operation, and formal operations require the subject to work with more than one binary operation at a time.

The use of the reciprocal, which is one of Collis' criteria of formal operational thought in mathematics, implies that a second operation is being used. The inverse implies only the 'negating' of a single operation. For instance, in an expression such as $a + b$, the use of the inverse is manifest if the subject simply subtracts b, thus: $a + b - b$. The reciprocal is manifest if he reasons that if $a + b = c$, then $a + b - b = c - b$. When faced with the problem of what to do after subtracting b from the lefthand side, he is able to refer to a second operation which, if used appropriately, enables him to preserve the truth of the equation.

The present account of formal operational thought has some consequences for the teaching of formal operations in the context of school mathematics. Formal operations constitute a system which consists of two or more binary operations, i.e. two or more concrete operational systems. It would follow, therefore, that concrete operations should be taught first, by ensuring that the subject has overlearned all the binary operations of arithmetic and can apply them in all reasonable situations. Formal operations can then be taught by introducing problems which require the subject to use two operations in combination. It is not necessary to use concrete representations for the individual operations at this stage because the operations themselves have already been internalized. As an example of a problem which would be taught this way, we can consider the following.

The rule $p/q = mp/mq$ has been found to require formal operational reasoning, as Collis points out in Chapter 8. The general principle which applies here is that a child can learn a formal operational performance if he already has the constituent binary operational systems and also the necessary information processing capacity to construct the larger level 3 system. This was illustrated earlier with respect to the level 3 task in Experiment 6.4. There we considered the problem of identifying the elements in the task, and it was found that the subject would have to match a set of three environment elements with a set of three symbol elements.

Learning to apply the rule $p/q = mp/mq$ requires the symbols, in this case the terms of the formula, to be matched to the specific numbers which figure in any given example of the rule. Consider an example such as $6/2 = 12/4$. Is this an instance of the rule? To answer this question, we must relate the numbers in the equation to the symbols in the formula. If the example was provided in a form which exactly matched the formula, this would be a purely mechanical task, devoid of cognitive demands. For instance, if the number were in the form $6/2 = (2 \times 6)/(2 \times 2)$, then the numbers can be matched with the symbols using only positional cues. Mathematical competence requires, however, that the matching be performed on a conceptual basis, so that instances of the rule can be recognized irrespective of form. Otherwise the subject becomes unable to apply the rule when the form of the example is varied, and the rule is virtually useless to him, perhaps even leading him into error. As Collis points out in Chapters 7 and 8, this kind of learning enables a child to apply algorithms mechanically, but does not enable them to recognize *when* to apply a particular algorithm, with sometimes bizarre results. Consequently, we need to analyse the basis of conceptual matching of formula to example.

Basically, the rule involves three ratios, which we will call R_1, R_2, and R_3. Essentially, it provides that R_1 must be identical to R_3 and R_2 must be equal to 1. That is, p/q is identical to p/q and $m/m = 1$. The subject must accordingly examine the set of numbers in any example to determine whether it conforms to that structure. The example $12/4 = 6/2$ can be expressed in this form; $6/2$ on the left-hand side is identical to $6/2$ on the right, and $2/2 = 1$. This matching task is of the same level of complexity as that which is necessary to perform the level 3 operator training task in Experiment 6.4. Recall the example which was given there, consisting of the three items: 'red, striped triangle → green', 'green, plain triangle → blue', and 'blue, plain triangle → green'. Here, instead of three ratios between numbers, we have three cues indicating movements from one colour to another. These three cues have to be matched to three operators in a way which is consistent with the structure of the system, just as the three ratios between numbers must be matched to the three ratios in the formula in such a way as to make the statement consistent with the rational number field.

The point is, of course, that the matching process cannot be broken down into simpler components in either case. Just as the level 3 system in Experiment 6.4 was defined in terms of mappings of ordered triples into single elements (ordered quadruples), so the formula $p/q = mp/mq$ cannot be expressed in simpler terms. In effect the simplest expression is equivalent to a mapping of three ratios into a fourth value which is the truth or falsity of the identity.

The general question of how we determine the complexity of any rule is thereby raised. In fact, any rule can be expressed as a set of ordered n-tuples. For instance, the rule $5X + 9$ might be expressed as the (infinite) set $\{(0,9), (1, 14), \dots\}$. To determine the level of complexity of a rule, we need to express the rule in terms of the simplest possible set of ordered n-tuples. If it is a set of ordered pairs, it is level 1; if it is a set of ordered triples, it is level 2; and if it is a set of ordered quadruples, it is level 3.

Most rules in common use are really compound rules, or several simpler rules combined. The compound rule can be applied by applying each of the simpler component rules in succession. Thus very few rules, when reduced to their simplest components, will be found to be beyond level 3.

DEVELOPMENT OF THOUGHT AND MEMORY

This chapter would not be complete without considering an important objection which might be raised to the notion, implied earlier, that the development of thought will be dependent on the development of memory. First, it should already be quite clear that it is not being argued that the growth of thought is simply a function of memory. Thought is not something which the subject simply learns or remembers. It requires the subject actively to construct a system of internal symbolic processes. This chapter has been mainly concerned with showing how systems can be defined which would produce the kinds of thought which are observed at three stages of cognitive development: the preoperational, concrete operational, and formal operational. It is also argued that information processing limitations would have the effect of determining the upper limit of complexity of the thought system which a subject could construct.

The most potent objection likely to be raised to this argument is that there is no such thing as a fixed information processing capacity, and that it is naive to suppose that a child can handle only a fixed number of chunks of information at a given age. It would be contended that memory development is found to be a function of the development of various strategies, such as clustering, coding, rehearsal, mnemonic devices, etc., and that memory capacity is not fixed. There is now a substantial literature concerned with both adult and child short-term memory (see, for instance, Flavell, 1970, 1971b; Norman, 1970, 1976), and it might be suggested that this literature is being ignored.

The answer to this objection is that it is not compelling. The child development literature has shown that memory development is a function of strategy. It has not been shown that it is entirely reducible to strategy. Consider the hypothesis that $R = f(S, C)$ where R is recall, S is strategy, and C is capacity, i.e. recall is a function of strategy and capacity. Capacity is difficult to investigate, whereas a variety of ingenious techniques are available for studying mnemonic strategies. If the equation $R = f(S, C)$ is valid, and if R and S are observable but C is not, then research will inevitably tend towards the conclusion that $R = f(S)$. In such a situation it is not possible to conclude, however, that memory capacity has no effect on recall. Furthermore, Case (1970) has reviewed the memory literature and pointed out that recall is only manipulable within narrow limits, which suggests that mnemonic performance cannot be accounted for solely in terms of strategies. To this it might be objected that the number of binary digits able to be recalled can be varied very widely by learning to recode into octal digits and then decode again (Miller, 1956). While such performances possibly upset the use of digit span as a measure of the number of chunks held in storage, they do not reflect on the concept of capacity *per se*. A person whose recall is increased in this way still has the same number of chunks in storage, and only the chunk size is changed. Thus it is entirely possible that the capacity to store a given number of chunks has remained constant.

Furthermore, it is doubtful whether children ever employ such powerful recording processes in everyday life. The mnemonic devices which have been demonstrated in the literature are of quite a different order.

Simon (1974), in an interesting and creative paper, has offered the speculation that apparent increase in memory with age may be attributed to growth in chunk size, with the number of chunks remaining constant. If true, this idea would put the present argument under strain, or would at least require it to be recast in terms of chunk size. At the present time there is insufficient evidence to determine whether Simon's thesis is likely to be correct, however. In any case, it is important to be clear that the only aspect of the present theory to be affected by theories of memory is the relation between information processing load and memory. The relation between the three levels of systems and information processing is not affected.

Lastly, there is evidence that capacity varies over and above development of strategies. For instance, Friedrich (1974) has shown that, while mnemonic strategies do increase in power with age, older children still have greater recall with strategy held constant. Furthermore, Huttenlocher and Burke (1976) have concluded that growth in memory span with age cannot be explained by strategies, since such strategies appear to be notably lacking in digit span performance. And in the final analysis it is very doubtful whether the extant theories about growth in memory strategies are applicable to the development of new cognitive systems. Recall strategies must be based on some sort of regularity within the material to be recalled. But if the nature of the task is to construct a symbol system which reflects that regularity, then the regularity itself cannot be used to enhance information processing. Thus it is doubtful whether information processing strategies could in fact influence the construction of the kinds of symbol systems which are under discussion here. It seems more likely that the process depends on capacity.

A further objection which might be raised is that memory is an active, dynamic process of coding, storage, and retrieval, not a static storage of items. The answer to this objection is that it is misplaced. Nothing in this chapter implies a static view of memory. All that has been said is that the subject must have a minimum number of chunks of information available in order to match symbols to task or environment elements in a system with a given level of complexity. Nothing has been said about how these chunks are stored; nor has it been said that the number of chunks which can be stored is necessarily constant. Digit span has been accepted as an approximate measure of the number of chunks available to average children under normal conditions. This in no way implies that the number of chunks could not be changed. It might be asked whether it should be possible to accelerate the progress of children through the stages by training their short-term memories so that they can construct systems of greater complexity earlier. There is as yet no information with which to answer this question. It depends on whether human subjects can be trained to increase their powers of recall in such a situation, without some compensating loss. The present literature on memory development gives no clue whatever about this. However, as pointed out above, it should be kept in mind that strategies which work to increase recall where the structure of the task is obvious or already familiar to the subject should not be assumed to work in cases where the structure of the task is what the subject is trying to learn.

SUMMARY AND CONCLUSIONS

It has been proposed that the four main stages of thought development, sensorimotor, preoperational, concrete operational and formal operational, can be characterized by four levels of system, level 0 to level 3. At level 0 there are no symbols, so there is no thought. At level 1 there are symbols which are defined one at a time with respect to elements of the environment ($S-E$ relations) and are also defined with respect to each other in a one-to-one fashion ($S-S$ relations). At level 2 the symbols are defined with respect to each other in pairs ($S \times S \to S$ relations), and pairs of symbols are defined with respect to pairs of environment elements ($S \times S \to E \times E$ relations). At level 3 the symbols are defined with respect to each other in triples ($S \times S \times S \to S$), and sets of the symbols can be defined with respect to sets of three environment elements ($S \times S \times S \to E \times E \times E$).

If a system in thought consists of symbols defined in sets of N, then the subject must have available $2N$ chunks of information in order to define the elements of that system with respect to environment elements. On the best information available so far, it appears that on average children have 2 chunks of information in immediate memory at the age of two, 4 at the age of five, and 6 at the age of eleven. Thus average children should be able to construct level 1 systems of symbols between the ages of two and five years, level 2 systems between the ages of five and eleven years, and level 3 systems after the age of eleven years.

The hypothetical thought systems have been illustrated with respect to a research paradigm. This makes it possible to study the learning of such systems. One of the major problems in this area has been the difficulty of developing learning paradigms which incorporate the kinds of processes which Piaget postulates. The present approach has been based on the belief that the way out of this difficulty was both to redefine Piaget's stages and to develop new learning paradigms.

Hopefully this might help to shed some light on the question of whether Piaget's stages really do exist by helping to understand why they exist. Much of the scepticism about the stage concept in cognitive development (e.g. Flavell, 1972; Kessen, 1962; Van den Daele, 1974) appears to be based on failure to find or understand any reason why stages should exist. If they exist in anything but a purely descriptive sense, it is presumably because learning is incapable of progressing beyond a particular level until the child reaches a certain age. Thus there must be clear limits to what a child can learn at a particular time, independent of the amount of training or experience given. The concept of limits to learning, once all but unthinkable, is slowly gaining acceptance (Hinde and Stevenson-Hinde, 1973). The problem, of course, is to define the nature of the limitation on learning which keeps a child locked within a particular stage, despite efforts to teach him the performance of the next stage. which is what the neo-Piagetian training studies have mostly failed to do (Beilin, 1971a; Halford, 1970a; Strauss, 1972). If the findings from the experiments reported in this chapter are confirmed by subsequent research, at least in broad terms, then it will appear to be quite likely that stages exist because there are limits to the complexity of the systems of symbols which a child can construct at any given age. These limitations might be describable in terms of the very simple principle enunciated above.

7

OPERATIONAL THINKING IN ELEMENTARY MATHEMATICS

K. F. Collis

For the school-age child (seven to seventeen years) Piaget's original theory notes only two main stages with ill-defined boundaries and a plethora of somewhat ambiguous criteria. This chapter is concerned with proposals, supported by some exploratory studies using elementary mathematical material, which aim to make up some of the deficiencies in the original Genevan work, especially with respect to the differences to be expected between concrete and formal operations. Although the discussion will be centred around mathematical items, it should be emphasized that the phenomena described are equally available in other subject matter areas (see Jurd, Chapters 9 and 10).

CONCRETE OPERATIONS

Concrete operational structures have been dealt with earlier in this book (Halford and Sheppard), but because of their importance for the ensuing discussion it is appropriate to recapitulate at this point. Let us look at certain important aspects of the notion of number and of the ability to classify according to given criteria.

It is clear that when Piaget writes on the concept of number he is not concerned with purely computational skills, rote counting, or the ability to give correct responses to tables of learned number facts. It is quite apparent that a child can memorize both the sequence of number names associated with counting and the elementary addition and subtraction facts without comprehending the basic concepts underlying them. For Piaget it is the mastery of these basic ideas which constitutes an understanding of number. Among these ideas are one-to-one correspondence and conservation. Piaget (1952) demonstrates that it is not until the child has reached the concrete operational level of reasoning that he can consistently construct two sets equivalent in number and conserve this equivalence despite changes in appearance. These would appear to be the essential minimum prerequisite abilities assumed for any type of learning experience which sets out to teach elementary mathematics at the concrete operational level.

Moreover, these abilities are basic to, and necessarily precede, the sequence of items which will be used to specify concrete operational thinking in this chapter. The ability to determine that $5 + 4 = 3 + 6$ by regarding the expressions as representing rearrangements of the same set of elements is fundamental to the ideas of closure and uniqueness which are described later as touchstones for concrete operational thinking.

An additional criterion for concrete operational thinking is the ability to make classifications. Piaget (e.g. 1952) demonstrates that a characteristic of concrete operational reasoning is the ability to reason correctly about elements of a given set on the basis of two attributes at once. This implies the ability to classify by two criteria simultaneously (logical multiplication). Further, the child understands the idea of a set with one attribute *or* another (logical addition), and is certain that the inclusive set is larger than either subset. These abilities, however, still leave the concrete operational level child with a limited strategy for dealing with the classification of sets of elements. The essential features of this aspect of concrete operational reasoning have been well set out by Halford (1968) and need not be repeated here.

In summary, then, it appears that the concrete operational child can handle a logical operation, as long as it is applied directly to a particular experience. Each application of the operation, taken alone, is quite sound, it is only when a number of such applications is examined that anomalies occur. *This stage, then, is one in which an operation can be applied to a direct reflection of experience, but in which operations cannot be related to one another nor can they constitute a system independently of direct experience* (Halford, 1968).

FORMAL OPERATIONS

Formal operational structures enable the adolescent to reason in terms of hypotheses. He is no longer confined in his thinking to physical reality but can see beyond this to possibility. He is able to develop theoretical systems and does not deal with an immediate problem in isolation from possible concomitant factors. Piaget developed an elaborate logical model to underpin these cognitive skills shown to be possessed by intelligent adolescents. Piaget's model has been criticized *in toto* on both psychological and logical grounds (Bruner, 1959; Parsons, 1960) and in part by Lunzer (1965), who doubted that it was legitimate to explain the phenomena by forcing the integration of the four group (*INRC* group) and the propositional calculus (sixteen binary propositions). At that time Lunzer felt that if one wished to have a characteristic common to all formal level functioning then it could best be seen as an elaboration of second-order relations, relations between relations. Concrete operations would be seen as at the level of first-order relations, relations between objects.

More recently Lunzer (1973) has been able to explicate his conception of formal reasoning more succinctly by taking the writer's formulation (Collis,

1972) of acceptance of lack of closure (ALC) and linking it to an ability to handle multiple interacting systems (MIS). It is in terms of these two concepts that it is probably most convenient to show the fundamental differences between the two levels of reasoning. Let us begin by considering what is meant by ALC and MIS.

ACCEPTANCE OF LACK OF CLOSURE (ALC)

In the context of this chapter the level of *closure* at which the child is able to work with arithmetical operations depends on his ability to regard the outcome of an operation (or series of operations) as unique and 'real'. At its lowest level this requires that two elements connected by the operation be *actually replaced* by a third element which is recognized as belonging to the same set. In terms of numbers this means that, at this level, the four operations of elementary arithmetic *can* be meaningful when used singly with small numbers within the child's experience. However, both the numbers and operations must be relatable, by the child, to the physical world with which he is familiar. He would be able to decide that $4 + 2 = 6$ and would consider the statement meaningful.

The next level involves the child in the ability to regard the outcome of performing an operation as necessarily unique without needing to make the actual replacement to guarantee this. The child may now use numbers beyond his empirically verified range (e.g. $374 + 463$). He may also use expressions involving (say) two operations which can be closed sequentially $(3 + 4 + 5)$. Later this ability to refrain from actual closure, so long as there is a guarantee that a unique familiar result is available at any time required, becomes general. The young adolescent has now moved on to what the writer has termed elsewhere the stage of *concrete generalization* (Collis, 1969). Now he is capable of working with formulae such as $V = L \times B \times H$, provided he is able to consider that each letter stands for a unique number and each binary operation involved may be closed at any stage.

The final stage of development so far as this concept is concerned enables the adolescent to consider closure in a formal sense because he is able to work on the operations themselves and does not need to relate either the elements or the operations to a physical reality. At this point he is capable of dealing with variables as such because he can hold back from drawing a final conclusion until he has considered various possibilities. This is an essential strategy for obtaining a relationship as distinct from obtaining a unique result. For example, if he is given a formula $V = L \times B \times H$, he would not only be able to obtain unique results by appropriate substitutions in the formula but would be able to discuss meaningfully the effect of various transformations on the formula. For example, what would one predict for 'V' if one increased 'L', decreased 'B', and held 'H' constant?

The development of ALC described above may be related to what Halford (1970a) pointed out when describing the acquisition of concrete operations.

Halford says that to acquire concrete operations children need to combine judgments (whether they be numbers or other units is of no consequence) two at a time and select those combinations which give unique results. In other words, they reorganize their judgments until they achieve closure on a unique result. To attain the level of formal operations the child must also be able to combine two units, but one of these units may itself be an operation. At the concrete operational level two numbers may be combined to give a unique result, e.g. $3 + 2 = 5$, whereas at the formal operational level the adolescent can work with a combination such as $(p \circ r) \circ q = c$, where $\circ$, p, r, q, and c are suitably defined. In this last case an operation $(p \circ r)$ is itself combined with another $(\circ q)$ to yield a unique result, the important point being that an operation is applied to something which is itself an operation. This implies that the initial operation must have meaning as a unit even though the individual cannot 'close' it arithmetically.

At this juncture the problem a child has in solving a simple equation such as $x + 3 = 8$ can serve two important purposes. First, it may help to clarify the notion of closure or uniqueness of the result of an operation, and, second, it can provide a vehicle for demonstrating a link between the level of closure available to the child and his notion of an inverse operation.

In terms of what has been said so far there would appear to be at least three levels at which children may be able to operate to find the value of x in the given equation. At the lowest level the problem is regarded as merely a counting task; to find x one counts on from 3 until 8 is reached and then records the number of units used. This can be done by reciting known addition tables, e.g. $1 + 3 = 4$, $2 + 3 = 5$; by the use of structured material; or by simply using the counting sequence. The operation sign is only required as a stimulus to set the child responding in terms of one of these procedures. It does not imply any understanding of the mathematical implications of the operation of addition. The reader will recognize that many children are quite capable of operating competently at this level in the infant-school classes.

At the second level the child regards both sides of the equation as representing a unique number and considers the 8 as the specific and only possible representation for the right-hand side of the equation. However, he also 'closes' $x + 3$. In other words, he now pays attention to the operation as indicating something performed on the two elements but must regard the outcome as unique. For this child, x is a unique number, like 8, but for the time being unknown; if one does the operation of 'plussing' 3 one still has a unique number even though one does not know what it is. This is an example of operational thought being tied to a specific empirical ikon (whether present or not) at the concrete operational stage. The child's work to this point has been closely linked to empirical experiences with objects; addition, for example, may be understood in terms of uniting sets of objects.

By this stage, too, the child is familiar with 'undoing' (or inverse) operations. From an early age he is familiar with this notion in the physical world. He knows, for example, that if one wraps up a piece of chalk one cannot see the chalk but the chalk can be made to reappear by unwrapping. In the same way subtracting can be seen as undoing adding. If he has made a union of two disjoint sets of blocks he can get back to his original state by 'taking away' one of the subsets. This notion of subtraction seems to be at a similar level to that of addition described in the last paragraph.

Given the points mentioned so far, the second-level child's problem in solving the equation $x + 3 = 8$ reduces to: x is an unknown but unique number and so is $x + 3$; the latter has been obtained by 'plussing' 3 to x and thus x can be found by subtracting 3 from $x + 3$, which *happens* to be equal to 8; thus, $x = 5$.

By the final stage the adolescent focuses on the operation and does not need to regard either side of the equation as unique and necessarily empirically constant. For him 8 could be replaced by any one of a number of expressions (e.g. $3 + 5$, $5 + 3$, $9 - 1$, etc.) and x could be variable or constant. The problem for him is to find the operation which will operate on the operation given so as to negate it. In the present case subtraction is the negating operation and it is convenient to use the subtraction of 3 in order to isolate x; likewise, he can work on the 8, replacing it by $5 + 3$ for convenience.

His reasoning in this stage might be recorded as follows:

$$x + 3 \quad = 8$$
$$x + 3 - 3 \quad = 8 - 3 \qquad \text{(negating the } + \text{ operation, choosing a convenient number and maintaining the relationships)}$$
$$x + (3 - 3) = 5 + (3 - 3) \quad \text{(replacing 8 by convenient expression and reassociating)}$$
$$x + 0 \quad = 5 + 0 \qquad \text{(inverse axiom)}$$
$$x \quad = 5 \qquad \text{(identity axiom)}$$

The difference between the negating mechanisms used by the concrete operational children and the formal operational adolescents is of major concern, as it highlights the difference between the two levels of reasoning. Figure 7.1 may help to illustrate the points to be made. The operation used on a, $+ b$ (say), giving $a + b$, can be negated by the use of either the inverse or the reciprocal. An operation applied to $(a + b)$, $+ c$ (say), giving $(a + b) + c$, can only be negated by the use of the reciprocal. Children at the first two levels described above appear to have only the inverse available and thus cannot manage an operation on an operation; the third level subjects, on the other hand, have both inverse and reciprocal available. If this model is looked at

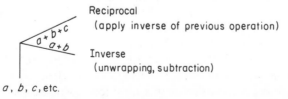

Reciprocal
(apply inverse of previous operation)

Inverse
(unwrapping, subtraction)

a, b, c, etc.

FIGURE 7.1

in terms of dimensions, the elements to be operated upon are one-dimensional; the introduction of an operation makes for two dimensions, while the introduction of an operation on an operation represents a third dimension. This implies an hierarchical order of some significance in the learning of mathematical operations.

It should be noted that this interpretation does not cut across Piaget's (Beth and Piaget, 1966; Inhelder and Piaget, 1958), but in fact supplements it. Piaget clearly distinguishes between the two concepts of inverse and reciprocal strategies and indicates that they may vary in form at various levels of behaviour and, implicitly, in various contexts. Essentially *negation* annuls the operation directly and the *reciprocal strategy* leaves the operation untouched while neutralizing its effect. In the beam balance experiment, for example, adding a weight to the left-hand pan is *negated* by removing it, but the same effect can be obtained by adding the same weight to the right-hand pan—a reciprocal strategy. Piaget also makes the point that, at the formal operational level, the adolescent has both strategies available.

In mathematical material there are many occasions in even elementary formal mathematics where the reciprocal strategy is essential rather than optional. Any attempt to use negation in such cases gives rise to serious errors.

From the theoretical orientation outlined so far two interesting deductions can be tested empirically. First, adolescents at the formal stage, because they have the reciprocal strategy available, would be able to cope with either two- or three-dimensional problems as defined above; concrete operational children, having available only the inverse operation, would be able to deal effectively only with problems which they are able to consider as two-dimensional (if necessary, reducing the number of elements to two upon which to use their typical *modus operandi*). Second, it seems reasonable to propose, in view of the apparent relationship of this work to cognitive structure theory, that the abilities involved form a hierarchy; specifically, individuals should be able to cope with two-dimensional problems before being able to move on to three-dimensional problems.

So far the development of higher levels of reasoning has been seen as closely related to the child's tolerance for unclosed operations. The closer to early concrete reasoning, the more the child depends on an immediate closure of the operation in order to make the situation meaningful to him. This phenomenon can be isolated in all the diversity of tests used by the various researchers who have worked in the area of concrete operations. For instance, concrete responses of Peel's (1967a) subjects, who select a particular aspect of a story for their explanation to the neglect of contributing factors clearly stated, may be seen as an example of 'premature closure'. However, the nearer one approaches the top level of adolescent thinking, the more it becomes apparent that the subject can withold closing while he considers the possible effect of the various variables in the problem. Peel's (1967a) evidence supports this also, and the phenomenon leads directly to a consideration of the concept of multiple interacting systems which was mentioned earlier.

MULTIPLE INTERACTING SYSTEMS (MIS)

Although ALC has a critical part to play in any consideration of the development of reasoning from the viewpoint being expressed in this chapter, it is clearly not the whole story. It is suggested that ALC has an enabling function to perform. But, more specifically, the level of tolerance of lack of closure in the individual largely determines the complexity of the system within which he can work meaningfully.

Lunzer (1973) distinguishes between simple and complex systems—the first available to concrete operational reasoners and the second to formal operational reasoners. With simple systems any solutions generated can be effected by assimilation to one set of covariants. Complex systems require more than one system of covariation, and any successful solution of a set problem depends upon working with the interaction of two (or more) systems.

The relevance of this concept to the many varieties of tasks used to distinguish formal reasoning, including those of Piaget and of Peel, is well brought out by Lunzer in his 1973 paper and does not need repeating here. It may be of value to take an illustration from school mathematics. Consider the formula for the area of a rectangle, $A = L \times B$.

It is suggested here, supported both by experimental evidence and classroom experience, that the child in the later concrete operational stage can work effectively with formulae of this kind at a particular level. He is able to recognize that, given *any rectangle* with specific units which measure L and B, he is able to find A. There is obviously a large number of possible rectangles and consequent A's. The idea is meaningful for him because it involves merely a single system of covariation: the area changes as the rectangle changes, $L \times B$ changes as the rectangle changes. What the child at this level cannot do is relate changes in one or more of the variables A, L, and B to changes in one (or more) of the others. He would not be able to solve problems of the following kind: if A is to stay constant and B is to be changed in some way (doubling, taking a fraction of the original, etc.), what must be done to length L? This type of problem involves the child in working with the interaction between two systems—B is varied and L must be varied in a compensatory way to keep the product, $L \times B$, constant.

The relevance of MIS to the idea of negation is readily seen also. The description of the difference between the 'inverse' and the 'reciprocal' as negating mechanisms may be seen as related to MIS. In brief, the use of the *inverse* can be seen as analogous to a simple system: it operates immediately and directly upon the latest operation performed without necessarily considering the effect on any other operation which may be interacting with it. Likewise, the *reciprocal* procedure may be said to involve a complex system: it takes into account interactions between the various variables involved. The reciprocal does not need to be applied directly to the last operation performed but may be applied to another part of the system (even other interacting variables) and may well involve compensatory action. This application of MIS is clear in the equation-solving illustration above, but is perhaps even more familiar in classical Piagetian experiments such as the beam balance experiment.

SOME EXPLORATORY STUDIES

The characteristics of the different levels of reasoning described thus far are best illustrated by reference to exploratory studies carried out by the writer over the last few years. The investigations have involved cross-sectional testing of groups of over thirty children at one-year age intervals beginning at the age of seven years and proceeding through to seventeen years. Throughout this age range two types of test were used. The first was concerned with the ability to handle (both singly and in combination) different kinds of *operation* on various types of *element* and the second with the ability to work with a *defined system*.

Preliminary experiments were exploratory and took in both types of test in order to obtain some basic data which could be used for the design of more specific probes at a later date. Test batteries were designed which attempted to explore in the two areas, elements × operations *per se* and elementary abstract mathematical systems.

The first study

To make a start in the first-named area it was decided to vary both elements and operations along a degree of abstraction dimension. In terms of the constructs set up in this chapter, this meant varying both the level of closure tolerance necessary and the level of inverse required to solve the problems.

Three group tests were devised. The items in these tests (see Table 7.1) were devised in such a way that (a) they were directly related to the kinds of mathematical stimulus with which the children would be familiar from the classroom and (b) they could be logically related to Piagetian concepts. Tests 1, 2, and 3 contained parallel items, the operations across tests were kept constant, while the elements related by the operations were varied by being made more abstract. Within the tests variation was obtained by using contrasting examples which changed the operation in the direction of greater complexity.

As the structure of the items is crucial to the whole experiment it is appropriate to examine their basis in more detail. Table 7.2 indicates the dimensions upon which the items varied.

TABLE 7.1. Item types in tests 1, 2, and 3

Instruction In each item replace Δ by a numeral (or pronumeral) which will make the statement true.

Item no.	Test 1	Test 2	Test 3
4	$8 \times 3 = 3 \times \Delta$	$1279 \times 783 = 783 \times \Delta$	$a \times b = b \times \Delta$
5	$12 \div 3 = \Delta \div 12$	$1232 \div 12 = \Delta \div 6$	$a \div b = \Delta \div a$

TABLE 7.2. Analysis of item types by dimension and level

		Operational structure dimension	
		Concrete level	Formal level
Element dimension	Concrete level	$8 \times 3 \quad = 3 \times \Delta$ $8 + 4 - 4 = \Delta$ (a)	$7 - 4 = \Delta - 7$ $4 + 3 = (4 + 2) + (3 - \Delta)$ (b)
	Formal level	$a \times b \quad\quad = b \times \Delta$ $4283 + 517 - 517 = \Delta$ (c)	$576 + 495 = (576 + 382) + (495 - \Delta)$ $a \div b \quad = 2a \div \Delta$ (d)

Items in cell (a) required, in most cases, only one operation for solution, the numeral which represented the solution to the question was nearly always on view in the statement, each operation was readily closed, and the numbers were small enough to leave no doubt as to the uniqueness of the result. When items in this category required an operation followed by an inverse for solution, the inverse was a simple negation which merely neutralized an operation by 'undoing' it.

Items in cell (b) raised the level of difficulty by requiring more than one operation for solution, necessitating the individual going beyond the numerals given and, in general, involving him in the ability to reverse by discriminating between two operations and weighing up their effects one against the other.

Items in cell (c) were parallel in structure to those in cell (a) but were made more difficult for the subjects by raising the level of abstraction of the elements in the question. The items in this cell were designed so that the binary operations involved would be difficult to close (in the case of test 3 impossible), and thus the students were forced to work with the operations themselves. For instance, in cell (a) an item might involve the expression, $15 \div 3$, and this can be readily replaced by 5 for further manipulation, while in cell (c) the item would involve $987 \div 47$ (in test 2) and $a \div b$ (in test 3).

Items in cell (d) were parallel to those in cell (b) in structure and to cell (c) in type of element.

Thus far two different classifications for the items have been indicated, namely the division into three tests and the categorization of items in terms of the dimensions 'operational structure × element type'. A third division was made of the test items within cells (c) and (d)—those using large numbers and those using letters. In the analysis, these divisions are indicated by use of the following nomenclature:

Test 1A:	test 1	items in cell (a)
Test 1B:	test 1	items in cell (b)
Test $2C_1$:	test 2	items in cell (c) with large numbers
Test $2D_1$:	test 2	items in cell (d) with large numbers

Test $3C_2$:   test 3   items in cell (c) with letters
Test $3D_2$:   test 3   items in cell (d) with letters

As the experimental details, including the statistical analyses, are set out elsewhere for both a preliminary study (Collis, 1971) and a more extensive follow-up (Collis, 1975), it is not proposed to repeat them here. Instead, an attempt will be made at this point to summarize the findings from the second study with a view to explicating the earlier theoretical framework.

An analysis of variance (ages × test, repeated measures) carried out on the data showed highly significant differences between ages, tests, and the interaction (ages × tests), the last result being a clear indication that there were genuine differences in the slopes of the growth curves for the different tests (Winer, 1962). As the interest in this experiment lies in the developmental trends revealed it is useful to examine a graph of the mean scores by ages. These are displayed in Figure 7.2.

Some interesting features of the developmental trends are revealed by this graph. The ages at which a significant proportion (0.70) of the children appear to achieve mastery of the item types catch the eye. Cell (a) type items appear to be well within the capability of 8 + year olds, while cell (b) type items are not handled well until 14 + years. Cell (c) items are apparently achieved earlier than those in cell (b) at about 11 + years. The most difficult of all items are those in cell (d), which are not well done until 16 + years. Perhaps the most striking feature of the results on these tests is the difference in the general shape of the curves. While tests 1A, 2C, and $3C_2$ tend to be convex towards the top of the page, the remaining tests tend to be concave towards the bottom of the page. This seems to point to an earlier development of the variables measured by the former tests and thus suggests support for an order of development different from what is normally implied by school curriculum and teaching methods. Classroom programmes imply that development appears in the order (a), (b), (c), (d), whereas these results show the order as (a), (c), (b), (d).

Test 1B is probably the critical test. It represents the items in cell (b) which were designed to have difficult operational structure together with simple elements—in this case small numbers. The graph shows that 1B items are much more poorly done in general than the items in tests 1A, $2C_1$, and $3C_2$, the latter two of which contain much more difficult elements than does test 1B. It is not until we reach the fourteen-year-old group of subjects that an average of 64 per cent. on test 1B items is achieved; the same average percentage is achieved by subjects on test $3C_2$ items by the ten-year-old group. This occurs in spite of the fact that test $3C_2$ contains what may be termed algebraic items, while test 1B contains only items of elementary arithmetic!

Average performance on all test items with low-level operational structure is better than that on items where the operational level is raised. However, the abstractness of the elements has some effect because both tests $2D_1$ and $3D_2$ seem to present much more difficulty than test 1B. For instance, thirteen to

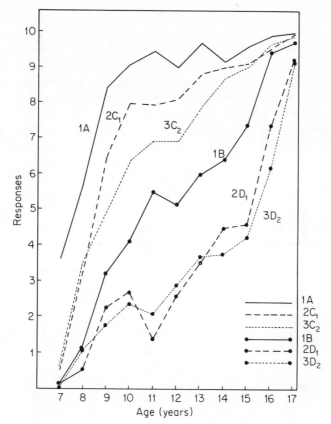

FIGURE 7.2 Average score by ages, tests 1A, 1B, $2C_1$, $2D_1$, $3C_2$, $3D_2$

fourteen year olds average over 60 per cent. on test 1B items, but it is not until the sixteen year-old groups that the subjects average as high on test $2D_1$ and $3D_2$ items. A reasonable deduction from this would be that the interaction between abstract elements and higher-level operational structure is an important determinant of the difficulty level of mathematical items.

The evidence presented so far seems to set aside objections which may be raised regarding the effects of school learning on the results. Two specific examples should suffice. First, consider the use of algebra. Test $3C_2$ consists of the kinds of items which would generally be considered as algebra, and neither the ten year olds nor the eleven year olds in this sample had experience in this area of mathematics. It can be seen from the data that the ten year olds obtain an average of 64 per cent. and eleven year olds 69 per cent. on these items. Both of these results are too high to be set down to chance where the subjects have to supply the answer. There is, of course, the rise in results after the children would have begun algebra at school (12 +) but, even if this increase was attributed to school experiences, it would not explain the earlier success. Second, the results on test 1B cannot be overlooked. The children had been dealing with exercises of this type from their early primary-school days and yet even at the age of thirteen years the average percentage result is only 60. It seems reasonable to assume that, although the investigator had not eliminated school learning from the items, the items were apparently tapping cognitive processes which transcended school experiences.

The application of appropriate t testing following the analysis of variance, mentioned above, shows that for tests with the elementary operational structure ($2C_1$ and $3C_2$) the use of more abstract elements does make a difference to achievement over the considerable age range from nine to thirteen years. Prior to the age of nine years the low scores obtained using either set of elements would prevent a difference showing up. In the case of the tests with the more difficult operational structure ($2D_1$ and $3D_2$) a similar pattern is discernible. In this latter case, achievement is quite low until the sixteen-year-old group, and thus any differences that the kind of element is making tends to be masked by the general low scoring. However, when the sixteen year olds begin to succeed, there is a significant difference between their achievement on the two types of element.

Thus it seems that before the operation problem has been overcome there is no difference between success on the items using differing elements. After the children begin to achieve items of a given operational difficulty, usually using small closable expressions, then the degree of abstractness of the elements begins to make a difference. For example, as soon as test 1A begins to be achieved well at the age of nine years, the difference between scores on test $2C_1$ and $3C_2$ is at a maximum. From that point on the differences begin to decrease. A similar pattern appears in the tests which raise the operational difficulty level. At the age sixteen years when average scores on test 1B have reached a high point, one can see the maximum difference occurring between the scores on tests $2D_1$ and $3D_2$.

To conclude this section, let us consider briefly some of the more important issues which are implicit in the data.

The logical analysis of the items in the tests gives some grounds for concluding that the tests were probing some cognitive phenomena which appear to develop consistently over the age range from seven to seventeen years. If this is the case, three aspects warrant some discussion, namely the nature of the phenomena, the timing of the achievement of the various levels of complexity, and the order of achievement.

The first aspect has been discussed earlier and relates to a child's developing ability to disentangle his thinking from the 'immediate' and 'real'. This has two sides which may, in the light of the study reported, appear to be closely related. On the one side, there is the necessity to have the elements with which the child works as 'real' things at the early stages followed by a gradual development of an ability to use abstractions as elements, these elements becoming more and more remote from the 'real' world; on the other, there is the notion of operations with these elements. The operation aspect begins with actual physical manipulation of objects and then develops through single operations, less physical but closely tied to the 'real' world, to a stage where operations are able to be applied to operations. In the investigation outlined above, items were set which ranged over the continuum. The level of element abstractness was seen as directly related to the child's ability to regard the result of an indicated operation as unique, e.g. even the youngest children in the study would so regard (say) $4 + 3$. However, when the elements appeared as (say) $576 + 495$ or $a + b$ there was little likelihood of the youngest children regarding these as certainly giving a unique result, as they were outside their empirically verifiable experience. Older children, however, would regard the result of the latter as likely to be unique because of their wider experience with numbers and because they would be further away from relying on direct empirical feedback from the environment to certify results. The structure of the mathematical operations on the elements was seen as reflecting the structure of cognitive operations necessary to solve the problem in each case. For instance, in an item such as $7 - 4 = \Delta - 7$, find Δ. To solve the problem, the subject needs to find a number such that, with 7 subtracted from it, the result is 3. His cognition here is required to maintain the 3 difference, obtained by subtraction, and perform a reversal, i.e. where subtraction has been used and is again suggested, he has to decide to add. The simpler operation structure is marked by an absence of *necessary* reversals and compensations—*necessary* because even the adolescents who were capable of operating at the highest cognitive level could have used the less sophisticated procedures and strategies if they so wished in a number of items which the youngest children were able to handle correctly.

In other words, the 'uniqueness' notion is not bound down to the nature of the elements only. When the operational level becomes more complex, where (say) two operations become involved, then the child might well be led to believe that this fact *per se* is relevant to achieving a unique result. Likewise, the structure of operations seems not to be bound entirely to the operation variable but interact with the element dimension.

Deductions concerning the ages at which the children attain the various levels of complexity on both dimensions, elements and operations, is bound up with the order in which these levels were attained and so will be discussed together. The simplest items were achieved well by the nine-year-old group. These items contained single operations and small numbers as elements. The next group of items, achieved well some year or two later, are the ones with elementary operational structure but large numbers. Later still, by a year or two, the group of items which contained more abstract elements but a similar operational structure was achieved. Between the ages of ten and fourteen years the achievement of this group of items goes from 60 to 70 per cent. to 80 to 90 per cent. of the age group.

The next set of items, in order of difficulty, was the first group in which the operational structure was raised. Although small numbers were used as elements it was not until the thirteen to fifteen year old group that we find success on these items. The final set of items, in which levels on both dimensions were raised, did not show signs of real achievement until the fifteen to seventeen year-old group.

The order of attainment of the various item types appears quite significant for cognitive developmental theory. It would seem that levels of abstraction of elements are far less important than the introduction of operational variables when consideration is being given to difficulty levels. This may be a function of the item types. It should be pointed out, at this stage, that young children often appear to show the ability to work with quite abstract elements and operations. However, a close investigation of their mode of reasoning usually shows that they are operating at a much lower level of cognition than is applied in their results. For example, if an adolescent has reached the stage of concrete generalization (Collis, 1969) he may appear to be operating at quite a formal level, whereas the same subject often displays his inability to work at a high level when asked to solve a parallel problem in a similar way but with unusual elements or operations. A more specific example can be used involving the solving of equations. Children are often able to give quite acceptable performances in the classroom without being aware of the notion of operating on operations as such. However, when asked to perform an analogous task with unusual operations they find themselves unable to succeed. Various aptitude-type tests (e.g. the Australian Council for Educational Research (ACER) quantitative thinking papers, 1968) seem to rely upon this phenomenon to separate the academic sheep from the academic goats. The study reported here is confined to mathematical items and thus one is unable to generalize with any safety beyond this type of item. However, certain studies (e.g. Jurd, 1970; Peel, 1967a, 1971) raise the same kind of problem in relation to non-mathematical material, and it would appear profitable to raise the question of generalizability across content areas in later investigations.

The evidence in this study for operations being the prime cause of difficulty in items is fairly clear, but must be considered in relation to the elements involved also. The results show that given the constant operational level the abstractness of the elements determines the difficulty. However, the operational difficulties are more readily overcome when the elements are simple. There is clearly an interaction involved and it is most noticeable in the data gathered on children between ten and fifteen years of age. The reasons for the pattern of achievement on the items with simple elements and complex operational structures are not clear from the data, but it appears certain that further investigation in this area could be quite rewarding. This is but one problem raised by this experiment; there are several others.

One of these is the apparent increase in difficulty which arose with cell (b) items when more than one operation was involved. It would seem that an increase in the operational difficulty could be obtained by increasing the number of reversals and compensations which had to be made in the one item. Moreover, the question as to why the increase in number of operations, *per se*, should result in raising the level of difficulty requires some thought. Several explanations come to mind in relation to the earlier theoretical orientation, and it is conceivable that they are interwoven. It is possible that, if at least two operations are involved, the student will have his notion of the uniqueness of an outcome disoriented to some extent. Where he might be prepared to grant a unique outcome to (say) 576 + 495 he may not be so willing to grant that the outcome to, say, (576 + 495) + 382 will necessarily be unique. If he regards the first operation, 576 + 495, as unique (but unknown) he is next presented with the problem of 'does unique (but unknown) added to 382 come to an unequivocal unique result?'. Also, even in the case of the use of smaller numbers a child must have the ability to retain what has been done in the short-term memory and relate it to another operation. Why should he be convinced, for example, that, in an expression such as $(4 + 3) + 2$, the replacement of $(4 + 3)$ by 7 should make no difference to the result. Is 7 really an adequate replacement for $(4 + 3)$ when it is to be operated upon again, i.e. by $+ 2$?

Alternatively, the necessary closure of $4 + 3$ to 7 may be retained as a whole in the available cognitive processing space (i.e. the 7 is not the only element retained after the initial closure). Thus more of the available processing space is being occupied than one would expect and a breakdown occurs because, in trying to process the $+ 2$, the capacity of the processing apparatus is exceeded.

The second study

The second area investigated was that concerned with elementary abstract mathematical systems.

Lunzer (1968) argues that the idea of the development from concrete to formal thinking, explicitly set up in Piaget's model of cognitive development, is analogous to the scientist's view of the transition from the notion of a systematic arrangement of reality to that of a closed system which is explained in terms of quite precise laws. It is in his search for a precise law that the formal operational subject displays the ability to handle the techniques generally associated with this level of thinking. The writer suggests that one may regard the ability to work within an arbitrarily defined mathematical system as analogous to being able to regard reality as a closed system governed by precise laws. From this point of view it seems reasonable to deduce that if a simple mathematical system is presented to children and they are asked to make certain deductions within it only formal operational reasoners will be able to cope.

Three tests, modelled on one of the tests used in the earlier study (Collis, 1971, test 9), were devised. Each test set up the same mathematical system by defining an operation, *, and indicating that the elements to be operated on were zero and the positive integers (0, 1, 2, ...). The children were asked to make deductions about the truth or falsity of five statements. The definition of the operation in each case was as follows: * is an operation such that $a * b = a + 2 \times b$. The five statements, set out in Table 7.3, were parallel items. From test to test they involved the same operations in the same order—the only

TABLE 7.3. Test items: elementary mathematical systems

Item	Test 1	Test 2	Test 3
1	$a * b = b * a$	$4 * 6 = 6 * 4$	$4728 * 8976 = 8976 * 4728$
2	$a * (b * c)$ $= (a * b) * c$	$5 * (4 * 6)$ $= (5 * 4) * 6$	$982 * (475 * 638)$ $= (982 * 475) * 638$
3	$a * x = a$	$4 * 5 = 4$	$4932 * 8742 = 4932$
4	$a * (b + c)$ $= (a * b) * c$	$3 * (4 + 6)$ $= (3 * 4) * 6$	$6836 * (935 + 2397)$ $= (6836 * 935) * 2397$
5	$a + (b * c)$ $= (b * c) + a$	$3 + (4 * 6)$ $= (4 * 6) + 3$	$572 + (865 * 749)$ $= (865 * 749) + 572$

changes were in the level of abstractness of the elements and the method of making responses. In test 1 the children were told to indicate when the statement would be true; in tests 2 and 3 they were asked to make the statement 'true' or 'false'. In all three tests provision was made for a third category of response, namely 'can't tell'.

Because the experimental details are fully reported elsewhere (Collis, 1973) there is no need to prolong this chapter by including them. It should suffice to point out that, on the basis of preliminary work, certain expectations could be listed and to report on the achievement of these expectations. Two of the expectations, set up as hypotheses in the original work, were as follows:

(1) Response to items in all three tests for children below sixteen years would show a tendency to ignore the given system and reason by analogy with a familiar system.

(2) Success on items 1 and 2 in test 1 would be preceded by success in the parallel items in tests 2 and 3.

The responses on the answer sheets revealed that a common approach to the items in test 1 up to about sixteen years of age was to ignore the defined operation and simply substitute the binary operations of elementary arithmetic. Children who did this usually responded to items 1 and 2 as 'true, when * means + or × ', item 3 as 'can't tell', and items 4 and 5 as 'true' or 'true, when * means + or × '. Apart from the correct responses which indicated an ability to work within the system as defined, two other categories of responses could be discerned. One of these was the 'can't tell' category. The other was defined by the group who showed that, although they were aware of the fact that they had to use the defined operation and not translate it into a more familiar operation, they did not have sufficient control of the system to be able to deduce the correct results. Examples of typical responses in this last category are shown in Table 7.4.

Table 7.5 shows the proportion of students in each age group in each of the four categories. The judgment as to which category a subject should be allotted was made on the basis of at least three of his responses to the five items in test 1. It can be seen that the results show strong support for the first expecta-

TABLE 7.4.　Examples of responses included in category (3) of Table 7.5. (Responses are copied from one subject's protocols for test 1 in each case)

Example 1
Item
1　　This will be true when $a = b$
2　　True when a and c are equal
3　　True when $A = 1$ or 0
4　　True when $(b + c) = (a * b)$ and $c = a$
5　　$(b * c) - a = a - (b * c)$

Note　Correct in item 1; an interesting confusion in items 2, 3, and 4; the response to item 5 appears to be an attempt to work it out.

Example 2
Item
1　　When $b * a = a + 2 \times b$
2　　When $a * b = b * c$
3　　When $a = a + 2x$
4　　True if $a + 2b = b + 2c$, that is $a * b = b * c$
5　　True if $a * b = b * c$

Note　Interesting confusion with same idea recurring.

Example 3
Item
1　　$a + 2 \times b = b + 2 \times a$
2　　$a + 2 (b + 2 \times c) = (a + 2 \times b) 2 \times c$
3　　$------------$
4　　$a + 2(b + c) = (a + 2 \times b) \times 2 \times c$
5　　$a + (b + 2 \times x) = (b + 2 \times c) + a$

Note　The student could work thus, but seemed unable or unwilling to draw a conclusion in any example.

tion listed above. By nine years of age a majority of children substituted a familiar system for the one given, and this approach continued up to the fourteen- and fifteen-year-olds. The latter groups made the first attempts to work with the defined system as such. By sixteen years of age there were 42 per cent. attempting to work within the given system, 26 per cent. of them successfully; by seventeen years these percentages had increased to 86 and 63 per cent. respectively.

Further consideration of the results of the sixteen- and seventeen-year-olds shows that, even at these levels, certain items are achieved much more readily than others. Items 1, 3, and 5 seem to be achieved before items 2 and 4 in all three tests. This last result is consistent with the hypothesis that individuals require a high level of abstract reasoning ability to perform operations on operations; items 2 and 4 are the only ones where this ability is tested. Both use different symbols in parentheses and so prevent a 'closure' of the more

TABLE 7.5. Proportion of subjects in response categories by age group

Age	Can't tell	+ or × substitution	Attempt to work with system defined	Worked correctly with system defined
	(1)	(2)	(3)	(4)
17	0·00	0·14	0·23	0·63
16	0·06	0·52	0·16	0·26
15	0·03	0·68	0·29	0·00
14	0·09	0·80	0·11	0·00
13	0·10	0·87	0·03	0·00
12	0·03	0·94	0·00	0·03
11	0·12	0·88	0·00	0·00
10	0·17	0·83	0·00	0·00
9	0·00	1·00	0·00	0·00
8	0·27	0·73	0·00	0·00
7	1·00	0·00	0·00	0·00

advanced type which solves the problem in item 5, where $b * c$ on both sides seems to imply for them that the result of the operation must be constant. In other words, the three items achieved first are ones where there was a need to work with only *one* defined operation; the other two items necessitated working with at least two defined operations.

Evidence on the second expectation was obtained from the protocols by counting the number of subjects who achieved an item on test 1 without first achieving both parallel items in tests 2 and 3. Although the expectation was concerned with items 1 and 2, all items were considered for both the sixteen- and seventeen-year-old group. The result of this count showed that only on two occasions did it occur that a student achieved a particular item in test 1 without first achieving *both* parallel items in the other tests.

Although the expectations, set up on the joint basis of earlier studies and of theoretical considerations, were shown to be justified by the results, certain features of the subjects' strategies and methods of work warrant serious consideration.

A significant feature of the strategy of the sixteen year olds in the study was their use of the general solutions from test 1 items to give correct responses to the parallel items in tests 2 and 3. Even with prompting from the investigator the younger groups in the study persisted in regarding each test as completely independent of its predecessor. Two pieces of evidence are available which would enable a viable hypothesis along these lines to be formulated and tested with less difficult items. First, the results of this study show the extreme difficulty that even the oldest subjects had in working *within* the abstract system in test 1 (50 per cent. of seventeen year olds with 4 or 5 items correct); it would be unlikely that they could relate these items to others in a different test until they had command of the items in the original test. Evidence on this can be seen in the results shown in Table 7.5. These seem to suggest that the only group with a sufficient command of test 1 to be able to apply the principles to tests 2 and 3 would be the seventeen year olds. Second, the investigator had testing assistants available. These were asked to observe and record examples of students referring back to their answers to test 1 while doing tests 2 and 3. The only group reported as having a significant number doing this was the seventeen year olds.

Another aspect requiring closer examination is the effect on the various age groups of the order of presentation of the tests. It is conceivable, on a small amount of evidence from part of the present study, that bright thirteen year olds begin to reconsider their reasoning by analogy with a known system when they recognize some inconsistencies arising in their responses. A revised order of testing (say test 2, test 3, test 1) might well allow children of these ages to use the earlier tests as a training experience which might enable them to achieve significantly better results on test 1.

The third study

Some interesting deductions can be made, and tested, if one links the results of the two studies just described with the introductory theoretical orientation. First of all, only adolescents at the formal operational level of reasoning should be able to cope with problems which involve two operations where the operations cannot be closed to a unique result, thus forcing the subject to work with an idea of reciprocity. Second, a child from about eleven to fourteen years of age who has the notion of inverse as an 'undoing' process should be able to solve problems with more than one operation involved when he is able to feel certain that the result of closing the first operation and using the result with the second gives a result which would be equivalent to the original expression. Third, children in the early concrete operational stage, that is up to about ten years of age, should not be able to work satisfactorily with exercises where more than one operation is involved. This should hold even if it is possible to close the operations in sequence and so reduce the exercise to a series of closures of single operations.

In addition, it seems reasonable to propose that the abilities described above form a hierarchy; children should be able to cope with the form of reasoning, designated above as more advanced concrete operational level, before being able to manage the form of reasoning described as requiring formal level cognitive capacity.

Expressing these notions in empirical terms, eleven- to fourteen-year-old children should be able to work effectively with exercises incorporating ideas such as:

$$\text{Given } (5 + 6) + 4 = (9 + 2) + 4$$
is it true or false to say that $(5 + 6) = (9 + 2)$?

Even the same type of exercise with larger numbers should cause little trouble for this group, e.g.

$$\text{Given } (579 + 685) + 294 = (533 + 535) + 490$$
$$\text{is it true or false to say that } (579 + 685) = (533 + 535)?$$

Another example of an item which should cause this upper-level concrete operational group little trouble would be:

$$\text{Given } (5 + 3) + x = (6 + 2) + x$$
$$\text{is it true or false to say that } (5 + 3) = (6 + 2)?$$

However, only adolescents at the formal level of reasoning could be expected to achieve well on items of the following types:

(1) Given $(a + 7) + 9 = (8 + 9) + 9$
   is it true or false to say that $(a + 7) = (8 + 9)$?
(2) Given $(a + b) + 6 = (c + d) + 7$
   is it true or false to say that $(a + b) = (c + d)$?
(3) Given $(4 \circ 2) \circ 6 = (6 \circ 1) \circ 6$ (where $\circ$ is suitably defined)
   is it true or false to say that $(4 \circ 2) = (6 \circ 1)$?
(4) Given $(x \circ y) \circ c = (p \circ r) \circ d$ (where $\circ$ and the symbols are suitably defined)
   is it true or false to say that $(x \circ y) = (p \circ r)$?

The implications of an hierarchical organization of the concepts involved would seem to indicate, on the basis of both the earlier studies described in this work and of the general theoretical orientation, that one would expect the first group of items to be necessary precursors to the second and, moreover, that within the second group success with the use of familiar operations would precede success with unfamiliar, but defined, operations.

Two group tests were devised. The items in each were designed to test the hypotheses implied above.

Test 1 was made up of six pairs of items in the following form:

$$\text{If } (a + b) + x = (c + d) + y$$
$$\text{is it true or false to say that } (a + b) = (c + d)?$$

Each was an equation consisting of a three-term expression on each side; the operation used to connect the terms was addition in all cases. Variation between the pairs of items was obtained by changing the terms from pair to pair in the direction of greater abstraction as illustrated immediately above. Thus as the child worked through the items he moved from items where closure was possible (and hence solvable with higher-level concrete reasoning) to items where he was forced to work with the operations themselves (i.e. formal reasoning). Within each pair one statement was true and the other false. To score on any one pair the subject had to have both responses correct.

Test 2 consisted of items parallel to those in test 1. The only difference was in the operation to be used: where test 1 used addition, test 2 used a defined operation symbolized by $\circ$ and thus required formal reasoning. Scoring was the same as for test 1.

A total of 330 children (170 boys, 160 girls) from schools in lower middle-class areas was tested. Thirty of average intelligence were taken at each age level and the age range covered was from 7 years to 17 years 11 months. Five hypotheses * were set up:

(1) Children under ten years of age would have little success with any item in either test.
(2) Children from ten to fourteen years would succeed on items 1 to 6 in test 1 but would have little success with any other item in either test.
(3) Adolescents of 15 + years would succeed in all items in both tests.
(4) Subjects would not succeed on items 7 to 12 of either test without first succeeding on items 1 to 6.
(5) Subjects would not succeed on test 2 without first succeeding on test 1.

Each subject had his response to each item recorded. These responses were then tallied to give scores by items to individual students and to make available totals achieved by item for an age group. Because of the nature of the tests and the method of making responses, a simple counting of marks in correct boxes could not be taken as sufficient evidence that the subject was able to handle the concept involved. In each test the items were paired 1 with 2, 3 with 4, ..., 11 with 12, and the child was required to have both items in the pair correct to score on that particular concept.

Table 7.6 summarizes the results on the two tests and sets out the proportion of children achieving the pairs of items in the two tests. The column headed T represents the proportion of the age groups obtaining either all items correct or only one item incorrect—this last allowance was made to take account of those who made one mistake for whatever reason. All students included in the total, however, had correctly responded to at least one of the item pairs where the mistake was made.

The table shows support for the first three hypotheses. Children of nine years and younger perform very poorly.

The expectation that children in the age range from ten to fourteen would succeed on items 1 to 6 of test 1, but not on the remaining items in either test, was well fulfilled if one accepts 0·60 of the age groups as a satisfactory criterion measure for subjects to be able to handle the concept involved. The few exceptions to this statement do not affect the trends shown in the table as a whole. The final hypothesis that adolescents of 15 + years would succeed on all items is borne out both by the body of the table and by the proportions indicated in T column.

It can be seen that, in general, clear-cut breaks appear in the proportions correct in the items between the ages of nine and eleven years and again between the ages of fifteen and sixteen years. Between these breaks and, in fact, both above and below them, there appears a reasonably stable set of proportions rarely significantly different from one another.

* The reader is reminded that, although many of the statements and hypotheses throughout this chapter are made in terms of ages, it should be clear that the basic theme is concerned with an hierarchy of task achievement—the ages are used for convenience of description and to orient the reader to the group of school children concerned.

TABLE 7.6. Proportion of subjects achieving item pairs in tests 1 and 2 by age groups

| | Test 1 | | | | | | Test 2 | | | | | | |
| | Item pairs | | | | | | | Item pairs | | | | | |
age	1 2	3 4	5 6	7 8	9 10	11 12	T	1 2	3 4	5 6	7 8	9 10	11 12
17	1·00	0·97	1·00	0·97	0·97	0·90	0·90	0·87	0·77	0·77	0·87	0·83	0·77
16	0·84	0·84	0·84	0·81	0·71	0·74	0·74	0·77	0·74	0·68	0·81	0·71	0·65
15	0·81	0·67	0·77	0·48	0·55	0·58	0·47	0·58	0·51	0·57	0·54	0·50	0·52
14	0·89	0·66	0·80	0·51	0·57	0·46	0·37	0·61	0·51	0·57	0·54	0·60	0·51
13	0·83	0·70	0·67	0·37	0·47	0·47	0·27	0·33	0·47	0·37	0·47	0·43	0·43
12	0·70	0·53	0·73	0·27	0·40	0·23	0·13	0·47	0·23	0·40	0·23	0·33	0·30
11	0·71	0·71	0·77	0·45	0·55	0·23	0·25	0·55	0·55	0·42	0·58	0·48	0·45
10	0·52	0·42	0·71	0·13	0·29	0·16	0·07	0·32	0·19	0·19	0·29	0·35	0·26
9	0·37	0·30	0·57	0·10	0·30	0·17	0·00	0·20	0·27	0·33	0·23	0·23	0·17
8	0·11	0·11	0·27	0·19	0·08	0·04	0·00	0·35	0·15	0·11	0·19	0·35	0·08
7	0·26	0·13	0·13	0·06	0·06	0·06	0·00	0·19	0·06	0·06	0·06	0·06	0·03

Table 7.7 relates to the last two hypotheses. Column (1) shows the proportions of students succeeding (5 or 6 correct) in items 7 to 12 without at the same time succeeding (5 or 6 correct) with items 1 to 6, the results being listed for both tests. Column (2) gives the proportion of subjects who scored 10 or more on test 2 without scoring at least 5 on items 1 to 6 in test 1. Column (3) takes this one stage further and gives the proportion of children scoring 10 or more on test 2 without scoring 10 or more on test 1. The criteria are quite restrictive but were designed to allow for some accidental mistakes without allowing children to be counted who did not have the concept involved. As the proportions in each of the three tables are of zero order, these results tend to confirm the hypotheses.

It appears that up till about ten years of age children cannot cope well with the use of more than one operation in an expression, even when there should be no difficulty in closing the operations in sequence. After ten years and up to about fourteen years the children seem to be able to work successfully with two operations unless a doubt is raised concerning the possible uniqueness of part or all of the expression. In this study this was done by either the introduction of a non-numerical element or of an unfamiliar operation. Adolescents over fifteen years of age seem to be able to handle all these problems.

Perhaps the most important notion explicated by the results is that concerning 'operating on operations'. The term 'operating on operations' or 'second-order operations' is common enough in the literature describing

TABLE 7.7. Proportion of children achieving formal items before concrete items: tests 1 and 2 by age group

	Column (1)		Column (2)	Column (3)
	Proportion achieving items 7 to 12 before items 1 to 6		Proportion achieving 10 + items in test 2 without achieving at least 5 of items 1 to 6 in test 1	Proportion achieving 10 + items in test 2 without achieving 10 + items in test 1
	(1)		(2)	(3)
Age level	Test 1	Test 2		
17	0·00	0·13	0·00	0·00
16	0·00	0·10	0·03	0·03
15	0·07	0·03	0·03	0·03
14	0·11	0·06	0·14	0·07
13	0·03	0·17	0·03	0·00
12	0·03	0·03	0·03	0·03
11	0·00	0·09	0·09	0·12
10	0·00	0·01	0·00	0·03
9	0·10	0·03	0·07	0·07
8	0·04	0·08	0·00	0·00
7	0·00	0·00	0·00	0·03

Piaget's idea of formal operational level thinking, but it is not always clear exactly what is meant by this term. This study has to some extent defined the term denotatively. In the early part of this chapter it was explained that in a three-term expression with two operations involved, i.e. of the general form $(a*b)*c$, the adolescent must be able to recognize that $(a*b)$ has a meaning and that it can be related to other expressions and operations before he can be said to be reasoning formally. It is suggested that this phenomenon is an example of 'operating on operations'. The age levels at which success is achieved would tend to support this idea.

In addition, it was mentioned earlier that children under ten years would not succeed with items where more than one operation was involved, and this was supported by the results obtained. It was also expected that eleven to fourteen year olds would succeed so long as the elements and operations in the expression were sufficiently reality-bound to guarantee uniqueness of result. It seems significant that the eleven to fourteen year olds did succeed on items where sequential closure was a viable strategy. In other words, in cases where it had to be realized that replacing $2 + 3$ by 5 (say) and combining it with another operation did not affect the value of the expression. It seems that this could be interpreted as early evidence of the development of formal operations and, if this were done, the approximate age level suggested by Piaget for the onset of this level of thinking would correspond to the results in the tables above. However, the writer has tended to regard this level of thinking as concrete operational, albeit of a more advanced kind, because it seems to be still well rooted in empirical reality as far as the concept of ALC is concerned. To say it another way and to use a term introduced earlier, this kind of thinking represents what the writer has called 'concrete generalization' (Collis, 1969). *The child remains convinced of the correctness of his deductions, not in terms of the structure itself remaining consistent at all times, but in terms of, 'it has worked for a number of specific examples and one can always return to an empirical ikon to justify a particular procedure'.*

The hypotheses with respect to the order of achievement of the various types of item were also supported by the results. Three broad categories of levels of thinking are represented in the discussion so far, namely concrete operations proper (to about ten years), concrete generalization (eleven to fourteen years), and formal operations proper. These seem to be achieved in the order named if one judges by the results of the studies described, and thus provides further general support for the Piagetian concept of stages of thinking and the notion of the invariance of the order of the stages.

The general inability of children to handle the items up to the age of nine years appears to be followed by a rapid improvement to the age of eleven years. From eleven to fourteen years there seems to be a time of relative stability followed by another of rapid improvement. From the kinds of thinking presumed to be involved in the items in this last study, as well as in the studies described earlier, it is as if the improvement to eleven years makes the child capable of concrete generalization-type thinking and then he settles on and develops this thinking for the next few years until, by some means, formal thinking becomes available to him. These deductions fit the general pattern of equilibrium as proposed by Piaget and his associates.

THE FOUR STAGES

In summary, it appears reasonable to suggest four levels of cognitive sophistication insofar as mathematical material is concerned at the age levels investigated. In the experiments described in this chapter the levels of cognition were related to specific criteria in terms of mathematical items. These items suggests that the level of cognition is closely bound to the elements involved, the operation(s) to be performed thereon, and the relationship that these two aspects bear to 'reality' as seen by the child.

The four stages which seem to emerge from the studies may be called early concrete operational (seven to nine years), middle concrete operational (ten to twelve years), late concrete operational, or concrete generalization (thirteen to fifteen years), and formal operational (over fifteen years). These stages correspond, in operational terms, to Piaget's stages IIA, IIB, IIIA, and IIIB. The various deductions which Piaget makes from the actions and statements of his subjects at each stage can be seen to parallel the achievement of the subjects in this work at the corresponding stage level. To conclude this chapter let us take each stage separately, sum up what Piaget says of the children's reasoning at that stage, and show how this relates to the ideas which come from the studies described above.

Early concrete operational children (Piaget's stage IIA)

The child at this stage is confined to operations upon immediately observable physical phenomena. The physical elements may change but the mental operation of knowing is related directly to the physical operation involved in making a particular physical change (Inhelder and Piaget, 1958).

In the context of this chapter it can be seen that these notions are implicit throughout the results of this age group. Specifically the studies indicate that:

(1) both elements and operations of ordinary arithmetic, to be meaningful, need to be related directly to physically available elements and operations; e.g.

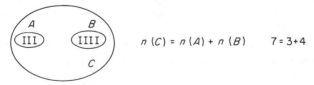

(2) again, to be meaningful to the child, there should be no more than two elements connected by one operation, and the results must be actually

closed (e.g. $3 + 4 = 7$) to avoid the problem of any doubt about the uniqueness of the result;

(3) the only notion of inverse is physical, e.g. what is put down can be taken up as a meaning for subtraction.

Middle concrete operational children (Piaget's stage IIB)

The child at this substage tends to work with qualitative correspondences, e.g. the closer, the bigger; and thus is still reality-bound and not capable of setting up a reliable system based on measurement. He is beginning to feel for a consistency between his qualitative compensations which leads him at times to consider quantitative compensations, but using additive procedures only (Inhelder and Piaget, 1958).

The studies reported here show, with respect to the corresponding level of development, that:

(1) children begin to work with operations as such, but only where uniqueness of result is guaranteed by their experience both with the operations and the elements operated upon. This in practice means two (or more) operations closed in sequence with small numbers or one familiar operation using numbers beyond the range which they might regard as physically verifiable.

(2) the developing notion of the inverse of an operation tends to be qualitative. They seem to regard subtracting as destroying the effect of addition without specifically relating to the operations themselves, e.g. to find the value of y in $y + 4 = 7$, they regard y as a unique number to which 4 has been added—subtracting 4 *happens* to destroy the effect of the original addition and the destroying notion makes the process involved non-reversible.

Late concrete operational children—concrete generalization period (Piaget's stage IIIA)

The child at this substage comes close to formal operations in many instances, but tends to fall short of the complete deduction which would make the full formal operational use of a transformation rule available. This fits in with the writer's argument that children at this level work on the basis of concrete generalizations where a few specific instances satisfy them of the reliability of a rule and where the result of an operation, even though it be on *apparent* variables, must necessarily be considered as unique (Inhelder and Piaget, 1958). In terms of the studies reported here this stage is marked by:

(1) the development of an apparent ability to work with operations and abstractions as such, but even in this stage the uniqueness of the outcome of an operation must be guaranteed in some way, e.g. the child might

very well be able to determine that

$$\frac{382 \times 743}{382}$$

is equivalent to

$$\frac{672 \times 743}{672}$$

but would not necessarily be able to understand and use meaningfully the generalization:

$$\frac{m.a}{m} = \frac{n.a}{n}$$

(2) the inverse process becomes an 'undoing' of an operation previously performed and generally can only be applied with familiar operations, e.g. in solving for y in $y + 4 = 7$, y and $y + 4$ are still regarded as unique, but unknown, numbers, but adding 4 can be 'undone' by subtracting 4—the undoing notion makes the process involved reversible.

Formal operational adolescents (Piaget's stage IIIB)

Adolescents develop transformation rules which completely solve the problem presented to them. Moreover, they come to the problem with a set of abstract hypotheses to test; they need no longer rely completely on reality for their ideas as they can envisage and manipulate abstract variables which may have a bearing on the solution to the problem. No longer are they satisfied that one or two specific demonstrations are a sufficient basis upon which to generalize (Inhelder and Piaget, 1958).

The studies reported here show that, at this stage of development adolescents:

(1) tend to look upon closure or uniqueness as being an abstract condition which makes certain things possible;
(2) regard the inverse process as working directly with the operations themselves in such a way as to balance or compensate without necessarily affecting the existence of the earlier operation, e.g. these students can handle well such items as: if $(p \circ r) \circ q = (a \circ b) \circ q$, then $p \circ r = a \circ b$;
(3) look upon the propositions and conditions themselves as the reality; they do not require that a link be established with the physical world prior to working on a problem where the system is defined.

The analysis of concrete operational and formal operational thinking in the terms outlined in this chapter brings forward for consideration the notion of intervening in the developmental continuum with training procedures designed to raise an individual's current level of cognition. By giving objective evidence for the existence of levels of cognition in terms of the mathematical items used here, one is able to hypothesize the kinds of procedure which are likely to be effective as one can at least see a specific example of higher-level reasoning. An attempt at finding such a procedure is described in the next chapter.

8

IMPLICATIONS OF THE PIAGETIAN MODEL FOR MATHEMATICS TEACHING

K. F. Collis

INTRODUCTION

The experimental work and theory in the previous chapter relates to an analysis of concrete and formal operations and ways of telling the difference between the two. To be able to see the difference is one thing, but a much more difficult task is to find out what experiences cause a child to move along the concrete-to-formal operational continuum. This latter knowledge, valuable in itself for theory-building purposes, has a direct practical application. It would allow intervention in the process of development should this be considered desirable. Moreover, in the light of a general lack of knowledge with respect to specific results of intervention and of the fact that the vast majority of pupils taught mathematics in the schools do not need to operate above the level of concrete generalization, it seems particularly appropriate for this chapter to include a section on presenting mathematics at a concrete level. This section may have the added advantage of clarifying the term 'concrete operational' with mathematical material.

Thus this chapter falls naturally into four sections. The first deals with the theory of how new levels of operational ability are attained; the second describes an experiment which attempts to apply these ideas in a training situation; the third presents a suggested procedure for teaching mathematics up to the late concrete operational stage; and the final section gives an overview which relates the Piagetian stages to children's ability to cope with elementary mathematical material.

ATTAINING NEW LEVELS OF OPERATIONAL ABILITY

A theory

It seems clear that formal operational reasoners can deal with operations as parts of a system, and not simply as reflections of objects, events, and experiences. For instance, it has been pointed out in the previous chapter that children from about seven years can cope with arithmetical operations in which two counting numbers are mapped uniquely into a third. Moreover, it has also been shown that it is not until about ten or eleven years that a significant number of children begin to work meaningfully with more than one operation where sequential closure is a viable strategy. This latter ability may be seen as a precursor to the stage called *concrete generalization* in Chapter 7. This last level may in turn be seen as an immediate forerunner to the ability to handle the transformation rule strategy set out below as the hallmark for formal operational level reasoning.

At this point it seems useful to discuss briefly one of the cognitive mechanisms which possibly enable individuals to attain the various levels of thinking described in the last chapter. Basically the phenomenon is concerned with the strategy used in order to achieve consistent dealings with one's environment. It was described by Bruner, Wallach, and Gallanter (1959) as 'scanning for recurrent regularities'. To relate this discussion more readily to the last chapter, let us consider this mechanism in relation to the key concept of 'closure'.

Much has been made in the previous chapter of the concept of closure, particularly with respect to arithmetical operations. How might this concept be derived from the child's experience? Flavell (1963) gives a summary of Piaget's view of the equilibration process by suggesting that development may be conceived as a succession of structures coming into equilibrium. Using the development of conservation as an example, Flavell draws attention to four major steps which seem to be involved.

Step 1. Child centres on one only of the variables x or y (e.g. length of column or thickness of column).

Step 2. Child alternates between choosing one of the variables x or y (a disjunction) in making a decision.

Step 3. Child *begins* to see x and y in relationship (a conjunction; e.g. as column becomes shorter it gets thicker).

Step 4. Child relates x to y consistently and is said to conserve in the particular field of experience.

Steps 1 and 2 give clear-cut, non-consistent results because each involves centering on one or other aspect of a situation and not relating them one to another. Step 4 gives completely consistent and coordinated results. Step 3, however, is a new type of behaviour—the individual hesitates among responses. It appears to mark a beginning coordination between the two strategies belonging to steps 1 and 2. Halford (1970a) has proposed a theory which gives far more specificity to what is happening in step 3. His proposal is that the acquisition of logical operations, considered basic to conservation of quantity, involves the principle that a child finds recurrent regularities which are consistent and subsequently discards judgments which are inconsistent. Since cognitive structures appropriate to conservation lead to more consistent judgments than do preconserving notions the child's tendency to select a consistent basis for his judgments leads him to conservation. The consistencies are a function of the individual's internal cognitive structure—the individual makes his own cognitions so that they are consistent with one another; the regularities are repeated occurrences which are presented to him.

At the concrete operational and formal operational levels of thinking any combination of judgments which lead to consistency are internalized and are available for application to any new situation which requires a similar performance. A mechanism whereby this could happen has been discussed by Mandler (1962) and considered further by Halford (1970a).

The development of a consistent basis for judgments depends on seeing that certain relationships occur consistently whereas others do not. In conservation, the child needs to discover that additions and subtractions always have a certain result, whereas mere transferrals from one vessel to another have a contrasting, but consistently different, type of result. For instance, transferral from one vessel to another means that if material is returned to the original vessel there will be the same amount as before. If, however, it is transferred to another vessel, and some more material is added, then there will be more when one returns the material to the original vessel. These relationships hold invariably and so represent regularities or consistencies relating to quantities. Halford (1970a) proposes that the child acquires the logical basis of conservation by discovering these regularities. It is suggested here that a similar problem exists with respect to the number operations of elementary arithmetic. The concept of closure (uniqueness) results from the recognition of 'recurrent regularities' which gives invariance, and hence consistency, to cognitions concerned with elementary number operations. This being so, judgments in new situations with similar stimuli are made on the basis of this internalized structure.

With this in mind, let us consider a set of objects in the physical environment. This set will have a number of attributes, among these the cardinal number of the set. The important point for our purpose is that this attribute will be the sole invariant across a large number of experiences with sets. In addition, it becomes clear that any one set has a unique cardinal number associated with it. This achievement could be expected soon after conservation of number. However, the main concern here is with the elementary operations on numbers and thus the need to consider initially the union of two disjoint sets.

Suppose two distinct sets of objects are put together, one set of five elements and the other of two. Is it possible for the result of this union to be characterized in a unique way? Or is the result dependent upon the views of the witnesses, some of whom may judge by simple appearances and others of whom may judge by selecting dimensions which will vary from occasion to occasion? A unique answer can only be obtained by finding a way of characterizing the set so that, for any pair of disjoint sets, their union can be characterized in one and only one way. This can be done if the sets are characterized in terms of their cardinal numbers. By taking any set of five objects and another set of two objects (the sets being mutually disjoint), the union of the two sets will always contain seven objects. The cardinal numbers of the individual sets are obtained by counting. If there is a need to record the numbers in the disjoint sets before union, then $5 + 2 = 7$ would be an appropriate statement in all cases. It is the regularity of this relationship which is its chief justification.

Thus there is a recurrent regularity, a consistent relationship, and this is a direct reflection of experience. However, it is not a copy of experience—the regularity depends on the child making certain constructions. In the case under discussion, he is required to combine sets and characterize them in a certain way. A set of such recurrent regularities may correspond to what we call a 'concrete operation', in this case addition. To sum up symbolically: a set A and a set B, where A and B are mutually disjoint:

$A \rightarrow n(A)$ (any set has a unique cardinal number)
$B \rightarrow n(B)$ (any set has a unique cardinal number)
$A \cup B \rightarrow n(A \cup B) = n(A) + n(B)$ (any set has a unique cardinal number)

The model described above can be generalized to concrete operational reasoning in all four of the operations of elementary arithmetic. Fundamentally, it requires that any pair of numbers can be mapped uniquely into another number and that the regularity thus implied corresponds to experienced reality. Addition has been described; multiplication can be discovered in a similar way, the sets of objects concerned being both disjoint and equivalent; a comparison between the cardinal number of one set and the cardinal number of another results in an excess of one over the other and this corresponds to a unique number (subtraction); a process of continuous subtraction of equivalent sets gives a meaning for division. It can be seen that at this stage the suggested paradigm excludes the possibility of subtraction and division being seen as inverse (or reciprocal) operations.

The achievement of the concepts in the manner described above must be distinguished from the learning of tables, i.e. from the learning of a set of mappings corresponding to a particular operation. It is clear that children may learn and use multiplication tables without having attached meaning to the multiplication operation. A good example of this last phenomenon can be seen in the teaching of the four operations with fractions. Children can learn to perform the motions by learning a sequence of standard procedures. However, they have no alternative to accepting the procedures on the authority of the teacher because they cannot see the mappings which constitute the discoverable regularities. Thus it is said that they do not 'understand' the topic. In terms of the argument presented here it is the recognition of the regularity to which the rule refers that is the prerequisite to understanding that rule or, in the case of mathematics, algorism.

It has been mentioned earlier that a child's recognition of a regularity which transcends various situations depends upon his attending to the relevant dimensions, in the present context, of the cardinal numbers of the sets. The obvious problem is what strategy does he use to discover the regularity? Certainly it is not an hypothesis-testing strategy because the regularity has not been anticipated; it would appear that he is using a scanning procedure since the child has no way of predicting the regularity prior to its discovery. A scanning strategy is implicit in the description given earlier, both of the child's way of discovering that the invariant attribute across sets is the cardinal number and of his realizing the significance of the addition operation in relation to the cardinal numbers associated with uniting disjoint sets. Moreover, it seems clear that once the regularity has been recognized it becomes internalized and thus part of the child's cognitive processing apparatus. It is this internalization of the detected regularity which makes for 'operational' as opposed to 'intuitive' behaviour. If the child merely notices that event x goes with event y then his level of functioning may be regarded as intuitive. To utilize the ideas of Halford (1970a) on the acquisition of conservation, one may say that the preconserving, intuitive child recognizes that if liquid is poured into a vessel, taller and narrower than the original vessel, it will rise higher than in the original vessel. However, when asked to pour liquid into the narrower vessel so as to have the same amount in both, he fills the narrower one to the same level as the wider one. He does not use the compensating relation between dimensions as a strategy for dealing with quantities, whereas the conserving child does. The conserving child uses the strategy of compensating relations between the dimensions and thus in this area exhibits operational behaviour.

Much of the foregoing reasoning implies that the concrete operational stage of reasoning requires recognition of regularity based on two sets of cues, or two dimensions. Specifically, it means that the same two cues are regularly associated with a given result, for example $n(A) + n(B) = n(A \cup B)$. The cues $n(A)$ and $n(B)$ may appear in many guises, e.g. the sets may be differently arranged, they may be made up of different sorts of objects, and so on. The child must still recognize that $n(A)$ and $n(B)$ on one occasion are associated with the same result as $n(A)$ and $n(B)$ on another. In general terms this means that the individual must recognize correspondences of the type '$a_1 b_1$ corresponds to $a_2 b_2$' ($a_1 b_1 \leftrightarrow a_2 b_2$).

The child has found, then, that there are two situations, each containing cues a and b, to which he can appropriately make the same response. A reasonable deduction from this is that he must have the information processing space and the immediate memory span to handle the items, a_1, b_1, a_2, b_2 simultaneously. It is clearly not sufficient for the child to notice that $a_1 b_1 \leftrightarrow a_2 \bar{b}_2$ (where $\bar{b} = $ not b), because this will not always be associated with the regularity of the same result. Nor is it possible for him to discover that $a_1 b_1 \leftrightarrow a_2 \Delta$ and then to search for Δ. This last technique presupposes an hypothesis-testing strategy and this, in turn, presumes that the regularity has been anticipated.

Halford (1972) has also made a proposal that the immediate memory span required to attain a given level of operational reasoning must equal twice the minimum number of information units needed to define the regularity underlying the operation. In addition, he suggests that each element involved in defining a regularity and any necessary transformation rule each contributes one unit. This implies that for concrete operations an individual requires a memory span of 4, as basically he must find a constancy between two sets of cues. In other words, when the early manifestations of concrete operations appear the child has developed his cognitive functioning level by coming upon and recognizing regularities between two empirical cues, firmly anchored to his dealings with his environment, which lead him to empirical constancies (physical consistencies). This means that a child at this stage is able to handle the arithmetic operation of addition, for example; i.e. he will be able to understand the kind of regularity underlying a statement such as $4 + 2 = 6$. This, in itself, brings forward other associated regularities of which he can become aware by scanning. For instance, the strategy of replacement, already available to the child in other activities, becomes associated with his arithmetic; 6 can be replaced by $4 + 2$, $3 + 3$, and so on. This last acquisition assists him in further developments at the same operational level, e.g. the problem of using large numbers and symbols at the concrete operational level.

Qualitatively examples such as the following:

$$3 + 2 = 5$$
$$274 + 475 = 749$$
$$a + b = c$$

are similar acquisitions if the elements in the statements are regarded as representing unique cardinal numbers. This is not to say that the three types of problem are necessarily of equal difficulty. It seems that the last two may be acquired later (Collis, 1971). This later acquisition, however, need not imply a separate stage of development. As long as they can be acquired using the model suggested above, they could be regarded as a substage of concrete operations.

The literature shows that there are a large number of tasks that seem to be beyond the capacity of children working at the concrete operational level, among them problems based on proportion (Inhelder and Piaget, 1958; Lovell and Butterworth, 1966; Lunzer, 1965; Pumfrey, 1968). It is suggested here that, in formal operational thinking, there are basically two variables as for the earlier level of development. However, the consistency between the two variables will not relate to a direct reflection of experience, but will require the intervention of a third variable related to the operation which connects the initial elements. This third variable, because of its purpose, will be called here a 'transformation rule'. To solve a problem at the formal operational level, an individual must be able to find and use this rule. The transformation rule may be thought of as that rule which consistently relates the operations and variables involved one to another. This rule becomes part of the 'recurrent regularity' in the relationship, which must be found in order to be able to operate at a formal operational level.

The common element in all formal operational tasks seems to be the abstract transformation rule which relates the variables consistently. The concrete operational reasoner, when faced with a task involving formal operations, is unable to anchor his scanning for consistency in direct reflections of experience—the transformation rule is simply not such a direct reflection. He may be able to recognize the other variables and see that changes in one or both induce changes in the system, but recognition of regularities underlying formal operations necessitates recognition of a triplet, the two variables plus the transformation rule. He cannot discover this if his reasoning is confined to the empirical domain. The classical Piagetian experiments are readily fitted into this model. A brief examination of the proportional schema in these terms is useful to clarify the point.

Suppose a child is given the problem of determining whether the following expressions are equal or not: $(3 + 7)/4$ and $(2 + 3)/2$. An obvious approach is to 'close' both numerators and consider $\frac{10}{4}$ and $\frac{5}{2}$. The transformation rule involved can be expressed in many ways, for example $p \propto p$, $p = kq$, $p/q = mp/mq$, but has to be achieved if the child is to be able to relate the two variables without intervention by empirical cues, i.e. in terms of the operations only. At the concrete level of reasoning he would be able to achieve equality of two ratios because he could use the fact that the measurement of one object can be recorded in more than one way, for instance, by using an ikon such as the following:

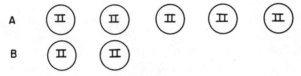

Measuring the number of elements in set A in terms of the number of elements in set B, a child could have either $\frac{10}{4}$ or, by grouping the elements in pairs, $\frac{5}{2}$. Both are true and accurate measures of the same number of elements and hence may be used as replacements one for the other, i.e. they are equal. Similar examples are innumerable in all elementary empirical measures, e.g. measuring the length of a one-metre string with a 5-cm rule and a 10-cm rule; measuring the capacity of a one-litre container successively with 100 cm³, 250 cm³, and 500 cm³ measuring flasks.

In terms of the original example, if the concrete operational child knows that $\frac{10}{4} = k$ and $\frac{5}{2} = k$, where k represents a measure of the same object, then he is able to deduce that $\frac{10}{4} = \frac{5}{2}$, but this may not bring him any closer to discovering the transformation rule itself. Just as a knowledge of addition facts does not indicate an understanding of the addition operation, the ability to 'simplify' $\frac{10}{4}$ to $\frac{5}{2}$ by 'cancelling' is no indication of an understanding of the rule, $a/b = (m \times a)/(m \times b)$.

The interesting question which arises is how does the individual see the significance of the transformation rule to begin with? If it is granted that he seeks consistency in his cognitions and that he has achieved this for the two-variable case at a concrete operational level, he will probably attempt to use the technique which proved successful in his past dealings with the environment. However, since this technique does not allow him to relate variables not directly reflected in the environment, he begins to achieve inconsistent results. Thus he seeks consistency by looking for a rule which governs the behaviour of the variables (see Scandura, 1970). Piaget's protocols have a number of examples of children trying to solve a formal level problem in this way. In the early stages the subject may interfere in the system himself, or he may suggest magical solutions, or he simply gives up after several failures to relate the variables. At a later stage he finds a rule which appears to work empirically (e.g. additive solutions in beam balance problems) but which breaks down if enough experiences with the system are given. At a later stage still he seeks a more adequate rule. It could be that this seeking for rule is identical with the hypothesis-testing strategy often given as a characteristic of formal operational thought (Flavell, 1963; Peel, 1968).

As the concrete operational thinker cannot be assumed to have an hypothesis-testing strategy he can only achieve his discovery of the regularity (transformation rule) by a scanning technique when he has the necessary prerequisites to go beyond the level of concrete operations.

What, then, are the necessary prerequisites for discovering regularities of the transformation rule kind? One condition, according to Halford's (1970a) suggestion on memory span, is that an individual would require a memory span of 6 because the minimum number of information units required at this level to arrive at consistency would be 3, viz. two variables and one transformation rule. This, of course, is proposed as a necessary but not sufficient condition, and there would certainly be other requirements necessary before an individual would be able to operate at the formal operational level.

As with concrete operations, once the person actually constructs the relevant transformation rule by noting the successive regularities which give him his consistency, he is then in a position to use this as a kind of internal model upon which he may build his future strategy with similar variables. The discovery of the regularity, in fact, justifies the rule. Just as, in concrete operations, the discovery of a regularity was the justification for the definition of a number operation, the discovery of a regularity with 3 units of information (which is of a different order from any concrete operational regularity) is the justification for a completely new concept—a transformation rule applying to an expression which is itself composed of operations.

Given a memory span of 6 and success on a number of occasions in defining a regularity in terms of a transformation rule, the adolescent may discover that this technique subsumes his previous concrete operational technique. It becomes clear that consistency can be achieved far more economically and efficiently by the use of the new strategy and thus it tends to become a general technique. Mathematics tends to reinforce this as so much of the work with symbols depends upon the definition of the variables and the transformation rules which define consistencies within the system.

The next obvious research step if one follows the line of reasoning just described is to investigate the viability of the proposal that movement along the presumed concrete operational to formal operational continuum can be influenced by an experimenter's intervention. In terms of the theoretical outline this intervention should be able to be seen as a presentation of regularities leading to a consistency through a process of scanning appropriate stimuli. However, it must be made clear from the outset that this can only be part of the story. For example, why should an individual raise his level of operational thinking?

Inhelder and Piaget (1958) suggest that the child moves from concrete to formal operations by realizing the shortcomings of the concrete operational methods of organizing and structuring the data. Gaps, uncertainties, and contradictions appear and the child begins to seek more adequate strategies for solving problems. This is not meant to imply that the movement from concrete operations to formal operations is an all-or-none process. Indeed, the bulk of the studies in the literature, and the basic theory, show explicitly that this is not likely to be so. For instance, it seems reasonable to consider that the development of the use of formal operations in mathematics depends on the construction of a *network* of relations within the child's cognitions which enable him to move freely about the developing structure of mathematics.

The implications which can be drawn for the purposes here are threefold.

First, raising the operational level of reasoning is likely to be a gradual process. An individual may become aware of a gap or contradiction appearing in his handling of a problem without being able to adjust his thinking level upwards in order to resolve it. In order to resolve the contradiction he needs to have an appropriate background and level of maturity and, in addition, receive certain experiences which highlight the means to a consistent response. This might mean that both positive and negative instances of the regularity involved need to be presented at the child's level of cognitive functioning.

Second, the higher the operational level of thinking the more efficient the child becomes at coping with problems associated with variables upon which he is expected to operate. Oddly enough, this means that, given the same problem, the lower-level reasoner has a more difficult task to perform with a less powerful tool than his counterpart who is operating at a higher level of reasoning.

Third, the strategies available to the higher-level reasoner subsume those available to the lower-level reasoner. It has been suggested in the previous chapter that the negation of an operation is replaced at a higher level by the principle of reciprocity in which the attention is directed to the operation itself and action taken to counterbalance the effect of the operation without destroying it. This subsumption process implies also that the higher-level reasoner has two strategies available where the lower-level reasoner has only one, and a much less sophisticated one at that.

It will be seen that the second and third implications are closely related, but a practical example may make the point clearer. Take three problems involving conservation of quantities in regular cylinders: one at the early concrete level and the others at a formal level.

To develop the concept of conservation of quantity a child has to realize that there is operating a compensating relation between dimensions. The liquid poured into a container will not change in quantity if it is merely transferred in toto to another vessel, although the latter may be of a different shape. The usual experiments of this kind use cylinders which vary in diameter and height. The child has to recognize that there is a compensating relation holding between the two variables, height and diameter. At the age involved, five to six years, this realization leads to conservation of quantity.

At the formal level, 15 + years, the adolescent becomes able to handle the same problem in terms of a rule, $V = \pi r^2 h$, and can see that if V is constant then any variations in h must be compensated for by a change in the value of r^2, and vice versa. Apart from the fact that this allows quantification of the problem, the rule, which expresses so precisely the relationship between the variables involved, subsumes the earlier notions and is clearly a much more powerful and efficient tool for coping with a wide variety of quantity (or volume) conservation problems.

Keeping what has been said above in view, it would be naive indeed to write of devising a training procedure which would cause a child to move from concrete operational reasoning as such to formal operational reasoning as such. Nevertheless, the analytical studies described in Chapter 7 show that there is scope for attempting to move children to a higher level within the various levels of reasoning generally described as concrete operational. For instance, the studies described earlier showed that a naive concept of uniqueness becomes inadequate when the operations become unfamiliar or when the elements operated upon go beyond the child's empirically verified range (see also Keats, 1955). To go beyond this level it would seem reasonable to deduce that the child needs to be placed in a position where (a) he realizes the inadequacy of his naive approach, (b) he can operate at a concrete level with empirical data, and (c) he can begin to build up a non-empirical category of uniqueness directly related to the operation involved.

A training procedure

Suppose one takes the operations of addition and subtraction. Let us have only two terms and consider what can be done to these terms in order to keep the result of the operation constant. To simplify the experience further, suppose only unity or zero changes to the terms are allowed. In order to keep the addition result constant one may do any of the following: add zero to both terms, subtract zero from both terms, subtract unity from the first term, and add unity to the second. By contrast, to keep the subtraction result constant, one needs to add zero to both terms, subtract zero from both terms, add unity to both terms, or subtract unity from both terms. These results can be set up and considered in tabular form. When this is done (as in Table 8.1) certain elements and relationships become clear. The table shows that the result of any pair of alterations to the terms is unique, the tables are symmetrical, and the table for subtraction is related to the table for addition by being the same table rotated clockwise through 90°.

TABLE 8.1. Results obtained by making unit or zero changes to addition and subtraction models

Addition				Subtraction			
	Second term				Second term		
	−1	0	1		−1	0	1
First term −1	−	−	0	First term −1	0	−	−
0	−	0	+	0	+	0	−
1	0	+	+	1	+	+	0

Note
> The − signs in the table refer to a decrease.
> The + signs in the table refer to an increase.
> The 0 signs in the table indicate no change.

It is suggested that to work successfully with the operations themselves (without using arithmetical closure), in the type of exercise shown below, implies an understanding of the relationships existing both within and between the tables. If the student is permitted to close off each binary operation involved, he can in effect turn the exercise into an elementary concrete achievement and obtain correct answers without attaining a knowledge of the relationships between constant sums and constant differences. This strategy seems impractical for the concrete operational-level child of about nine or ten years with large numbers and variables and leads to a search for and use of a pattern. The concrete operational child of this age typically finds a pattern that appears to work (perhaps with one operation only) and continues with it; it is only by upsetting his fixation on this one strategy that he will progress.

This is equivalent to saying that a child at this level is capable of using the addition model or the subtraction model. He finds it difficult to relate one to the other or, perhaps more correctly, is not even aware of the desirability of relating the operations. It seems reasonable to suggest that the ability to see these operations in relation to one another is a necessary step towards the development of formal operations. In other words, success in relating these operations means that the child is aware, implicitly at least, of the transformation which maps one table into the other. This, in itself, represents an upgrading of the level of cognitive functioning.

It is further suggested that the typical concrete operational child who is ready to make this move will be encouraged to do so under certain conditions. First, he must be able to examine the structures empirically by means appropriate to his level of cognitive functioning; second, he needs to return to experiences with 'greater than' and 'less than' in order to build up an identity category which, in this case, is the 'equals' relationship. The reason for the first condition is obvious—it is necessary to present the structures at a level at which the child is able to cope with them. The effect of presenting the material in this way is to reduce the cognitive load by reducing the number of variables which have to be taken into account at the one time. The second condition is derived from the basic idea that children come to the concept of equality by a consideration of inequalities. Halford (1969b, 1970a) offers evidence on this point with respect to training five year olds in conservation of quantity. He suggests that the child acquires conservation through learning a consistent classificatory system for quantities in which the child recognizes that container A = container B because he first recognizes that (for example) any container shorter than A (but of the same width) < container B, and any container taller than A (but of the same width) > container B, and so on.

A training experiment was conducted incorporating the ideas which are suggested above. As the full experimental details are given elsewhere (Collis, 1975) a summary of the method and results should suffice for the purposes envisaged here.

A training experiment

As the tests are crucial it is proposed to begin by describing them.

Test I was made up in two parallel forms, A and B. Half of each group was given form A as the pretest and the remainder form B. The procedure was reversed for the posttests. The test consisted of items which were alternately addition and subtraction. Larger numbers were used in order to discourage the students from using their tables to close each item and then making a simple comparison. Items were of the type shown below:

Item 4		Item 5	
	$95 - 46$ ☐		$564 + 487$ ☐
$94 - 47 =$	$93 - 46$ ☐	$567 + 486 =$	$568 + 485$ ☐
	$93 - 48$ ☐		$566 + 487$ ☐
	$95 - 48$ ☐		$566 + 485$ ☐

The instructions were for the subject to check ($\surd$) the response(s) which made the statement true.

In addition, two other tests were devised. Operation test I was given both as a pre- and posttest. It consisted, in one sense, of the reverse of test I in that it gave the relationships and asked the subject to indicate the operation(s) ($+$, $-$, or neither) for which the given relationship would be true. Items were of the following type:

$$\text{Item 3} \qquad 9*5 < 9*4 \ldots$$
$$9*5 > 9*4 \ldots$$
$$9*5 = 9*4 \ldots$$

Operation test II, also given as a pre- and posttest, was different from operation test I in only one respect. To discourage the children from arithmetically closing the operations, the numbers involved were made much larger, e.g.

Item 3
$$349*345 < 349*344 \dots$$
$$349*345 > 349*344 \dots$$
$$349*345 = 349*344 \dots$$

Test I (forms A and B) was designed to examine the students' ability to relate criteria for keeping the result of an addition operation constant to criteria for keeping the result of a subtraction operation constant. The second pretest (operation test I) set out to test the same kind of ability but differed in that the child had to select the appropriate operation which would make the statement true when the numbers in the exercise had been adjusted according to the criteria used in the previous test.

Sixty children were selected on the basis of their strategy for doing the exercises. Those selected had performed according to the one strategy in almost every one of the set of exercises. That is, they used *either* the appropriate approach for addition (constant sum) *or* the appropriate strategy for subtraction (constant difference), and did not vary their strategy according to the operation involved in the exercise.

The sixty pupils were randomly allocated to one of three groups of twenty and the groups so formed randomly allotted to three types of training.

The training procedures for all three groups began in the same way—with some introductory exercises. These were designed (a) to revise the use of the term 'sets' with concrete material, (b) to set up a criterion for concluding that two sets had an equal number of elements in each (matching in one-to-one correspondence), (c) to indicate that the union of two disjoint sets implied that the cardinal numbers of the sets were to be added in order to find the total number in the united set, and (d) to show that, if the number in one set was greater than the number in another set, the excess could be expressed using the operation of subtraction.

After this common introductory work was completed the training procedures diverged. The control group (C_1) concentrated on equality only and used concrete material to do exercises of the following kinds:

A	Exercise	Given
$2 + 4 = \boxed{}$		$4 + 2$
$2 + 4 = \boxed{}$		$3 + 3$
$2 + 4 = \boxed{}$		$1 + 5$
$2 + 4 = \boxed{}$		$6 + 0$

B	Exercise	Given
$8 - 3 =$ ☐		$5 - 0$
$8 - 3 =$ ☐		$7 - 2$
$8 - 3 =$ ☐		$9 - 4$
$8 - 3 =$ ☐		$8 - 3$

The children in this group were instructed to select an expression from those given on the right to make the statement true. They could do this by using the concrete material, 1×1 inch cardboard squares, or by whatever means, so long as they at some point verified their result with the cardboard squares, e.g.

$8 - 3 = 7 - 2$ would appear as

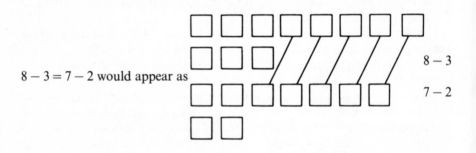

The experimental group (E) had similar exercises using the same material, but with two important differences. For each exercise they made up and kept a reference set at the top of their working space and each exercise forced a consideration of inequalities as well as equalities.

Exercises were of the types:

A	Exercise	Given
$2 + 4 =$ ☐		$3 + 5$
$2 + 4 =$ ☐		$1 + 5$
$2 + 4 >$ ☐		$3 + 3$
$2 + 4 <$ ☐		$1 + 3$

B		Exercise		Given
$8 - 3 =$	[ ]			$9 - 4$
$8 - 3 =$	[ ]			$7 - 4$
$8 - 3 >$	[ ]			$9 - 2$
$8 - 3 <$	[ ]			$7 - 2$

As they went about the exercises, experimental subjects became aware that, for addition, moving elements already in the sets left the union total constant and that the $>$ and $<$ relationships could only be obtained by bringing in more elements or removing some elements respectively. On the other hand, such was not the case for subtraction. Constancy of excess could be obtained by adding or subtracting matched pairs, whereas moving elements about within the sets was sufficient to give $<$ and $>$ relationships, as was the simple process of adding or subtracting one or more (unmatched) elements.

The experimental training procedures were intended to be analogous to the procedure used by Halford (1969b, 1970a) for training five year olds in the conservation of quantity. The subject began with two identical sets, one (I) was retained as a reference throughout each set of exercises and the other was subjected to various transformations, the results of each of which was readily referable to I. In fact, each transformation required such a reference to I in order to verify the relationship ($>$, $<$, or $=$). The procedure for group C_1, on the other hand, had no empirical identity set available and the concrete material was used simply to give an *ad hoc* representation of each expression of equality as it arose.

Group C_2 was intended as a control which received no specific training in exercises designed to assist students to relate the addition and subtraction models. They spent an equal amount of training time on topics irrelevant to the experiment.

All children did test I (form A or B), operation test I, and operation test II prior to the beginning of the first training session. The pretests were followed by six training sessions, each of one hour. The first hour with each group was taken up with preliminary work on sets. The remaining time was taken up for groups C_1 and E, with the appropriate training procedures. Group C_2 proceeded with further exploration of sets and modelling as a way of considering the relationship between various expressions using cardinal numbers. Finally, all three groups were given the posttests.

The results are shown graphically in Figure 8.1. Standard statistical analyses carried out on the data show that only the experimental group made significant gains from pretest to posttest in each area tested. Perhaps Table 8.2, which shows the actual gains and losses on test I, summarizes the results best. It can be seen that the experimental group makes the largest gains on both operations

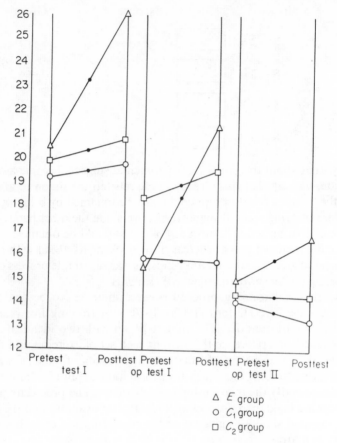

FIGURE 8.1 Graphs of means. Pretest, posttest

with the fewest losses on either operation. It appears that the control groups tend to make gains in one operation at the expense of losses in the other; they appear not to change strategy for keeping a constant result with a change in the operation.

These results lend some support to the hypothesis that the experimental training procedure assisted children to see the relationship between the addition and subtraction paradigm. The experimental training procedure aimed to

TABLE 8.2. Gain scores for test I

	E			C_1			C_2		
	+	−	Total	+	−	Total	+	−	Total
Gain	47	71	118	30	27	57	24	18	42
Loss	2	6	8	18	31	49	7	16	23

encourage the child to make judgmental responses and to use the arrangement of the concrete material to highlight any inconsistency in his judgment. The result of this training could indicate the construction of a system which put the two operations into relationship. It would be expected that, if this were done, the child would have made some acquisition of logical thinking which would result in the ability to perform better on the posttests. In these his judgment had to be made independently of the empirical support given during the training sessions. The procedure was designed to encourage children to learn relationships between responses appropriate to the stimulus operation rather that empirical 'facts'.

As the description suggests, the inverse relationship between the two operations is implicit in the training procedure for group E. The success of the experimental training procedure, indicated in the results, may be seen as a small step towards an understanding of the notion of an inverse relationship. It would seem to be a logical extension of this study to make explicit in the training procedure the inverse notion and to then test for its achievement. Moreover, it is clear that, in common with most training procedures using a Piagetian orientation (see Halford, 1972), further analytical experiments are necessary to determine precisely the operative factors.

It is of interest to note that the results of the control groups, both within and between the groups, show non-significant changes in performance after training. If anything, the results of group C_1 tend to indicate that any improvement which might take place naturally, as represented by no specific training (i.e. group C_2), may well be inhibited by attempts to train for 'understanding' of the processes without sufficient insight into the methods by which changes in cognition are induced. It was intended that the group C_1 training procedure typify the training given in most school situations; if one is training students to work with 'equalities' one trains them on this type of relationship and does not introduce others. If this type of training were to be successful in promoting the acquisition of genuine concepts (as opposed to an ability to obtain correct answers by algorism), it would negate the essence of Piaget's theory. Piaget makes clear that a number of variables must interact in a complex way to produce the development of a structure.

The experimental work just described gives some indication of the difficulties encountered when an attempt is made to raise an individual's cognitive functioning level. A vast amount of detailed basic research is required before one can reasonably expect appropriate general principles to be derived that can be applied in the typical classroom for this purpose. Nevertheless, sufficient analytical studies of concrete operational and formal operational reasoning have been done to enable a programme of mathematics education to be devised which would enable children of (say) nine to fourteen years to be able to grasp the basis of mathematical thinking without going beyond the typical cognitive functioning level of those years. Let us look briefly at the typical situation under the traditional programmes and then consider an experimental programme on which the writer worked for some years.

TEACHING MATHEMATICS AT THE CONCRETE OPERATIONAL LEVEL

Under what has become known as the 'traditional' scheme children seem to have been trained mainly in 'facts' and computational techniques. Little emphasis was placed either on forming judgments and problem solving at an appropriate level or on the understanding of the interrelationships between the various processes and procedures of elementary mathematics. In general, teachers followed textbooks which not only compartmentalized the subject matter into topics but also encouraged a method based on the presentation of a model example followed by a series of practice exercises designed to establish an appropriate algorism. The major concern seemed to be to teach the child to recognize a given stimulus and then for this stimulus to trigger off a chain of responses which ended with an answer. That the chain of responses was often quite meaningless in itself seemed to be of no account. For the average child, the outcome from this type of training seems to have been thoroughly bad (Allendoerfer, 1965; Biggs, 1962; Collis, 1967). At the very least it resulted in children coming to the secondary school already unable and/or unwilling to rely on their own capacity to reason in mathematics. Szeminska (1965) comments upon the same phenomenon occurring in her country; Allendoerfer (1965, p. 694) says:

> These pupils may be able to add and
> multiply but they do not know *when*
> to add and *when* to multiply.

One could not be surprised to find that these students often appeared to have tacitly assumed that mathematics *per se* was not meaningful and was not *really* related to reality. Instead, it appeared as a multiplicity of abstract (and often) apparently conflicting rules and procedures from which one was expected to make an appropriate response on being given a particular cue. Given the limitations of the child's cognitive capacity this approach led, very often, to students applying an inappropriate procedure to a problem. Examples of this latter are legion, many being of the 'schoolboy howler' type. Examiners have long been aware that a slight change in a customary cue will lead students astray.

Take a practical example (Collis, 1969). A common method of teaching the mensuration concerned with the area of a rectangle (under the 'traditional' approach) was for the teacher to hurry through some illustrations of what was meant by area and then to set up a formal model such as the following. If a surface is rectangular in shape, the area is found by the formula $A = L \times B$. The area will be in square measure and care must be taken to ensure that, when this formula is used, L and B are in the same units.

After several exercises to practise the application of the formula the lesson was complete. Periodically, the topic came up for revision with more practice of the same kind. However, later when the children came to early secondary

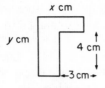

FIGURE 8.2

school many of them could not use their knowledge to find expressions for areas of figures shaped as shown in Figure 8.2. To this question many students responded $A = x\,y$

Another example which supports the Allendoerfer quotation above is as follows. Early secondary students when asked to answer the following problem, 'A snail crosses a sporting ground, which is $\frac{1}{4}$ kilometer wide, in 8 hours. What was his average speed in kilometers per hour?', often respond incorrectly. The typical incorrect responses to this question are 2 kilometers per hour and 32 kilometers per hour. This tendency for children to operate with numbers in the 'obvious' way to obtain an answer without regard for the underlying relationships is symptomatic of the phenomenon under discussion.

A contrast to the kind of assumption which seems to underlie the type of approach described, it does not appear unreasonable to suggest that, to be meaningful to the child, mathematics must relate to *his* reality. Mathematics provides a way of looking at, thinking about, and giving meaning to the environment which is unique. Dienes (1960) even suggests that its use in a general education to assist in personality development and integration can be seen as akin to the use of such creative activities as art and drama. Land (1963) goes even further. He writes that structure, relationship, regularity, and systematic variation constitute mathematics, and that, apart from the need for certain elementary skills, the subject of mathematics requires the use of imagination, the appreciation of order, structure and pattern, and, above all, a real interest in the changing, exciting world around the children.

If elementary mathematics is to provide a child with a way of thinking about his environment then he must construct his own structure. Thus the task for each child is different. A task analysis based on a logical analysis of the pure mathematical structure involved is most unlikely to relate closely to every individual child's developing cognitive structures (see Case, 1975). Ausubel (1963) distinguishes between logical and psychological meaning in this context and his views are relevant at this point.

Ausubel says that logical meaning implies that the material to be learnt consists, in itself, of possible non-arbitrary relationships which could be incorporated into a human cognitive structure given that it had the necessary prerequisites of a certain background and state of readiness. Logical meaning is transformed into psychological meaning when the logically meaningful propositions are subsumed into a particular cognitive structure. This means that when an individual learns material in a non-arbitrary, non-verbatim fashion he does not learn the logical meaning but a meaning that is personal

268

to him. Of course, as Ausubel indicates, these individual meanings, possessed by members of a group, are sufficiently similar to allow communication between group members.

The proposal to be put here is that elementary-school mathematics can be seen to form a structure, i.e. it has logical meaning *per se*, and the main object of teaching it in schools is to assist children to develop a psychological meaning for it from their own interactions with the environment. In the light of the analytical studies described in Chapter 7 and a broad interpretation of both Piaget's and Ausubel's theories it would seem that mathematics in the middle primary- to early secondary-school years needs to be presented as a *system* firmly anchored to a concrete operational model of reasoning. *

A system implies a set of relationships derived from a number of basic assumptions by means of some appropriate procedure for drawing conclusions. Basing the reasoning on a concrete operational model requires that the basic assumptions and reasoning procedure of the system be firmly established in the child's observable reality. At the age under consideration (nine to fourteen years), the assumptions of the system cannot be abstract, i.e. purely axiomatic, nor can the criteria of proof be abstract, i.e. purely deductive. Both must refer to observable realities, the things which the child can be certain of. This means that any mathematical system developed to cater for this group must be seen to develop from a concrete activity whose outcomes are clearly determinate and unambiguous. For example, the crosses in Figure 8.3 can be represented as five sets of two, or two sets of five. The symbolic expression of the outcome of this activity of structuring and restructuring this set of crosses is the mathematical statement, $5 \times 2 = 2 \times 5$.

Thus the child sees the relationships of mathematics to be merely representations of physical relationships which can be clearly and unambiguously observed in concrete reality. For the adult mathematician, mathematics, as such, may be abstract and formal. He may see the relationships between the elements of mathematics as relationships between abstractions. The weight of psychological evidence and theory suggests that most preadolescent children do not see relationships between abstractions and certainly cannot operate with them with any understanding. Unfortunately most primary mathematics curricula seem to be based on the proposition that mathematics exists and should be

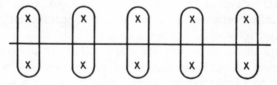

FIGURE 8.3

* A more detailed formulation of what follows has been described in various places, some of which include ANZAAS, Christchurch, N. Z., 1968 (Hubbard); AAMT Biennial Conference, Sydney, 1969 (Hubbard); N. S. W. Institute for Educational Research, Newcastle, 1968 (Collis); Canberra Mathematics Association, 1969 (Collis); *The Australian Mathematics Teacher*. **25**, No. 3, 1969 (Collis); *The Australian Mathematics Teacher*, **27**, No. 3, 1971 (Hubbard).

taught to the child. This results in conflict with both the child's experience and way of thinking, because for the *child* mathematics does not exist. Experience exists and thinking is in terms of this experience. Thus a mathematical system, to be meaningful for the child, must be devised in terms of his experience.

One activity, applied to a particular concrete model of reality, will engender a system of concrete operations. The scope of this system will depend on the number of specific activities that can be applied to the model. In the illustration given above the model is the representation of objects by neutral marks, and the activity is the discovery of significant set forms and their identification with corresponding numeral forms. The system resulting from this is very wide-ranging, inlcuding as it does the whole rational number system, so far as it is usually considered in elementary school.

A great deal of use has always been made of *ad hoc* concrete models for establishing mathematical relationships, e.g. the number line for negative numbers and fractions and sectors of circles for ratios. The problem in the past has been that teachers and texts have appealed to whichever referent seemed most easily to show the relationship being established. Often this involved taking more account of what was expedient rather than what was correct and of long-term benefit mathematically (for example $4x + 2x = 6x$ was suggested as analogous to 4 apples + 2 apples = 6 apples). With some reflection it becomes clear that different referents lead to different isolated systems, since a system is built on its referent. As it is typical of the concrete operational child to be unable to unify these separate systems into a single system on the basis of relationships between them it becomes necessary, in order to simulate a coherent and integrated mathematical system at the concrete operational level, for all number relationships to be developed as representations of physical relationships existing in a single referent. The single referent constitutes the essential framework and upon it a systematic procedure can be established by the use of rigorously applied, clearly defined, criteria.

A procedure based on this view would appear to be able to show several outcomes at the concrete operational level. Some of these, for the concrete operational child, might be:

(1) seeing mathematics develop as a coherent system because of the rigorous application of criteria;
(2) learning to have confidence in his own judgments;
(3) becoming aware of the interrelationships involved in mathematics with special emphasis on the number system itself;
(4) noting that the referent provided a model of the general realities of the environment; and
(5) giving experience of systematic procedure.

It should be clear also that, if a system were developed from relationships within the model suggested, then, to a large extent, the order of development of the system would be determined by the peculiarities inherent in the model itself. The sequence which may seem most appropriate mathematically and logically need not necessarily be the optimum sequence in a concrete operational system. Mathematically it may seem that addition, subtraction, multiplication, division is a desirable order. However, particular features of the model could well make this sequence undesirable or non-viable.

If a system of this kind is to begin with children aged eight or nine years, then even the most elementary operations (such as set equivalence and counting) need to be firmly established in terms of the chosen model. At no point must argument and uncertainty arise which cannot be resolved in terms of completely acceptable criteria.

Although not the only possibility, there appear to be considerable advantages in using sets as the basic field in which to operate. The concept of set can be seen as the base of the primary number system. It is also capable of ready interpretation in the light of both Piaget's concrete operational scheme and Ausubel's principle of progressive differentiation of a subject matter area. The *concrete activity* involved in what follows is measurement of the cardinal number of a set; the *concrete referent* is representation of sets by arrays of neutral marks. A numeral can be seen as the record of the measure of the cardinal number of a set, and particular numeral forms correspond to particular set structures. For instance, a sum is the numeral form which measures the number in a set structured as the union of disjoint sets; likewise, difference, product, and quotient can be related unambiguously to specially structured sets. The fundamental criterion for equality of numbers may be set up thus: if a set, structured to correspond to a cardinal number represented by the numeral N_1 is restructured, physically or mentally, into a structure corresponding to N_2, then $N_1 = N_2$. For example, Figure 8.4 could represent a restructuring process. Taking the top ties, the

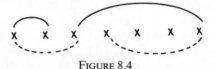

FIGURE 8.4

structured numeral representing the number of crosses in the array is $2 + 5$; the other structured numeral represented on the model is $3 + 4$. Both account for the same number of discrete marks; thus $2 + 5 = 3 + 4$.

This process can be generalized. If the cardinal number of a set A is represented by $n(A)$ and the cardinal number of a second set B by $n(B)$, A and B being any two mutually disjoint sets, then the cardinal number of the union is given by $n(A) + n(B)$, i.e.

$$n(A \cup B) = n(A) + n(B)$$

In terms of the outline so far this generalization must be regarded as a *concrete generalization*. This means that in the earlier preformal stages the children regard the statement, $n(A \cup B) = n(A) + n(B)$, A and B being two mutually disjoint sets, as true for any cardinal numbers within their empirically verifiable range—later in the same stage they may regard it as true for cardinal numbers which they can see as able to be closed. It would not be expected that they

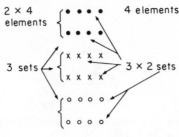

FIGURE 8.5

would regard the statement as a mathematical generalization requiring no connection with their empirical reality until they had reached the stage of formal operations.

The the children have a concrete criterion for testing the truth of a suggested equivalence relationship. For instance, are the expressions, $3 \times (2 \times 4)$ and $(3 \times 2) \times 4$, equivalent? To answer this question under the system suggested, the child could draw three sets each containing (2×4) elements and restructure the model so that it can be seen to consist of (3×2) sets each with four elements (see Figure 8.5). As the model can be restructured the expressions are equivalent and thus it is legitimate to write $3 \times (2 \times 4) = (3 \times 2) \times 4$. The fact that both expressions happen to equal 24 would be regarded in this context as not relevant to the question asked.

This notion of equivalence goes with the important mathematical idea of replacement. If two expressions are equivalent then one may be used to replace the other at any time. In the above example, $3 \times (2 \times 4)$ can replace $(3 \times 2) \times 4$ or, if one wishes, the counting number equivalent, 24, could be used to replace the expressions.

The operations and activities described above seem consistent with children's logic of classes, differences, and equivalences. The proofs, in particular, are based on concrete operations. They consist of:

(1) the classification of a visible set by structural form, together with the identification of the corresponding numeral, and vice versa; and
(2) the physical restructuring of a set.

Thus the approach would seem to satisfy, in general, both Piagetian criteria for concrete operational reasoners and cognitive structurist views on the development of meaningful knowledge in a particular area.

This system also has a great deal of flexibility built into it. The child can work in several different ways and come up with equivalent results, and can be asked *to prove* the equivalence. The criterion of reference to an appropriate set model is always available. An example may clarify this statement and assist to point up the difference between reasoning at the level suggested and formal operational reasoning. Suppose the question is to find a replacement for y in the following in such a way as to keep the statement true:

$$y + 4 = 9$$

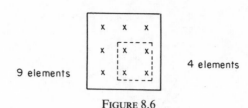

9 elements   4 elements

FIGURE 8.6

A number of responses would be correct, for example $4 + 1$, $2 + 3$, 5, and so on. However, in each case, the child could be required to prove that his result was true by reference to a model. One approach would be to look at the instruction as a question of restructuring a model with nine elements so that there is indicated at least one disjoint set with four elements in it, as shown in Figure 8.6. By counting one can obtain 5, or by making various ties, $3 + 1 + 1$ or $4 + 1$, and so on. If 5 is required as the response then the question would need to ask for the counting number replacement for y.

An essential aspect of this concrete operational approach is the finite nature of the elements; they are not variable and they are not movable. The child knows that $y + 4$ can be represented as a finite number of neutral marks and so can 9. He knows also that $y + 4$ must be able to be shown on the same set of neutral marks as the 9 in order for the equivalence statement to be made as a true statement.

The formal operational student, on the other hand, does not need these concrete props to his reasoning. He could approach the above exercise by reasoning thus: y and 4 are two elements operated on by addition; to isolate y, one finds the inverse operation, in this case subtraction, hence:

$$
\begin{aligned}
y + 4 &= 9 \\
y + 4 - 4 &= 9 - 4 \\
y + 0 &= 5 \\
y &= 5
\end{aligned}
$$

The formal operational child can work directly with the operation and needs no guarantee of the relationship of the expressions to an empirical reality; he could as easily work with $a \circ b = c$ where a, b, and c are defined as elements of some set and $\circ$ is a defined operation with an inverse defined as ϕ (say).

The following highly abbreviated sequence (Collis, 1969) gives an overall picture of part of the system which may be built up by the means suggested. The sequence presented is selected in order to illustrate the development of ratio numbers (fractions).

(1)   *   *   *   *   How many? $\Big\}$ Reduction of attributes of

     ×   ×   ×   ×   How many?   sets to those concerned with

                                         measuring and *recording* the

                                         number of the set.

Count—one-to-one correspondence—matching with counting sets.

(a) ×

(b) × ×

(c) × × ×

(d) × × × ×

(2) If two (or more) disjoint sets, how many?

Count right through—union of two sets. If counting number is not required, $3 + 4$, that is $n(A) + n(B) \to A \cup B$. (In this system the $+$ between the two numbers implies that one is considering the *union* of two *disjoint* sets.) Intersecting sets considered at this point.

(3) If the sets have the same number of elements in them (i.e. equivalent sets—one-to-one correspondence between elements) and they are disjoint, one still has $A \cup B \to n(A) + n(B)$ where $n(A) = n(B)$; but also one can express the number in the union as $x \times n(A)$ where $x =$ number of equivalent disjoint sets.

(4) Equivalence between expressions—expressions can be replaced by equivalent expressions and 'equals' (that is $=$) can be defined. Method of 'proof' of equivalence is to *match form of expression with model*, e.g.

$$\times \ \times \ \times \ \times \ \times \quad 16$$

$$\times \ \times \ \times \ \times \ \times \quad 5 \times 2 + 3 \times 2$$

$$\times \ \times \ \times \quad 10 + 6$$

$$\times \ \times \ \times \quad 2 + 2 + 2 + 2 + 2 + 2 + 2 + 2$$

$$2 \times 8, \text{ etc.}$$

By suitable indications on the model $5 \times 2 + 3 \times 2 = 10 + 6$ and/or 2×8, etc., can be used as a replacement for 16.

(5) Postulates of the real number field can be represented by models, e.g.

$$\times \ \times \ \times \ \times$$

$$\times \ \times \ \times \ \times \quad 4 \times 3 = 3 \times 4 \ (\text{CL} \times)$$

$$\times \ \times \ \times \ \times$$

(By reorientation of viewpoint with the same array)

(6) *Ratio numbers*

(a) *Measuring number in one set in terms of number in another set*

$$A \quad \times \times \times \times \times \times$$

$$B \quad \times$$

$$C \quad \times \times$$

$n(A)$ using $n(B)$ as unit of measure $= 6$ (or $\frac{6}{1}$)

$n(A)$ using $n(C)$ as unit of measure $= 3$ (or $\frac{3}{1}$ or $\frac{6}{2}$)

These 'new' numbers link with multiple counting and measuring in mensuration, and by the definition decided upon for 'equals' can be used as replacements for one another as they are different ways of measuring the same number. The 'new' numbers can be given a symbolism of their own, viz. $R(A, C)$ means the ratio number obtained when $n(C)$ is used as the measuring unit for $n(A)$. The reciprocal for $R(A, C)$ is $R(C, A)$, e.g.

$$\left. \begin{array}{l} R(A, C) = \frac{6}{2} \\[2mm] R(C, A) = \frac{2}{6} \end{array} \right\} \text{ (from model above)}$$

(b) *Equivalent ratio numbers*

$$A \quad \times \times \times \times \times \times$$

$$B \quad \times \times$$

$$R(A, B) = \frac{6}{2}$$
$$R(A, B) = \frac{3}{1}$$

that is

A	XX	XX	XX

B	XX

Hence, $\qquad\qquad \frac{6}{2} = \frac{3}{1}$

Note also from the model that $R(B, A) = \frac{2}{6}$ and $R(B, A)\frac{1}{3}$.

Hence $\qquad\qquad \frac{2}{6} = \frac{1}{3}$

Practice leads to the *concrete generalization*,

$$\frac{a}{b} = \frac{m \times a}{m \times b}$$

(c) *Addition*

$$A \quad \times \quad \times \quad \times \quad \times \quad \times \quad \times$$

$$B \quad \times \quad \times$$

$$C \quad \times \quad \times \quad \times \quad \times$$

$$R(A, B) \quad = \tfrac{3}{1} \text{ or } \tfrac{6}{2}$$
$$R(C, B) \quad = \tfrac{2}{1} \text{ or } \tfrac{4}{2}$$
$$R(A \cup C, B) = \frac{6+4}{2} = \frac{10}{2} \text{ or } \frac{3}{1} + \frac{2}{1} = \frac{5}{1}$$

Note that where the measuring set has one element one has the familiar counting number situation:

$$A \quad \times \quad \times \quad \times \quad \times$$

$$B \quad \times \quad \times \quad \times \quad \times \quad \times \quad \times$$

$$C \quad \times \quad \times \quad \times$$

$$R(A, B) \quad = \tfrac{2}{3} \text{ or } \tfrac{4}{6}$$
$$R(C, B) \quad = \tfrac{1}{2} \text{ or } \tfrac{3}{6}$$
$$R(A \cup C, B) = \frac{4+3}{6} = \frac{7}{6}$$

Notes: (*i*) Either $\dfrac{2}{3} = \dfrac{4}{6}$ from the model or $\dfrac{2}{3} = \dfrac{2 \times 2}{3 \times 2}$ from the equivalent

ratios.

(*ii*) Children also soon realize that

$$\tfrac{7}{6} = 1 + \tfrac{1}{6} = 1\tfrac{1}{6}, \text{ etc.}$$

Practice at the above addition leads to a further *concrete generalization*:

$$\frac{x}{a} + \frac{y}{a} = \frac{x+y}{a}$$

(d) *Multiplication*
A new criterion for x

$$A \quad \boxed{\times \quad \times \quad \times} \quad \boxed{\times \quad \times \quad \times}$$

$$B \quad \boxed{\times \quad \times \quad \times}$$

$$C \quad \boxed{\times}$$

$$R(A, B) = 2$$
$$R(B, C) = 3$$
$$R(A, C) = 3 \times 2$$

Let us define x for all ratio numbers thus:

$$\left. \begin{array}{l} R(A, B) = x \\ \\ R(B, C) = y \end{array} \right\} \rightarrow R(A, C) = x \times y$$

Note that this does not conflict with the definition of x for counting numbers. It follows that

$$\left. \begin{array}{l} R(A, B) = \tfrac{2}{3} \\ \\ R(B, C) = \tfrac{4}{5} \end{array} \right\} R(A, C) = \tfrac{2}{3} \times \tfrac{4}{5}$$

but as yet there is no way of expressing this product as a ratio number; one reasons as below using an empirical model.

Practice at the above leads to the concrete generalization,

$$\frac{x}{a} \times \frac{y}{b} = \frac{x \times y}{a \times b}$$

The example above (multiplication of ratio numbers) epitomizes the presentation of mathematics at the concrete operational level. It fits into the system of number, sets, models, measurement, and recording that the child has developed with counting numbers; it does not conflict with preceding work but extends and integrates previous structures in the number area. It illustrates the concrete operational model in that there are immediate concrete referents

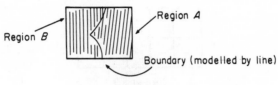

FIGURE 8.7

which the child can use. The referents require only classifying, reclassifying, and substituting to enable decisions to be made. The generalizations arrived at are plausible, not incompatible with the facts, and are geared into the system from which they arise. It may be argued, of course, that this is not 'mathematics' in the formal sense. However, it is reasonable to argue that the *child* learns mathematics by interacting with his environment in a special and unique way, and the teacher's task is to assist in this process by providing opportunities for meaningful experiences.

So far only one area of mathematics has been considered, number. However, application of the same principles in the field of geometry and mensuration and everyday applied mathematical problems is relatively straightforward. It is not proposed to develop these here in the detail given already to number, but it seems appropriate to indicate briefly how geometry and mensuration can be handled in terms of concrete referents.

Consider the geometrical concept of a point. The concrete development from a particular stage of discussion might go as follows:

(1) Surface is the part of objects one can see, touch, paint, etc. Kinds of surface are flat, round, rough, etc.

(2) A surface can be divided into regions. Two regions meet in a boundary, which is *modelled* by a *line* (Figure 8.7).

(3) Boundaries meet at a junction which is *modelled* by a *point* (Figure 8.8).

Thus it is clear that a boundary has the attribute of length but no breadth (see the Euclidean geometrical concept). The line, as a model which the child has to work with, exemplifies the essential attribute of length, but clearly must have some breadth in order to be seen. However, as with the models used in the number field, it serves as a concrete referent for an abstraction. Likewise, once the 'point' is accepted as a model for the meeting of two boundaries, it is a small step to regarding a 'set of points' as a 'line' and thus there is an obvious link with unions, intersections, subsets, and so on, of the number field.

Mensuration forms a convenient connection between number and geometry. For example, specially shaped regions (e.g. rectangles) abound in the environment and the need to measure these arises. Area as a measure of a region (or surface) can be obtained by covering with tiles (say) and then counting

FIGURE 8.8

278

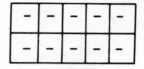

FIGURE 8.9

the tiles. In Figure 8.9 one can obtain the counting number, 10, by counting right through the set. Or one can obtain the expressions 2×5, 5×2, $5 + 5$, etc., by applying the technique learned when working in the number field.

ELEMENTARY MATHEMATICAL SYSTEMS AND PIAGETIAN STAGES—AN OVERVIEW

It is relevant at his stage to draw together some of the threads by looking more specifically at the relationship which exists between a child's ability to handle elementary mathematical material and the Piagetian stages.

A system may be said to consist of a structure of relationships which have as their bases a set of elements and a clearly defined method of operating thereon. If this definition is acceptable, consideration must be given to the two basic variables, the elements and the operations. Before looking at these from a psychological viewpoint, a brief excursion into what is involved for a competent mathematician working in the field of elementary mathematics seems warranted. The model in Figure 8.10 appears to cover most cases. The empirical field A represents the initial problem of measuring, predicting, or recording a measure of some empirical phenomenon. Let us think of the typical question: 'how many?' The subject maps the relevant aspects of the problem into the number field, operates according to the model which appears appropriate in the number field, and then maps the result of his calculation back into the empirical field. Alternatively, after mapping into the number field, the mathematician may find it necessary to make a further abstraction by mapping into field C. For instance, if the mapping into the number field indicates a need for the use of logarithms, the numbers are mapped into this field and the individual works with the operations appropriate to this field, returning to the empirical field via the number field. Occasionally the mapping might go directly from A to C. On other occasions, for instance cases where the problem is essentially associated with the relationship between the numbers themselves, as in the solving of equations, the mappings will take place only between fields B and C. Each of the fields A, B, and C represent a system with the elements and operations forming the basis for a number of interrelation-

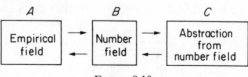

FIGURE 8.10

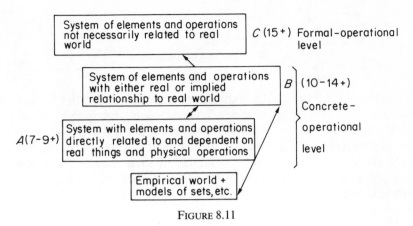

FIGURE 8.11

ships. The above may seem a reasonable logical breakdown of an exercise in elementary mathematics but, unfortunately, it does not seem to be isomorphic with the cognitive development shown by the child's ability to cope with certain kinds of mathematical material.

A psychological model, which takes better account of the Piagetian stages, may be summarized as shown in Figure 8.11. As the child emerges from the preoperational stage to the stage of concrete operations (seven to nine years) he is able to operate, in terms of the model, as far as stage *A*. From the age of ten years to fourteen years he gradually extends his ability to that represented by the highest level achievable in stage *B*, that is *concrete generalization*. Stage *C* represents a movement to formal operations proper. The model represents an hierarchical sequence of stages analogous to Piaget's concrete-to-formal operations continuum. Each stage in the hierarchy subsumes its predecessors. As the child moves up the sequence the stages become less reality-bound and, as a consequence, more flexible and efficient. The process of subsumption is such that the individual can return to working at a lower level in the sequence should he feel that the occasion warrants it.

Stages *A* and *B* represent what is generally considered the area of concrete operations, and are seen as a necessary precursor to the formal. thinking represented by stage *C*. Stage *A* begins when the basic conservation and classification skills are established and ends when the child seems to be able to cope with one arithmetic operation on two positive integers which remain within his empirically verifiable range. By the end of this stage the child is able to map from a narrowly specified reality to a positive integral number field, perform the arithmetic operation corresponding to elementary set operations, and map the result back into the real field. He needs, literally, to be able 'to see' a unique result before the operations either on sets or numbers mean anything to him. For example, $3 + 4 = 2 + 5$ *because* the following set of crosses:

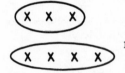 may be restructured thus: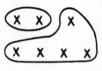

During stage B the child has the same basic skills to rely on, but the major advance is in the direction of less reliance upon 'seeing' uniqueness in the result of the operations. He is still bound to empirical evidence but is more content to infer beyond what can be demonstrated by model and to form a generalization by example from a number of specific cases. For instance, he can prove that $6 \times 54 = 3 \times 108$ by arguing from the partially completed model below:

$$54$$

```
  ┌ ┌ xxxxxxxxxxxxxxxxxxxxxxxxxxxxxxxxxxxxxxxxxxxxxxxxxxxxxx
  │ └ xxxxxxxxxxxxxxxxxxxxxxxxxxxxxxxxxxxxxx.................
  │ ┌ xxxxxxxxxxxxxxxxxxxxxxxxxxxxxxxx...... .. ......... ....
6 ⟨ └ xxxxxxxxxxxxxxxxxxxxxxxxxxxxxxx......................... 
  │ ┌ xxxxxxxxxxxxxxxxxxxxxxxxxxxxxxxxxxxxxxxxxx ...........
  └ └ xxxxxxxxxxxxxxxxxxxx ...............................
```

and, after a number of examples such as

$$\frac{2}{3} = \frac{2 \times 2}{2 \times 3} = \frac{3 \times 2}{3 \times 3} = \cdots$$

$$\frac{4}{5} = \frac{4 \times 5}{5 \times 5} = \cdots$$

he is willing to accept and to use the concrete generalization

$$\frac{a}{b} = \frac{m \times a}{m \times b}$$

In stage C, of course, he moves away completely from reliance on reality and works with abstract elements using the operations themselves.

Certain limitations are clearly built in to concrete operational thinking. A child at this level appears to be able to handle logical operations, provided they can be applied directly to particular experiences. He cannot relate operations to one another nor set up an abstract system independent of empirical experience. The ability to work with addition and multiplication operations at this stage would be tied initially to unions of sets of empirically available objects, either real or presented as ikons, developing to the stage where the real objects are not necessary but where the result of the operation must be regarded as unique, i.e. closed. In other words, the arithmetical operations must be seen as reflections of reality—the sums and products must refer to real sets of objects, whether present or not. This is the crux of the matter so far as concrete operations in elementary mathematics is concerned. For instance, both operations of addition and multiplication involve mapping two numbers into a unique third number belonging to the same set. If one derives from experience a formulae for finding the number of elements in the union of two disjoint sets (A and B say), $n(A) + n(B)$, the concrete operational child will be able to work meaningfully with it provided he can regard the result as unique. If there is any suspicion that $n(A)$ or $n(B)$, or the result, is variable, the child at this stage cannot be expected to cope with the problem. The formula may look abstract but he merely sees the symbols as 'names for', substitutions, or replacements for 'real' numbers which come from counting 'real' elements in 'real' sets, and the operation indicates a direct reflection of the experience of uniting two disjoint sets.

Thus the key to success in concrete operational-level reasoning with arithmetical operations can be related to the concept of 'closure' which was dealt with in the previous chapter. In this context, 'closure' means the ability to regard the outcome of an operation as unique and 'real', i.e. related to the individuals' reality. At its lowest level (apparent by the age of eight or nine years) this requires that two elements connected by the operation be replaced by a third number which is recognized as belonging to the same set. At a higher level (developed from ten to fourteen years of age) it involves regarding the outcome of performing the operation as necessarily unique, but it is not necessary to actually make the replacement to guarantee this.

There may be two levels involved within this latter stage also. First, the child may use numbers beyond his empirically verified range, including expressions involving multiple operations which can be closed sequentially. Then he might be expected to move on to what may be termed 'concrete generalizations' (Collis, 1969), where he has the capability of working with formulae such as $y = m \times s \times t$, provided he is able to consider that each letter stands for a unique number and each binary operation involved may be closed at any stage if necessary. This latter period would seem to be the appropriate time for the early signs of development of the proportional and correlational schemas. The final stage of development enables the adolescent to consider 'closure' in a formal sense, because he is able to operate on the operations and does not need to relate either the elements or the operations to reality.

From the above description one could reasonably expect that the eight or nine years old would be able to handle the four operations of elementary arithmetic using the small numbers within his experience. He should be able to show that the following pairs of expressions are equivalent:

(1) $3 + 6$ and $2 + 7$
(2) 4×3 and 6×2

As he moves into the next stage (ten to fourteen years) he should begin to succeed with items which require him to show that pairs of expressions such as the following are equivalent:

(1) $6 + 2 + 3$ and $3 + 6 + 2$
(2) $485 + 254$ and $486 + 253$

In addition, because uniqueness is guaranteed and trial closures possible, the child at this stage should find little difficulty with items of the type:

(1) If $9*5 = 4$ and $7*5 = 2$
what operation does $*$ stand for?
(2) If $6*3 = 18$ and $5*4 = 20$
what does $4*6$ equal?

Towards the end of this period it might be expected that these abilities come together to enable the young adolescent to cope with items where closure is guaranteed but where there are at least two operations involved and sequential closure is not a viable strategy—e.g. to decide whether the following pairs of expression are equivalent:

(1) $\dfrac{269 \times 416}{269}$ and $\dfrac{396 \times 416}{396}$

(2) $(467 + 362) - 258$ and $(469 + 363) - 261$

When adolescents have reached the final stage of development described above, i.e. where the ability to work without recourse to the uniqueness concept manifests itself, it could be expected that they could deal with items such as the following, where the subject is asked to decide on the equality or otherwise of pairs of expressions such as:

(1) $a + b$ and $(a + 1) + (b + 1)$
(2) $a + b$ and $(a + 1) + (b - 1)$
(3) $(a + 1) \times (b - 1)$ and $(a - 1) \times (b + 1)$
(4) $(a - b) \times (a + b)$ and $(a \times a) - (b \times b)$

The reader is reminded that the increasing level of difficulty is not regarded merely as a function of the degree of abstraction of the elements operated upon. The concept of 'closure' tends to mask the two aspects involved. One is certainly the abstractness of the elements themselves but the other, which appears more basic, is the structural properties characteristic of the operations themselves. The problem can be most easily explicated in terms of examples where combinations of two operations are required. For instance, if a child is presented with a problem such as:

$$\frac{4 + 8}{2} = ?$$

he can treat it as a series of operations to be closed successively, that is $4 + 8 = 12$; $12 \div 2 = 6$. Cases where combinations of operations cannot be broken down in this way represent a different level of functioning. Take, for example, cases where the expression as a whole must be considered. An obvious type of example involves Piaget's 'schema of proportionality', namely

$$\frac{A}{B} = \frac{xA}{xB}$$

If an individual is asked to verify the truth of statements such as:

$$\frac{4+8}{4} = \frac{2+4}{2}$$

$$\frac{224+122}{2} = \frac{448+244}{4}$$

$$\frac{a+b}{c} = \frac{2a+2b}{2c}$$

he is unable to do so (see Lovell, 1966) until he has reached the level of operation where the appropriate schema becomes available.

The theory of Halford (1970a) for the acquisition of concrete operations suggests that children combine judgments, numbers, or other units, two at a time, and select those combinations which yield unique results. Thus their judgments are restructured until closure is achieved. To attain formal operations they must be able to combine two units, one of which at least is itself an operation. For example, at the concrete operational level two numbers may be combined to give a unique result. At the formal operational level adolescents must be able to perform with a combination such as $(a + b) + x = c$. Here an operation $(a + b)$ is itself combined with another $(+ x)$ to yield a unique result. The key element in all such instances is that an operation is applied to something which is itself an operation. In other words, *the original operation* must have meaning as a unit even though the individual cannot close it arithmetically. For instance, if $(a + b) + x = (c + d) + x$, then $(a + b) = (c + d)$, even if $a \neq c$ and $b \neq d$.

9

CONCRETE AND FORMAL OPERATIONAL THINKING IN HISTORY

M. F. Jurd

In previous chapters it has been explained that Piaget's theory of development of the structures in thinking uses a logical operational model. The nature of this model has been one of the major factors influencing Piagetian research. Material which is easily described in terms of logical categories has been preferred, with the result that investigators of children's thinking, particularly those who hoped to show its relevance to school learning, have tended to use mathematical and scientific concepts and material. Yet Piaget's theory should have application to all kinds of material, and more recently interest has developed in its application to other school subject areas.

In this chapter the difficulty of using the logical model with other kinds of material is clarified by a brief, general view of the way in which the structure of the task is used in assessing the cognitive structures of the individual student. But the structure of the task must itself be compatible with the structure of the subject discipline. The structure of history is used as an example of the kinds of difficulty encountered in dealing with subject disciplines in which the emphasis is away from closed structures. The kinds of generalization used by historians and the kind of objectivity preferred by them requires that any investigator studying the development of thinking in that subject must modify his approach. Such modifications are rewarding, however, since research into cognitive development using social science material has demonstrated possible contributions to the clarification of the aims of teaching and the planning of sequences of learning activities.

How is the student's operational level assessed and how is this assessment dependent upon the task given? The question is considered in detail in relation to Inhelder and Piaget's own experiments in Chapter 11 (Seggie). In general, it may be said that when the operational level of individual students is being assessed, this level is defined in relation to the points of equilibrium which appear to occur in cognitive development. Such points of equilibrium are defined by structures or systems of logical operations. Piaget suggests a dynamic process in which a person gives meaning to his environment by assimilating objects and external data into existing cognitive structures or, where there is for him a noticeable discrepancy between the structures and the objects and data as he perceives them, he changes the structures to accommodate the new data in the environment. A state of equilibrium is said to be reached when there is a coordination of differentiated data and assimilatory structures. But as the person further differentiates the environment, the inadequacy of previous assimilatory structures is shown, and these are again modified to accommodate the newly recognized data until a further temporary equilibrium marks another stage of development.

The characteristic sets of logical operations used to define each stage are described elsewhere (Chapter 1). The stages mark a point of equilibrium for a person with regard to some aspect of his reasoning. Equilibrium exists within the person's experience when he is satisfied with the completeness of his explanation, irrespective of the correctness (in the mature adult's view) of that explanation. Thus the preoperational non-conserver of liquid is perfectly content that there is *more* lemonade in the tall glass, and the concrete operational conserver is content that the amount of lemonade is exactly the *same* since the glass is taller but thinner. Each of these children is at a point of equilibrium with regard to the concept of liquid quantity, and the thinking of each is adequately described by a closed structure in that his explanation has a certain completeness in itself. Such closed structures are stable.

By contrast, the transition from one stage to another is unstable and can only be understood in transformational terms if both of its termini are known (Piaget, 1970c, pp. 127–128). The child in a transition stage is likely to use first one explanation and then another, may contradict himself, and is likely to be more influenced by what the experimenter says or by modifications in the task. When he settles on an explanation it is only tentatively held, and he can be induced to change his mind. His thinking shows an unstable and comparatively open structure. He is not in a state of equilibrium and can only be described as transitional between, for example, concrete and formal operations.

These structural aspects of cognitive development are seen by Piaget (1973, pp. 15–16) as analogous to the structure and processes implicit in subject disciplines. Some disciplines seem to be more closely structured than others. The disciplines which use comparatively closed structures are said to include logico-mathematical structures, physical causality, and some social structures such as juridical structures. Other disciplines are those in which transformational processes are emphasized. Open structures are found where the process of constitution or reconstitution is an appropriate emphasis, such as in biological structures and social structures in the formative stages. Yet in all subjects the structures are constructed and may be transformed into new structures by some kind of dialectic process. Piaget mentions an inevitable progression once thought turns away from false absolutes. There is a recurrent historical process whose principle is that, 'given a completed structure, one negates one of its seemingly essential or at least necessary attributes' (Piaget, 1970c, p. 123). Such construction by negation is said to be a frequently used method in logic and mathematics, while similar constructions occur in other material. This process has parallels in individual development.

People working within disciplines and describing the nature of them tend to emphasize either the closed or open nature of the structure. In elementary mathematics and physical causality the use of closed structures tends to predominate, but in history the emphasis is frequently on the changes which occur over time and consequently the structures seem more open. Investigators of cognitive development usually provide a situation explicable in terms of a closed structure, e.g. one involving physical causality (Inhelder and Piaget, 1958), or mathematics (Collis Chapter 7), or isomorphic to a group or groupoid (Halford Chapter 6 and Sheppard Chapter 3) or a problem in logic (Seggie Chapter 11). In that situation the operations can be defined in two ways: first, in terms of the task, but second in terms of the person's thinking about the structure of the task. Since the characteristics of the cognitive stages are described at their points of equilibrium and in terms of logic, both of which provide closed structures, a more satisfactory match between the person's thinking and the theoretical model is possible if the task material also uses a closed structure.

Does that mean that the tasks also can be described as being at concrete or formal operational levels? Undoubtedly the complexity of the structure in the material as viewed by the experimenter defines the probable optimal operational level of the task. For example, if the INRC group is used the level may be called 'formal operational', whereas if the task is one of class inclusion with perceptible objects the level may be called 'concrete operational'. Conservation tasks are similar in that it is the structure of the particular concept or conservation which identifies the operational level. Though 'conservation' has usually been used to refer to concepts such as length, number, and quantity, and these are defined at the concrete operational level, conservation can be at either the concrete or the formal level (Inhelder and Piaget, 1958, p. 106). Each task has an operational level as defined by the investigator's view of it.

The operational level of the student's thinking is usually judged by his explanation of the task. His thinking about the structure of the task is matched against the theoretical model. If the student is given a formal-level task and gives a comprehensive explanation of it, his thinking is regarded as formal operational, but if he explains the problem by a limited substructure within the task, he is said to have made a premature closure at either a preoperational or concrete operational level.

Inhelder and Piaget have always insisted, however, that the definition of the student's operational level of thinking cannot be based upon any one explanation of a task, but that it is the whole process of his argument which reveals the operational level of his thinking—hence their use of clinical interviews. Collis has also demonstrated that formal operational-level thought processes can sometimes be identified in concrete operational-level tasks and, perhaps more importantly, that formal operational-level processes of thinking, e.g. systematic combination of variables, are sometimes displayed even when the 'best' explanation of the particular formal task is not given. Obviously, however, the task and the level of student's thinking are interactive. If the task can be adequately explained with concrete operational thinking, many 'normally' formal thinkers will not exert themselves beyond the concrete level. Again, when the particular material of a task is unfamiliar, formal processes may be displayed without an adequate explanation being found. A variety of other interactive effects may occur, for example, when the task matches the model, but seems artificial to the person attempting it.

In the context of this chapter the interactive effect of immediate concern is that between the nature of the questions which the experimenter may want to ask to get at the logical operations being used by the student and the nature of the questions which the subject specialist may regard as legitimate in a study of his subject. Social sciences, for example, are typically more open in structure, and it is important that the nature of the subject should not be grossly distorted to fit an inappropriate model. Consequently, the investigator must consider to what extent the logical operational model, which is reasonably applicable to closed structures, may be used in tasks with more open structures. Though open structures are recognized as part of Piaget's total theory, they are identified with transitional periods which tend to defy definition. It may be that as the process of transition is further investigated and more clearly described, new analogies with open structure tasks will become available. Riegel (1973) has already pointed out the need for investigation of dialectic thinking, and feels it has not been sufficiently recognized by Piaget. Meantime, however, it is useful to consider to what extent it is legitimate to treat more openly structured material as though it existed in a closed system.

With this problem in mind a brief study is made of the nature of history as described by historians and the extent to which cognitive development as reflected in logical operations may be investigated with history-type material. Particular consideration is given to the kinds of generalization possible and to the nature of objectivity.

THE NATURE OF HISTORY

The content of history is the account of man's activities in changing his society over a period of time. The purpose of the study of history is probably found in its contribution to the preservation and continued change of society. By explicating the origins of contemporary social institutions the study of history leads to an appreciation of the efforts of the various men and forces which made present society. It may also elucidate the values inherent in present institutional procedures. On the basis of such knowledge features of present society may be retained or changed. Contrast between societies demonstrates the variety and appropriateness of different activities in serving man's changing and unchanging needs. Awareness of past changes in societies, over varying periods of time, may indicate the nature and degree of change possible in relation to the stability or disruption of communities.

Marwick (1970, p. 14) sums up many of the above purposes by seeing history as providing a memory for present-day society, in the same way as memory provides stability and continuity within the life of a person. This memory society uses in order to know itself and to understand its relationship with the past and with other societies and cultures as they have developed over time. Yet, as happens in personal memory, each society or historian will select and interpret past experience in the light of his own needs and understanding. No age is ever completely and finally understood and interpreted.

Thus history tends not only to emphasize changes over time and to resist the close encapsulation of events in a closed system, but it also recognizes that explanations are relative to present insight and themselves are subject to changing interpretation. For these reasons history, by its nature, must retain an open structure.

How does this particularly affect the questions which may be asked by investigators of logical operational thinking? Among those aspects of history which have most immediate relation to logical operations are the use of concepts and generalizations and the achievement of objectivity. Both these aspects are also present in the physical sciences, but in slightly different form, and the comparison of the two may elucidate the modifications necessary in assessing operational thinking about historical material.

GENERALIZATIONS

Two forms of generalization are commonly considered important. These are generalization as found in law-giving hypotheses and generalization as reflected in concept formation or identification. A distinctive characteristic of formal operational thought is the ability to formulate and verify law-giving hypotheses. The differences between subject disciplines in the possibility of discovering such law-giving hypotheses and describing them in logical form which enables their verification may be seen by contrasting a school science experiment with an analysis of causal events in a social science or in history. In both situations the purpose is to produce a verifiable generalized statement.

In the physical sciences it is possible to isolate clearly an area for investigation, to enumerate and to define the relevant and irrelevant variables, to replicate the event and to note correspondences between events, logically to induce generalizations, and to verify these by the controlled manipulation of variables. In such an enclosed system it is possible to use logical argument with considerable stringency. Admittedly, within contemporary science there is a marked change away from viewing phenomena as occurring within closed systems where determinism, precise quantification, and impersonality are assumed, but to an even greater extent such assumptions are untenable in social sciences. Construction of structures and models, statements in probability terms, and the interaction of the scientist with his material are obvious necessities when complex social situations are examined. In social situations it is not as easy to isolate an area for investigation. It is also difficult to know which variables are relevant and which irrelevant at any one time, and it is particularly difficult to define them. If variables cannot be defined they cannot be satisfactorily used as terms in logical argument. Further, social events do not exactly repeat themselves and cannot easily be replicated, so correspondences between them are less easily observed; without such correspondences the logical induction of a generalized statement is not possible, and without the possibility of the controlled manipulation of variables the process of verifying the generalized statement is more difficult. A further factor which accentuates the differences between the physical and social sciences is that the actual material to be investigated becomes less concrete and perceptible, so that social scientists, more frequently than physical scientists, use hypothetical constructs as variables. In these ways, though the purpose is similar in all sciences, the nature of the material makes the use of precise logical argument more difficult within the social sciences.

Examples may explicate the contrast. Some of the science questions used by Inhelder and Piaget (1958) are: 'Why do some objects float and others not?', 'Why does a ball bounce from a wall in a certain direction?' and, 'Why do some rods bend more than others?'. Students who are asked a question about floating objects, for instance, are given a well-defined situation. The concrete material ia available to them in the form of a limited variety of objects of various definable sizes, shapes, and weights and a tank of water. Students can be reasonably sure that the answer is discoverable from the manipulation of the apparatus provided. For instance, they can try each object for its ability to float or sink, and they can try the same object as many times as they want to discover whether it is the shape, size, or weight which is important. It is quickly apparent that the colour of the objects is irrelevant. They can organize the material within the restricted number of relevant categories suggested by it, and look for correspondence among the various sequences of events. When it is apparent that neither the weight nor the size of the object alone accounts for the floating, they may guess that the weight and size combined may be important. Then they can retest to see whether this hypothesis, or any other they consider, is correct. The whole situation may be systematically and thoroughly investigated with the assurance that the main factors are all present and the behaviour of the objects will be consistent when the experiment is replicated. Hence it is possible to induce a general rule and conclude that an object will float if it is of less weight than the volume of water displaced by it. It is even possible to predict with a high degree of probability whether future objects of known weight and volume will float.

By contrast, when a question is asked about the cause of an event in history, e.g. 'Why were the British colonies established in North America in the eighteenth country?', there is no clearly isolated situation to be investigated. Britain's own position and her need for trade are important, but what of the influence of French colonization, or of the Dutch and Spanish? Documentary evidence could be found to support the idea that Britain wanted to increase her success in trade, but are such documents representative of the opinion of all the colonizing groups from Britain? Or is there other evidence suggesting different causes? What of the Puritans settling in Massachusetts Bay? Further, the evidence available is limited and preselected by the accident of documentation. In an open system the cause of an event may include many other events and/or the nature of the people involved in concurrent or preceding events. Even those purposes whose existence may not be identifiable until revealed by future events may be among the causes.

Apart from the problem of their relevance or irrelevance as causes, the actual isolating of variables is complicated by the fact that in historical situations these variables are not readily defined. For instance, how is 'the establishment of colonies' to be defined? Does it imply the settlement of a population from Europe or merely that trade relations were established? The definition of variables is important, since if different attributes are considered relevant when the same phrase is used on different occasions, then the terms are no longer the same for the purposes of logical argument. Sometimes measurement may aid in the definition of attributes, e.g. the number of settlers, but 'the establishment of colonies' cannot be defined only in terms of the number of settlers, though this factor may make an important difference to the kind of colony.

In history the imaginative reproduction of a situation for the purpose of testing the causal effect of variables is partly dependent on the use of analogy. Supposing trade were a variable, how would the British Parliament of today react to a problem of trade? Would merchants influence the Government decision? But the situation was different at that time. Would the Government have reacted in the same way in the eighteenth century as in the nineteenth century or as today? Since governments change, to what extent is a generalized statement possible?

When similar situations are identified in lieu of the replication of an experiment, i.e. as the establishment of other colonies is investigated, the relevant variables seem different; the opportunities for trade in New South Wales were non-existent at first. Trade may be a relevant variable at one time and not at another. Many interacting factors existed in ever-varying proportion. Establishing correspondences between series of events is difficult. It seems doubtful whether any general statement about the establishment of the British colonies can be proven.

In general, then, when variables, e.g. 'colonisation' and 'potential power', cannot be defined, when it is difficult to estimate their probable relevance as causes, and when situations cannot be replicated, so that there is at most only an approximate correspondence between sequences of events, the logical induction of a hypothesis may not seem appropriate. Hence there is reluctance and frequently refusal by historians to venture towards the statement of a law. Further, any deduction which might be made from a generalised hypothesis at the level of a law, and which would thus aid verification, is as likely to be either false or true through imprecise definition of terms as through matching against reality.

The process of verification is further inhibited by the impossibility of the controlled manipulation of variables. The outcome of each past situation is known. Only with the present can men attempt to change the proportional influence of various factors, and this they would do for purposes more complex than the systematic investigation of causal variables. Even then only one total manipulation of a situation is possible and the game is called 'politics', rather than 'history'.

In the past some teachers have overcomë this problem in history teaching by providing the preselected evidence of one textbook whose author has structured a closed system for the student. Variables are isolated and conclusions reached by the textbook writer. In such a situation the student does not have to think.

In order to avoid distorting the nature of historical study it is important to realize what is legitimate for historians. Historians themselves debate the use of generalizations in history. Whereas the purpose of science is to discover explanatory laws, many historians would deny this as a purpose of the study of history. Carr (1972) and Marwick (1970) see the tendency for historians to formulate or refuse to formulate laws as itself an historical phenomenon. Carr (1972, pp. 60–65) believes that generalizations, similar to scientific hypotheses, are necessary. He mentions the use of such fruitful hypotheses as 'Max Weber's famous diagnosis of a relation between Protestantism and capitalism'. He also quotes Elton's comment that 'what distinguishes the historian from the collector of historical facts is generalisation', and he further argues that hypotheses are gradually verified by scholarly concensus of opinion and adopted over time in the same way as scientists also adopt their hypotheses after further investigation. Carr concludes that 'history is concerned with the relation between the unique and the general. As a historian, you can no more separate them, or give precedence to one over the other, than you can separate fact and interpretation'. The scientist, however, would give precedence to the generalization.

Other historians deny the importance of generalizing laws. For Barbaum (1968), while the causal explanation in science is the relation between a particular fact and a universal law, the causal explanation in history is the relation between a particular fact and specific initial conditions. Similarly, Renier (1961, p. 76) rejects the possibility of historical laws, claiming that they are only tools which provide 'a point of view from which events, common origins, analogous motives, may be appreciated'. Again, both Burston and Dray stress the importance of history as lying in the particular event. Burston (1954, p. 17) suggests that 'the special characteristic of history is its preoccupation with the individual event and its desire to show, not why revolutions occur, but the special individual, non-recurrent reason why a particular revolution occurred when it did'. While many historians may classify events by similarities, their interest is said to be in the differences between that event and other events or conditions within the same classification. Dray (1957, p. 55) argues that 'collating a number of conditions, including supporting laws, is not applying a further covering law'. He suggests that such supporting laws as may be used in history are 'borrowed' from sociology, psychology, economics, or the historian's individual bias.

The debate apparently continues, but whether the generalizations made are elevated to the status of laws or whether they remain as comprehensive explanations some verification is needed for those probability statements and interpretations which the historian makes. Two possibilities in attempting the verification of causal relations have been suggested by Dray (1957). One is that in evaluating the suggested cause of an event the historian should 'think away' the suggested cause in order to judge what difference its non-occurrence might make. This is similar to the construction by negation mentioned earlier: "What would have happened if X were not so?" Thus the historian must do in thought what the scientist may do in reality. While the scientist may keep weight constant to judge whether it has an effect, the historian must imagine what would have happened if only a few British people had actually settled in North America. This is not so easy; it involves seeing the implications of a hypothesis.

The second possible method of verification which Dray (1957, p. 104) suggests is that where the scientist's conclusion carries the qualifying phrase 'all other things being equal', the qualifying phrase for the historian should be 'the situation being as it was'. The scientist ensures that all other things are equal by separating the variables and considering the effect of each separately. In stating the qualifier, 'the situation being as it was', the historian indicates that other mentioned and unmentioned features have been taken into account in arriving at a conclusion. An implicit assumption in the historian's qualifier would seem to be that if the situation were changed, the outcome might also be changed. The systematic verification of the necessary cause is not possible in history, but attempts may be made towards it, and it will be seen, in the next chapter, that these attempts may be useful to the investigator of logical operational thinking at the formal level.

While generalizations at the formal operational level are frequently tested in relation to law-giving hypotheses, at the concrete operational level generalizations have been considered as classifications, i.e. as concepts. As mentioned previously, however, concepts including conservation-type concepts may sometimes have structures which require formal operational thought. (See also Seggie, Chapter 12). Generalizations as concepts are useful since it would appear that while some historians debate the use of law-giving hypotheses, all are prepared to classify data and to talk of 'revolutions', of 'periods of time', and of 'democratic government'. Further, a particular categorization has been offered (Walsh, 1967) which may be regarded as a kind of conservation concept, since it 'corresponds to the property that is left unchanged across various transformations of the object' (Elkind and Flavell, 1969, p. 187), or, in this case, across transformations brought about through time. These are 'colligatory concepts' about which Walsh (1967, p. 73) says that they 'can be characterised as complex states of affairs which are systematically changing as the result of human effort'.

Colligatory concepts would encompass such things as 'the growth of democratic government' which might differ widely in the particularity of its occurrence in any one country or at different periods of time. The definition of the term is also likely to be markedly different at different times and places, yet the term has sufficient generality to go beyond the mere description of events and to aid in the formulation of interpretive hypotheses. Notice, however, that the concepts are said to 'interpret' or to 'aid' explanations, rather than to 'explain' history. They may be used to interpret actions such as the unfolding of a clearly defined purpose or policy, e.g. the struggle for political independence, but in doing this the historian is warned that no appearance of inevitability should be allowed. While a policy may, or may not, emerge as an accomplishment in time, the many accidents and irregularities which occur within the situation should also be recognized. Colligatory concepts may be used (Thompson in Burston and Thompson, 1967, p. 89) 'to separate happenings which have a specific connection, to aid in the explanation of the final event and to make the particular events more meaningful', e.g. the concept of the 'rise of the middle class'. Finally, they may also be used to 'single out the powerful forces operating in society at given times in the past', and so be able to state the essence of an age, e.g. the concept of the 'age of reason'. Such concepts do not include any notion of a necessary cause, but they do offer a further possible approach to the testing of logical operations in history-type material.

In summary, then, it may be said that in the matter of generalization history differs from science in that it does not see as its main purpose the production of verifiable law-giving hypotheses. Because historical events must be regarded as occurring within a more open system the logic which is legitimate in physical experiments is not as readily applied in history. Causal factors are multiple, complex probabilities. Events may be classified, but terms are not precisely definable. The invariant order of definable factors found in physical sciences is replaced in history by sequences of events having correspondences and by similarities between events which permit the naming of classes. Consequently, the induction and verification of laws which is appropriate with the physical sciences is replaced in history by a generalized interpretation which may be partially verified, and by classifications such as colligatory concepts. Research into logical operational thought with such open structure material must give implicit recognition to these facts and may result in the use of approximate parallels such as those indicated above. While the particular modifications suggested here are taken up in the next chapter, there is considerable research evidence available which has examined generalization as comprehensive explanation and as concepts.

RESEARCH ON GENERALIZATIONS AS HYPOTHESIS FORMATION AND COMPREHENSIVE EXPLANATION

Most research in the area of open structure material has concentrated on the comprehensiveness of explanations given by a student, i.e. the use made of evidence presented. Short stories of incidents such as a girl minding her brother or a pilot flying his plane into a cable were used by Peel (1965). Students' responses to questions were analysed into broad categories paralleling Piagetian stages. Peel (1965) described development in thinking as moving along a continuum from describer to explainer thinking, one of the differences between these two being that explanation involved deduction from a basis of hypotheses whereas 'description turns on inductive methods' (p.174). In general, he found that subjects were 14 + years before they gave comprehensive explanations.

Peel's work and the approximate categories he used have formed the basis of work by Case and Collinson (1962) in history, geography, and literature; by Lodwick (1965) and Hallam (1967) in history; and by Rhys (1972) in geography. The criteria used were based on Piagetian stages and were outlined most precisely by Hallam (1967, p. 85); they are included here (Table 9.1) to give an approximate idea of the levels of thinking involved. Using criteria similar to these it has been possible to identify a sequence of development with age, but without being able to describe exactly the stage of development for any one person.

The results of some of the investigations mentioned previously may be considered briefly. Lodwick (1959) gave three short passages of historical

TABLE 9.1. Criteria for stages of thinking used by Hallam (1967). (Reproduced by permission of *Educational Review*)

Stage	Some of the criteria used
Preoperational thinking	Not relating the question to the information provided. Not looking for possible contradictions in the thought processes. Isolated centerings on one feature only. Irreversibility of thought. Transductive and syncretic thinking.
Between preoperational and concrete operational thinking	More than one feature of the situation considered but the attempt to relate differing facts not too successful. Uncertainty of judgments; attempts at reversibility end in failure.
Concrete operational thinking	Able to give an organized answer but limited to what is apparent in the text; able to forecast a result from the evidence available; compensates one statement by another or negates a statement, but not able to coordinate negation and reciprocity.
Between concrete and formal operational thinking	Going outside the known data in the stories to form hypotheses, but not too successfully; beginning to relate different variables.
Formal operational thinking	Holds certain factors constant and varies others systematically in order to discover which explanations are true; hypotheses are postulated and then confirmed or not by the data; reasoning by implication at an abstract level; realizing a multiplicity of possible links.

interest and asked questions requiring inferential judgments. Since the passages and questions were of varying difficulty an attempt to combine scores and find one level for each pupil failed. Each child appeared to show a range of levels of answers, yet the sequence of development with age was apparent. Case and Collinson (1962) followed, and used passages with a variety of material. Again the questions were not similar to each other in difficulty, but all subjects from seven to seventeen years gave at least one answer at formal operational level. Hallam (1967) comments that Case and Collinson's criteria were surprisingly undemanding. Both studies attempted to match the operational stage with chronological or mental age, but children of similar mental age were not necessarily at the same operational stage, though there was a general trend in that direction.

The most substantial work of this kind in history was done by Hallam (1967) who presented three historical passages in interview to 100 volunteers between eleven and sixteen years, i.e. twenty students from each of the first five years of a coeducational school. Each of the passages given provided conflicting evidence on the question asked—questions such as 'Was William of Normandy a cruel man?', 'Why do you think so?'. The reasons for the answers given were categorized according to the criteria stated above. Because of variations in the pupil's level of thinking and variations in question difficulty, a global assessment was made of each pupil's level. Results indicated that formal operational thinking did not usually begin before sixteen years. While correlation of total scores was higher with mental than with chronological age, it was clear that operational thinking was not exactly the same as general intelligence reflected in mental age.

One of the distinctive contributions made by Rhys (1972) was the use of a variety of source material. In five different geographical case studies, maps and pictures as well as verbal material were used. Children (120) between 9 years 9 months and 16 years 3 months were tested in groups, except for the use of photographs which required individual presentation. Once again, scoring categories similar to those used by Peel (1965) were employed. The problems posed were carefully analysed and covered a variety of aspects of geographical study. In one problem a map, photograph and short text were used to depict rice-dominant, intensive subsistence tillage in an area of dense population. The questions focused on the contrast with British farming practices. One question related specifically to the map and asked: 'The British farmer normally lives away from the village with his land grouped around his home in a single piece. Why do you think the Japanese farmer lives in the village with his land scattered in a number of separate places?' (Rhys, 1972, p. 98). We may notice that in many ways the problem is similar to a history question which requires conditions in their own country with those of another culture or time.

The answers to this question, as to others, despite the spatial and pictorial material, displayed the same kinds of thinking that were identified by other investigators, and, of course, initially by Piaget. The most mature answers, involving a comprehensive judgment based on hypothetico-deductive reasoning, were not reached until a mental age of 15½ years approximately. Not until 13½ years were children able to 'orientate themselves spatially within that context-of-action' or to 'draw on concepts or generalisations beyond the test material'. The interpretation of photographs showed similar trends since abstracted aspects of the material were being used.

Rhys (1972) relates his findings to more general aspects of Piaget's theory. He discusses the tendency for individuals to judge from within their own frame of reference, the 'continual advance and retreat of ego-centric behaviour as the child progresses through the successive stages of his development, resurgence occurring whenever the child is confronted with some new cognitive challenge' (pp. 102–103). The process is that of decentring, which will be discussed later.

Like Peel, Rhys argues for a gradual development from 'describer' to 'explainer' thinking. Though he is able to identify different stages, he emphasizes the gradual process of change throughout adolescence. His comprehensive understanding of the factors involved in adolescent cognitive development, combined with his analysis of the nature of geographic knowledge, provides a very useful guide to teachers and typifies the kind of exploratory research which can aid in the clarification of both the aims of teaching and the sequences of understanding. In all these studies considerable variations were found within the scores of any individual student. This was not very surprising, since, as was mentioned earlier, Inhelder and Piaget (1958, pp. 278–279) have also commented that from any one answer it is nearly impossible to tell at what level the child is thinking. They recommend comparing all statements by a single student.

One consistent difference found between these results and those of Inhelder and Piaget (1958), however, was the apparently late age for beginning formal operational thinking when verbal material was used. As suggested earlier in discussion of the contrast between history questions and the physical science experiments, the abstract nature of the material and, Hallam adds, the fact that the experiences described are remote from that of the child's experience, may be sufficient explanation of the age difference. In this connection several interesting comparisons with results from mathematical material are possible. Piaget and Inhelder had noted earlier (1951, p. 248) that, as the child moved from working with small, familiar numbers to large numbers with more than twenty or thirty elements, there was a later age of attainment, even though the same operation was being used. They suggested that the ability to generalize to larger numbers marked the point of equilibrium with regard to probabilistic composition. Similar findings were made by Keats (1955) and further explored later by Collis (1975). Collis' work has shown a clear progression in the use of concrete operations from small to large numbers, then to letters in formulae. He identifies a stage he calls 'concrete generalisations' in which concrete operations are applied more generally. The description seems particularly apt for those concrete operations identified in verbal material beyond the child's immediate experience. Peel, who had previously refrained from precisely identifying Piagetian stages in his own material, has independently recognized the importance of the generalization of concrete operations and agrees with Collis' term (personal communication from Collis). A distinction is therefore made by Collis which enables him to use 'concrete generalisation' to replace 'formal operational IIIA'. This replacement of terms is probably not justified within a more general view of Piaget's theory. First, if the nature of the material serves to induce more probabilistic and hypothetical thinking then something approaching formal operations are involved. Second, the theory of stage development does not require the completion of one stage before the commencement of the next, and evidence is accumulating that an overlap of stages in different kinds of material and on different items is highly probable. It has been argued that 'it is the usual case that a stage-specific item continues to develop towards whatever eventually constitutes its functional maturity after one or more subsequent stages are in process' (Flavell, 1971a, p. 431). As was suggested earlier, the use of generalized terms and propositions instead of familiar objects results in late concrete operational activities beginning in early adolescence. The sequence of development is maintained in that the beginning of formal operational thought with the same social science material seems to be coincident with formal operational level IIIB in more concrete material.

A further comparison of indicators of logical operations in mathematical material with those found in social science is Collis' indicator of 'acceptance of lack of closure' (ALC). This first appears at the same age as Hallam's indicator of 'going outside the known data'. Both seem to be formal operational. The student refrains from making a closure at the point of simple inference and accepts a lack of closure until he can make a complete complex inference— in Hallam's example by adding material. The formal operational student is able to make a closure which he regards as adequate for the problem given, but the system is not permanently closed. This is the kind of closure acceptable to historians. If further discrepant information is made available the student is then willing to seek a new structure to account for the new information. Any closure he makes is regarded as only one of a number of possible closures. Such closure is said to be indicative of the change at the formal operational level from a focus on reality to one on possiblity. Similarly, if the information provided is inadequate to explain the problem this student will go beyond that information to seek material for a more comprehensive closed system. This latter situation is the one seen most clearly in material such as Peel's in which a relatively unstructured story contains insufficient information to answer the question asked. The formal operational thinker recognizes the discrepancies in the material and provides alternative offerings of additional information with which to form hypotheses. It would seem that effective use of ALC is a necessary part of thinking at a formal level with open structure material.

Research on generalization as hypothesis formation and as comprehensive explanation thus suggests that the sequence of cognitive development as outlined by Piaget may be discovered in a variety of material. Though the problems posed with open structure material have not required the identification of law-giving hypotheses which may be stringently verified, they have required the formulation of hypotheses which may be confirmed or not by a systematic consideration of the data available or by a recognition that it is necessary to go beyond the data given. The research studies have shown that it is possible to ask questions which relate thinking to the logical operational model without violating the structure that is implicit in the subject material.

Further exploration of the sequences of development and the concurrence of items of different kinds is necessary before clear conclusions on the nature of cognitive development are possible. Interrelations between cognitive items and their gradual, asynchronous development may be of particular interest (Flavell, 1971a, p. 451). For teachers there is clearly a need to recognize the kind of abstractions from concrete material which they are requiring their students to make, as well as to be aware of the operations involved in answering particular questions.

RESEARCH ON GENERALIZATIONS AS CONCEPTS

The second kind of generalization mentioned as possible with open structure material was that of classification as concepts. Though little previous research has shown explicit awareness of the logical operations implicit within social science concepts, a good deal of work has been concerned with the vocabulary or the labels for concepts.

Teachers are aware that the terms which label the concepts in any subject must be understood by the student. Even in history, which uses a minimum of technical language, terms may be confusing and there is the additional hazard that in history the meaning of words changes over time; 'democracy' is a notable example. Moreover, many historical terms may be shown to have different meanings in other contexts. 'Ruler', 'subject', 'church', 'party', and 'revolution' would be some words like this. The tendency is for children to use the word in the context which is most familiar to them.

This use of a familiar context was demonstrated by Milburn (1972), who tested 500 primary (eight to eleven years) and 500 secondary (eleven to sixteen years) children in England on 215 terms commonly used in geography. He found that pupils in the final year of both primary and secondary school knew approximately 62 per cent. of the terms used in the school subject. Among primary children in particular, but also with secondary, the child tended to adopt the meaning most related to his own experience. Consequently words were misread, e.g. 'more' for 'moor', 'good at painting' for 'artesian', 'going to another country' for 'irrigation'. Words were also interpreted within a known context, e.g. 'channel': 'where people go who can swim furthest', 'fault': 'it is your fault'.

This tendency to use the most familiar context for a word would be expected from what is known of assimilatory structures. The child would use the familiar context until a discrepancy in meaning was apparent to him and he would then be persuaded to accommodate his thinking to this new meaning. It is the teacher's task to highlight such discrepancies.

Analysing the vocabulary of geography textbooks, Milburn discovered that terms were frequently introduced without definition or with a partial definition.

Beside this inadequate intensive definition, the extensive definition given was often misleading, e.g. 27 out of 30 references to fiords referred to Norway. Milburn apparently did not analyse the kind of errors made by children at each age or relate them to cognitive theory, but he did note that despite a marked increase in verbal fluency during adolescence there was no equivalent increase in the understanding of the meanings of the words used.

The analysis of textbook material, as well as the testing of pupils' civic vocabulary, was undertaken in Australia by Rayner (1951). The results of testing gave the same general indication that pupils in schools were exposed to a vocabulary much of which had little meaning for them. Rayner also noted that the words used in textbooks were not those words about civic affairs which were most commonly used in newspapers. Consequently, the pupil was provided with only one general context, either textbook or newspaper, each of which was frequently inadequate, in which to form the meaning of words.

The problem of the language used and the level of cognitive development achieved is a recurrent one, particularly in Piagetian studies, for as Piaget maintains, and as is suggested by the above evidence, understanding does not necessarily accompany the use of words, and a greater contribution to thinking, at least before formal operations, is made by the internalization of actions rather than by the extension of vocabulary. The search for the usable meaning in words expressed seems a necessary supplement to the study of vocabulary levels. Dennis (1971) and Coltham (in Peel, 1967b) both attempted this task. The study by Dennis (1971) was on the use of political terms which, in the context given, were applicable to the present-day situation, but the words are also relevant to history.

Dennis tested 297 fifth, eighth, and ninth graders in Wisconsin asking them for the meaning of 'government', 'political parties', 'democracy', etc. He also interviewed 205 of their parents. The question was a simple one, e.g. 'When you think about "government" what comes to your mind?'. In this study Dennis noted the kind of changes which occurred in meaning; the word 'politics' was described first in terms of government structure and later in terms of processes, elections, and parties. Fifty-one per cent. of the fifth grade did not know the meaning of political parties; 20 per cent. of the eighth grade and 10 per cent. of the eleventh grade had the same ignorance. For 'government', 38 per cent. of fifth grade students understood this in terms of the President and 34 per cent. in terms of Congress, but by the eleventh grade 85 per cent. of students mentioned the law-making function of Congress. For this word parents tended to be more like eighth- than eleventh-grade students in their answers.

In the other investigation junior school children were asked by Coltham (in Peel, 1967b) to say verbally, and to draw, the meaning of the words 'king', 'early man', 'invasion', 'ruler', 'trade', and 'subject'. Coltham demonstrated a clear progression by age from king with pomp, through king with power, to king with power and change. Only in the last stage was there a reference to the important time dimension in kingship, and there were only a few mature answers such as 'kings used to have power but not now' (Peel, 1967b, pp. 169–170). Similar progression was found with 'trade', from a specific occupation (greengrocer) 'through ideas of retail, transport, on to the principle of exchange, then to exchange and commerce' (Peel, 1967b, pp. 169–170). Thus both Dennis and Coltham note a change from understanding in relation to position or place, to understanding in relation to function or process.

The measuring of the use of vocabulary against Piagetian stages was attempted by De Silva (1972), who used the developmental analysis suggested by Peel. The problem of historical terms was approached by presenting ten passages of historical interest in which a nonsense word was substituted for a key idea such as 'depression' or 'slump'. Students were asked to define the nonsense word and justify the use of the substitute word they gave. Scoring responses in categories very similar to Peel's and to Hallam's it was found that no real differences existed between twelve, thirteen, and fourteen year olds, but significant differences occurred between fourteen, fifteen, and sixteen year olds. Logically restricted responses and circumstantial conceptualizations using a single piece of evidence were typical of the younger ages. Then logical possibilities using two or more items of evidence were found. Some degree of generality and deductive conceptualization preceded the exploration of the whole passage in a deductive way, at which final stage the drawing of integrated and reasoned inferences was possible. The indications from this study are that the understanding of words as concepts might follow a similar course to the comprehension of verbal passages.

De Silva felt that since many historical terms are introduced mainly through contextual passages and without precise definition, erroneous concepts are likely to be formed. His study also recognized, as Hallam's had done, that the tendency of historians to write with 'style' can be a barrier to a student's understanding.

These studies of vocabulary clearly indicate that cognitive development in the understanding of terms is an important factor for the teacher of history to appreciate. There is evidence also that the kind of developments occurring are compatible with Piaget's theory. The same could be said of the comprehension of terms denoting time which are also used in history. The adult comprehension of terms, dates, and chronological sequences is reached at about the age of sixteen years. Though there is improvement with age, Gill (1964) found that for students between the fifth and eight grades, terms such as 'in colonial times' and 'the last decade' were loosely interpreted. Research on other aspects of time suggest some of the complexity involved in giving words meanings. In the study of history three aspects of time seem important: (a) the ordering of events into sequence, possibly similar to seriation, (b) the grouping of concurrent events in time, e.g. the Reformation, possibly similar to the forming of classes, and (c) the establishment of a sense of continuity in time between past and present.

An appreciation of the importance of chronology may reasonably be expected to be dependent upon seriation of number, yet ordering seems to be further delayed. Oakden and Sturt, and Bradley (reported in Jahoda, 1963) each found that it was not until eleven years that over 80 per cent. of pupils could order three events given with dates attached. Until that age all historical events belonged in 'the past', so that grouping of events into meaningful units was also not possible. After that approximate age there was an understanding of the reckoning of time, and time periods could then be differentiated. Recognition of time as a convention separated from actual events is generally held to occur at about $13\frac{1}{2}$ years (Jahoda, 1963, p. 93).

Rogers (1967) differentiated between 'historical' and 'integral' time. 'Historical' time included historical sequence, analogy, temporal absurdity, and the reconstruction of an historical account from scrambled data. 'Integral' time involved chronology. He found that whereas understanding of historical time showed a marked improvement between $12\frac{1}{2}$ and $13\frac{1}{2}$ years, significant improvement on integral time occurred between $13\frac{1}{2}$ and $14\frac{1}{2}$ years.

The concept of time, in the sense of events having a past cause or a future consequent, is apparently not appreciated until mid-adolescence (Adelson, 1971). Only by that age are leaders and others seen to make a choice between alternatives based on long-term consequences. Other aspects of thinking about time have been investigated, but these seem to have less immediate relevance to history. If these aspects are considered as part of the understanding of concepts of time, it is clear that generalizations about historical periods will not necessarily be meaningful at all ages.

Concepts as generalized statements of classifications are thus seen to have varying levels of difficulty depending upon the kind of abstraction required in selecting attributes, the structure of the relations between attributes, and the extent of the student's experience. The problem is analysed in more detail in the following chapter. It is sufficient here to note that teachers need to be aware of many difficulties arising in the use of technical vocabulary.

In summary, it seems possible to conclude that within the study of generalizations it is necessary to introduce some modifications from law-giving hypothesis formation and testing, but that in comprehensive explanations and in the understanding of concepts it is possible to find research evidence indicating the sequential development of logical operational thinking.

OBJECTIVITY AND DECENTRING

The second area of particular interest in relating history to the study of logical operations is the nature of objectivity. A measure of objectivity is commonly taken as the ability to answer the question 'Do we know what really happened?'. In both science and history a consensus of opinion among investigators is a good indicator of objectivity. Yet 'what really happened' involves, of necessity, some interpretation of facts, both in science and history. Here the comprehensiveness and simplicity of the explanation offered is assumed to be a valid indicator of the 'truth', even if the explanation is offered by only one person. Both consensus of opinion and adequacy of explanation are criteria of objectivity.

Historians value concensus of opinion with the same kind of reservation as they value generalization. It is desirable but the importance of the historian's particular point of view or interpretation of events (as to the individual event) gives coherence to an account which may otherwise be a chronology. Obviously the historian will try for an interpretation which is both comprehensive and compatible with the facts as he knows them. Yet he is under no obligation to justify his approach as the only one possible, i.e. to verify it as though it were law-giving hypothesis. The comprehensiveness and simplicity of the explanation may finally command some concensus of approval. Meantime, the historian's individual approach is so well recognized that some people maintain that in order to understand history it is necessary to know the historian.

In taking up his own particular point of view, it should be clear that no historian would deliberately distort the facts, or take up so biased a position that only one side of the argument is presented. Neither could he be an advocate of unsubstantiated rhetoric. He has an obligation to use the factual evidence available and he acknowledges the obligation of other historians, at least to be critical of his work. Yet he will present a case for a particular interpretation of events. At its most naive and unacceptable he may, through his interpretation, participate in the nation's self-delusions, and may present a case in terms of 'our glorious heritage'. Many of the older school textbooks have tended to present such a point of view in which, for example, Britain, as no other country, was invariably blameless.

The distortion is most likely to occur when the historian is closely identified with the situation. In these circumstances, even if so extreme a position as the 'glorious heritage' myth is avoided, there is likely to occur a point of view which unwittingly incorporates the myths of the parent nation. This is where the process of 'decentring' becomes necessary. What is involved in decentring from the material and producing a long-standing, useful interpretation of events?

Pieter Geyl (1967, p. 411) outlines the phenomena in relation to his own study of the Netherlands; he describes his own process of recognizing 'fact' as myth, and the later reluctance of others to accept the newly discovered reality:

I had been struck, when I came to be familiar with the particulars, by the astonishing partiality toward the stadholders prevailing in our historiography. Groen's religious philosophy would lead one to expect this of him, but I found the same attitude rampant even among the liberals. Later, after the second war, I have shown the effects of this bias somewhat haphazardly in the work of Fruin, and more systematically in that of Coenbrander. But it was in the early 'twenties that my opinions on this point took form. All the well-known assertions that Orange or the Orange party was identical with *national*, and States of Holland or regents' party with *egoistical, class, or provincial* interests; that the princes of Orange had prepared the way for unity while Holland did nothing but block it with her commercialism; that Orange was the people's protector, while the regents were no more than a group out for their own profit, a group outside the nation—all these assertions I learned to see as belonging to an Orange-myth at variance with past reality.

The historian's task is the destruction of myth—'in spite of those who do not like it. In this particular case too, most certainly, there were those who did not like it. The myth is, by its nature, intimately bound up with sentiment, and unyielding to reason' (1967, p. 411). As Geyl points out elsewhere (1967, p. 187) in relation to the French revolution, it is easier for a foreigner to detect the shortcomings in a country's historiography.

What process is Geyl describing? It seems that he has gradually come to recognize his own relationship to the position held and the events described. In doing this he simultaneously sees both himself and the events more clearly and objectively.

Piaget suggests that for all people this process of decentring is the process by which objectivity is achieved. In the process of decentring the person is involved in separating himself from some aspect of his environment. The baby learns to distinguish between himself and other objects, i.e. he separates himself from them and realizes that they have an identity of their own. Once their existence is seen as separate he is able to examine them and expect them to have an existence apart from his own actions. This is object constancy: the ball exists even when he cannot see it. Later children learn to distinguish their own perceptual field from that of someone else's, as Piaget has shown with his experiment with views of mountains. Until the child knows that things can be seen from another point of view he has not decentred from them. For this reason Piaget feels that the process of social interaction, particularly among peers, is vital in promoting decentring.

It is at a still later age that students learn to decentre themselves from other people sufficiently to realize that others may have different motives for behaviour. It consequently seems likely that one of the latest decentrings to be accomplished is that of separation from one's own society and one's own role so that each can be examined 'objectively'. This is one of the historian's tasks—to see himself as one person living at a particular time and under particular conditions. Until he can do this he cannot accurately examine the times or conditions of either the present or past.

Thus some of the difficulties and process of decentring are noted. In Geyl, the historian is seen using the most effective techniques to ensure that his interpretation is objective. He guards against bias by a constant reevaluation of the evidence, by learning to adopt alternative points of view and by noting the emotionalized, only partly substantiated, statements made. His final explanation has recognized his own place in history and his own previous viewpoint as only one of a number possible, all of which may be synthesized into a more comprehensive, objective, interpretation.

Marwick (1970, p. 21) recognizes that 'the historian who is aware of the limitations imposed upon him by his position in space and time can strive more successfully to counteract distortions caused by these limitations'. Carr (1972, p. 123) goes beyond interpretation in terms of the past and present and sees another mark of the historian's objectivity in his 'capacity to project his vision into the future in such a way as to give him a more profound and lasting insight into the past than can be attained by those historians whose outlook is entirely bounded by their own immediate situation'. He also recognizes that the historian's 'capacity to rise above the limited vision of his own situation in society and in history—is partly dependent on his capacity to recognise the extent of his involvement in that situation, to recognise, that is to say, the impossibility of total objectivity' (Carr, 1972, p. 123).

It is this kind of decentring that is important. Both the historian and the events achieve a fuller existence by the process. But it is not a dissociation of relationship; nor should it be confused with a false idea which equates objectivity with lack of emotional involvement. Under this false idea it has sometimes been assumed that events in the past will not be emotionally involving for the historian; thus he can be 'objective' and a 'true' pattern of events will emerge. This detached outlook and/or the pattern derived from remote events is then said to be superimposed upon other, often more recent events, and measurement made of the degree of match and mismatch in the pattern perceived so that a true account of both is achieved.

Two objections may be made which demonstrate the falsity of this notion. First, evidence that historians are without emotion would be hard to find, irrespective of the time they may be writing about. Their use of words is rarely technical and both evaluative and emotional words, phrases, and metaphors abound. Nor is the historian expected to remain aloof from human suffering, but he should be able to feel with a wide range of people in their various situations, not only with those to whom he feels immediately and unthinkingly responsive. Feeling and seeing the other's point of view is part of the process of decentring.

Second, no events, either remote or more recent, form themselves into a pattern without the interpretative perception of the historian who is most likely to use his present-day frame of reference, unless he is made aware both of alternative points of view and of the source of his own perceptions. The historian is required to identify his own situation in time and place and in relation to relevant experiences but, having seen that his own situation is only one of several possible ones, he is required and able simultaneously to see things from other points of view. By this process he achieves true objectivity.

RESEARCH ON DECENTRING IN RELATION TO PEOPLE

The research most relevant to the developmental process of decentring and to history is that which deals more directly with role-taking skills and with decentring in relation to people.

In this research, both affective and cognitive components are obviously relevant. While cognitive structure underlies the kind of thinking possible, emotional components also influence the ordering of material from which the student can decentre. As noted by Geyl, (1967), it is easier to decentre from things with which we are not closely identified, e.g. from other countries before our own. Flavell (1968) has found evidence of greater difficulty in thinking about oneself as object than in thinking about objects.

Research on role-taking was first linked to history-type material in Piaget and Wiel's (1951) study on nationality. From this study it seemed clear that because the child could only see things from his own point of view the pre-operational Swiss child could not see that he would be a foreigner if he were in France, or that it was possible to consider Switzerland as not always best and right. The difficulty lies in the child's inability to decentre himself from his own nation and to see himself and others in reciprocal relation. It is said to be overcome with the use of concrete operational thinking.

The replication in Australia of Piaget and Wiel's study by Knoche and Goldlust (in Davies, 1968) yielded similar results, but there were some interesting differences. Whereas Piaget's subjects had a clear idea of Geneva and only later could understand that Geneva was included in Switzerland, as an example of inclusion achieved with concrete operations, Melbourne children seemed to have a clearer idea of Australia than of either Melbourne or the state of Victoria. It appears that those aspects upon which the person centres, and from which decentration is later necessary, are determined primarily by the significant experiences which that person has. Connell (1970, p. 162) noted that when eleven to twelve year-old Australian children were asked to nominate a news story which interested them, more children mentioned overseas news than Australian news. Perhaps this links with Knoche and Goldlust's finding (in Davies, 1968) that Australian children saw their country in a world context and saw differences between countries as superficial. Knoche and Goldlust did not feel that this was an evidence of genuine reciprocity but rather an example of egalitarianism.

Further evidence on the nature of decentring was provided when children of 7 years 3 months, 9 years, and 11 years were tested by Middleton, Tajfel, and Johnson (1970). It was found that reciprocity developed first toward 'liked' countries and later towards 'neutral' or 'disliked' countries. Similarly, knowledge about those countries which were 'liked' by individuals was greater, irrespective of the availability of information in mass media. It appears that in school lessons students would learn most easily about other countries which were regarded as liked.

These results suggest an important point about the relationship between decentration and apparent reciprocity. It may be that a reciprocal relation appears to develop earlier with liked people or countries because complete decentration is not necessary. It is assumed that those liked will have the same preferences, motivations, and values; hence the different point of view is not so different. However, this is not complete reciprocity since, if it were discovered that the 'liked' differed on some points, a further act of decentration would be needed. Where the events in different countries or periods of time show only approximately parallel development, and where the value systems differ, the situation is one which clearly demands thinking about multiple interacting systems, which is a recognized aspect of formal operational thought.

Supplementary evidence relating to people's ability to see things from another point of view comes from recent work reported by Miller, Kessell, and Flavell

(1970) and demonstrates development in reciprocity beyond the concrete operational stage to higher levels of complexity. Whereas thinking about other people as social objects is comparatively easy, and 80 per cent. of the fourth grade can think about people talking to each other, only 50 per cent. of the sixth grade can 'think about X thinking'. To be able to do this would be a necessary preliminary to appreciating X's motivation, which is a necessary task in history. Indications that children of earlier age can appreciate people's motives are more likely to come from the children explaining others' actions in terms of their own purposes in such a situation. Even as adults we tend to imagine that other people will want the same things as we want. It seems likely that the more remote X's experience is from that of the child, the more difficult to understand his purposes in bringing about an event. It would thus be fairly difficult for an early adolescent to understand a political leader's motives. Adelson (1971) found that a deeper sense of motive was not apparent until about fifteen years.

Miller, Kessell, and Flavell (1970) also found that only 30 per cent. of sixth grade children could 'think about X thinking about Y thinking'. When history teachers expect students to understand that the source of evidence may be biased, either from documents of the times or from historian's accounts, they are asking the student to think about the historian (X) thinking about a historical personage (Y) who is considering his own future actions (Z). The process of decentring may also apply to the person's own role within an institution which itself has a function in society and which, within the study of history, may be comparable to other roles in social institutions of other times. This is speculative. Nevertheless, it is possible to see that the nature of decentring as a process in cognitive development is probably closely related to the process of achieving objectivity as it is viewed by the historian. Detailed sequences in such development may be made available in future research.

RESEARCH EVIDENCE INDICATING THE ROLE OF PERSONAL EXPERIENCE

Both the kinds of generalization possible and the nature of objectivity recognized in the study of history have been seen to influence the kind of investigation of logical operational thinking which may reasonably be regarded as legitimate. The research evidence into thinking about history and similar subjects reveals the apparently inevitable dominance of cognitive structure on the student's understanding. Two further studies are useful to consider. Both are more directly applicable to the current political scene than to history, but their implications for the study of history are clear. More importantly, both used semistructured interview techniques which enabled the meaning of the student's answers to be more thoroughly explored, and hence revealed material which is idiosyncratic and related to the student's own experience and values.

These contributions to the understanding of thinking about political concepts were undertaken by Adelson (1971) and Connell (1971). Initially in each it was possible to analyse the interviews so that the sequence of development in thinking described by Piaget was clearly shown. In addition, however, the way in which the individual's personal experience and interest contributed to his understanding was readily demonstrated.

In Adelson's team projects, adolescents in the United States, Great Britain, and West Germany were asked in an interview situation to consider the hypothetical migration of 1000 people to an island where a community had to be established. Many standardized questions presented dilemmas involving the function of legislation, political authority and processes, education, health, and the reciprocal obligations of citizen and state. Because the situation was imaginary, answers from the different national groups could be compared. More noticeable than minor differences between nationalities, however, were the marked similarities in the development of understanding. Connell also used individual interviews to explore, in less-structured fashion, the thinking of Sydney children aged between five and sixteen years on current political and social situations. Despite the difference in situations presented, e.g. hypothetical or actual, the major findings from these two studies support each other and are readily interpreted in terms of Piagetian theory. From a wealth of interesting evidence several illustrations of the development of thinking at different stages are selected.

Among some of Connell's findings with primary-school children those which could have been influenced by school learning may be of particular interest to the history teacher. It seemed clear that children became acquainted with the queen, the flag, and the national anthem in their earliest years at school and that in the final year of primary school some definite attempt to teach the nature of government in Australia was made. Yet what was 'learned' was markedly dependent on the child's own thinking. For the five year old, acquaintance with the Queen was likely to be with a lady who was like Mother, but who had more jewels. All information about political figures or events was put into the context of the child's own real or fantasy world. Particularly interesting was the apparent use of a task-pool by seven to nine year olds (Connell, 1971, pp. 19–37). From this 'pool of ideas about what public figures do' children 'draw more or less randomly' (p. 27) to answer the interviewer's questions about any particular public figure. The Queen 'rules London' and 'keeps the streets clean'; 'The Prime Minister is kind to people' and arranges for 'famous doctors to help those who are ill' (before a National Health Scheme was proposed).

From this preoperational level came the elements (e.g. special people and power) which combined to form later concepts (governmental). In such a formation some logical operation of classes (possibly multiplication) must have been used. By later childhood the territory of each political figure was known, but the same parallel tasks were performed in these different areas.

In early adolescence, evidence of late concrete operational thinking was given in the student's awareness of elementary hierarchies, e.g. the Prime

Minister and other ministers were differentiated. Political parties existed as parallel groups in conflict (Connell, 1971) and political slogans were used as labels of classes rather than as statements of the general principles which would have been more indicative of formal operations (Adelson, 1971). It seems likely that historical accounts of conflict at that stage of development might be seen in terms of 'goodies' and 'baddies'. Adelson (1971, p. 1015) regarded the most important change between early and mid-adolescence as the change from concrete to abstract, from 'if they had no laws, people could go around killing people' to laws are 'to limit what people can do'.

History has been said to emphasize the concrete, particular instance, so to this extent it is well suited to early adolescence, but in that the child denies any implications, understands conditions only in terms of opposing forces, and sees events as having an impact on specific individuals, rather than on society as a whole, he is not yet far advanced. In contrast, by mid-adolescence, minority rights were likely to receive consideration (Adelson, 1971, p. 1017). When asked to choose between alternatives, the pupil could 'break set' and say that neither alternative was necessary. He could order conditional arguments ('it depends on') and could understand reciprocal implication.

When formal operational thinking became possible at the next stage of development, then more complex structures were possible. It was possible to 'switch back and forth' between a 'generalisation and the use it covers' (Connell, 1971, p. 88). In history this ability would enable the appropriate use of colligatory concepts. At the same time also spontaneous use was made of comparison between different cultural situations, and judgments which were made in different times and places were seen as relative to those times and places. This being so, if teachers aim to have history students recognize the climate of other times and the difference in circumstances which influenced decisions taken by historical personages, this aim may not be fulfilled until formal operational thinking is available.

It is clear that the general sequences found in response to specifically school subject-oriented questions (Hallam, 1967; Peel, 1965; Rhys, 1972) were also present in material which was less formally acquired. Connell (1971) pointed to television as the major source of information on politics. The logical operations defining stages, as used by Piaget, were apparent in both kinds of studies, but the material available from interviews, as suggested earlier, also enabled the recognition of individual processes of thinking and of the interests and values which were from personal experience.

The influence of personal experience in relation to the development of concepts has received little specific attention in research, but the importance of the history student or historian identifying his own position and attitudes has been mentioned earlier in connection with attempts to achieve objectivity. Evidence that the basis of political ideas is strongly influenced by particular, personal considerations is given by Connell (1971). For example, Herda's view of the Vietnam war was constructed in collaboration with her sister; her views on social equality were based on experience with sickness, old age and death;

consequently they involved caring for the poor in quite practical ways (Connell, 1971, pp. 155–171).

Another individual student of particular interest was Howard (Connell, 1971) whose interest in America, originating in interest in the entertainment industry, seemed to have led to a political core of anticommunism. Part of the interviews illustrated the possibility, mentioned by Piaget (1972b), that where interest is involved higher levels of thinking are promoted. The following answer portrays a situation where a student has linked past and present in order to contrast conditions in different times and circumstances, incidentally giving evidence of the ability to see things from different points of view (Connell, 1971, p. 213).

Interviewer: 'Do you think this is something that the government ought to do, put money into film studios and T.V.?'

Student: 'No, not really,' cause although it is a form of entertainment, and you think of ancient times, in ancient Greece, the government was a centre of entertainment and they literally forced the people to go, well it's changed so much now, if the people don't want to go, they don't go, to pictures and that, and I think it's up to the companies themself to give the money.'

The same student, however, had numerous errors and inconsistencies in other material he presented which led Connell (1971) to hypothesize that these were 'signs of an unusually powerful assimilative activity (in Piaget's sense) by which elements of outside reality are subordinated to the stream of the person's thought. We may speculatively propose this as a force making for the ideological integration of political materials in adolescence, independent of social stimuli, and capable of substituting for them' (p. 226). Here is seen part of the development of a comprehensive and rational personal ideology. Is this an aim of history teaching?

Adelson (1971, p. 1033) gave another individual example from a longitudinal sample which showed the determinants in parental influence and respect for power contributing to the growth of a personal ideology which was consistent and increasingly integrated over a three-year period. Similarly, from a study of adults, Davies (1966, p. 250) has suggested that attitudes towards authority, sharing, and enemies and allies were established early in the child's life. He said that individuals 'commonly respond to novel political situations as if they were antique ones repeated'.

It is clear from Davies' studies, and to a considerable extent from Connell's and Adelson's, that basic attitudes are formed in direct response to active personal experience. These are then transferred or incorporated into attitudes toward similar political and social situations. In addition, Connell points out the influence of the family, e.g. in deciding what are 'our sort of people', and of television in providing both fact and opinion.

The exact process by which the student comes to incorporate within his own attitudes and ideology the material he learns in history lessons is not yet understood. Vicarious experience of characters and situations remote in time would not easily become personally relevant. Some history teachers hope that pupils will be inspired by a vision of great people or motivated to identify with particular causes, but the extent to which this actually occurs is problematic. The learning would, of necessity, be both cognitive and affective. Research specifically designed to see how far the broad aims of history teaching are accomplished is difficult.

Overall the review of research relevant to thinking in history shows the surprisingly wide applicability of Piagetian theory. While research which identifies stages of cognitive development has most weight, evidence is not lacking for the identification of specific operations at different ages, for the power of assimilatory structures influencing vocabulary usage, for the importance of decentration in achieving different points of view which contribute to objectivity, and for the interaction of personal experience with cognitive structure in producing political conceptions and personal-social ideologies. Despite the nature of history as different from mathematics and the physical sciences, applications of Piaget's theory may be found.

Consideration of the research evidence currently available and of the arguments relating history to the development of logical operations may now serve to clarify some of the more general aims of history teaching in schools.

THE AIMS OF HISTORY TEACHING IN SCHOOLS

The teaching of history in schools requires from the teacher both the recognition of the nature of history and an appreciation of the contribution which historical material may make to the pupil's understanding of society. The two processes are interactive since historical material is used in helping the student to understand the nature of history and of society. From this interaction the general aims of history teaching are derived.

History teachers have defined their aims on many occasions and, quite rightly, some of these may have little to do with the development of logical thinking as it has been reviewed here. Yet a study of thinking may serve to clarify most aims. Two aims with minimal reference to logical thought are mentioned, then a general aim which is dependent on formal operational thinking, and then three groups of aims associated with the nature of history, with generalizations and with objectivity, respectively.

Two aims of history teaching which are shared by many teachers but which are not directly connected to research reviewed here are the satisfaction of a need to know the origins of things and an appreciation of accurate prose. The first of these Marwick (1970 p. 14) calls the 'poetic necessity of history' in the sense 'that there is inborn in almost every individual a curiosity and sense of wonder about the past'. One suspects that this 'poetic necessity' is more apparent to historians than to others. The psychologist, but for his need for validation, could as easily conclude that there is an inborn need for people to understand each other's motives. While Marwick's view is shared in some measure by many other historians who assume a natural inquisitiveness about origins or a natural interest in biography and narrative, it should be realized that children will develop curiosity about anything presented in an interesting fashion.

Second, and derived largely from the recognition of the community's need for history as 'memory', many history teachers see it as an aim of their subject that students should learn to appreciate accurate communication in which fact and opinion are differentiated. The skill is not merely for the student to write well himself, but also to be able to analyse and evaluate the many written accounts which form the major substance of historical evidence. This aim is related to logical operational thinking through the recognition that the use of language is largely dominated by the understanding of the material. The relationship of language to thought has been more thoroughly explored in previous chapters (Keats and Keats in Chapters 4 and 5).

A general aim of history teaching which is more directly related to the study of logical thinking is that which seeks to modify both the thinking and attitude of the pupils. Elton (in Ballard, 1971) is possibly representative of many teachers who feel that the study of history will modify students' thinking in desirable ways. He feels that many of the present defects of youth could be overcome by an adequate study of history. Current intellectual faults in young people appear to him to be the 'excessive concentration on one line of thought, absence of understanding for other points of view, belief in simple solutions, lack of balance of mind, absence of imaginative understanding (empathy), intolerance, and an overriding concern with the present' (Ballard, 1971, p. 226).

In Elton's view, then, history should be taught in schools with the aim of making the student a different kind of person. His argument is appealing, since his expectation of the resulting student is of one who shows 'awe in the face of the magnitude of the past, some vision of ages not his own, and some ability to sink himself in minds and circumstances different from those with which he has been equipped by the accident of birth' (Ballard, 1971, p. 228). Elton correctly estimates that the thinking envisaged is most likely to be found in the sixth form-level students anticipating a tertiary education. With some conviction he declares that in teaching history to children under fifteen years of age, they 'should be excited by stories and descriptions distinguished from other similar tales by being about real people' in order to persuade them that history 'has point and could repay further attention' (Ballard, 1971, pp. 221–222), but *true* history cannot, in his opinion, be taught to the young.

For the history teacher, of course, the matter of what can be taught at various ages is important and the research outlined previously gives useful indications of progressive sequences in learning, while the analysis of the processes of thinking gives more precision to some aims. Three groups of aims may be recognized here: one centred around the recognition of the nature of history, a second associated with the kinds of generalization preferred, and a third concerned with the achievement of objectivity.

The recognition of the nature of history might well enable students to appreciate the different orders of data with which they come in contact. This aim has not, as yet, been widely recognized, but with increasing awareness of both the differences between disciplines and the need to integrate across subject boundaries in tackling many of society's problems, it may be that students will need to realize the variety of kinds of material dealt with, and the methods and purposes attached to different disciplines. The point may be illustrated even within the study of history where the use of statistics and the principles and techniques of economics, geography, anthropology, sociology, and psychology have been imported into historical studies to give new insight into past events (Marwick, 1970, pp. 107–129). In the context of interdisciplinary study the nature of history may itself be clarified. It could increasingly be regarded 'not as the mere reconstitution of events, but as interdisciplinary research dealing with the diachronic aspects of each of the fields studied by the various human sciences' (Piaget, 1973, p. 12).

As part of this first aim the teacher may clarify for senior students the differences between closed and open systems, the limitations imposed on the use of logical deductions in open systems, and hence the kinds of generalizations possible in history. Barcan (Barcan and coauthors, 1974) specifically outlines in a text for fourth-form students (approximately aged sixteen years) what he calls the 'lessons of history'. These include a discussion of generalizations or laws, the place of individual men in history, periodization in history, the question of history repeating itself, and current events as history. Making explicit the nature of the discipline being studied should enlighten the process of the study, at least for older adolescents.

Many aims are linked to an examination of the nature of generalization in history. Younger students might be expected to learn the process of ordering events into sequences and of grouping events, according to pertinent similarities and differences, into meaningful patterns and periods. Some of these groupings would be colligatory concepts.

In the process of establishing causal sequences the student may learn to understand that meaningful patterns arise from the interaction of many factors, not least from the purposive activity of people. From this he is led to appreciate the efforts of various men and forces which have produced a present society, or a society of a particular kind.

Contrasts between societies demonstrate to junior students the serving of men's needs in different ways and elucidate to seniors the significance of the qualifier 'the situation being as it was'. In this way students may reach an understanding of the significance of unique experiences or patterns of experience, both in the life of a society and in the life of an individual. A comparatively early appreciation of the continuity of events and the changes which occur over time may be linked later with an understanding of the balance of forces in a situation, which may indicate the nature and degree of change possible in relation to the stability of the community.

The third group of aims centres around the requirement of objectivity in history and indicates to the student his need to identify his own place in society and to empathize with others in order to learn their views of society. The material of history, by providing a contrast between societies of other times and places, should not only make the student aware of other ways of living and of alternative institutional structures but also of alternative value systems. Not only should he learn to identify multiple causes but also to identify multiple points of view on any event.

In the process of decentring to achieve objectivity, value judgments are recognized as part of the significant material of history. The teacher may help students to distinguish between facts and values and to recognize the significance of both to the community. The historian's commitment to a comprehensive, rational interpretation of events may also be used to encourage the students to examine their own value system and to attempt to make their own system as comprehensive and rational as possible. At the same time, they may realize that many historical events demonstrate that beliefs and irrational emotions are powerful agents in decision making. In general, the aim would be to help the student decentre from his own position in society so that he may achieve a fuller understanding of past events and the particular facets of those events relevant to his own time and to the future.

Thus, in fairly specific ways, the student's attitudes and thinking may be modified. Although, as in most disciplines, the full nature of the study is not possible before the level of formal operational thought (and this is unlikely to to occur before late adolescence), it is possible to recognize and teach for preliminary processes which later become integrated into the thinking required by a proper study of history. Research evidence on the development of logical thinking enables the clarification of some of the aims of history teaching and possible sequences towards fulfilling them.

10

AN EMPIRICAL STUDY OF OPERATIONAL THINKING IN HISTORY-TYPE MATERIAL

M. F. Jurd

In this chapter details are given of one study in which an attempt was made to identify aspects of Piaget's theory in the development of thinking about history-type material. Before considering the nature of the test devised and the results obtained from it, it may be useful to mention those selected aspects of Piaget's theory which were to be investigated.

THEORETICAL ISSUES

It was hoped to identify within adolescent's thinking about history-type material the stages of development which have been described previously as characterized by a set of logical operations and by concepts which incorporate those operations. Certain learning strategies have been said to exist within each stage and lead on to the following stage or point of equilibrium, but there has sometimes been dispute about the degree of discontinuity between stages and the extent to which equilibrium is made evident. Each of these aspects could be considered in the context of this research. Finally, the modifications of assessment induced by the nature of the history material, in particular the use and measurement of colligatory concepts as a substitute for verifiable generalizations, might be investigated. Each of these theoretical issues will be considered briefly.

Since the idea of a stage of development was to be investigated, the criteria as given by Piaget should be noted '(i) the order of succession; (ii) integration of acquisitions at one stage into the following stage; (iii) a whole characterising the total aspects of a stage; (iv) the fact that one stage prepares the following; and (v) that the new stage constitutes the culmination of what is prepared in the preceding stage, in other words the equilibrium step' (Tanner and Inhelder, 1960, pp. 120–121). While Piaget says that not all these criteria need be met, but may be regarded as degrees of the possible structuration of stages, the criteria mentioned are those which he feels can be found in a field where stages are clearest. Cognitive development is said to be such a field, in which Piaget considers that 'the concept of total structure takes on a precise sense which can be defined in terms of general algebra and symbolic logic' (Tanner and Inhelder, 1960, p. 12). By regarding symbolic logic as analogous to logical operations, those internalized, reversible actions which are agencies in establishing equilibrium, Piaget is able to demonstrate the fulfilment of all five criteria in the stages of cognitive development. A characteristic set of logical operations is used to define each stage. Coincidentally with the operations it is said that those concepts which embody such operations become attainable. The extent of this concurrence may be debated and limiting factors relating to particular task variables do exist (Flavell, 1971a,), but in general and applied to the student's thinking about history, it would be expected that the assimilatory structures which the student was using at any time would be reflected in his understanding of historical events. The stage of cognitive development reached would appear both in the logical operations he was able to use and in his understanding of historical concepts incorporating the relationships appropriate for particular stages.

Between each stage Piaget has identified recurrent strategies which lead to equilibrium at a higher level. These strategies are 'characterised by the progressive coordination of actions (overt or interiorised) that are at first isolated one from the other and centred on the results produced each time, rather than on the changes that link these results' (Pinard and Laurendeau in Elkind and Flavell, 1969, p. 152). Flavell and Wohlwill (in Elkind and Flavell, 1969, p. 91ff) have suggested that the strategies are linked with a probability model such that at the beginning of a movement towards each new equilibrium it may be predicted that the person concerned is likely to concentrate upon one aspect of the problem. The predictable probability of this particular aspect being chosen changes as the aspect is assimilated and then the observation of a different aspect becomes most probable. Next, the attention of the person is likely to alternate between those aspects previously considered singly. This is a kind of dialectic process. Following this alternating observation of varying aspects of the problem, the most probable change for any person is towards a synthesis in which there is realization of transformations but with the central concept conserved despite such transformations (Piaget in Tanner and Inhelder, 1960, pp. 102–104). Thus a new equilibrium, a more advanced stable structure, is formed. These strategies could be considered in this research in regard to the number and to the alternation of aspects of events which might be expected to lead to an integration of these aspects. Similarly, primary concentration by younger students on an end state or result would be expected to give way among older students to recognition of a process uniting a series of situations.

The degree of discontinuity between stages and the temporary nature of equilibrium are obviously two aspects of the same problem in that stages are successive steps of equilibrium and both are identified by the same scale of measurement. Piaget (in Tanner and Inhelder, 1960, p. 122) freely admits that the stages may be partly a reflection of the measuring scale used:

On the one hand we find stages which characterise a certain proportion of individuals at any given age. On the other hand we always find sub or intermediary stages, but as soon as we try to pin these intermediary stages down we enter a sort of cloud-dust of subintermediaries, because of their instability. Other organisational steps are relatively more stable and it is these that one can consequently consider as 'stages' .... Inhelder and I came up against the (same) objection of exaggerating a discontinuity and neglecting a continuity.

For Inhelder, as for others, some of the difficulty was in the widespread occurrence of décalages, the fact that some aspects of reality were more difficult to structure (with the same operations) than others, but she was finally persuaded by the 'surprising concordance of structural order' (Tanner and Inhelder, 1960, p. 125).

In this study group data could be used to measure discontinuity between ages in achieving particular tasks, while the equilibrium of stages could be considered in relation to the coincidence of achievement of theoretically similar tasks both for the group and the individual. The evidence of concordance of structural order might be found in the significant differences between grades on each item as it was scored in terms of structure and in the order of difficulty of items.

While for both Inhelder and Piaget the nature of the difference between stages is, by definition, qualitative, it has sometimes been suggested that quantitative differences are most significant. One possible connection between the two has been suggested by Flavell and Wohlwill (in Elkind and Flavell, 1969, p. 78) who postulate:

... ontogenetic stretches during which some segment of the child's intellectual programme changes only quantitatively, at the parameter level, and others during which that segment actually alters its basic character, setting the stage for renewed, qualitative change. Perhaps the relation between the two forms of change goes even deeper than mere temporal alternation. Maybe the quantitative element that an emergent undergoes is for one reason or another a necessary precondition for the advent of its successor. In fact, we read Piaget as implying this in his assimilation and accommodation equilibration model of cognitive development.

The possibly temporal relationship between quantitative and qualitative change could be investigated to some extent in the present study.

Finally, the modifications necessary in assessment because of the nature of the material have been mentioned in the previous chapter. The use of 'the situation being as it was' as a replacement for 'all other things being equal' and the recognition of the balance of forces in history have been sufficiently justified, but the method to be used in substituting a colligatory concept for the testing of a generalized hypothesis probably needs further explication.

MEASURING CONCEPT ATTAINMENT

A person's understanding of a concept may be measured by one of the ways in which he is found to define a concept. Traditionally a concept may be defined either extensively or intensively. Extensive definition involves the enumeration of all those examples seen as belonging to a specified group. Sometimes it may involve the matching of new objects with others in the group. Intensively a concept is defined by the statement of essential similarities between objects belonging to a group, such statement including both the relevant attributes and the relationship between these. Elkind (Elkind and Flavell, 1969) has pointed out that each kind of definition is estimated by a different task in psychological experiments. Extensive content is judged by object-sorting and classification-type tasks, while intensive content is assessed by verbal definitions or a statement of the criteria by which objects are classified. Elkind then relates Piaget's conservation problems to these other tasks by suggesting that conservation may be considered as a measure of intensive definition in that it 'corresponds to the property that is left unchanged across various transformations of the object' (Elkind and Flavell, 1969, p. 187).

For all persons who have attained the concept the intensive and extensive definitions of a concept are coordinated, since those characteristics which determine that objects belong to a class of objects are the same characteristics as define the nature of the particular object in that context. Yet Elkind suggested that 'there is little coordination between the extensive content of a concept as revealed by discriminative responses, and the intensive content of the same concept as revealed by verbal definition' (Elkind and Flavell, 1969, p. 180). Lovell, Mitchell, and Everett (1962), however, replicated experiments by Piaget and Inhelder on the classification of pictures and shapes and showed a progression towards the coordination of the extensive and intensive definitions which could be used to measure the degree of concept attainment. The important distinction between the experiments of Lovell, Mitchell, and Everett and those of others was that their classifications were concerned not only with the kind and number of the contents but with the relationships between them. The object sorting was on the basis of additive classification, multiplicative classification, seriation, and multiplication of asymmetrical transitive relations, among other operations. By giving all tests to the same children, they were able to show that operational mobility is achieved at about the same age in each, with a marked increase between the ages of seven and eight years. Before true classification there was found an emphasis on similarities and differences between elements with only partial coordination of intension and extension. When true classification was achieved, within the additive classification there were substages corresponding to the use of one, two, or three criteria as the basis for classification. Supporting evidence for a relationship between conservation tasks and coordinated classification is offered by Bruner, Olver, and Greenfield (1966).

It appeared from the above evidence that the possibility existed within classificatory tasks for using extensional definition and statements of similarities for tracing developments comparable to those in conservation problems. If the notion of a conservation concept as an intensive definition could be included in this measure by classification, there would be extensional and intensional definitions of a concept which might be expected to achieve greater coordination as the concept was more fully understood. Since within this context of coordinating concepts the need does not exist to verify the conservation concept, it seemed reasonable to substitute a colligatory concept as the third measure of definition.

Given the possibility of three definitions within the context of a classification task, it seemed advisable to consider those variables which would contribute to the difficulty of the task and hence would need to be controlled. Development in thinking has been demonstrated with respect to three main variables which could be expected to influence the attainment of a concept within this context. The first variable was seen to be the relations between attributes, i.e. the operations involved. Besides Piaget, research by Bruner, Goodnow, and Austin (1956), Seggie (1969), and Bourne and O'Banion (1971), among others, have shown that the relations between variables affect the difficulty of the concept. The second variable to be controlled in testing would be the number and nature of relevant attributes (one, two, or three criteria of the same or differing kinds). As mentioned earlier the number of attributes was shown to be important within stages by Lovell, Mitchell, and Everett (1962). Developmental changes, from perceptible to functional to nominal, in the kind of attribute preferred have been demonstrated by Olver and Hornsby (in Bruner, Olver and Greenfield, 1966). In this study the kind of attributes used would have to be at least functional, since the material used was verbal descriptions of events.

Apart from these two variables, which would directly affect the difficulty of the concept, it would be necessary to have a clear demarcation of the situation to which the concept was to be related so that the *same* concept would be examined by each definition. Without this demarcation it would be pointless to anticipate a coordination of definitions. Even with this it was expected that there would not be complete coordination of definitions until the concept was actually attained.

Since so many aspects of the development of thinking could be reflected in a defining task, it was decided that development in thinking in relation to concept level could be extended to a task in which the intensive definition of concepts was measured by the description of similarities both between groups of events and between series of events. Similarities between series of events were regarded as an approximation of a colligatory concept. Provided that consideration was given to the number and nature of the attributes, to the relations between them, and to the accurate demarcation of the situation to be considered, definitions should be increasingly coordinated. Comparisons would then be possible between such conceptual definitions and those other questions which were aimed at specific operations. Since the same population and the same material would be used for each kind of question, the attainment of stages related to both concepts and logical operations might be expected to coincide. This approach to concept attainment was aimed at providing some substitute, through the examination of colligatory concepts, for the verification of law-giving concepts.

In summary, it may be said that Piagetian theory is seen as concerned with processes of assimilation and accommodation governed by an equilibration tendency which results in temporary stages. In the present study evidence was sought within assimilatory structures for the existence of stages, not only as identified by sets of logical operations or by a certain level of concept, but also as a state of comparative equilibrium. It was anticipated that strategies could be identified and that there might be evidence of discontinuity between stages.

Those aspects of the nature of history and its relation to the investigation of logical operations which were mentioned in the previous chapter were also considered. It was thus recognized that the testing of the qualifier 'all other things being equal' should be replaced by the testing of 'the situation being as it was'. It was also recognized that the testing of a law-giving hypothesis was inappropriate in history, but that use might be made of the testing of aspects of concept attainment and, in particular, at the formal operational level, the attainment of a colligatory concept.

The test population

With the intention of demonstrating the relevance of these aspects of Piagetian theory to the development of thinking in history, a group test was devised which could be given to students from final-year primary school to final-year secondary school.

In deciding to use a group test it was recognized that it would not be possible to explore the individual meanings which students attached to concepts and the possible source of those meanings with their personal experience. Both of these might have been available in interview situations. Neither did the test allow for the exploration of personal value systems. Further, it was likely that pupils would work at their habitual assimilatory level rather than be extended to the limits of their thinking. Nevertheless, the importance of such assimilatory structures as instruments by which reality is organized should not be overlooked (Szeminska, 1965, p. 51). A pilot study indicated that much useful information could be gained within the group situation.

The population was chosen from an available area in which students came from various socioeconomic backgrounds. The area is only ten miles from the industrial city of Newcastle (Australia) to which many of the local population travel daily. People also work in local light industry, with the Water Board, with the Forestry Commission, on farms which are mostly dairying or vegetable growing, or they are Air Force personnel from a nearby RAAF base. The coeducational comprehensive high school serves all children in the area and three of the largest primary schools feeding into the high school were used for the final-year primary-school population.

One comprehensive study and a smaller follow-up study were undertaken. In the first study, a test was given to all fifth- and sixth-form students and to groups comparable in intelligence and attainments from fourth-form high school down to sixth-class primary school. This choice of subjects meant that the students were above average in ability, the mean IQ's of groups ranging from 112·1 to 115·7. The mean ages for groups ranged from 11 years 8 months in sixth class to 17 years 7 months in sixth form. This group will be called Total 1969 (T69) group.

In the follow-up study the same test was given approximately one year later to as many of the original group as were readily available. Unfortunately, sixth form, and of course the ex-sixth formers, were not available, so that only forms 1 to 5 of that year were retested. Movement of population, particularly from the RAAF. Base, resulted in a further depletion of numbers from the original 350 to 174, but the group did not differ significantly from the original group in age for grade or in ability. This group may be called Sample 1970 (S70). To enable some approach towards longitudinal data the results for this more restricted group were extracted from the 1969 data and these form the S69 group. Where data are used in the two-year grouping, e.g. sixth class 1969 with first form 1970, first form 1969 with second form 1970, etc., this grouping is called the 69/70 group. It is probably useful to keep in mind that both S69 and S70 had smaller numbers (about half) and a more limited range (sixth class to fourth form, and first form to fifth form). The age of the students and their general ability as measured by group verbal tests is given in Table 10.1.

The test and its rationale

The test consisted of three parallel series of events such as might have occurred in three countries, Adza, Mulba, and Nocha (see Figure 10.1 for events). The questions were divided into three sections. Question I, a vocabulary test, was designed to ensure that an inadequate knowledge of the words was not a reason for failing to answer questions. Second, a set of question (II to XV) was designed to test specific structures at particular operational levels, questions on one country being paralleled in structure by questions on the two other coun-

TABLE 10.1.   Age and general ability for subjects in the Total 1969 group grades

	Grades						
	6C	1	2	3	4	5	6F
Mean age (in years and months)	11.8	12.7	13.5	14.6	15.9	16.6	17.8
Age	11.0–	12.2–	12.10–	13.11–	14.10–	15.11–	16.11–
range (in years and months)	12.5	13.4	14.5	16.10	16.10	18.6	18.7
Mean IQ	112·1	115·5	115·7	114·4	114·3	115·3	113·9
IQ	97–	100–	100–	96–	91–	96–	90–
range	130	130	130	130	130	130	130
Boys	24	25	20	25	25	25	28
Girls	26	25	30	25	25	25	22
Totals	50	50	50	50	50	50	50

tries. A third section (XVI to XVIII, see Figure 10.1) required the extensive definition and intensive definition of concepts involving different levels of operational thought. All questions were marked in categories judged to reflect operational levels as defined by Piaget. Assuming that the use of particular operations rather than the nature of the material decides the stage reached, the stages discovered were expected to extend from preoperational to formal operational.

In general the test was concerned with the identification of one or more varaibles and the kinds of relations which might be thought to exist between them. Where only one variable was mentioned and where no genuine classification was found, the level was judged to be preoperational. With the identification of more than one variable which could be classified in terms of either classes or relations, or with the ordering of events, concrete operations were recognized. For the formal operational level, interest was centred on the possibility of examining 'the situation being what it was', the combination of cancellation and compensation, and the use of colligatory concepts. The difficulty, mentioned earlier of deciding the contribution made to the development of thinking in terms of quantitative criteria, i.e. whether more than two variables

XV. Here are the same events for Adza and Mulba set out in columns and rows. Events in Nocha were very similar. List the events in Nocha (as given opposite) in the rows 1 to 5 under 'Nocha'.

Adza	Mulba
1. After his father's death Henry became king.	1. Having led his people to victory against invaders, Richard became dictator.
2. Henry wanted to increase the number of large cargo ships, so that more goods would be imported.	2. Once he had power Richard desired more land and wealth.
3. Landowners' taxes were increased to pay for cargo ships.	3. All men between 18 and 25 years of age had to go into military service.
4. Landowners had little money to improve their farms.	4. Few young men were left in factories and on farms.
5. Farms produced less and landowners had no money to buy imported goods.	5. Production fell, goods could not be exported to nearby countries, and living conditions became worse.
6. Landowners refused to pay any more taxes.	6. There was a successful plot to kill Richard.
7. The king agreed to have an advisory council of representative landowners.	7. The people elected a group of other leaders.

Figure 10.1 Contd.

Events in Nocha (to be listed in correct order down the column)

A. Most money from taxes was spent on defence.
B. The leaders wanted to build up the army so Nocha would be safe.
C. Three military leaders were elected to rule Nocha together.
D. Standards of education declined and there were no more cultural festivals, which the people had enjoyed.
E. Less money was available for education, music and drama.

	Nocha	Similarities
1.		
2.		
3.		
4.		
5.		
6.		
7.		

XVI. Considering what happened in Adza and Mulba, fill in what might have happened next in Nocha (rows 6 and 7).

XVII. In the column headed 'Similarities', say in what way the events listed in each country (across rows) are similar (leave out row 5).

XVIII. Events in all three countries showed a change towards . . . .
. . . .

FIGURE 10.1 Some test items

were considered, recurred in the scoring of items in this test. In order to maintain the criteria of change in the structure of an answer being indicative of a new stage, rather than a mere increase in the number of variables, the use of three or more variables instead of two was rated as late concrete operational (IIB) rather than a new stage of formal operational.

This basic scale, as outlined above, underlaid the marking for all individual questions. Consequently, scores on different items could be compared and ages for the attainment of various stages could be noted. Chi-squares were used to indicate both statistically significant changes over all grades and significant changes between adjacent grades. The rationale and results of each of these three groups of questions will be presented with a distinction being made between those questions at concrete and those at formal operational level within both the second and third sections.

Vocabulary level

Because development of thinking about history is reflected in the understanding of words, as research mentioned in the previous chapter has indicated, it seemed important to ensure that answers to questions were not unduly influenced by lack of adequate vocabulary. Precautions against such a lack were taken both in the construction of the test and in the final test given.

The first precaution in constructing the test was taken by reading aloud the 'stories' of each of the three countries to a composite fifth/sixth primary class of normal ability range, who were not subjects in the investigation. These pupils were then asked to write the stories in their own words. Both the retold stories and the subjects' questions when seeking clarification of the test were used as a basis for the vocabulary and sentence structure of the test.

Second, a vocabulary test was included within the final test. The items for this vocabulary question were to be in multiple-choice form, so the distractors were devised after the manner of Rayner (1951, p. 31) by presenting the phrases and words in sentences similar to those actually included in the test to a second group of subjects comparable in age to the lowest group and with some children of lesser ability, viz. to approximately 60 sixth-class children. These children in the preliminary testing were required to explain in their own words what the underlined words and phrases meant, and from the frequency of common errors and the use of alternative meanings of the words the distractors were devised for question I of the final test. This vocabulary subtest of eight key words provided multiple-choice answers in which one was correct, two partially correct, and two wrong.

The results of this subtest indicated that all but four wrong answers and one partially correct answer were attractive distractors. Different grade groups showed development from partially to completely correct answers on five out of eight definitions of words used in the multiple-choice answer test, but only fifteen students in even the youngest group in T69 had a wrong answer on any one item. Since partially correct answers were considered adequate for the under standing of the test, it seemed unlikely that any student did poorly in the test because of the difficulty of the words used.

QUESTIONS INVOLVING SPECIFIC LOGICAL OPERATIONS

In the second section of the test, questions designed to reveal specific logical operational structures as related to history material were used. The rationale of these and the summary of results for both T69 and for S69 and S70 are presented and discussed. Questions whose upper level is concrete operational are considered first.

Concrete operational questions

(a) Questions on causes and negation of causes

In outlining the steps in the development of conservation, Piaget (1964, p. 14) describes the strategy used as follows. First, the child will focus on one dimension or another—for him, the two dimensions are independent at this stage. Second, he will focus on the alternative dimension, e.g. in conservation of quantity of plasticine 'he is thinking about width but he forgets about length'; at a third level he will oscillate between width and length and he will discover that the two are related. In discovering this relationship he comes to compensation, 'there's less in length and more in width'.

It seemed possible that thinking about the causes of an event in history might follow the same sequence. The recognition of one cause, preoperational, possibly followed by awareness of alternative causes, then recognition of more than one cause, early concrete operational, and finally of interdependence between the causes, of a reciprocal relationship between each other as well as the causal relationship to the event, might be anticipated. This would be late concrete operational. While there was no way of determining the awareness of alternative causes in a group test, the recognition of one cause, more than one cause, and the interdependence of causes was possible.

Whether there is awareness of a relationship between events rather than a mere juxtaposition of ideas may be partly decided by the subject's ability to reverse the relationship. Children use this operation in 'proving' the relationship they have stated, e.g. 'It must be, because you can make the sausage into a ball again.' If reversal is used to establish the relationship, the requirement of reversal should produce the same progression of answers as the development of the relationship.

In history the event could be reversed by asking what might have prevented it occurring. If a single cause had been given then the negation of a single cause should be sufficient to prevent the event, but if interdependent causes had been given, then both causes and the interdependence between them should be negated. As a form of negating the causes, an alternative to preventing the event could be a recognition of the expected consequences of an event. That is, if an event were designed to overcome some causal problem, such as legislation to overcome tax evasion, then the expected consequences of the event should parallel the causes, i.e. tax evasion should be prevented.

The questions designed to test the number and interdependence of causal factors offered as an explanation of why an event occurred were:

II Why did Adza get an advisory council?

and

VII Why did people plot to kill Richard?

The negation of these causes was provided by questions:

IV What differences might the advisory council make to Adza in the future?

and

IX In what ways might Richard have avoided being killed?

Each question was about a country in which the order of events had been given and in each the interdependence between events involved recognition of the interaction of ruler and people in the total situation within the country. The results indicated that the development of thinking on these questions followed the sequences predicted, from single to multiple to interdependent causes, and that differences over the total grades were highly significant in all questions and in both studies (see Table 10.2).

(b) Comparison of causes with the negation of causes

Since the overall sequence of development for both causes and the negation of causes seemed parallel, it was of interest to discover whether the same

TABLE 10.2. Order of difficulty of questions and level of significance of differences over grades

Level of questions	Total 1969(350) aged 11.8–17.8	Difference over grades	Sample 1969(174) aged 11.8–15.9	Difference over grades	Sample 1970(174) aged 12.7–16.6	Difference over grades
CO[a]	Completion 6	0·001	Completion 6	0·001	Completion 6	—
CO	Similarities 1	0·001	Similarities 1	—	Similarities 1	0·01
CO	XIV	0·001	VI	0·01	Similarities 6	—
CO	VI	0·01	XIV	—	Similarities 3	0·001
CO	XI	0·001	Similarities 2	—	Similarities 4	0·001
CO	Similarities 6	0·001	Similarities 6	0·001	XIV	—
CO	Completion 7	0·01	XI	0·01	XI	—
CO	Similarities 2	0·05	Completion 7	0·025	VI	—
CO	VII	0·001	Similarities 3	0·005	Similarities 2	0·001
CO	IX	0·001	Similarities 4	0·001	Completion 7	0·001
CO	Similarities 4	0·001	VII	0·01	IX	0·001
CO	II	0·001	IX	0·01	II	0·02
CO	Similarities 3	0·001	Similarities 7	—	Similarities 7	—
CO	IV	0·001	IV	0·001	VII	0·01
CO	Similarities 7	—	II	0·005	IV	0·05
FO[b]	XIII	0·001	XVIII	0·001	V	0·01
FO	V	0·001	VIII	—	VIII	—
FO	X	0·001	X	—	XVIII	0·001
FO	III	0·001	III	0·005	III	0·01
FO	XVIII	0·001	V	0·025	X	0·05
FO	VIII	0·001	XIII	0·025	XIII	0·001

[a] CO = concrete operational.
[b] FO = formal operational.

TABLE 10.3. Association of answers on causes and the negation of causes in the T 69 group

	Chi-square	df	P	Contingency coefficient
Questions II and IV	88·803	4	<0·001	0·45
Questions VII and IX	55·3162	4	< 0·001	0·37

individuals tended to use equivalent levels in their answers. A comparison was therefore made to find the degree of association between the causal question and the question negating the same causes, i.e. between questions II and IV, and VII and IX, for the T69 group only.

The significance of the chi squares in Table 10.3 indicates that both the contingency coefficients showed a low but significant degree of association between the levels at which causes and the negation of causes were answered. More than half of the students answered at the same level in each and very few combined preoperational and concrete operational IIB answers.

A comparison in terms of item difficulty suggested that in each instance the causes questions (II and VII) tended to be easier than the negation of the same cause (IV and IX) in T69, but this difference was not found in the S70 sample.

These results seemed to provide evidence that the sequence of steps in the development of thinking about the causes of an event was the same as that found in the development of Piaget's conservation concepts, in that it moved from a single factor to more than one factor, and then to the coordination of two factors. The fact that genuine causal relationships were recognized was confirmed by a similar and closely associated developmental sequence in the negation of the same causes.

(c) Making an evaluative judgment

At the same operational level a similar development in structure has been found when students are asked to make an evaluative judgment. As mentioned previously, Peel (1966), using verbal passages containing both conflicting evidence and irrelevant information, had found that students moved from the use of limited circumstantial evidence to the reconciliation of conflicting evidence by pleading extenuating circumstances, i.e. going beyond the data given.

In the present test the questions VI, XI, and XIV differed from Peel's in that subjects were required to say which of two apparently conflicting factors was more important. An adequate answer involved recognizing that the two factors were interdependent, thus achieving the required reconciliation.

The questions asked were:

VI Was farming or trade more important in Adza? What makes you think so?

    XI Was military expansion or high standard of living more important in Mulba? What makes you think so?

    XIV Was it more important in Nocha to keep up the standard of education or to defend the country? What makes you think so?

The categorical scoring was, of course, based on the reasons for the choice made rather than the nature of the choice itself. The sequence of development went from one piece of evidence for the choice made, preoperational (I), to the reason for the alternative to the choice being rejected, or to several reasons being given for the choice made, early concrete operational (IIA), before the level of reconciliation (IIB) was reached. Provision was also made in the scoring for formal operational (III) level thinking in which it was felt that a subject might state a generalized principle together with its application to the particular instance, but this kind of answer was not used sufficiently to form a separate category in the results. The development of thinking was as predicted in both studies and there were highly significant differences between grades in all three questions in T69, but the differences were not consistently significant with the smaller numbers and more-limited age range of the S69 and S70 groups.

Although the major interest in these questions was in the kinds of reason given for a choice, it was found that the actual making of a choice also presented some difficulty. The difficulty seemed to be caused by the disjunctive nature of the questions. Many subjects, particularly primary-school children, when asked which of two factors was more important, answered 'Yes' or 'No', as though only one factor could be considered by them even when the alternative was stated. Differences between grades were significant at the 0.001 level for questions VI and XI only.

Thus the consideration of only one factor, as opposed to more than one factor, which was found in questions on causes and the negation of causes, was present also in response to questions where a choice between alternatives was required. Similarly, the progression from more than one factor to a recognition of the interdependence of factors was found paralleled in the development towards the reconciliation of conflicting factors. The structures seemed the same and were parallel in development. The difficulty of considering two variables was further emphasized by the difficulty in seeing the need for stating a choice between alternatives. Answers to all these questions displayed the strategy typical of the development of conservation concepts.

(d) Putting events in order—questions XII and XV

Two further questions were primarily concerned with achievement at the concrete operational level. These required events to be put in order and should have been comparable to the operation of seriation.

The ability to place events in order is usually regarded as essential to the understanding of history. A difficulty with this kind of material is said to be a lack of time sense, so that dates have little meaning, but there is also some difficulty in ordering events even without comparisons of chronology or the seeking of anachronisms. As mentioned in the previous chapter, Rogers (1967, p. 103) suggests that the 'historical' concept of time includes 'events which are out of the proper chronological order (and have to be) ordered correctly from the information included in the scrambled account in the form of temporal cues and the indication of cause and effect'. In the present test the ordering of events was thought to be a probable prerequisite to the ability to answer questions involving causal sequence. It was therefore tested independently of other questions by asking for an ordering of events in Nocha (questions XII and XV). No specifically temporal cues were given but in ordering events students had to place a motivation before action (B before A) and to order two consequences in terms of immediate and remote effects (E before D). (See Figure 10.1.)

Results indicated little difference in the answers for the two questions, whether with (XV) or without (XII) the aid of the diagram of parallel events in the other two countries, but both questions showed highly significant changes ($P < 0.001$) over all grades in the T69 sample.

The highest number of errors occurred in the ordering of remote after immediate consequences, i.e. 'Less money was available for education' before 'The standard of education declined', but the whole process of ordering seemed more difficult than any particular aspect of it. Since correct answers were modal by the first form, the results were comparable both with those of Rogers and with other early concrete operational questions in this test. The process involved may be comparable to other kinds of seriation.

From the results of all questions designed to test concrete operational thinking in history, it seemed that the identification of interdependent causes and the negation of these, the making of an evaluative judgment between two issues, and the ordering of events in causal sequence were possible achievements which were illustrative of Piagetian theory.

Formal operational questions

Among questions designed to test specific structures at the formal operational level of thinking were two groups involving adaptations from science material. These were the use of the qualifier 'the situation being as it was' and the recognition of a balance of forces in history.

(a) 'The situation being what it was'

Inhelder and Piaget (1958, p. 59) suggest:

> ... that at substage IIIA two new forms of behaviour appear, resulting in three types of statement that distinguish the formal operation of implication from concrete correspondence. First, a more or less systematic effort is made to determine the consequences of eliminating or diminishing factor *A*, as compared to the simple search for association between factor *A* and its result *X*, which we found at the concrete level ... the second behaviour pattern new to substages IIIA and IIIB, (is) the formation and the utilisation of this total system ... manifested in the development of proof and notably in the schema 'all other things being equal'.

With regard to the first, it was felt that without the possibility of systematically testing hypotheses which the subject himself could initiate, it would not be possible to say whether the subject himself would undertake to judge the effect of diminishing or eliminating a factor. What was attempted in this test was to offer a situation in which one causal factor was diminished and to judge the extent to which the subject saw this diminution as affecting the whole system, or whether it appeared to him merely as a simple association between this new factor and one alternative result. The factor, in each series of events for each country, was diminished by suggesting a hypothetical compensation for its effect. In question V, for example, the subject was asked: 'What might have happened in Adza if Henry had been given a number of cargo ships by another country?' Question X asked: 'What might have happened in Mulba if many more women had been given work in factories?.'

As mentioned earlier in regard to the second behaviour pattern, Dray (1957, p. 104) had suggested that an equivalent in historical material for 'all other things being equal' is the qualifying phrase 'the situation being what it was'. The implication of this statement is that had the situation been altered in any particular way the pattern of events (as would be reflected in the historian's conclusion) might also have been altered. Thus the degree of organizational change envisaged as resulting from the change in one factor in the situation might be expected to reflect the degree of organizational interdependence within which the student had imagined the event to exist. In this way both forms of behaviour could be judged to some extent by responses to one situation. In response to the questions cited above, the extent of the perceived integration between events could be judged by the number of changed consequents described. Preoperational level was scored when subjects denied that the change could be made or that it would have any effect, e.g. 'Women should not go to work', or that it would only affect one item in the series of events. Early concrete operational level was judged as reached when two items in the sequence were changed, while at the highest level the whole sequence was involved, e.g. question V, 'The landowners' taxes wouldn't have been increased, production would have increased and there wouldn't have been an advisory council'.

In relation to these two questions (V and X) it should also be noted that the scoring levels reflect the same strategy as was found in concrete operational questions. That is, one factor is judged preoperational and two factors concrete operational, but instead of the interdependence of two factors, the interdependence of an extensive (at least three items) causal system is used to judge the highest level.

The results on these two questions were closely parallel and each showed significant changes over all grades in both studies. The ages at which higher levels were reached (about the fifth form) did suggest that answering the questions probably involved formal operations. Top-level answers did not become modal until the sixth form. The strategy by which the operations were attained seemed similar to those found for the attainment of concrete operations.

It seems at least reasonable to conclude that where the effect of some factor in a causal sequence is diminished by another event compensating some of the effect, the increasing number of implications envisaged reflects awareness of increasing organizational interdependence between events.

(b) Balances of forces in history

The second group of questions at the formal operational level was concerned with the recognition of a balance of forces in history. Peel (1967b, p. 160) has suggested that this concept of the balance of forces within a system in history could be analogous to the balance of forces in Inhelder and Piaget's (1958, p. 150) experiment with the hydraulic press. This possibility was tested in questions III, VIII, and XIII. In question III, for example, 'How could Henry have helped the landowners to buy imported goods?', the problem was for the student to understand that the forces exerted by increased taxation affected the whole balance of the country's economy. Instead of the weight of the piston the weight of increased taxation was given, instead of the opposing density of the liquid the postulated desire of the landowners to buy imports was given, and instead of the concept of pressure the concept of a balance of resources and expenditure was given.

A basic requirement in answering these questions remained the recognition of the essential sequence of events, but beyond this the questions were also a test of reversibility which could be achieved either by the inversion of action previously taken, e.g. reducing the landowners' taxation, or by supplementary action directed at compensating a cause and thus negating an effect, e.g. subsidizing farm production. Not only could both forms of reversibility, inversion or compensation, be used to answer the questions, but in a complete answer the two might be combined, revealing an approximation of the reciprocity of formal operational thinking, for instance, 'By lowering taxes and importing less goods so as to create a balance of consumption and supply'.

Results from all groups were scored in terms of operational levels, but since the data would give a less than precise approximation of processes it was decided to summarize the scored responses for T69 in two ways. These ways would enable a comparison between (a) the supposed use of different kinds of operations and (b) grouping by counting of the number of factors considered, irrespective of the logical operation involved. In this way some light might be shed on whether the changes in thinking with this material were initially quantitative and later qualitative.

In both categorizations of data, 'wrong' answers (which failed to see the problem) and answers offering one negation or one compensation were judged to be at the preoperational level. However, in the first method of grouping (a), scores were given on the basis of those using multiple negations or multiple compensations being scored at the concrete operational level (II); those combining both a negation and a compensation were called formal operational (IIIA); while those which specifically mentioned a balance of forces were called late formal operational (IIIB). The second method (b) relied simply on

332

counting the number of factors considered irrespective of their function of either negation or compensation, on the assumption that the more items that were mentioned the more of the total system was seen to be involved. Thus double negations, or double compensations, or one negation combined with one compensation were called *doubles*, while three negations, three compensations, (the latter did not occur) or any combination of compensations and negations which exceeded two were scored as *triples*.

If, as Flavell and Wohlwill (in Elkind and Flavell, 1969, p. 78) suggested, an increase in the number of variables considered is a prerequisite for movement to a new stage, then two variables should be used before operations which combined cancellation and compensation. It was also a matter of interest to notice to what extent formal operations as judged by IIIA should coincide with triples. Though the results from this test would not necessarily have had general implications, it was decided to note whether negation tended to precede the use of compensation. The various combinations of the same scores were designed to clarify these possibilities.

The results of question III are presented in detail in Table 10.4 for group T69. Results on all questions by both methods of scoring showed a highly significant change with age for T69. For group S69 and S70, scored on logical

TABLE 10.4. Questions on the balance of forces with alternative grouping of scores
Question III

(a) Grouping by logical operations

				Grades				
	6C	1	2	3	4	5	6F	Totals
Formal operational (IIIB)							4	4
Formal operational (IIIA)	1	1	7	11	11	16	12	59
Concrete operational (II)	3	9	7	9	9	15	11	63
Preoperational (I)	46	40	36	30	30	19	23	224

Chi-square = 51·3558, df = 12, $P < 0.001$.
Fourth and fifth chi-square = 30·0, $df = 2$, $P < 0.001$.

(b) Grouping by numbers

				Grades				
	6C	1	2	3	4	5	6F	Totals
Triples			1	0	3	3	6	13
Doubles	4	10	13	20	17	28	21	113
Singles	37	31	30	28	26	18	21	191
Wrong	9	9	6	2	4	1	2	33

Pooling triples with doubles and singles with wrong.
Chi-square = 46·3541, $df = 6$, $P < 0.001$.
Pooling triples with doubles and singles with wrong.
Fourth and fifth chi-square = 4·0016, $df = 1$, $P < 0.05$ (single to double).

operations only, significant changes were found in questions III and XIII. On examining the nature of transitions between grades it was found that the transitions which occurred on all these questions showed a move from preoperational to concrete operational between 6C and form 1, and either from concrete operational to formal operational or from doubles to triples between forms 4 and 5. It thus appeared to make little difference whether numbers of factors or logical operations were considered in tracing general trends and marked transitions in development.

When the detailed scores were examined it was, of course, found that many doubles were a combination of cancellation and compensation, but some were double cancellations or double compensations. Double and triple scores were examined separately in order to clarify this position, but there was no real evidence that double negation occurred before the combination of negation and compensation.

Thus the suggestion of Flavell and Wohlwill, mentioned earlier, that quantitative change might be a prerequisite for more basic changes, does not receive support from this test. Though it is recognized that cancellation and compensation combined, as measured here, was not a stringent measure of formal operational thinking, the question remains whether the change to the use of an additional variable may not be at least as indicative of development in thinking as the use of a different operation.

The more stringent requirement of the explicit expression of a sense of balance between forces, indicated by Peel as typical of formal operations, was given by very few students, and all of these were in the sixth form. Here, as was anticipated, appreciation of such a balance did seem to indicate a development in structure.

From all the results in the second section of the test, it seemed that it was possible to ask questions about history-type material where answers would reveal the use of logical operations at both concrete and formal levels, and that the same strategies might be used in gaining those operational levels. Upon such knowledge of developmental sequence the history teacher can base a sequence of learning experiences.

Testing the conceptual level

The third section was designed to test the kind of historical concepts likely to be available to students at different levels of thinking. Piaget suggests that at each level concepts may be formed which incorporate the logical operations available. In this way, conservation concepts are the product of a system of propositional logic in which several classes or simple propositions stating relations may be combined.

In this test the development in thinking in relation to concept level could be judged by a task in which the extensive definition of concepts was measured by the supplying of additional exemplars and the intensive definition was measured by the description of similarities both between groups of events and between series of events. Similarities between series of events were regarded as an approximation of a colligatory concept. Provided that consideration was given to the number and nature of the attributes, to the relations between them, and to the accurate demarcation of the situation to be considered, definitions should be increasingly coordinated. Comparisons would then be possible between such conceptual definitions and those other questions which were aimed at specific operations. Since the same population and the same material would be used for each kind of question, the attainment of stages related to both concepts and logical operations might be expected to coincide.

The intensive definition by similarities between sets of events will be considered first, as this directs particular attention to the differences caused by the number and kind of relationships involved.

(a) Intensive definitions—relationships in similarities

In the previous discussion on the nature of concepts it was suggested that one of the important variables contributing to the difficulty of a concept was the kind of relationships required between the relevant attributes. It was further suggested that these relationships, as they might occur within descriptions of similarities, would probably show a similar progression to those found in answers to questions involving the same logical operations on the same material.

The setting out of events in the three countries into rows and columns (see Figure 10.1) was assumed to clarify for students the classes of events both between and within countries which could be defined in terms of their similarities. The criteria for judging these similarities had been contrived to resemble the logical operations of addition of classes (grouping I), bi-univocal multiplication of class (grouping V), and bi-univocal multiplication of relations (grouping VIII). It was assumed that the degree to which a subject would choose to describe the similarity in terms of the criteria would reflect the degree to which he used such a logical operation within an assimilatory structure. All criteria were at the concrete operational level (IIB), but involved different groupings and different numbers and types of operations; hence they need not be coincident in difficulty. Itemized answers were scored at the preoperational level and partially valid generalizations were all scored at the concrete operational level (IIA).

The criteria for logical operations selected as valid for each row are briefly described to enable interpretation of results. I am indebted to Sheppard for clarifying these groupings, some of which had been previously interpreted otherwise (Jurd, 1973).

Similarities for rows 1, 2, and 6 Addition of classes (grouping I, level IIB). These were scored on the selection of several relevant attributes in combination. It was expected that they would not necessarily be of equal difficulty since row 1 required only the statement of two attributes (new + leadership), while row 2, with two attributes also, had as one attribute a motivation or plan which

	Leader's Policy
Unfortunate events	Unfortunate consequences of leader's Policy

FIGURE 10.2

might be expected to be more difficult than an event (leader + plan for country). Row 6 required a combination of three attributes (*action* by the *people* against the *leaders*). In each item the abstracting of common attributes was seen as an example of grouping I, which is sometimes studied by asking children to put together those objects which are alike.

Similarities for rows 3 and 4 Bi-univocal multiplication of classes (grouping IV, level IIB). The criteria for these two items required both a similarity across a row (between countries) and another down a column (within countries). The similarity was thus an intersection of classes, e.g. row 3 (see Figure 10.2).

Similarities for row 7 Bi-univocal multiplication of relations (grouping VIII, level IIB). This grouping is used to describe coseriation, which is what is being required in this item. Within each country, i.e. down each column, there was a change of government to one which was more representative of people. The statement of similarity required the recognition of this relationship between row 1 and row 7 as it occurred in each of the three countries.

The results from these items supported the assumed operational levels in that similarities 1, requiring the addition of two attributes, was easiest. Similarities 2, also requiring the addition of two attributes, but with one of those attributes a motivation, was slightly more difficult, but for both these similarity items the late concrete operational level (IIB) was modal by form 1. With similarities 6, which involved the addition of three attributes, level IIB was not modal until form 3. Similarities 3 and 4, on the bi-univocal multiplication of classes, also showed significant increase in operational levels over grades, but achievement of this grouping did not become modal in the T69 group until forms 5 and 4 respectively, which was later than would be expected. Only one item failed to show a significant development on the description of similarities. This was similarities 7, the multiplication of relations, in which the majority of students scored only a partial generalization, early concrete operational (IIA) level.

From these results it seemed that the requirements of a statement of similarities between events varied in difficulty as the number of attributes and the logical operations involved in the similarities also varied. The use of an adequate intensive definition of a concept is apparently dependent on the availability of appropriate logical operations. It would appear advisable for teachers to analyse the concepts they hope to teach in terms of their attributes and relationships so that the concept is not too far removed from the pupil's level of thinking.

(b) Extensive definition

In the questions involving the extensive definition of a concept, the student was required to appreciate the course of events in each country and to extend the series of particular events in Nocha to match those of the other two countries. It was assumed that this would involve him in isolating the common attributes of events in rows 6 and 7 for Adza and Mulba in order to invent similar events. The criteria for scoring were the same as those for similarities across the same row.

Results indicated that the completion of row 6, except in group S70, and of row 7 both showed significant differences in levels over grades. Not only the generalization, as in similarities, but the ability to give instances of a concept seemed dependent upon the ability to use the logical operations involved.

(c) Intensive definition as in a colligatory concept

Question XVIII was designed to require subjects to identify the process of change in events in all three countries. It was hoped that this question might approximate the use of a colligatory concept. The results indicated a significant development with age in all groups. Furthermore, the highest-level answers were not modal until the sixth form, a pattern which suggested that such colligatory concepts might require formal operations. Insofar as the use of a colligatory concept may be said to approach the postulation of a covering law, it would be reasonable to argue for the formal operational level, but the criterion used was precisely the same as for the completion and similarities row 7. In the following comparison of the three test items, the possible difference in processes of thinking involved is discussed.

(d) Comparing the three kinds of definition

It has been argued previously that the degree of the attainment of a concept may be measured by the coordination of the extensive and intensive definitions. Such a measure was possible with both row 6 and row 7 in that completion (extensive definition) and similarity (intensive definition) used the same material and had the same criteria for a correct answer. In the case of row 7 the definitions could be further extended to include question XVIII which, it was hoped, would be equivalent to a colligatory concept, and the same criterion for a correct answer could be used.

Three comparisons were made in relation to each of these rows for T69 data only. First, the likelihood of coordination of definitions being a measure of attainment of the concept may be judged by the number of subjects in each grade who were able to fulfil the correct criteria on none, one, two, or three of the definitions. Second, the degree of association between individual students' answers over all grades may indicate whether the answers to questions are closely related to each other, and third, the comparative difficulty of the items may serve to indicate a progression in the difficulty of the kind of definitions.

The use of the coordination of definitions as a measure of the attainment of a concept was examined first for row 6 similarities and extension. Here the common criterion was 'action by the people against the leaders'. The coordination of correct answers did increase significantly with age, the levels of answers being closely associated for all individuals, and the definitions appeared to be equally difficult.

With row 7 there were several differences to be noted. As was indicated, there were three definitions for this concept, the criterion of which was 'change of government with increasing representation of the people'. These definitions were the extensive definition (XVI), intensive definition by similarities (XVII), and intensive definition by colligatory concept (XVIII). A complete understanding of the concept was expected to lead to the coordination of all three definitions. However, results for similarities, row 7, showed no significant change with age, most subjects continuing to give only partially correct answers. The increased difficulty of the relationships involved within the criterion and the multiplication of relationships as opposed to addition of classes probably influenced attempts at all three definitions for row 7, so that comparatively few subjects were able to coordinate even two of the definitions. This does not invalidate the use of such a measure, however, but merely indicates that the concept concerned may have been a more difficult one than that in row 6. Only a small number of subjects (in T69, 18 out of 350) actually succeeded in giving correct answers on all three definitions, i.e. most were not able to coordinate the definitions. If concept attainment can be measured by coordination of definitions, it seems clear that a concept such as 'the growth of democracy' is unlikely to be achieved before late adolescence. The number of subjects achieving three definitions was so small in fact that it had to be combined with those giving correct answers on two definitions in order to calculate chi-square. When this was done, results showed a significant increase in the coordination of definitions with increasing age ($P < 0.001$).

The degree of association between individual students' answers over grades for questions XVI, XVII, and XVIII was found to be high and indicated that answers were closely related to each other. With row 7 there was also a significant difference in the difficulty of all three items, completion being simpler than similarities, which, in turn, was simpler than the colligatory concept. That these differences were not entirely due to the lack of development in row 7 similarities was indicated by the still greater difference between completion 7 and the colligatory concept (XVIII).

Since the relationships and material involved in the criteria were the same within each row, the differences in the difficulty of the questions needs further examination. This difference in questions may resolve itself into a consideration of the extent of the material to be scanned as indicated by the question. Although the same material was available for consideration for each question not all of it may have been used. It is speculated that the completion of events within a single country might possibly be accomplished by matching of each attribute with corresponding attributes, without abstracting the similarity. In abstracting similarities some attempt could be made without considering the total progress of all events in each country, but in question XVIII the subject was specifically directed to consider all events in all three countries. In directing attention to increasingly wide areas for consideration, the questions did differ. Hence, while the identity of the answers and the relationships involved in the answers were the same, the actual process of thinking by the subjects in each context may have differed.

Another interesting aspect of the difference in difficulty between the questions may be found in the fact that similarities require a statement of a state, whereas the colligatory concept in XVIII required the statement of a process. Even with the use of the same criterion for each, the widening of the context, if this did occur, would carry with it this change from end state to process. In this aspect there seems to be a parallel with the strategy found within the acquisition of a conservation concept. As we postulated, the colligatory concept has many similarities to a conservation concept, except that it is concerned with relations between propositions rather than between concrete material. It is possible that the neglect of areas of material available for consideration in questions XVI, XVII, and XVIII, and the consequent reduction in the number of variables, is a reflection of the subject's inability to cope with more propositional material.

The whole of this explanation for the increase in difficulty, from extensive definition to similarities intension to colligatory concept intension, would need verification with further independent evidence, but while no firm conclusions can be drawn it is interesting that Taba and Elzey (1964, p. 532) identified a similar progression in learning from their examination of children's strategies in classroom interactions. They say (p. 533) that:

> ... a strategy representing an effective pacing of shifting the thought onto higher levels seems to follow a characteristic course. The level of seeking information is sustained for a considerable time during the first portion of the discussion. Grouping is requested only after a large amount of information has been accumulated. The result is that in a fairly brief period children transcend from grouping to labelling and then to providing reasons for labelling and then to inferences.

Since this strategy, recommended to teachers, is based on information gained from observation of the actual process of learning, it is clear that from grouping to labelling to explication of the relationships involved is a natural progression in learning.

The strategy of grouping, labelling, and explication of relationships is so apparently similar to that which shows a movement from gathering of additional exemplars to statement of similarities to explication of relations, as in a colligatory or conservational concept, that it seems reasonable to wonder whether the same strategy provides another aspect of the series of developments which might be recurrently discovered in the development of concepts. In this instance the use of a colligatory concept implies that the strategy is identified as pertinent for the formal operational level, though the initial step was possible with concrete operations. Annett (1959, p. 229), in a study of class concepts with both children and adults, also found a progression, both in terms of age and in terms of the Mill Hill Vocabulary score, in which 'contiguities preceded similarities which in turn preceded class names'. Despite the logically necessary coordination of definitions of various kinds (extensive, intensive similarity, and intensive conservational), complete coordination would appear to be unlikely until intensive definition in the conservational sense is possible.

This consideration of strategies in the development of concepts leads to a consideration of some of the more general aspects of Piagetian theory.

RESULTS RELATED TO MORE GENERAL ASPECTS OF PIAGETIAN THEORY

Having examined individual questions and groups of questions, each of which highlighted a particular logical operation or concept involving operations, we may now give consideration to the more general aspects of Piaget's theory which appeared in an overall examination of results on all questions. These general aspects were the existence of stages and the nature of stages as an equilibrium step. The identification of stages as a coincidence in time of the attainment of sets of logical operations, the order in which stages appeared, and the degree and kind of discontinuity between stages, were all considered in relation to the results of the present study. It was also thought that the nature of a stage as a temporary equilibrium might be reflected in the degree of variability found in individual subjects' answers at different ages.

Identification of stages

In identifying the existence of stages it was necessary to establish that there did occur within the results of the test an invariant order in the sets of logical operations by which the stages were defined. The possibility for such recognition existed in the ranking in difficulty of the twenty-one questions in sections 2 and 3 of the test, which gave specific consideration to particular logical operations. If such rankings were both grouped according to the expected logical operations and graded in difficulty according to the expected order, there would be evidence of a basis for stages.

By attributing scores of 1, 2, 3, and 4 for levels I, IIA, IIB, and III, it was possible to find a total score on each question for each grade. Where no distinction was made in marking within level II, the answer was scored 2 as for IIA. Questions could then be ranked in order of difficulty for each grade and the rankings compared by means of Kendall's coefficient of concordance. When this was done it was found that the difficulty of questions was highly consistent, irrespective of grades. Using formula (9.16) in Siegel (1956, p. 234) which allows for tied observations, $W = 0.704$. The significance of this coefficient was calculated using chi-square $= K(N-1)W$. For T69 chi-square $= 103.488$, which had a probability well below $< .001$. This result suggested that the questions and their operational levels were reliable over different grades.

The only partial exceptions to this order were similarities 3 and 4, supposedly representing the multiplication of classes. In group T69 these questions presented comparable difficulty until about the fourth form, ranking about 17, but from the fourth form onwards both questions moved to about rank 2. A similar sudden change from difficult to easy was found in group S70, though here it occurred about the third form. As mentioned, all other questions in the test retained a comparatively stable position.

In order to consider the importance of the rank order discovered, in terms of the logical operations represented by the questions, an estimate of true rank was needed. Kendall (Siegel, 1956, p. 238) suggests that the 'best estimate of the "true" ranking of the N objects is provided, when W is significant, by the order of the various sums of rank, R_j'. On this basis the ranking of difficulty of questions was considered for the present test, though it was necessary to realize that the ranks were not equidistant. Equivalence in difficulty could not be judged by other means since not all the questions were marked on the same part of the scale.

In Table 10.2 the questions are listed in order of difficulty for all three population groups, while the accompanying columns show the overall level of significance of differences between grades for each question. The first column shows the theoretical level of questions (i.e. concrete or formal) in the order they are listed for the T69 study.

A number of comments may be made on these data. In general it may be said that there appear to be three groups of question: (a) the formal operational questions, which are all grouped together as the most difficult, (b) concrete operational questions on causes and the negation of causes, and similarities 3, 4, and 7, and (c) easier concrete operational questions.

More detailed examination of Table 10.2 suggests the increasing difficulty from extensive definition (completion 6 and 7) to intensive similarity (questions 6 and 7) to colligatory concept (question XVIII), which is apparent for all groups, even to the extent of the colligatory concept appearing to be suitably placed at the formal operational level of thinking. It may also be noted that evaluative judgments between two factors (VI, XIV, and XI) remain easier than statements of causes and negation of causes of events (II, IV, VII, IX), possibly because the available two alternatives were actually stated in the evaluative judgment questions. The recurrent conservation strategy mentioned by Piaget had been identified in each of these groups of question. In addition to this, the same strategy had been found at the formal operational level in questions V and X.

Those other formal operational questions (III, VII, and XIII), which had also been adaptations required by the nature of historical material, had resulted in those questions being ranked among the more difficult, so the adaptations appeared to have been effective. Overall, it seemed that the order of difficulty grouped questions according to the theoretical level of the logical operations involved and thus supported Piaget's use of defining operational levels.

Apart from the comparative difficulty of questions within the test, the modal

TABLE 10.5. Numbers of questions at different modal levels

Modal Levels	6C		1		2		3		4		5		6F	
	T69	S70	T69	S70	T69	S70	T69	S70	T69	S70	T69	S70	T69	S70
Formal operational (III)						1		1	2	2	2		—	2
Concrete operational (IIB)	2	—	6	4	5	8	8	9	10	9	10	9	—	12
Concrete operational (IIA)	7	—	11	11	11	8	9	11	8	9	8	9	—	5
Preoperational (I)	12	—	4	6	5	4	4	1	2	1	1	1	—	2

level at which questions were answered in various grades indicated a reasonable degree of homogeneity within different groups (T69 and S70), with concrete operations appearing before formal logical operations (Table 10.5).

The total number of questions modal at a particular level is deceptive to some extent in that 15 out of 21 questions could not be answered at any level higher than concrete operational. It should be remembered, however, that these concrete operations were being used on material which was remote from the student's own experience and was expressed verbally. The attributes used for categorizing were abstract. Thus the 'stage' reached is probably most usefully described as 'concrete general'. The results are comparable with research on similar material cited in the previous chapter or with the concrete general level in mathematics. As an alternative to defining a stage as concrete general, it is possible to describe the same phenomena in terms of horizontal décalages.

Szeminska (1965) has undertaken the systematic and comprehensive study of horizontal décalages such as these, and her studies indicate the complexity of the many factors which influence development in thinking. Among these factors are differences in content, differences in type of activity, and differences in the situations in which material is learned.

A relevant illustration of this complexity was found in the wide décalage which occurred with minor changes of material. Szeminska (1965) said that 'with the (classification of) geometric forms in three sizes and four colours, we obtained at the age of five to six, 100% of stage V conceptualisation ... however ... in the classification of irregular forms or images evoking many functional schemas, among which a choice was necessary, the conceptual stage was reached later, about the age of thirteen or fourteen' (p. 51). 'Stage V was defined as conceptual schemas, anticipation of the whole class but without trying to coordinate the different classes' (p. 50). Such wide variations in age with similar types of material make it less surprising that in the present study with verbal descriptions of events, which presumably also evoke many functional schemas and among which a choice is necessary, a conceptual stage in classifying similar to Szeminska's stage V is not reached until about 12 years 7 months.

From the order of difficulty of questions in this test it appeared that the logical operations were used in the sequence suggested by Piaget's theory. Whether the stages might be regarded as distinct within the same material was another problem.

Discontinuity of stages

The possibility of identifying discontinuity between stages of thinking was approached in several different ways. First, significant differences between adjacent grades in any question in any group were noted (T69, S69, and S70). Second, it was possible to note significant differences between grades for S69/70 groups where the same subjects had been involved in each. Table 10.6 shows the total number of significant differences ($p < 0.05$) between adjacent grades for each group as well as the type of questions in which the transitions occurred.

It may be seen that in the T69 group ($N = 350$) there were ten marked transitions between the sixth class and first form, nine between the fourth and fifth forms and very few between other adjacent grades. These results suggested that there might be some discontinuity in the stages of development and supported evidence from other investigators with this material, who have found discontinuity at the same ages and approximately the same levels (Case and Collinson, 1962; Hallam, 1967). In all groups any transitions which occurred in formal operational questions at earlier grades were between preoperational and concrete operational levels. Not all transitions, however, clearly belonged to the same theoretical level at each age, even within one question, e.g. in question IX the transition between the sixth class and first form was contributed to by preoperational to early concrete and early concrete to late concrete operational.

Not surprisingly, the number of transitions changed for groups other than

TABLE 10.6. Number of questions with significant differences between adjacent grades

Group	Level of question	6C–1	1–2	Grades 2–3	3–4	4–5
T69	Concrete operational	6	1	2	0	2
(350)	Formal operational	4	0	0	0	7
S69	Concrete operational	4	1	2	0	X
(174)	Formal operational	3	0	0	1	
S70	Concrete operational	X	4	1	2	1
(174)	Formal operational		1	0	0	2
S69/70	Concrete operational	6	3	1	0	1
(174)	Formal operational	1	0	4	6	3

T69, since in these groups there were fewer subjects and fewer grades, but the pattern of transitions also changed. This was particularly noticeable in group S69/70. Where the scores of the same people were compared as groups in two consecutive years, there was no clear evidence of a pattern of more transitions between some grades than between others. What does seem evident from the S69/70 data is that transitions tend to occur at the ages appropriate to the level of the question, i.e. there are significant differences between early adjacent grades on questions theoretically at the concrete operational level while formal operational questions discriminate answers from the second or third forms upwards. One may only conclude that the evidence from group data for discontinuity between stages is not clear, particularly when a longitudinal approach is used.

Equilibrium

Piaget's insistence on the importance of equilibrium in judging the attainment of stages in thinking led to an attempt at a second, different measure for discontinuity. According to the theory, as a new stage is reached there is a general stability in the logical operations used on that material. It was hypothesized that if an individual had just achieved a new level of thinking, i.e. a temporary equilibrium, there should be fewer deviations from his own modal score than if he were, for example, in the phase of oscillation before the establishment of a stage. The modal score was found for each student and the total deviation from this score calculated for each individual. The totals of these scores were then used to estimate an average deviation score for each grade. Presumably deviations should have been less where a marked transition was found in operational levels of answers.

Some support for this notion was found in the T69 group, where it was evident that the average deviation score was less at form 5, where it was also shown that for that group there were a number of recent transitions to a new level. The same support was not available at the first form for T69, but neither was it refuted since little deviation was possible in the sixth class primary where the majority of subjects could only give preoperational answers. In other group data, however, particularly with the S69/70 group, the pattern of deviation scores did not match the number of significant differences between grades (Table 10.7). Thus, while both the pattern of transitions and the use of deviation scores compared with that pattern gave limited support for discontinuity in

TABLE 10.7. Average deviation scores at each grade

Groups	6C	1	2	Grades 3	4	5	6F
T69	11·4	13·06	13·31	15·7	15·3	13·7	14·5
S69	11·4	13·35	13·5	15·78	14·8	—	—
S70	—	12·7	10·08	13·57	14·57	13·7	—

group T69, the support was less evident in S70 and disappeared entirely when a longitudinal approach was used.

The existence of scores for the same subjects in two consecutive years did enable another, individually based, approach to the problem of equilibrium. If the attainment of a new stage for each individual is preceded by increased deviation and followed by decreased deviation, this should be apparent from deviation scores for those subjects whose modal score remained the same or those whose modal score increased over the year. One difficulty with testing only at a yearly interval, however, is that there is no way of telling at what time of the year the modal score may have changed. The results were inconclusive so that this rather gross use of changes in deviation scores also failed to support the notion that stages of thinking may be identified by changes in the stability of answers.

Considering the measures of discontinuity, then both the fact that the transitions which do occur are not necessarily between the same levels and the fact that the same pattern is not found with longitudinal data suggest that the use of group data may not be satisfactory in judging discontinuity between stages of development. Further, the lack of stability, irrespective of the kind of material, found in the operational levels used by any one subject suggests that an individual pattern of variation over time might be a more effective measure. A longitudinal study with a more frequent use of measures at clearly defined levels of operation is probably needed to elucidate the problem of equilibrium and of discontinuity in stages of development. The present study did not succeed in finding a suitable measure of discontinuity between stages of development, or of equilibrium within the thinking of individual students.

SUMMARY OF CONCLUSIONS

In summarizing the results it may be said that the study here has shown that the stages defined by logical operations and the strategies within those stages may be identified in history-type material. The sequence of development found in science and mathematics material is confirmed in history material when appropriate modifications are made to the questions asked.

Three main modifications were used in this study. In the first modification, the combination of cancellation and compensation which is typical of formal reciprocal relations was tested with historical material when, as had been suggested by Peel (1967b, p. 160), a recognition of the balance of forces within a system was sought. For the second, 'the situation being what it was' provided a substitute for the scientist's qualifying phrase of 'all other things being equal', and it was possible to test the degree of complex interdependence of variables by evaluating the extent of the effects imagined when one causal variable was modified by compensation. Both these adaptations were added to other possible logical operations which could be applied to history. In the third modification, also at the formal operational level, a substitute was needed for the law-giving hypothesis of science. An approximation for this seemed to be Walsh's (1967, p. 63) notion of a colligatory concept, which was found to resemble a conservational approach to concept attainment.

The measure of the degree of attainment of a concept by means of the degree of coordination of the extensive and intensive definitions which had been suggested by Lovell, Mitchell, and Everett (1962) was extended to include the notion of conservation as an intensive definition. The test provided for each kind of definition as measured by additional exemplars, statements of similarities, and explicit statement of both attributes and relationship as in a conservational or colligatory concept. The necessity for controlling the number, kind, and relations of attributes within a concept, a control which also involved the specification of a context for the concept, was recognized. In particular, the importance of the different relationships involved in a concept was shown by measuring these relationships as found in statements of similarity and comparing results with those on other questions using equivalent logical operations.

Given this adapted approach to the measurement of logical operations, it became possible to consider the evidence for 'stages' in cognitive development as defined by Piaget (Tanner and Inhelder, 1960, pp. 120–121). The first criterion for stages is the invariable order of succession of certain aspects of thinking. Following Piaget's theory, both the strategies within stages and the groupings of logical operations appropriate for the ordering of stages had formed the basis for criteria for marking each question. Within the concrete operational level, questions included the statement of causes of events, the negation of these causes, and the reconciliation of conflicting evidence. In results of all three questions it was found possible to identify the strategy which is typical of conservation experiments, viz. the concentration on one aspect, on alternating or multiple aspects, and, finally, the integration of both aspects. The recurrence of this strategy at the formal operational level was also shown in answers to the three questions on the balance of forces. Another apparent strategy, not specifically mentioned by Piaget but similar in kind, was found in questions concerned with similarities and in questions requiring completion of a series. In these answers there seemed to be an order from specific instance to partial generalization, with recognition of similarities and differences, to coordination of the definition in the description of attributes and the relations between them. The existence of such strategies lent weight to the existence of stages as described by Piaget. The order of stages was confirmed in that, in all questions permitting measurement at the formal operational level, the answers at that level did appear at later ages, though in most instances the number of students reaching that level was not high.

The second criterion is the assimilation of one stage into a later one. This criterion was supported in that in the more extensive population, T69, all but one of the total twenty-one questions showed highly significant increases in the level of cognitive operations over the seven grades. That one question was similarities 7, which seemed to be a very poor discriminator with all groups. If the similarities 7 question is discarded, then within the more limited samples S69, testing the sixth class to the fourth form, showed fifteen significant differences, eleven on concrete operational questions and the remainder at the same level though in formal operational questions, while S70, testing the first to fifth forms, showed sixteen significant differences, five on the formal operational level questions. It was noted that with each question there was a marked diminution of preoperational answers from the sixth class onwards, particularly between the sixth class and the first form, and a later increase in the number of concrete operational level (IIB) answers. This change in level of thinking did suggest that one stage became integrated into the next, although the remnants of preoperational thinking could be found even at the sixth form level and there was considerable variability of level within each student's answers.

The third criterion requires that a whole, in this case groups of logical operations, may be used to characterize a stage. When questions were grouped according to the logical operations involved, it was found that like questions were closest to each other in terms of difficulty and that groups of questions which could be characterized as either concrete or formal operational levels were also grouped together; for instance, causes of an event and the negation of such causes were closely associated. Concepts which presented the stabilization of logical operations seemed to coincide with questions involving operations at the same level; similarities involving the addition of classes coincided with concrete operational questions such as the reconciliation of conflicting evidence. At the formal operational level, it was found that results based on the qualifying phrase 'the situation being as it was', on the equilibrium of cancellation and compensation found in the balance of forces, and on the attainment of a colligatory concept were closely associated. Thus the characterization of stages by sets of logical operations and by concepts involving those operations, as described by Piaget, did seem to be effective.

The fourth and fifth criteria for the existence of stages, namely one stage preparing for the following and each new stage being a culmination of preceding development, were met in that the increasingly complex logical operations used as the defining characteristics of a stage imply such a development. Apart from this implied fulfilment, the evidence cannot be easily demonstrated in a cross-sectional or group data approach. Thus some evidence was found to support all five criteria for the existence of stages in the development of thinking.

It would seem that it is possible to identify aspects of Piaget's theory of cognitive development within history-type material. That the initial differences noted in the previous chapter on the nature of the material are not such as to preclude the application of the theory has been demonstrated both in the research reviewed and in this present study. The specific implications of these findings for the teaching of history in schools have yet to be adequately investigated, but some limited suggestions may be made.

IMPLICATIONS FOR TEACHING

When the implications of Piaget's theory and the research related to it are considered for the teaching of history, it seems that the major contribution of the theory may come from the confirmation of the sequence of logical operations. To this may be added a knowledge of the strategies and problems involved in learning concepts and an awareness of some of the aspects of thinking needed in adequate historical study.

From a knowledge of the sequence of development in logical operations, teachers may plan realistic sequences in understanding historical material. The process of putting events into causal order, of understanding simple interdependent causes of events, of reconciling conflicting events, or of understanding concepts involving the addition of classes might reasonably be expected to precede an understanding of the balance of forces in history, the use of a colligatory concept, the use of the qualifying idea 'the situation being as it was', or the modification of laws. When considering the concepts to be taught, teachers who can analyse these concepts in terms of both the kind and number of attributes and the operational level of the relationship between those attributes may determine the difficulty level of the concept.

Once the ordered sequence is established the notion of 'pacing' is important in that it recognizes the progress of the individual child against that ordered sequence of development. The teacher aims to provide the next appropriate experience at the time when the child shows readiness for it. The size of the step may vary with each child. The fact that groups of operations seem to occur together, i.e. concrete and formal operations, suggests that learning may not appear as smoothly incremental. But the dangers of not pacing teaching with the learning of operations have been shown by Szeminska (1965, p. 55), who found that 'poorly assimilated information had become a mnemonic burden' and even prevented later understanding.

A knowledge of the strategies involved in learning concepts or arriving at particular ideas may assist in teaching the process by which learning occurs, so that the learner learns how to learn. The possibilities exist of teaching Taba's observed strategy of gathering particular instances before making a generalization and deliberately searching for consequences or implications. Similarly, it may be possible to recognize in teaching a sequence which proceeds from building up a series of events to defining similarities between events to formulating a colligatory concept.

Some teaching programmes have made deliberate use of an inquiry technique, with questions specifically designed to help the student feel the process of being a historian using source material such as documents, pictures, etc. Such programmes have been widely debated, but two aspects which may be relevant to the present study are the use of original sources and 'being an historian'. Of the first aspect Hallam (in Ballard, 1971, p. 170) points out that since formal operational thinking does not usually appear until mid-adolescence with history material, the use of concrete material such as pictures, artifacts, newspaper reports, etc., may be particularly appropriate before that age. The material itself is not the crucial element in relation to difficulty, but the use that can be made of it by the student is important. As was noted in the studies of vocabulary, and in those by Hallam (1967) and by Rhys (1972), the interpretation of the documents, maps, or pictures will be largely dependent upon the cognitive structure of the student. However, where the material enables the initial use of concrete operations and may later lead on to meaningful understanding at a higher level, its use may be important. Szeminska (1965, p. 56) reports that Putkiewicz has used:

> ... graphic schemas in the solution of arithmetic problems, permitting him to substitute concrete operations for the formal operations of which the students were not capable. He has obtained substantial results. Students could solve different problems on the semi-concrete, graphic level, but, in addition, after a certain amount of time (3 months) they could also solve the task on the abstract level using a system of formal operation.

Unfortunately, no indication is given as to whether the students were approaching transition to the formal operational stage in any case.

The second aspect, the aim that students should experience the process of being an historian, is commendable in that inquiry into realistic problem situations most frequently generates real interest. The idea is criticized by Elton (in Ballard, 1971) on the grounds that the scholarly analysis required is too demanding for school children and that the kinds of topic which can be researched from local original sources and sites are likely to be too limited. Certainly the student's analysis will be limited by his cognitive level, and certainly if the study is to be entirely restricted to the local scene and to first-hand sources in that locality the topics would be limited, but this would be an extreme interpretation. Within the use of such methods is found more opportunity for self-regulation and active assimilation without which, in Piaget's (1964, pp. 17–18) opinion there is 'no possible didactic or pedagogy which significantly transforms the subject'. The activity of the individual learner is paramount, but the planning of sequenced material must be based on a knowledge of strategies and of the order of operations.

The importance of the pupil's own activity is emphasized by two other factors noted in the research reviewed. One was the contribution made to the understanding of a concept by the student's own experience. This being so, the teacher needs to know his students personally and to some extent realize their likely sources of both interest and difficulty in acquiring new ideas. The other was the development of understanding of various points of view. Hallam (in Ballard, 1971, p. 171) suggests that the teacher may assist the student, who tends to judge every incident and character from a twentieth-century point of view, by posing other points of view and teaching the students how to use reversibility. The associated process of decentring, mentioned earlier, is slightly more complicated and involves the attitudes and values of the student, but a study of this process may well assist the teacher to develop this aspect of objectivity in the study of history.

Finally, it has been suggested that knowledge of the structures and methods of various disciplines might assist students to understand the appropriateness of methods used with different kinds of material and the kinds of generalization which can be made from them. In general, there are many aspects of the teaching of history which could be clarified and enlivened by the application of Piagetian theory and research.

11

FORMAL OPERATIONAL THOUGHT

J. L. Seggie

In the past decade the literature of scientific psychology has revealed a burgeoning growth in studies dealing with the Piagetian model of the development of intelligence. Yet to the disinterested observer the emphasis on the work of Piaget has had a peculiar, lopsided quality in that the vast majority of studies deal with the transition from intuitive to concrete operations. Such has been the paucity of independent effort expended in the transition from concrete to formal thought that the neophyte scholar, who neglects original sources, must be forgiven for the belief that Piaget's life has been spent exclusively in the study of young children. With relatively few exceptions two important aspects of the Piagetian model have received scant attention. First, there is little data available on the operational *details* of the transition from concrete to formal operational thought. Second—and perhaps more relevant— little is known of the *extent* to which adolescents in Western Society make the transition from concrete to formal operational thought. An additional implicit aspect of the developmental model which lies fallow but potentially fertile is the fact that the end stage of the model—the description of formal operational thought—purports to describe the behaviour of adults in problem-solving situations.

For over sixty years psychologists have laboured to capture the essence of complex cognitive processes through the study of learning, problem solving and concept attainment. Critics could be forgiven for the jibe that never in the history of science have so many laboured so mightily with such little success. However, if subsequent study shows that the formal operational aspect of Piaget's model is as accurate in its description of adult cognitive processes as is the concrete operational aspect in its description of the cognitive processes of childhood, then Piaget's contribution to the understanding of adult thinking may go some way towards rectifying the balance.

The reasons for the relative neglect of the formal operational stage could be many. Among them may be the fact that there is no empirically dramatic diagionistic criteria which allow statements to be made on the presence or absence of formal thought, as is the case with concrete operational thought.

For example, the attainment of the conservations is a demonstrably dramatic change in the quality of the child's reasoning which requires no formal training in psychology to appreciate. For the naive adult the display of an example of non-conservation is readily appreciated and represents yet another example of the young child's weird way of reasoning. The same adult can just as readily comprehend the change in the thought processes which comes about when the child conserves, say, quantity or weight in the face of transformations of shape. Unfortunately, the transition from concrete to formal thought is not marked by any such empirical drama and the diagnosis of the transition is consequently made much more difficult.

A more probable reason for the relative lack of attention paid to the formal stage lies in Piaget's medium of communication—symbolic logic. Piaget's developmental model of intelligence is a logico-mathematical model, and in the student without benefit of a mathematical or a formal logical background the seemingly abstruse and esoteric symbols are efficient in provoking a marked avoidance response. The problem is that while the empirical demonstrations of the transition from intuitive to concrete thought can be savoured without reference to the strictly formal aspects of the model, so far this has not been the case with the transition from concrete to formal thought. The symbols of the algebraic logic represent both the barrier and the road to an appreciation of the formal model's evaluation of complex cognitive processes in adolescents and adults. However, in recent years many excellent expositions of the formal model have contributed to the attrition of the barriers (Baldwin, 1967; Boyle, 1969; Ginsburg and Opper, 1969; Hunt, 1961; Lunzer, 1965, 1968; Mays, 1953). This chapter attempts to follow and, hopefully, extend the example of these authors.

Following an attempt to clarify the propositional calculus, some of Piaget's empirical work is examined through the use of elementary truth tables. Before a brief discussion of work which has been done independently of the Genevan School, an examination is made of some of the serious theoretical problems associated with the model.

SYMBOLIC LOGIC AND THE PROPOSITIONAL CALCULUS

The last stage in the development of intelligence is essentially described in terms of the sixteen binary operations of propositional logic. Hunt (1961) describes the limitations of the concrete phase in dealing with these operations with the following example. He assumes that the propositions concern the class of animals which is divided into vertebrates (V) and invertebrates (I). The class of animals is also divided into those which live on land and are terrestrial (T) and those which live in water and are aquatic (A). If a child in the concrete operational stage is given the task of describing the population of animals on a newly discovered planet, he would be limited to the empirical task of searching for animals and assigning them to the four classes based on a two-way classification with the following entries in the 2×2 contingency table:

$$VT \qquad VA$$
$$IT \qquad IA$$

But if an adolescent or adult in the stage of formal operations were given the same task he would be capable, theoretically, of generating all the various combinations of classes of animals which were possible, and would be able to set out these possibilities without benefit of empirical support (see Table 11.1, for example).

In generating these classes, and combinations of classes, no consideration need be given to (a) the relations between any of the classes *within* any of the eleven combinations with two or more classes, or (b) the relations *between* any of the combinations themselves. However, each of these sixteen combinations of classes corresponds to one of the sixteen logical relations of binary propositional logic, and when dealing with propositions *qua* propositions the above relations referred to in (a) and (b) become important. In the case of (a) the relations are described in terms of the conventions of symbolic logic, and in the case of (b) the relations are described in terms of a mathematical group, known as the *INRC* group. To begin with, the (a) case will be considered.

Logicians normally use the letters p and q as an economical method of symbolizing propositions which are simply statements which have specific meanings. The relations between the propositions are described by another set of symbols, the main symbols being shown in Table 11.2.

The − symbol refers to the fact that each and every proposition can be negated. If, for example, we have the proposition that 'the moon is blue' (symbolized by p), the negation of the proposition is 'the moon is not blue' (symbolized by $\bar{p}$—not p).

In symbolic logic there is a form of simple addition and multiplication as there is in arithmetic. The symbols which denote these operations are (·) and

TABLE 11.1. Possible combinations of classes of animals

---

1. No animals at all
2. Only VA
3. Only VT
4. Only IA
5. Only IT
6. VA and VT but no IA or IT
7. VA and IA but no VT or IT
8. VT and IT but no VA or IA
9. IA and IT but no VA or VT
10. VA and IT but no VT or IA
11. VT and IA but no VA or IT
12. VA, VT, and IA but no IT
13. VA, VT, and IT but no IA
14. VA, IA, and IT but no VT
15. VT, IA, and IT but no VA
16. All four classes

TABLE 11.2.   Symbols used to show the relations between propositions

Symbol	Meaning
$-$	not (negation)
$\cdot$	and (conjunction)
v	or (disjunction—either or both)
$\supset$	if ... then (implication)

(v). Consider the case in which we have another proposition—'the moon is made of cheese' (q). The addition, or conjunction, of the two propositions becomes $p \cdot q$ and obviously means that 'the moon is blue and the moon is made of cheese'. The multiplication of the two propositions produces $p \vee q$ which means that 'either the moon is blue or is made of cheese, or both'. The economy of the algebraic logic can be seen by teasing out the meaning of the multiplication of the two propositions which produces the disjunctive relationship $p \vee q$. According to this relationship the following alternative statements are true.

(1) The moon is blue and is made of cheese.

or

(2) The moon is blue and is not made of cheese.

or

(3) The moon is not blue and is made of cheese.

This simply means that under this system we have various types of moon, excluding one which is not blue and not made of cheese. Yet how much more economical it is to use the algebraic form:

$$p \vee q = p \cdot q \vee p \cdot \bar{q} \vee \bar{p} \cdot q$$

The last of the chief symbols describes the implicatory relationship $p \supset q$, which means that if p is true then q is true, or in terms of the above propositions 'if the moon is blue then it is made of cheese'. Again we can tease the meaning out of this statement and find that the following alternative statements are true.

(1) The moon is blue and is made of cheese.

or

(2) The moon is not blue and is made of cheese.

or

(3) The moon is not blue and is not made of cheese.

Under the implication the type of moon which is not possible is one which is blue and is not made of cheese or, put more succinctly:

$$p \supset q = p \cdot q \vee \bar{p} \cdot q \vee \bar{p} \cdot \bar{q}$$

By now it is obvious that when we have two propositions p and q the four possible conjunctions which can arise are $p \cdot q$, $p \cdot \bar{q}$, $\bar{p} \cdot q$, and $\bar{p} \cdot \bar{q}$. It is equally obvious that these conjunctions may occupy the cells of a 2×2 contingency table

	p	$\bar{p}$
q	$p \cdot q$	$\bar{p} \cdot q$
$\bar{q}$	$p \cdot \bar{q}$	$\bar{p} \cdot \bar{q}$

FIGURE 11.1

(see Figure 11.1), as in the case of the classifications described by Hunt (1961). And, as in the case of the classification, sixteen combinations of these basic conjunctive relationship may be generated; these are referred to by Piaget as the sixteen binary operations of propositional logic. They are shown in Table 11.3.

In our examination of disjunction and implication we have already come across two of these binary operations. In the disjunction $p \vee q = p \cdot q \vee p \cdot \bar{q} \vee \bar{p} \cdot q$ we have an example of operation 12, and in the implication $p \supset q = p \cdot q \vee \bar{p} \cdot q \vee \bar{p} \cdot \bar{q}$ we have an example of operation 13. Needless to say, the majority of the operations in Table 11.1 may be similarly simplified. The simplification may be clarified by the use of the 2×2 tables as shown by Boyle (1969).

1. The first operation—the null operation—is represented by an empty table and means precisely that—the absence of anything:

	p	$\bar{p}$
q		
$\bar{q}$		

2. Under the second operation, we have an entry in the first cell of the table

TABLE 11.3. Sixteen binary operations of propositional logic

1.	0
2.	$p \cdot q$
3.	$p \cdot \bar{q}$
4.	$\bar{p} \cdot q$
5.	$\bar{p} \cdot \bar{q}$
6.	$p \cdot q \vee p \cdot \bar{q}$
7.	$p \cdot q \vee \bar{p} \cdot q$
8.	$p \cdot q \vee \bar{p} \cdot \bar{q}$
9.	$p \cdot \bar{q} \vee \bar{p} \cdot q$
10.	$p \cdot \bar{q} \vee \bar{p} \cdot \bar{q}$
11.	$\bar{p} \cdot q \vee \bar{p} \cdot \bar{q}$
12.	$p \cdot q \vee p \cdot \bar{q} \vee \bar{p} \cdot q$
13.	$p \cdot q \vee \bar{p} \cdot q \vee \bar{p} \cdot \bar{q}$
14.	$p \cdot q \vee p \cdot \bar{q} \vee \bar{p} \cdot \bar{q}$
15.	$\bar{p} \cdot q \vee p \cdot \bar{q} \vee \bar{p} \cdot \bar{q}$
16.	$p \cdot q \vee p \cdot \bar{q} \vee \bar{p} \cdot q \vee \bar{p} \cdot \bar{q}$

$(+)$ which indicates that the conjunction $p \cdot q$ is true, while each of the remaining cells have an entry $(-)$ which indicates that all of the conjunctions $p \cdot \bar{q}$, $\bar{p} \cdot q$, and $\bar{p} \cdot \bar{q}$ are false:

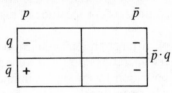

The meaning of operations 3 to 5 is similar.

3.

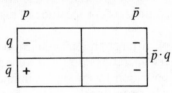

4.

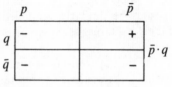

5.

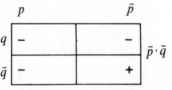

6. The sixth operation states $p \cdot q \vee p \cdot \bar{q}$, which in terms of the 2×2 table is represented as follows:

$$p \cdot q \vee p \cdot \bar{q} = p$$

In terms of the propositions this means that either
  (a) The moon is blue and is made of cheese
                    or
  (b) The moon is blue and is not made of cheese
The table shows that both of these statements are true $(+)$ which simply means that the truth of the proposition 'the moon is blue' (p) is independent of the truth of the proposition 'the moon is made of cheese' (q). As a result, $p \cdot q \vee p \cdot \bar{q} = p$. That is, the moon is blue irrespective of the material which is unspecified.
Operations 7 to 11 are similar in that two of the cell entries are $(+)$ and two

are $(-)$. However, only in the case of 7 does the simplification lead to the independence of a proposition.

7.

	p	$\bar{p}$
q	+	+
$\bar{q}$	−	−

$$p \cdot q \vee \bar{p} \cdot q = q$$

8. Under operation 8, $p \cdot q \vee \bar{p} \cdot \bar{q}$, the patterns of $(+)$'s and $(-)$'s in the 2×2 table are as follows:

	p	$\bar{p}$
q	+	−
$\bar{q}$	−	+

$$p \cdot q \vee \bar{p} \cdot \bar{q} = (p = q)$$

In other words:
(a) The moon is blue and is made of cheese
or
(b) The moon is not blue and is not made of cheese.

This means there can be no moon which is blue and not made of cheese or not blue and made of cheese. This leads to what is known as an equivalence relationship between p and q ($p = q$), which we shall encounter later when considering Piaget's empirical work.

9. The ninth operation, $p \cdot \bar{q} \vee \bar{p} \cdot q$, is the opposite of the eighth:

	p	$\bar{p}$
q	−	+
$\bar{q}$	+	−

$$p \cdot \bar{q} \vee \bar{p} \cdot q = p \vee\vee q$$

This establishes the truth of the propositions:
(a) The moon is blue and is not made of cheese
or
(b) The moon is not blue and is made of cheese.

Consequently, under this operation we can never have a blue moon made of cheese or a not-blue moon not made of cheese. The symbol used in the $p \vee\vee q$ simplification of this operation means that p and q are incompatible and never the two shall meet. Piaget defines the operation as one of reciprocal exclusion.

Operations 10 and 11 are similar in that they lead to the independence of the negation of a proposition. The reasoning behind the simplification is similar to that of operations 6 and 7.

10.

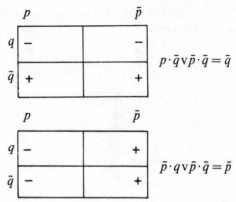

	p	$\bar{p}$
q	−	−
$\bar{q}$	+	+

$$p\cdot\bar{q}\vee\bar{p}\cdot\bar{q}=\bar{q}$$

11.

	p	$\bar{p}$
q	−	+
$\bar{q}$	−	+

$$\bar{p}\cdot q\vee\bar{p}\cdot\bar{q}=\bar{p}$$

As we have seen, operation 13 is an example of an implicatory relationship. It can be shown that operations 12, 13, 14, and 15 can all be reduced to implications.

12.

	p	$\bar{p}$
q	+	+
$\bar{q}$	+	−

$$p\cdot q\vee p\cdot\bar{q}\vee\bar{p}\cdot q=\bar{p}\supset q=p\vee q$$

13.

	p	$\bar{p}$
q	+	+
$\bar{q}$	−	+

$$p\cdot q\vee\bar{p}\cdot q\vee\bar{p}\cdot\bar{q}=p\supset q=\bar{p}\vee q$$

14.

	p	$\bar{p}$
q	+	−
$\bar{q}$	+	+

$$p\cdot q\vee p\cdot\bar{q}\vee\bar{p}\cdot\bar{q}=\bar{p}\supset\bar{q}=p\vee\bar{q}$$

15.

	p	$\bar{p}$
q	−	+
$\bar{q}$	+	+

$$\bar{p}\cdot q\vee p\cdot\bar{q}\vee\bar{p}\cdot\bar{q}=p\supset\bar{q}=\bar{p}\vee\bar{q}$$

16. The last operation is one in which all cells of the 2×2 table are true, indicating that p and q are truly independent, and either can and does occur in both the absence and presence of the other. This is known as a tautology and is symbolized $p*q$:

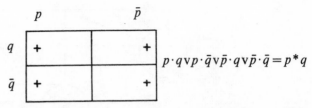

$$p \cdot q \vee p \cdot \bar{q} \vee \bar{p} \cdot q \vee \bar{p} \cdot \bar{q} = p * q$$

The simplification of the sixteen binary operations reduces them to what is known in the symbolic logic as propositional relations. These are summarized in Table 11.4.

By now the reader who is familiar with Wertheimer's (1964) criticism on the inability of formal symbolic logic to account for the unpredictable flights of creative thought may be justified in wondering precisely what the sixteen binary operations have to do with problem solving, intelligence, or any of the complex cognitive processes. So before we consider the theoretical aspects of the relations *between* the sixteen binary operations we will make a foray against the problem of relating the operations to the performance of subjects in problem-solving situations.

PIAGET'S EMPIRICAL WORK

The Growth of Logical Thinking (Inhelder and Piaget, 1958) is seen by Bruner (1959) and Lunzer (1968) as a landmark in the study of the processes of higher reasoning and as a culmination of Piaget's efforts. The experiments in the text fall into two groups. The first include the problems of the pendulum and the flexibility of a rod and are concerned with the development of the propositional logic. It is this development which is of immediate interest.

In the experiments with the pendulum the subjects are presented with a stimulus situation consisting of four independent variables and one dependent

TABLE 11.4.   The sixteen binary operations expressed as propositional relations

1. Null
2. $p \cdot q$
3. $p \cdot \bar{q}$
4. $\bar{p} \cdot q$
5. $\bar{p} \cdot \bar{q}$
6. p
7. q
8. $p \equiv q$
9. $p \text{ vv } q$
10. $\bar{q}$
11. $\bar{p}$
12. $\bar{p} \supset q \equiv p \vee q$
13. $p \supset q \equiv \bar{p} \vee q$
14. $\bar{p} \supset \bar{q} \equiv p \vee \bar{q}$
15. $p \supset \bar{q} \equiv \bar{p} \vee \bar{q}$
16. $p * q$

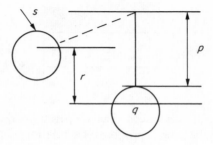

FIGURE 11.2

variable. The independent variables are the length of the string, the weight of the attached object, the height from which the pendulum is released, and the force used to impel the pendulum. The dependent variable is the frequency of oscillation of the pendulum. Essentially the task of the subject is to find which of the four independent variables affects the dependent variable. According to Piaget the method used by the subjects is the operational strategy of holding the value of all independent variables constant except one; by varying the value of this one independent variable its relationship with the dependent variable can be established. By systematically working through each of the independent variables the corresponding relationship with the dependent variable for length, weight, height, and force is found.

It will make matters easier if we denote each of the independent variables by a letter as follows:

$$p \equiv \text{a given length of string}$$
$$\bar{p} \equiv \text{any modification in the length of string}$$
$$q \equiv \text{a given weight}$$
$$\bar{q} \equiv \text{any modification of that weight}$$
$$r \equiv \text{a given height}$$
$$\bar{r} \equiv \text{any modification of that height}$$
$$s \equiv \text{a given force}$$
$$\bar{s} \equiv \text{any modification of that force}$$

And, of course, we have the dependent variable:

$$x = \text{a given observed frequency}$$
$$\bar{x} = \text{any modification of that frequency}$$

The situation faced by the subject is shown in Figure 11.2. According to Piaget the formal operational subject attacks the problem quite systematically by holding three of these variables constant while studying the affect of the fourth on the frequency of the pendulum (x). The steps in such an ideal strategy can be shown diagrammatically as follows.

First of all we may assume that the subject will establish the frequency of the pendulum, x, dangling on the length of string p, with a weight of q and impelled by a force s from the height r. So we have step A.

Combinations of independent variables	Affect on dependent variable

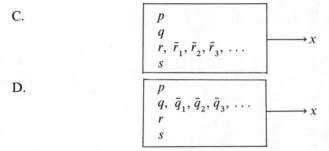

A.

$$\begin{array}{c} p \\ q \\ r \\ s \end{array} \longrightarrow x$$

As a second step the subject may decide to vary the force while keeping the length of string constant together with the height and weight. The outcome will be as follows:

B.

$$\begin{array}{c} p \\ q \\ r \\ s, \bar{s}_1, \bar{s}_2, \bar{s}_3, \ldots \end{array} \longrightarrow x$$

The different forces used in conjunction with p, q, and r are symbolized by $\bar{s}_1, \bar{s}_2, \bar{s}_3, \ldots$, and the subject finds that no matter how he varies the force the value of the frequency remains constant. The next two steps may be as follows:

C.

$$\begin{array}{c} p \\ q \\ r, \bar{r}_1, \bar{r}_2, \bar{r}_3, \ldots \\ s \end{array} \longrightarrow x$$

D.

$$\begin{array}{c} p \\ q, \bar{q}_1, \bar{q}_2, \bar{q}_3, \ldots \\ r \\ s \end{array} \longrightarrow x$$

Steps C and D have shown that when the height (r) and weight (q) are varied, independently, then the variations have no effect on the frequency of the pendulum, which still oscillates at the rate which was originally measured (x).

But this strategy leads to results in the fifth step; when the subject starts varying the length of string he observes measurable changes in the frequency of the pendulum:

E.

$$\begin{array}{c} p, \bar{p}_1, \bar{p}_2, \bar{p}_3, \ldots \\ q \\ r \\ s \end{array} \longrightarrow x, x_1, x_2, x_3, \ldots$$

Given this state of affairs the subject notes that $\bar{p}_1 \rightarrow \bar{x}_1$, $\bar{p}_2 \rightarrow \bar{x}_2$, $\bar{p}_3 \rightarrow \bar{x}_3$, and he may very well try other lengths of string $\bar{p}_4 \rightarrow \bar{x}_4$, $\bar{p}_5 \rightarrow \bar{x}_5$, ..., and so on, because now he is in a position to formulate a hypothesis: the frequency of the pendulum is related to the length of the string. The next step will depend

360

on the operational level of the subject. For the subject at the concrete operational stage the demonstration of the change in frequency associated with changes in the length of string, as seen in step E, will be sufficient evidence for the support of the hypothesis. Not so for the formal operational subject, who theoretically will go on to test the other possiblities thus:

F.

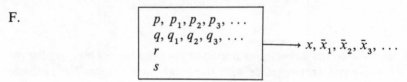

$$p, p_1, p_2, p_3, \cdots$$
$$q, q_1, q_2, q_3, \cdots$$
$$r$$
$$s$$
$$\longrightarrow x, \bar{x}_1, \bar{x}_2, \bar{x}_3, \cdots$$

Step F represents the concomitant variation of both length of string and weight of pendulum. The remaining combinations of independent variables to be tested are:

G.

$$p, \bar{p}_1, \bar{p}_2, \bar{p}_3, \cdots$$
$$q$$
$$r, \bar{r}_1, \bar{r}_2, \bar{r}_3, \cdots$$
$$s$$
$$\longrightarrow x, \bar{x}_1, \bar{x}_2, \bar{x}_3, \cdots$$

H.

$$p, \bar{p}_1, \bar{p}_2, \bar{p}_3, \cdots$$
$$q$$
$$r$$
$$s, \bar{s}_1, \bar{s}_2, \bar{s}_3, \cdots$$
$$\longrightarrow x, \bar{x}_1, \bar{x}_2, \bar{x}_3, \cdots$$

I.

$$p$$
$$q, \bar{q}_1, \bar{q}_2, \bar{q}_3, \cdots$$
$$r, \bar{r}_1, \bar{r}_2, \bar{r}_3, \cdots$$
$$s$$
$$\longrightarrow x$$

J.

$$p$$
$$q, \bar{q}_1, \bar{q}_2, \bar{q}_3, \cdots$$
$$r$$
$$s, \bar{s}_1, \bar{s}_2, \bar{s}_3, \cdots$$
$$\longrightarrow x$$

K.

$$p$$
$$q$$
$$r, \bar{r}_1, \bar{r}_2, \bar{r}_3, \cdots$$
$$s, \bar{s}_1, \bar{s}_2, \bar{s}_3, \cdots$$
$$\longrightarrow x$$

L.

$$p, \bar{p}_1, \bar{p}_2, \bar{p}_3, \cdots$$
$$q, \bar{q}_1, \bar{q}_2, \bar{q}_3, \cdots$$
$$r, \bar{r}_1, \bar{r}_2, \bar{r}_3, \cdots$$
$$s$$
$$\longrightarrow x, \bar{x}_1, \bar{x}_2, \bar{x}_3, \cdots$$

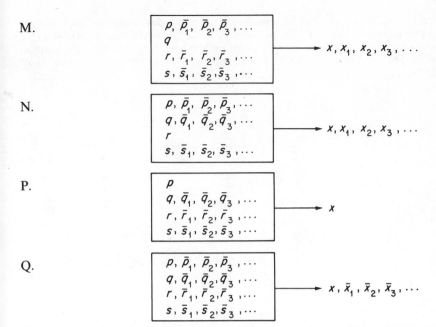

M. $p, \bar{p}_1, \bar{p}_2, \bar{p}_3, \ldots$
q
$r, \bar{r}_1, \bar{r}_2, \bar{r}_3, \ldots$
$s, \bar{s}_1, \bar{s}_2, \bar{s}_3, \ldots$
$\longrightarrow x, x_1, x_2, x_3, \ldots$

N. $p, \bar{p}_1, \bar{p}_2, \bar{p}_3, \ldots$
$q, \bar{q}_1, \bar{q}_2, \bar{q}_3, \ldots$
r
$s, \bar{s}_1, \bar{s}_2, \bar{s}_3, \ldots$
$\longrightarrow x, x_1, x_2, x_3, \ldots$

P. p
$q, \bar{q}_1, \bar{q}_2, \bar{q}_3, \ldots$
$r, \bar{r}_1, \bar{r}_2, \bar{r}_3, \ldots$
$s, \bar{s}_1, \bar{s}_2, \bar{s}_3, \ldots$
$\longrightarrow x$

Q. $p, \bar{p}_1, \bar{p}_2, \bar{p}_3, \ldots$
$q, \bar{q}_1, \bar{q}_2, \bar{q}_3, \ldots$
$r, \bar{r}_1, \bar{r}_2, \bar{r}_3, \ldots$
$s, \bar{s}_1, \bar{s}_2, \bar{s}_3, \ldots$
$\longrightarrow x, \bar{x}_1, \bar{x}_2, \bar{x}_3, \ldots$

It is only after having tested all these combinations that the formal operational subject will confidently assert that the only relevant independent variable is the length of the string; it is the string and only the string which governs the frequency of the pendulum; force, height, and weight are irrelevant and there are no interactions between any of the variables.

In this description of the ideal strategy used by our hypothetical subject no mention has been made of the sixteen binary relations of propositional logic. Some may claim that none need be made, and in his description of complex cognitive processes in terms of the sixteen binary relations Piaget does not assert that his subjects have any knowledge of these relations. Propositional thought does not depend upon this knowledge of the formal relations as outlined in Table 11.4, and the formal operational subject can systematically work through the steps A to Q outlined as the ideal strategy in happy ignorance of the relations (Ihnelder and Piaget, 1958, p. 310).

However, the symbolic logic is used as a method and a model for explaining the cognitive processes which are capable of producing such an ideal strategy in the problem-solving situation. One of the confusing aspects of the use of symbolic logic in the exposition of formal thought in *The Growth of Logical Thinking* is that it is used both to explain the cognitive processes of the subjects and to examine the stimulus structure of the problems presented to the subjects. The confusion arises because the distinction between stimulus structure and cognitive process *vis à vis* the symbolic logic is never made explicit. Paradoxically, when made explicit it leads to a simplification or an aid to the understanding of the model and the place of the symbolic logic in the problem-solving strategies of formal operational subjects.

TABLE 11.5. Truth table for all combinations of independent variables (p,q,r,s) in the Piagetian pendulum problem. The appropriate value of the dependent variable (x) is shown, as is the logical relationship between each independent variable and dependent variable. The step in the ideal strategy corresponding to each combination is also shown

Row	p	q	r	s	x	Step
1	1	1	1	1	1	A
2	1	1	1	0	1	B
3	1	1	0	1	1	C
4	1	1	0	0	1	K
5	1	0	1	1	1	D
6	1	0	1	0	1	J
7	1	0	0	1	1	I
8	1	0	0	0	1	P
9	0	1	1	1	0	E
10	0	1	1	0	0	H
11	0	1	0	1	0	G
12	0	1	0	0	0	M
13	0	0	1	1	0	F
14	0	0	1	0	0	N
15	0	0	0	1	0	L
16	0	0	0	0	0	Q

Logical relations between dependent and independent variables

$$p \cdot x \; v \; p \cdot \bar{x} \; v \; \bar{p} \cdot x \; v \; \bar{p} \cdot \bar{x} \equiv p = x$$
$$8 \quad\quad - \quad\quad - \quad\quad 8$$

$$p \cdot x \; v \; p \cdot \bar{x} \; v \; \bar{q} \cdot x \; v \; \bar{q} \cdot \bar{x} \equiv p*x$$
$$4 \quad\quad 4 \quad\quad 4 \quad\quad 4$$

$$r \cdot x \; v \; r \cdot \bar{x} \; v \; \bar{r} \cdot x \; v \; \bar{r} \cdot \bar{x} \equiv r*x$$
$$4 \quad\quad 4 \quad\quad 4 \quad\quad 4$$

$$s \cdot x \; v \; s \cdot \bar{x} \; v \; \bar{s} \cdot x \; v \; \bar{s} \cdot \bar{x} \equiv s*x$$
$$4 \quad\quad 4 \quad\quad 4 \quad\quad 4$$

To begin with we will examine the stimulus structure of the pendulum problem in terms of the relationships which exist between independent variables and dependent variables. An indispensable tool in the clarification of the stimulus structure lies in the truth tables of symbolic logic.

STIMULUS STRUCTURE AS REFLECTED BY TRUTH TABLES

As before we have the four independent variables p, q, r, and s, together with the dependent variable x, and, of course, their negations. In this case we will simplify matters further by assuming that there is only one value for each of p, $\bar{p}$ (length), q, $\bar{q}$ (weight), r, $\bar{r}$ (height), and s, $\bar{s}$ (force). This means that x and $\bar{x}$ represent two different frequencies. The truth table of Table 11.5 shows all possible combinations of the independent variables and their negations. The result of these combination of stimuli on the dependent variable x is also shown. In the body of the table the symbol 1 represents the truth of a proposition, the symbol 0 its negation. In this case the 'propositions' represent the variables p, q, r, s, and x. For example, the combination of row 7 reads p, $\bar{q}$, $\bar{r}$, s (each of which had a specific value), which results in the frequency of oscillation x.

If we return for a moment to the diagrammatic representation of the subjects' ideal strategy, we can see that row 7 in fact represents step I. When the subject decides to vary weight (q) and height (r) concomitantly he is in fact constructing row 7 of the truth table. Obviously each of the sixteen combinations shown in the truth table is a representation of each of the steps taken by the subject who performs the ideal strategy. In Table 11.5 the step number is shown beside each row. The appropriate value of the dependent variable (x) is shown, as is the logical relationship between each independent variable and dependent variable. The step in the ideal strategy corresponding to each combination is also shown.

From Table 11.5 it is possible to calculate the frequency of occurrence of the conjunction of each value of each independent variable with each value of the dependent variable. These frequencies are shown on the right of the table. A rather striking symmetry emerges in the frequencies of occurrence of all possible conjunctions. For example, in the case of the irrelevant variable q the component conjunctions of the tautology $q*x$ are $q \cdot x$, $q \cdot \bar{x}$, $\bar{q} \cdot x$, and $\bar{q} \cdot \bar{x}$ (see combination 16 of Table 11.4). It can be seen from Table 11.5 that, when the subject employs the ideal strategy systematically, each of these conjunctions occur with equal frequency; q is associated with x four times and with $\bar{x}$ four times, and similarly for the other two conjunction $\bar{q} \cdot x$ and $\bar{q} \cdot \bar{x}$. Table 11.5 also shows that a similar tautologous relationship exists between the other two irrelevant variables (r and s) and x. In the case of the relevant variable, the length of string p, the relationship with x is seen to differ. There is an equality of the frequency of occurrence of the conjunctions $p \cdot x$ and $\bar{p} \cdot \bar{x}$ while the conjunctions $\bar{p} \cdot x$ and $p \cdot \bar{x}$ do not occur. The fact that the latter do not exist shows that the relationship between p and x is one of equivalence, $p \equiv x$ (combination 8 of Table 11.4).

Table 11.5 shows precisely the problem which is faced by the subject in the pendulum problem. He must detect the tautologies which exist between the irrelevant variables and x, that is $q*x$, $r*x$, and $s*x$; in the case of the relevant variable he must learn that the relationship which exists between p and x is one of logical equivalence, $p \equiv x$. According to Piaget this is done by verifying the falsehood of the reciprocal exclusion $p \mathbin{\text{v}\kern-0.3em\text{v}} x$; this is something which we shall return to when we discuss some of the theoretical problems associated with the model.

The stimulus structure of any of Piaget's problems involving the propositional logic may be analysed in terms of the truth table. As with the pendulum problem, such an analysis points precisely to the relations between independent and dependent variables which must be learned. In the flexible rods problem, for example, Piaget studies the method by which the subject separates the variables involved. In that problem the subject is presented with a number of different rods which vary with respect to material, length, cross-section, and thickness of cross-section. He is also given some weights and is shown that when some of these weights are placed on the ends of cantilevered rods, the rods bend and touch the surface of a bowl of water placed strategically beneath the free ends of the cantilevered rods. Not all of the rods bend and the subject is asked to find the factors involved. Again we have a situation in which the subject is presented with four independent variables. To simplify analysis we will assume that these variables have two values as follows:

$p \equiv$ a given length of rod > 300 mm
$\bar{p} \equiv$ a given length of rod < 300 mm
$q \equiv$ a given weight > 50 g

$$\bar{q} \equiv \text{a given weight} < 50 \text{ g}$$
$$r \equiv \text{a given material, steel}$$
$$\bar{r} \equiv \text{a given material, brass}$$
$$s \equiv \text{a given diameter of rod} > 10 \text{ mm}$$
$$\bar{s} \equiv \text{a given diameter of rod} < 10 \text{ mm}$$

When all possible combination of these variables are constructed they lead to one of two outcomes, x or $\bar{x}$—flexibility or non-flexibility of the rod, the dependent variable. That is, when the combination of independent variables is such that the rod bends and touches the water, then this flexibility is represented by x. Naturally $\bar{x}$ means that the rod remains inflexible and does not touch the water under a given combination of independent variables.

Again, to clarify analysis, we will assume that in this particular problem two independent variables are relevant to producing the flexibility of the rods— that is p and q, the length of the rod and the size of the weight; a long rod in conjunction with a large weight will always bend (irrespective of the material or cross-section).

As before, we can imagine the subject at the formal operational stage who attacks the problem by means of an ideal strategy. This attack will result in the production of all possible combinations of independent variables which reveals the relationship between each independent variable and dependent variable. The truth table of Table 11.6 shows all combinations of independent variables and the effect of these on the flexibility of the rod (x). The logical relationship between each independent and the dependent variable is also shown.

TABLE 11.6. Truth table for all combinations of independent variables (p,q,r,s) in the Piagetian rods problem, together with the appropriate binary value of the dependent variable (x). The logical relationship between each independent and the dependent variable is also shown

Row	p	q	r	s	x
1	1	1	1	1	1
2	1	1	1	0	1
3	1	1	0	1	1
4	1	1	1	0	1
5	1	0	1	1	0
6	1	0	0	0	0
7	1	0	1	1	0
8	1	0	1	0	0
9	0	1	0	1	0
10	0	1	1	0	0
11	0	1	1	1	0
12	0	1	0	0	0
13	0	0	1	1	0
14	0	0	1	0	0
15	0	0	0	1	0
16	0	0	0	0	0

Logical relations between dependent and independent variables

$$p \cdot x \text{ v } p \cdot \bar{x} \text{ v } \bar{p} \cdot x \text{ v } \bar{p} \cdot \bar{x} = \bar{p} \supset \bar{x}$$
$$\quad 4 \quad\quad 4 \quad\quad - \quad\quad 8$$
$$q \cdot x \text{ v } q \cdot \bar{x} \text{ v } \bar{q} \cdot x \text{ v } \bar{q} \cdot \bar{x} \equiv \bar{q} \supset \bar{x}$$
$$\quad 4 \quad\quad 4 \quad\quad - \quad\quad 8$$
$$r \cdot x \text{ v } r \cdot \bar{x} \text{ v } \bar{r} \cdot x \text{ v } \bar{r} \cdot \bar{x} \equiv r * x$$
$$\quad 2 \quad\quad 2 \quad\quad 6 \quad\quad 6$$
$$s \cdot x \text{ v } s \cdot \bar{x} \text{ v } \bar{s} \cdot x \text{ v } \bar{s} \cdot \bar{x} \quad s * x$$
$$\quad 2 \quad\quad 2 \quad\quad 6 \quad\quad 6$$

Again it is possible to consider the conjunction of each value of each independent variable with each value of the dependent variable. A striking symmetry again emerges in the frequencies of the conjunctions. However, it is a symmetry which differs in potentially important respects from the logical representation of the stimulus structure of the pendulum problem.

Considering the irrelevant variables first, we find that the stimulus structure contains the binary relations $r*x$ and $s*x$. But comparison of Tables 11.5 and 11.6 shows that the uniformity of frequency of the component conjunctions of the tautologous relations of Table 11.5 does not exist in Table 11.6. It can be seen that the existence of the second relevant variable in Table 11.6 produces different frequencies of the conjunctions making up $r*x$ and $s*x$. It could well be that this could contribute to greater difficulty in detecting the tautologous relationships indicating the irrelevant variables in the rods problem. However, there is little evidence on the comparative difficulty of Piaget's problems.

Perhaps more interesting are the logical relations which emerge from considering the binary relations of the relevant variables, p and q, with the dependent variable, x. By comparing the conjunctions which occur—$p \cdot x$, $p \cdot \bar{x}$, $\bar{p} \cdot \bar{x}$ and $q \cdot x$, $q \cdot \bar{x}$, $\bar{q} \cdot \bar{x}$—with Tables 11.3 and 11.4 it can be seen that the negation of p and q each is in the relation of implication with the negation of x, that is $\bar{p} \supset \bar{x}$ and $\bar{q} \supset \bar{x}$. From the analysis of Table 11.6 it is apparent that the task of the subject is to distinguish the tautologies involving the irrelevant variables and the implications involving the negations of the relevant variables.

The probability that the rods problem may be more difficult than the pendulum can be appreciated by examining the outcome of the initial stages of the ideal strategy used by the formal operational subjects. The first step is to find if any of the independent variables, in isolation, affect the flexibility of the rod and consequently the variables will be altered one at a time thus:

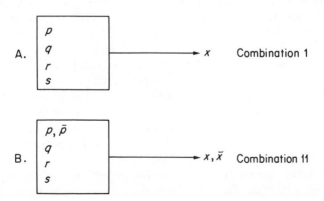

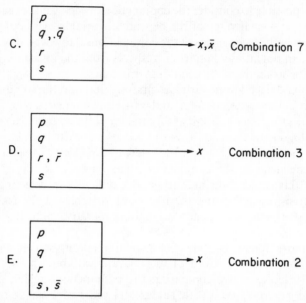

C. $x, \bar{x}$ Combination 7

D. x Combination 3

E. x Combination 2

Having altered each of the variables singly, while holding the others constant, the subject is able to establish that none of the variables, *in isolation*, affects the flexibility of the rod. When *both p* and *q* are altered independently a change of frequency results. Unlike the pendulum problem in which, at this stage in the strategy there is evidence to support a single, relatively simple hypothesis, the rods problem presents a pattern which is somewhat more complicated. At the very least this is likely to be conducive to the production of some degree of cognitive strain of the type described by Bruner, Goodnow, and Austin (1956).

The analysis of the stimulus structure of the pendulum and rods problems has a number of advantages. Tables 11.5 and 11.6 show precisely the nature of the logical relationships involved between dependent and independent variables. Comparison of the tables in both problems shows that the relationship between irrelevant variables and dependent variables is one of tautology. Examination of Tables 11.3 and 11.4 reveals that this tautologous relationship corresponds directly with the sixteenth of the operations of binary propositional logic. In the case of the relevant variables Tables 11.5 and 11.6 show that different relations are involved. But again they correspond directly to operations shown in Tables 11.3 and 11.4. In the case of the pendulum problem the equivalence relation between the length of string and frequency of oscillation corresponds to the *eight* operation of Tables 11.3 and 11.4. In the case of the rods problem each of the relevant variables, the length of rod and size of weight, is in an implicatory relationship with the flexibility of the rod, which corresponds to the *fourteenth* operation of Tables 11.3 and 11.4.

The truth table examination of the stimulus structure of these problems followed directly from the analysis of the relations *within* the sixteen combinations which can be generated from the conjunctions $p \cdot q$, $p \cdot \bar{q}$, $\bar{p} \cdot q$, and $\bar{p} \cdot \bar{q}$. The truth tables have shown that the terms of symbolic logic which describe these relations are not introduced merely to add to the difficulty of the student. It has been shown that these relations actually exist within the stimulus structure of the problems analysed and before the subject can solve the problems successfully he has to differentiate between the various logical relations—*notwithstanding* the fact that he is very unlikely at all to have any knowledge about the logical meaning of such terms as tautology, equivalence, or implication between negated propositions. But the analysis of the logical relations which describe the sixteen combinations of conjunctions of Table 11.3 is but half the story. The reader will recall that the relations *between* the combinations are also said to constitute an important part of Piaget's theory of formal operational thought. The relations between the combinations are described, in part, in terms of a group of operators, which are the transformations which can take place on each of the binary relations of Tables 11.3 and 11.4. The group of operators is known as the *INRC* group, which will now be examined.

FURTHER CHARACTERISTICS OF FORMAL THOUGHT

Earlier it was stated that formal operational thought can be described *essentially* in terms of the propositional logic. The use of the qualifier *essentially* was deliberate as the attainment of formal thought is also characterized by other structural changes in the thought processes. Piaget (1953b, p. 22) stated:

> This fourth period (acquisition of formal operations) therefore includes two important acquisitions. Firstly the logic of propositions, which is both a formal structure holding independently of content and a general structure coordinating the various logical operations into a single system. Secondly, a series of operational schemata which have no apparent connection with each other nor with the logic of propositions.

The acquisition of formal operations is also characterized by the structural creation of the *INRC* group which, Piaget claims, results from the union of the two great systems of reversibility developed during the concrete operational stage. With the development of concrete operational thought the child develops the ability to perform reversible operations on both classes (inversions) and relations (reciprocities). But it is not until the formal operational stage is reached that there is a synthesis between the two forms of reversibility and the cognitive structures acquire a new mobility, the direct result of the acquisition of the *INRC* operators. Piaget claims that the *INRC* group is related to both the propositional logic and the operational schemata. However, before the nature of the *INRC* group is examined in relation to the propositional logic we must first of all look briefly at an example of the schemata which are said to develop in formal operational thought.

It has been stated that the experiments in the *Growth of Logical Thinking* fall into two parts. We have already dealt with the rods and pendulum problems as representative of the first part of the text. In the second part Piaget studies the development of what he calls 'operational schemata'. These are individual schemes which allow the subject to deal with the problems involved in such areas as probabilities, ratios and proportions, correlations, and in particular with systems involving reciprocal actions. The activities of the *INRC* group can be most clearly seen in problems involving such reciprocal actions. An excellent example is the case in which the subject is presented with an apparatus consisting of a U-shaped tube containing liquid. On one arm of the U is a piston which exerts pressure on the liquid and on which weights can be placed. Variation in the weights exerts differing forces on the liquid, which results in different levels of the liquid in the other arm of the U-tube. Yet the weights are not the only source of varying the level of the liquid. By holding the weight of the piston constant and varying the density of the liquids in the U-tube the same effect can be achieved. In short, counteracting the force of the piston and weight on the liquid is a reciprocal force, the density of the liquid itself. The types of cognitive operation allowed by the *INRC* group are as follows.

Let us consider that the U-tube apparatus is in front of us and the level of the liquid is at level x_0. It is a simple operation to vary x_0 by adding a weight to the piston; we will define this operation as the identity operation (I) which results in level x_1. The previous level x_0 may be restored by the opposite or inverse (N) operation of removing the added weight. But to get the level back to x_0 other means are available, namely the reciprocal (R) operation which is equivalent to N and which involves altering the density of the liquid. If this is done, and level x_0 is again reached, we can get back to x_1 by the inverse or opposite of the reciprocal, which is known as the correlate (C). These four operations or transformations, *INRC*, make up a mathematical group within which the following relations hold true:

$$I^2 = N^2 = R^2 = C^2 = I$$

$$IN = RC = I$$

The *INRC* group is also held to be of great importance to the sixteen binary relations of propositional logic and it is through the medium of the *INRC* group that Piaget explains the relations between the combinations of Tables 11.3 and 11.4. Each of the combinations has an inverse, a reciprocal, and a correlate. The general rules for operating on the binary relations of propositional logic in terms of the *INRC* group are as follows:

(1) Inverse (N): in this case both propositions are negated and the conjunction changed to disjunction, or vice versa. For example, if the relation is $p \cdot q$ then $N(p \cdot q) \equiv \bar{p} \vee \bar{q}$.

(2) Reciprocal (R): in this case both propositions are simply negated. For example $R(p \cdot q) \equiv \bar{p} \cdot \bar{q}$.

(3) Correlate (C): this is obtained by substituting (v) for ($\cdot$) and vice versa. For example $C(p \cdot q) \equiv p \vee q$.

(4) Identity (I): this is the identity operator and the maintenance of the status quo, $I(p \cdot q) \equiv p \cdot q$.

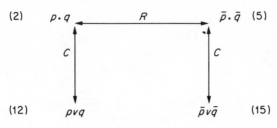

FIGURE 11.3

According to Piaget each and every one of the sixteen binary operations of Table 11.3 and 11.4 may be expressed in terms of its inverse, reciprocal, or correlate. As an example we can start with the second binary operation of Tables 11.3 and 11.4, $p \cdot q$.

The reciprocal (R) of $p \cdot q$ is defined above as $\bar{p} \cdot \bar{q}$ (operation 5), and vice versa, and this can be expressed as follows:

$$(2)\, p \cdot q \xleftarrow{\hspace{3cm} R \hspace{3cm}} \bar{p} \cdot \bar{q}\, (5)$$

The correlate (C) of both these operations is as follows: $C(p \cdot q) \equiv p \vee q$; $C(\bar{p} \cdot \bar{q}) = \bar{p} \vee \bar{q}$. It can be seen that when this transformation is applied to the second and fifth binary operations we end up with the twelfth and fifteenth, which can be expressed diagrammatically as shown in Figure 11.3.

The reciprocal of $p \vee q$ is $\bar{p} \vee \bar{q}$ and, in terms of the above rules, the following inverse relationships exist between the operations dealt with so far: $N(p \cdot q) \equiv \bar{p} \vee \bar{q}$; $N(\bar{p} \cdot \bar{q}) \equiv p \vee q$. As a result the diagram can be completed, as shown in Figure 11.4.

It can be seen that starting with the second operation ($p \cdot q$) we can move freely between the second, fifth, twelfth, and fifteenth through the transformations involved in the $INRC$ group. (Needless to say, in Figure 11.4 $p \cdot q$ is defined as the identity I.) The particular route we take in travelling between (2), (5), (12), and (15) may be varied and an examination of alternative variations brings to light an essential aspect of the $INRC$ group. We may, for example, go from (2) through (15) to (5). In terms of the transformations involved we first of all take the inverse of (2), symbolized as $N(p \cdot q)$, followed by the correlate of the result which can be symbolized as $C[N(p \cdot q)]$. This gets us to the fifth operation which, of course, is the reciprocal of (2), or $R(p \cdot q)$. Consequently

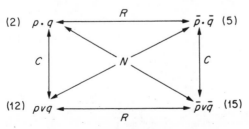

FIGURE 11.4

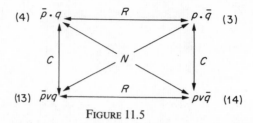

(4) $\bar{p} \cdot q$ R $p \cdot \bar{q}$ (3)

C N C

(13) $\bar{p} v q$ R $p v \bar{q}$ (14)

FIGURE 11.5

$CN = R$. The point to note is that any combination of the transformations of the *INRC* group has other equivalent transformations which happen to be important in terms of the mathematical nature of the group. We can start, for example, with the identity (I) $(p \cdot q)$ and end up in the same spot by first of all finding its correlate, then the reciprocal of the correlate, followed by the inverse of the reciprocal. In short, $CRN = I$. Similarly, $NRC = I$, $RCN = I$ and $RNC = I$.

So far we have seen the transformations possible between four of the sixteen binary operations. The operations (2) $p \cdot q$, (5) $\bar{p} \cdot \bar{q}$, (12) $p v q$, and (15) $\bar{p} v \bar{q}$ are interconnected through the *INRC* group. It can be shown that the sixteen binary operations of Tables 11.3 and 11.4 can be divided into six separate divisions in terms of the transformations made possible by the *INRC* group. We may, for example, start with operation (4) $\bar{p} \cdot q$ and construct the diagram shown in Figure 11.5.

As can be seen, Figure 11.5 accounts for the operations (3) $p \cdot \bar{q}$, (4) $\bar{p} \cdot q$, (13) $\bar{p} v q$, and (14) $p v \bar{q}$. As before, the transformations of the *INRC* group allow us to move between these four binary operations which leaves eight operations to be accounted for, and a slight problem. The general rules quoted above describe the transformations possible between the operations which are defined in terms of the conjunction or disjunction of two propositions. The

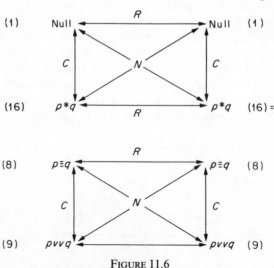

FIGURE 11.6

attempt to apply these rules to the remaining eight propositions runs into difficulty simply because they are not defined in terms of the conjunction or disjunction of two propositions. The remaining binary operations to be accounted for are (Table 11.3 and 11.4):

(1) Null	(7) q	(9) $p\,\mathrm{vv}\,q$	(11) $\bar{p}$
(6) p	(8) $p \equiv q$	(10) $\bar{q}$	(16) $p*q$

Piaget (1953b) defines the transformations involving four of these binary operations as shown in Figure 11.6. In both diagrams of Figure 11.6 it can be seen that the reciprocal of the identity are one and the same, for example $R(\text{Null}) = \text{Null}$ and $R(p \equiv q) = p \equiv q$; it can also be seen that both the correlate and inverse transformations are identical, for example $R(\text{Null}) = C(\text{Null}) = p*q$ and $R(p \equiv q) = C(p \equiv q) = p\,\mathrm{vv}\,q$. Consequently, the relations between operations (1) Null and (16) $p*q$ and between operations (8) $p \equiv q$ and (9) $p\,\mathrm{vv}\,q$ are marked by the fact that $I = R$ and $C = N$. This would seem to involve a marked reduction in mobility between the binary operations involved.

A similar lack of mobility is evident in the defined relations (Piaget, 1953b) between the remaining binary operations, which are shown in Figure 11.7. In the case of operations (6) p, (7) q, (11) $\bar{p}$, and (10) $\bar{q}$ it can be seen that the correlate and the identity are one and the same, for example $C(p) = p$, $C(q) = q$, while the reciprocal and inverse transformations are identical, for example $R(p) = N(p) = \bar{p}$ and $R(q) = N(q) = \bar{q}$. Consequently, the relations between (6) p and (11) $\bar{p}$ and the relations between (7) q and (10) $\bar{q}$ are marked by the fact that $I = C$ and $R = N$.

The six separate divisions within the sixteen binary operations of propositional logic arise from the fact that the operations within each of the divisions are related in terms of the transformations of the *INRC* group. Within each of the divisions one may transform any individual binary operation in terms

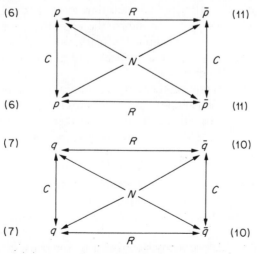

FIGURE 11.7

TABLE 11.7. The sixteen binary operations of propositional logic classified in terms of the relationships between the operations as defined by the *INRC* group

Division	Binary operations			
1	(2) $p \cdot q$	(5) $\bar{p} \cdot \bar{q}$	(12) $p \vee q$	(15) $\bar{p} \vee \bar{q}$
2	(3) $p \cdot \bar{q}$	(4) $\bar{p} \cdot q$	(13) $\bar{p} \vee q$	(14) $p \vee \bar{q}$
3	(1) Null	(16) $p * q$	$[I = R, \ C = N]$	
4	(8) $p \equiv q$	(9) $p \vee\vee q$	$[I = R, \ C = N]$	
5	(6) p	(11) $\bar{p}$	$[I = C, \ R = N]$	
6	(7) q	(10) $\bar{q}$	$[I = C, \ R = N]$	

of the rules of the group and the result will be another of the binary operations within the group. The six divisions are summarized in Table 11.7.

THE PROPOSED THEORY AND THE ACTUAL STRATEGY

The analysis of the relationship between the theory and the strategy can be made in terms of two of the problems already discussed, the rods and pendulum problems. In the case of the pendulum problem it will be recalled that Piaget claims that the formal operational subject finds the relevant variable through the operations of equivalence and reciprocal exclusion. From Table 11.5 we have seen that the relevant variable, the length of string (p), is in an equivalence relationship with the observed frequency $(x) - p \cdot x \vee \bar{p} \cdot \bar{x}$ $(p \equiv x)$. According to Piaget the problem is solved when the subject establishes the falsehood of the reciprocal exclusion, $\bar{p} \cdot x \vee p \cdot \bar{x}$ $(p \vee\vee x)$. The fact that there is no *empirical* opportunity to establish the truth value of $p \vee\vee x$ is a matter which will be dealt with later. What is of importance at the moment is the relationship between the equivalence $p \equiv x$ and reciprocal exclusion $p \vee\vee x$. From Table 11.7 it can be seen that $N(p = x) = p \vee\vee x$. In short, the cognitive operation which the subject must perform in establishing the truth value of $p \vee\vee x$ is the inverse (or, since in this case $N = C$, the correlate), and in doing so he is said to be making use of the *INRC* group.

It may be objected, of course, that concrete operational subjects can successfully utilize the inverse in isolation, and this is true. The objection would lend weight to Piaget's consistent emphasis of the fact that formal operational thought cannot be diagnosed reliably on the presence of one operation alone; the subject's total strategy, preferably on a number of problems, must be analysed carefully. So the operation of $N(p \equiv q) = p \vee\vee q$ is part of a total pattern which allows the subject to generate the steps of the strategy analysed earlier in the chapter. Yet the precise part played in the pattern by the *INRC* group must be analysed more closely. We can have another look at the rods problem.

In the simplified rods problem as analysed by the truth table of Table 11.6 it can be seen that the relations between both of the relevant independent

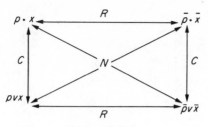

FIGURE 11.8

variables and the dependent variable is in terms of implication. (It has further been shown that any implication may be expressed in terms of its equivalent disjunction.) The appropriate relationships are $\bar{p} \supset \bar{x} \equiv p \vee \bar{x}$ and $\bar{q} \supset \bar{x} \equiv q \vee \bar{x}$, where p symbolizes the length of rod, q symbolizes the weight, and x symbolizes the flexibility of the rod.

Consider the subject who sets out on the rods problem by hypothesizing $p \cdot x$, that is that a rod of given length will always be associated with flexibility. The subject will be able to test out a number of possibilities as a result of the *INRC* group (e.g. Figure 11.8).

In terms of the 2×2 contingency table used earlier the group will allow him to test empirically the truth value of these relationships (see Figure 11.9). (The symbol ∘ indicates that the binary relation of the 2×2 table is transformed in terms of the *INRC* group, the particular transformation denoted by the appropriate letter.)

By creating the appropriate experimental conditions the subject will then be able to establish the truth or falsity of $p \cdot x$, $\bar{p} \cdot \bar{x}$, $p \vee x$, and $\bar{p} \vee \bar{x}$. Under the conditions of the experiment described by the truth table of Table 11.6 he will find none of these relations to be true and it will be necessary to construct additional hypotheses before a solution is possible. He may hypothesize $p \supset x (\bar{p} \vee x)$ which allows him access to other possibilities (see Figure 11.10).

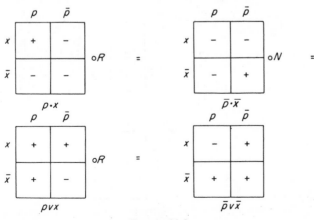

FIGURE 11.9

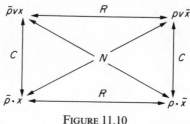

FIGURE 11.10

Again in terms of the 2×2 contingency tables the following possibilities may be tested empirically (see Figure 11.11).

In this case it can be seen that as a result of the group transformations on the hypothesis $\bar{p} \cdot x$ the subject can find, empirically, that while the relations $\bar{p} \cdot x$, $\bar{p}vx$, and $p \cdot \bar{x}$ are false the disjunctive relationship $pv\bar{x}$ is true—an important step on the way to a solution of the rods problem. However, this analysis has highlighted at least two important theoretical problems which must be dealt with. To begin with there is the problem of whether the subjects actually use the *INRC* group and the propositional logic as described in the above analysis—most unlikely, but that is an empirical problem which will be conveniently ignored until later. The most immediate problem which the analysis raises is concerned with the relations *between* the sixteen binary operations of propositional logic.

It has been claimed that the relations *between* these operations can be described in terms of the *INRC* group and that the transformations of this group provide mobility of thought between the sixteen operations. But it is a strictly limited mobility; from Table 11.7 we have seen that the sixteen binary operations can be classified into six separate divisions in terms of the transformations which can be applied through the medium of the *INRC* group. The problem we face at the moment is how the subject travels, in thought, between

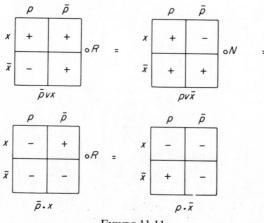

FIGURE 11.11

one division and another. It cannot be done with the help of the *INRC* group as was made obvious in the above analysis of the rods problem.

There we assumed that the first hypothesis drawn up by the subject was $p \cdot x$. The group structure then allowed him to establish the truth value of $p \cdot x$, $R(p \cdot x) = \bar{p} \cdot \bar{x}$, $C(\bar{p} \cdot \bar{x}) = \bar{p} \vee \bar{x}$, $R(\bar{p} \vee \bar{x}) = p \vee x$. Under the rods problem none of these operations occur. We then assumed that the subject created the hypothesis $\bar{p} \vee x$ which, through the *INRC* group, allowed him to establish that $p \vee \bar{x}$ was true. The great leap, which is so far unexplained, is concerned with how the subject goes from the first hypothesis $p \cdot x$ to the second $\bar{p} \vee x$. In other words, there is the theoretical problem of how the subject travels between the six divisions of Table 11.7. According to Piaget the complete mobility between the sixteen binary operations is provided by another characteristic of formal operational thought which is described in terms of the mathematical concept of the lattice.

MATHEMATICAL LATTICES AND FORMAL OPERATIONAL THOUGHT

A brief search through any library of mathematical textbooks will uncover many tomes dedicated to the elucidation, analysis, and development of the concept of the lattice. Like complex cognitive processes lattices are far from simple—hence the numerous tomes. However, it is possible to glimpse the theoretical importance of the lattice to the propositional logic without delving into the technical aspects of the mathematics which provides the foundation for the concept of the lattice.

According to Piaget the development of intelligence involves the ever-increasing construction, differentiation, and elaboration of existing cognitive structures. The foundations of these structures begin to be laid down as soon as the individual starts interacting with his environment—at birth. In the same way as every act of intelligence presupposes a structure which has been built up over a long period of time, so the emergence of the cognitive operations made possible by the lattice presupposes the development in concrete thought of operations made possible by semilattices.

Semilattices and lattices both refer to the elements of a structure and the relation between the elements of the structure. The structure in this case may be a classification system or it may be the sixteen binary operations of Tables 11.3 and 11.4. In the first case the elements which make up the structure are the various classes in the classification system. In the second case the elements which make up the structure are each of the sixteen binary operations themselves.

One of the necessary foundations for the development of propositional logic is the increasing competence during the concrete operational phase to deal with the relations between classes. The semilattice is said to be important in this respect. For example, at some time in the life of the child he is aware of the existence of flowers, without necessarily being aware of the relationship

376

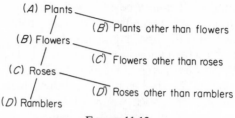

FIGURE 11.12

between flowers and plants. Eventually this does develop, as will the classification of some of the more common flowers. The type of classification system which could be constructed is shown in Figure 11.12.

The two classes D and D' can be said to join at C; C and C' at B, and so on. C is defined as the least upper bound (l.u.b.) of D and D' because it is the smallest class in the system which contains both D and D'. (Classes A and B also contain D and D', but they are larger than C.) A semilattice is defined as a system in which any two of the elements have an l.u.b.

For the semilattice to develop into a lattice another condition must be fulfilled. Broadly speaking this is the condition in which any two elements of the system may be combined because they have something in common. We can ask, for example, what type of plant is both flower and rose—obviously the rose. And the class of roses (C) is the largest class the members of which are both roses and flowers; C is defined as the greatest lower bound (g.l.b.) of B and C. A lattice is defined as a system in which any two of the elements have both an l.u.b. and a g.l.b. We can see that the above classification system does not conform to this definition if we consider the classes D and B'. The l.u.b. of these two classes is A, but they do not have a g.l.b. Class B', for example, could consist of aquatic plants. In this case there is no g.l.b. for B' and D because there is no plant in existence recognized as an aquatic rambling rose. It is claimed, in fact, that the only systems which have the properties of the lattice exist in the field of abstract symbolism (Boyle, 1969). An example is the system made up from the sixteen binary operations of Tables 11.3 and 11.4. The lattice structure is shown diagrammatically by Baldwin (1967) and Boyle (1969) through the 2×2 contingency tables as in Figure 11.13.

For any two of the binary operations of Figure 11.13 there is an l.u.b. These can be found through the lines connecting the 2×2 contingency tables. For example, the l.u.b. of operations 6 and 7 is operation 12, as this is the smallest of the binary operators which contains both operations 6 and 7. On the other hand, the g.l.b. of operations 6 and 7 is operation 1, since this operation is the 'largest' which contains $p \cdot q$, which operations 6 and 7 have in common. In the same way, the l.u.b. and g.l.b. of any two of the operations may be found. The l.u.b. of operations 12 and 13 is operation 16 and the g.l.b. is operation 7. Theoretically, the lattice structure of the sixteen binary operations provides the complete mobility between the operations, a mobility which Piaget sees as being of paramount importance in formal operational thought. Yet it is a

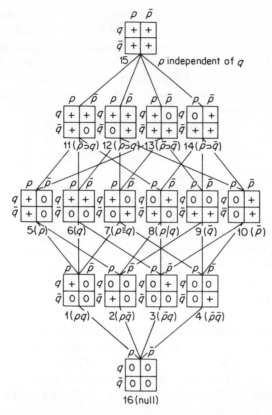

FIGURE 11.13 Completed relations between 16
binary operations of propositional logic. (Reproduced from Baldwin, 1967, by Permission of
John Wiley and Sons, Inc.)

mobility which may seem rather artificial when related to possible thought
patterns employed by subjects.

SOME THEORETICAL PROBLEMS OF THE FORMAL
OPERATIONAL MODEL

The difficulties involved in accepting the alliance of the lattice structure and
the *INRC* group as accounting for the systematic unity of the sixteen binary
operations may be highlighted by returning, once again, to our analysis of
the rod problem.

We may recall that our subject decided to test the hypothesis $p \cdot x$, and
through the transformations of the *INRC* group was able to construct the
binary operations shown in Figure 11.9. It will also be recalled that when the
subject, empirically, had established that each of these operations were false
he went on to hypothesize that $p \supset x \, (\bar{p} \vee x)$ was a possible relationship between
the independent variable p and dependent variable x. The problem was to

explain his additional hypothesis which is part of the sixteen binary operations of propositional logic, but which could not have been arrived at through the transformations of the *INRC* group. Theoretically the construction of the hypothesis may be explained as follows. The operations $p \cdot x$ and $\bar{p} \cdot \bar{x}$, shown in the above 2×2 tables, are equivalent to operations 2 and 5 of Figure 11.13. Having established that his original hypothesis, $p \cdot x$, was not tenable, he then hypotheses $p \supset x$ (operation 13, Figure 11.13). It can be seen from Figure 11.13 that, as a result of the lattice structure of the sixteen binary operations, there is a direct link between operation 13 and operations 2 and 5, through operation 8. Operation 8 is the l.u.b. of operations 2 and 5, while operation 13 is the l.u.b. of operations 7 and 8.

While such a link may be established through the unity of the model it would be rash to claim that there is a direct isomorphism between the theory and the cognitive operation of the subject. Even as far as the sixteen binary operations themselves are concerned, Inhelder and Piaget (1958, p. 310) state quite plainly that the non-specialist adult subjects who can calculate all sixteen combinations are few and far between. Lunzer (1965) analysed the relationship of the *INRC* group to the propositional logic and quite justifiably expressed sceptism as to the possibility of the subject carrying out the transformations described by the group. These theoretical problems are reflected in the independent empirical work which has attempted to establish the validity of the model. On the one hand, we have a series of studies which suggest that adolescent subjects do not think in the formal operational terms described by Piaget. On the other hand, we have a series of studies which point to the heuristic value of the model both in the development of thought and in the description of adolescent and adult thought.

INDEPENDENT EMPIRICAL WORK

The empirical work based on the formal operational model has taken a number of forms. A proportion of studies has focused on replicating some of the Genevan problems. Representative of this line of enquiry are the experiments reported by Lovell (1961), Berzonsky (1971), and Dulit (1972). Although such work concentrates on different aspects of the model the finding common to the quoted and unquoted work is that formal operational thought as described by Piaget is a rare commodity which is difficult to identify outside of Geneva. The unanimity of the results of the replications is such that Piaget (1972b) has seen fit to clarify his position. He admits that the findings reported in *The Growth of Logical Thinking* are based on the performances of a biased sample of bright Swiss adolescents. However, he still maintains his essential position on the reality of formal operations and speculates on the possibility of an interaction between such operations and the developing aptitudes and attitudes of the adolescent. His latest position seems to be that the basic formal operational structures are a natural biological development, the manifestation of which depends upon the interests and social environment of the individual.

Given the possibility of the existence of basic structures, the problem exists of developing the experimental conditions which will allow the subject to operate to his potential capacity on the material provided. Only under such conditions (perhaps naively ideal) can meaningful diagnoses be made on the operational level of any population. The very real difficulties which are involved in such an endeavour may be seen in an interesting series of studies which has been concerned with the problem of whether adult subjects have a formal understanding of the truth—functional properties of the types of logical relationship described in Tables 11.3 and 11.4.

The implication $p \supset x$ may be stated verbally as 'if p, then x'. The logician regards this as a material implication; sentences of the form 'if it is fine, then I'm going to the cinema' have the logical structure of material implication. In logic $p \supset x$ has four components. We have seen that three of these are true, $p \cdot x$, $\bar{p} \cdot x$, $\bar{p} \cdot \bar{x}$. The remaining component $p \cdot \bar{x}$ is false; consequently, logically valid inferences can only be made from p and $\bar{x}$. Peel (1967c) enumerates these as follows:

$$p \; x \qquad\qquad\qquad p \; x$$
$$p \qquad\qquad\qquad\qquad \bar{x}$$

.$\dot{}$. What? (x) .$\dot{}$. What? ($\bar{p}$)

modus ponendo ponens *modus tollendo tollens*

Modus tollens is also known as the contrapositive (Wason, 1968).

Fallacious inferences are possible from $\bar{p}$ and x simply because $p \cdot x$, $\bar{p} \cdot x$, and $\bar{p} \cdot \bar{x}$ are all true. For example, if from $\bar{p}$ one infers $\bar{x}$, the inference is fallacious because $\bar{p}$ is also associated with x. Wason (1968) regards the latter as 'denial of the antecedent'. He gives an example of the other fallacious inference to be 'affirmation of the consequent', which occurs when p is inferred from the presence of x.

In a series of studies with adult subjects Wason and Johnson-Laird (1972) have been concerned with the valid and fallacious inferences made by subjects when presented with sentences constructed on the basis of material implication. These studies produce interesting evidence on the subjects' understanding of the relations within the conjunctions which make up the material implication. Wason (1966) reports a study in which the subjects were presented with four cards and the following sentence: 'If there is a vowel on one side of the card, then there is an even number on the other side.' On front of the first card was a vowel (p), on front of the second a consonant ($\bar{p}$), on front of the third an even number (x), and on front of the fourth an odd number ($\bar{x}$). The task of the subject was to select *only* those cards which would have to be selected in order to discover whether the experimenter was lying.

Each subject had the choice of four cards as follows:

1. $\boxed{p}$ 2. $\boxed{\bar{p}}$ 3. $\boxed{x}$ 4. $\boxed{\bar{x}}$

Consider the subject who assumes that the experimenter is telling the truth. He must restrict his choice to only those cards which will establish the truth of the statement. If he selects the second card ($\bar{p}$), he will be in error, because in terms of the implication $p \supset x$ both $\bar{p} \cdot x$ and $\bar{p} \cdot \bar{x}$ are true. So to assume that the experimenter is telling the truth and then to select $\bar{p}$ leads to a situation in which no information can be gained on the status of the assumption. The same situation holds for the choice of the third card (x) because both $p \cdot x$ and $\bar{p} \cdot x$ are true in terms of the implication. The only logically valid choices are the first (p) and fourth cards ($\bar{x}$). If $\bar{x}$ appears on the back of the first card (p) then the experimenter lies. Similarly, if p appears on the back of the fourth card ($\bar{x}$), he lies.

The results are interesting in the context of the previous discussion on the importance of the transformations made possible on the sixteen binary operations by the *INRC* group. It was found that very few subjects selected the $\bar{x}$ or $\bar{p}$ cards. Almost all subjects selected p and above 60 per cent. selected x. Consequently there were two types of error: the consequent was fallaciously affirmed and the contrapositive ignored. On the basis of his results Wason assumed that his subjects were not constrained by the rules of the propositional calculus—a serious blow, perhaps, to the validity of the formal operational model. Apparently Wason's subjects looked upon the conditional sentence, constructed on the basis of the implication, as having three outcomes or truth values: $p \cdot x$ was generally regarded as true, $p \cdot \bar{x}$ as false, while $\bar{p} \cdot x$ and $\bar{p} \cdot \bar{x}$ were dismissed as irrelevant (a finding of relevance to a more direct test of one of the formal operational schemata to be discussed later). The reason why x is erroneously selected lies in the subjects interpretation that only $p \cdot x$ is true; they selected x to see if it is in fact associated with p. If this was found to be the case then they regarded the conditional sentence to be true.

Wason's (1968, p. 274) explanation of the infrequent selection of $\bar{x}$ is of relevance. He states:

> ... that individuals are biased through a long learning process to expect a relation of truth, correspondence or match to hold between sentences and states of affairs. In adult experience truth is encountered more frequently than falsity, and we seldom use a proposition or judgment that something is false in order to make a deduction. The semantic concept of falsity is logically equivalent to the syntactic concept of negation ...

In other words, having convinced themselves that $p \cdot x$ was true, subjects rarely used the transformation $R(p \cdot x) \equiv \bar{p} \cdot \bar{x}$ to test the truth value of $\bar{p} \cdot \bar{x}$; apparently they regarded the association of an odd number with a consonant as being irrelevant.

Wason's (1968) study was concerned specifically with correcting the bias for establishing the association of $p \cdot x$. It was designed to encourage subjects to make the transformation $R(p \cdot x)$ involved in the contrapositive. It was not successful; the 'therapies' designed by Wason to facilitate the act of making the $R(p \cdot x)$ transformation to test the contrapositive inference did not do so.

The work of Wason (1966, 1968) was extended by Johnson-Laird and Tagart (1969). These authors examined the extent to which the interpretation of implication was influenced by the manner in which it was expressed. The statements

(1) If p, then x.
(2) There isn't a p, if there isn't x.
(3) Either there isn't p, or there is x (or both).
(4) There is never p without there being x.

are logically equivalent. Sentences were constructed which conformed to the logical form of the statements.

The results of the experiment confirmed the basic finding of Wason in that sentences of the form 'if p, then x' were not classified in a truth functional way. The only sentences which were classified in accordance with the truth value of implication were those cast in the disjunctive form 'either there isn't p or there is x (or both)', and then only by a third of the subjects.

Both Wason (1966) and Johnson-Laird and Tagart (1969) relate their results to Piagetian theory. They point out that according to the theory their subjects should have reached the stage of formal operations and should have been capable of dealing with the logical relations presented to them. The formal operational subject should take account of the possible and hypothetical and be capable of formulating propositions about them. Wason (1968) points out that this is precisely what his subjects failed to do.

Wason and Johnson-Laird (1972) comment on the problem presented by the consistent failure of their subjects in the four-card task; the authors also describe the problem presented by the inability of the subjects to respond to the therapies and programmes designed to improve performance on the task. The search for the source of the difficulty centred on the verbal guise of the implication 'if p, then x', on the assumption that difficulty lay there, rather than in the concept of implication *per se*. The search was unproductive; however, later investigation has shown that an important variable in the performance of the task lies in the form of the material which is presented to the subject. In the early studies this was said to be 'abstract'. It has been found that when subjects are given the conditional rule in a 'thematic' form there is a significant rise in performance when compared with the 'abstract' material. Wason and Shapiro (1971) presented their subjects with the statement 'every time I go to Manchester I go by car', and invited them to test the truth of the statement in a procedure directly analogous to the four-card task. The improvement in performance was significant and the results have been confirmed by others (Johnson-Laird, Legrenzi, and Legrenzi, 1972; Lunzer, Harrison, and Davey, 1972). These studies have led Wason and Johnson-Laird to make the statement that in the four-card problem 'content is crucial'.

However, in citing the content of the material as being the crucial variable in the performance of the subjects, Wason and Johnson-Laird (1972) gainsay somewhat the contribution of Legrenzi (1971) which is quoted in their text. Legrenzi has shown that abstract material may be dealt with quite efficiently in the context of the four-card task. The evidence for Legrenzi's study would indicate that a variable which is also crucial to performance is the prior experience of the subject in dealing with the relationships involved between antecedent and consequent before introduction to the four-card task. In Legrenzi's two experiments the subjects were shown the classification of all possible conjunctions between antecedent and consequent which were classified according to a statement of the form 'if p, then x'. In effect the subjects learned the classification system of the following truth table:

Conjunction	Classification
$p \cdot x$	$+$
$p \cdot \bar{x}$	$-$
$\bar{p} \cdot x$	$+$
$\bar{p} \cdot \bar{x}$	$+$

In the first experiment the subjects were then invited to express verbally the nature of the relationship between p and x. Because so few subjects expressed the relationship in the form 'if p, then x', the second experiment compelled the subjects to express the relationship in that form. In both experiments, following the verbal expression of the relationship, the subjects were asked to test the truth of the statement 'if p, then x' in the four-card task. The groups who discovered the rule by themselves, i.e. learned the classification system and then expressed it verbally, made significantly more correct choices than the appropriate control groups.

The ability of Legrenzi's subjects to deal efficiently with abstract material is related to the fact that the subject's were forced to express verbally the relationship between antecedent and consequent. This was said to constitute the 'discovery' of the conditional. However, a recently completed study by Brown and Seggie (in preparation) provides evidence that adolescent subjects can make correct selections in the four-card task involving abstract material, without being forced to express the relationship verbally.

The work of Brown and Seggie unites two independent streams of work involving the propositional logic. In a series of studies Seggie (1970a, 1970b, 1971a, 1973) has shown that adult subjects can learn the relationships involved between antecedent and consequent described by the conditional statement. Much more important is the fact of the evidence that adult subjects can make use of the relationships so learned in a concept-learning task. The initial evidence shows that young adolescents (twelve or thirteen years) have difficulty in using the relationships in concept learning. This work is described in detail in the following chapter.

In the Brown and Seggie study subjects learned to classify, individually, four binary-valued stimuli prior to a concept-learning task. Experimental subjects were told that the classification of the individual stimuli would help them in the concept-learning task; in the case of the control group, the classification of individual stimuli and the concept-learning problem were presented as two different tasks.

The classification of the individual stimuli (p,q,r,s) is described as follows:

Conjunction	Classification		Conjunction	Classification
$p \cdot x$	$+$		$q \cdot x$	$+$
$p \cdot \bar{x}$	$-$		$q \cdot \bar{x}$	$-$
$\bar{p} \cdot x$	$+$		$\bar{q} \cdot x$	$+$
$\bar{p} \cdot \bar{x}$	$+$		$\bar{q} \cdot \bar{x}$	$+$

Conjunction	Classification		Conjunction	Classification
$r \cdot x$	$+$		$s \cdot x$	$+$
$r \cdot \bar{x}$	$+$		$s \cdot \bar{x}$	$+$
$\bar{r} \cdot x$	$+$		$\bar{s} \cdot x$	$+$
$\bar{r} \cdot \bar{x}$	$+$		$\bar{s} \cdot \bar{x}$	$+$

It can be seen that the relationship between p, q, and x is one of implication, while the relationship between r, s, and x is one of tautology.

Following the learning of these relationships the subjects completed the concept-learning task before moving on to the second phase of the experiment. The subjects were informed that the main objective of this phase was, again, a concept-learning task in which the same rule was involved. However, the relevant attributes may or may not have changed. Prior to the concept-learning task the subjects were presented with the Wason four-card problem as follows: four sentences were presented to the subject together with four groups of four cards:

Sentence form	Cards
If p, then x.	$p \; \bar{p} \; x \; \bar{x}$
If q, then x.	$q \; \bar{q} \; x \; \bar{x}$
If r, then x.	$r \; \bar{r} \; x \; \bar{x}$
If s, then x.	$s \; \bar{s} \; x \; \bar{x}$

The subjects were informed that two of the sentences were true and two false. They were asked to find out which sentences were true and which false by selecting the appropriate cards only. The control and experimental groups differed only in that the experimental group was told that the task was relevant to the subsequent concept-leaning problem, in that the stimuli described in the true sentences were relevant to the concept-learning task while the stimuli described in the false sentences were irrelevant. In the case of the control group the subjects were merely asked to find out which sentences were true and which false; no mention was made of any relationship between the four-card tasks and the concept-learning problem.

When the subjects had selected the cards for all four sentences, they were invited to state which sentences were true and which false. If they could not do so they were asked to revise their selections. Each testing of a sentence was regarded as a trial, and a measure of performance was the number of trials completed before appropriate selections were made in the case of all four sentences. Large differences in favour of the experimental groups were recorded, indicating a rapidly evolving competence in dealing with the four-card problem. A number of features of the Brown and Seggie study should be noted. First, the material used was 'abstract' as defined by Wason. Second, at no time during the initial classification task involving the individual stimuli were the subjects asked to state verbally the relationships which they had learned. Third, during the four-card problem the subjects were unaware of the actual logical relationships between antecedents and consequents, which was not the case in the Legrenzi experiment.

The above results highlight the difficulties involved in the diagnosis of formal thought. The evidence of Legrenzi and Brown and Seggie indicates that content may not be as crucial as was originally thought. Previous experience with the classification system of the logical relationship may be of importance. As yet, the evidence is not available to enable precise statements to be made on the nature of the important variables.

The difficulties involved in the development of an appropriate methodology can be seen in the attempt to replicate the findings of Inhelder and Piaget on the development of one of their formal operational schemata—the concept of correlation.

A FORMAL OPERATIONAL SCHEMATA—THE CONCEPT OF CORRELATION

Inhelder and Piaget claim that the concept of correlation is an integral part of formal operational thought. They present evidence to support their contention that the development of the concept results in the ability to form the ratio of the diagonal frequencies of a 2×2 contingency table. The evidence was derived from the attempts of subjects, between the ages of ten and fifteen years, to judge the relationship between eye and hair colour. The subjects were shown cards, each with a face drawn on it. The faces had blond or dark hair and blue or brown eyes. The four possible pairs of eye and hair colour may be arranged in a 2×2 table as follows:

A relationship existed between eye and hair colour in that the frequency of the a and d cases, the confirming cases, was greater than the frequency of the b and c cases, the non-confirming cases. The subjects were claimed to be using

Hair colour
blond   dark

	blond	dark
blue	a	b
brown	c	d

eye colour

a concept of correlation if their judgments were based on the difference between $a+d$ and $b+c$. If the frequency of the $a+d$ cells exceeds the frequency of the $b+c$ cells a positive correlation exists; if the frequency of the $b+c$ cells exceeds the frequency of the $a+d$ cells a negative correlation exists; and if $a+d=b+c$ there is no correlation.

Jenkins and Ward (1965) have shown that this formulation is restricted to certain cases in which two states of at least one of the variables appear equally often. For example, it is possible for the confirming cases to outnumber the non-confirming cases when no correlation exists. If, in the above table, we let $a=40$, $b=10$, $c=20$, and $d=5$, then there are more confirming cases ($a+d=45$) than non-confirming ($b+c=35$). However, the probability of dark hair given either blue or brown eyes is identical and no correlation exists. This is an important point but one which is peripheral to the central issue of our present concern which is methodological.

One of the most prolific workers in the field of Piagetian studies is Professor Jan Smedslund, who for well over a decade has provided valuable insights into the development of concrete operations. Smedslund (1963) constructed an experiment to test hypotheses derived from the formal operational model, in particular from the development of the concept of correlation. He asked nurses to estimate the strength of a relationship between a symptom (A) and a disease (F). Five groups of subjects were given a pack of cards—one pack to each subject—and each of the cards described the state of a patient. An $A.F$ card indicated that the patient had both the symptom and the disease; an $A.\bar{F}$ card, the symptom but no disease; an $\bar{A}.F$ card, no symptom but had the disease; and an $\bar{A}.\bar{F}$ card showed that the patient had neither the symptom nor the disease. The frequency of the four different cards in the packs varied for each of the five groups. The data in the cards of two groups showed a relationship between A and F: for one group the relationship was positive, for the other the relationship was negative. The remaining three groups were given data which showed that there was no relationship between A and F.

According to Smedslund, his adult subjects were unable to detect any relationship or lack of relationship between A and F on the basis of the information in the cards. Even when the data were presented in table form, and when a perfect relationship existed between A and F, the subjects could not reliably estimate the strength of the relationship. Significantly it was reported that his subjects regarded the $\bar{A}.\bar{F}$ cases as being irrelevant in estimating the relationship, a finding which is of relevance to the later work by Wason who found that his subjects regarded $\bar{p} \cdot \bar{x}$ as irrelevant to the truth of the implication $p \cdot x$. Needless to say, Smedslund was forced to the conclusion that his adult subjects did not have a cognitive structure isomorphic with the concept of correlation.

Further work was carried out by Jenkins and Ward (1965) and Ward and Jenkins (1965). The results were similar to those of Smedslund, which led Peterson and Beach (1967) to suggest that there are special difficulties for the adult subject when dealing with the data of the 2×2 table. Unfortunately the nature of the difficulties were neither specified nor explored—unfortunate, as the suggestion has serious operational implications. These can best be drawn out by referring to the more widely known limitation of pre-concrete operational thought in children.

As an example we can take the case of the child who cannot conserve number. The operational consequences of this are that the child cannot discriminate between the spatial arrangement of a set of objects and the actual number of objects in the set. This can be demonstrated quite easily by placing two sets of objects before the child, with equal numbers of objects in each set. Before the stage of concrete operations the child's judgment of equality or inequality of numbers in each of the two sets depends upon the spatial arrangement of the sets. If one of the sets is spaced out in a long, straight line, while the other set occupies a small circular space, then the preoperational child will state that the latter has fewer objects than the set which is spaced out in the straight line. Without the ability to conserve number the child cannot make a logical decision based on number alone; his decisions are based on such irrelevant dimensions as space. The same can be shown in the conservation of quantity, weight, volume, and so on. The non-conservation subject in each area does not have the cognitive structure necessary to operate logically in empirical situations.

This being the case, surely it may be assumed that the absence of a formal operational structure would preclude logical thought in an empirical situation designed to utilize such a structure. If, as is maintained by Smedslund, Jenkins and Ward, and Peterson and Beach, adult subjects do not have a cognitive structure isomorphic with the concept of correlation, then it is difficult to imagine that they would be capable of the empirical utilization of correlated variables. Like the pre-concrete subject, the pre-formal subject's performance in the absence of the formal structure is likely to be distorted by irrelevant factors. This was the rationale which provoked the study by Seggie and Endersby (1972), who designed an empirical task logically isomorphic to those employed by Jenkins and Ward (1965), Smedslund (1963), and Ward and Jenkins (1965). It was assumed that only subjects with a concept of correlation would be successful in its solution.

Basically the subjects in the Seggie and Endersby study were asked to make an important decision between two alternatives which could lead to one of two outcomes. To help them make the decision they were given the frequency with which both outcomes had followed each alternative in the past. These frequencies, for five of the groups of the study, were taken directly from the frequencies used by Smedslund (1963). In effect these data allowed the subjects to establish whether or not a correlation existed between the two binary variables. As in Smedslund's experiment the performance of the subjects (also nurses) was examined under two conditions. In the first the subjects were required to extract the relevant information from the cards; in the second the information was supplied in the tables.

The information given to the subjects was on the recovery rates of 100 patients who had suffered a rare disease. The subjects were told whether each patient had recovered or died and whether treatment had been carried out in hospital or at home. Consequently, each of the patients could be placed in one cell of the 2 × 2 table.

		Treatment	
		Hospital	Home
Recovery	Yes		
	No		

The nurses were asked to imagine that they had a patient who was suffering from the disease, and they were asked to decide whether to treat the patient at home or in hospital. They were required to use the information on past recovery rates if this would help them make a correct decision. This they did with accuracy. When a positive correlation existed between hospitalization and recovery, there was a significant tendency to send patients to hospital. When a negative correlation existed between hospitalization and recovery, there was a significant tendency to treat patients at home. And when no correlation existed, the decisions were made at random. The difficulties suggested by Peterson and Beach (1967) did not exist for the nurses of the Seggie and Endersby study. As suggested by Halford (1972), the problem seems rather to have been one of finding the conditions under which formal operational thought may be exhibited. In a later developmental study the writer administered the same decision-making task to children ($9\frac{1}{2}$ to $10\frac{1}{2}$ years age range), adolescents (14 to 15 years age range), and adults. Significant differences were found between the three age ranges which would support the contention that the task requires the formal operational structure as described by Inhelder and Piaget. However, caution must be exercised since in a later study (Seggie, 1975) with adult subjects evidence was found that the decision-making task may not have required formal operations in a strictly logical sense.

SUMMARY

The theoretical problems associated with the model are formidable and likely to prove enduring in the absence of the development of an appropriate methodology. In the model there are four separate areas, supposedly united:

(1) sixteen binary operations of propositional logic,
(2) *INRC* group,
(3) lattice structure of (1), and
(4) formal operational schemata.

The work of Wason and his colleagues has shown that empirical tasks can be constructed ostensibly on the basis of the propositional logic. Adult subjects, who theoretically should be operating formally, show important qualitative differences in their thought processes from those which perhaps could be expected from an analysis of the model. It is also possible to devise empirical measures of the existence of the *INRC* group as has been done by Wermus (1971). And, of course, it is possible to replicate the original Genevan experiments which show the existence, or absence, of the various operational schemata. Yet the development of an empirical correlate of the lattice structure remains elusive, while the theoretical and empirical unity of the four parts of the model is more than elusive. As Lunzer (1965) points out, the importance of the transformations of the *INRC* group to the sixteen binary operations, as claimed by Piaget, is problematical. While the propositional logic may be utilized as an explanatory device in the study of the subjects' empirical strategies—and so be related, however tenuously, to the formal operational schemata—the relationship of the lattice structure to either the *INRC* group or the schemata is one characterized by infinite obscurity, a factor which no doubt contributes to an even more serious criticism on the lack of unity in the formal model by Lunzer (1973). As the reader no doubt will by now appreciate, these factors may well correspond to the relative lack of attention paid to the formal operational part of Piaget's overall model.

Yet despite the difficulties and obscurities, and despite the esoteric symbolism and the use of symbolic logic which attracts trenchant criticism from formal logicians (Parsons, 1960), the formal model goes some way in describing the essential nature of adult thought and its advantages over the thought patterns of the child. The advantages are essentially in the areas of mobility and fluidity, of systematization and discipline. The adult can think in terms of possibilities and can construct hypotheses independent of empirical material, and when thinking within a closed system can do so systematically so that all possibilities may be explored. As stated by Boyle (1969, p. 13): 'The child in the concrete operations phase is concerned with the actual; the adolescent in the formal operations phase is concerned with the possible and its relation to the actual.' This is seen as the fundamental difference between the concrete and formal stages.

12

CONCEPT LEARNING AND THE FORMAL OPERATIONAL MODEL

J. L. Seggie

In his review of Inhelder and Piaget (1958), Bruner (1959, p. 368) makes the important point that:

> Good correspondence between a formal model and a process ... presupposes that the model will, by appropriate manipulation, yield descriptions (or predictions) of how behaviour will occur and will even suggest forms of behaviour to look for that have not yet been observed—that are merely possible.

The relevance of the formal model to the field of mathematics and history has been examined in the previous chapters. That work will now be extended to show that the truth table analysis of the Piagetian tasks (Chapter 11) is a manipulation of direct relevance to the classic work of Bruner, Goodnow, and Austin (1956). Unlike the Piagetian approach the work of Bruner and associates has more firm foundations within the tradition of experimental psychology. However, it can be shown that the model of formal thought suggests forms of behaviour to be studied in the traditional field of concept learning. This is possible because of the communalities which exist between the apparently dissimilar problems used by Bruner and Piaget in their study of complex cognitive processes.

In his 1956 study Bruner is concerned with concept attainment which is defined as the process of 'finding predictive defining attributes that distinguish exemplars from non-exemplars of the class one seeks to discriminate' (p. 22). This is an interesting definition and one which can be applied to the experimental problems of Piaget. The pendulum problem, for example, could be regarded as one in which the task of the subject is to find the exemplars of the class of independent variables which alter the frequency of the pendulum. The exemplars of the class may be regarded as the relevant variables (in the case of the pendulum problem, one relevant variable); the non-exemplars may be regarded as the irrelevant variables. The predictive defining attributes are merely those stimulus characteristics which allow the subject to discriminate between, say, the length of the string (exemplar) and the weight of the pendulum (non-exemplar).

These are basic matters; it is the *process* which is of real importance in finding points of contact between the work of Piaget and Bruner. It is of significance that a large part of Bruner's work is concerned with the comparative study of the attainment of conjunctive and disjunctive concepts. In terms of the Piagetian model these logical concepts represent two of the sixteen binary operations of propositional logic.

CONJUNCTIVE AND DISJUNCTIVE CONCEPTS

The typical Bruner, Goodnow, and Austin experiment required the subjects to classify given combinations of a finite stimulus population into positive and negative categories. The stimulus population consisted of a series of cards on which appeared geometrical figures which varied in *colour*, *number*, and *form*; the *number of borders* also varied. These are the dimensions or attributes. The concepts were defined in terms of these dimensions, each of which could be relevant or irrelevant. For example, a simple concept could be defined by the presence or absence of a triangle. An instance or combination would be called positive when a triangle was present and negative when no triangle appeared. In this case *forms* would be the relevant dimension and *colour*, *number of figures*, and *number of borders* irrelevant. This would be so because the concept would be defined by the presence or absence of a triangle, and the category (positive or negative) of any instance could not be predicted from the dimensions of *colour*, *number of figures*, or *number of borders*.

Bruner defined a conjunctive concept as the joint presence of the appropriate value of several attributes. An example of a conjunctive concept, in which *forms* and *colour* are the relevant attributes or variables, is all cards containing a circle or circles (*form*) which are red (*colour*). Cards which have such attributes are termed positive; cards which do not contain such attributes are regarded as negative. The irrelevant attributes in this case would be *number of figures* and *number of borders*.

The attributes shown on the cards used by Bruner were ternary in value; there were three types of figure: crosses, circles, and squares; any card had one, two, or three of such figures together with one, two, or three borders; and the figures could be one of three colours: red, green, or black. Some instances of the conjunctive concept 'red circles' would be, in the terms of Bruner, Goodnow, and Austin (1956, p. 87):

Instances	Classification	Description
3 R 0 2 b	+	Three red circles, two borders
2 R 0 2 b	+	Two red circles, two borders
3 G 0 2 b	−	Three green circles, two borders
3 R + 1 b	−	Three red crosses, one border
1 R 0 1 b	+	One red circle, one border

The two negative instances are the ones in which a red circle or circles do not appear. An example of a disjunctive concept based on the two attributes of form and colour is as follows:

Instances	Classification	Description
3 R + 1 b	+	Three red crosses, one border
3 G + 1 b	−	Three green crosses, one border
1 G + 3 b	−	One green cross, three borders
2 B 0 1 b	+	Two black circles, one border
2 B □ 1 b	−	Two black squares, one border
1 R 0 1 b	+	One red circle, one border

In this example the *form* of the figures and their *colour* are relevant. Any instance is positive which contains either circles (of any colour) or red figures (of any form) or red circles.

Considered in the light of the Piagetian tasks it can be claimed that in the concept attainment situation of Bruner the subject is faced with a similar problem. He is concerned with the effect on the dependent variable (the classification of positive or negative) on the independent variables (the attributes). This can be seen from an analysis of Bruner's concept attainment tasks in terms of the truth tables which have already been applied to the Piagetian problems in Chapter 11. As with the latter, the analysis will be simplified by considering a binary stimulus population, rather than the ternary as employed by Bruner and associates. While this simplification is used to clarify the analysis, it must be pointed out that this approach of describing the stimulus structure of concepts in terms of truth tables is not restricted to binary stimulus populations. It has been shown (Seggie, 1971b) that this method of analysis is also applicable to ternary stimulus populations.

TRUTH TABLE ANALYSIS OF CONJUNCTIVE AND DISJUNCTIVE CONCEPTS

Consider a stimulus population of four binary attributes, *form, colour, number of figures*, and *number of borders*, which can be symbolized as follows:

$p \equiv$ circle
$\bar{p} \equiv$ non-circle (square)
$q \equiv$ red
$\bar{q} \equiv$ non-red (black)
$r \equiv$ one figure
$\bar{r} \equiv$ not one figure (two)
$s \equiv$ one border
$\bar{s} \equiv$ not one border (two)

Combinations of these stimuli constitute instances which may be classified

TABLE 12.1. Truth table for all combinations of four binary stimuli (p, q, r, s) showing classifications (x) for the conjunctive concept $p \cdot q$

Row	p	q	r	s	x				
1	1	1	1	1	1				
2	1	1	1	0	1				
3	1	1	0	1	1				
4	1	1	0	0	1				
5	1	0	1	1	0	$p \cdot x$	$p \cdot \bar{x}$	$\bar{p} \cdot x$	$\bar{p} \cdot \bar{x}$
6	1	0	1	0	0	4	4	–	8
7	1	0	0	1	0				
8	1	0	0	0	0	$q \cdot x$	$q \cdot \bar{x}$	$\bar{q} \cdot x$	$\bar{q} \cdot \bar{x}$
9	0	1	1	1	0	4	4	–	8
10	0	1	1	0	0				
11	0	1	0	1	0	$r \cdot x$	$r \cdot \bar{x}$	$\bar{r} \cdot x$	$\bar{r} \cdot \bar{x}$
12	0	1	0	0	0	2	6	2	6
13	0	0	1	1	0				
14	0	0	1	0	0	$s \cdot x$	$s \cdot \bar{x}$	$\bar{s} \cdot x$	$\bar{s} \cdot \bar{x}$
15	0	0	0	1	0	2	6	2	6
16	0	0	0	0	0				

as positive (x) or negative ($\bar{x}$). The truth table showing all possible instances which can be generated from such a stimulus population is shown in Table 12.1. The Table also defines the conjunctive concept 'red circle(s)'.

As before, the symbol 1 in the truth table represents the truth of a 'proposition', these being the attributes p, q, r, s, and the classification x. The symbol 0 represents the negation of these 'propositions' which, of course, are the remaining values of the attributes $\bar{p}$, $\bar{q}$, $\bar{r}$, and $\bar{s}$; 0 also represents the alternative classification, $\bar{x}$. Consequently, the fifth row of the table, for example, represents the instance p, $\bar{q}$, r, s which contains one black circle within one border and which is classified as negative.

As in the earlier analysis of the Piagetian problems the frequency with which each value of each attribute is associated with each classification may be tabulated. As before, the frequencies are shown to the right of the truth table. It can be seen that the relationships between attributes and classification (independent and dependent variables) are precisely those which emerged in Table 11.6. The relationship between the relevant attributes (p and q) and classification (x) is one of implication; the relationship between the irrelevant attributes (r and s) and classification (x) is one of tautology. The finding of these relationships could represent no small matter. An initial comparison of the strictly controlled laboratory concept-learning task with the loosely controlled Piagetian tasks could justifiably lead to the conclusion that they have little, if anything, in common. Yet the truth table analyses give the hint of a different story; the ostensibly dissimilar problems have similar logical relationships embedded within their respective stimulus structures. These similarities are not confined to conjunctive concepts. The relationships described in the sixteen binary operations of propositional logic which were shown to exist in

TABLE 12.2. Truth table for all combinations of four binary stimuli (p, q, r, s) showing classification (x) for the disjunctive concept $p \vee q$

Row	p	q	r	s	x
1	1	1	1	1	1
2	1	1	1	0	1
3	1	1	0	1	1
4	1	1	0	0	1
5	1	0	1	1	1
6	1	0	1	0	1
7	1	0	0	1	1
8	1	0	0	0	1
9	0	1	1	1	1
10	0	1	1	0	1
11	0	1	0	1	1
12	0	1	0	0	1
13	0	0	1	1	0
14	0	0	1	0	0
15	0	0	0	1	0
16	0	0	0	0	0

Auxiliary counts (aligned with rows):

	$p{\cdot}x$	$p{\cdot}\bar{x}$	$\bar{p}{\cdot}x$	$\bar{p}{\cdot}\bar{x}$
	8	–	4	4

	$q{\cdot}x$	$q{\cdot}\bar{x}$	$\bar{q}{\cdot}x$	$\bar{q}{\cdot}\bar{x}$
	8	–	4	4

	$r{\cdot}x$	$r{\cdot}\bar{x}$	$\bar{r}{\cdot}x$	$\bar{r}{\cdot}\bar{x}$
	6	2	6	2

	$s{\cdot}x$	$s{\cdot}\bar{x}$	$\bar{s}{\cdot}x$	$\bar{s}{\cdot}\bar{x}$
	6	2	6	2

conjunctive concepts, again emerge when disjunctive concepts based on binary attributes are analysed. The truth table of Table 12.2 shows the classification of all instances of the disjunctive concept $(p \vee q)$, under which instances containing either circles, red figures, or red circles are all classified as positive.

Again it can be seen that under the disjunctive concept the relationship between the relevant attributes and classification is one of implication, while a tautologous relationship exists between the irrelevant attributes and classification. The question naturally arises as to the ability of subjects to utilize such relationships in concept-attainment tasks. To study this ability a method, known as the *search procedure* (SP), was developed. This was designed to study the extent to which subjects were able to utilize the logical relationships embedded within the stimulus structure of concept-learning tasks. Before the SP is described we will examine some of the more common experimental paradigms in the laboratory study of concept learning.

THE EMPIRICAL STUDY OF CONCEPT LEARNING

The issues investigated in the scientific study of concept learning have been many. Bruner and associates were concerned with the strategies of their subjects under various experimental conditions and with the comparative difficulties of various types of concept. Later workers have taken up these themes (Bourne, 1967; Byers, 1963; Laughlin, 1968; Neisser and Weene, 1962). With few exceptions the broad findings of Bruner and associates have been replicated and the extensions fit comfortably into the framework originally set up.

Difficulty in a concept-learning situation may be manipulated in two ways. In the first place the number of irrelevant attributes (independent variables) may be varied. Perhaps not surprisingly, given the same concept to be learned, the greater the number of irrelevant attributes involved the more difficult is the concept to be learned (Bourne and Bunderson, 1963). The second method of studying the dimension of difficulty is the comparative study of the different types of concept possible. Bruner and associates established, for example, that disjunctive concepts are more difficult than conjunctive. While Seggie (1969) has shown that disjunctive and conjunctive concepts under binary-valued attributes are logically equivalent, both in structure and difficulty of learning, Bruner's broad finding has been replicated many times with ternary-valued stimuli. Since the original work it has been established that a hierarchy of difficulty exists within the various types of concept studied. It is invariably found, for example, that conditional concepts are more difficult than disjunctive, which are more difficult than conjunctive. The hierarchy is documented in Bourne (1966, 1967).

The study of strategies in concept learning is the study of the methods used by the subject during the learning of any particular concept. Again the work of Bruner and associates has become a classic in its description of the strategies used under various experimental conditions. Needless to say, the conditions under which concepts may be learned are numerous. However, to the reader familiar with the work of Inhelder and Piaget (1958) some of the descriptions of Bruner and associates have a peculiar *déja vu* quality. In a series of studies Bruner's subjects were allowed freedom in their selection of instances to be tested. That is, after having been told that their job was to find the rule (concept) by which the cards could be classified reliably, they were then presented with the complete array of stimulus combinations (instances) and allowed to select any instance at all. Under these conditions there appeared a dominant and persuasive strategy which Bruner and associates labelled *conservative focusing*. This involved the selection of an 'anchor' instance and then the systematic variation of single attributes within that instance in order to study the effects of the variation on the classification of the instance. Such a strategy was used to find the relevant attributes in the situation, and it is difficult not to draw the conclusion that the behaviour exhibited in the selection strategy of conservative focusing is similar to behaviour described by Inhelder and Piaget. They describe the emergence of the scientific approach which involves holding all variables constant except one, and then varying the values of the one independent variable to study the effect of this on the dependent variable. It would seem that the two approaches have independently discovered a problem-solving technique common to both European and American subjects. Yet, as is known, Bruner and associates did not describe the performance of their subjects in terms of the formal operational model; nor did their analysis take into account the possibility that the logical relations described in Tables 12.1 and 12.2 were of importance in the strategies of their subjects. The SP was developed to look into this possibility.

THE DEVELOPMENT OF THE SEARCH PROCEDURE

As has been shown by Haygood and Bourne (1965) the subject faced with a concept-learning task has, in effect, two different problems to solve. First of all, he must establish which of the attributes are irrelevant and which relevant. Then, having established the relevant attributes he must learn the rule which relates the relevant attributes to the classification system to be learned. When both problems are presented together it is described as a *complete learning* (CL) situation. However, the experimental conditions may be manipulated so that the problems are distinctly separated. The subject, for example, may be given prior practice on the specific rule to be learned; consequently when introduced to the concept-learning situation his task is merely that of finding the relevant attributes, which is known as *attribute identification* (AI). Alternatively, the subject may be told which attributes are relevant, in which case his task is merely that of *rule learning* (RL). The SP is a method which allows the subject to find for himself which attributes are relevant and which irrelevant prior to concept learning. It is a method which utilizes the logical relations between each of the stimuli and the classification as shown in Tables 12.1 and 12.2.

A series of studies has established that adult subjects can use these logical relations to assist them in a concept-learning task (Seggie 1970a, 1970b, 1971b). In the earliest study (Seggie, 1970a) evidence was found that adults were more efficient in the utilization of these relations than children in the age range of 12 years to 13 years 11 months. The SP as used in that experiment involved a fair degree of subject/experimenter interaction. To reduce this interaction the procedure was modified and the SP as employed in the later studies will be described (Seggie 1970b, 1971a).

In the concept-learning tasks the subjects were presented with four, binary-valued geometric figures. The four figures were diamond (p), circle (q), triangle (r), and square (s), which could be white (p, q, r, s) or shaded ($\bar{p}$, $\bar{q}$, $\bar{r}$, $\bar{s}$). The subjects were presented with the sixteen combinations of stimuli (photographed on slides) and informed that each of the combinations could be classified reliably on the basis of a rule and that their job was to learn how to classify the stimulus combinations. To familiarize the subjects with the general type of task involved they were given examples of possible concepts and required to classify the stimulus combinations under these rules. An important part of this familiarization procedure was that the subjects became aware of the importance of distinguishing between relevant and irrelevant figures. They were also informed that the rule or concept which they had to learn could involve only one relevant figure or a combination of more than one relevant figure. Subjects who were involved in the SP were then told that they were going to be given the opportunity to find out which were the relevant and irrelevant figures. The SP was introduced with the following instructions:

> In front of you there are eight separate packs of cards. You can see that there are diamonds, circles, squares and triangles all of which can be white or shaded and which are in separate packs. The slides were photographed from these cards. What I want you to do is to select one card at a time and then guess whether the figure on the card you select can be x or y. After you've done that I'll pick up the card you've selected and show you the letter on the back of the card. You'll find that on the back of each

of the cards is a letter, x or y, and these are what the figures *can be according to the rule you've got to learn*. In other words it's the rule you've eventually got to learn which has dictated what these figures can be. Through finding out what these figures can be you can find out which figure or figures are important to the rule you have to learn.

You can pick any figure you like, any number of times you like. When I've shown you what's on the back of the card you pick I'll put it to the bottom of the pack. But when you're pretty sure what's important let me know and we'll get on to the rule learning part. Work at your own speed.

The subjects recorded their choices and guesses as to whether a card could be an x or a y on a response proforma of the following form:

Diamond	Circle	Square	Triangle	Your guess	It can be
w s	w s	w s	w s		
☐ ☐	☐ ☐	☐ ☐	☐ ☐		

The subjects selected the figures one at a time and recorded their choice on one row of the proformas. For example, if the choice was a white circle the subject was required to tick the 'w' box beneath the 'circle' column and then write his estimation of whether it could be an x or a y under the 'your guess' column. After the subject had done this the experimenter picked up the top card on the pack, showed the subject the letter printed on the reverse side of the pack, and then replaced the card at the bottom of the pack. When the subject read the letter on the reverse side he recorded this under the 'it can be' column.

In the completed studies it has been common for the initial administration of the instructions for the SP to provoke many questions from the subjects. Such questions have been answered by repeating the instructions and emphasizing that their task was to find out what the figures 'could be'. It was possible to discover this from the letters printed on the reverse side of the cards. Emphasis was also placed on the fact that the ultimate task was to learn how to classify the slides as x or y, and that by finding out what the individual figures could be they could find out which were the important figure or figures, and which irrelevant.

Each of the 2×2 inch cards in front of the subject had a single figure printed on the face side. Each of the eight packs consisted of thirty cards having one of the binary-valued stimuli on the face side, i.e. one pack contained thirty white circles, another thirty shaded circles, and so on. The presence of the letter x or y on the reverse sides of these cards was based on the following rationale. Consider the subject whose subsequent task is to learn the conjunctive concept $(p \cdot q)$ in which combinations containing the figures p (white diamond) and q (white circle) are classified as x, while the remaining combinations are classified as y. The relations between each of the geometric figures and the classification can be seen from Table 12.1, which shows the truth table for a stimulus population of four binary stimuli and the conjunctive concept $(p \cdot q)$. It can be seen that the following conjunctions between the relevant figures (p, q) and the classification occur: $p \cdot x, p \cdot \bar{x}, \bar{p} \cdot \bar{x}$ in the case of the diamond and

$q \cdot x$, $q \cdot \bar{x}$, $\bar{q} \cdot \bar{x}$ in the case of the circle. In neither case does $\bar{p} \cdot x$ or $\bar{q} \cdot x$ occur. In terms of symbolic logic the occurrence of these conjunctives represent the implications $p \cdot x \vee p \cdot \bar{x} \vee \bar{p} \cdot \bar{x}$ and $q \cdot x \vee q \cdot \bar{x} \vee \bar{q} \cdot \bar{x}$. As it is these relationships which dictate what letters will appear on the reverse sides of the cards, the packs containing white diamonds and white circles would be assembled so that 50 per cent. of the cards would have x printed on the reverse side and 50 per cent. y. This would be so because both the white diamond (p) and the white circle (q) are associated with x and $\bar{x}$ under the concept ($p \cdot q$). The implicatory relationships show that shaded diamonds and shaded circles are only associated with $\bar{x}$. As a result the packs of shaded diamonds and shaded circles would be assembled from cards with the letter y printed on the reverse side.

In the case of the irrelevant figures, square and triangle, it can be seen from Table 12.1 that the following conjunction occur: $r \cdot x$, $r \cdot \bar{x}$, $\bar{r} \cdot x$, $\bar{r} \cdot \bar{x}$ and $s \cdot x$, $s \cdot \bar{x}$, $\bar{s} \cdot x$, $\bar{s} \cdot \bar{x}$. These represent the tautologies $r \cdot x \vee r \cdot \bar{x} \vee \bar{r} \cdot x \vee \bar{r} \cdot \bar{x}$ and $s \cdot x \vee s \cdot \bar{x} \vee \bar{s} \cdot x \vee \bar{s} \cdot \bar{x}$. Consequently, the packs of cards for both values of square and triangle would be assembled so that each pack consisted of cards, 50 per cent. of which had x printed on the reverse side and 50 per cent. y.

As has been stated earlier, it has been found over a series of studies that adult subjects are capable of the utilization of such logical relations in concept learning through the SP. In the investigation of this aspect of concept learning a number of issues have been investigated; these have included (a) the strategies used by subjects during the SP, (b) the effect of the SP on concepts of differing levels of difficulty, and (c) a comparison of concept-learning performance in subjects working under SP and RL experimental procedures. Each of these areas will be considered in turn.

Strategies used during the SP

The SP was designed to establish the extent to which subjects are capable of the utilization of the logical relations described by Piaget's sixteen binary operations of propositional logic (Tables 11.3 and 11.4) in a concept learning set-up. The concern of Inhelder and Piaget has been with the operational nature of thought and its development. They have not been overly concerned with the part played by learning in the genesis of operational thought; it could well be important. Consider, for example, the subject involved in the simplified rods problem described in Chapter 11 (which, of course, is structurally isomorphic to the conjunctive concept ($p \cdot q$) described in Table 12.1). It is the contention of the Genevan school that the subject actively constructs hypotheses with respect to the relationships between independent and dependent variables —and so they may. These hypotheses and relationships are described by the sixteen binary operations. What is obscure is the nature of the activity which may be a prerequisite for the construction of the hypothesis. It could well be that the subject has got to undergo some initial learning on the possible relationships involved before he actively constructs hypotheses. In the rods problem the subject may initially construct the following four combinations of independent variables (p, q, r, s) and examine the effect they have on the flexibility of the rod (x):

p	q	r	s	x
1	1	1	1	1
1	1	0	0	0
1	0	0	1	0
0	1	1	0	0

From this initial sample of the possible combinations of independent variables, he would find that the following conjunctions between individual independent variables and dependent variable occur:

$p \cdot x$	$p \cdot \bar{x}$	$\bar{p} \cdot x$	$\bar{p} \cdot \bar{x}$
2	1	—	1
$q \cdot x$	$q \cdot \bar{x}$	$\bar{q} \cdot x$	$\bar{q} \cdot \bar{x}$
2	1	—	1
$r \cdot x$	$r \cdot \bar{x}$	$\bar{r} \cdot x$	$\bar{r} \cdot \bar{x}$
1	1	1	1
$s \cdot x$	$s \cdot \bar{x}$	$\bar{s} \cdot x$	$\bar{s} \cdot \bar{x}$
1	1	1	1

From the occurrence of these component conjunctions it is possible to distinguish the implicatory relationship between the relevant independent variables, p and q, and the dependent variable, x. It is also possible to distinguish the tautologous relationship between the irrelevant independent variables, r and s, and the dependent variable, x. What is not known is whether the subject would actively hypothesize the existence of the implication and tautology involved, on the basis of the examination of only four combinations of independent variable, and then set out to systematically test the hypotheses. It would seem reasonable to assume that the component conjunctions would have to be established with greater frequency before the subject would be willing to act on the relationships which they form. Boyle (1969) may well be referring to this aspect of behaviour when he differentiates between the actualizing of existing structures and the formation or development of new operational structures. The actualizing could involve learning of a more basic type than that involved in the development of the structures. The studies involving the SP would indicate that this is not so.

Few of the subjects involved in the SP, in the series of studies referred to, were completely at ease when the instructions introducing the SP were administered. Of necessity the instructions, as can be seen, were somewhat nebulous, merely asking the subjects to find out what the individual figures 'could be' and providing the information that the presence of the letters on the reverse sides of the cards had been dictated by the rule to be learned. Initial hypotheses or guesses were often made tentatively and the choices were made with a great deal of hesitation. The sense of perplexity frequently provoked by the instructions were often compounded if the subjects' initial choices involved cards which could be classified as both x and y. During the early part of the SP the majority of subjects obviously had difficulty in relating such a dual classification to the question of the relevance or irrelevance of the figure to the rule to be learned. However, over the series of choices the difficulty characteristically became less and certain patterns were revealed in the subjects' hypotheses as to the classifications of the individual figures.

It will be recalled that the SP required the subject to select a single value of one of the attributes and then guess or hypothesize whether this single value could be x or y. The subject's hypothesis was recorded before he was shown the letter, on the back of the card selected, which revealed what the selection could be according to the rule to be learned. The patterns which are of interest are those which appeared in the hypotheses made by the subjects as to the classifications of their choices.

Consider the case in which the subject is presented with the stimulus population of four, binary-valued figures of diamond (p), circle (q), triangle (r), and square (s), which may be white (p, q, r, s) or shaded ($\bar{p}, \bar{q}, \bar{r}, \bar{s}$). This stimulus population is described in Tables 12.1 and 12.2. Imagine that we set some subjects the task of learning the conjunctive concept described in Table 12.1. The table shows that the relevant dimensions are p and q and the irrelevant are r and s. If we assume the binary classification system of x and y the table shows that slides containing $p \cdot q$ are classified as x while slides containing $p \cdot \bar{q}$, $\bar{p} \cdot q$, and $\bar{p} \cdot \bar{q}$ are classified as y. This concept determines the letters which appear on the backs of the SP cards which will be presented to the subjects prior to concept learning proper.

From Table 12.1 it can be seen that the logical relationships between the individual figures and classification are as follows: in the case of the relevant figures p and q:

$$p \cdot x \vee p . \bar{x} \vee \bar{p} \cdot \bar{x}$$
$$q \cdot x \vee q \cdot \bar{x} \vee \bar{q} \cdot \bar{x}$$

and in the case of the irrelevant figures r and s:

$$r \cdot x \vee r \cdot \bar{x} \vee \bar{r} \cdot x \vee \bar{r} \cdot \bar{x}$$
$$s \cdot x \vee s \cdot \bar{x} \vee \bar{s} \cdot x \vee \bar{s} \cdot \bar{x}$$

Consequently the letters appearing on the individual cards in the packs presented to the subjects are as follows:

It will be recalled that each pack of cards in past studies has contained thirty cards. In the concept under consideration the above shows that the packs of cards with white diamonds, white circles, white triangles, shaded triangles, white squares, and shaded squares would contain cards, 50 per cent. of which would have x on the reverse side and 50 per cent y. In the case of the shaded diamond, and shaded circles the packs of cards would only contain cards having the letter y on the reverse side.

On the basis of past studies it could be expected that the subjects involved in a SP based on the above conjunctive concept $(p \cdot q)$ would begin to learn that a choice of shaded diamond or shaded circle will always produce the letter y on the reverse side of such cards. Under these circumstances it could be expected that the subjects would hypothesize that the choice of white diamond or white circle will always produce the letter x on the back of these cards. This pattern of choices has appeared in past studies (Seggie 1970a, 1971b) and the reasoning seems to be as follows: if shaded diamond always produces y, then white diamond should always produce x; similarly for the two values of the circle. Moreover, in past studies this pattern has generalized to the irrelevant dimensions, the values of which are associated with both x and y.

These choices are interesting in that they can be assumed to represent a search for logical relationships which are simpler than those present. The subject who hypothesizes the occurrence of $p \cdot x$ and $\bar{p} \cdot \bar{x}$ significantly more frequently than $\bar{p} \cdot x$ and $p \cdot \bar{x}$ may be assumed to be searching for the simple equivalence pattern $(p \equiv x) = (p \cdot x \vee \bar{p} \cdot \bar{x})$. It would appear from the initial studies that the search for simple relations takes precedence over the eventual appreciation that more complex relationships are involved. The results of the past studies have been related to the work of Peel (1967c) who has shown that under certain conditions children interpret the logical relations of implication as equivalence. They may also be related to the 'weak' form of the formal operational model as proposed in a paper by Lunzer, Harrison, and Davey (1972). These authors, on the basis of the overall evidence to date, contend that the majority of adults do not spontaneously apply the propositional calculus when faced with problems involving the calculus. However, they may eventually be induced to employ the propositional logic described by Piaget. The subjects in the studies referred to above who were involved in the SP did not, on the whole, give evidence of an initial search for the more complicated relations empirically in the subsequent concept-learning task.

On the basis of the present evidence—rather sparse—the indications are that subjects will search for equivalence during the SP only under a given range of conditions. This means, of course, that there is evidence available on the conditions under which this type of behaviour does not appear. It has failed to appear under conditions in which there is a greater variety of logical relations between individual dimensions and classifications. Under the conjunctive concept $(p \cdot q)$ the relationship between both relevant dimensions and classification is one of implication. This is not the case with all concepts, as can be seen from the truth table of Table 12.3.

TABLE 12.3. Truth table for all combinations of four binary stimuli (p, q, r, s) showing classification (x) for the conditional concept $p \cdot \bar{q}$

Row	p	q	r	s	$p \cdot \bar{q}(x)$				
1	1	1	1	1	0				
2	1	1	1	0	0				
3	1	1	0	1	0				
4	1	1	0	0	0	$p \cdot x$ v $p \cdot \bar{x}$ v $\bar{p} \cdot x$ v $\bar{p} \cdot \bar{x}$			
5	1	0	1	1	1	4	4	–	8
6	1	0	1	0	1				
7	1	0	0	1	1	$q \cdot x$ v $q \cdot \bar{x}$ v $\bar{q} \cdot x$ v $\bar{q} \cdot \bar{x}$			
8	1	0	0	0	1	–	8	4	4
9	0	1	1	1	0				
10	0	1	1	0	0	$r \cdot x$ v $r \cdot \bar{x}$ v $\bar{r} \cdot x$ v $\bar{r} \cdot \bar{x}$			
11	0	1	0	1	0	2	6	2	6
12	0	1	0	0	0				
13	0	0	1	1	0	$s \cdot x$ v $s \cdot \bar{x}$ v $\bar{s} \cdot x$ v $\bar{s} \cdot \bar{x}$			
14	0	0	1	0	0	2	6	2	6
15	0	0	0	1	0				
16	0	0	0	0	0				

Table 12.3 shows the classification under the conditional concept $p \cdot \bar{q}$, together with the relationships which occur between each individual figure and classification. It can be seen that in the case of the relevant dimensions (p, q) there are two different relationships involved; there is an implicatory relationship between p and x ($x \supset p$) and a disjunctive relationship between the negations of q and x ($\bar{q}$ v $\bar{x}$). Consequently, if the cards used in the SP reflected the relationships involved in the conditional concept $p \cdot \bar{q}$ the following letters would appear on the reverse sides:

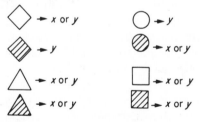

Following the studies which detected the search for equivalence when conjunctive concepts were involved, studies were carried out in which subjects were required to learn conditional concepts (Seggie 1971b, 1973). As before, part of the rationale of the studies was the investigation of the subject behaviour during the search procedure. Prior to the collection of data the following possibilities were considered: it was thought possible that the search for equivalence may still make itself evident in the case of the implicatory relationship between p and x. That is, when subjects began to learn that the shaded diamond was always associated with y, they would begin to hypothesize that the white diamond was always associated with x ($p \cdot x$ v $\bar{p} \cdot \bar{x}$). However, in the disjunctive relationship between q and x the possibility existed that the mirror image of such behaviour would be manifested. That is, when the subjects began to learn that the white circle was always associated with y, then the shaded circle was always associated with x ($q \cdot \bar{x} \vee \bar{q} \cdot x$). In other words, the possibility existed that the presence of the disjunctive relationship would provoke a search for reciprocal exclusion.

As to what would occur in the case of the irrelevant dimensions r and s—that was problematical.

From the two studies which have been carried out involving conditional concepts the following generalization may be hazarded. The result of the increase in the variety of the logical relationships between individual figures and classification is a decrease in the tendency to search for the simpler logical relations of equivalence and reciprocal exclusion. The majority of subjects hypothesized x or y at random after their selection of both relevant and irrelevant figures prior to learning which figures were relevant and which irrelevant.

Apart from the guesses and hypotheses made by the subjects after their selection of cards there are other issues of interest arising from the performance of the subjects during the SP. One is related to the experimental conditions imposed on the subjects and the effect of these conditions on behaviour; another is related to the ideal strategy which may be employed in the search for relevant and irrelevant dimensions.

The conditions under which the SP has been studied to date have not allowed the subjects to refer back to the actual classifications of previous choices they had made. This placed a great strain on memory which could only have been reduced by the employment of the ideal strategy. This would have involved the repeated selection of both values of a single dimension until the relevance or irrelevance of that dimension had been established. These repeated choices of a single figure or dimension would have been carried out on each separate dimension in turn under an ideal strategy. This behaviour was rarely manifested by the subjects employed in the studies, all of whom were of above-average intelligence. The characteristic behaviour of the subjects was to select one value of a given figure once, twice, or thrice before changing the selection to a different figure. This meant that subjects had to make, on average, well over a hundred choices before being able to discriminate between the relevant and irrelevant dimensions. It is doubtful if such behaviour would be manifested under conditions which allowed subjects to refer back to the results of previous choices. While such a change of conditions may not result in the universal appearance of the ideal strategy, it is reasonable to assume that it would be more prevalent and allied to a significant decrease in the number of selections made.

The role of experience in the SP situation also represents an area about which nothing is known. The existing data on the SP comes from subjects who were totally unfamiliar with the procedure and who were involved with it but once. It is not unlikely that familiarization with the procedure would lead to changes in the subjects' patterns of selections. Again, it could be predicted that experience in the procedure would be likely to lead to a reduction in the number of choices necessary, and perhaps the appearance of strategies closely approximating the ideal. However, these are matters which are the concern of the not-too-distant future. What has been well established is the fact that adult subjects are capable of the empirical utilization of the logical relations involved in the SP. The effect of this behaviour on other aspects of concept learning remains to be examined.

Effect of the SP on concepts of differing levels of difficulty

From the first study involving the SP (Seggie, 1970a) it was obvious that not only could subjects utilize logical relations in concept learning but that involvement in the SP significantly reduced the number of errors made. The following studies investigated other aspects of the concept-learning process following the SP, among these aspects being its effect on concepts of differing levels of difficulty.

The hierarchy involved in the differences in difficulty of different types of concept has been well established (Neisser and Weene, 1962). The difference in difficulty between disjunctive and conjunctive concepts has already been mentioned. Even more difficult than the disjunctive concept is the conditional, an example of which has been presented in Table 12.3. The comparative difficulty of conditional and conjunctive concepts was one of the variables investigated in two studies (Seggie 1970b, 1971b). As in previous work both studies found the conditional concept to be significantly more difficult than the conjunctive. However, the comparative difficulty of the concepts was a function of the conditions under which they were learned. In each of the studies one of the conditions required the subjects (a) to identify the relevant attributes and (b) to learn the concept involving these attributes—the complete learning (CL) procedure. Another involved the SP which allowed the subjects to establish the logical relationships which existed between the attributes and classification prior to concept learning. The average number of errors made in the learning of both types of concept under both conditions can be seen in Table 12.4.

The significant and dramatic reduction in the number of errors in the case of the subjects who learned the concepts following the SP is obvious. For these subjects the well-established comparative difficulty of the conditional has been

TABLE 12.4. Average number of errors made by subjects of two studies (Seggie, 1970b, 1971b) working under SP and CL in concept-learning tasks

	Study 1 Concept		Study 2 Concept	
	Conjunctive	Conditional	Conjunctive	Conditional
SP	1·5	2·6	1·9	2·3
CL	13·3	40·2	31·7	56·7

eliminated. It would seem that rather important processes have taken place during the SP, a supposition which is reinforced by an examination of some of the other variables involved in the studies.

From Table 12.4 it can be seen that the subjects of the second study who worked under the CL condition made many more errors than the subjects of the first study who worked under the same condition. This was the result of an additional variable which was studied. In the first study the subjects were allowed to work at their own pace during the concept-learning task. On the presentation of a slide no time limit was placed on the interval between the appearance of the slide and the subject's classification of it. Once the subject had classified the slide it was he who decided when the next slide should appear; again no time limit was placed on this interval. This freedom of action was not enjoyed by the subjects of the second study who worked under somewhat more rigorous and controlled conditions.

The important events during any given trial in a concept learning task are as follows:

(1) the appearance of a stimulus combination,
(2) the classification of that combination by the subject,
(3) the informative feedback (IF) which provides the subject with the information as to the correct classification of the stimulus combination, and
(4) the postinformative feedback (PIF) interval which occurs between the delivery of IF and the presentation of the next stimulus combination.

The importance of the temporal variables involved in these events has been made the scrutiny of Bourne and his associates (Bourne and Bunderson, 1963; Bourne and coauthors, 1965). Briefly, it has been found that variations in the IF interval have no effect on concept learning but that the PIF interval is a rather more important variable. By increasing the length of the PIF interval from 1 to 9 sec the efficiency of concept learning is increased. Perhaps of greater importance is the finding that the effect of the PIF interval was related to task complexity in that greater facilitation was found in the more complex problems. Bourne and associates varied problem complexity by increasing the number of irrelevant dimensions in the stimulus populations presented to the subjects. Seggie (1971b) has shown that an increase in the PIF interval also has a facilitatory effect when difficulty is varied by learning method—the more difficult the learning method the greater the facilitation in learning which is found with a 15-sec as opposed to a 2-sec PIF interval. But of far greater relevance to the present discussion is the effect of varying the PIF interval on subjects who have to learn the concept after involvement in the SP. Again the results are unequivocal in their clarity. In the second study it was found that, while an increase in the PIF interval reduced errors under the CL condition, there was absolutely no effect for subjects working under the SP. SP subjects who were allowed a 2-sec PIF interval found the concept-learning task just as easy as subjects who were allowed a 15-sec PIF interval. A comparison of the basic results of the first and second study also reveals the efficiency of the

SP subjects in both studies. Imposing the conditions of the strictly controlled PIF interval has had no effect on subjects working under the SP conditions, and this is not the case for subjects working under CL conditions. The results show that under both conjunctive and conditional concepts, the loss of freedom entailed by controlling the PIF interval has resulted in an increase in the number of errors for these subjects working under CL conditions.

The genesis of the SP was founded in the sixteen binary operations of propositional logic, as described in the Piagetian model of formal operational thought. With the detection of the logical structure underlying the relationships between attributes and classification in the type of concepts used in the laboratory study of concept learning, the logical step was the development of a method which allowed investigation as to the subject's ability to utilize such relationships empirically. The result of that step was the development of the SP. From the initial studies it would appear that fundamental processes take place during the subject's involvement with the SP. It has been established that adult subjects are indeed capable of the empirical utilization of such logical relations as implication, disjunction, and tautology. It has been seen that the evidence which supports this position takes the form of data which seem contrary to well established findings. The comparative difficulty of conditional concepts does not exist following experience with the SP; the imposition of the strict temporal controls involved in the PIF interval does little to impair the concept-learning efficiency of SP subjects. Yet the operations which result in this efficiency remain to be established.

It will be recalled from the instructions given to SP subjects that they were informed that the procedure would allow them to distinguish between relevant and irrelevant attributes with respect to the concept to be learned. If the knowledge imparted by the SP had been restricted to this distinction then SP subjects would be placed in a position analogous to that of subjects serving under the RL condition in concept learning. This possibility is one of the issues which has been examined.

Comparison of concept-learning performance under SP and RL conditions

Haygood and Bourne (1965) differentiated between attribute and rule learning in conceptual behaviour. In attribute learning the subject receives prior instruction in the particular concept to be learned. Consequently, in the concept-learning situation the task of the subject is merely one of identifying the attributes or dimensions which are relevant. In the case of RL no prior instructions in the concept to be learned are given. But before the learning task the subject is *told* which particular dimensions are relevant; from this it is a simple step to deduce which are irrelevant. Prior to the series of studies which are being reviewed in this chapter the possibility existed that the subjects who identified relevant and irrelevant attributes by means of the SP would have no particular advantage over RL subjects in the subsequent concept-learning task.

The second possibility was that subjects who serve under the SP may have been able to deduce the nature of the concept to be learned from the logical relations between the relevant attributes and classification. Consider the subject who is required to learn the conjunctive concept $p \cdot q$ as shown in Table 12.1. As has been shown, the logical relationships which exist between relevant attributes, (p, q) and classification (x) are as follows:

$$p \cdot x \vee p \cdot \bar{x} \vee \bar{p} \cdot \bar{x}$$

and

$$q \cdot x \vee q \cdot \bar{x} \vee \bar{q} \cdot \bar{x}$$

During the SP the subject would learn that both p and q are associated with both x and $\bar{x}$. He would also learn that $\bar{p}$ and $\bar{q}$ are associated with $\bar{x}$ and only $\bar{x}$. From this analysis it is obvious that the subjects may have been able to deduce that the conjunction of $\bar{p}$ and $\bar{q}$ would always produce x in the rule to be learned. If such a deduction were made then the hypothesis which emerges is that subjects who work under the SP conditions would be more efficient in the concept-learning situation than subjects serving under the RL condition. This hypothesis was examined under the conditions of both of the studies previously referred to (Seggie 1970b, 1971b). The average number of errors made in the learning of conditional and conjunctive concepts under the SP and RL conditions can be seen in Table 12.5.

It is evident from Table 12.5 that, under the conditions of both studies, the SP subjects were more efficient during concept learning than the RL subjects. As a result it may be assumed that the SP experience led to more than the ability to distinguish between relevant and irrelevant attributes. The utility of learning the logical relations embedded within the stimulus structure of the concepts to be learned was not restricted to the separation of the relevant and irrelevant attributes. The details of the cognitive operations which have led to the ease of concept learning following the SP remain to be established. However, it is likely that the learning involved in the SP leads to a significant reduction in errors for particular combinations of the values of the relevant attributes (e.g. the $p \cdot \bar{q}$ combination under the conjunctive concept $p \cdot q$).

THE RELEVANCE OF FORMAL OPERATIONAL THOUGHT TO CONCEPT LEARNING (AND VICE VERSA)

Writers such as Baggaley (1955), Bourne (1966), and Haygood and Devine (1967) have touched on the possibility of the existence of complex cognitive

TABLE 12.5. Average number of errors made by subjects of two studies (Seggie 1970b, 1971b) working under SP and RL conditions in concept-learning tasks

| | Study 1 Concept | | Study 2 Concept | |
	Conjunctive	Conditional	Conjunctive	Conditional
SP	1·5	2·6	1·9	2·3
RL	7·8	10·7	13·9	23·8

processes which may be used in concept learning. However, as Saltz (1971) has pointed out, the majority of concept-learning studies are firmly based in the methodological tradition which gave rise to the discrimination model of concept learning. One of Saltz's complaints would appear to be that this type of model encourages the study of perceptual rather than complex cognitive processes in concept learning. The fact that subjects will exercise cognitive economy by the use of perceptual processes is well documented (Bruner, Goodnow, and Austin, 1956; Haygood and Bourne, 1965; Seggie, 1969). The problem is then one of creating the experimental conditions which will encourage the use of cognitive operations which by-pass the perceptual. The further development of the SP presents one possibility in this direction.

So far the studies involving the SP have involved stimulus populations having three or four binary-valued attributes. However, the findings from these studies have relevance for the model of formal thought.

In the review of the work of Wason and his associates in Chapter 11 it was seen that subjects were not capable of evaluating the truth value of conditional sentences. On the basis of this work, Wason was forced to conclude that his subjects were not capable of the type of reasoning described by Piaget's formal model. What is not a little remarkable is the fact that Wason's subjects were called upon to deal with precisely the same logical relation (conditional implication) as were the subjects in the concept-learning studies discussed in this chapter. On the one hand, the subjects of Wason found the task beyond them; on the other, the subjects in the concept-learning tasks were capable of the empirical utilization of the logical relations. The two series of studies are paralleled by the work done on the concept of correlation. Smedslund (1963), Jenkins and Ward (1965), Ward and Jenkins (1965), and Petersen and Beach (1967) found no evidence that subjects had a concept of correlation when dealing with the data of a 2×2 table. The empirical implications of these findings have been spelled out elsewhere (Seggie and Endersby, 1972), and it has been shown that in spite of a remarkable incompetence, as evidenced by the former studies, adults subjects are perfectly capable of making logically correct decisions on the basis of the data contained in the 2×2 contingency table. As is pointed out by Halford (1972), one of the big problems in the field of formal operational thought is the specification and creation of the conditions under which it will be manifested.

This was the concern of Lunzer, Harrison, and Davey (1972) who developed procedures based on the work of Wason. Lunzer and associates displayed that the performance of subjects in the evaluation of the truth value of conditional sentences can be markedly improved under the appropriate conditions. By presenting the material in familiar form and by providing the appropriate experience subjects have been shown to manifest a greater ability than was evident in earlier subjects. The findings of Lunzer and associates resulted in the proposal of a weaker form of the formal model which suggests that subjects who have attained the level of formal reasoning can be 'led to apply the propositional calculus correctly'—a proposition which is relevant to the performance of subjects under the SP.

As has been stated earlier, few of the subjects who participated in the SP found the task easy. However, by repeated selections of the cards which re-presented the values of the attributes in the concept-learning task, strategies began to emerge under some conditions. There was evidence of a search for simpler logical relations which indicated that learning was taking place. More important, there was the efficient utilization of what was learned in the sub-sequent concept-learning task. Yet the performance of the subjects was such as to lend support by Lunzer's 'weaker form' of the model. Subjects did not spontaneously apply the ideal strategy and they did not spontaneously hypothe-size the existence of particular logical relations and then test for their existence. They had, on the whole, to be led to the application of the logical relations which they were dealing with.

The early studies have indicated the difficulty of the SP, in spite of the fact that the stimuli used were restricted to binary values. It is more than likely that ternary-valued stimuli would render the task extremely stressful and beyond the ability of a number of, if not most, subjects. Yet again we have the relevance of the work of Lunzer and associates since it could well be hypothesized that the probable difficulty with ternary-valued stimuli would be markedly reduced by prior experience with SP using binary-valued stimuli. These are fields which have still to be explored and are some indication of the heuristic value of Piaget's model in the field of concept learning. In this field the model does appear to satisfy Bruner's (1959) criterion of good correspondence between theory and process. This chapter has been an attempt to show that appropriate manipulations of the model do yield descriptions of how behaviour can occur and, in addition, suggest new forms of behaviour to look for which are as yet unobserved.

13

AN INTEGRATION

G. S. Halford and J. A. Keats

The aim of this book, as outlined in Chapter 1, was to develop and investigate various structural descriptions of the main stages of cognitive development. Since the book is devoted to thóse stages which are cognitive, in the sense that they involve symbolic or representational processes, the sensorimotor stage has been excluded. The book is therefore concerned with Piaget's stages I, II, and III, generally called the preoperational, concrete operational, and formal operational stages respectively.

All the authors of Chapters 1 to 12 have in common the belief that Piaget's stages I, II, and III correspond to meaningfully different sets of structural properties, although they differ with Piaget as to what these structural properties are. Sheppard, for instance, deals with the weaknesses of Piaget's account of concrete operations in terms of groupings in Chapter 3. Most of the present authors have defined structural properties of stages in a way which is appropriate to the particular subject matter or material under investigation. Thus the underlying structures of formal operations are defined in different ways by Collis, Seggie, and Jurd so as to fit the content areas of school mathematics, laboratory studies of concept attainment, and comprehension of history respectively. Nevertheless, any but the most cursory examination of the studies contained in this book shows that there are common underlying themes. It is the main purpose of this last chapter to define the structural stage properties which are common to all the approaches.

At stage I, or the preoperational stage, Sheppard defines the underlying structure, by implication, as the absence of a groupoid. Halford, in Chapter 6, defines it as a binary relation or a functional relation, the latter term being in line with Piaget and coauthors (1968). We can say that stage I, or preoperational structures, therefore have a maximum complexity as defined by mappings of the form:

$$a \rightarrow b$$

That is, stage I structures cannot be more complex than ordered pairs. This is consistent with Sheppard's view, because a set of ordered pairs is the only possible level of structure which is less complex than a groupoid, a set with a single binary operation.

At stage II, or the concrete operational stage, Sheppard and Halford are in basic agreement about the nature of the underlying structure. Sheppard calls it a groupoid, a set with a single binary operation, which is a particular case of Halford's level 2 structure, which is any structure which can be mapped in the form:

$$a, b \rightarrow c$$

This mapping corresponds to the form of a binary operation, which is the defining property of a groupoid. Thus there is no basic conceptual difference between Halford and Sheppard at this point. Each is merely stating the theory in a way which is most appropriate to his research aims.

Sheppard is primarily concerned with using groupoid structures to bring about the transition from one stage to another, specifically in the areas of conservation and class inclusion. In the first case the groupoid used is Piaget's grouping VIII, whereas in the latter case it is a structure defined by Halford (1970a). In both cases Sheppard is able to show that mastery of the groupoid structure is associated with successful acquisition of the appropriate Piagetian concept. The acquistion was of a kind which was consistent with the idea of assimilation to a self-regulating internal system, as evidenced by his finding that improvement continues after training has ceased.

Sheppard in Chapter 3 also reports a very extensive investigation of young children's ability to learn the structure of the three-group. At this point the distinction between his notion of a groupoid and Piaget's approach using the concept of a grouping can be highlighted. On the one hand, Piaget argues that a child becomes concrete operational because he acquires a specific set of structures—the eight groupings (groupement) (Piaget, 1957). Sheppard, on the other hand, argues that the concrete operational stage corresponds to the ability to learn any structure in a given class—the class of groupoids, which includes the group structure. Piaget, on the other hand, would argue that the group would be beyond the capability of the concrete operational child. Sheppard's data clearly establish that his own point of view is correct in this respect. Furthermore, Sheppard has been able to show that acquisition of a simple group is closely associated with successful performance on a number of traditional concrete operational tasks.

Halford's work on concrete operations emphasizes the acquisition of a system of symbolic processes. The system can be represented by sets of ordered pairs mapped into single elements. He is primarily concerned with doing three things. His first aim is to spell out the properties which are characteristic of a system at this level but are absent in lower-level organizations such as binary relations or ordered pairs. These properties are: generality across tasks with the same form but different content, ability to draw inferences, recognition of invariance, and integration of the elements of a situation into a unified system.

Halford's second aim in Chapter 6 is to show how the concept of a system is relevant to the concept of conservation. He postulates a system for organizing quantities and the relations between them, so that an ambiguous quantity, such as one resulting from a transformation which changes the dimensions of the material, can be interpreted in a way which is consistent with the system as a whole.

Halford's third aim is to develop learning set tasks (in the sense used by Halford, 1975b) as a means of investigating the acquisition of systems. Learning sets are particularly suitable because they constitute a kind of learning which is independent of specific task elements. Learning set tasks have been devised which allow the complexity of the system to be varied while holding the procedure and the number of items to be learned (elements) constant. It was found that level I systems, corresponding to the ordered pairs or stage I structures discussed above, can be mastered by four-year-old children. Level 2 systems, corresponding to the stage II mappings discussed above, were mastered by children of five years and older. Level 3 systems, corresponding to the stage III structures to be discussed below, were first mastered by eleven-year-old children. These findings would indicate that children are potentially concrete operational at the age of five, and potentially formal operational at the age of eleven as these stages are defined in this book.

Considerable integration can be seen here in the way concrete operational tasks are defined. Conservation, inclusion, acquisition of horizontality, learning a simple group structure, and the acquisition of certain learning sets all have in common a particular level of structural complexity. The methods of study vary widely, and thereby give confidence that the correspondence between age and ability to master a structure of a given level of complexity is not an artifact of one particular method.

Probably the most serious challenge to the view that cognitive development depends on the development of structures comes from those theorists who believe that it depends on the acquisition of specific linguistic processes. The literature on this question which is most directly relevant to the concerns of this book was reviewed by Keats and Keats in Chapter 4. At the empirical level, the problem has been dealt with in this book in three ways.

Halford distinguishes in Chapter 6 between structures or systems, which consist of relationships (expressed as mappings) between elements, and elements themselves. The structure or system is the same irrespective of the elements which happen to comprise it. It follows, of course, that a structure cannot be changed to a higher-level structure by changing the elements, as would be proposed by (say) Bruner (1964) or Bruner, Olver, and Greenfield (1966). That is, a change from non-linguistic to linguistic elements may influence performance in some ways, but it cannot of itself produce a higher-level system.

Collis, in Chapters 7 and 8, develops a distinction between an element dimension and a structure dimension within mathematical tasks. He shows that children can operate with elements which are in a sense formal without having formal operational structure. In this respect, Halford's and Collis' work are entirely consistent.

Keats and Keats' empirical work, summarized in Chapter 5, adds to the weight of evidence favouring the independence of cognitive and language development by showing that concrete operational concepts are not encoded in a way which is specific to a particular language. Using bilingual children, they show that training in one language carries over to another language, which shows that the concept is either encoded in a non-linguistic form, or is encoded in a way which is not specific to the language in which it was taught.

Stage III, the formal operational stage, is treated by Halford in Chapter 6, by Collis in Chapters 7 and 8, by Jurd in Chapters 9 and 10, and by Seggie in Chapters 11 and 12. Here the variety of materials and techniques is very wide and the theoretical formulations are in all cases quite complicated. Nevertheless, there are common underlying themes.

Halford defines level 3 systems in Chapter 6 as mappings of the form:

$$a, b, c \rightarrow d$$

The examples he uses are compositions of two level 2 systems, just as the level 2 systems are compositions of level 1 systems. The level 3 structure contains no more elements than the level 2 structure used in the same experiment; nor are the elements different in kind. The level 3 structure is distinguished by the greater complexity of relationships between the elements.

Collis defines formal operational thinking in school mathematics as a composition of two binary operations. There are formal operational tasks which require two binary operations to be coordinated simultaneously into a single move. He gives an example in Table 7.2 of an item which requires level 3 structure but with elements which might well appear in a stage II task: $7 - 4 = \Delta - 7$, find Δ. At the risk of grossly oversimplifying, this performance might be thought of as requiring the child to arrive at an expression equivalent to: $\Delta = 7 - 4 + 7$. This means that, whatever specific form his reasoning may take, the child must find a statement which contains two operations and preserves the truth of the original expression. Thus the situation is one where the invariant is not an operation, but a set of operations, and it has this point of contact with the level 3 tasks used by Halford in Chapter 6. Collis also uses tasks in which the subject is specifically required to relate one binary operation to another: in Chapter 7 he reports a training study in which the ability to recognize the relation between the binary operations of addition and subtraction was found to be characteristic of formal operational reasoning.

Collis notes that, although each of the arithmetical operations is closed for the set of numbers on which it is defined, children differ in the extent to which they can accept lack of closure at this level, and operate on combinations of operations so as to achieve closure at a higher level. This ability to accept lack of closure at the lower level becomes a generalized tendency which applies to other content areas, as Jurd found in history.

Collis sees formal operations in school mathematical tasks as requiring the child to see a system of operations as an invariant, as opposed to seeing the operation itself as an invariant, as would be true of stage II. Acceptance of lack of closure, which Collis sees as a prerequisite to formal operations, would be a concomitant of a level of functioning in which the system of operations was an invariant. Furthermore, Lunzer's (1973) belief that multiple interacting systems are basic to formal operations also requires that a system of operations remains invariant.

One contribution which Collis' work does not share with the other chapters in this book is his distinction between early and late concrete and formal operations in school mathematics. This is entirely consistent with Piaget's stage IIA and IIB, IIIA and IIIB respectively, as Collis points out, but Collis' unique contribution has been to work out systematically what mathematical performances belong to each of these levels. On the other hand, Halford's formulations, at the present stage at least, are incapable of distinguishing between early and late stage II or stage III.

A variation of the closure theme can be seen in Chapters 9 and 10 where Jurd has applied the colligatory concept (Walsh, 1967) to an analysis of historical thinking. For example, a colligatory concept such as the growth of democratic government implies that the person has synthesized a number of complex events or processes into a single idea. She notes the need for acceptance of lack of closure in order to ensure that the generalizations developed are based on a sufficiently extensive set of historical facts. The wider the range of data the subject takes into account, the more general the conceptual system he develops and the more readily new facts can be accommodated.

Jurd also develops a new approach to the analysis of historical thinking, which takes several fictional 'historical' events which are paralleled in three different places. The subject is then required to relate events both within and across places. In this way the subject's ability to relate events to one another in a sufficiently complex manner to be called formal operational (compare multiple interacting systems) can be tested, independently of any knowledge the subject might have of the specific events themselves.

Seggie, in Chapters 11 and 12, has attempted an integration of two fields of work which formerly were so far apart that few people would have thought an integration would be possible. He has applied the concept of psycho-logic in a quasi-Piagetian sense to the kind of concept formation studied by Bruner, Goodnow, and Austin (1956) or Haygood and Bourne (1965). He has shown how subjects could attain concepts by constructing models of contingencies between events in the task. For instance, relevant dimensions may be distinguished from irrelevant dimensions by constructing a model of the constraints between the attributes of the dimension and the classification criterion. Consider three dimensions a, b, and c such that a and $\bar{a}$ are the two values of one relevant dimension, b and $\bar{b}$ are the two values of another relevant dimension, while c and $\bar{c}$ are values of an irrelevant dimension. Now consider a disjunctive concept such that a or b is x, while not-a ($\bar{a}$) and not-b ($\bar{b}$) are not-x ($\bar{x}$); that is a, $b \rightarrow x$, a, $\bar{b} \rightarrow x$, $\bar{a}$, $b \rightarrow x$, and $\bar{a}$, $\bar{b} \rightarrow \bar{x}$. We find that the contingencies between the dimensions a, b, c and the criterion x are as follows:

$$
\begin{array}{cccc}
a \cdot x & a \cdot \bar{x} & \bar{a} \cdot x & \bar{a} \cdot \bar{x} \\
1 & 0 & 1 & 1
\end{array} \quad (a \text{ relevant})
$$

$$b \cdot x \quad b \cdot \bar{x} \quad \bar{b} \cdot x \quad \bar{b} \cdot \bar{x}$$
$$1 \qquad 0 \qquad 1 \qquad 1 \qquad (b \text{ relevant})$$

$$c \cdot x \quad c \cdot \bar{x} \quad \bar{c} \cdot x \quad \bar{c} \cdot \bar{x}$$
$$1 \qquad 1 \qquad 1 \qquad 1 \qquad (c \text{ irrelevant})$$

where $1 = $ 'it does occur' and $0 = $ 'it does not occur'.

These two contingencies are equivalent to the truth tables for a implies x and b implies x ($a \supset x$ and $b \supset x$) respectively. Seggie finds that the subjects interpret the contingencies as equivalences; that is a implies x and x implies a ($a \propto x$), and $b \propto x$, rather than as the implications which they should be. This is interesting, but it is probably even more important in the present context that Seggie has demonstrated that concept attainment can be analysed in these terms. His analysis has further consequences, of which we will give one illustration here.

A central problem in concept attainment research has been to explain why the biconditional concept $(a \cdot b) \vee (\bar{a} \cdot \bar{b})$ is more difficult to learn than other two-dimensional concepts such as disjunction, conjunction, or the conditional (implication). A clear explanation falls right out of Seggie's (1971) analysis. Let us consider the conditional concept $a \cdot b \rightarrow x$ and $\bar{a}\bar{b} \rightarrow x$ (that is x is either a and b or not-a and not-b). We now set up the tables for the contingencies between a and x and b and x as before:

$$a \cdot x \quad a \cdot \bar{x} \quad \bar{a} \cdot x \quad \bar{a} \cdot \bar{x}$$
$$1 \qquad 1 \qquad 1 \qquad 1$$

$$b \cdot x \quad b \cdot \bar{x} \quad \bar{b} \cdot x \quad \bar{b} \cdot \bar{x}$$
$$1 \qquad 1 \qquad 1 \qquad 1$$

We find that although a and b are both relevant dimensions, there is no association between them and the criterion. In fact, the contingencies we obtain between a and x, and between b and x, are the same as those we would obtain for an irrelevant dimension. The implication is that relevant dimensions cannot be distinguished from irrelevant dimensions, if taken one at a time. Relevant dimensions can be distinguished only if we take both relevant dimensions together, thus:

$$a \cdot b \cdot x \quad a \cdot \bar{b} \cdot x \quad \bar{a} \cdot b \cdot x \quad \bar{a} \cdot \bar{b} \cdot x \quad a \cdot b \cdot \bar{x} \quad a \cdot \bar{b} \cdot \bar{x} \quad \bar{a} \cdot b \cdot \bar{x} \quad \bar{a} \cdot \bar{b} \cdot \bar{x}$$
$$1 \qquad 0 \qquad 0 \qquad 1 \qquad 0 \qquad 1 \qquad 1 \qquad 0$$

The biconditional and the exclusive disjunctive, out of all the possible two-dimensional concepts, require that two dimensions be found to be relevant simultaneously. In Seggie's terms, this is a considerably more difficult job than discovering the relevance of one dimension at a time. Thus if subjects do attain concepts in the way Seggie suggests, it becomes very clear why the biconditional and exclusive disjunctive are more difficult than the conjunctive, etc.

The notions expressed immediately above provide a fine example of acceptance of lack of closure and multiple interacting systems. The subject must suspend judgment on the relevance of dimensions a or b separately (equivalent to accepting lack of closure) until he has information about the two dimensions acting jointly. This is tantamount to switching from individual systems to multiple interacting systems. An untested prediction arising from this would be that whereas concrete operational children can attain all other two-dimensional concepts, only formal operational subjects should be capable of attaining the biconditional and exclusive disjunctive concepts.

Another basis for this prediction would be that the contingency shown above for determining the joint relevance of two dimensions in the biconditional concept (for example) consists of a set of mappings of the form: $a \cdot b \cdot x \to 1$, $a \cdot \bar{b} \cdot x \to 0$, etc. Each contingency $a \cdot x$ with the truth values 1 or 0 and $b \cdot x$ with 1 or 0 itself constitutes a binary operation. (The correspondence between a truth table with two variables and a binary operation was established in Chapter 1.) The contingency required for determining the relevance of the two variables in the biconditional concept therefore consists of a composition of binary operations, and would therefore be a stage III task in terms of the common strand of theory which underlies this work.

An implication of the closure concept would be that performance on any task requires the child to take into account (i.e. to 'close') a certain number of elements of the problem before making any decision. Furthermore, the level of the problem is defined by the number of elements which need to be closed in order to make a particular decision. A simple example may help: in a task which involves only one operation, say the operation of addition, then the interpretation of a set of elements such as the following requires only two elements to be taken into account at a time: 3, 4, 2, 5 → Δ. We can interpret this sequence by first adding 3 and 4, yielding 7. Then we add 7 and 2, and then add the result, 9, to 5, yielding 14. Although there are four elements to be interpreted, it is only a level 2 problem because the elements can be interpreted, or closed, in pairs. In contrast, a problem which involves two or more operations requires one more element, corresponding to the operation itself, to be taken into account; for example $3 + 4 \to 7$ but $3 \times 4 \to 12$. Here three elements must be taken into account in making each decision. This is because this problem has reference to a larger system, in which the elements are defined in triples and in which the operation itself is a variable.

Acceptance of lack of closure, then, is broadly consistent with the idea of ability to process adequate information. Halford shows how processing of only one element leads to error on a level 2 task, and processing only two elements leads to error on a level 3 task. Ultimately, then, the levels of thinking which a child can attain are probably limited by information processing capacity. Some support for this was found by Collis in work being done currently (personal communication). One of the most challenging tasks for the future therefore might be to spell out this relationship between stages of development and information processing capacity. Halford has drawn attention to a correspondence between stages and the traditional digit-span measure, such that levels 1, 2, 3 require spans of 2, 4, 6 respectively. While some reasons for this correspondence have been suggested, it is for the future to determine whether or not it is merely a coincidence.

INFORMATION PROCESSING, STAGES, AND LEARNING

The purpose of this section is to develop briefly one of the consequences of the kind of stage notion which has been developed in this book. A stage results, not from the possession of a specific structure or set of structures but from possession of sufficient information processing capacity to organize symbolic systems at a particular level of complexity. This would mean that information processing capacity, in some form, would be a necessary but not sufficient condition for successful performance at a given level. Once sufficient information processing capacity was attained, performance would be a function of experience and task variables—in a word, of learning. We can therefore distinguish two regions in the development of any cognitive ability: an information processing capacity-limited region and a learning-limited region. These are shown in Figure 13.1.

Most concrete operational tasks are known to develop at different rates. Conservation of number develops before mass conservation, which in turn develops before weight, etc. The logic of the tasks is much the same, but the procedural details vary. We may therefore provisionally attribute the different rates of development to different rates of learning. On the other hand, we would predict that under no circumstances would any of these performances develop before information processing capacity reached the minimum required level. Halford suggests this would be at the age of five for average subjects.

This would mean that correlations between these tasks would be difficult to interpret. If data were sampled in the learning-limited region (i.e. from the ages of five to ten for concrete operational tasks), the size of the correlations would depend on task variables, since these would influence the learning rate. We can predict that, within this region, the correlations would be entirely independent of stage-related ability factors, and would be a function of the

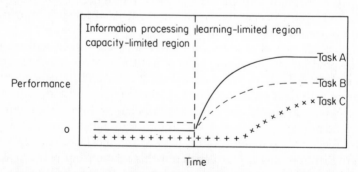

FIGURE 13.1 Relationships between time and performance in three cognitive development tasks

degree to which the materials and procedures used were similar across the different tasks.

If, on the other hand, we sampled data in the information processing capacity-limited region, all tasks would be failed and correlations would become indeterminate. In effect 'stage' is defined in the Piagetian tradition as a set of tasks on which all subjects *fail* during a given period of development. Thus the normal procedure of obtaining correlations among tasks chosen so that some subjects fail while others pass does not apply.

If, on the other hand, we sampled data from both the information processing capacity-limited region and the learning-limited region (as, for instance, if we chose children ranging from two to ten years), the size of the correlation would depend on the relative proportions of data from the two regions.

From this model it is clear that simple correlations are likely to be of little use in the study of stages. The correlation could be raised or lowered by manipulating task similarity, or by taking greater or smaller proportions of subjects from within one region or the other, with no significance for the stage concept. Most correlational studies use subjects from five to eight years of age, and report low positive correlations (e.g. Goldschmidt, 1967; Tuddenham, 1970). So far no one appears to have systematically investigated the degree of correlation as a function of task similarity.

The crucial test of this formulation would not come from correlational studies at all, but from determining whether it is possible to teach concepts to children in the information processing capacity-limited region. The problem is to determine the boundaries of this region precisely. One possibility is that the proportion of children who succeed at any age would not exceed the proportion who have the memory span which Halford suggests in Chapter 6 to be a prerequisite for that performance. For instance, the proportion of four year olds who would succeed on concrete operational tasks should not exceed the proportion who have a memory span of four items.

At the formal operational stage, too, it has been found that successful performance depends very much on task variables and previous experience of the participant, as Seggie points out in Chapter 11 with respect to his own work on understanding of the concept of correlation and Lunzer, Harrison, and Davey's (1972) investigation of the four-card problem. Thus formal operations evidently should not be thought of as 'structures' which develop automatically, as Piaget implies, but rather as a capacity to form cognitive systems with a certain level of complexity. Piaget's contention that formal operations would be independent of problem content should therefore be no more true than it is of concrete operations.

TOWARDS A QUANTIFICATION OF STAGE DEVELOPMENT

One of the characteristics used here to define concrete and formal operational stages has been that of the ability of the person to learn a task with a particular type of structure. It has been suggested further that one of the limitations that prevents a person at an earlier stage from learning a task with a structure more complex than those which can be learned at that stage is a lack of information processing capacity. This information processing capacity may be simply a matter of the amount of information that can be stored in immediate memory as suggested by McLaughlin (1963) and Halford (1968), and also by Jenson (1974) in his level I intelligence, or it may be a more complex ability as proposed by Carroll (1963, 1973). These approaches all assume a more basic ability, increasing steadily with age, which must reach a certain level before tasks of a particular structural complexity can be learned.

There is no generally accepted quantitative model for the development of ability. In fact most of the standardized deviation measures currently used are such as to discourage the study of the development of ability, since they fix the mean and standard deviation of scores at each age level.

A simple non-linear representation of development will be presented which distinguishes between present and ultimate ability level and introduces a separate rate of growth parameter. The proposed development formula relates A_{ij}, the ability of child i at time t_j, to his ultimate ability M_i and a growth parameter k_i such that:

$$A_{ij} = \frac{M_i t_j}{t_j + k_i} \tag{1}$$

The formula assumes that time is measured from the latest time at which ability is zero. Whether that time is at conception or birth, or somewhere in between, or even some time after birth could be investigated by methods described below. Because $t_j/(t_j + k_i) = \frac{1}{2}$ when $t_j = k_i$, it is obvious that k_i indicates the time at which development will reach (or has reached) half of the maximum value, M_i. As time increases the maximum value M_i will be approached but

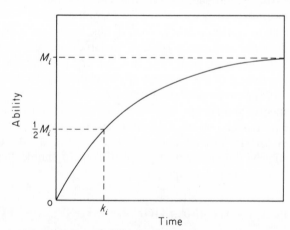

FIGURE 13.2 Graphical relationship between ability and time

never reached. In Figure 13.2 ability develops rapidly at first and then slowly as the maximum is approached. As noted in the Appendix, it is possible to define a group curve of the same form by taking the harmonic mean of the abilities of persons at each of the age levels and plotting these means against age.

To account for the appearance of (say) concrete operational thinking, it must be assumed that a minimum ability A_0 is required for even the *possibility* of a performance satisfying the criteria for (say) concrete operational thinking. If this ability is attained at the age t_0 by a typical child, then at some time after this age the typical child will begin to satisfy the criteria for concrete operational thinking on at least some tasks. Thus if B_{ij} is a measure of performance on a particular task by child i at time j, then

$$B_{ij} = \frac{N_i(t_j - t_{io})}{t_j - t_{i_0} + l_i}, \text{ for } t_j > t_{i0}$$

$= 0$, otherwise where N_i is the maximum performance on such tasks and l_i is a growth parameter.

This proposal is very similar to that made by Carroll (1963), except that he proposed that development is linear. However, the ratio (mean B/mean A) as defined by Carroll is perspective on time, as would be the ratio of the harmonic means in the present model; with minor restrictions and data quoted by him (Carroll, 1973) support this deduction. Carroll used his formulation to distinguish between achievement in school tasks and required ability.

Figure 13.3 indicates that successful performance on a task requiring a minimum ability level A_0 is possible after time t_0 for the average child, but will be possible at an earlier age, $t_{io} < t_0$ for a child of superior ability. Thus the model proposed here accounts for both steady development in ability and stage-wise development in certain kinds of task. The tasks referred to in

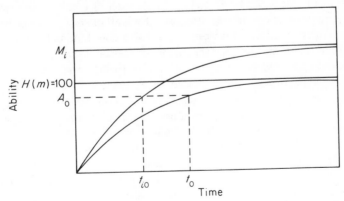

FIGURE 13.3 Age of achieving ability A_0 for average person and person (i)

420

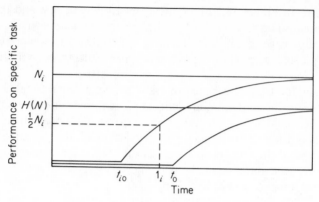

FIGURE 13.4 Performance on specific task of person (i) and average person

Piaget's theory as concrete and formal operational become possible for the child after he has developed the necessary ability to acquire certain structures. Obviously a higher minimum ability will be required for formal operational structures than for concrete.

The concept of horizontal decalage used by Piaget to describe the fact that success on one concrete operational task does not necessarily imply success on another is depicted in the present model by allocating to these tasks different A_0 values corresponding to t_0 values within the range of six to ten years, as shown in Figure 13.1. Concrete operational tasks of the kind invented by Piaget would typically have very sharply rising developmental curves, that is $l_i - t_{i0}$ would be very small. However, this would not be true for the tasks defined by Collis (Chapter 7) as concrete generalization because such tasks usually require more complicated sequences of concrete operations. Similarly, some of the tasks invented by Piaget to examine formal operational thinking also require not only more sophisticated concepts such as combinatorial concepts but also sequences of operations, any one of which may or may not be formal in nature. An error at any stage of the sequence could indicate, wrongly, that the child or adult has not reached the formal operational level.

The model proposed here covers, in a more formal way, ideas which have not always been expressed very precisely by Piaget and by other writers in this area. The concept of stage in these terms is *not* inconsistent with the notion of a steady increase in information processing capacity; in fact it is suggested here that the stage concepts can be derived by postulating such a capacity. The present formulation would predict problems in attempting to apply standard psychometric procedures to items based on the present stage theory. These problems seem to have been met but not overcome by those working in this way. A more promising approach would appear to be to try to obtain measures of ability against which performance on (say) concrete operational tasks can be assessed. As noted in the Appendix, a development of the Rasch (1960) approach could help here.

SOME FURTHER PROBLEMS

The present volume has investigated ways in which a structural approach can be applied to cognitive development in various areas. Some structures such as groupoids are advocated over others as being more scientifically useful. Two kinds of problem suggest themselves in the approach. First, there are the problems of discovering and investigating other kinds of structures, e.g. those arising from operators in differential geometry. The questions of which structures will prove most useful and how many will be required for a comprehensive treatment of cognitive development cannot be answered yet.

Finally, there is the deeper question of the possible neurological basis for the structures and the stages which they define. Too little is known yet about the functioning of the cortex to know whether there are neurological analogies of the structures or whether limitations in cognitive development are simply those of the amount of information that can be processed at any one time. Collaboration with physiologists will be necessary to investigate this question.

APPENDIX

A PROPOSED FORM FOR A DEVELOPMENTAL FUNCTION

J. A. Keats

The purpose of this appendix is to present some of the mathematical properties of the form of the curve representing the development of ability with time proposed in Chapter 13. The notes will be of interest to readers who wish to apply this developmental function to data or who wish to have a more precise statement of the developmental processes for theoretical purposes.

THE MEAN DEVELOPMENTAL CURVE

The proposed developmental curve relating ability (A_{ij}) of person i at time t_j to time is:

$$A_{ij} = \frac{M_i t_j}{t_j + k_i} \tag{1}$$

where M_i represents the maximum ability for person i and k_i represents the growth rate.

It is common practice (see, for example, Bayley, 1955) to represent mean developmental curves by simply taking the arithmetic average of ability values for a representative sample of subjects at each of a number of age levels. With the above formula this practice would result in an average curve which would very often be of a different mathematical form from that of equation (1). However, if the *harmonic* mean, $H(A_{ij})$, of A_{ij} is taken to define the average curve, then the form of equation (1) is preserved since

$$H(A_{ij}) = \frac{H(M_i)t_j}{t_j + E}$$

where $H(M_i)$ is the harmonic mean of the individual maximum values and E is a growth parameter of the average curve. This result arises from rewriting equation (1) in the form

$$\frac{t_j}{A_{ij}} = \frac{t_j}{M_i} + \frac{k_i}{M_i}$$

RELATIONSHIP OF A_{ij} TO TRADITIONAL MEASURES

The measures of ability most usually reported have been in one of the following forms: mental age, ratio IQ, or standardized deviation score (or IQ). None of these indices can be used to study development because they fix the average value for each age level. It is clear that A_{ij} is a measure of *ability* as yet unrelated to observed performance; it is not a *raw* score. It is tempting to use equation (1) to define mental age (t_e) by finding the value of t_j for which $H(A_{ij})$ equals the A_{ij} for the particular person at a given time. With this approach

$$t_e = \frac{A_{ij}t_j}{H(M_i) - A_{ij}}$$

but this leads to a ratio IQ = $100 \times t_e/t_j$ which could be infinite and later negative for subjects whose M_i value is greater than $H(M_i)$. A second approach on similar lines leads to

$$t_e = \frac{A_{ij}E}{M_i - A_{ij}}$$

and this expression leads to a ratio IQ = $100 \times E/k_i$ which stresses the *rate* of development aspect of the ratio IQ but is independent of the maximum value M_i. Finally, one can find a transformation which would transform $H(A_{ij})$ into an expression which would be linear in time (t) for persons whose $A_{ij} = H(A_{ij})$ for all t_j. This approach leads to

$$t_e = \frac{t_j + E}{H(M_i)} A_{ij}$$

If $H(M_i)$ is set at 100, as it may be without loss of generality, then

$$\text{Ratio IQ} = \frac{M_i(t_j + E)}{t_j + k_i}$$

Thus, in general, this expression for IQ converges to M_i as t_j becomes large, but equals M_i only if $k_i = E$, i.e. for a person with a rate of development equal to that of the (harmonic) average curve. These are properties that an IQ value has been expected to have, but they do not appear to have been specified precisely before.

RELATIONSHIP TO RASCH'S THEORY

Rasch (1960) has developed a theoretical approach which leads to measurement of ability in a strict sense, from the basic equation

$$P_{ij} = \frac{A_i}{A_i + D_j}$$

in which p_{ij} is the probability of a correct response on an item of difficulty D_j for a person of ability A_i. This formulation can be extended to include the present developmental approach by noting that A_i must be considered at a particular time t_m, in which case

$$P_{ijm} = \frac{A_{im}}{A_{im} + D_j} = \frac{M_i t_m}{(M_i + D_j)t_m + D_j k_i}$$

At least two values of A_{im} would be needed to estimate M_i and k_i for a particular person. Unfortunately, measures of ability obtained in this way are not available from longitudinal studies. In principle it would be possible to obtain estimates for M_i and k_i and to test the model if a large number of subjects were tested at two separate times, t_1 and t_2, in the same way as the simpler Rasch model is currently applied. This does not seem to have been done as yet.

TESTING THE MODEL

It is possible to obtain a test of the above assumptions using data collected in longitudinal studies. Most of these studies report either ratio IQ's or mental ages, both of which can be converted to ability scores. Skodak and Skeels (1947) provide data for nineteen subjects tested at the ages of 26, 51, 84, and 162 months. If E is taken as approximately 80 months it is possible to convert the IQ values they provide to ability estimates and to apply the cross-ratio test to these estimates. This test is applicable because equation (1) implies that ability is projectively related to time, so that the cross-ratios of four corresponding values of A and t must be equal where the cross-ratio is defined as

$$\frac{(A_1 - A_2)(A_3 - A_4)}{(A_2 - A_3)(A_4 - A_1)} = \frac{(t_1 - t_2)(t_3 - t_4)}{(t_2 - t_3)(t_4 - t_1)}$$

For sixteen of the nineteen subjects the average cross-ratio is -0.441 compared with -0.437 for the numbers 26, 51, 84, and 162. The remaining three subjects give unstable values because of irregular growth rates. If ability is assumed to develop from birth, then the cross-ratio (-0.216) of the numbers 0, 26, 84, and 162 should equal the average of the cross-ratios of ability scores at these ages. On the other hand, if ability were assumed to develop from conception, the four numbers would be 0, 35, 93, and 171, with a cross-ratio of -0.275. The same data yield a value of -0.226 which is significantly greater than -0.275 with a chi-square test, but not significantly different from -0.216.

The ability estimates at each of the four age levels can be used to estimate M_i and k_i for each of the subjects. The simplest way to estimate these parameters is to note that by rearranging equation (1) it may be found that $t_j/A_{ij} =$

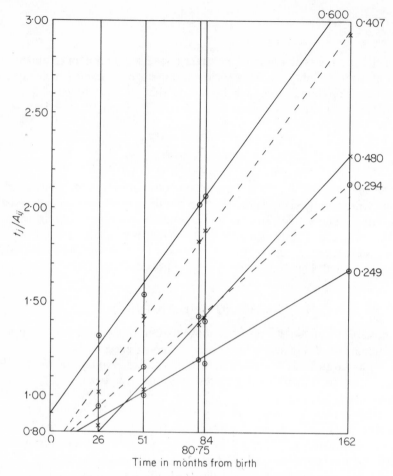

FIGURE A.1 Graphical estimates of M_i and K_i

$t_j/M_i + k_i/M_i$, i.e. that t_j/A_{ij} is linearly related to t_j with slope $1/M_i$ and intercept k_i/M_i. If the four values of t_j/A_{ij} for a particular subject are very nearly linear, then the corresponding estimates of M_i and k_i can be accepted with some confidence. Figure A.1 presents graphs for five subjects from the data of Skodak and Skeels (1947). In all cases the graph of t_j/A_{ij} is sufficiently close to linearity to yield stable estimates of M_i and k_i. The five cases were chosen because they provide a wide range of values for M_i and k_i. The developmental curves for each of these subjects are presented in Figure A.2. In cases where the k_i value departs considerably from the value of 80 months, the IQ at any of the ages considered would be misleading as an index of ultimate ability.

RELATIONSHIP OF B_{ij} TO ABILITY MEASURES

Performance B_{ij} at time t_j, on a particular task requiring a minimum ability A_0 which is reached at time t_{i_0} by individual i, was written in Chapter 13 as

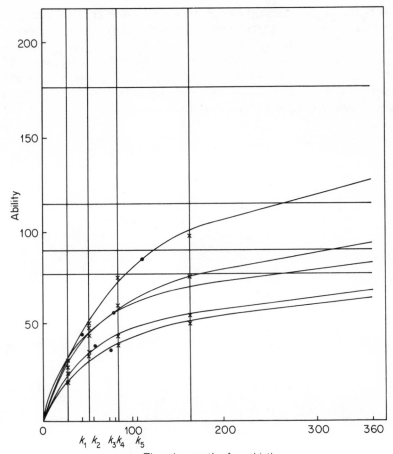

FIGURE A.2 Individual development curves

$$B_{ij} = \frac{N_i(t_j - t_{io})}{t_j - t_{io} + l_i}, \text{if } t_j > t_{io}$$

$$= 0, \text{otherwise}$$

where N_i is maximum performance and l_i is a growth parameter for individual i.

If $M_i > A_{ij} > A_0$ for individual i,

$$B_{ij} = \frac{N_i M_i k_i (A_{ij} - A_0)}{A_{ij}[M_i(k_i - l_i) + l_i A_0] + M_i[l_i M_i - A_0(k_i + l_i)]}$$

In the special case when $l_i = k_i + t_{i0}$

$$B_{ij} = \frac{N_i(A_{ij} - A_o)}{M_i - A_o}$$

that is B_{ij} and A_{ij} are linearly related when the growth curve of performance on the task is the same as that of ability, but displaced by a constant amount t_{i_0}.

Thus the development of performance on a task requiring a minimum ability A_0 before success is possible can be related to the development of the ability or information processing capacity itself. In this way it is possible to link performance on intellectual tasks which exhibit development in stages to the continuous development of an underlying ability.

REFERENCES

Adelson, J. (1971). The Political imagination of the young adolescent. *Daedalus*, **100** (4), 1013–1050.

Alberts, E., and Ehrenfreund, D. (1951). Transposition in children as a function of age. *Journal of Experimental Psychology*, **41**, 30–38.

Allendoerfer, C. B. (1965). The second revolution in mathematics. *The Mathematics Teacher*, **58**, 690–695.

Angyal, A. (1941). *Foundations of a Science of Personality*, Harvard University Press, Cambridge, Massachusetts.

Annett, M. (1959). The classification of instances of four common class concepts by children and adults. *British Journal of Educational Psychology*, **29**, 223–236.

Apostel, L. (1963). Structure et genèse. In L. Apostel, J. B. Grize, S. Papert, and J. Piaget, La filiation des structures, *Etudes d'épistémologie génétique*, Vol. XV. Presses Universitaires de France, Paris.

Australian Council for Educational Research (1968). *Commonwealth Secondary Scholarships Examination, Quantitative Thinking*, ACER, Melbourne. 168ff.

Ausubel, D. P. (1963). *The Psychology of Meaningful Verbal Learning*, Grune and Stratton, New York.

Baggaley, A. R. (1955). Concept formation and its relation to cognitive variables. *Journal of General Psychology*, **52**, 297–306.

Bain, B. (1974). Bilingualism and congnition: towards a general theory. In S. Cary (Ed.), *Bilingualism Biculturalism, and Education*, University of Alberta Press, Edmonton.

Baldwin, A. L. (1967). *Theories of Child Development*, Wiley, New York.

Ballard, M. (1971). *New Movements in the Study and Teaching of History*, Cheshire, Melbourne.

Bandura, A. (1969). Social learning theory of identification processes. In D. A. Goslin (Ed.), *Handbook of Socialization Theory and Research*, Rand-McNally, Chicago.

Bandura, A., Grusec, J. E., and Menlove, F. L. (1966). Observational learning as a function of symbolization and incentive set. *Child Development*, **37**, 499–506.

Barbaum, G. (1968). Sociology and contemporary history. *Educational Review*, **120** (3), 191–203.

Barcan, A., Blunden, T., Dwight, A., and Shortus, S. (1974). *A Nation Emerges*, Macmillan, Melbourne.

Barr, M. (1975). *Implied Meaning and Language Acquisition*. Paper read to the Australian National Conference on Cognitive Development, Canberra, February 1975.

Bart, W. M. (1971). A generalization of Piaget's logical-mathematical model for the stage of formal operations. *Journal of Mathematical Psychology*, **8**, 539–553.

Baylor, G. W., and Gascon, J. (1974). An information processing theory of aspects of the development of weight seriation in children. *Cognitive Psychology*, **6**, 1–40.

Baylor, G. W., Gascon, J., Lemoyne, G., and Pothier, N. (1973). An information-processing model of some seriation tasks. *Canadian Psychologist*, **14**, 167–196.

430

Beard, R. M. (1969). *An Outline of Piaget's Developmental Psychology*, Routledge and Kegan Paul, London.

Bearison, D. J. (1969). Role of measurement operations in the acquisition of conservation. *Developmental Psychology*, **1**, 654–660.

Beilin, H. (1965). Learning and operational convergence in logical thought development. *Journal of Experimental Child Psychology*, **2**, 317–339.

Beilin, H. (1969). Stimulus and cognitive transformation in conservation. In D. Elkind, and J. H. Flavell (Eds.), *Studies in Cognitive Development. Essays in Honor of Jean Piaget*, Oxford University Press, New York.

Beilin, H. (1971a). Developmental stages and developmental processes. In D. R. Green, M. P. Ford., and G. B. Flamer (Eds.), *Measurement and Piaget*, McGraw-Hill, New York.

Beilin, H. (1971b). The training and acquisition of logical operations. In M. F. Rosskopf, L. P. Steffe, and S. Taback (Eds.), *Piagetian Cognitive-Developmental Research and Mathematical Education*, National Council of Teachers of Mathematics, Washington.

Bellugi, U., and Brown, R. (Eds.) (1964). The acquisition of language. *Monographs for the Society of Research in Child Development*, **29**(1).

Belmont, J. M., and Butterfield, E. C. (1969). The relation of short-term memory to development and intelligence. In H. Reese (Ed.), *Advances in Child Development and Behaviour*, Academic Press, New York.

Berlyne, D. E. (1965). *Structure and Direction in Thinking*, Wiley, New York.

Berlyne, D. E. (1975). Behaviourism? Cognitive theory? Humanistic psychology—to Hull with them all. *Canadian Psychological Review*, **1**, 69–80.

Bernstein, B. (1958). Some sociological determinants of perception: an enquiry into sub-cultural differences. *British Journal of Sociology*, **9**, 159–174.

Bernstein, B. (1959). Public language: some sociological implications of a linguistic form. *British Journal of Sociology*, **10**, 311–326.

Bernstein, B. (1960). Language and social class. *British Journal of Society*, **11**, 271–276.

Bernstein, B. (1965). A socio-linguistic approach to social learning. In J. Gould (Ed.), *Penguin's Survey of the Social Sciences*, Cox and Wyman, London.

Bernstein, B. (1971). Language and roles. In R. Huxley and E. Ingram (Eds.), *Language Acquisition: Models and Methods*, Academic Press, London.

Bernstein, B. (1973). *Class, Codes and Control*, Vol. 1. Paladin, St. Albans, Herts.

Berzonsky, M. (1971). Interdependence of Inhelder and Piaget's model of logical thinking. *Developmental Psychology*, **4**, 469–476.

Beth, E. W., and Piaget, J. (1966). *Mathematical Epistemology and Psychology*, Reidel, Dordrecht.

Biggs, J. B. (1962). *Anxiety, Motivation and Primary School Mathematics*, NFER Occasional Publication No. 7.

Biggs, J. B. (1968). *Information and Human Learning*, Cassell, Melbourne. p. 328.

Binet, A., and Simon, T. (1916). *The Development of Intelligence in Children* (E. S. Kite, trans.), Publication of the Training School No. 11, Vineland, N. J. p. 336.

Bitterman, M. E. (1960). Toward a comparative psychology of learning. *American Psychologist*, **15**, 704–712.

Bitterman, M. E., Wodinsky, J., and Candland, D. K. (1958). Some comparative psychology. *American Journal of Psychology*, 1958, **71**, 94–110.

Bloom, L. (1970). *Language Development: Form and Function in Emerging Grammars*, M. I. T. Press, Cambridge, Massachusetts.

Boon, Jean-Paul. (1973). Acceptability, interpretation and knowledge of the world. Remarks on the verb PLANTER (to plant). *Cognition*, **2**, 183–211.

Bourne, L. E. (1966). *Human Conceptual Behaviour*, Allyn & Bacon, Boston.

Bourne, L. E. (1967). Learning and utilization of conceptual rules. In B. Kleinmuntz (Ed.), *Concepts and the Structure of Memory*, Wiley, New York.

Bourne, L. E., and Bunderson, C. V. (1963). Effects of delay of information feedback and length of postfeedback interval on concept identification. *Journal of Experimental Psychology*, **65**, 1–5.

Bourne, L. E., Guy, D. E., Dodd, D. H., and Justesen, D. R. (1965). Concept identification: the effects of varying lengths and informational components of the inter-trial interval. *Journal of Experimental Psychology*, **69**, 624–629.

Bourne, L. E., and O'Banion, K. (1971). Conceptual rule learning and chronological age. *Developmental Psychology*, **5**, 3, 525–534.

Boyle, D. G. (1969). *A Student's Guide to Piaget*, Pergamon Press, London.

Brainerd, C. J. (1972). *Structures of Thought in Middle-Childhood: Recent Research on Piaget's Concrete-Operational Groupements*. Paper presented at the Third Annual Meeting on Structural Learning, Philadelphia.

Brainerd, C. J., and Allen, T. W. (1971). Experimental inductions of the conservation of 'first-order' quantitative invariants. *Psychological Bulletin*, **75**, 128–144.

Brenner, S. O., and Hjelmquist, E. (1974). Psycholinguistics: foundations and research approaches II, from Chomsky (1965) to Chomsky (1971). *Göteborg Psychological Reports*, **4**, 18.

Broadbent, D. E. (1970). In defence of empirical psychology. *Bulletin of the British Psychological Society*, **23**, 87–96.

Bronckart, J. P. (1973). The regulating role of speech: a cognitivist approach. *Human Development*, **16**, 417–439.

Brown, Ann L., and Scott, Marcia S. (1972). Transfer between the oddity and relative size concepts: reversal and extradimensional shifts. *Journal of Experimental Child Psychology*, **13**, 350–367.

Brown, R. W. (1973). *A First Language: The Early Stages*, Harvard University Press, Cambridge, Massachusetts.

Brown, R. W., and Lenneberg, E. H. (1954). A study in language and cognition. *Journal of Abnormal and Social Psychology*, **49**, 454–462.

Bruner, J. S. (1959). Inhelder and Piaget's *The Growth of Logical Thinking*. 1. A Psychologist's viewpoint. *British Journal of Psychology*, **50**, 363–370.

Bruner, J. S. (1964). The course of cognitive growth. *American Psychologist*, **19**, 1–5.

Bruner, J. S. (1966). On cognitive growth II. In J. S. Bruner, R. R. Olver and P. M. Greenfield (Eds.), *Studies in Cognitive Growth*, Wiley, New York.

Bruner, J. S., Goodnow, J., and Austin, G. A. (1956). *A Study in Thinking*, Wiley, New York.

Bruner, J. S., Olver, R. R., and Greenfield, P. M. (1966). *Studies in Cognitive Growth*. Wiley, New York.

Bruner, J. S., Wallach, M. A., and Gallanter, E. H. (1959). The identification of recurrent regularity. *American Journal of Psychology*, **72**, 200–209.

Bryant, P. E., and Trabasso, T. (1971). Transitive inferences and memory in young children. *Nature*, **232**, 456–458.

Burnham, R. W., and Clark, J. R. (1955). A test of hue memory. *Journal of Applied Psychology*, **39**, 164–172.

Burston, W. H. (1954). *Social Studies and the History Teacher*, Teaching of History Leaflet No. 15, Historical Association.

Burston, W. H., and Thompson, D. (Eds.) (1967). *Studies in the Nature and Teaching of History*, Routledge and Kegan Paul, London.

Byers, J. L. (1963). Strategies and learning set in concept attainment. *Psychological Reports*, **12**, 623–634.

Carr, E. H. (1972). *What is History*, Pelican, London.

Carroll, J. B. (1963). A model of school learning. *Teachers College Record*, **64**, 723–733.

Carroll, J. B. (1973). *Fitting a Model of School Learning to Aptitude and Achievement Data over Grade Levels* (ETS RB. 73–51), Educational Testing Service, Princeton, N. J.

Carroll, J. B., and Casagrande, J. B. (1958). The function of language classifications in behaviour. In E. E. Maccoby, T. M. Newcombe, and E. L. Hartley (Eds.), *Readings in Social Psychology*, 3rd ed. Holt, Rinehart and Winston, New York.

Case, R. (1970). *A New Look at the Limitations of the Process of Human Learning*. Unpublished paper, University of California, Berkeley.

Case, R. (1972a). Validation of a neo-Piagetian mental capacity construct. *Journal of Experimental Child Psychology*, 14, 287–302.

Case, R. (1972b). Learning and development: a neo-Piagetian interpretation. *Human Development*, 15, 339–358.

Case, R. (1975). Gearing the demands of instruction to the developmental capacities of the learner. *Review of Educational Research*, 45, 59–87.

Case, D., and Collinson, J. M. (1962). The development of formal thinking and verbal comprehension. *British Journal of Educational Psychology*, 32, 103–112.

Chomsky, N. (1957). *Syntactic Structures*, Morton, The Hague.

Chomsky, N. (1965). *Aspects of the Theory of Syntax*. M.I.T. Press, Cambridge, Massachusetts.

Chomsky, N. (1968). *Language and Mind*, Harcourt, Brace and World, New York.

Chomsky, N. (1971). Deep structure, surface structure and semantic interpretation. In D. D. Steinberg and L. A. Jacobovitz (Eds.), *Semantics*, Cambridge University Press, Cambridge.

Chomsky, N. (1972). *Language and Mind*, enlarged ed. Harcourt Brace, Jovanovich, New York.

Chomsky, N., and Halle, M. (1968). *The Sound Pattern of English*, Harper and Row, New York.

Clark, E. (1973). Non-linguistic strategies in the acquisition of word meanings. *Cognition*, 2, 161–182.

Clark, R. (1974). Performing without competence. *Journal of Child Language*, 1, 1–10.

Coates, B., and Hartup, W. W. (1969). Age and verbalization in observational learning. *Developmental Psychology*, 1, 556–567.

Cole, M. (1973). A developmental study of factors influencing discrimination transfer. *Journal of Experimental Child Psychology*, 16, 126–147.

Cole, M., and Medin, D. (1973). On the existence and occurrence of mediation in discrimination transfer: a critical note. *Journal of Experimental Child Psychology*, 15, 352–355.

Collis, K. F. (1967). *The Relationship between Textbook Orientation and Mathematics Achievement and Attitude*. Unpublished M.Ed. thesis, University of Queensland.

Collis, K. F. (1969). Concrete-operational and formal-operational thinking in mathematics. *The Australian Mathematics Teacher*, 25, 77–84.

Collis, K. F. (1971). A study of concrete and formal reasoning in school mathematics. *Australian Journal of Psychology*, 23, 289–296.

Collis, K. F. (1972). *A Study of Concrete and Formal Operations in School Mathematics*. Unpublished Ph.D. thesis, University of Newcastle, N.S.W.

Collis, K. F. (1973). A study of children's ability to work with elementary mathematical systems. *Australian Journal of Psychology*, 25, 121–130.

Collis, K. F. (1975). *A Study of Concrete and Formal Operations in School Mathematics: A Piagetian Viewpoint*, ACER, Melbourne.

Connell, R. W. (1970). Class consciousness in childhood. *Australian and New Zealand Journal of Sociology*, 6, 87–99.

Connell, R. W. (1971). *A Child's Construction of Politics*, Melbourne University Press, Melbourne.

Davies, A. F. (1966). *Private Politics*, Melbourne University Press, Melbourne.

Davies, A. F. (1968). The child's discovery of nationality. *Australian and New Zealand Journal of Sociology*, 4(2), 107–124.

De Boysson-Bardies, B., and O'Regan, K. (1973). What children do in spite of adults' hypotheses. *Nature*, **246**, 531–534.

de Lacey, P. R. (1970). A cross-cultural study of classificatory ability. *Journal of Cross-Cultural Psychology*, **1**, 293–304.

Dennis, J. (1971). *Political Learning in Childhood and Adolescence: A Study of 5th, 7th and 11th graders in Milwaukee, Wisconsin*, Educational Research Information Centre, Bethesda, Maryland (ERIC Document Reproduction Service No. ED 040 117).

De Silva, W. A. (1972). The formation of historical concepts through contextual cues. *Educational Review*, **24**, 174–182.

Dienes, Z. P. (1960). *Building up Mathematics*, Hutchinson, London.

Dienes, Z. P., and Jeeves, M.A. (1965). *Thinking in Structures*, Hutchinson, London.

Dienes, Z. P., and Jeeves, M. A. (1970). *The effect of Structural Relations on Transfer*, Hutchinson, London.

Donaldson, M. (1971). Preconditions of inference. In *Nebraska Symposium on Motivation*, University of Nebraska Press, pp. 81–106.

Dray, W. (1957). *Laws and Explanation in History*, Oxford University Press, London.

Drinkwater, B. A. (1976). Visual memory skills of medium contact Aboriginal children. *Australian Journal of Psychology*, **28**(1), 37–43.

Dulit, E. (1972). Adolescent thinking à la Piaget: the formal stage. *Journal of Youth and Adolescence*, **4**, 281–301.

Dunn, L. M. (1965). *Expanded Manual for the Peabody Picture Vocabulary Test*, American Guidance Service, Circle Pines.

Edwards, D. (1973). Sensory-motor intelligence and semantic relations in early child grammar. *Cognition*, **2**, 395–434.

Eisenson, J. (1970). Developmental aphasia: differential diagnosis. *Journal of the Australian College of Speech Therapists*, **20**, 15–21.

Elkind, D., and Flavell, J. H. (1969). *Studies in Cognitive Development: Essays in Honor of Jean Piaget*, Oxford University Press, New York.

Emery, F. E. (1969). *Systems Thinking*, Middlesex, Harmondsworth.

Evans, R. I. (1973). *Jean Piaget: The Man and His Ideas*, Dutton, New York.

Farnham-Diggory, S. (1972). *Information Processing in Children*, Academic Press, New York.

Fenelon, B. (1976). *Brain Responses in Children Exhibiting Severe Reading Disability: A Neuropsychological Approach to Diagnosis*. Unpublished Ph.D. thesis, University of Newcastle.

Ferreiro, E., and Sinclair, H. (1971). Temporal relationships in language. *International Journal of Psychology*, **6**, 39–47.

Ficken, F. A. (1967). *Linear Transformations and Matrices*, Prentice Hall, Englewood Cliffs, N.J.

Fillmore, C. J. (1971). Types of lecical information. In D. D. Steinberg and L. A. Jakobovitz (Eds.), *Semantics*, Cambridge University Press, Cambridge.

Fishman, J. A. (1960). A systemization of the Whorfian hypothesis. *Behavioural Science*, **5**, 323–339.

Flavell, J. H. (1963). *The Developmental Psychology of Jean Piaget*, Van Nostrand, Princeton, N.J.

Flavell, J. H. (1968). *The Development of Role-taking and Communication Skills in Children*. Wiley, New York.

Flavell, J. H. (1970). Developmental studies of mediated memory. In H. Reese and L. P. Lipsitt (Eds.), *Advances in Child Development and Behaviour*, **5**, 181–211.

Flavell, J. H. (1971a). Stage related properties of cognitive development. *Cognitive Psychology*, **2**, 421–453.

Flavell, J. H. (1971b). What is memory development the development of? *Human Development*, **14**, 225–288.

434

Flavell, J. H. (1972). An analysis of cognitive developmental sequence. *Genetic Psychology Monographs*, **86**, 279–350.

Flavell, J. H. (1977). *Cognitive Development*, Prentice-Hall, Englewood Cliffs, N.J.

Flavell, J. H., and Wohlwill, J. F. (1969). Formal and functional aspects of cognitive development. In D. Elkind and J. H. Flavell (Eds.), *Studies in Cognitive Development*: *Essays in Honor of Jean Piaget*, Oxford University Press, New York.

French, J. W. (1951). *The Description of Aptitude and Achievement Tests in Terms of Rotated Factors*, Psychometric Monographs No. 5, University of Chicago Press.

Friedrich, D. (1974). Developmental analysis of memory capacity and information-encoding strategy. *Developmental Psychology*, **10**, 559–563.

Furth, H. G. (1961). Influence of language on the development of concept formation in deaf children. *Journal of Abnormal and Social Psychology*, **63**, 386–389.

Furth, H. G. (1964). Research with the deaf: implications for language and cognition. *Psychological Bulletin*, **62**, 142–164.

Furth, H. G. (1966). *Thinking without Language: Psychological Implications of Deafness*, Free Press, New York.

Furth, H. G. (1969). *Piaget and Knowledge: Theoretical Foundations*, Prentice-Hall, Englewood Cliffs, N.J.

Furth, H. G. (1970). *Piaget for Teachers*, Prentice-Hall, Englewood Cliffs, N.J.

Furth, H. G. (1971). Linguistic deficiency and thinking. Research with deaf subjects 1964–1969. *Psychological Bulletin*, **76**, 58–72.

Furth, H. G., and Milgram, N. A. (1965). The influence of language on classification: A theoretical model applied to normal, retarded and deaf children. *Genetic Psychology Monographs*, **72**, 317–351.

Furth, H. G., and Youniss, J. (1971). Formal operations and language: a comparison of deaf and hearing adolescents. *International Journal of Psychology*, **6**, 49–64.

Furth, H. G., Youniss, J., and Ross, B. M. (1970). Children's utilization of logical symbols: an interpretation of conceptual behavior based on Piagetian theory. *Developmental Psychology*, **3**, 36–57.

Gagne, R. M. (1968). Contributions of learning to human development. *Psychological Review*, **75**, 177–191.

Gallagher, G. (1971). *Some Findings on the Role of Language in the Acquisition of Operational Structures: Performance on Piagetian Conservation Tasks by Bilingual Greek Children* (R.R.5/71), Victorian Education Department, Melbourne.

Gazzaniga, M. S. (1972). One brain—two minds? *American Scientist*, **60**, 311–317.

Gazzaniga, M. S., and Sperry, R. W. (1967). Language after section of the cerebral commissures. *Brain*, **90**, 131–148.

Gelman, R. (1969). Conservation acquisition: a problem of learning to attend to relevant attributes. *Journal of Experimental Child Psychology*, **7**, 167–187.

Gelman, R. (1972). Logical capacity of very young children: number invariance rules. *Child Development*, **43**, 75–90.

Geyl, P. (1967). *Encounters in History*, Fontana Library, London.

Gill, C. C. (1964). Fractured facts: how high school students interpret indefinite quantitative concepts in U.S. history. *Clearing House*, **39**, 35–39.

Ginsburg, H., and Opper, S. (1969). *Piaget's Theory of Intellectual Development*, Prentice-Hall, Englewood Cliffs, N.J.

Gleitman, L. R., Gleitman, H., and Shipley, E. F. (1972). The emergence of the child as grammarian. *Cognition*, **1**, 137–164.

Goldschmidt, M. L. (1967). Different types of conservation and nonconservation and their relation to age, sex, I.Q., M.A. and vocabulary. *Child Development*, **38**, 1229–1246.

Goodnow, J. J., and Bethon, G. (1966). Piaget's tasks: the effects of schooling and intelligence. *Child Development*, **37**, 573–581.

Granger, G. (1965). Un problème d'axiomatisation en psychologie. *Logique et Analyse*, **29**, 72–83.

Greenfield, P. M. (1966). On culture and cognitive growth. In J. S. Bruner, R. R. Olver, and P. M. Greenfield, *Studies in Cognitive Growth*, Wiley, New York.

Greenfield, P. M., and Bruner, J. S. (1966). Culture and cognitive growth. *International Journal of Psychology*, **1**(2), 89–107.

Greeno, J. G. (1973). The structure of memory and the process of solving problems. In R. L. Solso (Ed.), *Contemporary Issues in Cognitive Psychology*, Winston, Washington, D.C.

Grize, J. B. (1960). Du groupement au nombre: essai de formalisation. In P. Gréco, J. B. Grize, S. Papert, and J. Piaget, Problèmes de la construction du nombre, *Etudes d'Epistémologie Génétique*, Vol. XI. Presses Universitaires de France, Paris.

Grize, J. B. (1963). Des groupements à l'algèbre de Boole: essai de filiation des structures logiques. In L. Apostel, J. B. Grize, S. Papert, and J. Piaget, La filiation des structures, *Etudes d'épistémologie Génétique*, Vol. XV. Presses Universitaires de France, Paris.

Grize, J. B. (1967). Remarques sur l'épistémologie mathematique des nombres naturels. In J. Piaget (Ed.), *Logique et Connaissance Scientifique*, Gallimard, Dijon.

Grize, J. B. (1969). Note sur la notion de groupement. *Archieves de Psychologie*, **40**, 51–54.

Guilford, J. P. (1967). *The Nature of Human Intelligence*, McGraw-Hill, New York.

Hagen, J. W. (1972). Strategies for remembering. In S. Farnham-Diggory (Ed.), *Information Processing in Children*, Academic Press, New York.

Halford, G. S. (1968). *An Investigation of Concept Learning*. Unpublished Ph.D. thesis, University of Newcastle.

Halford, G. S. (1969a). On the validity of the S-R mediation explanation of the ease of reversal concept shifts. *Australian Journal of Psychology*, **21**, 49–54.

Halford, G. S. (1969b). An experimental analysis of the criteria used by children to judge quantities. *Journal of Experimental Child Psychology*, **8**, 314–327.

Halford, G. S. (1970a). A theory of the acquisition of conservation. *Psychological Review*, **77**, 302–316.

Halford, G. S. (1970b). A classification learning set which is a possible model for conservation of quantity. *Australian Journal of Psychology*, **22**, 11–19.

Halford, G. S. (1972). The impact of Piaget on psychology in the seventies. In P. C. Dodwell (Ed.), *New Horizons in Psychology 2*, Penguin, Harmondsworth.

Halford, G. S. (1975a). Children's ability to interpret transformations of a quantity. I. An operational system for judging two transformations. *Canadian Journal of Psychology*, **29**, 38–55.

Halford, G. S. (1975b). Effect of structure on learning and transfer: a possible link between learning and thinking. *Australian Journal of Psychology*, **27**, 237–240.

Halford, G. S., and Galloway, W. R. (1977). Children who fail to make transitive inferences can remember comparisons. *Australian Journal of Psychology*, **29**, 1–5.

Halford, G. S., and Macdonald, C. (1977). Children's pattern construction as a function of age and complexity. *Child Development*, **48**(3), in Press.

Hallam, R. N. (1967). Logical thinking in history. *Educational Review*, **119**, 182–202.

Halliday, M. A. K. (1973). *Explorations in the Functions of Language*, Edward Arnold, London.

Hartig, M., and Kanfer, F. H. (1973). The role of verbal self instructions in children's resistance to temptation. *Journal of Personality and Social Psychology*, **25**, 259–267.

Hayes, J. R. (1970). *Cognition and the Development of Language*, Wiley, New York.

Haygood, R. C., and Bourne, L. E. (1965). Attribute and rule learning aspects of conceptual behaviour. *Psychological Review*, **72**, 175–195.

Haygood, R. C., and Devine, J. V. (1967). Effects of composition of the positive category on concept learning. *Journal of Experimental Psychology*, **74**, 230–235.

Heron, A., and Simonsson, M. (1969). Weight conservation in Zambian children. A non-verbal approach. *International Journal of Psychology*, **4**, 281–292.

Hinde, R. A., and Stevenson-Hinde, J. (1973). *Constraints on Learning: Limitations and Predispositions*, Academic Press, London.

436

Hockett, C. F. (1954). Chinese versus English: an exploration of the Whorfian hypothesis. In H. Hoijer (Ed.), *Language and Culture*, University of Chicago Press, Chicago.

Hoefler R. (1927). Ueber die Bedeutung der abstraktion fuer die geistige Entwicklung des taubstummen kindes. *Z. Kinderforsch*, **33**, 414–444. (Cited in H. G. Furth. Research with the deaf. *Psychological Bulletin*, 1964, **62**, 145–164).

Holt, R. R. (1964). Imagery: the return of the ostracized. *American Psychologist*, **12**, 254–264.

Hubbard, G. L. (1971). Preparing the junior secondary student for formal mathematics. *The Australian Mathematics Teacher*, **27**, 81–87.

Hunt, J. McV. (1961). *Intelligence and Experience*, Ronald Press, New York.

Huttenlocher, J., and Burke, D. (1976). Why does memory span increase with age? *Cognitive Psychology*, **8**, 1–31.

Hyde, D. M. G. (1973). *Piaget and Conceptual Development*, Holt, Rinehart and Winston, London.

Hymes, D. H. (1964). *Language in Culture and Society: A Reader in Linguistics and Anthropology*, Harper and Row, New York.

Hymes, D. H. (1966). Two types of linguistic relativity. In W. Bright (Ed.), *Sociolinguistics*, Mouton, The Hague.

Hymes, D. H. (1967). Models of the interaction of language and social setting. *Journal of Social Issues*, **23**, 8–28.

Inhelder, B., and Piaget, J. (1958). *The Growth of Logical Thinking from Childhood to Adolescence*, Routledge and Kegan Paul, London.

Inhelder, B., and Piaget, J. (1964). *The Early Growth of Logic in the Child*, Routledge and Kegan Paul, London.

Inhelder, B., Sinclair, H., and Bovet, M. (1974). *Learning and the Development of Cognition*, Routledge and Kegan Paul, London.

Jahoda, G. (1963). Children's concept of time and history. *Educational Review*, **15**(2), 87–104.

Jenkins, H. M., and Ward, W. C. (1965). Judgment of contingency between responses and outcome. *Psychological Monographs*, **79** (Whole No. 594).

Jenkins, J. J. (1969). Language and thought. In J. Voss (Ed.), *Approaches to Thought*, Merrill Palmer, Columbus, Ohio.

Jensen, A. R. (1974). Interaction of level I and level II abilities with race and socioeconomic status. *Journal of Educational Psychology*, **66**, 99–111.

Johnson, R. J., and White, R. M. (1967). Concept of dimensionality and reversal shift performance in children. *Journal of Experimental Child Psychology*, **5**, 223–227.

Johnson, W., and Halford, G. S. (1975). Children's ability to interpret transformations of a quantity, II: Judgment and memory for series of one to seven unambiguous transformations. *Canadian Journal of Psychology*, **29**, 142–150.

Johnson-Laird, P. N. (1972). The three-term series problem. *Cognition*, **1**, 57–82.

Johnson-Laird, P. N., Legrenzi, P., and Legrenzi, M. S. (1972). Reasoning and a sense of reality. *British Journal of Psychology*, **63**, 395–400.

Johnson-Laird, P. N., and Tagart, J. (1969). How implication is understood. *American Journal of Psychology*, **82**, 367–373.

Jurd, M. (1970). *Structure of Adolescent Thought with History-type Material*. Unpublished M.A. thesis, University of Newcastle, N.S.W.

Jurd, M. (1973). Adolescent thinking in history-type material. *Australian Journal of Education*, **17**, 1, 2–17.

Katz, J. J., and Fodor, J. A. (1963). The structure of a semantic theory. *Language*, **39**, 170–210.

Kearins, J. (1975). Skills of desert children. In G. E. Kearney and D. W. McElwain (Eds.), *Aboriginal Cognition—Prospect*, Canberra Institute of Aboriginal Studies, A.C.T.

Keats, D. M., and Keats, J. A. (1974). The effect of language on concept acquisition in bilingual children. *Journal of Cross-Cultural Psychology*, **5**, 80–99.

Keats, D. M., Keats, J. A., and Wan Rafaei Abdu Rahman (1974). Performan dalam ujian-ujian perbendaharaan kata dan operational dalam dua bahasa di kalagan kanak-Kanak Malayua dan China. *Akademika*, **4**, 15–26.

Keats, D. M., Keats, J. A., and Wan Rafaei Abdul Rahman (1974–76). Perolahan konsep di kalangan kanak-kanak Malaysia yang bertutur dua bahasa. *Akademika*, **5**, 31–42.

Keats, D. M., Keats, J. A., and Wan Rafaei (1976). Concept acquisition in Malaysian bilingual children. *Journal of Cross-Cultural Psychology*, **1**, 87–99.

Keats, D. M., Keats, J. A., and Wan Rafaei (1977). The performance of Malay and Chinese children in vocabulary and operational tasks in two languages. *Australian Psychologist* (in press).

Keats, J. A. (1955). *Formal and Concrete Thought Processes* (ETS RB55–17), Educational Testing Service Princeton, N.J.

Kelly, M. R. (1970). *Some Findings in the Area of Language and Cognition*. Paper read to the Australian Association for Research in Education, Founding Conference.

Kelly, M. R. (1971). Some aspects of conservation of quantity and length in Papua/New Guinea in relation to language, sex and years at school. *Papua and New Guinea Journal of Education*, **7**(1), 55–66.

Kemp, B. M., and Perry, D. G. (1976). *Children's Coding Strategies in Observational Learning*. Paper given to the Australian Social Psychology Conference, Sydney, May 1976.

Kendler, H. H., and Kendler, T. S. (1962). Vertical and horizontal processes in problem solving. *Psychological Review*, **69**, 1–16.

Kendler, H. H., Kendler, T. S., and Ward, J. W. (1972). An ontogenetic analysis of optional intradimensional and extradimensional shifts. *Journal of Experimental Psychology*, **95**, 102–109.

Kess, J. F. (1976). *Psycholinguistics: Introductory Perspectives*, Academic Press, New York.

Kessen, W. (1962). 'Stage' and 'structure' in the study of children. *Monographs of the Society for Research in Child Development*, **27**(2), 65–81.

Klahr, D. (1973). An information-processing approach to the study of cognitive development. In A. D. Pick (Ed.), *Minnesota Symposium on Child Psychology*, **7**, 141–177.

Klahr, D., and Wallace, J. G. (1970). An information-processing analysis of some Piagetian experimental tasks. *Cognitive Psychology*, **1**, 358–387.

Klahr, D., and Wallace, J. G. (1972). Class inclusion processes. In S. Farnham-Diggory (Ed.), *Information-processing in Children*, Academic Press, New York.

Klahr, D., and Wallace, J. G. (1973). The role of quantification operators in the development of conservation of quantity. *Cognitive Psychology*, **4**, 301–327.

Kohlberg, L., Yaeger, J., and Hjertholm, E. (1968). Private speech: four studies and a review of theories. *Child Development*, **39**, 691–735.

Kolers, P. A. (1968). Bilingualism and information processing. *Scientific American*, **218**, 357–376.

Kreutzer, M. A., Leonard, Sister Catherine, and Flavell, J. H. (1975). An interview study of children's knowledge about memory. *Monographs of the Society for Research on Child Development*, **40**, Serial No. 159.

Kuenne, M. R. (1946). Experimental investigation of the relation of language to transposition behaviour in young children. *Journal of Experimental Child Psychology*, **36**, 471–490.

Kuhn, T. S. (1962). *The Structure of Scientific Revolutions*, University of Chicago Press, Chicago.

Labov, W. (1972). *Language in the Inner City*, University of Pennsylvania Press, Philadelphia.

Lakoff, G. (1971). On generative semantics. In D. D. Steinberg and L. A. Jacobovitz (Eds.), *Semantics*, Cambridge University Press, Cambridge.

Lakoff, R. (1972). Language in context. *Language*, **48**, 907–927.

Lambert, W. E. (1972). *Language, Psychology and Culture*, Stanford, University Press, Stanford.

Lambert, W. E., and Macnamara, J. (1969). Some cognitive consequences of following a first-grade curriculum in a second language. *Journal of Educational Psychology*, **60**, 86–96.

Lamon, W. (1969). An experimental study of the levels of learning of an abstract structure by elementary school children. *Journal of Structural Learning*, **2**, 27–51, 65–87, 59–73.

Land, F. W. (1963). The need for new approaches. In F. W. Land (Ed.), *New Approaches to Mathematics Teaching*, Macmillan, London.

Lantz, De L., and Stefflre (1964). Language and cognition revisited. *Journal of Abnormal and Social Psychology*, **69**, 472–481.

Laughlin, P. R. (1968). Focusing strategy for eight concept rules. *Journal of Experimental Psychology*, **77**, 661–669.

Lawton, D. (1963). Social class differences in language development: a study of some samples of written work. *Language and Speech*, **6**, 120–143.

Lawton, D. (1964). Social class language differences in group discussions. *Language and Speech*, **7**, 183–204.

Lawton, D. (1968). *Social Class, Language and Education*, Routledge and Kegan Paul, London.

Legrenzi, P. (1971). Discovery as a means to understanding. *Quarterly Journal of Experimental Psychology*, **23**, 417–422.

Lenneberg, E. H. (1967). *Biological Foundations of Language*, Wiley, New York.

Lenneberg, E. H., and Roberts, I. M. (1956). *The Language of Experience: A Study in Methodology*, Memoir 13. Indiana University Publications in Anthropology and Linguistics, Baltimore.

Loban, W. D. (1963). *The Language of Elementary School Children*, National Council of Teachers of English, Champaign, Illinois.

Lodwick, A. R. (1959). Experimental examination of some of Piaget's schemata concerning children's perception and thinking and a discussion of their educational significance. *British Journal of Educational Psychology*, **29**, 89–103.

Lovell, K. (1961). A follow-up study of Inhelder and Piaget's *The Growth of Logical Thinking*. *British Journal of Psychology*, **52**, 143–153.

Lovell, K. (1966). Concepts in mathematics. In H. J. Klausmeier and C. W. Harris (Eds.), *Analyses of Concept Learning*, Academic Press, New York.

Lovell, J., and Butterworth, I. B. (1966). Abilities underlying the understanding of proportionality. *Mathematics Teaching*, **37**, 5–9.

Lovell, K., Mitchell, B., and Everett, I. R. (1962). An experimental study of the growth of some logical structures. *British Journal of Educational Psychology*, **53**, 175–188.

Lunzer, E. A. (1960). *Recent Studies in Britain Based on the Work of Jean Piaget*, NFER, Bucks.

Lunzer, E. A. (1965). Problems of formal reasoning in test situations. *Monographs of the Society for Research in Child Development*, **30**, 19–46.

Lunzer, E. A. (1968). Formal reasoning. In E. A. Lunzer and J. F. Morris (Eds.), *Development in Human Learning*, Staples, London.

Lunzer, E. A. (1973). *Formal Reasoning: A Re-appraisal*. Keynote paper delivered at the Jean Piaget Society Symposium, Philadelphia, Spring 1973.

Lunzer, E. A., Harrison, C., and Davey, M. (1972). The four-card problem and the generality of formal reasoning. *Quarterly Journal of Experimental Psychology*, **24**, 326–339.

Luria, A. R. (1961). In J. Tizard (Ed.), *The Role of Speech in the Regulation of Normal and Abnormal Behaviour*, Pergammon Press, London.

Luria, A. R. (1967). The directive function of speech in development and dissolution. Part 1. Development of the directive function of speech in early childhood. In Salzinger and Salzinger, *Research in Verbal Behaviour and Some Neurophysiological Implications*, Academic Press, New York.

Luria, A. R. (1970). *Traumatic Aphasia*, Mouton, The Hague.

Macandrew, H. (1948). Rigidity and isolation: a study of the deaf and the blind. *Journal of Abnormal and Social Psychology*, **43**, 476–494. (Cited in H. G. Furth. Research with the deaf. *Psychological Bulletin*, 1964, **62**, 145–164.)

Maclay, H. (1971). Overview. In D. D. Steinberg and L. A. Jacobovitz (Eds.), *Semantics*, Cambridge University Press, Cambridge.

McCawley, J. D. (1971). Where do noun phrases come from? In D. D. Steinberg and L. A. Jacobovitz (Eds.), *Semantics*, Cambridge University Press, Cambridge.

McLaughlin, G. H. (1963). Psycho-logic: a possible alternative to Piaget's formulation. *British Journal of Educational Psychology*, **33**, 61–67.

McNally, D. W (1968). *The Nature of the Sociometric Choice Process*. Unpublished Ph.D. thesis, University of Sydney.

McNally, D. W. (1973). *Piaget, Education and Teaching*, Angus and Robertson, Sydney.

McNeill, D. (1966). Developmental psycholinguistics. In F. Smith and G. A. Miller (Eds.), *The Genesis of Language: A Psycholinguistic Approach*, M.I.T. Press, Cambridge, Massachusetts.

McNiell, D. (1970). *The Acquisition of Language*, Harper, New York. Mandelbaum, D. G. (Ed.) (1949). *Selected Writings of Edward Sapir in Language, Culture and Personality*, University of California Press, Berkeley.

Mandler, G. (1962). From association to structure. *Psychological Review*, **69**, 415–427.

Mann, L. (1970). *Social Psychology*, Wiley, Sydney.

Marshall, J. C. (1973). Language, learning and laterality. In R. A. Hinde and J. Stevenson-Hinde (Eds.), *Constraints on Learning*, Academic Press, London.

Marwick, A (1970). *The Nature of History*, Macmillan, London.

Mays, W. (1953). An elementary introduction to Piaget's logic. In J. Piaget, *Logic and Psychology*, Manchester University Press, Manchester.

Middleton, M. R., Tajfel, H., and Johnson, N. B. (1970). Cognitive and affective aspects of children's national attitudes. *British Journal of Social and Clinical Psychology*, **9**, 122–134.

Milburn, D. Children's vocabulary. In N. Graves (Ed.), *New Movements in the Study and Teaching of Geography*, Cheshire, Melbourne.

Miller, G. A. (1956). The magical number seven, plus or minus two: some limits on our capacity for processing information. *Psychological Review*, **63**, 81–97.

Miller, G. A., and McNeill, D. (1968). Psycholinguistics. In G. Lindzey and E. Aronson (Eds.), *The Handbook of Social Psychology*, Vol. 3. Addison-Wesley, Reading.

Miller, P. H., Kessel, F. S., and Flavell, J. H. (1970). Thinking about people thinking about people thinking about . . . a study of social cognitive development. *Child Development*, **41**, 613–23.

Milner, B. (1971). Interhemispheric differences and psychological processes. *British Medical Bulletin*, **27**, 272–277.

Miron, M. S., and Osgood, C. E. (1966). Language behavior: the multivariate structure of qualification. In R. B. Cattell (Ed.), *Handbook of Multivariate Experimental Psychology*, Rand-McNally, Chicago.

Moscovitch, M. (1973). Language and the cerebral hemispheres: reaction-time studies and their implications for models of cerebral dominance. In P. Pliner, L. Krames, and T. Alloway (Eds.), *Communication and Affect: Language and Thought*, Academic press, New York.

Neimarck, E. D. (1970). Model for a thinking machine: an information-processing framework for the study of cognitive development. *Merrill-Palmer Quarterly*, **16**, 345–368.

Neisser, U., and Weene, P. (1962). Hierarchies in concept attainment. *Journal of Experimental Psychology*, **64**, 640–645.

Nelson, K. E., and Bonvillian, J. D. (1973). Concepts and words in the 18 month old: acquiring concept names under controlled conditions. *Cognition*, **2**, 435–450.

Newell, A., and Simon, H. A. (1972). *Human Problem Solving*, Prentice-Hall, Englewood Cliffs, N.J.

Newton, P. W. (1972). *Residential Mobility: a Process in the Differentiation of Urban Structure*. Unpublished M.A. thesis, University of Newcastle, N.S.W.

Nordenstreng, K. (1970). Changes in the meaning of semantic differential scales: measurement of subject-scale interaction effects. *Journal of Cross-Cultural Psychology*, **1**, 217–237.

Norman, D. A. (Ed.) (1970). *Models of Human Memory*. Academic Press, New York.

Norman, D. A. (1976). *Memory and Attention*, 2nd ed. Wiley, New York.

Oléron, P. (1951). Pensée conceptuelle et langage: performances comparées de sourds-muets et d'entendants dans des epreuves de classement multiple. *Année Psychologie*, **51**, 89–120. (Cited in H. G. Furth. Research with the deaf. *Psychological Bulletin*, 1964, **62**, 145–64.)

Oléron, P. (1953). Conceptual thinking of the deaf. *American Annals of the Deaf*, **98**, 304–310. (Cited in H. G. Furth. Research with the deaf. *Psychological Bulletin*, 1964, **62**, 145–164.)

Oléron, P. (1957). *Recherches sur le Développement Mental des Sourdsmuets*, Centre National de la Recherche Scientifique, Paris. (Cited in H. G. Furth. Research with the deaf. *Psychological Bulletin*, 1964, **62**, 145–164.)

Oléron, P. (1962). Le développement des responses à le relation identité-dissemblance: Ses rapports avec le langage. *Psychologie Française*, **7**, 4–16. (Cited in H. G. Furth. Research with the deaf. *Psychological Bulletin*, 1964, **62**, 145–164.)

Oléron, P. (1971). Langage et pensée: quelques évidences. *International Journal of Psychology*, **6**, 1–11.

Oléron, P., and Herren, H. (1961). L'acquisition des conservations et de language: étude comparative sur des enfants sourds et entendants. *Enfance*, 201–219, Cited in H. Furth (1964). Research with the deaf: implications for language and cognition. *Psychological Bulletin*, **62**, 145–164.

Olson, D. R. (1970). *Cognitive Development*, Academic Press, New York.

Osgood, C. E. (1953). *Method and Theory in Experimental Psychology*, Oxford University Press, New York.

Osgood, C. E. (1964). The semantic differential technique in the comparative study of cultures. *American Anthropologist*, **66**, 171–200.

Osgood, C. E. (1965). Cross-cultural compatibility in attitude measurement via multilingual semantic differentials. In I. D. Steiner and M. Fishbein (Eds.), *Current Studies in Social Psychology*, Holt, Rinehart and Winston, New York.

Osgood, C. E., Suci, G. J., and Tannenbaum, P. H. (1957). *The Measurement of Meaning*, University of Illinois Press, Urbana, Illinois.

Osherson, D. N. (1974). *Logical Abilities in Children*, Vol. 1. Wiley, New York.

Overton, W. F. (1975). General systems, structure and development. In K. F. Riegel and G. C. Rosenwald (Eds.), *Structure and Transformation: Developmental and Historical Aspects*, Wiley, New York.

Owens, L. (1976). Syntax in children's written composition, socioeconomic status, and cognitive development. *Australian Journal of Education*, **20**(2), 202–222.

Page, S. C. (1970). *The Transition from Concrete to Formal Thinking*. Unpublished Ph.d. Thesis, Australian National University, Canberra.

Paivio, A. (1975). Neomentalism. *Canadian Journal of Psychology*, **29**, 263–291.

Parsons, C. (1960). Inhelder and Piaget's *The Growth of Logical Thinking*, II. A logician's viewpoint. *British Journal of Psychology*, **51**, 75–84.

Pascual-Leone, J. A. (1970). Mathematical model for the transition rule in Piaget's developmental stages. *Acta Psychologica*, **32**, 301–345.

Pascual-Leone, J., and Smith, J. (1969). The encoding and decoding of symbols by children: a new experimental paradigm and a neo-Piagetian model. *Journal of Experimental Child Psychology*, **8**, 328–355.

Pavlov, I. P. (1949). *Natural Science and the Brain: Collected Works*, Vol. 3. Academy of Pedagogical Sciences U.S.S.R. Press, Moscow-Leningrad. (Cited in A. N. Sokolov, *Inner Speech and Thought*, Blenheim Press, New York, 1972.)

Peel, E. A. (1965). Intellectual growth during adolescence. *Educational Review*, **17**(3), 169–180.

Peel, E. A. (1966). A study of the difference in the judgements of adolescent pupils. *British Journal of Educational Psychology*, **36**, 77–86.

Peel, E. A. (1967a). *The Pupil's Thinking*, 2nd ed. Oldbourne, London.

Peel, E. A. (1967b). Some problems of the psychology of history teaching. In W. H. Burston and D. Thompson (Eds.), *Studies on the Nature and Teaching of History*, Routledge and Kegan Paul, London.

Peel, E. A. (1967c). A method for investigating children's understanding of certain logical connectives used in binary propositional thinking. *British Journal of Mathematical and Statistical Psychology*, **20**, 81–92.

Peel, E. A. (1968). Conceptual learning and explainer thinking. In E. A. Lunzer and J. F. Morris (Eds.), *Development in Human Learning*, Staples, London.

Peel, E. A. (1971). *The Nature of Adolescent Judgment*, Staples, London.

Peill, E. J. (1975). *Invention and Discovery of Reality*, Wiley, London.

Peterson, C. R., and Beach, L. R. (1967). Man as an intuitive statistician. *Psychological Bulletin*, **68**, 29–46.

Phillips, J. L. (1975). *The Origins of Intellect: Piaget's Theory*, 2nd ed. Freeman, San Francisco.

Philp, H., and Kelly, M. (1974). Product and process in cognitive development: Some comparative data on the performance of school-age children in different cultures. *British Journal of Educational Psychology*, **44**, 248–265.

Piaget, J. (1923). *Le Langage et la Pensée chez l'Enfant*, Delachaux et Niestlé, Neuchâtel-Paris.

Piaget, J. (1926). *The Language and Thought of the Child*, Routledge and Kegan Paul, London.

Piaget, J. (1942). *Classes, Relations et Nombres: Essai sur les 'groupments' de la Logistique et la Réversibilité de la Pensée*, Vrin, Paris.

Piaget, J. (1947). *The Psychology of Intelligence*, Routledge and Kegan Paul, London.

Piaget, J. (1949). *Traité de Logique*, Colin, Paris.

Piaget, J. (1950). *The Psychology of Intelligence*, Routledge and Kegan Paul, London.

Piaget, J. (1951). *Play, Dreams and Imitation in Childhood*, Heinemann, London.

Piaget, J. (1952). *The Child's Conception of Number*, Routledge and Kegan Paul, London.

Piaget, J. (1953a). *The Origin of Intelligence in the Child*, Routledge and Kegan Paul, London.

Piaget, J. (1953b). *Logic and Psychology*, Manchester University Press, Manchester. (Reprinted 1957, Basic Books, New York.)

Piaget, J. (1954a). Le langage et la pensée du point de vue génétique. *Acta Psychologica*, **10**, 51–60.

Piaget, J. (1954b). *The Construction of Reality in the Child*, Basic Books, New York.

Piaget, J. (1963). Le langage et les opérations intellectuelles. In *Problèmes de Psycholinguistique: Symposium de l'Association de Psychologie Scientifique de Langue Francaise* Presses Universitaires de France, Paris. (Translated by H. G. Furth, in H. G. Furth, *Piaget and Knowledge: Theoretical Foundations*, Prentice-Hall, Englewood Cliffs, N.J., 1969.)

Piaget, J. (1964). Learning and development. In R. E. Ripple and V. N. Rockcastle (Eds.), *Piaget Rediscovered: A Report of the Conference on Cognitive Studies and Curriculum Development*, Cornell University Press, Ithaca.

Piaget, J. (1966). General psychological problems of logico-mathematical thought. A. The problem of structures. In E. W. Beth and J. Piaget, *Mathematical Epistemology and Psychology*, Reidel, Dordrecht.

442

Piaget, J. (1967). *Six Psychological Studies*, Random House, New York.

Piaget, J. (1969). *The Child's Conception of Time*, Routledge and Kegan Paul, London.

Piaget, J. (1970a). *The Child's Conception of Movement and Speed*, Routledge and Kegan Paul, London.

Piaget, J. (1970b). *Genetic Epistemology*, Columbia University Press, New York.

Piaget, J. (1970c). *Structuralism*, Harper and Row, New York. (Reprinted 1971, Routledge and Kegan Paul, London.)

Piaget, J. (1972a). *Essai de Logique Opératoire*, Dunod, Paris.

Piaget, J. (1972b). Intellectual evolution from adolescence to adulthood. *Human Development*, **15**, 1–12.

Piaget, J. (1973). *Main Trends in Interdisciplinary Research*, George Allen and Unwin, London.

Piaget, J., Grize, J. B., Szeminska, A., and Vinh Bang (1968). *Epistémologie et Psychologie de la Fonction*, Presses Universitaires de France, Paris.

Piaget, J., and Inhelder, B. (1951). *La Genèse de l'Idée de Hussard chez l'Fanfant*, Presses Unitaires de France, Paris. (Partly translated by T. Brown, French Department, Newcastle University, N.S.W.)

Piaget, J., and Inhelder, B. (1956). *The Child's Conception of Space*, Routledge and Kegan Paul, London.

Piaget, J., and Inhelder, B. (1969). *The Psychology of the Child*, Routledge and Kegan Paul, London.

Piaget, J., and Inhelder, B. (1971). *Mental Imagery in the Child*, Routledge and Kegan Paul, London.

Piaget, J., Inhelder, B., and Szeminska, A. (1960). *The Child's Conception of Geometry*, Routledge and Kegan Paul, London.

Piaget, J., and Wiel, A. J. (1951). The development in children of the idea of the homeland and of relations with other countries. *International Social Science Bulletin*, **3**, 561–578.

Pick, A. D., and Frankel, G. W. (1973). A study of strategies of visual attention in children. *Developmental Psychology*, **9**, 348–357.

Poole, M. E. (1971). Social class differences in code elaboration. A study of oral communication at the tertiary level. *Australian Journal of Education*, **15**, 152–160.

Poole, M. E. (1972a). Social class and language predictability. *British Journal of Educational Psychology*, **42**, 127–136.

Poole, M. E. (1972b). Social class differences in code elaboration. A study of written communication at the tertiary level. *Australian and New Zealand Journal of Sociology*, **8**, 46–55.

Poole, M. E. (1973). Social class differences in language predictability: written. *Australian Journal of Education*, **17**, 300–313.

Průcha, J. (1974). Research on child language in East European countries. *Journal of Child Language*, **1**, 77–88.

Pumfrey, P. (1968). The growth of the schema of proportionality. *British Journal of Educational Psychology*, **38**, 202–204.

Rasch, G. (1960). *Probabilistic Models for Some Intelligence and Attainment Tests*, Danmarks Paedogogishe Institut, Copenhagen.

Ray, N. F. (1953). Human color perception and behavioral response. *Transactions of the New York Academy of Science*, **16**, 98–104. [Reprinted in T. Al-Issa and W. Dennis, *Cross-Cultural Studies of Behaviour*, Holt, Rinehart and Winston, New York, 1970.)

Rayner, S. A. (1951). *The Special Vocabulary of Civics*, University Press, Melbourne.

Renier, G. J. (1961). *History, Its Purpose and Method*, George Allen and Unwin, London.

Rhys, W. T. (1972). Geography and the adolescent. *Education Review*, **24**, 3, 183–196.

Richmond, P. G. (1970). *An Introduction to Piaget*, Routledge and Kegan Paul, London.

Riegel, K. F. (1973). Dialectic operations: the final period of cognitive development. *Human Development*, **16**, 346–370.

Riegel, K. F., and Rosenwald, G. C. (Eds.) (1975). *Structure and Transformation: Developmental and Historical Aspects*, Wiley, New York.

Rimoldi, H. J. A. (1971). Logical structures and languages in thinking processes. *International Journal of Psychology*, **6**, 65–77.

Robertson, A., and Youniss, J. (1969). Anticipatory visual imagery in deaf and hearing children. *Child Development*, **40**, 123–135.

Robinson, W. P. (1965). The elaborated code in working class language. *Language and Speech*, **8**, 243–52.

Robinson, W. P., and Rackstraw, S. J. (1972). *A Question of Answers*, Vol. I. Routledge and Kegan Paul, London.

Robinson, W. P., and Rackstraw, S. J. (1975). *Questioning and Answering of School Children*, Macquarie University, Joseph Rowntree Memorial Trust Fund, Sydney.

Rogers, K. W. (1967). Concepts of time in secondary school children of above average I.Q. *British Journal of Educational Psychology*, **37**, 1, 99–109.

Rommetveit, R. (1960). Studies in concept formation and levels of cognitive functioning. *Scandinavian Journal of Psychology*, **1**, 115–124.

Royce, J. R. (1973). A conceptual framework for a multi-factor theory of individuality. In J. R. Royce (Ed.), *Multivariate Analysis and Psychological Theory*, Academic Press, London.

Saltz, E. (1971). *The Cognitive Bases of Human Learning*, The Dorsey Press, Homewood.

Sapir, E. (1915). *Abnormal Types of Speech in Nootka*. Geological Survey of Canada, Anthropological Series No. 5, Government Printing Bureau, Ottawa. (Cited in D. G. Mandelbaum (Ed.), *Selected Writings of Edward Sapir in Language, Culture and Personality*, University of California Press, Berkeley, 1949.)

Sapir, E. (1921). *Language: An Introduction to the Study of Speech*, Harcourt Brace and and World, New York.

Sapir, E. (1929). Male and female forms of speech in Yana. In St. W. J. T. Teeuwen (Ed.), *Donum Natalicium Schrijen*, Nijemegen-Utrecht, 79–85. Cited in D. C. Mandelbaum (Ed.) (1949). *Selected Writings of Edward Sapir in Language, Culture and Personality*. University of California Press, Berkeley.

Scandura, J. M. (1970). Role of rules in behaviour: toward an operational definition of what (rule) is learned. *Psychological Review*, **77**, 516–533.

Scandura, J. M. (1973). *Structural Learning: I. Theory and Research*, Gordon and Breach, New York.

Seggie, J. L. (1969). Levels of Learning Involved in Conjunctive and Disjunctive Concepts. *Australian Journal of Psychology*, **21**, 325–333.

Seggie, J. L. (1970a). The utilization by children and adults of binary propositional thinking in concept learning. *Journal of Experimental Child Psychology*, **10**, 235–247.

Seggie, J. L. (1970b). Variables involved in confirming the consistency of a learned concept. *Australian Journal of Psychology*, **22**, 225–235.

Seggie, J. L. (1971a). Relationship of the post-feedback interval to concept difficulty and methods of learning. *Australian Journal of Psychology*, **23**, 267–278.

Seggie, J. L. (1971b). *An Investigation of Formal Operational Thought*. Unpublished Ph.D. thesis, University of Newcastle, N.S.W.

Seggie, J. L. (1973). The utilization of Piaget's binary logical relations in concept learning. *Journal of Behavioural Science*, **1**, 337–347.

Seggie, J. L. (1975). The empirical observation of the Piagetian concept of correlation. *Canadian Journal of Psychology*, **29**, 32–42.

Seggie, J. L., and Endersby, H. (1972). The empirical implications of Piaget's concept of correlation. *Australian Journal of Psychology*, **24**, 3–8.

Sheppard, J. L. (1973). Conservation of part and whole in the acquisition of class inclusion. *Child Development*, **44**, 380–383.

Sheppard, J. L. (1974a). Concrete operational thought and developmental aspects of solutions to a task based on a mathematical three-group, *Developmental Psychology*, **10**, 116–123.

Sheppard, J. L. (1974b). Compensation and combinatorial systems in the acquisition and generalization of conservation. *Child Development*, **45**, 717–730.

Sheppard, J. L. (1974c). The child's concept of horizontality with water levels: A training study. *Australian Journal of Psychology*, **26**, 191–198.

Sheppard, J. L. (1975a). Verbal analogies and concrete operations. *Australian Journal of Education*, **19**, 26–37.

Sheppard, J. L. (1975b). Children's performance on a test of the concept of horizontality, using water levels. *Australian Journal of Education*, **19**, 191–192.

Sheppard, J. L. (1976). Cognitive development in the primary school child: the relationship between tests of combinations and tests of concrete operations. *Australian Journal of Education*, **20**, 77–87.

Siegal, S. (1956). *Non-Parametric Statistics for the Behavioural Sciences*. McGraw-Hill, New York.

Sigel, I. E., and Hooper, F. H. (1968). *Logical Thinking in Children*. Holt, Rinehart and Winston, New York.

Simon, H. A. (1962). An information-processing theory of intellectual development. *Monographs of the Society for Research in Child Development*, **27**, (S, Serial No. 83).

Simon, H. A. (1972). Complexity and the representation of patterned sequences of symbols. *Psychological Review*, **79**, 369–382.

Simon, H. A. (1974). How big is a chunk? *Science*, **183**, 482–488.

Sinclair, H. (1971). Sensori-motor action patterns as a condition for the acquisition of syntax. In R. Huxley and E. Ingram (Eds.), *Language Acquisition: Models and Methods*, Academic Press, London.

Sinclair, H. (1973). Some remarks on the Genevan point of view on learning with special reference to language learning. In R. A. Hinde and J. Stevenson-Hinde (Eds.), *Constraints on Learning*, Academic Press, London.

Sinclair-de-Zwart, H. (1967). *Acquisition du Language et Développement de la Pensée*, Dunod, Paris.

Sinclair-de-Zwart, H. (1969). Developmental psycholinguistics. In D. Elkind and J. Flavell (Eds.), *Studies in Cognitive Development: Essays in Honour of Jean Piaget*, Oxford University Press, New York.

Skemp, R. R. (1961). Reflective intelligence and mathematics. *British Journal of Educational Psychology*, **31**, 45–55.

Skinner, B. F. (1957). *Verbal Behaviour*, Appleton, New York.

Skodak, M., and Skeels, H. M. (1949). A final follow-up study of one hundred adopted children. *The Journal of Genetic Psychology*, **75**, 85–125.

Slobin, D. I. (1971). *Psycholinguistics*, Scott Foresman, Illinois.

Slobin, D. I. (1973). Cognitive prerequisites for the development of grammar. In C. A. Ferguson and D. I. Slobin (Eds.), *Studies in Child Language Development*, Holt, Rinehart and Winston, New York.

Smedslund, J. (1963). The concept of correlation in adults. *Scandinavian Journal of Psychology*, **4**, 165–173.

Sokolov, A. N. (1972). *Inner Speech and Thought*, Plenum Press, New York-London.

Spearman, C. (1904). 'General intelligence', objectively determined and measured. *American Journal of Psychology*, **15**, 201–292.

Stevenson, H. W. (1970). Learning in children. In P. H. Mussen (Ed.), *Carmichael's Manual of Child Psychology*, 3rd ed. Wiley, New York.

Strauss, S. (1972). Inducing cognitive development and learning A review of short-term training experiments. I. The organismic developmental approach. *Cognition*, **1**, 329–357.

Szeminska, A. (1965). The evolution of thought: some application of research findings to educational practice. *Monographs of the Society for Research in Child Development*, **30**(2). 47–57.

445

Taba, H., and Elzey, F. E. (1964). Teaching strategies and thought processes. *Teachers' College Record*, **65**, 6.

Tanaka, Y. (1967). Cross-cultural compatibility of the affective meaning systems (measured by means of multilingual semantic differentials). *Journal of Social Issues*, **3**, 27–47.

Tanaka, Y. (1972). The cross-cultural generality of psycho-logic in the perception of national stereotypes. In H. C. Triandis, V. G. Vassiliou, Y. Tanaka, and A. V. Shanmugan (Eds.), *The Analysis of Subjective Outline*, Wiley, New York.

Tanaka, M., Campbell, J. T., and Helmick, J. S. (1970). Piaget for first-grade teachers: written exercises for assessing intellectual development. In I. J. Athey and D. O. Rubadeau (Eds.), *Educational Implications of Piaget's Theory*, Ginn-Blaisdell, Waltham, Massachusetts.

Tanaka, Y., and Osgood, C. E. (1965). Cross-culture, cross-concept and cross-subject generality of affective meaning systems. *Journal of Personality and Social Psychology*, **2**, 143–153.

Tanner, J. M., and Inhelder, B. (Eds.) (1960). *Discussions on Child Development*, Vol. 4. Tavistock, London.

Tenezakis, M. D. (1975). Linguistic subsystems and concrete operations. *Child Development*, **46**, 430–436.

Trotter, J. R. (1972). Review of structuralism, by J. Piaget. *Australian Journal of Psychology*, **24**, 119–121.

Tuddenham, R. D. (1970). Psychometricizing Piaget's methode clinique. In I. J. Athey and D. O. Rubadeau (Eds.), *Educational implications of Piaget's theory*, Ginn-Blaisdell, Waltham, Massachusetts.

Turner, J. (1975). *Cognitive Development*. Methuen, London.

Van den Daele, L. O. (1974). Infrastructure and transition in developmental analysis. *Human Development*, **17**, 1–23.

Vygotsky, L. S. (1962). *Thought and Language*, M.I.T. Press, Cambridge, Massachusetts.

Wadsworth, B. J. (1971). *Piaget's Theory of Cognitive Development*, McKay, New York.

Wallach, L. (1969). On the bases of conservation. In E. Elkind and J. H. Flavell (Eds.), *Studies in Cognitive Development*, Oxford University Press, New York.

Wallach, L., Wall, A. J., and Anderson, L. (1967). Number conservation: the roles of reversibility, addition-subtraction and misleading perceptual cues. *Child Development*, **38**, 425–442.

Walsh, W. H. (1967). Colligatory concepts in history. In W. H. Burston and D. Thomson (Eds.), *Studies in the Nature and Teaching of History*, Routledge and Kegan Paul, London.

Ward, W. C., and Jenkins, H. M. (1965). The display of information and the judgment of contingency. *Canadian Journal of Psychology*, **19**, 231–241.

Wason, P. C. (1966). Reasoning. In B. Foss (Ed.), *New Horizons in Psychology*, Penguin, Harmondsworth.

Wason, P. C. (1968). Reasoning about a rule. *Quarterly Journal of Psychology*, **20**, 273–281.

Wason, P. C., and Johnson-Laird, P. N. (1972). *Psychology of Reasoning: Structure and Content*, Harvard University Press, Cambridge.

Wason, P. C., and Shapiro, D. (1971). Natural and contrived experience in a reasoning problem. *Quarterly Journal of Experimental Psychology*, **23**, 63–71.

Weinreb, N., and Brainerd, C. J. (1975). A developmental study of Piaget's groupement model of the emergence of speed and time concepts. *Child Development*, **46**, 176–185.

Wermus, H. (1971). The insolutive (reciprocal) transformations of propositional logic. *Archives de Psychologic*, **41**, 153–171. (also in *Psychological Abstracts*, 1974, **52**, No. 221).

Wermus, H. (1972). Formalisation de quelques structures initiales de la psychogenese. *Archives de Psychologie*, **41**, 271–288.

Wertheimer, M. (1964). The syllogism and productive thinking. In J. M. Mandler and G. Mandler (Eds.), *Thinking: From Association to Gestalt*, Wiley, New York.

446

White, R. M., and Johnson, R. J. (1968). Concept of dimensionality and optional shift performance in nursery school children. *Journal of Experimental Child Psychology*, **6**, 113–119.

White, S. H. (1965). Evidence for a hierarchical arrangement of learning processes. *Advances in Child Development and Behaviour*, **2**, 187–220.

Whorf, B. L. (1956). *Language, Thought and Reality*, M.I.T. Press, Cambridge, Massachusetts.

Winer, B. J. (1962). *Statistical Principles in Experimental Design*, McGraw-Hill, New York.

Wittmann, E. (1973). The concept of grouping in Jean Piaget's psychology—formalization and applications. *Educational Studies in Mathematics*, **5**, 125–146.

Witz, K. G. (1969). On the structure of Piaget's grouping I. *Archives de Psychologie*, **159**, 37–49.

Wolff, J. L. (1967). Concept shift and discrimination reversal learning in humans. *Psychological Bulletin*, **68**, 369–408.

Wozniak, R. H. (1972). Verbal regulation of motor behaviour—Soviet research and non-Soviet replications. *Human Development*, **15**, 13–57.

Youniss, J., and Robertson, A. (1970). Projective visual imagery as a function of age and deafness. *Child Development*, **41**, 215–234.

Zangwill, O. L. (1960). *Cerebral Dominance and Its Relation to Psychological Function*, Oliver and Boyd, Edinburgh.

AUTHOR INDEX

SUBJECT INDEX